SECOND EDITION

The Norton Field Guide to Writing
with handbook

SECOND EDITION

The Norton
Field Guide
to Writing

with handbook

Richard Bullock

WRIGHT STATE UNIVERSITY

Francine Weinberg

W. W. NORTON & COMPANY

New York • London

W. W. Norton & Company has been independent since its founding in 1923, when William Warder Norton and Mary D. Herter Norton first published lectures delivered at the People's Institute, the adult education division of New York City's Cooper Union. The Nortons soon expanded their program beyond the Institute, publishing books by celebrated academics from America and abroad. By mid-century, the two major pillars of Norton's publishing program—trade books and college texts—were firmly established. In the 1950s, the Norton family transferred control of the company to its employees, and today—with a staff of four hundred and a comparable number of trade, college, and professional titles published each year—W. W. Norton & Company stands as the largest and oldest publishing house owned wholly by its employees.

Editor: Marilyn Moller
Associate Editor: Erin Granville
Editorial Assistant: Ana Cooke
Project Editor: Rebecca A. Homiski
Copy Editor: Mark Gallaher
Managing Editor: Marian Johnson
Electronic Media Editor: Eileen Connell
Production Manager: Jane Searle
Manufacturing: R.R. Donnelley, Crawfordsville
Composition: Matrix Publishing Services
Text Design: Anna Palchik
Cover Design: Debra Morton Hoyt

Library of Congress Cataloging-in-Publication Data

Bullock, Richard H.
  The Norton Field guide to writing : with handbook /
Richard Bullock, Francine Weinberg. — 2nd ed.
     p. cm.
  Includes bibliographical references and index.
  ISBN: 978-0-393-93247-8 (pbk.)
  1. English language—Rhetoric—Handbooks, manuals, etc. 2. English language—
Grammar—Handbooks, manuals, etc. 3. Report writing—Handbooks, manuals, etc.
I. Weinberg, Francine. II. Title. III Title: Field guide to writing, with handbook.
  PE1408.B8838243 2009
  808'.042—dc22   2008040628

W. W. Norton & Company, Inc., 500 Fifth Avenue, New York, N.Y. 10110
www.wwnorton.com

W. W. Norton & Company Ltd., Castle House, 75/76 Wells Street, London W1T 3QT

1 2 3 4 5 6 7 8 9 0

Preface

The Norton Field Guide to Writing began as an attempt to offer the kind of writing guidelines found in the best rhetorics in a format as user-friendly as the most popular handbooks, and on top of that to be as brief as could be. It was to be a handy guide to help college students with all their written work. Just as there are field guides for bird watchers and accountants, this would be one for writers. The book touched a chord with many instructors, and it quickly became the most widely used brief rhetoric. At the same time, many instructors asked for more on grammar and punctuation. So we are happy now to offer this second edition of the *Field Guide* in a version that includes a brief handbook.

The Norton Field Guide still aims to offer the guidance new teachers and first-year writers need and the flexibility many experienced teachers want. From our experiences as teachers and WPAs, we know that explicit writing guides work well for students and novice teachers. Many instructors chafe at the structure imposed by such books, however, and students complain about having to buy books that have much more detail than they need. So we've tried to provide enough structure without too much detail — to give the information college writers need to know, and to resist the temptation to tell them everything there is to know.

Most of all, we've tried to keep the book brief and easy to use. To that end, it includes menus, directories, and a glossary/index to make it easy for students to find what they're looking for — and color-coded links to help them navigate the book. These links are also the key to keeping the book brief: chapters are short, but the links point to pages elsewhere in the book *if* students need more detail.

Students can access much of the *Field Guide* and the complete handbook on the Web, and a color-coded Writing Toolbar provides online access when students most need it: *as they write.*

What's in the Book

The Norton Field Guide covers 15 kinds of writing often assigned to college students. Much of the book is in the form of guidelines, designed to help students consider the choices they have as writers. Most chapters are brief, in response to students' complaints about books with too much detail—but color-coded links send them to places in the book where they can find more information if they need it. The book has 7 parts:

1. **RHETORICAL SITUATIONS.** Chapters 1–5 focus on purpose, audience, genre, stance, and media and design. In addition, most chapters include tips to help students focus on their particular rhetorical situation.

2. **GENRES.** Chapters 6–20 offer guidelines for fifteen kinds of writing, from abstracts to lab reports to memoirs. Literacy narrative, textual analysis, report, and argument are treated in greater detail.

3. **PROCESSES.** Chapters 21–28 offer advice on generating ideas, drafting, revising, editing, proofreading, compiling portfolios, collaborating, and writing as inquiry.

4. **STRATEGIES.** Chapters 29–41 cover familiar ways of developing and organizing text—writing effective beginnings and endings, coming up with good titles and developing effective thesis statements, comparing, describing, using dialogue, and other essential writing strategies. Chapters 40–41 offer useful strategies for reading and essay exams.

5. **RESEARCH / DOCUMENTATION.** Chapters 42–50 offer advice on how to do academic research; work with sources; quote, paraphrase, and summarize source materials; and document sources using MLA and APA styles.

6. **MEDIA / DESIGN.** Chapters 51–53 give general guidance on designing and presenting texts for print, spoken, and electronic media.

7. **HANDBOOK.** At the end of the book is a handbook to help students edit what they write. We've organized the handbook around the intuitive categories of sentences, words, and punctuation to make it easy for students to find the help they need.

What's on the Website

A free and open website provides instant access to much of *The Norton Field Guide* online. Visit the site at **wwnorton.com/write/fieldguide**.

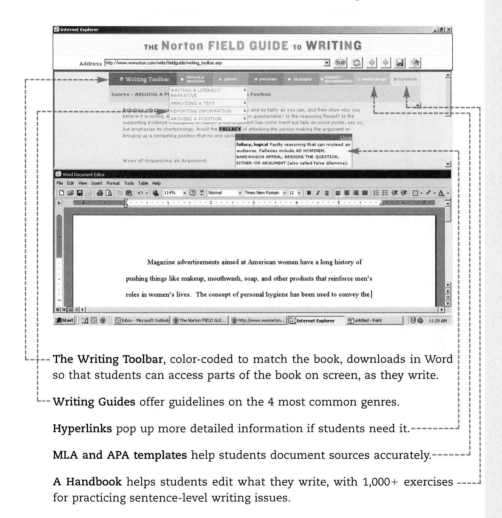

The Writing Toolbar, color-coded to match the book, downloads in Word so that students can access parts of the book on screen, as they write.

Writing Guides offer guidelines on the 4 most common genres.

Hyperlinks pop up more detailed information if students need it.

MLA and APA templates help students document sources accurately.

A Handbook helps students edit what they write, with 1,000+ exercises for practicing sentence-level writing issues.

Highlights

It's easy to use. Color-coding, menus, directories, and a glossary / index make it easy for students to find what they're looking for; a minimum of jargon makes it easy to understand. Color-coded templates even make MLA and APA documentation easy.

It has just enough detail, with short chapters that include color-coded links sending students to more detail *if* they need more.

It's uniquely flexible for teachers, with explicit assignment sequences if you want them — or you can create your own. See the facing page for ways of teaching with this book.

A user-friendly handbook, with an intuitive organization around sentences, words, and punctuation to make it easy for students to find what they need. And we go easy on the grammatical terminology, with links to the glossary for students who need detailed definitions.

What's New

11 new readings, from a textual analysis of 24 to a report on the inevitability of air turbulence to a proposal for controlling the prices of textbooks.

Documentation maps, showing students where to look for publication information in books, magazines, journals, databases, and websites.

A new chapter on synthesizing ideas, helping students connect ideas in multiple sources and use them in their own writing. (Chapter 45)

A new chapter on mixing genres, showing how to combine a number of genres in a single text, as is done in much real-world writing. (Chapter 20)

A new chapter on writing as inquiry, helping students approach writing projects with curiosity and providing strategies to help them get beyond what they already know about their topic. (Chapter 21)

A new chapter on arguing, with strategies for articulating a position, giving good reasons and evidence, considering other positions, and more. (Chapter 32)

A new chapter on taking essay exams (Chapter 41)

Ways of Teaching with *The Norton Field Guide to Writing*

The Norton Field Guide is designed to give you both support and flexibility. It has clear assignment sequences if you want them, or you can create your own. If, for example, you assign a position paper, there's a full chapter. If you want students to use sources, add the appropriate research chapters. If you want them to submit a topic proposal or an annotated bibliography, add those chapters.

If you're a new teacher, the genre chapters offer explicit assignment sequences — and the color-coded links will remind you of other detail that you may want to bring in. The *Instructor's Manual* is designed for new teachers, with advice on creating a syllabus, responding to writing, balancing graduate work with teaching responsibilities, and more.

If you focus on genres, there are complete chapters on 15 genres college students are often assigned. Color-coded links will help you bring in details about research or other writing strategies as you wish.

If you organize your course thematically, you might start with Chapter 22 on generating ideas to get students thinking about a theme. You can also assign them to do research on the theme, starting with Chapter 43 on finding sources, or perhaps with Chapter 21 on writing as inquiry. If they then write in a particular genre, there will be a chapter to guide them.

If you want students to do research, there are 8 chapters on the research process, along with guidelines and sample papers demonstrating MLA and APA documentation. If you want them writing particular genres, each genre chapter includes links to the research chapters.

If you focus on particular strategies, you'll find full chapters on narration, description, and so on. The chapters assume these to be strategies that a writer might use for many writing purposes, and each chapter points out genres where that strategy is particularly useful. If you wish to assign essays organized around a particular strategy, each chapter ends with links that lead students through the process of doing so.

If you teach online, much of the book is on the Web, with a Writing Toolbar that downloads into Word to give students access as they write.

Acknowledgments

Writing never takes place in isolation; from start to finish, it is always a collaborative venture. In writing our acknowledgments, we struggled thinking about whom to include and how far back we should go in recognizing the many people who have influenced what we do as writers and teachers, and as authors of this book. Even as we offer our gratitude here by naming those who have most directly contributed to making *The Norton Field Guide to Writing, with handbook* a reality, we are aware that many others have been instrumental as well.

Marilyn Moller, the editor of the *Field Guide*, tops our list of those we want to thank, for her keen instincts, creative thinking, and unflagging assistance. She is one of the finest editors we've had the good fortune to work with. The quality of this book is due in large part to her knowledge of the field of composition, her formidable editing and writing skills, and her sometimes uncanny ability to see the future of the teaching of writing.

The second edition has benefited from the steady editorial hand of Erin Granville, who shepherded it (and Rich) through its revisions. Her deft editing and insightful suggestions have been especially valuable for the new parts—and in fact have improved the entire book.

Many others have contributed. Thanks to project editor Rebecca Homiski for her energy, patience, and great skill. Ana Cooke has coordinated a flurry of manuscripts and other materials, as did Cat Spencer before her. I thank Anna Palchik for the user-friendly (and award-winning) interior design and Debra Morton Hoyt for the whimsical cover. Jane Searle (and Diane O'Connor before her) transformed a scribbled-over manuscript into a finished product in record time—and to high standards. Mark Gallaher copyedited and Barbara Necol proofread, both with great attention to detail. Megan Jackson cleared text permissions, and Stephanie Romeo researched and cleared permission for the images. Eileen Connell, Jack Lamb, and Cliff Landesman planned, designed, and produced the sensational website. Steve Dunn helped us all keep our eyes on the market, and Mike Wright, Katie Hannah, and now Doug Day have worked enthusiastically and skillfully to introduce the book to the market. Thanks to all, and to Roby Harrington, Drake McFeely, and Julia Reidhead for supporting this project in the first place.

At Wright State, Rich has many, many people to thank for their support and assistance over the many years he's been working on the *Norton Field Guide*; among them Brady Allen, Debbie Bertsch (now at Columbus State Community College), Vicki Burke, Jane Blakelock, Adrienne Cassel (now at Sinclair Community College), Jimmy Chesire, Carol Cornett, Byron Crews, Catherine Crowley, Deborah Crusan, Sally DeThomas, Stephanie Dickie, Scott Geisel, Beth Klaisner, Peggy Lindsey, Nancy Mack, Marty Maner, Cynthia Marshall, Sarah McGinley, Michelle Metzner, Kristie Rowe, Bobby Rubin, Cathy Sayer, David Seitz, Caroline Simmons, Tracy Smith, Rick Strader, Mary Van Loveren, and A.J. Williams. He also thanks Henry Limouze, chair of the English Department, and Lynn Morgan and Becky Traxler, the secretaries to the writing programs. And thanks especially to the more than 200 graduate teaching assistants and 9,000 first-year students who have class-tested, taught, and studied with the various editions of the *Field Guide* and whose experiences have helped shape it.

Thanks to the many teachers across the county who have reviewed various versions and offered valuable input and encouragement: Alan Ainsworth, Houston Community College; Jonathan Alexander, University of California at Irvine; Althea Allard, Community College of Rhode Island; James Allen, College of DuPage; Cathryn Amdahl, Harrisburg Area Community College; Jeff Andelora, Mesa Community College; Anne Beaufort, University of Washington, Tacoma; Sue Beebe, Texas State University; Patrick Bizzaro, East Carolina University; Kevin Brooks, North Dakota State University; Ron Brooks, Oklahoma State University; Cheryl Brown, Towson University; Gina Caison, University of Alabama, Birmingham; Jill Channing, Mitchell Community College; Ron Christiansen, Salt Lake Community College; Susan Cochran-Miller, North Carolina State University at Raleigh Durham; Billye Currie, Samford University; Paul C. Davis, Northland Community and Technical College; Pat Densby, San Jacinto College Central; Marvin Diogenes, Stanford University; Sarah Duerdan, Arizona State University; Russel Durst, University of Cincinnati; Sylvia Edwards, Longview Community College; Karen Fitts, West Chester University; Paul Formisano, University of New Mexico; Lloren A. Foster, Hampton University; Ivonne M. Garcia, Ohio State University; Anne Gervasi, DeVry University; Gregory Glau, Arizona State University; Emily Golson, University of Northern Colorado; Richard Hansen, California State Fresno; Susanmarie Harrington,

University of Vermont; Lory Hawkes, DeVry Institute of Technology; Gary Hawkins, Warren Wilson College; Paul Heilker, Virginia Polytechnic Institute and State University; Hal Hellwig, Idaho State University; Michael Hennessy, Texas State University; Cheryl Huff, Germanna Community College; Maurice Hunt, Baylor University; Teresa James, South Florida Community College; Kim Jameson, Oklahoma City Community College; Peggy Jolly, University of Alabama, Birmingham; Mitzi Walker Jones, University of Arkansas, Fort Smith; Jeanne Kelly, Holmes Community College; Rhonda Kyncl, University of Oklahoma; Sally Lahmon, Sinclair Community College; Erin Lebacqz, University of New Mexico; Paul Lynch, Purdue University; T. Michael Mackey, Community College of Denver; Magdalena Maczynska, Marymount Manhattan College; Leigh A. Martin, Community College of Rhode Island; Deborah McCollister, Dallas Baptist University; Miles McCrimmon, J. Sargeant Reynolds Community College; Jeanne McDonald, Waubonsee Community College; Jacqueline McGrath, College of DuPage; Pat McQueeny, Johnson County Community College; Shellie Michael, Volunteer State Community College; Thomas Miller, University of Arizona; Bryan Moore, Arkansas State University; Mary Ellen Muesing, University of North Carolina, Charlotte; Roxanne Munch, Joliet Junior College; Terry Novak, Johnson & Wales University; Peggy Oliver, San Jacinto College; Amy Patrick, Western Illinois University; Ann Pearson, San Jacinto College; Irv Peckham, Louisiana State University; K. J. Peters, Loyola Marymount University; Deirdre Pettipiece, University of the Sciences; Donna Qualley, Western Washington University; Daniela Ragusa, Southern Connecticut State University; Dana Resente, Montgomery County Community College; Nedra Reynolds, University of Rhode Island; Althea Rhodes, University of Arkansas, Fort Smith; Mauricio Rodriguez, El Paso Community College; Gardner Rogers, University of Illinois at Urbana-Champaign; Tony Russell, Purdue University; Matthew Samra, Kellogg Community College; Lisa L. Sandoval, Joliet Junior College; Lisa M. Schwerdt, California University of Pennsylvania; Michelle Sidler, Auburn University; William H. Smith, Weatherford College; Leah Sneider, University of New Mexico; Jeffrey Larsen Snodgrass, Prince George's Community College; Jean Sorensen, Grayson County College; Brady J. Spangenberg, Purdue University; Candace Stewart, Ohio University; Jennifer Stewart, Indiana University–Purdue University, Fort Wayne; Amy Ferdinandt Stolley, Purdue University; Mary

Stripling, Dallas Baptist University; Martha Swearingen, University of District Columbia; Elyssa Tardiff, Purdue University; Linda Tetzlaff, Normandale Community College; John M. Thomson, Johnson County Community College; Monica Parrish Trent, Montgomery College, Rockville Campus; Griselda Valerio, University of Texas at Brownsville; Jarica Watts, University of Utah; Scott Weeden, Indiana University–Purdue University Fort Wayne; Candice Welhausen, University of New Mexico; Carol Westcamp, University of Arkansas, Fort Smith; Barbara Whitehead, Hampton University; Melissa E. Whiting, University of Arkansas, Fort Smith; and Anne-Marie Yerks, University of Michigan. Thanks especially to Avon Crismore's students at Indiana University–Purdue University Fort Wayne for their thoughtful (and well-written) evaluations.

The *Norton Field Guide* has also benefited from the good advice and conversations Rich has had with writing teachers across the country, including (among many others) Maureen Mathison, Susan Miller, Tom Huckin, Gae Lyn Henderson, and Sundy Watanabe at the University of Utah; Christa Albrecht-Crane, Doug Downs, and Brian Whaley at Utah Valley State College; Anne Dvorak and Anya Morrissey at Longview Community University; Jeff Andelora at Mesa Community College; Robin Calitri at Merced College; Lori Gallinger, Rose Hawkins, Jennifer Nelson, Georgia Standish, and John Ziebell at the Community College of Southern Nevada; Stuart Blythe at Indiana University–Purdue University Fort Wayne; Janice Kelly at Arizona State University; Jeanne McDonald at Waubonsee Community College; Web Newbold, Mary Clark-Upchurch, Megan Auffart, Matt Balk, Edward James Chambers, Sarah Chavez, Desiree Dighton, Ashley Ellison, Theresa Evans, Keith Heller, Ellie Isenhart, Angela Jackson-Brown, Naoko Kato, Yuanyuan Liao, Claire Lutkewitte, Yeno Matuki, Casey McArdle, Tibor Munkacsi, Dani Nier-Weber, Karen Neubauer, Craig O'Hara, Martha Payne, Sarah Sandman, and Kellie Weiss at Ball State University.

I wouldn't have met most of these people without the help of the Norton travelers, the representatives who spend their days visiting faculty, showing and discussing the *Field Guide* and Norton's other fine textbooks. Thanks to Kathy Carlsen, Michelle Church, John Darger, Erin Lizer, Brita Mess, and all the other Norton travelers. And I'd especially like to thank Mike Wright, Katie Hannah, and Doug Day for promoting this book so enthusiastically and professionally.

It's customary to conclude by expressing gratitude to one's spouse and family, and for good reason. Writing and revising *The Norton Field Guide* over the past several years, we have enjoyed the loving and unconditional support of our spouses, Barb and Larry, who provide the foundation for all we do. Thank you. We couldn't have done it without you.

How to Use This Book

There's no one way to do anything, and writing is no exception. Some people need to do a lot of planning on paper; others write entire drafts in their heads. Some writers compose quickly and loosely, going back later to revise; others work on one sentence until they're satisfied with it, then move on to the next. And writers' needs vary from task to task, too: sometimes you know what you're going to write about and why, but need to figure out how to do it; other times your first job is to come up with a topic. *The Norton Field Guide to Writing* is designed to allow you to chart your own course as a writer—to offer you guidelines that suit your writing processes and needs. It is organized in seven parts:

1. **RHETORICAL SITUATIONS:** No matter what you're writing, it will always have some purpose, audience, genre, stance, and medium and design. This part will help you consider each of these elements.

2. **GENRES:** Use these chapters for help with specific kinds of writing, from abstracts to lab reports to memoirs and more. You'll find more detailed guidance for four especially common assignments: literacy narratives, analyzing texts, reporting information, and arguing a position.

3. **PROCESSES:** These chapters offer general advice for all writing situations—from generating ideas and text to drafting, revising and rewriting, compiling a portfolio—and more.

4. **STRATEGIES:** Use the advice in this part to develop and organize your writing—to write effective beginnings and endings, to guide readers through your text, and to use comparison, description, dialogue, and other strategies as appropriate.

5. **RESEARCH / DOCUMENTATION:** Use this section for advice on how to do research, work with sources, and compose and document research-based texts using MLA and APA styles.

6. **MEDIA / DESIGN:** This section offers guidance in designing your work and working with visuals, and in delivering what you write on paper, on screen, or in person.

7. **HANDBOOK:** Look here for help with sentence-level editing.

Ways into the Book

The Norton Field Guide gives you the writing advice you need, along with the flexibility to write in the way that works best for you. Here are some of the ways you can find what you need in the book.

Brief menus.   Inside the front cover you'll find a list of all the chapters; start here if you are looking for a chapter on a certain kind of writing or a general writing issue. Inside the back cover is a menu of all the topics covered in the **HANDBOOK**.

Complete contents.   Pages xix–xxv contain a detailed table of contents. Look here if you need to find a reading or a specific section in a chapter.

Guides to writing.   If you know the kind of writing you need to do, you'll find guides to writing 15 common genres in Part 2. These guides are designed to help you through all the decisions you have to make — from coming up with a topic to organizing your materials to editing and proof-reading your final draft.

Color-coding.   The parts of this book are color-coded for easy reference: red for **RHETORICAL SITUATIONS,** green for **GENRES,** lavender for **PROCESSES,** orange for **STRATEGIES,** blue for **RESEARCH / DOCUMENTATION,** gold for **MEDIA / DESIGN,** and yellow for the **HANDBOOK.** You'll find a key to the colors on the front cover flap and also at the foot of each left-hand page. When you see a word highlighted in a color, that tells you where you can find additional detail on the topic.

Glossary / index.   At the back of the book is a combined glossary and index, where you'll find full definitions of key terms and topics, along with a list of the pages where everything is covered in detail.

Directories to MLA and APA documentation.   A brief directory inside the back cover will lead you to guidelines on citing sources and composing a list of references or works cited. The documentation models are color-coded so you can easily see the key details.

The website.   You can also start at **wwnorton.com/write/fieldguide.** There you'll find a Writing Toolbar that provides electronic access to some of what's in the book, including writing guides for several genres, MLA and APA guidelines, the glossary, the complete handbook, exercises, and more.

Ways of Getting Started

If you know your genre, simply turn to the appropriate genre chapter. There you'll find model readings, a description of the genre's Key Features, and a Guide to Writing that will help you come up with a topic, generate text, organize and write a draft, get response, revise, edit, and proofread. The genre chapters also point out places where you might need to do research, use certain writing strategies (comparison, description, and so on), design your text a certain way—and direct you to the exact pages in the book where you can find help doing so.

If you know your topic, you might start with some of the activities in Chapter 23, Generating Ideas and Text. From there, you might turn to Chapter 43, for help Finding Sources on the topic. When it comes time to narrow your topic and come up with a thesis statement, Chapter 30 can help. If you get stuck at any point, you might turn to Chapter 22, Writing as Inquiry; it provides tips that can get you beyond what you already know about your topic. If your assignment or your thesis defines your genre, turn to that chapter; if not, consult Chapter 3 for help determining the appropriate genre, and then turn to that genre chapter. The genre chapters point out places where you might need to do more research, use certain writing strategies, design your text a certain way—and direct you to the exact pages in the book where you can find help doing so.

Contents

Part 3   Processes   *209*

Part 4   Strategies   *259*

Part 5   Doing Research   *373*

Part 6   Media / Design   *521*

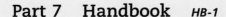

Part 7   Handbook   *HB-1*

SECOND EDITION

The Norton Field Guide to Writing
with handbook

part 1

Rhetorical Situations

Whenever we write, whether it's an email to a friend or a toast for a wedding, an English essay or a résumé, we face some kind of rhetorical situation. We have a **PURPOSE**, a certain **AUDIENCE**, a particular **STANCE**, a **GENRE**, and a **MEDIUM** to consider—and often as not a **DESIGN**. All are important elements that we need to think about carefully. The following chapters offer brief discussions of those elements of the rhetorical situation, along with questions that can help you make the choices you need to as you write. See also the fifteen **GENRES** chapters for guidelines for considering your rhetorical situation in each of these specific kinds of writing.

Rhetorical Situations

Purpose 1

All writing has a purpose. We write to explore our thoughts and emotions, to express ourselves, to entertain; we write to record words and events, to communicate with others, to try to persuade others to believe as we do or to behave in certain ways. In fact, we often have several purposes at the same time. We may write an essay in which we try to persuade an audience of something, but as we write, we may also be exploring our thoughts on the subject. Look, for example, at this passage from a 2002 *New York Times Magazine* essay by economist and editorial columnist Paul Krugman about the compensation of chief executive officers:

> Is it news that C.E.O.'s of large American corporations make a lot of money? Actually, it is. They were always well paid compared with the average worker, but there is simply no comparison between what executives got a generation ago and what they are paid today.
>
> Over the past 30 years most people have seen only modest salary increases: the average annual salary in America, expressed in 1998 dollars (that is, adjusted for inflation), rose from $32,522 in 1970 to $35,864 in 1999. That's about a 10 percent increase over 29 years — progress, but not much. Over the same period, however, according to *Fortune* magazine, the average real annual compensation of the top 100 C.E.O.'s went from $1.3 million — 39 times the pay of an average worker — to $37.5 million, more than 1,000 times the pay of ordinary workers.
>
> The explosion in C.E.O. pay over the past 30 years is an amazing story in its own right, and an important one. But it is only the most spectacular indicator of a broader story, the reconcentration of income and wealth in the U.S. The rich have always been different from you and me, but they are far more different now than they were not long ago — indeed, they are as different now as they were when F. Scott Fitzgerald made his famous remark.
>
> — Paul Krugman, "For Richer"

rhetorical situations   genres   processes   strategies   research mla/apa   media/ design   handbook

Krugman is reporting information here, outlining how top business executives' pay has increased over the last thirty years. He is also making an argument, that their pay is far greater than it was not too long ago and that this difference between their income and the average worker's resembles the disparity that characterized the United States right before the Great Depression. (Krugman, writing for a magazine, is also using a style — dashes, contractions, rhetorical questions that he then answers — that strives to be entertaining while it informs and argues.)

Even though our purposes may be many, knowing our primary reason for writing can help us shape that writing and understand how to proceed with it. Our purpose can determine the genre we choose, our audience, even the way we design what we write.

Identify your purpose.   While writing often has many purposes, we usually focus on one. When you get an assignment or see a need to write, ask yourself what the primary purpose of the writing task is: to entertain? to inform? to persuade? to demonstrate your knowledge or your writing ability? What are your own goals? What are your audience's expectations, and do they affect the way you define your purpose?

Thinking about Purpose

- *What do you want your audience to do, think, or feel?* How will they use what you tell them?

- *What does this writing task call on you to do?* Do you need to show that you have mastered certain content or skills? Do you have an assignment that specifies a particular **STRATEGY** or **GENRE** — to compare two things, perhaps, or to argue a position?

- *What are the best ways to achieve your purpose?* What kind of **STANCE** should you take? Should you write in a particular genre? Do you have a choice of **MEDIUM,** and does your text require any special format or **DESIGN** elements?

259 ◆
19 ▲
12–14 ◼
521 ◻

Audience   2

Who will read (or hear) what you are writing? A seemingly obvious but crucially important question. Your audience affects your writing in various ways. Consider a piece of writing as simple as a note left on the kitchen table:

Jon—
Please take the chicken out to thaw,
and don't forget to feed Annye.
Remember: Dr. Wong at 4.
Love,
Mom

On the surface, this brief note is a straightforward reminder to do three things. But in fact it is a complex message filled with compressed information for a specific audience. The writer (Mom) counts on the reader (her son) to know a lot that can be left unsaid. She expects that Jon knows that the chicken is in the freezer and needs to thaw in time to be cooked for dinner; she knows that he knows who Annye is (a pet?), what he or she is fed, and how much; she assumes that Jon knows who (and where) Dr. Wong is. She doesn't need to spell any of that out because she knows what Jon knows and what he needs to know—and in her note she can be brief. She understands her audience. Think how different such a reminder would be were it written to another audience—a babysitter, perhaps, or a friend helping out while Mom is out of town.

What you write, how much you write, how you phrase it, even your choice of **GENRE** (memo, essay, email, note, speech)—all are influenced by the audience you envision. And your audience will interpret your writing according to their expectations and experiences.

9–11

When you are a student, your teachers are most often your audience, so you need to be aware of their expectations and know the conventions (rules, often unstated) for writing in specific academic fields. You may make statements that seem obvious to you, not realizing that your instructors may consider them assertions that must be proved with evidence of one sort or another. Or you may write more or less formally than teachers expect. Understanding your audience's expectations—by asking outright, by reading materials in your field of study, by trial and error—is important to your success as a writer.

This point is worth dwelling on. You are probably reading this text for a writing course. As a student, you will be expected to produce essays with few or no errors. If as part of your job or among friends you correspond using email, you may question such standards; after all, much of the email you get at work or from friends is not grammatically perfect. But in a writing class, the instructor needs to see your best work. Whatever the rhetorical situation, your writing must meet the expectations of your audience.

Identify your audience. Audiences may be defined as *known, multiple,* or *unknown. Known audiences* can include people with whom you're familiar as well as people you don't know personally but whose needs and expectations you do know. You yourself are a known, familiar audience, and you write to and for yourself often. Class notes, to-do lists, reminders, and journals are all written primarily for an audience of one: you. For that reason, they are often in shorthand, full of references and code that you alone understand. Other known, familiar audiences include anyone you actually know—friends, relatives, teachers, classmates—and whose needs and expectations you understand. You can also know what certain readers want and need, even if you've never met them personally, if you write for them within a specific shared context. Such a known audience might include computer gamers who read instructions that you have posted on the Internet for beating a game; you don't know those people, but you know roughly what they know about the game and what they need to know, and you know how to write about it in ways they will understand.

You often have to write for *multiple audiences.* Business memos or reports may be written initially for a supervisor, but he or she may pass them along to others. Grant proposals are a good example: the National Cancer Institute website advises scientists applying for grants to bear in

rhetorical situations   genres   processes   strategies   research mla/apa   media/ design   handbook

mind that the application may have six levels of readers — each, of course, with its own expectations and perspectives. Even writing for a class might involve multiple audiences: your instructor and your classmates.

Unknown audiences can be the most difficult to address since you can't be sure what they know, what they need to know, how they'll react. Such an audience could be your downstairs neighbor, whom you say hello to but with whom you've never had a real conversation. How will she respond to your letter asking her to sponsor you in an upcoming charity walk? Another unknown audience — perhaps surprisingly — might be many of your instructors, who want — and expect! — you to write in ways that are new to you. While you can benefit from analyzing any audience, you need to think most carefully about those you don't know.

Thinking about Audience

- *Whom do you want to reach?* To whom are you writing (or speaking)?

- *What is your audience's background — their education and life experiences?* It may be important for you to know, for example, whether your readers attended college, fought in a war, or have young children.

- *What are their interests?* What do they like? What motivates them? What do they care about?

- *Is there any demographic information that you should keep in mind?* Consider whether race, gender, sexual orientation, disabilities, occupations, religious beliefs, economic status, and so on should affect what or how you write. For example, writers for *Men's Health*, *InStyle*, and *Out* must consider the particular interests of each magazine's readers.

- *What political circumstances may affect their reading?* What attitudes — opinions, special interests, biases — may affect the way your audience reads your piece? Are your readers conservative, liberal, or middle of the road? Politics may take many other forms as well — retirees on a fixed income may object to increased school taxes, so a letter arguing for such an increase would need to appeal to them differently than would a similar letter sent to parents of young children.

- *What does your audience already know — or believe — about your topic? What do you need to tell them? What is the best way to do so?* Those retirees who oppose school taxes already know that taxes are a burden for them; they may need to know why schools are justified in asking for more money every few years when other government organizations do not. A good way to explain this may be with a bar graph showing how good schools with adequate funding benefit property values. Consider which **STRATEGIES** will be effective — narrative, comparison, something else?

259 ◆

- *What's your relationship with your audience, and how does it affect your language and tone?* Do you know them, or not? Are they friends? Colleagues? Mentors? Adversaries? Strangers? Will they likely share your **STANCE?** In general, you need to write more formally when you're addressing readers you don't know, and you may address friends and colleagues more informally than you would a boss.

15–17 ■

- *What does your audience need and expect from you?* Your history professor, for example, may need to know how well you can discuss the economy of the late Middle Ages in order to assess your learning; that same professor may expect you to write a carefully reasoned argument, drawing conclusions from various sources, with a readily identifiable thesis in the first paragraph. Your boss, on the other hand, may need an informal email that briefly lists your sales contacts for the day; she may expect that you list the contacts in the order in which you saw them, that you clearly identify each one, and that you give a few words about how well each contact went. What **GENRE** is most appropriate?

19 ▲

- *What kind of response do you want?* Do you want to persuade readers to do or believe something? To accept your information on a topic? To understand why an experience you once had matters to you?

521 ☐

- *How can you best appeal to your audience?* Is there a particular **MEDIUM** that will best reach them? Are there any **DESIGN** requirements? (Elderly readers may need larger type, for instance.)

Genres are kinds of writing. Letters, profiles, reports, position papers, poems, Web pages, instructions, parodies — even jokes — are genres. Genres have particular conventions for presenting information that help writers write and readers read. For example, here is the beginning of a **PROFILE** ▲ 161–70 of a mechanic who repairs a specific kind of automobile:

> Her business card reads Shirley Barnes, M.D., and she's a doctor, all right—a Metropolitan Doctor. Her passion is the Nash Metropolitan, the little car produced by Austin of England for American Motors between 1954 and 1962. Barnes is a legend among southern California Met lovers—an icon, a beacon, and a font of useful knowledge and freely offered opinions.

A profile offers a written portrait of someone or something that informs and sometimes entertains, often examining its subject from a particular angle — in this case, as a female mechanic who fixes Nash Metropolitans. While the language in this example is informal and lively ("she's a doctor, all right"), the focus is on the subject, Shirley Barnes, "M.D." If this same excerpt were presented as a poem, however, the new genre would change our reading:

> Her business card reads
> Shirley Barnes, M.D.,
> and she's a doctor, all right
> —a Metropolitan Doctor.
> Her passion is the Nash Metropolitan,
> the little car produced by Austin of England
> for American Motors between 1954 and 1962.
> Barnes is a legend
> among southern California Met lovers
> — an icon,

a beacon,
and a font of useful knowledge and
freely offered opinions.

The content and words haven't changed, but the presentation invites us to read not only to learn about Shirley Barnes but also to explore the significance of the words and phrases on each line, to read for deeper meaning and greater appreciation of language. The genre thus determines how we read and how we interpret what we read.

Genres help us write by establishing features for conveying certain kinds of information. They give readers clues about what sort of information they're likely to find and so help them figure out how to read ("Ah! A letter from Brit!" or "Thank goodness! I found the instructions for programming this DVD player"). At the same time, writers sometimes challenge genre conventions, reshaping them as communicative needs and technologies change. For example, computers have enabled us to add visuals to texts that we never before thought to illustrate.

19 ▲ **Identify your genre.** Does your writing situation call for a certain GENRE? A memo? A report? A proposal? A letter? Academic assignments generally specify the genre ("take a position," "analyze the text"), but if the genre isn't clear, ask your instructor.

Thinking about Genre

- **What is your genre, and does it affect what content you can or should include?** Objective information? Researched source material? Your own opinions? Personal experience?

259 ◆
133–42 ▲
- **Does your genre call for any specific STRATEGIES?** Profiles, for example, usually include some narration; LAB REPORTS often explain a process.

171–79 ▲
- **Does your genre require a certain organization?** Most PROPOSALS, for instance, first identify a problem and then offer a solution. Some genres leave room for choice. Business letters delivering good news might be organized differently than those making sales pitches.

- *Does your genre affect your tone?* An abstract of a scholarly paper calls for a different TONE than a memoir. Should your words sound serious and scholarly? Brisk and to the point? Objective? Opinionated? Sometimes your genre affects the way you communicate your STANCE.

13

12–14

- *Does the genre require formal (or informal) language?* A letter to the mother of a friend asking for a summer job in her bookstore calls for more formal language than does an email to the friend thanking him for the lead.

- *Do you have a choice of medium?* Some genres call for print; others for an electronic medium. Sometimes you have a choice: a résumé, for instance, can be mailed (in which case it must be printed), or it may be emailed. Some teachers want reports turned in on paper; others prefer that they be emailed or posted to a class website. If you're not sure what MEDIUM you can use, ask.

521

- *Does your genre have any design requirements?* Some genres call for paragraphs; others require lists. Some require certain kinds of typefaces—you wouldn't use **Impact** for a personal narrative, nor would you likely use DrSeuss for an invitation to Grandma's sixty-fifth birthday party. Different genres call for different DESIGN elements.

521

4 Stance

Whenever you write, you have a certain stance, an attitude toward your topic. The way you express that stance affects the way you come across as a writer and a person. This email from a college student to his father, for example, shows a thoughtful, reasonable stance for a carefully researched argument:

> Hi Dad,
> I'll get right to the point: I'd like to buy a car. I saved over $2500 from working this summer, and I've found three different cars that I can get for under $2000. That'll leave me $400 to cover the insurance. I can park in Lot J, over behind Monte Hall, for $75 for both semesters. And I can earn gas and repair money by upping my hours at the cafeteria. It won't cost you any more, and if I have a car, you won't have to come and pick me up when I want to come home.
> Love,
> Michael

While such a stance can't guarantee that Dad will give permission, it's more likely to produce results than this version:

> Hi Dad,
> I'm buying a car. A guy in my Western Civ course has a cool Chevy he wants to get rid of. I've got $2500 saved from working this summer, it's mine, and I'm going to use it to get some wheels. Mom said you'd blow your top if I did, but I want this car.
> Michael

The writer of the first email respects his reader and offers reasoned arguments and evidence of research to convince him that buying a car is an action that will benefit them both. The writer of the second, by contrast, seems impulsive, ready to buy the first car that comes along, and defiant—he's picking a fight. Each email reflects a certain stance that shows the writer as a certain kind of person dealing with a situation in a certain way and establishing a certain relationship with his audience.

Identify your stance. What is your attitude about your topic? Objective? Critical? Curious? Opinionated? Passionate? Indifferent? Your stance may be affected by your relationship to your **AUDIENCE.** How do you want them to see you? As a colleague sharing information? As a good student show- ■ 5–8 ing what you can do? As an advocate for a position? Often your stance is affected by your **GENRE:** for example, lab reports require an objective, ▲ 19 unemotional stance that emphasizes the content and minimizes the writer's own attitudes. Memoir, by comparison, allows you to reveal your feelings about your topic. Your stance is also affected by your **PURPOSE,** as ■ 3–4 the two letters about cars show. Your stance in a piece written to enter- tain will likely differ from the stance you'd adopt to persuade. As a writer, you communicate your stance through your tone.

Tone is created through the words you use and the way you approach your subject and audience. For example, in an academic essay you would state your position directly—"*America's Next Top Model* reflects the values of American society today"—demonstrating a confident, assertive tone and stance. In contrast, using qualifiers like "might" or "I think" can give your writing a wishy-washy, uncertain tone: "I think *America's Next Top Model* might reflect some of the values of American society today." The following paragraph, from an essay analyzing a text, has a sarcastic tone that might be appropriate for a note to a friend, but that isn't right for an academic essay:

> In "Just Be Nice," Stephen M. Carter complains about a boy who wore his pants too low, showing his underwear. Is that really something peo- ple should worry about? We have wars raging and terrorism happen- ing every day, and he wants to talk about how inconsiderate it is for someone to wear his pants too low? If by that boy pulling his pants up, the world would be a better place and the Iraq War would end, I'm sure everyone would buy a belt.

This writer clearly thinks Carter's example is trivial in comparison with the larger issues of the day, but her sarcastic tone belittles Carter's argument instead of answering it with a serious counterargument. Like every other element of writing, your tone must be appropriate for your rhetorical situation.

Just as you likely alter what you say depending on whether you're speaking to a boss, an instructor, a parent, or a good friend, so you need to make similar adjustments as a writer. It's a question of appropriateness: we behave in certain ways in various social situations, and writing is a social situation. You might sign an email to a friend with an x and an o, but in an email to your supervisor you'll likely sign off with a "Many thanks" or "Regards." To write well, you need to write with integrity, to say what you wish to say; yet you also must understand that in writing, as in speaking, your stance needs to suit your purpose, your relationship to your audience, the way in which you wish your audience to perceive you, and your medium. In writing as in other aspects of life, the Golden Rule applies: "Do unto audiences as you would have them do unto you." Address readers respectfully if you want them to respond to your words with respect.

Thinking about Stance

- *What is your stance, and how can you best present it to achieve your purpose?* If you're writing about something you take very seriously, be sure that your language and even your typeface reflect that seriousness. Make sure your stance is appropriate to your **PURPOSE.**

  3–4 ▪

- *What tone will best convey your stance?* Do you want to be seen as reasonable? Angry? Thoughtful? Gentle? Funny? Ironic? What aspects of your personality do you want to project? Check your writing for words that reflect that tone—and for ones that do not (and revise as necessary).

- *How is your stance likely to be received by your audience?* Your tone and especially your attitude toward your **AUDIENCE** will affect how willing they are to take your argument seriously.

  5–8 ▪

- *Should you openly reveal your stance?* Do you want or need to announce your own perspective on your topic? Will doing so help you reach your audience, or would it be better to make your **ARGUMENT** without saying directly where you're coming from?

  283–99 ◆

In its broadest sense, a *medium* is a go-between: a way for information to be conveyed from one person to another. We communicate through many media, verbal and nonverbal: our bodies (we catch someone's eye, wave, nod), our voices (we whisper, talk, shout, groan), and various technologies, including handwriting, print, telephone, radio, CD, film, and computer.

Each medium has unique characteristics that influence both what and how we communicate. As an example, consider this message: "I haven't told you this before, but I love you." Most of the time, we communicate such a message in person, using the medium of voice (with, presumably, help from eye contact and touch). A phone call will do, though most of us would think it a poor second choice, and a handwritten letter or note would be acceptable, if necessary. Few of us would break such news on a website or during a radio call-in program.

By contrast, imagine whispering the following sentence in a darkened room: "By the last decades of the nineteenth century, the territorial expansion of the United States had left almost all Indians confined to reservations." That sentence starts a chapter in a history textbook, and it would be strange indeed to whisper it into someone's ear. It is available in the medium of print, in the textbook, but it may also be read on a website, in promotional material for the book, or on a PowerPoint slide accompanying an oral presentation. Each medium has different uses and takes different forms, and each has distinctive characteristics. As you can see, we can choose various media depending on our purpose and audience. *The Norton Field Guide* focuses mostly on three media: **PRINT**, **SPOKEN**, and **ELECTRONIC**.

523–33
534–45
546–56

Because we now do most of our writing on computers, we are increasingly expected to pay close attention to the look of the material we write. No matter the medium, a text's *design* affects the way it is received and understood. A typed letter on official letterhead sends a different message than the same letter handwritten on pastel stationery, whatever the words on the page. Classic type sends a different message than *flowery italics*. Some genres and media (and audiences) demand **PHOTOS, DIAGRAMS,** color. Some information is easier to explain—and read—in the form of a **PIE CHART** or a **BAR GRAPH** than in the form of a paragraph. Some reports and documents are so long and complex that they need to be divided into sections, which are then best labeled with **HEADINGS.** Those are some of the elements to consider when you are thinking about how to design what you write.

528–32

526–28

Identify your media and design needs.   Does your writing situation call for a certain medium and design? A printed essay? An oral report with visual aids? A website? Academic assignments often assume a particular medium and design, but if you're unsure about your options or the degree of flexibility you have, check with your instructor.

Thinking about Media

523–33
534–45
546–56

- *What medium are you using—* **PRINT? SPOKEN? ELECTRONIC?**—*and how does it affect the way you will write your text?* A printed résumé is usually no more than one page long; a scannable résumé sent via email has no length limits. An oral presentation should contain detailed information; accompanying PowerPoint slides should provide only an outline.

259

- *Does your medium affect your organization and* **STRATEGIES?** Long paragraphs are fine on paper but don't work well on the Web. On PowerPoint slides, phrases or key words work better than sentences. In print, you need to define unfamiliar terms; on the Web, you can sometimes just add a link to a definition found elsewhere.

- *How does your medium affect your language?* Some print documents require a more formal voice than spoken media; email often invites greater informality.

- *Should you use a combination of media?* Should you include audio or video in Web text? Do you need PowerPoint slides, handouts, or other visuals to accompany an oral presentation?

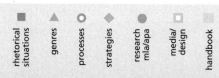

■ rhetorical situations　▲ genres　○ processes　◆ strategies　● research mla/apa　□ media/design　▨ handbook

Thinking about Design

- *What's the appropriate look for your* RHETORICAL SITUATION? Should your text look serious? Whimsical? Personal? Something else? What design elements will suit your audience, purpose, genre, and medium?

1

- *Does your text have any elements that need to be designed?* Is there any information you would like to highlight by putting it in a box? Are there any key terms that should be boldfaced?

- *What typeface(s) are appropriate* to your audience, purpose, genre, and medium?

- *Are you including any illustrations?* Should you? Is there any information in your text that would be easier to understand as a chart or graph? Will your AUDIENCE expect or need any?

5–8

- *Should you include headings?* Would they help you organize your materials and help readers follow the text? Does your GENRE require them?

9–11

part 2

Genres

When we make a shopping list, we automatically write each item we need in a single column. When we email a friend, we begin with a salutation: "Hi, Brian." Whether we are writing a letter, a résumé, a lab report, or a proposal, we know generally what it should contain and what it should look like because we are familiar with each of those genres. Genres are kinds of writing, and texts in any given genre share goals and features—a proposal, for instance, generally starts out by identifying a problem and then suggests a certain solution. The chapters in this part provide guidelines for writing in fifteen common academic genres. First come detailed chapters on four genres often assigned in writing classes: LITERACY NARRATIVES, essays ANALYZING TEXTS, REPORTS, and ARGUMENTS, followed by brief chapters on TEN OTHER GENRES and one on MIXING GENRES.

Genres

Writing a Literacy Narrative   6

Narratives are stories, and we read and tell them for many different purposes. Parents read their children bedtime stories as an evening ritual. Preachers base their Sunday sermons on Bible stories to teach lessons about moral behavior. Grandparents tell how things used to be (sometimes the same stories year after year). Schoolchildren tell teachers that their dog ate their homework. College applicants write about significant moments in their lives. Writing students are often called upon to compose literacy narratives to explore their experiences with reading and writing. This chapter provides detailed guidelines for writing a literacy narrative. We'll begin with three good examples.

MARJORIE AGOSÍN

Always Living in Spanish: Recovering the Familiar, through Language

Marjorie Agosín, a Spanish professor at Wellesley College, wrote this literacy narrative for Poets & Writers *magazine in 1999. Originally written in Spanish, it tells of Agosín's Chilean childhood and her continuing connection to the Spanish language.*

> In the evenings in the northern hemisphere, I repeat the ancient ritual that I observed as a child in the southern hemisphere: going out while the night is still warm and trying to recognize the stars as it begins to grow dark silently. In the sky of my country, Chile, that long and wide stretch of land that the poets blessed and dictators abused, I could eas-

rhetorical situations

genres

processes

strategies

research mla/apa

media/ design

handbook

ily name the stars: the three Marias, the Southern Cross, and the three Lilies, names of beloved and courageous women.

But here in the United States, where I have lived since I was a young girl, the solitude of exile makes me feel that so little is mine, that not even the sky has the same constellations, the trees and the fauna the same names or sounds, or the rubbish the same smell. How does one recover the familiar? How does one name the unfamiliar? How can one be another or live in a foreign language? These are the dilemmas of one who writes in Spanish and lives in translation.

Since my earliest childhood in Chile I lived with the tempos and the melodies of a multiplicity of tongues: German, Yiddish, Russian, Turkish, and many Latin songs. Because everyone was from somewhere else, my relatives laughed, sang, and fought in a Babylon of languages. Spanish was reserved for matters of extreme seriousness, for commercial transactions, or for illnesses, but everyone's mother tongue was always associated with the memory of spaces inhabited in the past: the shtetl, the flowering and vast Vienna avenues, the minarets of Turkey, and the Ladino whispers of Toledo. When my paternal grandmother sang old songs in Turkish, her voice and body assumed the passion of one who was there in the city of Istanbul, gazing by turns toward the west and the east.

Destiny and the always ambiguous nature of history continued my family's enforced migration, and because of it I, too, became one who had to live and speak in translation. The disappearances, torture, and clandestine deaths in my country in the early seventies drove us to the United States, that other America that looked with suspicion at those who did not speak English and especially those who came from the supposedly uncivilized regions of Latin America. I had left a dangerous place that was my home, only to arrive in a dangerous place that was not: a high school in the small town of Athens, Georgia, where my poor English and my accent were the cause of ridicule and insult. The only way I could recover my usurped country and my Chilean childhood was by continuing to write in Spanish, the same way my grandparents had sung in their own tongues in diasporic sites.

5   The new and learned English language did not fit with the visceral emotions and themes that my poetry contained, but by writing in Spanish I could recover fragrances, spoken rhythms, and the passion of my own identity. Daily I felt the need to translate myself for the

strangers living all around me, to tell them why we were in Georgia, why we are different, why we had fled, why my accent was so thick, and why I did not look Hispanic. Only at night, writing poems in Spanish, could I return to my senses, and soothe my own sorrow over what I had left behind.

This is how I became a Chilean poet who wrote in Spanish and lived in the southern United States. And then, one day, a poem of mine was translated and published in the English language. Finally, for the first time since I had left Chile, I felt I didn't have to explain myself. My poem, expressed in another language, spoke for itself . . . and for me.

Sometimes the austere sounds of English help me bear the solitude of knowing that I am foreign and so far away from those about whom I write. I must admit I would like more opportunities to read in Spanish to people whose language and culture is also mine, to join in our common heritage and in the feast of our sounds. I would also like readers of English to understand the beauty of the spoken word in Spanish, that constant flow of oxytonic and paraoxytonic syllables (*Vérde qué té quiéro vérde*),* the joy of writing — of dancing — in another language. I believe that many exiles share the unresolvable torment of not being able to live in the language of their childhood.

I miss that undulating and sensuous language of mine, those baroque descriptions, the sense of being and feeling that Spanish gives me. It is perhaps for this reason that I have chosen and will always choose to write in Spanish. Nothing else from my childhood world remains. My country seems to be frozen in gestures of silence and oblivion. My relatives have died, and I have grown up not knowing a young generation of cousins and nieces and nephews. Many of my friends were disappeared, others were tortured, and the most fortunate, like me, became guardians of memory. For us, to write in Spanish is to always be in active pursuit of memory. I seek to recapture a world lost to me on that sorrowful afternoon when the blue electric sky and the

---

*"*Vérde qué té quiéro vérde*" ("Green, how I want you, green") is the opening line of a famous Spanish poem that demonstrates the interplay of words with the main stress on the final syllable (oxytonic) and those with the main stress on next-to-last syllable (paroxytonic) in Spanish. [Editor's note]

Andean cordillera bade me farewell. On that, my last Chilean day, I carried under my arm my innocence recorded in a little blue notebook I kept even then. Gradually that diary filled with memoranda, poems written in free verse, descriptions of dreams and of the thresholds of my house surrounded by cherry trees and gardenias. To write in Spanish is for me a gesture of survival. And because of translation, my memory has now become a part of the memory of many others.

Translators are not traitors, as the proverb says, but rather splendid friends in this great human community of language.

Agosín's narrative uses vivid detail to bring her childhood in Chile to life for her readers. Her love for her homeland and its people is clear, as is the significance of her narrative—with her childhood home gone, to write in Spanish is a "gesture of survival."

RICHARD BULLOCK

How I Learned about the Power of Writing

I wrote this literacy narrative, about my own experience learning to read, as a model for my students in a first-year writing course.

When I was little, my grandmother and grandfather lived with us in a big house on a busy street in Willoughby, Ohio. My grandmother spent a lot of time reading to me. She mostly read the standards, like *The Little Engine That Could,* over and over and over again. She also let me help her plant African violets (I stood on a chair in her kitchen, carefully placing fuzzy violet leaves into small pots of soil) and taught me to tell time (again in her kitchen, where I watched the minute hand move slowly around the dial and tried in vain to see the hour hand move). All that attention and time spent studying the pages as Grandma read them again and again led me to start reading when I was around three years old.

My family was blue-collar, working-class, and—my grandmother excepted—not very interested in books or reading. But my parents took pride in my achievement and told stories about my precocious literacy,

such as the time at a restaurant when the waitress bent over as I sat in my booster chair and asked, "What would you like, little boy?" I'm told I gave her a withering look and said, "I'd like to see a menu."

There was a more serious aspect to reading so young, however. At that time the murder trial of Dr. Sam Sheppard, a physician whose wife had been bludgeoned to death in their house, was the focus of lurid coverage in the Cleveland newspapers. Daily news stories recounted the grisly details of both the murder and the trial testimony, in which Sheppard maintained his innocence. (The story would serve as the inspiration for both *The Fugitive* TV series and the Harrison Ford movie of the same name.) Apparently I would get up early in the morning, climb over the side of my crib, go downstairs and fetch the paper, take it back upstairs to my crib, and be found reading about the trial when my parents got up. They learned that they had to beat me to the paper in the morning and remove the offending sections before my youthful eyes could see them.

The story of the Sheppard murder had a profound effect on me: it demonstrated the power of writing, for if my parents were so concerned that I not see certain things in print, those things must have had great importance. At the same time, adults' amazement that I could read was itself an inducement to continue: like any three-year-old, I liked attention, and if reading menus and the *Plain Dealer* would do it, well then, I'd keep reading.

As I got older, I also came to realize the great gift my grandmother had given me. While part of her motivation for spending so much time with me was undoubtedly to keep me entertained in a house isolated from other children at a time when I was too young for nursery school, another part of her motivation was a desire to shape me in a certain way. As the middle child in a large family in rural West Virginia, my grandmother had received a formal education only through the eighth grade, after which she had come alone to Cleveland to make a life for herself, working as a seamstress while reading the ancient Greeks and Etruscans on her own. She had had hopes that her daughter (my mother) would continue her education as she herself hadn't been able to, but Mom chose instead to marry Dad shortly after graduating from high school, and Dad hadn't even gotten that far — he had dropped out of school three days before graduation. So Grandma decided that I was going to be different, and she took over much of my preschool life to promote the love of learning that she herself had always had. It worked, and at ninety she got to see me graduate from college, the first in our family to do so.

In my literacy narrative, the disconnect between my age and my ability to read provides a frame for several anecdotes. The narrative's significance comes through in the final paragraph, in which I explore the effects of my grandmother's motivation for teaching me.

SHANNON NICHOLS

"Proficiency"

In the following literacy narrative, Shannon Nichols, a student at Wright State University, describes her experience taking the standardized writing proficiency test that high school students in Ohio must pass to graduate. She wrote this essay for a college writing course, where her audience included her classmates and instructor.

The first time I took the ninth-grade proficiency test was in March of eighth grade. The test ultimately determines whether students may receive a high school diploma. After months of preparation and anxiety, the pressure was on. Throughout my elementary and middle school years, I was a strong student, always on the honor roll. I never had a GPA below 3.0. I was smart, and I knew it. That is, until I got the results of the proficiency test.

Although the test was challenging, covering reading, writing, math, and citizenship, I was sure I had passed every part. To my surprise, I did pass every part—except writing. "Writing! Yeah right! How did I manage to fail writing, and by half a point, no less?" I thought to myself in disbelief. Seeing my test results brought tears to my eyes. I honestly could not believe it. To make matters worse, most of my classmates, including some who were barely passing eighth-grade English, passed that part.

Until that time, I loved writing just as much as I loved math. It was one of my strengths. I was good at it, and I enjoyed it. If anything, I

thought I might fail citizenship. How could I have screwed up writing? I surely spelled every word correctly, used good grammar, and even used big words in the proper context. How could I have failed?

Finally I got over it and decided it was no big deal. Surely I would pass the next time. In my honors English class I worked diligently, passing with an A. By October I'd be ready to conquer that writing test. Well, guess what? I failed the test again, again with only 4.5 of the 5 points needed to pass. That time I did cry, and even went to my English teacher, Mrs. Brown, and asked, "How can I get A's in all my English classes but fail the writing part of the proficiency test twice?" She couldn't answer my question. Even my friends and classmates were confused. I felt like a failure. I had disappointed my family and seriously let myself down. Worst of all, I still couldn't figure out what I was doing wrong.

I decided to quit trying so hard. Apparently — I told myself — the 5 people grading the tests didn't have the slightest clue about what constituted good writing. I continued to excel in class and passed the test on the third try. But I never again felt the same love of reading and writing.

This experience showed me just how differently my writing could be judged by various readers. Obviously all my English teachers and many others enjoyed or at least appreciated my writing. A poem I wrote was put on television once. I must have been a pretty good writer. Unfortunately the graders of the ninth-grade proficiency test didn't feel the same, and when students fail the test, the state of Ohio doesn't offer any explanation.

After I failed the test the first time, I began to hate writing, and I started to doubt myself. I doubted my ability and the ideas I wrote about. Failing the second time made things worse, so perhaps to protect myself from my doubts, I stopped taking English seriously. Perhaps because of that lack of seriousness, I earned a 2 on the Advanced Placement English Exam, barely passed the twelfth-grade proficiency test, and was placed in developmental writing in college. I wish I knew why I failed that test because then I might have written what was expected on the second try, maintained my enthusiasm for writing, and continued to do well.

Nichols's narrative focuses on her emotional reaction to failing a test that she should have passed easily. The contrast between her demonstrated writing ability and her repeated failures creates a tension that captures readers' attention. We want to know what will happen to her.

Key Features / Literacy Narratives

A well-told story.   As with most narratives, those about literacy often set up some sort of situation that needs to be resolved. That need for resolution makes readers want to keep reading. We want to know whether Nichols ultimately will pass the proficiency test. Some literacy narratives simply explore the role that reading or writing played at some time in someone's life — assuming, perhaps, that learning to read or write is a challenge to be met.

Vivid detail.   Details can bring a narrative to life for readers by giving them vivid mental images of the sights, sounds, smells, tastes, and textures of the world in which your story takes place. The details you use when describing something can help readers picture places, people, and events; dialogue can help them hear what is being said. We get a picture of Agosín's Chilean childhood when she writes of the "blue electric sky" and her "little blue notebook" in which she described her "house surrounded by cherry trees and gardenias." Similarly, we can picture a little boy standing on a stool planting African violets — and hear a three-year-old's exasperation through his own words: "I'd like to see a menu." Dialogue can help bring a narrative to life.

Some indication of the narrative's significance.   By definition, a literacy narrative tells something the writer remembers about learning to read or write. In addition, the writer needs to make clear why the incident matters to him or her. You may reveal its significance in various ways. Nichols does it when she says she no longer loves to read or write. Agosín points out that she writes in Spanish because "nothing else from my childhood world remains . . . To write in Spanish is for me a gesture of survival." The trick is to avoid tacking onto the end a brief statement about your narrative's significance as if it were a kind of moral of the story. My narrative would be less effective if, instead of discussing my grandmother's background and my graduation, I had simply said, "She taught me to be a lifelong reader."

A GUIDE TO WRITING LITERACY NARRATIVES

Choosing a Topic

In general, it's a good idea to focus on a single event that took place during a relatively brief period of time. For example:

- any early memory about writing or reading that you recall vividly

- someone who taught you to read or write

- a book or other text that has been significant for you in some way

- an event at school that was interesting, humorous, or embarrassing

- a writing or reading task that you found (or still find) especially difficult or challenging

- a memento that represents an important moment in your literacy development (perhaps the start of a LITERACY PORTFOLIO) ○ 257–58

- the origins of your current attitudes about writing or reading

- learning to write instant messages, learning to write email appropriately, learning to construct a website, creating and maintaining a Facebook page

Make a list of possible topics, and then choose one that you think will be interesting to you and to others — and that you're willing to share with others. If several seem promising, try them out on a friend or classmate. Or just choose one and see where it leads; you can switch to another if need be. If you have trouble coming up with a topic, try FREEWRITING, LISTING, CLUSTERING, or LOOPING. ○ 219–22

Considering the Rhetorical Situation

| PURPOSE | Why do you want to tell this story? To share a memory with others? To fulfill an assignment? To teach a lesson? To explore your past learning? Think about the reasons for your choice and how they will shape what you write. | ■ 3–4 |

5–8 **AUDIENCE** Are your readers likely to have had similar experiences? Would they tell similar stories? How much explaining will you have to do to help them understand your narrative? Can you assume that they will share your attitudes toward your story, or will you have to work at making them see your perspective? How much about your life are you willing to share with this audience?

12–14 **STANCE** What attitude do you want to project? Affectionate? Neutral? Critical? Do you wish to be sincere? serious? humorously detached? self-critical? self-effacing? something else? How do you want your readers to see you?

15–17 **MEDIA / DESIGN** Will your narrative be in print? presented orally? on a website? Would photos, charts, or other illustrations help you present your subject? Is there a typeface that conveys the right tone? Do you need headings?

Generating Ideas and Text

Good literacy narratives share certain elements that make them interesting and compelling for readers. Remember that your goals are to tell the story as clearly and vividly as you can and to convey the meaning the incident has for you today. Start by writing out what you remember about the setting and those involved, perhaps trying out some of the methods in the chapter on **GENERATING IDEAS AND TEXT.** You may also want to **INTERVIEW** 219–25 394–95 a teacher or parent who figures in your narrative.

Describe the setting. Where does your narrative take place? List the places where your story unfolds. For each place, write informally for a few minutes, **DESCRIBING** what you remember: 324–32

- **What do you see?** If you're inside, what color are the walls? What's hanging on them? What can you see out any windows? What else do you see? Books? Lined paper? Red ink? Are there people? Places to sit? A desk or a table?

- **What do you hear?** A radiator hissing? Leaves rustling? The wind howling? Rain? Someone reading aloud? Shouts? Cheers? Children playing? Music? The zing of an instant message arriving?
- **What do you smell?** Sweat? Perfume? Incense? Food cooking?
- **How and what do you feel?** Nervous? Happy? Cold? Hot? A scratchy wool sweater? Tight shoes? Rough wood on a bench?
- **What do you taste?** Gum? Mints? Graham crackers? Juice? Coffee?

Think about the key people.   Narratives include people whose actions play an important role in the story. In your literacy narrative, you are probably one of those people. A good way to develop your understanding of the people in your narrative is to write about them:

- **Describe each person in a paragraph or so.** What do the people look like? How do they dress? How do they speak? Quickly? Slowly? With an accent? Do they speak clearly, or do they mumble? Do they use any distinctive words or phrases? You might begin by **DESCRIBING** their movements, their posture, their bearing, their facial expressions. Do they have a distinctive scent?

  324–32

- **Recall (or imagine) some characteristic dialogue.** A good way to bring people to life and move a story along is with **DIALOGUE,** to let readers hear them rather than just hearing about them. Try writing six to ten lines of dialogue between two people in your narrative. If you can't remember an actual conversation, make up one that could have happened. (After all, you are telling the story, and you get to decide how it is to be told.) Try to remember (and write down) some of the characteristic words or phrases that the people in your narrative used.

  333–37

Write about "what happened."   At the heart of every good **NARRATIVE** is the answer to the question "What happened?" The action in a literacy narrative may be as dramatic as winning a spelling bee or as subtle as a conversation between two friends; both contain action, movement, or change that the narrative tries to capture for readers. A good story dramatizes the action. Try **SUMMARIZING** the action in your narrative in a paragraph — try to capture what happened. Use active and specific verbs (*pondered*, *shouted*, *laughed*) to describe the action as vividly as possible.

343–51

360–61

Consider the significance of the narrative. You need to make clear the ways in which any event you are writing about is significant for you now. Write a page or so about the meaning it has for you. How did it change or otherwise affect you? What aspects of your life now can you trace to that event? How might your life have been different if this event had not happened or had turned out differently? Why does this story matter to you?

Ways of Organizing a Literacy Narrative

223–24 ◐

Start by **OUTLINING** the main events in your narrative. Then think about how you want to tell the story. Don't assume that the only way to tell your story is just as it happened. That's one way—starting at the beginning of the action and continuing to the end. But you could also start in the middle—or even at the end. Shannon Nichols, for example, could have begun her narrative by telling how she finally passed the proficiency test and then gone back to tell about the times she tried to pass it, even as she was an A student in an honors English class. Several ways of organizing a narrative follow.

[Chronologically, from beginning to end]

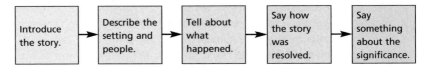

Introduce the story. → Describe the setting and people. → Tell about what happened. → Say how the story was resolved. → Say something about the significance.

[Beginning in the middle]

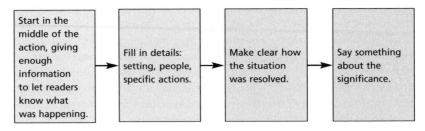

Start in the middle of the action, giving enough information to let readers know what was happening. → Fill in details: setting, people, specific actions. → Make clear how the situation was resolved. → Say something about the significance.

[Beginning at the end]

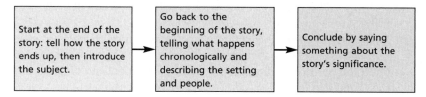

| Start at the end of the story: tell how the story ends up, then introduce the subject. | → | Go back to the beginning of the story, telling what happens chronologically and describing the setting and people. | → | Conclude by saying something about the story's significance. |

Writing Out a Draft

Once you have generated ideas and thought about how you want to organize your narrative, it's time to begin **DRAFTING**. Do this quickly—try to write a complete draft in one sitting, concentrating on getting the story on paper or screen and on putting in as much detail as you can. Some writers find it helpful to work on the beginning or ending first. Others write out the main event first and then draft the beginning and ending.

○ 226–28

Draft a beginning.   A good narrative grabs readers' attention right from the start. Here are some ways of beginning; you can find more advice in the chapter on **BEGINNING AND ENDING.**

◆ 261–71

- *Jump right in.* Sometimes you may want to get to the main action as quickly as possible. Nichols, for example, begins as she takes the ninth-grade proficiency test for the first time.

- *Describe the context.* You may want to provide any background information at the start of your narrative, as I decided to do, beginning by explaining how my grandmother taught me to read.

- *Describe the setting, especially if it's important to the narrative.* Agosín begins by describing the constellations in her native Chile.

Draft an ending.   Think about what you want readers to read last. An effective **ENDING** helps them understand the meaning of your narrative. Here are some possibilities:

◆ 266–70

- *End where your story ends.* It's up to you to decide where a narrative ends. Mine ends several years after it begins, with my graduation from college.

- *Say something about the significance of your narrative.* Nichols observes that she no longer loves to write, for example. The trick is to touch upon the narrative's significance without stating it too directly, like the moral of a fable.

- *Refer back to the beginning.* My narrative ends with my grandmother watching me graduate from college; Nichols ends by contemplating the negative effects of failing the proficiency test.

- *End on a surprising note.* Agosín catches our attention when she tells us of the deaths and disappearances of her friends and relatives.

272–73 ◆ **Come up with a title.**   A good **TITLE** indicates something about the subject of your narrative—and makes readers want to take a look. Nichols's title states her subject, "Proficiency," but she also puts the word in quotes, calling it into question in a way that might make readers wonder—and read on. I focus on the significance of my narrative: "How I Learned about the Power of Writing." Agosín makes her title an expression of her sense of identity: "Always Living in Spanish."

Considering Matters of Design

You'll probably write your narrative in paragraph form, but think about the information you're presenting and how you can design it to enhance your story and appeal to your audience.

524–25 ☐ - What would be an appropriate **TYPEFACE**? Something serious, like Times Roman? Something whimsical, like *Comic Sans*? Something else?

526–27 ☐ - Would it help your readers if you added **HEADINGS** in order to divide your narrative into shorter sections?

528–32 ☐ - Would photographs or other **VISUALS** show details better than you can describe them with words alone? If you're writing about learning to

rhetorical situations   genres   processes   strategies   research mla/apa   media/ design   handbook

read, for example, you might scan in an image of one of the first books you read in order to help readers picture it. Or if your topic is learning to write, you could include something you wrote.

Getting Response and Revising

The following questions can help you study your draft with a critical eye. **GETTING RESPONSE** from others is always good, and these questions can guide their reading, too. Make sure they know your purpose and audience.

235–36

- Do the **TITLE** and first few sentences make readers want to read on? If not, how else might you **BEGIN**?

272–73
261–66

- Does the narrative move from beginning to end clearly? Does it flow, and are there effective **TRANSITIONS**? Does the narrative get sidetracked at any point?

277

- Is anything confusing?

- Is there enough detail, and is it interesting? Is there enough information about the setting and the people? Can readers picture the characters and sense what they're like as people? Would it help to add some **DIALOGUE,** so that readers can "hear" them? Will they be able to imagine the setting?

333–37

- Have you made the situation meaningful enough to make readers wonder and care about what will happen?

- Do you narrate any actions clearly? vividly? Does the action keep readers engaged?

- Is the significance of the narrative clear?

- Is the **ENDING** satisfying? What are readers left thinking?

266–70

The preceding questions should identify aspects of your narrative you need to work on. When it's time to **REVISE,** make sure your text appeals to your audience and achieves your purpose as successfully as possible.

236–39

Editing and Proofreading

242–45 ○
Readers equate correctness with competence. Once you've revised your draft, follow these guidelines for **EDITING** a narrative:

343–51 ◆
277 ◆
- Make sure events are **NARRATED** in a clear order and include appropriate time markers, **TRANSITIONS,** and summary phrases to link the parts and show the passing of time.

HB-33 ▨
- Be careful that **VERB TENSES ARE CONSISTENT** throughout. If you write your narrative in the past tense ("he *taught* me how to use a computer"), be careful not to switch to the present ("So I *look* at him and *say* . . . ") along the way.

HB-12–14 ▨
- Check to see that **VERB TENSES** correctly indicate when an action took place. If one action took place before another action in the past, for example, you should use the past perfect tense: "I forgot to dot my i's, a mistake I *had made* many times."

333–37 ◆
- Punctuate **DIALOGUE** correctly. Whenever someone speaks, surround the speech with quotation marks ("No way," I said.). Periods and commas go inside quotation marks; exclamation points and question marks go inside if they're part of the quotation, outside if they're part of the whole sentence:

  INSIDE   Opening the door, Ms. Cordell announced, "Pop quiz!"
  OUTSIDE   It wasn't my intention to announce "I hate to read"!

245–46 ○
- **PROOFREAD** your finished narrative carefully before turning it in.

Taking Stock of Your Work

- How well do you think you told the story?
- What did you do especially well?
- What could still be improved?
- How did you go about coming up with ideas and generating text?

- How did you go about drafting your narrative?
- Did you use photographs or any other graphics? What did they add? Can you think of graphics you might have used?
- How did others' responses influence your writing?
- What would you do differently next time?

IF YOU NEED MORE HELP

See also **MEMOIRS** (Chapter 15), a kind of narrative that focuses more generally on a significant event from your past, and **REFLECTIONS** (Chapter 18), a kind of essay for thinking about a topic in writing. See Chapter 28 if you are required to submit your literacy narrative as part of a writing **PORTFOLIO.**

▲ 153–60
180–88

● 247–58

7 Analyzing a Text

Both *Time* and *U.S. News and World Report* cover the same events, but each magazine interprets them differently. All toothpaste ads claim to make teeth "the whitest." Saddam Hussein was supporting terrorists—or he wasn't, depending on which politician is speaking. Those are but three examples that demonstrate why we need to be careful, analytical readers of magazines and newspapers, ads, political documents, even textbooks. Not only does text convey information, but it also influences how and what we think. We need to read, then, to understand not only what texts say but also how they say it. Because understanding how texts say what they say is so crucial, assignments in many disciplines ask you to analyze texts. You may be asked to analyze sensory imagery in James Joyce's story "Araby" for a literature class or, for an art history course, to analyze the use of color and space in Edward Hopper's painting *Nighthawks*. In a statistics course, you might analyze a set of data—a numerical text—to find the standard deviation from the mean. This chapter offers detailed guidelines for writing an essay that closely examines a text both for what it says and for how it does so, with the goal of demonstrating for readers how—and how well—the text achieves its effects. We'll begin with three good examples.

GINIA BELLAFANTE

In the 24 World, Family Is the Main Casualty

In this 2007 analysis of the TV show 24, Ginia Bellafante, a reporter at the New York Times, explores the show's depiction of family and relationships.

The frenetic, labyrinthine, exhausting counterterrorism drama *24* concludes its sixth year on Monday night with its ratings slipping and its

fans in revolt. With each season of the series transpiring over a single day, this one, detractors lament, has felt like 70. The producers themselves have acknowledged the challenges of maintaining the story line's intensity and focus. Recently in his blog on *24*, the humorist Dave Barry expressed a wish for Congressional hearings into the show's crimes against narrative cohesiveness.

Until two weeks ago I had included myself among the dissenters, complaining that digressions and strange forays into cold war nostalgia had subsumed the larger plot and proclaiming, to the walls in my living room, that *24* ought to become *12* — or *8* or *6*. But during Hour 21, Agent Jack Bauer's father, Phillip (played by the gifted James Cromwell), re-emerged to subject members of his family to renewed acts of twisted venality. And the effect was intense and chilling, a reminder that *24* has always sustained its tension by operating in two genres, not one, deploying the conventions of domestic horror in the language of an apocalyptic thriller.

Since it first appeared in 2001, *24* has successfully woven the terrors of intimate life through its narrative of an America facing potential annihilation. Parents kill children. Husbands abuse wives. Sisters try to kill sisters. Wives fire husbands — or stab them, as Martha Logan, ex-wife of Charles Logan, the former president, did earlier this year, plunging a knife into his shoulder as recompense for his treacheries, both personal and civic.

Discussions of *24* have long concentrated on its depiction of torture — elaborate to the point of parody this season — as the source of its controversy. But it is the show's treatment of family as an impossible and even dangerous illusion that truly challenges our complacency. The anxious gloom of watching *24* comes not from wondering whether the world will blow up (obviously it won't; Jack Bauer — played by Kiefer Sutherland — is protection against all that) but from knowing that the bonds that hold people together will eventually be imperiled or destroyed, perfidy and neglect so often the forces.

The introduction of Phillip Bauer early in the season quickly established that Jack did not inherit his rectitude from his father. Shortly after he appeared, Phillip suffocated his son Graem, forced his daughter-in-law to endanger the lives of federal agents, and threatened Jack. When he reappeared, weeks later, Phillip was kidnapping his grandson, Josh, for the second time in a single day.

Parenthood, untouchably sacrosanct in so much of our culture, is 5
on *24* a grotesquely compromised institution. During Season 4 we witnessed the show's defense secretary subject his son to torture for refus-
ing to divulge information that might help track down a terrorist. At
the same time we observed the director of the Counter Terrorist Unit
labor to thwart a nuclear attack despite the deterioration of her men-
tally disturbed daughter in a nearby room.

That each child was portrayed as a petulant nuisance made it easier to see that the country's security imperatives had to come first. The
perverse brilliance of *24* lies, at least in some part, in its capacity to
elicit our sympathies for heinous miscalculations of judgment. In the
end we feel less for the troubled girl than we do for her beleaguered
mother, who after all has been making sound decisions every step of
the way.

The most enduring relationships on *24* are not between parents
and children, boyfriends and girlfriends, spouses or siblings, but between
individuals and their governments and causes. And in this way the show
seems committed not to the politics of the left or right, but to a kind
of quasi-totalitarianism in which patriotism takes precedence over everything else and private life is eroded, undermined, demeaned. Privacy
isn't even a viable concept in a world in which there is no taco stand,
phone booth, laptop, or S.U.V. that isn't immediately accessible to the
advanced surveillance systems of the ever-vigilant Counter Terrorist Unit.

Human connection is forever suffocated. Totalitarianism, Hannah
Arendt, wrote, "bases itself on loneliness, on the experience of not
belonging to the world at all." And above and beyond everything else,
the universe of *24* is a very lonely place.

Friendship can barely be said to exist beyond the parameters of
bureaucracy: the offices of the Los Angeles division of the unit and the
halls of the White House. And when men and women become involved,
it is not only with each other but also with the greater American purpose. Ordinary social intercourse simply doesn't exist. The idea that two
people might sit down for a cup of coffee is as contrary to the show's
internal logic as the idea that polar bears might someday learn to sing.

On *24* the choice to forfeit all that and respond to your country's 10
call is never the wrong choice, no matter how regrettable the personal
consequences. Five seasons ago Jack was a married man who played
chess with his teenage daughter. Since then he has lost his wife (at the

rhetorical situations ■

genres ▲

processes ○

strategies ◆

research mla/apa ●

media/ design □

handbook ▨

hands of a unit mole), his daughter (to his own emotional inattention), and various girlfriends to his unfailing devotion to eradicating the state's enemies, whatever the cost. He has killed colleagues who have impeded his pursuit of justice, lost his identity, and acquired a heroin addiction combating drug lords. The price of a safe world is considerable, *24* tells us: love and the rest of it mortgaged for some other lifetime.

Bellafante analyzes the depiction of relationships on 24 and concludes that on the show, "human connection is forever suffocated." She cites several plotlines and events to support this interpretation, painting a bleak picture of the show's family relationships, and suggests that the show is making a larger statement about what we sacrifice for duty.

WILLIAM SAFIRE

A Spirit Reborn

Just before the first anniversary of September 11, 2001, New York Times columnist William Safire analyzed the Gettysburg Address for what it meant to Americans after 9/11.

Abraham Lincoln's words at the dedication of the Gettysburg cemetery will be the speech repeated at the commemoration of September 11 by the governor of New York and by countless other speakers across the nation.

The lips of many listeners will silently form many of the famous phrases. "Four score and seven years ago" — a sonorous way of recalling the founding of the nation eighty-seven years before he spoke — is a phrase many now recite by rote, as is "the last full measure of devotion."

But the selection of this poetic political sermon as the oratorical centerpiece of our observance need not be only an exercise in historical evocation, nonpolitical correctness, and patriotic solemnity. What makes this particular speech so relevant for repetition on this first anniversary of the worst bloodbath on our territory since Antietam Creek's waters ran red is this: now, as then, a national spirit rose from the ashes of destruction.

Here is how to listen to Lincoln's all-too-familiar speech with new ears.

In those 236 words, you will hear the word *dedicate* five times. The first two times refer to the nation's dedication to two ideals mentioned in the Declaration of Independence, the original ideal of "liberty" and the ideal that became central to the Civil War: "that all men are created equal."

The third, or middle, *dedication* is directed to the specific consecration of the site of the battle of Gettysburg: "to dedicate a portion of that field as a final resting place." The fourth and fifth times Lincoln repeated *dedicate* reaffirmed those dual ideals for which the dead being honored fought: "to the unfinished work" and then "to the great task remaining before us" of securing freedom and equality.

Those five pillars of dedication rested on a fundament of religious metaphor. From a president not known for his piety—indeed, often criticized for his supposed lack of faith—came a speech rooted in the theme of national resurrection. The speech is grounded in conception, birth, death, and rebirth.

Consider the barrage of images of birth in the opening sentence. The nation was "conceived in liberty" and "brought forth"—that is, delivered into life—by "our fathers" with all "created" equal. (In the nineteenth century, both "men" and "fathers" were taken to embrace women and mothers.) The nation was born.

Then, in the middle dedication, to those who sacrificed themselves, come images of death: "final resting place" and "brave men, living and dead."

Finally, the nation's spirit rises from this scene of death: "that this nation, under God, shall have a new birth of freedom." Conception, birth, death, rebirth. The nation, purified in this fiery trial of war, is resurrected. Through the sacrifice of its sons, the sundered nation would be reborn as one.

An irreverent aside: All speechwriters stand on the shoulders of orators past. Lincoln's memorable conclusion was taken from a fine oration by the Reverend Theodore Parker at an 1850 Boston antislavery convention. That social reformer defined the transcendental "idea of freedom" to be "a government of all the people, by all the people, for all the people."

rhetorical situations genres processes strategies research mla/apa media/ design handbook

Lincoln, thirteen years later, dropped the "alls" and made the phrase his own. (A little judicious borrowing by presidents from previous orators shall not perish from the earth.) In delivering that final note, the Union's defender is said to have thrice stressed the noun "people" rather than the prepositions "of," "by," and "for." What is to be emphasized is not rhetorical rhythm but the reminder that our government's legitimacy springs from America's citizens; the people, not the rulers, are sovereign. Not all nations have yet grasped that.

Do not listen on September 11 only to Lincoln's famous words and comforting cadences. Think about how Lincoln's message encompasses but goes beyond paying "fitting and proper" respect to the dead and the bereaved. His sermon at Gettysburg reminds "us the living" of our "unfinished work" and "the great task remaining before us" — to resolve that this generation's response to the deaths of thousands of our people leads to "a new birth of freedom."

Safire's analysis focuses on patterns of specific words and images — he identifies dedicate *as a key term and analyzes how its meaning changes and develops each time it is used. He shows how Lincoln shaped his text around images of birth, death, and resurrection to assert that although a nation's soldiers die, their deaths permit the rebirth of the nation. In doing so, Safire builds an argument linking Lincoln's words to current circumstances.*

DOUG LANTRY

"Stay Sweet As You Are": An Analysis of Change and Continuity in Advertising Aimed at Women

Doug Lantry wrote this analysis of three print ads for a first-year writing course at the University of Akron.

Magazine advertisements aimed at American women have a long history of pushing things like makeup, mouthwash, soap, and other products that reinforce men's roles in women's lives. The concept of personal hygiene has been used to convey the message that "catching" a man or becoming a wife is a woman's ultimate goal, and in advertisements from the 1920s, 1930s, and 1950s this theme can be traced through verbal and visual content.

For example, a 1922 ad for Resinol soap urges women to "make that dream come true" by using Resinol (see Fig. 1). The dream is marriage. The premise is that a bad complexion will prevent marriage even if a woman has attributes like wit and grace, which the ad identifies as positive. Blotchy skin, the ad says, will undermine all that. The word *repellent* is used for emphasis and appears in the same sentence as the words *neglected* and *humiliated*, equating the look of the skin with the state of the person within. Of course, Resinol can remedy the condition, and a paragraph of redemption follows the paragraph about being repellent. A treatment program is suggested, and the look and feel of "velvety" skin are only "the first happy effects," with eventual marriage (fulfillment) implied as the ultimate result of using Resinol soap.

Visual content supports the mostly verbal ad. In a darkened room, a lone woman peers dreamily into a fireplace, where she sees an apparition of herself as a bride in a white veil, being fulfilled as a person by marriage to a handsome man. She lounges in a soft chair, where the glow of the image in the fireplace lights her up and warms her as much as the comforting fire itself. A smaller image shows the woman washing with Resinol, contentedly working her way toward clear skin and marriage over a water-filled basin suggestive of a vessel of holy water. This image is reinforced by her closed eyes and serene look and by the ad's suggestion that "right living" is a source of a good complexion.

A somewhat less innocent ad appeared more than a decade later, in 1934 (see Fig. 2). That ad, for Lux soap, like the one for Resinol, prescribes a daily hygiene regimen, but it differs significantly from the Resinol message in that it never mentions marriage and uses a clear-skinned movie star as proof of Lux's effectiveness. Instead of touting marriage, Lux teaches that "a girl who wants to break hearts simply must have a tea-rose complexion." Romance, not marriage, is the woman's goal, and competition among women is emphasized because "girls who want to make new conquests . . . [are] *sure* to win out!" by using Lux. Lux's pitch is more sophisticated than Resinol's, appealing to a more emancipated woman than that of the early 1920s and offering a kind of evidence based on science and statistics. The text cites "9 out of 10 glamorous Hollywood stars" and scientists who explain that Lux slows aging, but it declines to cite names, except that of Irene

Fig. 1. 1922 Resinol soap ad.

Fig. 2.   1934 Lux soap ad.

Dunne, the ad's star. The unnamed stars and scientists give the ad an
air of untruthfulness, and this sense is deepened by the paradox of the
ad's title: "Girls who know this secret always win out." If Lux is a secret,
why does it appear in a mass-media publication?

Like Resinol, Lux urges women to seek love and fulfillment by   5
enhancing their outward beauty and suggests that clear skin means
having "the charm men can't resist."

The Lux ad's visual content, like Resinol's, supports its verbal message. Several demure views of Irene Dunne emphasize her "pearly-

rhetorical
situations

genres

processes

strategies

research
mla/apa

media/
design

handbook

smooth skin," the top one framed by a large heart shape. In all the photos, Dunne wears a feathery, feminine collar, giving her a birdlike appearance: she is a bird of paradise or an ornament. At the bottom of the ad, we see a happy Dunne being cuddled and admired by a man.

The visual and verbal message is that women should strive, through steps actually numbered in the ad, to attain soft, clear skin and hence charm and hence romance. Not surprisingly, the ad uses the language of battle to describe the effects of clear skin: girls who use Lux will "make new conquests!" and "win out!" Similar themes are developed for a younger audience in a 1954 ad for Listerine mouthwash (see Fig. 3). This time the target is no longer grown women but teenage girls: "If you want to win the boys . . . Stay Sweet As You Are!" Because attracting men would be inappropriate for teenagers, boys are the catch of the day in the Listerine ad. The idea of staying sweet means on the surface that girls should have nice breath, but the youthful context of the ad means that for women to be attractive they must stay young and "stay adorable," preferably with the girlish innocence of a teenager. The consequences of not staying sweet are clear: if you don't use Listerine every morning, every night, and before every date, "you're headed for boredom and loneliness." If you do use Listerine, there are "good times, good friends, and gaiety ahead."

Like Lux, Listerine relies on science as well as sex. With talk of "the bacterial fermentation of proteins," research, and clinical tests, the mouthwash props up its romantic and sexual claims by proclaiming scientific facts. Listerine is "4 times better than any tooth paste," the ad proclaims. "With proof like this, it's easy to see why Listerine belongs in your home."

Visuals contribute to the message, as in the other ads. The central image is a photo of a perky, seemingly innocent teenage girl playing records on a portable phonograph. A vision of midcentury American femininity, she wears a fitted sweater, a scarf tied at the neck (like a wrapped present?), and a full, long skirt. She sits on the floor, her legs hidden by the skirt; she could be a cake decoration. Leaning forward slightly, she looks toward the reader, suggesting by her broad smile and submissive posture that perhaps kissing will follow when she wins the boys with her sweet breath. The record player affirms the ad's teenage target.

The intended consumers in the Resinol, Lux, and Listerine ads are 10 women, and the message of all three ads is that the product will lead

LISTERINE ANTISEPTIC STOPS BAD BREATH
4 times better than any tooth paste

Fig. 3.   1954 Listerine mouthwash ad.

to—and is required for—romantic or matrimonial success. Each ad implies that physical traits are paramount in achieving this success, and the ads' appearance in widely circulated magazines suggests that catching a man (whether or not she marries him) is the ultimate goal of

every American woman. While there is a kind of progress over time, the ads' underlying assumptions remain constant. There is evidence of women's increasing sophistication, illustrated in the later ads' use of science and "objective" proof of the products' effectiveness. Women's development as individuals can also be seen in that marriage is not presupposed in the later ads, and in the case of Lux a single woman has a successful career and apparently has her pick of many partners.

Still, one theme remains constant and may be seen as a continuing debilitating factor in women's struggle for true equality in the world of sex roles: pleasing men is the prerequisite for happiness. Despite apparent advances on other levels, that assumption runs through all three ads and is the main selling point. The consumer of Resinol, Lux, and Listerine is encouraged to objectify herself, to become more physically attractive not for her own sake but for someone else's. The women in all three ads are beautifying themselves because they assume they must "make new conquests," "win the boys," and "make that dream come true."

Lantry summarizes each ad clearly and focuses his analysis on a theme running through all three ads: the concept that to find happiness, a woman must be physically attractive to men. He describes patterns of images and language in all three ads as evidence.

Key Features / Textual Analysis

A summary of the text. Your readers may not know the text you are analyzing, so you need to include it or tell them about it before you can analyze it. Because Safire's text is so well-known, he describes it only briefly as "Abraham Lincoln's words at the dedication of the Gettysburg cemetery." Texts that are not so well-known require a more detailed summary. Lantry includes the texts — and images — he analyzes and also describes them in detail.

Attention to the context. Texts don't exist in isolation: they are influenced by and contribute to ongoing conversations, controversies, or debates, so to understand the text, you need to understand the larger context. Bellafante opens by describing fans' critical response to the sixth season of 24. Safire notes the source of the phrase "of the people, by the people, for the people" and is clearly writing in the context of the United States after 9/11.

A clear interpretation or judgment.　Your goal in analyzing a text is to lead readers through careful examination of the text to some kind of interpretation or reasoned judgment, generally announced clearly in a thesis statement. When you interpret something, you explain what you think it means, as Lantry does when he argues that the consumers of the three beauty products are encouraged to "objectify" themselves. He might instead have chosen to judge the effectiveness of the ads, perhaps noting that they promise the impossible, that no mouthwash, soap, or other product can guarantee romantic "success."

Reasonable support for your conclusions.　Written analysis of a text is generally supported by evidence from the text itself and sometimes from other sources. The writer might support his or her interpretation by quoting words or passages from a written text or referring to images in a visual text. Safire, for example, looks at Lincoln's repetition of the word "dedicate" in the Gettysburg Address as a way of arguing that the speech was still relevant in 2002, on the anniversary of the 9/11 attacks. Lantry examines patterns of both language and images in his analysis of the three ads. Bellafante describes several scenes and plotlines from 24. Note that the support you offer for your interpretation need only be "reasonable" — there is never any one way to interpret something.

A GUIDE TO WRITING TEXTUAL ANALYSES

Choosing a Text to Analyze

Most of the time, you will be assigned a text or a type of text to analyze: a poem in a literature class, the work of a political philosopher in a political science class, a speech in a history or communications course, a painting or sculpture in an art class, a piece of music in a music the-

rhetorical situations

genres

processes

strategies

research mla/apa

media/ design

handbook

ory course. If you must choose a text to analyze, look for one that suits the demands of the assignment—one that is neither too large or complex to analyze thoroughly (a Dickens novel or a Beethoven symphony is probably too big) nor too brief or limited to generate sufficient material (a ten-second TV news brief or a paragraph from *Fast Food Nation* would probably be too small). You might also choose to analyze three or four texts by examining elements common to all. Be sure you understand what the assignment asks you to do, and ask your instructor for clarification if you're not sure.

Considering the Rhetorical Situation

PURPOSE	Why are you analyzing this text? To demonstrate that you understand it? To persuade readers that the text demonstrates a certain point? Or are you using the text as a way to make some other point?	3–4
AUDIENCE	Are your readers likely to know your text? How much detail will you need to supply?	5–8
STANCE	What interests you about your analysis? Why? What do you know or believe about your topic, and how will your own beliefs affect your analysis?	12–14
MEDIA / DESIGN	Are you writing an essay for a class? To be published in a journal or magazine? Something for the Web? If you are analyzing a visual text, you will probably need to include an image of the text.	15–17

Generating Ideas and Text

In analyzing a text, your goal is to understand what it says, how it works, and what it means. To do so, you may find it helpful to follow a certain sequence: read, respond, summarize, analyze, and draw conclusions from your analysis.

Read to see what the text says.   Start by reading carefully, to get a sense of what it says. This means first skimming to **PREVIEW THE TEXT,** rereading for the main ideas, then questioning and **ANNOTATING.**

353
354–55
354

Consider your **INITIAL RESPONSE.** Once you have a sense of what the text says, what do you think? What's your reaction to the argument, the tone, the language, the images? Do you find the text difficult? puzzling? Do you agree with what the writer says? Disagree? Agree *and* disagree? Your reaction to a text can color your analysis, so start by thinking about how you react—and why. Consider both your intellectual and any emotional reactions. Identify places in the text that trigger or account for those reactions. If you think that you have no particular reaction or response, try to articulate why. Whatever your response, think about what accounts for it.

416–17
324–32
223–24

Next, consolidate your understanding of the text by **SUMMARIZING** (or, if it's a visual text, **DESCRIBING**) what it says in your own words. You may find it helpful to **OUTLINE** its main ideas. See, for instance, how Lantry carefully described what a soap ad he was analyzing shows and says. Some of this analysis ended up in his essay.

> Several demure views of Irene Dunne emphasize her "pearly-smooth skin," the top one framed by a large heart shape. In all the photos, Dunne wears a feathery, feminine collar, giving her a birdlike appearance: she is a bird of paradise or an ornament. At the bottom of the ad, we see a happy Dunne being cuddled and admired by a man.

Decide what you want to analyze.   Having read the text carefully, think about what you find most interesting or intriguing, and why. Does the language interest you? The imagery? The structure? The argument? The larger context? Something else? You might begin your analysis by exploring what attracted your notice.

Study how the text works.   Texts are made up of several components— words, sentences, images, even punctuation. Visual texts might be made up of images, lines, angles, color, light and shadow, and sometimes words. All these elements can be used in various ways. To analyze them, look for patterns in the way they're used and try to decide what those patterns

reveal about the text. How do they affect its message? See the sections on **THINKING ABOUT HOW THE TEXT WORKS** and **IDENTIFYING PATTERNS** for specific guidelines on examining patterns this way.

358–60
361–63

Then write a sentence or two describing the patterns you've discovered and how they contribute to what the text says.

Analyze the argument.   Every text makes an argument. Both verbal and visual texts make certain assertions and provide some kind of support for those claims. An important part of understanding any text is to recognize its argument—what the writer or artist wants the audience to believe, feel, or do. Consider the text's purpose and audience, identify its thesis, and decide how convincingly it supports that thesis. See the section on **ANALYZING THE ARGUMENT** for help doing so.

364

Then write a sentence or two summarizing the argument the text makes, along with your reactions to or questions about that argument.

Think about the larger context.   Texts are always part of larger, ongoing conversations. To analyze a text's role in its **LARGER CONTEXT,** you may need to do additional **RESEARCH** to determine where the text was originally published, what else was happening or being discussed at the time the text was published or created, and whether or not the text responded directly to other ideas or arguments.

365–66
373

Then write a sentence or two describing the larger context surrounding the text and how that context affects your understanding of the text.

Consider what you know about the writer or artist.   What you know about the person who created a text can influence your understanding of that text. His or her **CREDENTIALS,** other work, reputation, stance, and beliefs are all useful windows into understanding a text.

401

Then write a sentence or two summarizing what you know about the writer and how that information affects your understanding of the text.

Come up with a thesis.   When you analyze a text, you are basically **ARGUING** that the text should be read in a certain way. Once you've studied the text thoroughly, you need to identify your analytical goal: do you

283–99

want to show that the text has a certain meaning? Uses certain techniques to achieve its purposes? Tries to influence its audience in particular ways? Relates to some larger context in some significant manner? Should be taken seriously—or not? Something else? Come up with a tentative 273–75 **THESIS** to guide your thinking and analyzing—but be aware that your thesis may change as you continue to work.

Ways of Organizing a Textual Analysis

Examine the information you have to see how it supports or complicates your thesis. Look for clusters of related information that you can use to 223–24 structure an **OUTLINE.** Your analysis might be structured in at least two ways. You might, as Safire does, discuss patterns or themes that run through the text. Alternatively, you might analyze each text or section of text separately, as Bellafante and Lantry do. Following are graphic representations of some ways of organizing a textual analysis.

[Thematically]

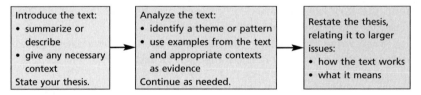

[Part by part, or text by text]

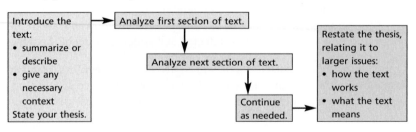

Writing Out a Draft

In drafting your analysis, your goal should be to integrate the various parts into a smoothly flowing, logically organized essay. However, it's easy to get bogged down in the details. Consider writing one section of the analysis first, then another and another until you've drafted the entire middle; then draft your beginning and ending. Alternatively, start by summarizing the text and moving from there to your analysis and then to your ending. However you do it, you need to support your analysis with evidence: from the text itself (as Lantry's analysis of advertisements and Bellafante's analysis of 24 do), or from **RESEARCH** on the larger context of the text (as Safire does).

373

Draft a beginning. The beginning of an essay that analyzes a text generally has several tasks: to introduce or summarize the text for your readers, to offer any necessary information on the larger context, and to present your thesis.

- *Summarize the text.* If the text is one your readers don't know, you need to give a brief **SUMMARY** early on that introduces it to them and shows that you understand it fully. For example, Lantry begins each analysis of a soap advertisement with a brief summary of its content.

416–17

- *Provide a context for your analysis.* If there is a larger context that is significant for your analysis, you might mention it in your introduction. Safire does this when he frames his analysis of the Gettysburg Address as a "centerpiece" of 9/11 commemorations.

- *Introduce a pattern or theme.* If your analysis centers on a certain pattern of textual or contextual elements, you might begin by describing it, as Bellafante does when she writes of 24 as "deploying the conventions of domestic horror in the language of an apocalyptic thriller."

- *State your thesis.* Lantry ends his first paragraph by stating the **THESIS** of his analysis: "The concept of personal hygiene has been used to convey the message that 'catching' a man or becoming a wife is a woman's

273–75

ultimate goal, and in advertisements from the 1920s, 1930s, and 1950s this theme can be traced through verbal and visual content."

261–71 • See Chapter 29 for more advice on **BEGINNING AND ENDING.**

Draft an ending.   Think about what you want your readers to take away from your analysis, and end by getting them to focus on those thoughts.

- *Restate your thesis — and say why it matters.* Lantry, for example, ends by pointing out that "one theme remains constant" in all the ads he analyzes: that "pleasing men is the prerequisite for happiness."

- *Say something about the implications of your findings.* If your analysis has any general implications, you might end by stating them as Safire does: "[Lincoln's] sermon at Gettysburg reminds 'us the living' of our 'unfinished work' and 'the great task remaining before us' — to resolve that this generation's response to the deaths of thousands of our people leads to 'a new birth of freedom.'"

261–71 • See Chapter 29 for more advice on ways of **BEGINNING AND ENDING.**

272–73 **Come up with a title.**   A good **TITLE** indicates something about the subject of your analysis — and makes readers want to see what you have to say about it. Bellafante's title makes her point that 24 depicts family relationships as unsustainable. And Lantry's title uses an eye-catching headline from one ad with a clear statement of his essay's content: " 'Stay Sweet As You Are': An Analysis of Change and Continuity in Advertising Aimed at Women."

Considering Matters of Design

425–27 • If you cite written text as evidence, be sure to set long quotations and **DOCUMENTATION** according to the style you're using.

526–27 • If your essay is lengthy, consider whether **HEADINGS** would make your analysis easier for readers to follow.

- If you're analyzing a visual text, you may need to include a reproduction, along with a caption identifying it.

Getting Response and Revising

The following questions can help you and others study your draft with a critical eye. Make sure that anyone you ask to read and **RESPOND** to your text knows your purpose and audience.

235–36

- Is the **BEGINNING** effective? Does it make a reader want to continue?

261–66

- Does the introduction provide an overview of your analysis and conclusions? Is your **THESIS** clear?

273–75

- Is the text described or **SUMMARIZED** clearly and sufficiently?

416–17

- Is the analysis well organized and easy to follow? Do the parts fit together coherently? Does it read like an essay rather than a collection of separate bits of analysis?

- Does each part of the analysis relate to the thesis?

- Is anything confusing or in need of more explanation?

- Are all **QUOTATIONS** accurate and correctly **DOCUMENTED**?

410–13
425–27

- Is it clear how the analysis leads to the interpretation? Is there adequate **EVIDENCE** to support the interpretation?

287–93

- Does the **ENDING** make clear what your findings mean?

266–70

Then it's time to **REVISE.** Make sure your text appeals to your audience and achieves your purpose as successfully as possible.

236–39

Editing and Proofreading

Readers equate correctness with competence. Once you've revised your draft, edit carefully:

- Is your **THESIS** clearly stated?

273–75

- Check all **QUOTATIONS, PARAPHRASES,** and **SUMMARIES** for accuracy and form. Be sure that each has the required **DOCUMENTATION**.

408–19
425–27

277
- Make sure that your analysis flows clearly from one point to the next and that you use **TRANSITIONS** to help readers move through your text.

245–46
- **PROOFREAD** your finished analysis carefully before turning it in.

Taking Stock of Your Work

Take stock of what you've written and learned by writing out answers to these questions:

- How did you go about analyzing the text? What methods did you use — and which ones were most helpful?
- How did you go about drafting your essay?
- How well did you organize your written analysis? What, if anything, could you do to make it easier to read?
- Did you provide sufficient evidence to support your analysis?
- What did you do especially well?
- What could still be improved?
- Did you use any visuals, and if so, what did they add? Could you have shown the same thing with words?
- How did other readers' responses influence your writing?
- What would you do differently next time?
- Are you pleased with your analysis? What did it teach you about the text you analyzed? Did it make you want to study more works by the same writer or artist?

143–52

247–58
> **IF YOU NEED MORE HELP**
>
> See also Chapter 14 on **LITERARY ANALYSES** if you are analyzing a work of poetry, fiction, or drama. See Chapter 28 if you are required to submit your analysis as part of a writing **PORTFOLIO.**

Reporting Information 8

Many kinds of writing report information. Newspapers report on local and world events; textbooks give information about biology, history, writing; websites provide information about products (jcrew.com), people (johnnydepp.com), institutions (smithsonian.org). We write out a lot of information ourselves, from a note we post on our door saying we've gone to choir practice to an essay we're assigned to write for a history class, reporting what we've learned about the state of U.S. diplomacy in the days before the bombing of Pearl Harbor. This chapter focuses on reports that are written to inform readers about a particular topic. Very often this kind of writing calls for some kind of research: you need to know your subject in order to report on it! When you write to report information, you are the expert. Before offering guidelines for writing essays that inform, we'll begin with three good examples.

SUSAN STELLIN

The Inevitability of Bumps

In this article, which appeared in the New York Times *in 2007, reporter and travel writer Susan Stellin explains the causes of turbulence and its effects on airplanes and passengers.*

> People who fly a lot tend to be nonchalant about the experience — until the plane hits a patch of choppy air. Then, as cups start skidding across tray tables and luggage jostles overhead, even some frequent fliers admit to gripping the armrest with fear.

"Logically and rationally, I know that planes are designed to withstand pretty severe amounts of turbulence before anything bad would happen," said Lawrence Mosselson, who works for a commercial real estate company in Toronto and flies about 50 times a year. "And yet I find that at the first sign of any turbulence, I'm almost paralyzed in my seat."

Industry experts say turbulence rarely causes substantial damage to an aircraft, especially as systems to detect and respond to it have improved. Most of the injuries caused by turbulence, they say, could have been prevented by a decidedly low-tech measure: a seat belt.

"The airplane is designed to take a lot more aggressive maneuvering than we are," said Nora Marshall, chief of aviation survival factors at the National Transportation Safety Board. "We see people getting injured in turbulent events because they're not restrained."

Because of the way the safety board defines an accident—an event involving substantial damage to the aircraft, a death, or a serious injury—the agency has officially investigated 94 accidents in the past decade involving turbulence as a cause or factor. Almost all were classified as accidents because 119 people (mostly flight attendants) suffered serious injuries, ranging from broken bones to a ruptured spleen. Only one of the accidents involved substantial damage to the aircraft.

The safety board attributed one death to turbulence over that time. In 1997, a Japanese passenger on a United Airlines flight from Tokyo to Honolulu was jolted out of her seat when the plane encountered turbulence; she suffered fatal injuries when she hit the armrest on the way back down. According to Ms. Marshall, who participated in the investigation, the woman was not wearing her seat belt, perhaps because the announcement advising passengers to keep seat belts fastened while the seat belt sign was off was not translated into Japanese.

That announcement is required by the Federal Aviation Administration. But Ms. Marshall said most passenger injuries still involve people seated without being buckled in. Including minor injuries, like a cut or a twisted ankle, safety board data indicates that about 50 people a year suffer turbulence-related injuries. But that is only the number of accidents the agency investigates, so the true figure is higher.

Now for the reassuring part: the plane should be able to handle the turbulence.

"People really shouldn't be too concerned about the airplane having difficulty in turbulence — it's designed for turbulence," said Jeff Bland, senior manager for commercial airplane loads and dynamics at Boeing, adding that structural failures because of turbulence are rare.

Although there have been airplane crashes where turbulence was 10 a factor, accidents typically involve multiple factors so it is often impossible to say that turbulence caused a crash. Industry and safety officials agree that such accidents have become unlikely as more has been learned about turbulence.

According to Mr. Bland, aircraft manufacturers have been collecting data since the 1970s to determine the maximum stress that planes experience in turbulence, and they then design aircraft to withstand one and a half times that. In fact, a video clip available on YouTube shows Boeing's test of the wing of a 777; using cables, the wing is bent upward about 24 feet at the tip before it breaks.

Systems to detect and respond to turbulence have also improved, including the technology that automatically adjusts to lateral gusts of wind. And Boeing's 787 aircraft will have a new vertical gust suppression system to minimize the stomach-churning sensation of the plane suddenly dropping midair.

Pilots say those drops are typically no more than 50 feet — not the hundreds of feet many passengers perceive. They also emphasize that avoiding turbulence is mostly a matter of comfort, not safety.

"The mistake that everybody makes is thinking of turbulence as something that's necessarily abnormal or dangerous," said Patrick Smith, a commercial pilot who also writes a column called "Ask the Pilot" for Salon.com. "For lack of a better term, turbulence is normal."

A variety of factors can cause turbulence, which is essentially a dis- 15 turbance in the movement of air. Thunderstorms, the jet stream, and mountains are some of the more common natural culprits, while what is known as wake turbulence is created by another plane. "Clear air turbulence" is the kind that comes up unexpectedly; it is difficult to detect because there is no moisture or particles to reveal the movement of air.

Pilots rely on radar, weather data, and reports from other aircraft to spot turbulence along their route, then can avoid it or at least minimize its effect by slowing down, changing altitude, or shifting course. But even with advances in technology, it is not always possible to predict rough air.

"We still don't have a really good means in the cockpit of seeing turbulence up ahead," said Terry McVenes, a pilot who serves as executive air safety chairman for the Air Line Pilots Association. "Sometimes we can prepare ourselves; other times it does sneak up on us."

Yet that has not deterred some fearful fliers from trying to gauge whether they are going to have a bumpy ride. Peter Murray, a computer network administrator from Lansing, Michigan, created TurbulenceForecast.com to offer nervous fliers like himself a way to view potential turbulence along their flight path.

At the time, he was frequently flying to Baltimore to visit his girlfriend and would sometimes change his flight if it looked as if he would encounter choppy air. "I have never been in anything that could even be considered light turbulence because I could avoid it so well," he said.

But for those unable to avoid a shaky situation, technology also 20 offers more ways to cope. That is why Tim Johnson, a frequent flier who works for a satellite phone company in Washington, posted a question on the forums at Flyertalk.com asking other travelers about their favorite turbulence tunes. (His choice was the "Theme From *Rawhide*" on *The Blues Brothers* soundtrack. Other suggestions included "I Will Survive" by Gloria Gaynor and "Free Fallin' " by Tom Petty.)

"I was on an A340 and it was flying all over the place," Mr. Johnson said, recalling a particularly bumpy flight. "But something about that song had me laughing out loud."

At least these days, he added, "You've got a lot more tools to distract you."

That is, as long as your iPod does not fly out of your hand.

This report focuses on turbulence during airline flights and how it affects passengers. Stellin interviews various authorities — frequent fliers, a researcher at the National Transportation Safety Board, an engineer at Boeing, pilots — and defines several key terms to provide an in-depth account of her subject. Notice how she balances statistical information with anecdotes about passengers' reactions to turbulence.

■ rhetorical situations　▲ genres　○ processes　◆ strategies　● research mla/apa　□ media/ design　▨ handbook

JAMES FALLOWS

Throwing Like a Girl

In the following report, Atlantic Monthly *correspondent James Fallows explores the art of throwing a baseball and the misconceptions that lead to the phrase "throwing like a girl."*

Most people remember the 1994 baseball season for the way it ended — with a strike rather than a World Series. I keep thinking about the way it began. On opening day, April 4, Bill Clinton went to Cleveland and, like many Presidents before him, threw out a ceremonial first pitch. That same day Hillary Rodham Clinton went to Chicago and, like no First Lady before her, also threw out a first ball, at a Cubs game in Wrigley Field.

The next day photos of the Clintons in action appeared in newspapers around the country. Many papers, including the *New York Times* and the *Washington Post*, chose the same two photos to run. The one of Bill Clinton showed him wearing an Indians cap and warm-up jacket. The President, throwing lefty, had turned his shoulders sideways to the plate in preparation for delivery. He was bringing the ball forward from behind his head in a clean-looking throwing action as the photo was snapped. Hillary Clinton was pictured wearing a dark jacket, a scarf, and an oversized Cubs hat. In preparation for her throw she was standing directly facing the plate. A right-hander, she had the elbow of her throwing arm pointed out in front of her. Her forearm was tilted back, toward her shoulder. The ball rested on her upturned palm. As the picture was taken, she was in the middle of an action that can only be described as throwing like a girl.

The phrase "throwing like a girl" has become an embattled and offensive one. Feminists smart at its implication that to do something "like a girl" is to do it the wrong way. Recently, on the heels of the O. J. Simpson case, a book appeared in which the phrase was used to help explain why male athletes, especially football players, were involved in so many assaults against women. Having been trained (like most American boys) to dread the accusation of doing anything "like a girl," athletes were said to grow into the assumption that women were valueless, and natural prey.

I grant the justice of such complaints. I am attuned to the hurt caused by similar broad-brush stereotypes when they apply to groups I belong to — "dancing like a white man," for instance, or "speaking foreign languages like an American," or "thinking like a Washingtonian."

Still, whatever we want to call it, the difference between the two 5 Clintons in what they were doing that day is real, and it is instantly recognizable. And since seeing those photos I have been wondering, Why, exactly, do so many women throw "like a girl"? If the motion were easy to change, presumably a woman as motivated and self-possessed as Hillary Clinton would have changed it. (According to her press secretary, Lisa Caputo, Mrs. Clinton spent the weekend before opening day tossing a ball in the Rose Garden with her husband, for practice.) Presumably, too, the answer to the question cannot be anything quite as simple as, Because they *are* girls.

A surprising number of people think that there is a structural difference between male and female arms or shoulders — in the famous "rotator cuff," perhaps — that dictates different throwing motions. "It's in the shoulder joint," a well-educated woman told me recently. "They're hinged differently." Someday researchers may find evidence to support a biological theory of throwing actions. For now, what you'll hear if you ask an orthopedist, an anatomist, or (especially) the coach of a women's softball team is that there is no structural reason why men and women should throw in different ways. This point will be obvious to any male who grew up around girls who liked to play baseball and became good at it. It should be obvious on a larger scale this summer, in broadcasts of the Olympic Games. This year [1996], for the first time, women's fast-pitch softball teams will compete in the Olympics. Although the pitchers in these games will deliver the ball underhand, viewers will see female shortstops, center fielders, catchers, and so on pegging the ball to one another at speeds few male viewers could match.

Even women's tennis is a constant if indirect reminder that men's and women's shoulders are "hinged" the same way. The serving motion in tennis is like a throw — but more difficult, because it must be coordinated with the toss of the tennis ball. The men in professional tennis serve harder than the women, because they are bigger and stronger. But women pros serve harder than most male amateurs have ever done, and the service motion for good players is the same for men and women

rhetorical situations

genres

processes

strategies

research mla/apa

media/ design

handbook

alike. There is no expectation in college or pro tennis that because of their anatomy female players must "serve like a girl." "I know many women who can throw a lot harder and better than the normal male," says Linda Wells, the coach of the highly successful women's softball team at Arizona State University. "It's not gender that makes the difference in how they throw."

At a superficial level it's easy to tick off the traits of an awkward-looking throw. The fundamental mistake is the one Mrs. Clinton appeared to be making in the photo: trying to throw a ball with your body facing the target, rather than rotating your shoulders and hips ninety degrees away from the target and then swinging them around in order to accelerate the ball. A throw looks bad if your elbow is lower than your shoulder as your arm comes forward (unless you're throwing sidearm). A throw looks really bad if, as the ball leaves your hand, your wrist is "inside your elbow" — that is, your elbow joint is bent in such a way that your forearm angles back toward your body and your wrist is closer to your head than your elbow is. Slow-motion film of big-league pitchers shows that when they release the ball, the throwing arm is fully extended and straight from shoulder to wrist. The combination of these three elements — head-on stance, dropped elbow, and wrist inside the elbow — mechanically dictates a pushing rather than a hurling motion, creating the familiar pattern of "throwing like a girl."

It is surprisingly hard to find in the literature of baseball a deeper explanation of the mechanics of good and bad throws. Tom Seaver's pitching for the Mets and the White Sox got him into the Hall of Fame, but his book *The Art of Pitching* is full of bromides that hardly clarify the process of throwing, even if they might mean something to accomplished pitchers. His chapter "The Absolutes of Pitching Mechanics," for instance, lays out these four unhelpful principles: "Keep the Front Leg Flexible!" "Rub Up the Baseball!" "Hide the Baseball!" "Get It Out, Get It Up!" (The fourth refers to the need to get the ball out of the glove and into the throwing hand in a quick motion.)

A variety of other instructional documents, from *Little League's* [10] *Official How-to-Play Baseball Book* to *Softball for Girls & Women*, mainly reveal the difficulty of finding words to describe a simple motor activity that everyone can recognize. The challenge, I suppose, is like that of writing a manual on how to ride a bike, or how to kiss. Indeed, the most useful description I've found of the mechanics of throwing comes from a man whose specialty is another sport: Vic Braden made his name as a tennis coach, but he has attempted to analyze the physics of a wide variety of sports so that they all will be easier to teach.

Braden says that an effective throw involves connecting a series of links in a "kinetic chain." The kinetic chain, which is Braden's tool for analyzing most sporting activity, operates on a principle like that of crack-the-whip. Momentum builds up in one part of the body. When that part is suddenly stopped, as the end of the "whip" is stopped in crack-the-whip, the momentum is transferred to and concentrated in the next link in the chain. A good throw uses six links of chain, Braden says. The first two links involve the lower body, from feet to waist. The first motion of a throw (after the body has been rotated away from the target) is to rotate the legs and hips back in the direction of the throw, building up momentum as large muscles move body mass. Then those links stop—a pitcher stops turning his hips once they face the plate—and the momentum is transferred to the next link. This is the torso, from waist to shoulders, and since its mass is less than that of the legs, momentum makes it rotate faster than the hips and legs did. The torso stops when it is facing the plate, and the momentum is transferred to the next link—the upper arm. As the upper arm comes past the head, it stops moving forward, and the momentum goes into the final links—the forearm and wrist, which snap forward at tremendous speed.

This may sound arcane and jerkily mechanical, but it makes perfect sense when one sees Braden's slow-mo movies of pitchers in action. And it explains why people do, or don't, learn how to throw. The implication of Braden's analysis is that throwing is a perfectly natural action (millions and millions of people can do it), but not at all innate. A successful throw involves an intricate series of actions coordinated among muscle groups, as each link of the chain is timed to interact with the next. Like bike riding or skating, it can be learned by anyone—male or female. No one starts out knowing how to ride a bike or throw a ball. Everyone has to learn.

Fallows describes in detail what distinguishes a successful baseball throw from an awkward-looking one, concluding with the point that throwing a baseball effectively is a learned activity. He draws on various sources—including a women's softball coach, a tennis coach, and his own observations — to support his claim. Notice how he establishes the context for his essay by focusing on the differences between the stances of the Clintons when photographed throwing a baseball.

JEFFREY DeROVEN

The Greatest Generation: The Great Depression and the American South

The following essay was written in 2001 by a student for a history course at the Trumbull Campus of Kent State University. It was first published in Etude *and* Techne, *a journal of Ohio college writing.*

Tom Brokaw called the folks of the mid-twentieth century the greatest generation. So why is the generation of my grandparents seen as this country's greatest? Perhaps the reason is not what they accomplished but what they endured. Many of the survivors feel people today "don't have the moral character to withstand a depression like that."[1] This paper will explore the Great Depression through the eyes of ordinary Americans in the most impoverished region in the country, the American South, in order to detail how they endured and how the government assisted them in this difficult era.

President Franklin D. Roosevelt (FDR) announced in 1938 that the American South "represented the nation's number one economic problem." He commissioned the National Emergency Council to investigate and report on the challenges facing the region. Though rich in physical and human resources, the southern states lagged behind other parts of the nation in economic development.[2]

Poor education in the South was blamed for much of the problem. Young children attending school became too costly for most families. In the Bland family, "when Lucy got to the sixth grade, we had to stop her because there was too much to do."[3] Overcrowding of schools, particularly in rural areas, lowered the educational standards. The short school terms further reduced effectiveness. As Mrs. Abercrombie recalls, "Me and Jon both went to school for a few months but that wa'n't enough for us to learn anything."[4] Without the proper education, the youth of the South entered the work force unprepared for the challenges before them.

Southern industries did not have the investment capital to turn their resources into commodities. Manufacturers were limited to producing goods in the textile and cigarette industries and relied heavily on the cash crops of cotton and tobacco for the economy. Few facilities existed in the South for research that might lead to the development of new industries. Hampered by low wages, low tax revenue, and a high interest rate, Southerners lacked the economic resources to compete with the vast industrial strength of the North. The National Emergency Council report concluded, "Penalized for being rural, and handicapped in its efforts to industrialize, the economic life of the South has been squeezed to a point where the purchasing power of the southern people does not provide an adequate market for its own industries nor an attractive market for those of the rest of the country."[5] The South had an untapped market for production and consumption. However, without adequate capital, it did not have the means to profit from them.

Southern industries paid their employees low wages, which led ⁵ to a low cost of living. "You could live very cheaply because . . . you couldn't make a great deal of money," remembers Rita Beline."[6] Most families did not have much left for themselves after bills and living expenses. "Nobody had much money, you know," recalls June Atchetce. "Everybody kind of lived at home, had gardens and raised their own produce, raised their own meat and had chickens and eggs and such as that." The needs of the families "were very small as far as purchases were concerned." What they could not grow, they did not have a need for, except for basic staples such as coffee, flour, sugar, and honey. To save on the cost of clothes, families "had a lot of hand-me-downs from the oldest to the baby. We did not throw them away. We patched them up and sent them down the line."[7] Luxury items, like radios, cost too much money, and "only the [aristocrats] had radios because the poor did not stay at home long enough to enjoy them."[8] The fact was that Southerners wanted modern consumer items but did not have the purchasing power to pay for them. "The people of the South need to buy, they want to buy, and they would buy—if they had the money."[9] Without paying laborers a fair wage, industry had

Franklin Delano Roosevelt (1882–1945)
Photo from Bettmann / Corbis

forced upon itself a lower living standard, thus perpetuating losses in local revenue resulting in a decline in purchasing power.[10]

The Federal government had to step in and help, as the National Emergency Council's report noted:

> Some of the South's credit difficulties have been slightly relieved in recent years . . . by the Public Works Administration, . . . the Works Progress Administration, [and] the Soil Conservation Service, [which] have brought desperately needed funds into the South.[11]

Along with other New Deal projects like the Tennessee Valley Authority (TVA) and the Civilian Conservation Corps [CCC], President Roosevelt was able to prime the pump into a seemingly dead Southern economy.

Other ways the federal government primed the pump was with the WPA [Works Progress Administration]. This New Deal measure gave jobs to those who wanted to work. Local governments benefited too. The WPA provided new roads, buildings, hospitals, and schools. Rita Beline remembers her "father came very short of money, . . . took a job with the WPA, in which he helped in building a road across a lagoon."[12] President Roosevelt knew "cheap wages mean low buying power."[13] The WPA ensured a fair wage for good work. Warren Addis remembers that "workers were tickled to death with it because it gave so many people jobs. It started out at eight cents an hour for common labor, and it finally went to thirty cents an hour."[14]

FDR also created the CCC. The concept of putting the American youth to work yielded an economic stimulus by having them send home twenty-five dollars a month. That money worked itself back into local economies as families spent the money on needed goods. Young men across the South "left home to go and do this work. They got paid a little bit of money, which they sent home to their families."[15] The CCC created recreation habitats as well. Jefferson Brock recalls, "They came and built brush poles for the fish to live in the lake near my cottage."[16] The CCC became an outlet for young men who could not find work in their hometowns. Jesse Brooks remembers:

> They did a great lot of good. For instance, they built Vogel State Park and raised the wall up on the national cemetery. Just put people to work. Gave them their pride back. A man's not going to feel very good about himself if he can't feed his family. So, that was the New Deal itself — to put people back to work and get the economy growing again.[17]

The South did not enjoy the United States' economic successes in the early part of the twentieth century and in many ways was a third world country within our own nation. The federal action that fueled the Southern economy during the Great Depression changed the way of life for the better and helped Southerners endure a time of great despair. Programs like the TVA, WPA, and CCC planted the seeds for a prosperous future. I still do not know if they were the greatest generation, but they did overcome tremendous obstacles to bring forth other "greatest generations."

Notes

1. Allen Furline in Kenneth J. Bindas, "Oral History Project," Kent State University, Trumbull Campus, Trumbull, OH. Dr. Bindas has a collection of 476 oral-history interviews from western Georgia and eastern Alabama, from which the information for this paper is derived. (Hereafter cited in Notes as BOHP.)

2. David L. Carlton and Peter A. Coclanis, eds., *Confronting Southern Poverty in the Great Depression: The Report on Economic Conditions of the South with Related Documents* (New York: Bedford/St. Martin's Press, 1996), 92.

3. Vera Bland in BOHP.

4. M. Abercrombie in BOHP.

5. Carlton and Coclanis, *Confronting Southern Poverty*, 76–78.

6. Rita Beline in BOHP.

7. June Romero Atchetce in BOHP.

8. Ruby Girley in BOHP.

9. Carlton and Coclanis, *Confronting Southern Poverty*, 78.

10. Ibid., 64–65.

11. Ibid., 73.

12. Rita Beline in BOHP.

13. David M. Kennedy, *Freedom from Fear: The American People in Depression and War, 1929–1945* (New York: Oxford University Press, 1999), 346.

14. Warren Addis in BOHP.

15. Jane Berry in BOHP.

16. Jefferson Brock in BOHP.

17. Jesse Brooks in BOHP.

DeRoven's essay reports information about how the American South got through the Great Depression. His information is based on both library research and recorded interviews with people who lived through the period he describes. He documents his sources according to The Chicago Manual of Style, *the preferred style in history classes.*

Key Features / Reports

A tightly focused topic.   The goal of this kind of writing is to inform readers about something without digressing—and without, in general, bringing in the writer's own opinions. All three examples focus on a particular topic—air turbulence, throwing a baseball, and the Great Depression in the American South—and present information about the topics evenhandedly.

Accurate, well-researched information.   Reports usually require some research. The kind of research depends on the topic. Library research to locate scholarly sources may be necessary for some topics—DeRoven, for example, uses an archive available only at his university's library. Other topics may require field research — interviews, observations, and so on. Fallows interviewed two coaches in addition to reading several books on pitching baseballs.

Various writing strategies.   Presenting information usually requires various organizing patterns — defining, comparing, classifying, explaining processes, analyzing causes and effects, and so on. Stellin explains the causes of turbulence and its effects; Fallows explains the process governing throwing a baseball and classifies different ways of throwing. DeRoven analyzes some of the causes of the Great Depression in the South.

Clear definitions.   Reports need to provide clear definitions of any key terms that their audience may not know. Stellin defines three types of air turbulence as well as what constitutes an accident.

Appropriate design.   Reports often combine paragraphs with information presented in lists, tables, diagrams, and other illustrations. When

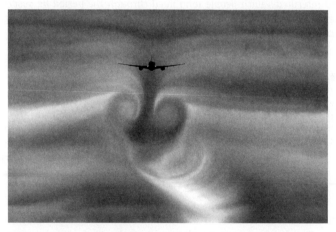

Wake turbulence was captured in this photo of a British Airways flight descending through thin clouds near London last July.

you're presenting information, you need to think carefully about how to design it—numerical data, for instance, can be easier to understand and remember in a table than in a paragraph. Often a photograph can bring a subject to life, as does the photo on page 72, which accompanied "The Inevitability of Bumps." The caption provides important information that is explained more fully in the essay itself.

A GUIDE TO WRITING REPORTS

Choosing a Topic

If you are working with an assigned topic, see if you can approach it from an angle that interests you. If you get to choose your topic, the following guidelines should help:

If you get to choose.   What interests you? What do you wish you knew more about? The possible topics for informational reports are limitless, but the topics that you're most likely to write well on are those that engage you. They may be academic in nature or reflect your personal interests or both. If you're not sure where to begin, here are some places to start:

- an intriguing technology: hybrid cars, cell phones, roller coasters
- sports: soccer, snowboarding, ultimate Frisbee, basketball
- an important world event: 9/11, the fall of Rome, the Black Death
- a historical period: the African diaspora, the Middle Ages, the Ming dynasty, the Great Depression
- a common object: hooded sweatshirts, gel pens, mascara, Post-it notes
- a significant environmental issue: Arctic oil drilling, the Clean Air Act, mercury and the fish supply
- the arts: hip-hop, outsider art, the J. Paul Getty Museum, Savion Glover, Mary Cassatt

220–21
LIST a few possibilities, and then choose one that you'd like to know more about—and that your audience might find interesting, too. You might start out by phrasing your topic as a question that your research will attempt to answer. For example:

> How is Google different from Yahoo!?
>
> How was the Great Pyramid constructed?
>
> Why did the World Trade Center towers collapse on themselves rather than fall sideways?
>
> What kind of training do football referees receive?

If your topic is assigned.   Some assignments are specific: "Explain the physics of roller coasters." If, however, your assignment is broad— "Explain some aspect of the U.S. government"—try focusing on a more limited topic within the larger topic: federalism, majority rule, political parties, states' rights. Even if an assignment seems to offer little flexibility, your task is to decide how to research the topic—and sometimes even narrow topics can be shaped to fit your own interests and those of your audience.

Considering the Rhetorical Situation

3–4
PURPOSE   Why are you presenting this information? To teach readers about the subject? To demonstrate your research and writing skills? For some other reason?

5–8
AUDIENCE   Who will read this report? What do they already know about the topic? What background information do they need in order to understand it? Will you need to define any terms? What do they want or need to know about it? Why should they care? How can you attract their interest?

12–14
STANCE   What is your own attitude toward your subject? What interests you most about it? What about it seems important?

rhetorical situations

genres

processes

strategies

research mla/apa

media/ design

handbook

MEDIA / DESIGN What medium are you using? What is the best way to present the information? Will it all be in paragraph form, or is there information that is best presented as a chart or a table? Do you need headings? Would diagrams, photographs, or other illustrations help you explain the information?

15–17

Generating Ideas and Text

Good reports share certain features that make them useful and interesting to readers. Remember that your goal is to present information clearly and accurately. Start by exploring your topic.

Explore what you already know about your topic. Write out whatever you know or want to know about your topic, perhaps by **FREEWRITING**, **LISTING,** or **CLUSTERING.** Why are you interested in this topic? What questions do you have about it? Such questions can help you decide what you'd like to focus on and how you need to direct your research efforts.

219–22

Narrow your topic. To write a good report, you need to narrow your focus — and to narrow your focus, you need to know a fair amount about your subject. If you are assigned to write on a subject like biodiversity, for example, you need to know what it is, what the key issues are, and so on. If you do, you can simply list or brainstorm possibilities, choose one, and start your research. If you don't know much about the subject, though, you need to do some research to discover focused, workable topics. This research may shape your thinking and change your focus. Start with **SOURCES** that can give you a general sense of the subject, such as an encyclopedia entry, a magazine article, an Internet site, perhaps an interview with an expert. Your goal at this point is simply to find out what issues your topic might include and then to focus your efforts on an aspect of the topic you will be able to cover.

384–99

Come up with a tentative thesis. Once you narrow your topic, write out a statement that explains what you plan to report or explain. A good **THESIS** is potentially interesting (to you and your readers) and limits your

273–75

topic enough to make it manageable. Stellin presents her thesis, that plane accidents caused by turbulence "have become more unlikely as more has been learned about turbulence," after establishing a context for passengers' concern about it. DeRoven lays out exactly what will be discussed, using a format acceptable in some disciplines but frowned on in others: "This paper will explore the Great Depression through the eyes of ordinary Americans in the most impoverished region in the country, the American South, in order to detail how they endured and how the government assisted them in this difficult era." At this point, however, you need only a tentative thesis that will help focus any research you do.

223–24 ◔
375–83 ●

Do any necessary research, and revise your thesis. To focus your research efforts, **OUTLINE** the aspects of your topic that you expect to discuss. Identify any aspects that require additional research and **DEVELOP A RESEARCH PLAN.** Expect to revise your outline as you do your research, since more information will be available for some aspects of your topic than others, some may prove irrelevant to your topic, and some may turn out to be more than you need. You'll need to revisit your tentative thesis once you've done any research, to finalize your statement.

Ways of Organizing a Report

Reports can be organized in various ways. Here are three common ones:

[Reports on topics that are unfamiliar to readers]

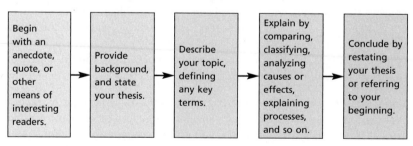

Begin with an anecdote, quote, or other means of interesting readers. → Provide background, and state your thesis. → Describe your topic, defining any key terms. → Explain by comparing, classifying, analyzing causes or effects, explaining processes, and so on. → Conclude by restating your thesis or referring to your beginning.

rhetorical situations ■　genres ▲　processes ○　strategies ◆　research mla/apa ●　media/design □　handbook ◩

[Reports on an event]

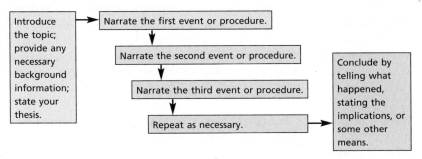

[Reports that compare and contrast]

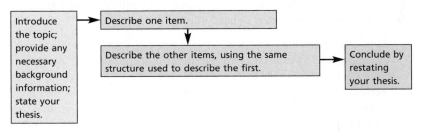

Many reports use a combination of organizational structures; don't be afraid to use whatever method of organization best suits your material and your purpose.

Writing Out a Draft

Once you have generated ideas and thought about how you want to organize your report, it's time to start **DRAFTING.** Do this quickly — try to write a complete draft in one sitting, concentrating on getting the report on paper or screen and on putting in as much detail as you can.

○ 226–28

Writing that reports information often calls for certain writing strate-

338–42
278–82
306–13

gies. The report on throwing a baseball, for example, **EXPLAINS THE PROCESS** of throwing, whereas the report on turbulence **ANALYZES THE CAUSES** of turbulence. When you're reporting on a topic your readers aren't familiar with, you may wish to **COMPARE** it with something more familiar; you can find useful advice on these and other writing strategies in Part 4 of this book.

Draft a beginning. Essays that report information often need to begin in a way that will get your audience interested in the topic. Here are a few ways of **BEGINNING**:

261–66

- *Simply state your thesis.* DeRoven begins his essay about "the greatest generation" this way. Opening with a thesis works well when you can assume your readers have enough familiarity with your topic that you don't need to give detailed background information.

- *Start with something that will provoke readers' interest.* Stellin begins by noting that people who fly often can become fearful when their plane hits turbulence, before she moves on to an overview of the actual safety risks involved. She knows that most readers will have experienced air turbulence and will likely want to read on to learn about how pilots and aircraft manufacturers—and other passengers— deal with it.

- *Begin with an illustrative example.* Fallows uses the contrasting photographs of the Clintons throwing baseballs as a way of defining "throwing like a girl."

Draft an ending. Think about what you want your readers to read last.

266–70

An effective **ENDING** leaves them thinking about your topic.

- *Summarize your main points.* This is a good way to end when you've presented several key points you want readers to remember. DeRoven ends this way, summarizing the South's poverty and the government's successful actions to alleviate it.

- *Point out the implications of your report.* Although Stellin's report on turbulence is reassuring, she ends by acknowledging that many air travelers still find rough air unsettling and describes some of their ways of coping.

- *Frame your report by referring to its introduction.* DeRoven begins and ends his report by mentioning "the greatest generation."

- *Tell what happened.* If you are reporting on an event, you could conclude by telling how it turns out.

Come up with a title. You'll want a title that tells readers something about your subject—and makes them want to know more. Stellin, for instance, gets our interest in her report on turbulence with the title "The Inevitability of Bumps," which generates interest first by its ambiguity (Is this about skin? Roads?) and then by its relevance to anyone who flies. See the chapter on **GUIDING YOUR READER** for tips on coming up with titles that are informative and enticing enough to make readers wish to read on.

272–77

Considering Matters of Design

You'll probably write your report in paragraph form, but think about the information you're presenting and how you can design and format it to make it as easy as possible for your readers to understand. You might ask yourself these questions:

- What is an appropriate **TYPEFACE**? Something serious like Times Roman, something traditional like `Courier`, something else?

524–25

- Would it help your readers if you divided your report into shorter sections and added **HEADINGS**?

526–27

- Is there any information that would be easier to follow in a **LIST**?

525–26

- Could any of your information be summarized in a **TABLE**?

528–32

- Do you have any data that readers would more easily understand in the form of a bar **GRAPH,** line graph, or pie chart?

528–30 ☐

528–32 ☐

- Would **ILLUSTRATIONS** — diagrams, photos, drawings, and so on — help you explain anything in your report?

Getting Response and Revising

The following questions can help you study your draft with a critical eye.

235–36 ◉

GETTING RESPONSE from others is always good, and these questions can guide their reading, too. Make sure they know your purpose and audience.

272–73 ◆

- Do the **TITLE** and opening sentences get readers' interest? If not, how might they do so?

3–4 ■

- What information does this text provide, and for what **PURPOSE?**

- Does the introduction explain why this information is being presented? Does it place the topic in a larger context?

- Are all key terms defined?

- Do you have any questions? Is more information or explanation needed? Where might an example help you understand something?

528–32 ☐

- Is any information presented **VISUALLY,** with a chart, graph, table, drawing, or photograph? If so, is it clear how these illustrations relate to the larger text? Is there any text that would be more easily understood if it were presented visually?

259 ◆

- Does the organization help make sense of the information? Does the text include description, comparison, or any other writing **STRATE-GIES?** Does the topic or rhetorical situation call for any particular strategies?

408–19 ●

425–27

- If the report cites any sources, are they **QUOTED, PARAPHRASED,** or **SUM-MARIZED** effectively (and with appropriate **DOCUMENTATION**)?

266–70 ◆

- Does the report **END** in a satisfying way? What are readers left thinking?

These questions should identify aspects on your report you need to work on. When it's time to **REVISE**, make sure your report appeals to your audience and achieves your purpose as successfully as possible.

◯ 236–39

Editing and Proofreading

Readers equate correctness with the writer's competence. Once you've revised your draft, follow these guidelines for **EDITING** a report:

◯ 242–45

- Check your use of key terms. Repeating key words is acceptable in reports; synonyms for unfamiliar words may confuse readers while the repetition of key words or the use of clearly identified **PRONOUNS** can be genuinely helpful.

HB-24–28

- Check your use of **TRANSITIONS** to be sure you have them where you need them.

◆ 277

- If you have included **HEADINGS**, make sure they're parallel in structure and consistent in design.

◻ 526–27

- Make sure that any photos or other **ILLUSTRATIONS** have captions, that charts and graphs have headings—and that all are referred to in the main text. Have you used white space effectively to separate sections of your report and to highlight graphic elements?

◻ 528–32

- Check any **DOCUMENTATION** to see that it follows the appropriate style without mistakes.

● 425–27

- **PROOFREAD** and spell-check your report carefully.

◯ 245–46

Taking Stock of Your Work

- How well did you convey the information? Is it complete enough for your audience's needs?
- What strategies did you rely on, and how did they help you achieve your purpose?

- How well did you organize the report?
- How did you go about researching the information for this piece?
- How did you go about drafting this piece?
- Did you use any tables, graphs, diagrams, photographs, illustrations, or other graphics effectively?
- How did others' responses influence your writing?
- What did you do especially well?
- What could still be improved?
- What would you do differently next time?

247–58 ○
111–15 ▲
133–42
161–70

IF YOU NEED MORE HELP

See Chapter 28 if you are required to submit your report in a writing **PORTFOLIO.** See also Chapter 10 on **ABSTRACTS** if your report requires one; Chapter 13 on **LAB REPORTS,** a kind of report written in the sciences; and Chapter 16 on **PROFILES,** a report based on firsthand research.

rhetorical situations
genres
processes
strategies
research mla/apa
media/ design
handbook

Arguing a Position   **9**

Everything we say or do presents some kind of argument, takes some kind of position. Often we take overt positions: "Everyone in the United States is entitled to affordable health care." "The university needs to offer more language courses." "Sean Combs shouldn't have gone into acting." Some scholars claim that everything makes some kind of argument, from yellow ribbons that honor U.S. troops to a yellow smiley face, which might be said to argue for a good day. In college course work, you are constantly called on to argue positions: in an English class, you may argue for a certain interpretation of a poem; in a business course, you may argue for the merits of a flat tax; in a linguistics class, you may argue that English should not be made the official language of the United States. All of those positions are arguable—people of goodwill can agree or disagree with them and present reasons and evidence to support their positions. This chapter provides detailed guidelines for writing an essay that argues a position. We'll begin with three good examples.

GARY TAUBES
What If It's All Been a Big Fat Lie?

In this text, science writer Gary Taubes argues that the root of the so-called obesity epidemic is our consumption of carbohydrates. It first appeared in the New York Times in 2002.

> One of the reasonably reliable facts about the obesity epidemic is that it started around the early 1980s. According to Katherine Flegal, an epidemiologist at the National Center for Health Statistics, the percentage

of obese Americans stayed relatively constant through the 1960s and 1970s at 13 percent to 14 percent and then shot up by 8 percentage points in the 1980s. By the end of that decade, nearly one in four Americans was obese. That steep rise, which is consistent through all segments of American society and which continued unabated through the 1990s, is the singular feature of the epidemic. Any theory that tries to explain obesity in America has to account for that. Meanwhile, overweight children nearly tripled in number. And for the first time, physicians began diagnosing Type 2 diabetes in adolescents. Type 2 diabetes often accompanies obesity. It used to be called adult-onset diabetes and now, for the obvious reason, is not.

So how did this happen? The orthodox and ubiquitous explanation is that we live in what Kelly Brownell, a Yale psychologist, has called a "toxic food environment" of cheap fatty food, large portions, pervasive food advertising and sedentary lives. By this theory, we are at the Pavlovian mercy of the food industry, which spends nearly $10 billion a year advertising unwholesome junk food and fast food. And because these foods, especially fast food, are so filled with fat, they are both irresistible and uniquely fattening. On top of this, so the theory goes, our modern society has successfully eliminated physical activity from our daily lives. We no longer exercise or walk up stairs, nor do our children bike to school or play outside, because they would prefer to play video games and watch television. And because some of us are obviously predisposed to gain weight while others are not, this explanation also has a genetic component—the thrifty gene. It suggests that storing extra calories as fat was an evolutionary advantage to our Paleolithic ancestors, who had to survive frequent famine. We then inherited these "thrifty" genes, despite their liability in today's toxic environment.

This theory makes perfect sense and plays to our puritanical prejudice that fat, fast food, and television are innately damaging to our humanity. But there are two catches. First, to buy this logic is to accept that the copious negative reinforcement that accompanies obesity—both socially and physically—is easily overcome by the constant bombardment of food advertising and the lure of a supersize bargain meal. And second, as Flegal points out, little data exist to support any of this. Certainly none of it explains what changed so significantly to start the epidemic. Fast-food consumption, for example, continued to grow

steadily through the 70s and 80s, but it did not take a sudden leap, as obesity did.

As far as exercise and physical activity go, there are no reliable data before the mid-80s, according to William Dietz, who runs the division of nutrition and physical activity at the Centers for Disease Control; the 1990s data show obesity rates continuing to climb, while exercise activity remained unchanged. This suggests the two have little in common. Dietz also acknowledged that a culture of physical exercise began in the United States in the 70s — the "leisure exercise mania," as Robert Levy, director of the National Heart, Lung and Blood Institute, described it in 1981 — and has continued through the present day.

As for the thrifty gene, it provides the kind of evolutionary rationale for human behavior that scientists find comforting but that simply cannot be tested. In other words, if we were living through an anorexia epidemic, the experts would be discussing the equally untestable "spendthrift gene" theory, touting evolutionary advantages of losing weight effortlessly. An overweight homo erectus, they'd say, would have been easy prey for predators.

It is also undeniable, note students of Endocrinology 101 [the science behind the idea that carbohydrates cause obesity], that mankind never evolved to eat a diet high in starches or sugars. "Grain products and concentrated sugars were essentially absent from human nutrition until the invention of agriculture," Ludwig says, "which was only 10,000 years ago." This is discussed frequently in the anthropology texts but is mostly absent from the obesity literature, with the prominent exception of the low-carbohydrate-diet books.

What's forgotten in the current controversy is that the low-fat dogma itself is only about 25 years old. Until the late 70s, the accepted wisdom was that fat and protein protected against overeating by making you sated, and that carbohydrates made you fat. In *The Physiology of Taste*, for instance, an 1825 discourse considered among the most famous books ever written about food, the French gastronome Jean Anthelme Brillat-Savarin says that he could easily identify the causes of obesity after 30 years of listening to one "stout party" after another proclaiming the joys of bread, rice, and (from a "particularly stout party") potatoes. Brillat-Savarin describes the roots of obesity as a natural predisposition conjuncted with the "floury and feculent substances

5

which man makes the prime ingredients of his daily nourishment." He added that the effects of this fecula—i.e., "potatoes, grain, or any kind of flour"—were seen sooner when sugar was added to the diet.

This is what my mother taught me 40 years ago, backed up by the vague observation that Italians tended toward corpulence because they ate so much pasta. This observation was actually documented by Ancel Keys, a University of Minnesota physician who noted that fats "have good staying power," by which he meant they are slow to be digested and so lead to satiation, and that Italians were among the heaviest populations he had studied. According to Keys, the Neopolitans, for instance, ate only a little lean meat once or twice a week, but ate bread and pasta every day for lunch and dinner. "There was no evidence of nutritional deficiency," he wrote, "but the working-class women were fat."

By the 70s, you could still find articles in the journals describing high rates of obesity in Africa and the Caribbean where diets contained almost exclusively carbohydrates. The common thinking, wrote a former director of the Nutrition Division of the United Nations, was that the ideal diet, one that prevented obesity, snacking, and excessive sugar consumption, was a diet "with plenty of eggs, beef, mutton, chicken, butter, and well-cooked vegetables." This was the identical prescription Brillat-Savarin put forth in 1825.

Few experts now deny that the low-fat message is radically over- 10 simplified. If nothing else, it effectively ignores the fact that unsaturated fats, like olive oil, are relatively good for you: they tend to elevate your good cholesterol, high-density lipoprotein (H.D.L.), and lower your bad cholesterol, low-density lipoprotein (L.D.L.), at least in comparison to the effect of carbohydrates. While higher L.D.L. raises your heart-disease risk, higher H.D.L. reduces it.

What this means is that even saturated fats—a k a, the bad fats—are not nearly as deleterious as you would think. True, they will elevate your bad cholesterol, but they will also elevate your good cholesterol. In other words, it's a virtual wash. As Walter Willett, chairman of the department of nutrition at the Harvard School of Public Health, explained to me, you will gain little to no health benefit by giving up milk, butter, and cheese and eating bagels instead.

But it gets even weirder than that. Foods considered more or less deadly under the low-fat dogma turn out to be comparatively benign

rhetorical situations · genres · processes · strategies · research mla/apa · media/ design · handbook

if you actually look at their fat content. More than two-thirds of the fat in a porterhouse steak, for instance, will definitely improve your cholesterol profile (at least in comparison with the baked potato next to it); it's true that the remainder will raise your L.D.L., the bad stuff, but it will also boost your H.D.L. The same is true for lard. If you work out the numbers, you come to the surreal conclusion that you can eat lard straight from the can and conceivably reduce your risk of heart disease. . . .

After 20 years steeped in a low-fat paradigm, I find it hard to see the nutritional world any other way. I have learned that low-fat diets fail in clinical trials and in real life, and they certainly have failed in my life. I have read the papers suggesting that 20 years of low-fat recommendations have not managed to lower the incidence of heart disease in this country, and may have led instead to the steep increase in obesity and Type 2 diabetes. I have interviewed researchers whose computer models have calculated that cutting back on the saturated fats in my diet to the levels recommended by the American Heart Association would not add more than a few months to my life, if that. I have even lost considerable weight with relative ease by giving up carbohydrates on my test diet, and yet I can look down at my eggs and sausage and still imagine the imminent onset of heart disease and obesity, the latter assuredly to be caused by some bizarre rebound phenomena the likes of which science has not yet begun to describe.

This is the state of mind I imagine that mainstream nutritionists, researchers and physicians must inevitably take to the fat-versus-carbohydrate controversy. They may come around, but the evidence will have to be exceptionally compelling. Although this kind of conversion may be happening at the moment to John Farquhar, who is a professor of health research and policy at Stanford University and has worked in this field for more than 40 years. When I interviewed Farquhar in April, he explained why low-fat diets might lead to weight gain and low-carbohydrate diets might lead to weight loss, but he made me promise not to say he believed they did. He attributed the cause of the obesity epidemic to the "force-feeding of a nation." Three weeks later, after reading an article on Endocrinology 101 by David Ludwig in the *Journal of the American Medical Association*, he sent me an e-mail message asking the not-entirely-rhetorical question, "Can we get the low-fat proponents to apologize?"

Taubes offers evidence from many sources to support his argument that fat is actually better for you than carbohydrates. His matter-of-fact, objective tone helps readers take his unorthodox argument seriously. Because this text appeared in the New York Times, *Taubes does not document his sources—standard practice in journalism.*

LAWRENCE LESSIG

Some Like It Hot

This essay on electronic piracy appeared in Wired *magazine in March 2004. Lawrence Lessig is an authority on copyright law. He teaches at Stanford Law School, where he founded its Center for Internet and Society.*

If piracy means using the creative property of others without their permission, then the history of the content industry is a history of piracy. Every important sector of big media today—film, music, radio, and cable TV—was born of a kind of piracy. The consistent story is how each generation welcomes the pirates from the last. Each generation—until now.

The Hollywood film industry was built by fleeing pirates. Creators and directors migrated from the East Coast to California in the early twentieth century in part to escape controls that film patents granted the inventor Thomas Edison. These controls were exercised through the Motion Pictures Patents Company, a monopoly "trust" based on Edison's creative property and formed to vigorously protect his patent rights.

California was remote enough from Edison's reach that filmmakers like Fox and Paramount could move there and, without fear of the law, pirate his inventions. Hollywood grew quickly, and enforcement of federal law eventually spread west. But because patents granted their holders a truly "limited" monopoly of just seventeen years (at that time), the patents had expired by the time enough federal marshals appeared. A new industry had been founded, in part from the piracy of Edison's creative property.

Meanwhile, the record industry grew out of another kind of piracy. At the time that Edison and Henri Fourneaux invented machines for

reproducing music (Edison the phonograph; Fourneaux the player piano), the law gave composers the exclusive right to control copies and public performances of their music. Thus, in 1900, if I wanted a copy of Phil Russel's 1899 hit, "Happy Mose," the law said I would have to pay for the right to get a copy of the score, and I would also have to pay for the right to perform it publicly.

But what if I wanted to record "Happy Mose" using Edison's ⁵ phonograph or Fourneaux's player piano? Here the law stumbled. If I simply sang the piece into a recording device in my home, it wasn't clear that I owed the composer anything. And more important, it wasn't clear whether I owed the composer anything if I then made copies of those recordings. Because of this gap in the law, I could effectively use someone else's song without paying the composer anything. The composers (and publishers) were none too happy about this capacity to pirate.

In 1909, Congress closed the gap in favor of the composer and the recording artist, amending copyright law to make sure that composers would be paid for "mechanical reproductions" of their music. But rather than simply granting the composer complete control over the right to make such reproductions, Congress gave recording artists a right to record the music, at a price set by Congress, after the composer allowed it to be recorded once. This is the part of copyright law that makes cover songs possible. Once a composer authorizes a recording of his song, others are free to record the same song, so long as they pay the original composer a fee set by the law. So, by limiting musicians' rights — by partially pirating their creative work — record producers and the public benefit.

A similar story can be told about radio. When a station plays a composer's work on the air, that constitutes a "public performance." Copyright law gives the composer (or copyright holder) an exclusive right to public performances of his work. The radio station thus owes the composer money.

But when the station plays a record, it is not only performing a copy of the *composer's* work. The station is also performing a copy of the *recording artist's* work. It's one thing to air a recording of "Happy Birthday" by the local children's choir; it's quite another to air a recording of it by the Rolling Stones or Lyle Lovett. The recording artist is adding to the value of the composition played on the radio station.

Both photos from Bettmann/Corbis

And if the law were perfectly consistent, the station would have to pay the artist for his work, just as it pays the composer.

But it doesn't. This difference can be huge. Imagine you compose a piece of music. You own the exclusive right to authorize public performances of that music. So if Madonna wants to sing your song in public, she has to get your permission.

Imagine she does sing your song, and imagine she likes it a lot. 10 She then decides to make a recording of your song, and it becomes a top hit. Under today's law, every time a radio station plays your song, you get some money. But Madonna gets nothing, save the indirect effect on the sale of her CDs. The public performance of her recording is not a "protected" right. The radio station thus gets to pirate the value of Madonna's work without paying her a dime.

No doubt, one might argue, the promotion artists get is worth more than the performance rights they give up. Maybe. But even if that's the case, this is a choice that the law ordinarily gives to the creator. Instead, the law gives the radio station the right to take something for nothing.

rhetorical
situations

genres

processes

strategies

research
mla/apa

media/
design

handbook

Cable TV, too: When entrepreneurs first started installing cable in 1948, most refused to pay the networks for the content that they hijacked and delivered to their customers—even though they were basically selling access to otherwise free television broadcasts. Cable companies were thus Napsterizing broadcasters' content, but more egregiously than anything Napster ever did—Napster never charged for the content it enabled others to give away.

Broadcasters and copyright owners were quick to attack this theft. As then Screen Actors Guild president Charlton Heston put it, the cable outfits were "free riders" who were "depriving actors of compensation."

Copyright owners took the cable companies to court. Twice the Supreme Court held that the cable companies owed the copyright owners nothing. The debate shifted to Congress, where almost thirty years later it resolved the question in the same way it had dealt with phonographs and player pianos. Yes, cable companies would have to pay for the content that they broadcast, but the price they would have to pay was not set by the copyright owner. Instead, lawmakers set the price so that the broadcasters couldn't veto the emerging technologies of cable. The companies thus built their empire in part upon a piracy of the value created by broadcasters' content.

As the history of film, music, radio, and cable TV suggest, even if 15 some piracy is plainly wrong, not all piracy is. Or at least not in the sense that the term is increasingly being used today. Many kinds of piracy are useful and productive, either to create new content or foster new ways of doing business. Neither our tradition, nor any tradition, has ever banned all piracy.

This doesn't mean that there are no questions raised by the latest piracy concern—peer-to-peer file sharing. But it does mean that we need to understand the harm in P2P sharing a bit more before we condemn it to the gallows.

Like the original Hollywood, P2P sharing seeks to escape an overly controlling industry. And like the original recording and radio industries, it is simply exploiting a new way of distributing content. But unlike cable TV, no one is selling the content that gets shared on P2P services. This difference distinguishes P2P sharing. We should find a way to protect artists while permitting this sharing to survive.

Much of the "piracy" that file sharing enables is plainly legal and good. It provides access to content that is technically still under copyright but that is no longer commercially available — in the case of music, some four million tracks. More important, P2P networks enable sharing of content that copyright owners want shared, as well as work already in the public domain. This clearly benefits authors and society.

Moreover, much of the sharing — which is referred to by many as piracy — is motivated by a new way of spreading content made possible by changes in the technology of distribution. Thus, consistent with the tradition that gave us Hollywood, radio, the music industry, and cable TV, the question we should be asking about file sharing is how best to preserve its benefits while minimizing (to the extent possible) the wrongful harm it causes artists.

The question is one of balance, weighing the protection of the law 20 against the strong public interest in continued innovation. The law should seek that balance, and that balance will be found only with time.

Lessig argues that the "piracy" that Napster and other peer-to-peer music-sharing services are accused of is similar to that practiced by every other electronic medium in the last one hundred years. He offers a clear definition of piracy and carefully supports his assertions with historical evidence for each one.

JOANNA MACKAY

Organ Sales Will Save Lives

In this essay, written in 2004 for a class on ethics and politics in science, MIT student Joanna MacKay argues that the sale of human organs should be legal.

There are thousands of people dying to buy a kidney and thousands of people dying to sell a kidney. It seems a match made in heaven. So why are we standing in the way? Governments should not ban the sale of human organs; they should regulate it. Lives should not be wasted; they should be saved.

About 350,000 Americans suffer from end-stage renal disease, a state of kidney disorder so advanced that the organ stops functioning altogether. There are no miracle drugs that can revive a failed kidney, leaving dialysis and kidney transplantation as the only possible treatments (McDonnell and Mallon, pars. 2 and 3).

Dialysis is harsh, expensive, and, worst of all, only temporary. Acting as an artificial kidney, dialysis mechanically filters the blood of a patient. It works, but not well. With treatment sessions lasting three hours, several times a week, those dependent on dialysis are, in a sense, shackled to a machine for the rest of their lives. Adding excessive stress to the body, dialysis causes patients to feel increasingly faint and tired, usually keeping them from work and other normal activities.

Kidney transplantation, on the other hand, is the closest thing to a cure that anyone could hope for. Today the procedure is both safe and reliable, causing few complications. With better technology for confirming tissue matches and new anti-rejection drugs, the surgery is relatively simple.

But those hoping for a new kidney have high hopes indeed. In the year 2000 alone, 2,583 Americans died while waiting for a kidney transplant; worldwide the number of deaths is around 50,000 (Finkel 27). With the sale of organs outlawed in almost every country, the number of living donors willing to part with a kidney for free is small. When no family member is a suitable candidate for donation, the patient is placed on a deceased donors list, relying on the organs from people dying of old age or accidents. The list is long. With over 60,000 people in line in the United States alone, the average wait for a cadaverous kidney is ten long years.

Daunted by the low odds, some have turned to an alternative solution: purchasing kidneys on the black market. For about $150,000, they can buy a fresh kidney from a healthy, living donor. There are no lines, no waits. Arranged through a broker, the entire procedure is carefully planned out. The buyer, seller, surgeons, and nurses are flown to a predetermined hospital in a foreign country. The operations are performed, and then all are flown back to their respective homes. There is no follow-up, no paperwork to sign (Finkel 27).

The illegal kidney trade is attractive not only because of the promptness, but also because of the chance at a living donor. An organ from a cadaver will most likely be old or damaged, estimated to function for about ten years at most. A kidney from a living donor can last over twice as long. Once a person's transplanted cadaverous kidney stops functioning, he or she must get back on the donors list, this time probably at the end of the line. A transplanted living kidney, however, could last a person a lifetime.

While there may seem to be a shortage of kidneys, in reality there is a surplus. In third world countries, there are people willing to do anything for money. In such extreme poverty these people barely have enough to eat, living in shacks and sleeping on dirt floors. Eager to pay off debts, they line up at hospitals, willing to sell a kidney for about $1,000. The money will go towards food and clothing, or perhaps to pay for a family member's medical operation (Goyal et al. 1590–1). Whatever the case, these people need the money.

There is certainly a risk in donating a kidney, but this risk is not great enough to be outlawed. Millions of people take risks to their health every day for money, or simply for enjoyment. As explained in *The Lancet*, "If the rich are free to engage in dangerous sports for pleasure, or dangerous jobs for high pay, it is difficult to see why the poor who take the lesser risk of kidney selling for greater rewards . . . should be thought so misguided as to need saving from themselves (Radcliffe-Richards et al. 1951). Studies have shown that a person can live a healthy life with only one kidney. While these studies might not apply to the poor living under strenuous conditions in unsanitary environments, the risk is still theirs to take. These people have decided that their best hope for money is to sell a kidney. How can we deny them the best opportunity they have?

Some agree with Pope John Paul II that the selling of organs is 10 morally wrong and violates "the dignity of the human person" (qtd. in Finkel 26), but this is a belief professed by healthy and affluent individuals. Are we sure that the peasants of third world countries agree? The morals we hold are not absolute truths. We have the responsibility to protect and help those less fortunate, but we cannot let our own ideals cloud the issues at hand.

In a legal kidney transplant, everybody gains except the donor. The doctors and nurses are paid for the operation, the patient receives a new kidney, but the donor receives nothing. Sure, the donor will have the warm, uplifting feeling associated with helping a fellow human being, but this is not enough reward for most people to part with a piece of themselves. In an ideal world, the average person would be altruistic enough to donate a kidney with nothing expected in return. The real world, however, is run by money. We pay men for donating sperm, and we pay women for donating ova, yet we expect others to give away an entire organ for no compensation. If the sale of organs were allowed, people would have a greater incentive to help save the life of a stranger.

While many argue that legalizing the sale of organs will exploit the poorer people of third world countries, the truth of the matter is

that this is already the case. Even with the threat of a $50,000 fine and five years in prison (Finkel 26), the current ban has not been successful in preventing illegal kidney transplants. The kidneys of the poor are still benefiting only the rich. While the sellers do receive most of the money promised, the sum is too small to have any real impact on their financial situation. A study in India discovered that in the long run, organ sellers suffer. In the illegal kidney trade, nobody has the interests of the seller at heart. After selling a kidney, their state of living actually worsens. While the $1,000 pays off one debt, it is not enough to relieve the donor of the extreme poverty that placed him in debt in the first place (Goyal et al. 1591).

These impoverished people do not need stricter and harsher penalties against organ selling to protect them, but quite the opposite. If the sale of organs were made legal, it could be regulated and closely monitored by the government and other responsible organizations. Under a regulated system, education would be incorporated into the application process. Before deciding to donate a kidney, the seller should know the details of the operation and any hazards involved. Only with an understanding of the long-term physical health risks can a person make an informed decision (Radcliffe-Richards et al. 1951).

Regulation would ensure that the seller is fairly compensated. In the illegal kidney trade, surgeons collect most of the buyer's money in return for putting their careers on the line. The brokers arranging the procedure also receive a modest cut, typically around ten percent. If the entire practice were legalized, more of the money could be directed towards the person who needs it most, the seller. By eliminating the middleman and allowing the doctors to settle for lower prices, a regulated system would benefit all those in need of a kidney, both rich and poor. According to Finkel, the money that would otherwise be spent on dialysis treatment could not only cover the charge of a kidney transplant at no cost to the recipient, but also reward the donor with as much as $25,000 (32). This money could go a long way for people living in the poverty of third world countries.

Critics fear that controlling the lawful sale of organs would be too 15 difficult, but could it be any more difficult than controlling the unlawful sale of organs? Governments have tried to eradicate the kidney market for decades to no avail. Maybe it is time to try something else. When "desperately wanted goods" are made illegal, history has shown that there is more opportunity for corruption and exploitation than if those goods were allowed (Radcliffe-Richards et al. 1951). (Just look at the effects of the prohibition of alcohol, for example.) Legalization of organ sales would give governments the authority and the opportunity to closely monitor these live kidney operations.

Regulation would also protect the buyers. Because of the need for secrecy, the current illegal method of obtaining a kidney has no contracts and, therefore, no guarantees. Since what they are doing is illegal, the buyers have nobody to turn to if something goes wrong. There is nobody to point the finger at, nobody to sue. While those participating in the kidney market are breaking the law, they have no other choice. Without a new kidney, end-stage renal disease will soon kill them. Desperate to survive, they are forced to take the only offer available. It seems immoral to first deny them the opportunity of a new kidney and then to leave them stranded at the mercy of the black market. Without laws regulating live kidney transplants, these people are subject to possibly hazardous procedures. Instead of turning our backs, we have the power to ensure that these operations are done safely and efficiently for both the recipient and the donor.

Those suffering from end-stage renal disease would do anything for the chance at a new kidney, take any risk or pay any price. There are other people so poor that the sale of a kidney is worth the profit. Try to tell someone that he has to die from kidney failure because selling a kidney is morally wrong. Then turn around and try to tell another person that he has to remain in poverty for that same reason. In matters of life and death, our stances on moral issues must be reevaluated. If legalized and regulated, the sale of human organs would save lives. Is it moral to sentence thousands to unnecessary deaths?

Works Cited

Finkel, Michael. "This Little Kidney Went to Market." <u>New York Times Magazine</u> 27 May 2001: 26–33, 40, 52, 59.

Goyal, Madhav, Ravindra L. Mehta, Lawrence J. Schneiderman, and Ashwini R. Sehgal. "Economic and Health Consequences of Selling a Kidney in India." <u>Journal of the America Medical Association</u> 288 (2002): 1589–92.

McDonnell, Michael B., and William K. Mallon. "Kidney Transplant." <u>eMedicine Health</u>. 18 Aug. 2008. WebMD. 30 Nov. 2008 <http://www.emedicinehealth.com/articles/24500-1.asp.>.

Radcliffe-Richards, J., A.S. Daar, R.D. Guttmann, R. Hoffenberg, I. Kennedy, M. Lock, R.A. Sells, and N. Tilney. "The Case for Allowing Kidney Sales." <u>The Lancet</u> 351 (1998): 1950–2.

MacKay clearly states her position at the beginning of her text: "Governments should not ban the sale of human organs; they should regulate it." Her argument appeals to her readers' value of fairness; when kidney sales are legalized and regulated, both sellers and buyers will benefit from the transaction. MacKay uses MLA style to document her sources.

Key Features / Arguments

A clear and arguable position.   At the heart of every argument is a claim with which people may reasonably disagree. Some claims are not arguable because they're completely subjective, matters of taste or opinion ("I hate sauerkraut"), because they are a matter of fact ("The first *Star Wars* movie came out in 1977"), or because they are based on belief or faith ("There is life after death"). To be arguable, a position must reflect one of at least two points of view, making reasoned argument necessary: Internet file sharing should (or should not) be considered fair use; selling human organs should be legal (or illegal). In college writing, you will often argue not that a position is correct but that it is plausible — that it is reasonable, supportable, and worthy of being taken seriously.

Necessary background information.   Sometimes we need to provide some background on a topic we are arguing so that readers can understand what is being argued. MacKay establishes the need for kidney donors before launching her argument for legalizing the selling of organs; Taubes describes the rise in obesity before he takes a position on its cause.

Good reasons.   By itself, a position does not make an argument; the argument comes when a writer offers reasons to back the position up. There are many kinds of good reasons. Lessig makes his argument by comparing, showing many examples of so-called piracy in other media. Taubes points out that people didn't evolve to eat refined grains and that data show carbohydrates to be more fattening than fat. MacKay bases her argument in favor of legalizing the sale of human organs on the fact that kidney transplants save lives and that regulation would protect impoverished people who currently sell their organs on the black market.

Convincing evidence.   It's one thing to give reasons for your position. You then need to offer evidence for your reasons: facts, statistics, expert testimony, anecdotal evidence, case studies, textual evidence. All three arguments use a mix of these types of evidence. MacKay cites statistics about Americans who die from renal failure to support her argument for legalizing organ sales; Lessig offers facts from the history of the broadcast media to support his argument for file sharing.

Appeals to readers' values.   Effective arguers try to appeal to readers' values and emotions. Both MacKay and Lessig appeal to basic values—MacKay to the value of compassion, Lessig to the value of fairness. These are deeply held values that we may not think about very much and as a result may see as common ground we share with the writers. And some of MacKay's evidence appeals to emotion—her descriptions of people dying from kidney disease and of poor people selling their organs are likely to evoke an emotional response in many readers.

A trustworthy tone.   Arguments can stand or fall on the way readers perceive the writer. Very simply, readers need to trust the person who's making the argument. One way of winning this trust is by demonstrating that you know what you're talking about. Lessig offers plenty of facts to show his knowledge of copyright history—and he does so in a self-assured tone. There are many other ways of establishing yourself (and your argument) as trustworthy—by showing that you have some experience with your subject, that you're fair, and of course that you're honest.

Careful consideration of other positions.   No matter how reasonable and careful we are in arguing our positions, others may disagree or offer counterarguments or hold other positions. We need to consider those other views and to acknowledge and, if possible, refute them in our written arguments. MacKay, for example, acknowledges that some believe that selling one's organs is unethical, but she counters that it's usually healthy, affluent people who say this—not people who need the money they could get by selling one.

A GUIDE TO WRITING ARGUMENTS

Choosing a Topic

A fully developed argument requires significant work and time, so choosing a topic in which you're interested is very important. Students find that widely debated topics such as "animal rights" or "gun control" can be difficult to write on because they seldom have a personal connection to them. Better topics include those that

- interest you right now,
- are focused, but not too narrowly,
- have some personal connection to your life.

One good way to **GENERATE IDEAS** for a topic that meets those three criteria is to explore your own roles in life.

219–25

Start with your roles in life. On a piece of paper, make four columns with the headings "Personal," "Family," "Public," and "School." Then **LIST** the roles you play that relate to it. Here is a list one student wrote:

220–21

Personal	Family	Public	School
gamer	son	voter	college student
dog owner	younger	homeless-shelter	work-study
old-car owner	brother	volunteer	employee
male	grandson	American	dorm resident
white		resident	primary-education
middle-class		of Ohio	major

Identify issues that interest you.   Think, then, about issues or controversies that may concern you as a member of one or more of those groups. For instance, as a primary-education major, this student cares about the controversy over whether kids should be taught to read by phonics or by whole language methods. As a college student, he cares about the costs of a college education. Issues that stem from these subjects could include the following: Should reading be taught by phonics or whole language? Should college cost less than it does?

Pick four or five of the roles you list. In five or ten minutes, identify issues that concern or affect you as a member of each of those roles. It might help to word each issue as a question starting with *Should*.

Frame your topic as a problem.   Most position papers address issues that are subjects of ongoing debate — their solutions aren't easy, and people disagree on which ones are best. Posing your topic as a problem can help you think about the topic, find an issue that's suitable to write about, and find a clear focus for your essay.

For example, if you wanted to write an argument on the lack of student parking at your school, you could frame your topic as one of several problems: What causes the parking shortage? Why are the university's parking garages and lots limited in their capacity? What might alleviate the shortage?

Choose one issue to write about.   Remember that the issue should be interesting to you and have some connection to your life. It is a tentative choice; if you find later that you have trouble writing about it, simply go back to your list of roles or issues and choose another.

Considering the Rhetorical Situation

3–4 ■ | **PURPOSE** | Do you want to persuade your audience to do or think something? Change their minds? Consider alternative views? Accept your position as plausible — see that you have thought carefully about an issue and researched it appropriately?

AUDIENCE Who is your intended audience? What do they likely know and believe about this issue? How personal is it for them? To what extent are they likely to agree or disagree with you? Why? What common ground can you find with them?

5–8

STANCE How do you want your audience to perceive you? As an authority on your topic? As someone much like them? As calm? Reasonable? Impassioned or angry? Something else? What's your attitude toward your topic, and why?

12–14

MEDIA / DESIGN What media will you use, and how do your media affect your argument? If you're writing on paper, does your argument call for photos or charts? If you're giving an oral presentation, should you put your reasons and support on slides? If you're writing on the Web, should you add links to counterarguments?

15–17

Generating Ideas and Text

Most essays that successfully argue a position share certain features that make them interesting and persuasive. Remember that your goal is to stake out a position and convince your readers that it is plausible.

Explore what you already know about the issue. Write out whatever you know about the issue by freewriting or as a **LIST** or **OUTLINE**. Why are you interested in this topic? What is your position on it at this point, and why? What aspect do you think you'd like to focus on? Where do you need to focus your research efforts? This activity can help you discover what more you need to learn. Chances are you'll need to learn a lot more about the issue before you even decide what position to take.

220–21
223–24

Do some research. At this point, try to get an overview. Start with one **GENERAL SOURCE** of information that will give you a sense of the ins and outs of your issue, one that isn't overtly biased. *Time, Newsweek,* and other national weekly newsmagazines can be good starting points on current

388

394–95

issues; encyclopedias are better for issues that are not so current. For some issues, you may need to **INTERVIEW** an expert. For example, one student who wanted to write about chemical abuse of animals at 4H competitions interviewed an experienced show competitor. Use your overview source to find out the main questions raised about your issue and to get some idea about the various ways in which you might argue it.

Explore the issue strategically.　Most issues may be argued from many different perspectives. You'll probably have some sense of the different views that exist on your issue, but you should explore multiple perspectives before deciding on your position. The following methods are good ways of exploring issues:

314–23

- As a matter of **DEFINITION**. What is it? How should it be defined? How can *organic* or *genetically modified food* be defined? How do proponents of *organic food* define it — and how do they define *genetically modified food*? How do advocates of *genetically modified food* define it — and how do they define *organic*? Considering such definitions is one way to identify different perspectives on the topic.

300–305

- As a matter of **CLASSIFICATION**. Can the issue be further divided? What categories might it be broken into? Are there different kinds and different ways of producing organic foods and genetically modified foods? Do different subcategories suggest particular positions or perhaps a way of supporting a certain position? Are there other ways of categorizing foods?

306–13

- As a matter of **COMPARISON**. Is one subject being considered better than another? Is organic food healthier or safer than genetically modified food? Is genetically modified food healthier or safer than organic? Is the answer somewhere in the middle?

338–42

- As a matter of **PROCESS**. Should somebody do something? What? Should people buy and eat more organic food? More genetically modified food? Should they buy and eat some of each?

Reconsider whether the issue can be argued.　Is this issue worth discussing? Why is it important to you and to others? What difference will it make if one position or another prevails? Is it **ARGUABLE**? At this point, you want to be sure that your topic is worth arguing about.

283–99

Draft a thesis. Having explored the possibilities, decide your position, and write it out as a complete sentence. For example:

> Pete Rose should not be eligible for the Hall of Fame.
>
> Reading should be taught using a mix of whole language and phonics.
>
> Genetically modified foods should be permitted in the United States.

Qualify your thesis. Rather than taking a strict pro or con position, in most cases you'll want to **QUALIFY YOUR POSITION**—in certain circumstances, with certain conditions, with these limitations, and so on. This is not to say that we should settle, give in, sell out; rather, it is to say that our position may not be the only "correct" one and that other positions may be valid as well. **QUALIFYING YOUR THESIS** also makes your topic manageable by limiting it. For example:

285

274–75

> Pete Rose should not be eligible for the Hall of Fame, though he should be permitted to contribute to major league baseball in other ways.
>
> Reading should be taught using a mix of phonics and whole language, but the needs of individual students, not a philosophy, should be the primary focus.
>
> Genetically modified foods should be permitted in the United States if they are clearly labeled as such.

Come up with good reasons. Once you have a thesis, you need to come up with good **REASONS** to convince your readers that it's plausible. Write out your position, and then list several reasons. For instance, if your thesis is that Pete Rose should not be eligible for the Hall of Fame, two of your reasons might be:

286–87

> He bet on professional games, an illegal practice.
>
> Professional athletes' gambling on the outcome of games will cause fans to lose faith in professional sports.

Think about which reasons are best for your purposes: Which seem the most persuasive? Which are most likely to be accepted by your audience? Which seem to matter the most now? If your list of reasons is short or you think you'll have trouble developing them enough to write an appropriate essay, this is a good time to rethink your topic—before you've invested too much time in it.

Develop support for your reasons.   Next, you have to come up with
287–93 **EVIDENCE** to support your reasons: facts, statistics, examples, testimony by
authorities and experts, anecdotal evidence, scenarios, case studies and
observation, and textual evidence.

What counts as evidence varies across audiences. Statistical evidence may be required in certain disciplines but not in others; anecdotes
may be accepted as evidence in some courses but not in engineering.
Some audiences will be persuaded by emotional appeals while others
will not. For example, if you argue that Pete Rose should be eligible for
the Baseball Hall of Fame because he's one of the greatest baseball players of all time, you could support that reason with *facts*: he played well in
five different positions during his career. Or you could support it with *statistics*: Rose holds Major League records for the most career hits, most
games played, and most career at bats. *Expert testimony* might include a
plea on his behalf by former President Jimmy Carter, who wrote in 1995,
"Pete Rose should at least be declared eligible for later consideration" for
election to the Hall of Fame.

Identify other positions.   Now, think about positions that differ from
yours and about the reasons people are likely to give for those positions.
Be careful to represent their points of view as accurately and fairly as you
can. Then decide whether you need to acknowledge or refute the position.

Acknowledging other positions.   Some positions can't be refuted, but still
294 you need to **ACKNOWLEDGE** potential doubts, concerns, and objections to
show that you've considered them. Doing so shows that you've considered other perspectives. For example, in an essay arguing that vacations
are necessary to maintain good health, medical writer Alina Tugend
acknowledges that "in some cases, these trips — particularly with entire
families in tow — can be stressful in their own way. The joys of a holiday
can also include lugging around a ridiculous amount of paraphernalia,
jet-lagged children sobbing on airplanes, hotels that looked wonderful
on the Web but are in reality next to a construction site." Tugend quali-
fies her assertions to moderate her position and make her stance appear
reasonable.

rhetorical situations

genres

processes

strategies

research mla/apa

media/ design

handbook

Refuting other positions.   State the position as clearly and as fairly as you can, and then **REFUTE** it by showing why you believe it is wrong. Perhaps the reasoning is faulty, or the supporting evidence inadequate. Acknowledge the merits of the argument, if any, but emphasize its short-comings. Avoid the **FALLACY** of attacking the person making the argument or bringing up a competing position that no one seriously entertains.

◆ 295

◆ 296–98

Ways of Organizing an Argument

Readers need to be able to follow the reasoning of your argument from beginning to end; your task is to lead them from point to point as you build your case. Sometimes you'll want to give all the reasons for your argument first, followed by discussion of any other positions. Alternatively, you might discuss each reason and any counterargument together.

[Reasons to support your argument, followed by counterarguments]

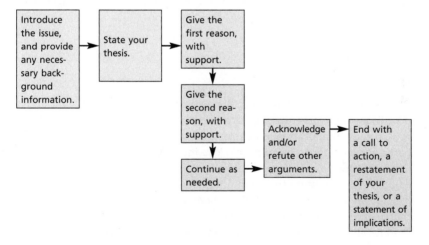

[Reason / counterargument, reason / counterargument]

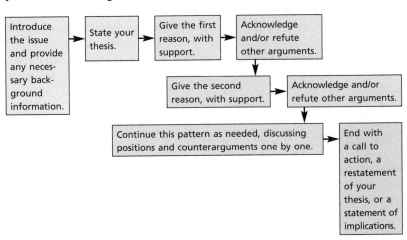

Consider the order in which you discuss your reasons. Usually what comes last is the most emphatic and what comes in the middle is the least emphatic, so you might want to put your most important or strongest reasons first and last.

Writing Out a Draft

Once you have generated ideas, done some research, and thought about how you want to organize your argument, it's time to start **DRAFTING**. Your goal in the initial draft is to develop your argument—you can fill in support and transitions as you revise. You may want to write your first draft in one sitting, so that you can develop your reasoning from beginning to end. Or you may write the main argument first and the introduction and conclusion after you've drafted the body of the essay; many writers find that beginning and ending an essay are the hardest tasks they face. Here is some advice on how you might **BEGIN AND END** your argument:

226–28

261–71

Draft a beginning. There are various ways to begin an argument essay, depending on your audience and purpose. Here are a few suggestions.

- *Offer background information.* You may need to give your readers information to help them understand your position. Taubes establishes that the obesity rate has risen in the past twenty years and states the conventional explanation before making his argument that carbohydrates, not fats, are to blame.

- *Define a key term.* You may need to show how you're using certain key words. Lessig, for example, defines piracy as "using the creative property of others without their permission" in his first sentence, a **DEFINITION** that is central to his argument.

314–23

- *Begin with something that will get readers' attention.* MacKay begins emphatically: "There are thousands of people dying to buy a kidney and thousands of people dying to sell a kidney . . . So why are we standing in the way?"

- *Explain the context for your position.* All arguments are part of a larger, ongoing conversation, so you might begin by showing how your position fits into the arguments others have made. Taubes does this in his second paragraph when he explains how scientists have traditionally explained the rise in obesity.

Draft an ending. Your conclusion is the chance to wrap up your argument in such a way that readers will remember what you've said. Here are a few ways of concluding an argument essay.

- *Summarize your main points.* Especially when you've presented a complex argument, it can help readers to **SUMMARIZE** your main point. MacKay sums up her argument with the sentence "If legalized and regulated, the sale of human organs would save lives."

416–17

- *Call for action.* Lessig does this when he concludes by saying the law should seek a balance between copyright law and the need for continued innovation.

- *Frame your argument by referring to the introduction.* MacKay does this when she ends by reiterating that selling organs benefits both seller and buyer.

Come up with a title. Most often you'll want your title to tell readers something about your topic—and to make them want to read on. MacKay's "Organ Sales Will Save Lives" tells us both her topic and position. Taubes's title is a little unclear until you read the first paragraph, but "What If It's All Been a Big Fat Lie" makes us want to read that paragraph. See the chapter on **GUIDING YOUR READER** for more advice on composing a good title.

272–77

Considering Matters of Design

You'll probably write your essay in paragraph form, but think about the information you're presenting and how you can design it in such a way as to make your argument as easy as possible for your readers to understand. Think also about whether any visual elements would be more persuasive than plain words.

524–25
- What would be an appropriate **TYPEFACE?** Something serious like Times Roman? Something traditional like Courier? Something else?

526–27
- Would it help your readers if you divided your argument into shorter sections and added **HEADINGS?**

525–26
- If you're making several points, would they be easier to follow if you set them off in a **LIST?**

528–30
- Do you have any supporting evidence that would be easier to understand in the form of a bar **GRAPH**, line graph, or pie chart?

528–32
- Would **ILLUSTRATIONS**—photos, diagrams, or drawings—add support for your argument?

Getting Response and Revising

235–36
At this point you need to look at your draft closely, and if possible **GET RESPONSE** from others as well. Following are some questions for looking at an argument with a critical eye.

- Is there sufficient background or **CONTEXT?** 262–63
- Is the **THESIS** clear and appropriately qualified? 274–75
- Are the **REASONS** plausible? 286–87
- Is there enough **EVIDENCE** to support these reasons? Is that evidence appropriate? 287–93
- Have you cited enough **SOURCES,** and are these sources credible? 384–99
- Can readers follow the steps in your reasoning?
- Have you considered potential objections or **OTHER POSITIONS?** Are there any others that should be addressed? 294–95
- Are source materials **DOCUMENTED** carefully and completely, with in-text citations and a works cited or references section? 425–27

Next it's time to **REVISE,** to make sure your argument offers convincing evidence, appeals to readers' values, and achieves your purpose. 236–39

Editing and Proofreading

Readers equate correctness with competence. Once you've revised your draft, follow these guidelines for **EDITING** an argument: 241–45

- Check to see that your tone is appropriate and consistent throughout, reflects your **STANCE** accurately, and enhances the argument you're making. 12–14
- Be sure readers will be able to follow the argument; check to see you've provided **TRANSITIONS** and summary statements where necessary. 277
- Make sure you've smoothly integrated **QUOTATIONS, PARAPHRASES,** and **SUMMARIES** from source material into your writing and **DOCUMENTED** them accurately. 408–19 425–27
- Look for phrases such as "I think" or "I feel" and delete them; your essay itself expresses your opinion.
- Make sure that **ILLUSTRATIONS** have captions and that charts and graphs have headings — and that all are referred to in the main text. 528–32
- **PROOFREAD** and spell-check your essay carefully. 245–46

Taking Stock of Your Work

Take stock of what you've written by writing out answers to these questions:

- What did you do well in this piece?
- What could still be improved?
- How did you go about researching your topic?
- How did others' responses influence your writing?
- How did you go about drafting this piece?
- Did you use graphic elements (tables, graphs, diagrams, photographs, illustrations) effectively? If not, would they have helped?
- What would you do differently next time?
- What have you learned about your writing ability from writing this piece? What do you need to work on in the future?

247–58
125–32
143–52
171–79

> **IF YOU NEED MORE HELP**
>
> See Chapter 28 if you are required to submit your argument as part of a writing **PORTFOLIO.** See also Chapter 12 on **EVALUATIONS,** Chapter 14 on **LITERARY ANALYSES,** and Chapter 17 on **PROPOSALS** for advice on writing those specific types of arguments.

rhetorical situations

genres

processes

strategies

research mla/apa

media/ design

handbook

Abstracts **10**

Abstracts are summaries written to give readers the gist of a report or presentation. Sometimes they are published in conference proceedings or databases. In some academic fields, you may be required to include an abstract in a **REPORT** or as a preview of a presentation you plan to give at an academic or professional conference. Abstracts are brief, typically 100–200 words, sometimes even shorter. Three common kinds are *informative abstracts*, *descriptive abstracts*, and *proposal abstracts*.

59–82

INFORMATIVE ABSTRACTS

Informative abstracts state in one paragraph the essence of a whole paper about a study or a research project. That one paragraph must mention all the main points or parts of the paper: a description of the study or project, its methods, the results, and the conclusions. Here is an example of the abstract accompanying a seven-page essay that appeared in 2002 in *The Journal of Clinical Psychology*:

> The relationship between boredom proneness and health-symptom reporting was examined. Undergraduate students (N = 200) completed the Boredom Proneness Scale and the Hopkins Symptom Checklist. A multiple analysis of covariance indicated that individuals with high boredom-proneness total scores reported significantly higher ratings on all five subscales of the Hopkins Symptom Checklist (Obsessive–Compulsive, Somatization, Anxiety, Interpersonal Sensitivity, and Depression). The results suggest that boredom proneness may be an important element to consider when assessing symptom reporting. Implications for determining the effects of boredom proneness on psychological- and physical-health symptoms, as well as the application in clinical settings, are discussed.
>
> —Jennifer Sommers and Stephen J. Vodanovich,
> "Boredom Proneness"

The first sentence states the nature of the study being reported. The next summarizes the method used to investigate the problem, and the following one gives the results: students who, according to specific tests, are more likely to be bored are also more likely to have certain medical or psychological symptoms. The last two sentences indicate that the paper discusses those results and examines the conclusion and its implications.

DESCRIPTIVE ABSTRACTS

Descriptive abstracts are usually much briefer than informative abstracts and provide much less information. Rather than summarizing the entire paper, a descriptive abstract functions more as a teaser, providing a quick overview that invites the reader to read the whole. Descriptive abstracts usually do not give or discuss results or set out the conclusion or its implications. A descriptive abstract of the boredom-proneness essay might simply include the first sentence from the informative abstract plus a final sentence of its own:

> The relationship between boredom proneness and health-symptom reporting was examined. The findings and their application in clinical settings are discussed.

PROPOSAL ABSTRACTS

Proposal abstracts contain the same basic information as informative abstracts, but their purpose is very different. You prepare proposal abstracts to persuade someone to let you write on a topic, pursue a project, conduct an experiment, or present a paper at a scholarly conference. This kind of abstract is not written to introduce a longer piece but rather to stand alone, and often the abstract is written before the paper itself. Titles and other aspects of the proposal deliberately reflect the theme of the proposed work, and you may use the future tense, rather than the past, to describe work not yet completed. Here is a possible proposal for doing research on boredom:

rhetorical situations

genres

processes

strategies

research mla/apa

media/ design

handbook

Undergraduate students will complete the Boredom Proneness Scale and the Hopkins Symptom Checklist. A multiple analysis of covariance will be performed to determine the relationship between boredom-proneness total scores and ratings on the five subscales of the Hopkins Symptom Checklist (Obsessive–Compulsive, Somatization, Anxiety, Interpersonal Sensitivity, and Depression).

Key Features / Abstracts

A summary of basic information. An informative abstract includes enough information to substitute for the report itself, a descriptive abstract offers only enough information to let the audience decide whether to read further, and a proposal abstract gives an overview of the planned work.

Objective description. Abstracts present information on the contents of a report or a proposed study; they do not present arguments about or personal perspectives on those contents. The informative abstract on boredom proneness, for example, offers only a tentative conclusion: "The results *suggest* that boredom proneness *may* be an important element to consider."

Brevity. Although the length of abstracts may vary, journals and organizations often restrict them to 120–200 words — meaning you must carefully select and edit your words.

A BRIEF GUIDE TO WRITING ABSTRACTS

Considering the Rhetorical Situation

PURPOSE   Are you giving a brief but thorough overview of a completed study? Only enough information to create interest? Or a proposal for a planned study or presentation? ▮ 3–4

AUDIENCE   For whom are you writing this abstract? What information about your project will your readers need? ▮ 5–8

12–14 ■   **STANCE**   Whatever your stance in the longer work, your abstract must be objective.

15–17 ■   **MEDIA / DESIGN**   How will you set your abstract off from the rest of the text? If you are publishing it online, will you devote a single page to it? What format does your audience require?

Generating Ideas and Text

Write the paper first, the abstract last. You can then use the finished work as the guide for the abstract, which should follow the same basic structure. *Exception:* You may need to write a proposal abstract months before the work it describes will be complete.

Copy and paste key statements. If you've already written the work, highlight your **THESIS,** objective, or purpose; basic information on your methods; your results; and your conclusion. Copy and paste those sentences into a new document to create a rough version of your abstract.

274–75 ◆

416–17 ●   **Pare down the information to key ideas.**   **SUMMARIZE** the report, editing out any nonessential words and details. In your first sentence, introduce the overall scope of your study. Also include any other information that seems crucial to understanding your paper. Avoid phrases that add unnecessary words, such as "It is concluded that." In general, you probably won't want to use "I"; an abstract should cover ideas, not say what you think or will do.

Conform to any requirements. In general, an informative abstract should be at most 10 percent as long as the original and no longer than the maximum length allowed. Descriptive abstracts should be shorter still, and proposal abstracts should conform to the requirements of the organization calling for the proposal.

Ways of Organizing an Abstract

[An informative abstract]

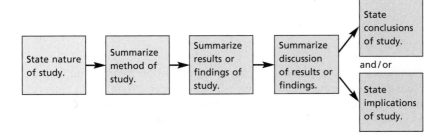

[A descriptive abstract]

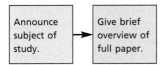

[A proposal abstract]

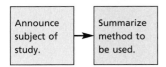

IF YOU NEED MORE HELP

See Chapter 24 for guidelines on **DRAFTING**, Chapter 25 on **ASSESSING YOUR OWN WRITING**, Chapter 26 on **GETTING RESPONSE AND REVISING**, and Chapter 27 on **EDITING AND PROOFREADING**.

226–28
235–41
242–46

11 Annotated Bibliographies

Annotated bibliographies describe, give publication information for, and sometimes evaluate each work on a list of sources. When we do research, we may consult annotated bibliographies to evaluate potential sources. You may also be assigned to create annotated bibliographies to weigh the potential usefulness of sources and to document your search efforts so that teachers can assess your ability to find, describe, and evaluate sources. There are two kinds of annotations, *descriptive* and *evaluative*; both may be brief, consisting only of phrases, or more formal, consisting of sentences and paragraphs. Sometimes an annotated bibliography is introduced by a short statement explaining its scope.

Descriptive annotations simply summarize the contents of each work, without comment or evaluation. They may be very short, just long enough to capture the flavor of the work, like the following excerpt from a bibliography of books and articles on teen films, published in 1997 in the *Journal of Popular Film and Television*.

MICHAEL BENTON, MARK DOLAN, AND REBECCA ZISCH

Teen Film$

In the introduction to his book *The Road to Romance and Ruin*, Jon Lewis points out that over half of the world's population is currently under the age of twenty. This rather startling fact should be enough to make most Hollywood producers drool when they think of the potential profits from a target movie audience. Attracting the largest demographic group is, after all, the quickest way to box-office success.

rhetorical situations

genres

processes

strategies

research mla/apa

media/ design

handbook

In fact, almost from its beginning, the film industry has recognized the importance of the teenaged audience, with characters such as Andy Hardy and locales such as Ridgemont High and the 'hood.

Beyond the assumption that teen films are geared exclusively toward teenagers, however, film researchers should keep in mind that people of all ages have attended and still attend teen films. Popular films about adolescents are also expressions of larger cultural currents. Studying the films is important for understanding an era's common beliefs about its teenaged population within a broader pattern of general cultural preoccupations.

This selected bibliography is intended both to serve and to stimulate interest in the teen film genre. It provides a research tool for those who are studying teen films and their cultural implications. Unfortunately, however, in the process of compiling this list we quickly realized that it was impossible to be genuinely comprehensive or to satisfy every interest.

Doherty, Thomas. <u>Teenagers and Teenpics: The Juvenilization of American Movies in the 1950s</u>. Boston: Unwin Hyman, 1988. Historical discussion of the identification of teenagers as a targeted film market.

Foster, Harold M. "Film in the Classroom: Coping with Teen Pics." <u>English Journal</u> 76 (1987): 86–88. Evaluation of the potential of using teen films such as <u>Sixteen Candles</u>, <u>The Karate Kid</u>, <u>Risky Business</u>, <u>The Flamingo Kid</u>, and <u>The Breakfast Club</u> to instruct adolescents on the difference between film as communication and film as exploitation.

Washington, Michael, and Marvin J. Berlowitz. "Blaxploitation Films and High School Youth: Swat Superfly." <u>Jump Cut</u> 9 (1975): 23–24. Marxist reaction to the trend of youth-oriented black action films. Article seeks to illuminate the negative influences the films have on high school students by pointing out the false ideas about education, morality, and the black family espoused by the heroes in the films.

These annotations are purely descriptive; the authors express none of their own opinions. They describe works as "historical" or "Marxist" but do not indicate whether they're "good." The bibliography entries are documented in MLA style.

Evaluative annotations offer opinions on a source as well as describe it. They are often helpful in assessing how useful a source will be for your own writing. The following evaluative annotations are from a bibliography by Jessica Ann Olson, a student at Wright State University.

JESSICA ANN OLSON

Global Warming

Parmesan, Camille, and Hector Galbraith. "Executive Summary." <u>Observed Impacts of Global Climate Change in the U.S.</u> Nov. 2004. Pew Center on Global Climate Change. 17 Jan. 2007 <http://www.pewclimate.org/ global-warming-in-depth/all_reports/observedimpacts/execsumm.cfm>. This report summarizes recent scientific findings that document the impact changes in the climate have had on the distribution of plants and animals in the United States and on how they interact within their communities. For example, it explains how a shift has taken place in the blooming period for plants and the breeding period for animals caused by global warming. Because of changes in their geographic range, species may interact differently, possibly resulting in population declines. For example, the red fox is now found in areas dominated by the arctic fox and is threatening its survival. The report stresses that such shifts can harm the world's biodiversity. Plants and animals that are rare now face extinction. The annual cycle of carbon dioxide levels in the atmosphere has also changed, largely due to the lengthening of the growing season, affecting basic ecosystem processes. I did not find this report as helpful as other sources because its information is based only on observations made in the United States. The information appears reliable, though, because it is based on scientific evidence. This essay will be helpful to my essay because it focuses on how plants and animals are currently affected, such as their shifting communities and how they are clashing. I could use this to explain human changes by providing evidence of what is happening to other species. This source will not be as helpful in explaining the climate's effects on human biological function in particular, but it will provide some framework. For example, I could explain how the plants that help convert carbon dioxide into oxygen are being harmed and relate that to how the humans will suffer the consequences.

Gore, Al. <u>An Inconvenient Truth: The Planetary Emergency of Global Warming and What We Can Do About It</u>. New York: Rodale, 2006.

This publication, which is based on Gore's slide show on global warming, stresses the urgency of the global warming crisis. It centers on how the atmosphere is very thin and how greenhouse gases such as carbon dioxide are making it thicker. The thicker atmosphere traps more infrared radiation, causing warming of the Earth. Gore argues that carbon dioxide, which is created by burning fossil fuels, cutting down forests, and producing cement, accounts for eighty percent of greenhouse gas emissions. He includes several examples of problems caused by global warming. Penguins and polar bears are at risk because the glaciers they call home are quickly melting. Coral reefs are being bleached and destroyed when their inhabitants overheat and leave. Global warming is now affecting people's lives as well. For example, the highways in Alaska are only frozen enough to be driven on fewer than eighty days of the year. In China and elsewhere, record-setting floods and droughts are taking place. Hurricanes are on the rise. This source's goal is to inform its audience about the ongoing global warming crisis and to inspire change across the world. It is useful because it relies on scientific data that can be referred to easily and it provides a solid foundation for me to build on. For example, it explains how carbon dioxide is produced and how it is currently affecting plants and animals. This evidence could potentially help my research on how humans are biologically affected by global warming. It will also help me structure my essay, using its general information to lead into the specifics of my topic. For example, I could introduce the issue by explaining the thinness of the atmosphere and the effect of greenhouse gases, then focus on carbon dioxide and its effects on organisms.

These annotations not only describe the sources in detail, but also evaluate their usefulness for the writer's own project. They show that the writer understands the content of the sources and can relate it to her own anticipated needs as a researcher and writer.

Key Features / Annotated Bibliographies

A statement of scope. You need a brief introductory statement to explain what you're covering. The authors of the bibliography on teen films introduce their bibliography with three paragraphs establishing a context for the bibliography and announcing their purpose for compiling it.

Complete bibliographic information. Provide all the information about the source following one documentation system (MLA, APA, or another one) so that your readers or other researchers will be able to find each source easily.

A concise description of the work. A good annotation describes each item as carefully and objectively as possible, giving accurate information and showing that you understand the source. These qualities will help to build authority — for you as a writer and for your annotations.

Relevant commentary. If you write an evaluative bibliography, your comments should be relevant to your purpose and audience. The best way to achieve relevance is to consider what questions a potential reader might have about the sources. Your evaluation might also focus on the text's suitability as a source for your writing, as Olson's evaluative annotations do.

Consistent presentation. All annotations should follow a consistent pattern: if one is written in complete sentences, they should all be. Each annotation in the teen films bibliography, for example, begins with a phrase (not a complete sentence) characterizing the work.

A BRIEF GUIDE TO WRITING ANNOTATED BIBLIOGRAPHIES

Considering the Rhetorical Situation

3–4   **PURPOSE**   Will your bibliography need to demonstrate the depth or breadth of your research? Will your readers actually track down and use your sources? Do you need or want to convince readers that your sources are good?

rhetorical situations   genres   processes   strategies   research mla/apa   media/design   handbook

AUDIENCE	For whom are you compiling this bibliography? What does your audience need to know about each source?	5–8
STANCE	Are you presenting yourself as an objective describer or evaluator? Or are you expressing a particular point of view toward the sources you evaluate?	12–14
MEDIA / DESIGN	If you are publishing the bibliography online, will you provide links from each annotation to the source itself? Online or off, do you need to distinguish the bibliographic information from the annotation by using a different font?	15–17

Generating Ideas and Text

Decide what sources to include.   You may be tempted to include in a bibliography every source you find or look at. A better strategy is to include only those sources that you or your readers may find potentially useful in researching your topic. For an academic bibliography, you need to consider these qualities:

- *Appropriateness.* Is this source relevant to your topic? Is it a primary source or a secondary source? Is it aimed at an appropriate audience? General or specialized? Elementary, advanced, or somewhere in between?

- *Credibility.* Is the author reputable? Is the publication or publishing company reputable? Do its ideas more or less agree with those in other sources you've read?

- *Balance.* Does the source present enough evidence for its assertions? Does it show any particular bias? Does it present countering arguments fairly?

- *Timeliness.* Is the source recent enough? Does it reflect current thinking or research about the subject?

If you need help **FINDING SOURCES,** see Chapter 43.   384–99

MLA 428–76 ●
APA 477–519

Compile a list of works to annotate. Give the sources themselves in whatever documentation style is required; see the guidelines for **MLA** and **APA** styles in Chapters 49 and 50.

Determine what kind of bibliography you need to write. Descriptive or evaluative? Will your annotations be in the form of phrases? Complete sentences? Paragraphs? The form will shape your reading and note taking. If you're writing a descriptive bibliography, your reading goal will be to understand and capture the writer's message as clearly as possible. If you're writing an evaluative bibliography, your annotations must also include your own comments on the source.

Read carefully. To write an annotation, you must understand the source's argument, but when you are writing an annotated bibliography as part of a **PROPOSAL,** you may have neither the time nor the need to read the whole text. Here's a way of quickly determining whether a source is likely to serve your needs:

171–79 ▲

- Check the publisher or sponsor (university press? scholarly journal? popular magazine? website sponsored by a reputable organization?).

- Read the preface (of a book), abstract (of a scholarly article), introduction (of an article in a nonscholarly magazine or a website).

- Skim the table of contents or the headings.

- Read the parts that relate specifically to your topic.

Research the writer, if necessary. If you are required to indicate the writer's credentials, you may need to do additional research. You may find information by typing the writer's name into a search engine or looking up the writer in *Contemporary Authors*. In any case, information about the writer should take up no more than one sentence in your annotation.

324–32 ◆

Summarize the work in a sentence or two. **DESCRIBE** it as objectively as possible: even if you are writing an evaluative annotation, you can evaluate the central point of a work better by stating it clearly first. *If you're writing a descriptive annotation, you're done.*

Establish criteria for evaluating sources. If you're **EVALUATING** sources for a project, you'll need to evaluate them in terms of their usefulness for your project, their **STANCE,** and their overall credibility.

▲ 125–32

■ 12–14

Write a brief evaluation of the source. If you can generalize about the worth of the entire work, fine. You may find, however, that some parts are useful while others are not, and what you write should reflect that mix.

Be consistent—in content, sentence structure, and format.

- **Content.** Try to provide about the same amount of information for each entry; if you're evaluating, evaluate each source, not just some sources.

- **Sentence structure.** Use the same style throughout—**COMPLETE SEN- TENCES,** brief phrases, or a mix.

HB-4–7

- **Format.** Use one documentation style throughout; use consistent **TYPE** for each element in each entry—for example, italicize or underline all book titles.

□ 524–25

Ways of Organizing an Annotated Bibliography

Depending on their purpose, annotated bibliographies may or may not include an introduction. Most annotated bibliographies cover a single topic and so are organized alphabetically by author's or editor's last name. When a work lacks a named author, alphabetize it by the first important word in its title. Consult the documentation system you're using for additional details about alphabetizing works appropriately.

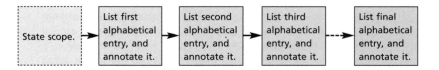

State scope. → List first alphabetical entry, and annotate it. → List second alphabetical entry, and annotate it. → List third alphabetical entry, and annotate it. ⇢ List final alphabetical entry, and annotate it.

Sometimes an annotated bibliography needs to be organized into several subject areas (or genres, periods, or some other category) and the entries are listed alphabetically within each category. For example, a bibliography about terrorism breaks down into subjects such as "Global Terrorism" and "Weapons of Mass Destruction."

[Multi-category bibliography]

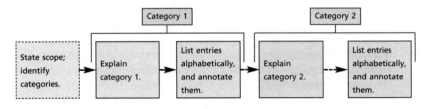

IF YOU NEED MORE HELP

See Chapter 24 for guidelines on **DRAFTING,** Chapter 25 on **ASSESSING YOUR OWN WRITING,** Chapter 26 on **GETTING RESPONSE AND REVISING,** and Chapter 27 on **EDITING AND PROOFREADING.** See Chapter 28 if you are required to submit your bibliography in a writing **PORTFOLIO.**

Evaluations 12

Consumer Reports evaluates cell phones and laundry detergents. The *Princeton Review* and *US News & World Report* evaluate colleges and universities. You probably consult such sources to make decisions, and you probably evaluate things all the time—when you recommend a film (or not) or a teacher (ditto). An evaluation is at bottom a judgment; you judge something according to certain criteria, supporting your judgment with reasons and evidence. You need to give your reasons for evaluating it as you do because often your evaluation will affect your audience's actions: they must see this movie, needn't bother with this book, should be sure to have the Caesar salad at this restaurant, and so on. In the following review, written for a first-year writing class at Wright State University, Ali Heinekamp offers her evaluation of the film *Juno*.

ALI HEINEKAMP

Juno: Not Just Another Teen Movie

It all starts with a chair, where Juno (Ellen Page) has unprotected sex with her best friend Bleeker (Michael Cera). Several weeks later, she's at a convenience store, buying a pregnancy test. Only sixteen, Juno faces the terrifying task of telling her parents that she is pregnant. With their support, Juno moves forward in her decision to give birth and give the child to Mark (Jason Bateman) and Vanessa (Jennifer Garner), a wealthy and seemingly perfect married couple looking to adopt. Although the situations *Juno*'s characters find themselves in and their dialogue may be criticized as unrealistic, the film, written by Diablo Cody and directed by Jason Reitman, successfully portrays the emotions of a teen being shoved into maturity way too fast.

Much of the time, *Juno* seems unrealistic because it seems to treat the impact of teen pregnancy so lightly. The consequences of Juno's pregnancy are sugar-coated to such an extent that in many cases, they are barely apparent. The film downplays the emotional struggle that a pregnant woman would feel in deciding to give birth and then put that child up for adoption, and it ignores the discomforts of pregnancy, such as mood swings and nausea.

Likewise, *Juno*'s dialogue is too good to be true — funny and clever, but unrealistic. For example, Juno tells Mark and Vanessa "If I could just have the thing and give it to you now, I totally would. But I'm guessing it looks probably like a sea monkey right now, and we should let it get a little cuter." At another point, talking about her absent mother, Juno says, "Oh, and she inexplicably mails me a cactus every Valentine's Day. And I'm like, 'Thanks a heap, coyote ugly. This cactus-gram stings even worse than your abandonment.'" As funny as they are, the creatively quirky one-liners often go a bit too far, detracting from both the gravity of Juno's situation and the film's believability.

But although the situations and dialogue are unrealistic, the emotional heart of the movie is believable — and moving. Despite the movie's lack of realism in portraying her pregnancy, Juno's vulnerability transforms her character and situation into something much more believable. Juno mentions at various times that her classmates stare at her stomach and talk about her behind her back, but initially she seems unconcerned with the negative attention. This façade falls apart, however, when Juno accuses Bleeker, the baby's father, of being ashamed of the fact that he and Juno have had sex. The strong front she is putting up drops when she bursts out, "At least you don't have to have the evidence under your sweater." This break in Juno's strength reveals her vulnerability and makes her character relatable and believable.

The juxtaposition of Juno's teenage quirks and the adult situation she's in also remind us of her youth and vulnerability. As a result of the adult situation Juno finds herself in and her generally stoic demeanor, it's easy to see her as a young adult. But the film fills each scene with visual reminders that Juno is just a kid being forced into situations beyond her maturity level. At a convenience store, Juno buys a pregnancy test along with a licorice rope. She calls Women Now, an abortion clinic, on a phone that looks like a hamburger. And while she is giving birth, she wears long, brightly striped socks. These subtle visual

5

cues help us remember the reality of Juno's position as both physically an adult and emotionally an adolescent.

While the dialogue is too clever to be realistic, in the end it's carried by the movie's heart. Scott Tobias from the entertainment Web site *The A.V. Club* says it best when he writes that the colorful dialogue is often "too ostentatious for its own good, but the film's sincerity is what ultimately carries it across." In fact, intensely emotional scenes are marked by their *lack* of witty dialogue. For example, when Juno runs into Vanessa at the mall, Vanessa, reluctantly at first, kneels down to talk to the baby through Juno's stomach. Vanessa's diction while talking to the baby is so simple, so expected. She simply starts with, "Hi baby, it's me. It's Vanessa," and then continues, "I can't wait to meet you." This simple, everyday statement stands out in comparison to the rest of the well-crafted, humorous script. For her part, Juno simply stares admiringly at Vanessa. She doesn't have to say anything to transform the scene into a powerful one. Another scene in which the dialogue stops being clever is the one in which Juno and Bleeker lie in side by side in a hospital bed after Juno has given birth, Juno in tears and Bleeker lost in thought. They don't need to say anything for us to feel their pain at the realization that although the pregnancy is over, it will never truly be in the past. The absence of dialogue in scenes such as these actually contributes to their power. We finally see more than stoicism and sarcasm from Juno: we see caring and fear, which are feelings most would expect of a pregnant teen.

There has been much concern among critics that as a pregnant teenager, Juno doesn't present a good role model for teen girls. Worrying that teens may look up to Juno so much that being pregnant becomes "cool," Dana Stevens writes in *Slate*, "Let's hope that the teenage girls of America don't cast their condoms to the wind in hopes of becoming as cool as 16-year-old Juno MacGuff." But it is not Juno's pregnancy that makes her cool: it is her ability to overcome the difficult obstacles thrown at her, and that strength does make her a good role model. Another critic, Lisa Schwarzbaum from *Entertainment Weekly*, feels that the movie might have been more realistic had Juno chosen to go through with an abortion. It's true that Juno may have chosen the more difficult answer to a teen pregnancy, but she is far from alone in her decision. Perhaps Schwarzbaum underestimates teens in thinking that they would not be able to cope with the emotionally difficult situation Juno chooses. Again, in her strength, Juno is a role model for young women.

Although *Juno* is a comedy filled with improbable situations, exaggerations, and wit, its genuine emotion allows us to connect with and relate to the film. The reality of the characters' emotions in controversial and serious situations allows *Juno* to transcend its own genre. It reaches depths of emotion that are unusual for teenage comedies, proving that *Juno* is not just another teen movie.

Works Cited

Cody, Diablo. <u>Juno</u>. Dir. Jason Reitman. Perf. Ellen Page, Michael Cera, Jennifer Garner, Jason Bateman. Fox Searchlight, 2007.

Schwarzbaum, Lisa. Rev. of <u>Juno,</u> dir. Jason Reitman. <u>EW.com</u> 28 Nov. 2007. 14 Apr. 2008 <http://www.ew.com/ew/article/0,,20163026,00.html>.

Stevens, Dana. "Superpregnant: How <u>Juno</u> Is <u>Knocked Up</u> from the Girl's Point of View." Rev. of <u>Juno,</u> dir. Jason Reitman. <u>Slate</u> 5 Dec. 2007. 12 Apr. 2008 <http://www.slate.com/id/2179273/fr/flyout>.

Tobias, Scott. Rev. of <u>Juno,</u> dir. Jason Reitman. <u>The A. V. Club</u> 6 Dec. 2007. 13 Apr. 2008 <http://www.avclub.com/content/cinema/juno>.

Heinekamp quickly summarizes Juno's plot and then evaluates the film according to clearly stated criteria. In the process, she responds to several reviewers' comments, joining the critical conversation about the film. She documents her sources according to MLA style.

Key Features / Evaluations

A concise description of the subject.   You should include just enough information to let readers who may not be familiar with your subject understand what it is; the goal is to evaluate, not summarize. Heinekamp briefly describes *Juno*'s main plot points in her first paragraph, only providing what readers need to understand the context of her evaluation.

Clearly defined criteria.   You need to determine clear criteria as the basis for your judgment. In reviews or other evaluations written for a broad audience, you can integrate the criteria into the discussion as reasons for

rhetorical situations | genres | processes | strategies | research mla/apa | media/design | handbook

your assessment, as Heinekamp does in her evaluation of *Juno*. In more formal evaluations, you may need to announce your criteria explicitly. Heinekamp evaluates the film based on the power of its emotion and the realism of its situations, characters, and dialogue.

A knowledgeable discussion of the subject. To evaluate something credibly, you need to show that you know it yourself and that you've researched what other authoritative sources say. Heinekamp cites many examples from *Juno*, showing her knowledge of the film. She also cites reviews from three Internet sources, showing that she's researched others' views as well.

A balanced and fair assessment. An evaluation is centered on a judgment. Heinekamp concedes that *Juno*'s situations and dialogue are unrealistic, but she says it nevertheless "reaches depths of emotion that are unusual for teenage comedies." It is important that any judgment be balanced and fair. Seldom is something all good or all bad. A fair evaluation need not be all positive or all negative; it may acknowledge both strengths and weaknesses. For example, a movie's soundtrack may be wonderful while the plot is not. Heinekamp criticizes *Juno*'s too-witty dialogue and unrealistic situations, even as she appreciates its heart.

Well-supported reasons. You need to argue for your judgment, providing reasons and evidence. Heinekamp gives several reasons for her positive assessment of *Juno*—the believability of its characters, the intensely emotional scenes, the strength of the main character as a role model—and she supports these reasons with many quotations and examples from the film.

A BRIEF GUIDE TO WRITING EVALUATIONS

Choosing Something to Evaluate

You can more effectively evaluate a limited subject than a broad one: review certain dishes at a local restaurant rather than the entire menu; review one film or episode rather than all the films by Alfred Hitchcock or all eighty *Star Trek* episodes. The more specific and focused your subject, the better you can write about it.

Considering the Rhetorical Situation

3–4 **PURPOSE**   Are you writing to affect your audience's opinion of a subject? Do you want to evaluate something to help others decide what to see, do, or buy?

5–8 **AUDIENCE**   To whom are you writing? What will your audience already know about the subject? What will they expect to learn from your evaluation of it? Are they likely to agree with you or not?

12–14 **STANCE**   How will you show that you have evaluated the subject fairly and appropriately? Think about the tone you want to use: should it be reasonable? Passionate? Critical?

15–17 **MEDIA / DESIGN**   How will you deliver your evaluation? In print? Online? As a speech? Can you show an image or film clip? If you're submitting your text for publication, are there any format requirements?

Generating Ideas and Text

219–20 **Explore what you already know.**   **FREEWRITE** to answer the following questions: What do you know about this subject or subjects like it? What are your initial or gut feelings, and why do you feel as you do? How does this subject reflect or affect your basic values or beliefs? How have others evaluated subjects like this?

Identify criteria.   Make a list of criteria you think should be used to evaluate your subject. Think about which criteria will likely be important to your **AUDIENCE.** You might find **CUBING** and **QUESTIONING** to be useful
5–8
222–23 processes for thinking about your topic.

Evaluate your subject.   Study your subject closely to determine if it meets your criteria. You may want to list your criteria on a sheet of paper with space to take notes, or you may develop a grading scale for each criterion to help stay focused on it. Come up with a tentative judgment.

Compare your subject with others.   Often, evaluating something involves **COMPARING AND CONTRASTING** it with similar things. We judge movies in comparison with the other movies we've seen and french fries with the other fries we've tasted. Sometimes those comparisons can be made informally. For other evaluations, you may have to do research—to try on several pairs of jeans before buying any, for example—to see how your subject compares.

306–13

State your judgment as a tentative thesis statement.   Your **THESIS STATEMENT** should be one that balances both pros and cons. "*Fight Club* is a great film—but not for children." "Of the five sport-utility vehicles tested, the Toyota 4Runner emerged as the best in comfort, power, and durability, though not in styling or cargo capacity." Both of these examples offer a judgment but qualify it according to the writer's criteria.

273–75

Anticipate other opinions.   I think Will Ferrell is a comic genius whose movies are first-rate. You think Will Ferrell is a terrible actor who makes awful movies. How can I write a review of his latest film that you will at least consider? One way is by **ACKNOWLEDGING** other opinions—and **REFUTING** those opinions as best I can. I may not persuade you to see Will Ferrell's next film, but I can at least demonstrate that by certain criteria he should be appreciated. You may need to **RESEARCH** how others have evaluated your subject.

294
295
373

Identify and support your reasons.   Write out all the **REASONS** you can think of that will convince your audience to accept your judgment. Review your list to identify the most convincing or important reasons. Then review how well your subject meets your criteria and decide how best to **SUPPORT** your reasons: through examples, authoritative opinions, statistics, or something else.

286–87
287–93

Ways of Organizing an Evaluation

Evaluations are usually organized in one of two ways. One way is to introduce what's being evaluated, followed by your judgment, discussing your criteria along the way. This is a useful strategy if your audience may not be familiar with your subject.

[Start with your subject]

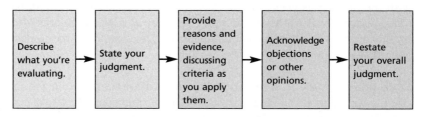

Describe what you're evaluating. → State your judgment. → Provide reasons and evidence, discussing criteria as you apply them. → Acknowledge objections or other opinions. → Restate your overall judgment.

You might also start by identifying your criteria and then follow with a discussion of how your subject meets or doesn't meet those criteria. This strategy foregrounds the process by which you reached your conclusions.

[Start with your criteria]

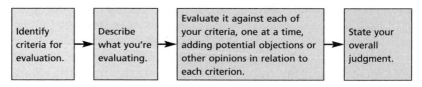

Identify criteria for evaluation. → Describe what you're evaluating. → Evaluate it against each of your criteria, one at a time, adding potential objections or other opinions in relation to each criterion. → State your overall judgment.

IF YOU NEED MORE HELP

See Chapter 24 for guidelines on **DRAFTING**, Chapter 25 on **ASSESSING YOUR DRAFT**, Chapter 26 on **GETTING RESPONSE AND REVISING**, and Chapter 27 on **EDITING AND PROOFREADING**. See Chapter 28 if you are required to submit your report in a writing **PORTFOLIO**.

226–28
229–34
235–41
242–46
247–58

rhetorical situations   genres   processes   strategies   research mla/apa   media/ design   handbook

Lab reports describe the procedures and results of experiments in the natural sciences, the social sciences, and engineering. We write reports of lab work in school to show instructors that we have followed certain procedures, achieved appropriate results, and drawn accurate conclusions. On the job, lab reports not only describe what we did and what we learned; they may also present data and interpretations to attempt to persuade others to accept our hypotheses, and they become a record that others may refer to in the future. As an example, here is a lab report written by a student for a psychology class at Wittenberg University.

SARAH THOMAS

The Effect of Biofeedback Training on Muscle Tension and Skin Temperature

Purpose
The purpose of this lab was for subjects to train themselves to increase their skin temperature, measured on the index finger of their non-dominant hand, and to decrease their muscle tension, measured over the frontalis muscle, by using biofeedback training. This study is based on the research of Miller and Brucker (1979), which demonstrated that smooth muscles could experience operant conditioning.

Methods
Subjects
Seven subjects were used in this study: five female and two male. The subjects were the undergraduate students of Dr. Jo Wilson in her hon-

ors psychophysiology class at Wittenberg University in Springfield, Ohio. All subjects were in their early twenties.

Apparatus

Equipment used in this lab included an Apple Microlab system config- ured to measure (1) skin temperature through a thermode taped with paper surgical tape onto the index finger of the subjects' nondominant hand and (2) frontalis muscle tension via three electrodes placed over the frontalis. When subjects' skin temperatures were more than the means for the previous 90-second intervals, the computer emitted a tone. It also emitted a tone when muscle tension in the frontalis was less than the mean of the previous interval. See the procedure section for exact electrode placement specifications.

Materials

Materials used in this lab included paper surgical tape, alcohol to clean off the forehead, conducting gel, wire, electrode collars, and a chair.

Procedure

Upon arriving at the lab, the researchers turned on the Apple Micro-　5 lab computer. With the aid of Dr. Wilson, subjects had either electrodes attached to their forehead or a thermode attached to the nondomi- nant hand's index finger. The treatment order was random for each subject, and it was reversed for his or her second biofeedback session. The forehead was swiped with alcohol to clean the skin. Electrodes with conducting gel were placed over the frontalis muscle by putting the ground electrode in the center of the forehead and the white elec- trodes two inches on either side of the center of the forehead. Pre- measured electrode collars allowed the researchers to place the conducting gel on the electrodes, peel off the backing on the collar, and place it on the subjects' forehead. The researchers still made sure the electrodes were placed properly. The wire running from the elec- trodes to the computer was then taped to the subjects' back so it would be out of the way. Subjects were then seated in a comfortable chair with their back to the computer.

　　Depending on the experimental condition, subjects were told to reduce their frontalis muscle tension by relaxing and even thinking of holding something warm in their hands. They were told that they

rhetorical situations

genres

processes

strategies

research mla/apa

media/ design

handbook

would know they were meeting the goal when they heard a tone emitted by the computer.

Each session began with a 90-second baseline period, followed by fifteen 90-second trial periods. During each trial period, a tone was emitted by the computer each time the subjects' frontalis muscle tension was below their mean tension for the previous trial; the tone served as the rewarding stimulus in the operant conditioning paradigm.

When skin temperature was to be measured, a thermode was attached to the index finger of the subjects' nondominant hand with surgical tape. The wire running from the thermode to the computer was taped to the back of their hand so it would be out of their way. Then a 90-second baseline period occurred, followed by fifteen 90-second trial periods. During each trial period, a tone was emitted by the computer each time the subjects' skin temperature was above their mean temperature for the previous trial; once again, the tone served as the rewarding stimulus in the operant conditioning paradigm.

Results

The results of this lab were generally similar (Tables 1 and 2). All subjects demonstrated the ability to increase their skin temperature and decrease the tension in their frontalis muscle in at least one of their sessions. Five subjects were able to increase their skin temperature in both sessions; the same number decreased their muscle tension in both trials.

The majority of subjects (five) were able to both increase the skin   10
temperature of the index finger of their nondominant hand and decrease the tension of their frontalis muscle more during the second trial than the first.

Specifically, subject 7 had atypical results. This subject's overall average skin temperature was less than the baseline value; the subject's overall average muscle tension was more than the baseline value.

Discussion

The bulk of the data collected in this study validated the research of Neal Miller; the subjects appeared to undergo operant conditioning of their smooth muscles in order to relax their frontalis muscles and increase their skin temperatures. Subjects 3 and 6 each failed to do this in one session; subject 7 failed to do this several times. This finding is difficult to explain precisely. It is possible that for subjects 3 and 6, this

Table 1:   Skin Temperature in Degrees Fahrenheit during Sessions 1 and 2

	Subject 1	Subject 2	Subject 3	Subject 4	Subject 5	Subject 6	Subject 7
Baseline, Session 1	75.2	77.3	78.5	74.3	78.0	67.7	75.1
Mean skin temp, Session 1	79.3	85.6	78.5	74.4	83.2	73.5	72.6
Mean minus baseline, Session 1	4.1	8.3	0.0	0.1	5.2	5.8	−2.5
Baseline, Session 2	77.9	80.1	69.5	80.9	67.2	73.7	88.0
Mean skin temp, Session 2	79.9	86.3	70.7	84.6	76.8	79.7	88.8
Mean minus baseline, Session 2	2.0	6.2	1.2	3.7	9.6	6.0	0.8
Overall average of mean skin temp minus baseline	3.1	7.3	0.6	1.9	7.4	5.9	−0.85

data was a fluke. For subject 7, it is likely that the subject was simply stressed due to outside factors before arriving for the first trials of EMG and skin temperature, and this stress skewed the data.

The effect of biofeedback training was generally greater as the operant conditioning became better learned. Learning was indicated by the finding that the majority of the subjects performed better on the second trials than on the first trials. This finding shows the effectiveness of

Table 2: EMG of the Frontalis Muscle in Microvolts for Sessions 1 and 2

	Subject 1	Subject 2	Subject 3	Subject 4	Subject 5	Subject 6	Subject 7
Baseline, Session 1	4.4	4.5	2.8	3.8	7.9	3.1	2.4
Mean EMG, Session 1	2.1	1.4	1.7	3.2	2.0	3.7	3.2
Baseline minus mean, Session 1	2.3	3.1	1.1	0.6	5.9	−0.6	−0.8
Baseline, Session 2	4.1	2.3	3.0	2.9	11.1	6.5	1.9
Mean EMG, Session 2	1.3	1.3	1.4	2.3	2.5	3.2	1.4
Baseline minus mean, Session 2	2.8	1.0	1.6	0.6	8.6	3.3	0.5
Overall average of mean EMG minus baseline	2.6	2.1	1.4	0.6	7.3	1.4	−0.15

biofeedback on reducing factors associated with stress, like muscle tension and low skin temperature; biofeedback's impact is even greater when it is administered over time. The implications of this information are without limits, especially for the treatment of a variety of medical disorders.

There were a few problems with this lab. The subjects all were at different levels of relaxation to begin with. It is impossible to determine the effects of outside events, like exams or other stresses, on their EMG and skin temperature levels. Skin temperature itself could have been altered by cold outside temperatures. Being in a lab may have altered the stress level of some subjects, and noises from outside the lab may have had an effect as well.

If this study were repeated, it would be a good idea to let sub-   15 jects simply be in the lab for a period of time before measures are taken. This would allow the effect of outside temperature to be minimized. It would also reduce the effect of getting used to the lab, decreasing the orienting response. Finally, it would also be good to do the experiment in a soundproof room.

Reference

Miller, N. E., & Brucker, B. S. (1979). A learned visceral response apparently independent of skeletal ones in patients paralyzed by spinal lesions. In N. Birnbaumer & H. D. Kimmel (Eds.), *Biofeedback and self-regulation* (pp. 287–304). Hillsdale, NJ: Erlbaum.

This report includes sections commonly part of lab reports in the natural and social sciences: purpose, method, results, discussion, and references. Some reports keep results and discussion in one section; some reports include an abstract; and some reports include one or more appendices containing tables, calculations, and other supplemental material, depending on the audience and publication. In this example, the author assumes that her audience understands basic terms used in the report, such as frontalis muscle and biofeedback.

Key Features / Lab Reports

An explicit title.   Lab report titles should describe the report factually and explicitly to let readers know exactly what the report is about and to provide key words for indexes and search engines. Avoid phrases like "an Investigation into" or "a Study of" and titles that are clever or cute. Thomas's title, "The Effect of Biofeedback Training on Muscle Tension and Skin Temperature," clearly describes the report's subject and includes the key words needed for indexing (*biofeedback training, muscle tension, skin temperature*).

Abstract. Some lab reports include a one-paragraph, 100–200-word abstract, a summary of the report's purpose, method, and discussion.

Purpose. Sometimes called an "Introduction," this section describes the reason for conducting the study: Why is this research important, and why are you doing it? What has been done by others, and how does your work relate to previous work? What will your research tell us?

Methods. Here you describe how you conducted the study, including the materials and equipment you used and the procedures you followed. This is usually written as a narrative, explaining the process you followed in order to allow others to repeat your study, step-by-step. Your discussion should thoroughly describe the following:

- subjects studied and any necessary contextual information
- apparatus—equipment used, by brand and model number
- materials used
- procedures—including reference to the published work that describes any procedures you used that someone else had already followed; the techniques you used and any modifications you made to them; any statistical methods you used

Results and discussion. Here you analyze the results and present their implications, explain your logic in accepting or rejecting your initial hypotheses, relate your work to previous work in the field, and discuss the experiment's design and techniques and how they may have affected the results: what did you find out, and what does it mean? In longer reports, you may have two separate sections. "Results" should focus on the factual data you collected by doing the study; "Discussion" should speculate about what the study means: why the results turned out as they did, and what the implications for future studies may be.

References. List works cited in your report, alphabetized by author's last name and using the appropriate documentation style.

Appendices. Appendices are optional, presenting information that is too detailed for the body of the report.

Appropriate format. The design conventions for lab reports vary from discipline to discipline, so you'll need to check to see that yours meets the appropriate requirements. Find out whether any sections need to start their own page, whether you need to include a list of figures, whether you need to include a separate title page—and whether there are any other conventions you need to follow.

A BRIEF GUIDE TO WRITING LAB REPORTS

Considering the Rhetorical Situation

3–4 **PURPOSE** Why are you writing? To demonstrate your ability to follow the appropriate methods and make logical inferences? To persuade others that your hypotheses are sound and your conclusions believable? To provide a record of the experiment for others?

5–8 **AUDIENCE** Can you assume that your audience is familiar with the field's basic procedures? How routine were your procedures? Which procedures need to be explained in greater detail so your audience can repeat them?

12–14 **STANCE** Lab reports need to have an impersonal, analytical stance. Take care not to be too informal, and don't try to be cute.

15–17 **MEDIA / DESIGN** Are you planning to deliver your report in print or online? All lab reports have headings; choose a typeface that includes bold or italics so your headings will show clearly.

rhetorical situations   genres   processes   strategies   research mla/apa   media/ design   handbook

Generating Ideas and Text

Research your subject.   Researchers do not work in isolation; rather, each study contributes to an ever-growing body of information, and you need to situate your work in that context. **RESEARCH** what studies others have done on the same subject and what procedures they followed.

● 373

Take careful notes as you perform your study.   A lab report must be repeatable. Another researcher should be able to duplicate your study exactly, using only your report as a guide, so you must document every method, material, apparatus, and procedure carefully. Break down procedures and activities into discrete parts, and record them in the order in which they occurred. **ANALYZE CAUSES AND EFFECTS;** think about whether you should **COMPARE** your findings with other studies. Take careful notes so that you'll be able to **EXPLAIN PROCESSES** you followed.

◆ 278–82
306–13
338–42

Draft the report a section at a time.   You may find it easiest to start with the "Methods" or "Results" section first, then **DRAFT** the "Discussion," followed by the "Purpose." Do the "Abstract" last.

◎ 226–28

- Write in **COMPLETE SENTENCES** and paragraphs.

HB-4–7

- Avoid using the first person *I* or *we*; keep the focus on the study and the actions taken.

- Use the **ACTIVE VOICE** as much as possible ("the rats pushed the lever" rather than "the lever was pushed by the rats").

HB-18–19

- Use the **PAST TENSE** throughout the report.

HB-12

- Place subjects and verbs close together to make your sentences easy to follow.

- Use **PRECISE TERMS** consistently throughout the report; don't alternate among synonyms.

HB-38–40

- Be sure that each **PRONOUN** refers clearly to one noun.

HB-24–26

Organizing a Lab Report

Lab reports vary in their details but generally include these sections:

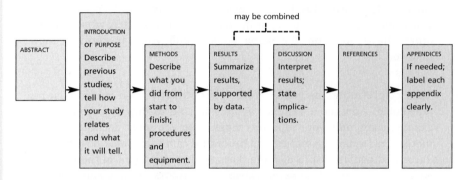

IF YOU NEED MORE HELP

See Chapter 25 on **ASSESSING YOUR OWN WRITING,** Chapter 26 on **GETTING RESPONSE AND REVISING,** and Chapter 27 on **EDITING AND PROOFREADING.** See Chapter 28 if you are required to submit your report in a writing **PORTFOLIO.**

229–34 ○
235–41
242–46
247–58

Literary Analyses **14**

Literary analyses are essays in which we examine literary texts closely to understand their messages, interpret their meanings, and appreciate their writers' techniques. You might read *Macbeth* and notice that Shakespeare's play contains a pattern of images of blood. You could explore the distinctive point of view in Ambrose Bierce's story "An Occurrence at Owl Creek Bridge." Or you could point out the differences between Stephen King's *The Shining* and Stanley Kubrick's screenplay based on that novel. In all these cases, you use specific analytical tools to go below the surface of the work to deepen your understanding of how it works and what it means. Here is a sonnet by the nineteenth-century English Romantic poet Percy Bysshe Shelley, followed by one student's analysis of it written for a literature course at Wright State University.

PERCY BYSSHE SHELLEY

Sonnet: "Lift not the painted veil which those who live"

Lift not the painted veil which those who live
Call Life: though unreal shapes be pictured there,
And it but mimic all we would believe
With colours idly spread, — behind, lurk Fear
And Hope, twin Destinies; who ever weave   5
Their shadows, o'er the chasm, sightless and drear.
I knew one who had lifted it — he sought,
For his lost heart was tender, things to love,
But found them not, alas! nor was there aught

The world contains, the which he could approve. 10
Through the unheeding many he did move,
A splendour among shadows, a bright blot
Upon this gloomy scene, a Spirit that strove
For truth, and like the Preacher found it not.

STEPHANIE HUFF

Metaphor and Society in Shelley's "Sonnet"

In his sonnet "Lift not the painted veil which those who live," Percy Bysshe Shelley introduces us to a bleak world that exists behind veils and shadows. We see that although fear and hope both exist, truth is dishearteningly absent. This absence of truth is exactly what Shelley chooses to address as he uses metaphors of grim distortion and radiant incandescence to expose the counterfeit nature of our world.

The speaker of Shelley's poem presents bold assertions about the nature of our society. In the opening lines of the poem, he warns the reader to "Lift not the painted veil which those who live / Call Life" (1–2). Here, the "painted veil" serves as a grim metaphor for life. More specifically, the speaker equates the veil with what people like to *call* life. In this sense, the speaker asserts that what we believe to be pure reality is actually nothing more than a covering that masks what really lies beneath. Truth is covered by a veil of falsehood and is made opaque with the paint of people's lies.

This painted veil does not completely obstruct our view, but rather distorts what we can see. All that can be viewed through it are "unreal shapes" (2) that metaphorically represent the people that make up this counterfeit society. These shapes are not to be taken for truth. They are unreal, twisted, deformed figures of humanity, people full of falsities and misrepresentations.

Most people, however, do not realize that the shapes and images seen through the veil are distorted because all they know of life is the veil—this life we see as reality only "mimic[s] all we would believe" (3), using "colours idly spread" (4) to create pictures that bear little resemblance to that which they claim to portray. All pure truths are covered up and painted over until they are mere mockeries. The lies that cloak the truth are not even carefully constructed, but are created

rhetorical situations

genres

processes

strategies

research mla/apa

media/ design

handbook

idly, with little attention to detail. The paint is not applied carefully, but merely spread across the top. This idea of spreading brings to mind images of paint slopped on so heavily that the truth beneath becomes nearly impossible to find. Even the metaphor of color suggests only superficial beauty—"idly spread" (4)—rather than any sort of pure beauty that could penetrate the surface of appearances.

What really lies behind this facade are fear and hope, both of which "weave / Their shadows, o'er the chasm, sightless and drear" (5–6). These two realities are never truly seen or experienced, though. They exist only as shadows. Just as shadows appear only at certain times of day, cast only sham images of what they reflect, and are paid little attention, so too do these emotions of hope and fear appear only as brief, ignored imitations of themselves when they enter the artificiality of this chasmlike world. Peering into a chasm, one cannot hope to make out what lies at the bottom. At best one could perhaps make out shadows and even that cannot be done with any certainty as to true appearance. The world is so large, so caught up in itself and its counterfeit ways, that it can no longer see even the simple truths of hope and fear. Individuals and civilizations have become sightless, dreary, and as enormously empty as a chasm.

This chasm does not include *all* people, however, as we are introduced to one individual, in line 7, who is trying to bring to light whatever truth may yet remain. This one person, who defies the rest of the world, is portrayed with metaphors of light, clearly standing out among the dark representations of the rest of mankind. He is first presented to us as possessing a "lost heart" (8) and seeking things to love. It is important that the first metaphor applied to him be a heart because this is the organ with which we associate love, passion, and purity. We associate it with brightness of the soul, making it the most radiant spot of the body. He is then described as a "splendour among shadows" (12), his purity and truth brilliantly shining through the darkness of the majority's falsehood. Finally, he is equated with "a bright blot / Upon this gloomy scene" (12–13), his own bright blaze of authenticity burning in stark contrast to the murky phoniness of the rest of the world.

These metaphors of light are few, however, in comparison to those of grim distortion. So, too, are this one individual's radiance and zeal too little to alter the warped darkness they temporarily pierce. This one person, though bright, is not bright enough to light up the rest of civilization and create real change. The light simply confirms the dark falsity that comprises the rest of the world. Shelley gives us one flame of hope, only to reveal to us what little chance it has under the suffocating veil. Both the metaphors of grim distortion and those of radiant incandescence work together in this poem to highlight the world's counterfeit nature.

Huff focuses her analysis on patterns in Shelley's imagery. In addition, she pays careful attention to individual words and to how, as the poem unfolds, they create a certain meaning. That meaning is her interpretation.

Key Features / Literary Analyses

An arguable thesis. A literary analysis is a form of argument; you are arguing that your analysis of a literary work is valid. Your thesis, then, should be arguable, as Huff's is: "[Shelley] uses metaphors of grim distortion and radiant incandescence to expose the counterfeit nature of our world." A mere summary — "Shelley writes about a person who sees reality and seeks love but never finds it" — would not be arguable and therefore is not a good thesis.

Careful attention to the language of the text. The key to analyzing a text is looking carefully at the language, which is the foundation of its meaning. Specific words, images, metaphors — these are where analysis begins. You may also bring in contextual information, such as cultural, historical, or biographical facts, or you may refer to similar texts. But the words, phrases, and sentences that make up the text you are analyzing are your primary source when dealing with texts. That's what literature teachers mean by "close reading": reading with the assumption that every word of a text is meaningful.

Attention to patterns or themes. Literary analyses are usually built on evidence of meaningful patterns or themes within a text or among several texts. These patterns and themes reveal meaning. In Shelley's poem, images of light and shadow and artifice and reality create patterns of meaning, while the poem's many half rhymes (*live/believe, love/approve*) create patterns of sound that may contribute to the overall meaning.

A clear interpretation.   A literary analysis demonstrates the plausibility of its thesis by using evidence from the text and, sometimes, relevant contextual evidence to explain how the language and patterns found there support a particular interpretation. When you write a literary analysis, you show readers one way the text may be read and understood; that is your interpretation.

MLA style.   Literary analyses usually follow MLA style. Even though Huff's essay has no works-cited list, it refers to line numbers using MLA style.

A BRIEF GUIDE TO WRITING LITERARY ANALYSES

Considering the Rhetorical Situation

PURPOSE	What do you need to do? Show that you have examined the text carefully? Offer your own interpretation? Demonstrate a particular analytical technique? Or some combination? If you're responding to an assignment, does it specify what you need to do?	▮ 3–4
AUDIENCE	What do you need to do to convince your readers that your interpretation is plausible and based on sound analysis? Can you assume that readers are already familiar with the text you are analyzing, or do you need to tell them about it?	▮ 5–8
STANCE	How can you see your subject through interested, curious eyes — and then step back in order to see what your observations might *mean*?	▮ 12–14
MEDIA / DESIGN	Will your analysis focus on a print text and take the form of a print text? If your subject is a visual or electronic medium, will you need to show significant elements in your analysis? Are you required to follow MLA or some other style?	▮ 15–18

Generating Ideas and Text

Look at your assignment.   Does it specify a particular kind of analysis? Does it ask you to consider a particular theme? To use any specific critical approaches? Look for any terms that tell you what to do, words like *analyze, compare, interpret,* and so on.

Study the text with a critical eye.   When we read a literary work, we often come away with a reaction to it: we like it, we hate it, it made us cry or laugh, it perplexed us. That may be a good starting point for a literary analysis, but students of literature need to go beyond initial reactions, to think about HOW THE TEXT WORKS: What does it *say,* and what does it *do?* What elements make up this text? How do those elements work together or fail to work together? Does this text lead you to think or feel a certain way? How does it fit into a particular context (of history, culture, technology, genre, and so on)?

358–60

Choose a method for analyzing the text.   There are various ways to analyze your subject. Three common focuses are on the text itself, on your own experience reading it, and on other cultural, historical, or literary contexts.

314–23
324–32
343–51

- *The text itself.* Trace the development and expression of themes, characters, and language through the work. How do they help to create the overall meaning, tone, or effect for which you're arguing? To do this, you might look at the text as a whole, something you can understand from all angles at once. You could also pick out parts from the beginning, middle, and end as needed to make your case, DEFINING key terms, DESCRIBING characters and settings, and NARRATING key scenes. The example essay about the Shelley sonnet offers a text-based analysis that looks at patterns of images in the poem. You might also examine the same theme in several different works.

- *Your own response as a reader.* Explore the way the text affects you or develops meanings as you read through it from beginning to end. By doing such a close reading, you're slowing down the process to notice how one element of the text leads you to expect something, confirming earlier suspicions or surprises. You build your analysis on your experience of reading the text—as if you were pretending to drive somewhere for the first time, though in reality you know the way intimately. By closely examining the language of the text as you experience it, you explore how it leads you to a set of responses, both intellectual and emotional. If you were responding in this way to the Shelley poem, you might discuss how its first lines suggest that while life is an illusion, a veil, one might pull it aside and glimpse reality, however "drear."

- *Context.* Analyze the text as part of some **LARGER CONTEXT**—as part of a certain time or place in history or as an expression of a certain culture (how does this text relate to the time and place of its creation?), as one of many other texts like it, a representative of a genre (how is this text like or unlike others of its kind? how does it use, play with, or flout the conventions of the genre?). A context-based approach to the Shelley poem might look at Shelley's own philosophical and religious views and how they may have influenced the poem's characterization of the world we experience as illusory, a "veil." 365–66

Read the work more than once. Reading literature, watching films, or listening to speeches is like driving to a new destination: the first time you go, you need to concentrate on getting there; on subsequent trips, you can see other aspects—the scenery, the curve of the road, other possible routes—that you couldn't pay attention to earlier. When you experience a piece of literature for the first time, you usually focus on the story, the plot, the overall meaning. By experiencing it repeatedly, you can see how its effects are achieved, what the pieces are and how they fit together, where different patterns emerge, how the author crafted the work. To analyze a literary work, then, plan to read it more than once, with the assumption that every part of the text is there for a reason. Focus on details, even on a single detail that shows up more than once: Why is it there? What can it mean? How does it affect our experience of reading or studying the text? Also, look for anomalies, details that *don't* fit the patterns: Why are they part of the text? What can they mean? How do they affect the experience of the text? See the **READING STRATEGIES** chapter for several different methods for reading a text. 352–66

273–75 ◆

Compose a strong thesis. The **THESIS** of a literary analysis should be specific, limited, and open to potential disagreement. In addition, it should be analytical, not evaluative: avoid thesis statements that make overall judgments, such as a reviewer might do: "Virginia Woolf's *The Waves* is a failed experiment in narrative" or "No one has equaled the achievement of *The Matrix* trilogy." Rather, offer a way of seeing the text: "The choice presented in Robert Frost's 'The Road Not Taken' ultimately makes no difference"; "The plot of *The Matrix Reloaded* reflects the politics of America after 9/11."

Do a close reading. When you analyze a text, you need to find specific, brief passages that support your interpretation. Then you should interpret those passages in terms of their language, their context, or your reaction to them as a reader. To find such passages, you must read the text closely, questioning it as you go, asking, for example:

- What language provides evidence to support your thesis?
- What does each word (phrase, passage) mean exactly?
- Why does the writer choose *this* language, *these* words? What are the implications or connotations of the language? If the language is dense or difficult, why might the writer have written it that way?
- What images or metaphors are used? What is their effect on the meaning?

361–63 ◆

- What **PATTERNS** of language, imagery, or plot do you see? If something is repeated, what significance does the repetition have?
- How does each word, phrase, or passage relate to what precedes and follows it?
- How does the experience of reading the text affect its meaning?

365–66 ◆

- What words, phrases, or passages connect to a larger **CONTEXT?** What language demonstrates that this work reflects or is affected by that context?
- How do these various elements of language, image, and pattern support your interpretation?

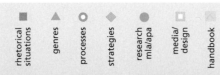

Your analysis should focus on analyzing and interpreting your subject, not simply summarizing or paraphrasing it. Many literary analyses also use the strategy of **COMPARING** two or more works.

◆ 306–13

Find evidence to support your interpretation. The parts of the text you examine in your close reading become the evidence you use to support your interpretation. Some think that we're all entitled to our own opinions about literature. And indeed we are. But when writing a literary analysis, we're entitled only to our own *well-supported* and *well-argued* opinions. When you analyze a text, you must treat it like any other **ARGUMENT**: you need to discuss how the text creates an effect or expresses a theme, and then you have to show **EVIDENCE** from the text—significant plot or structural elements; important characters; patterns of language, imagery, or action—to back up your argument.

◆ 283–99

◆ 287–93

Pay attention to matters of style. Literary analyses have certain conventions for using pronouns and verbs.

- In informal papers, it's okay to use the first person: "I believe Frost's narrator has little basis for claiming that one road is 'less traveled.'" In more formal essays, make assertions directly; claim authority to make statements about the text: "Frost's narrator has no basis for claiming that one road is 'less traveled.'"

- Discuss textual features in the **PRESENT TENSE** even if quotations from the text are in another tense: "When Nick finds Gatsby's body floating in the pool, he says very little about it: 'the laden mattress moved irregularly down the pool.'" Describe the historical context of the setting in the **PAST TENSE**: "In the 1920s, such estates as Gatsby's were rare."

▫ HB-12–14

▫ HB-12–14

Cite and document sources appropriately. Use **MLA** citation and documentation style unless told otherwise. Format **QUOTATIONS** properly, and use **SIGNAL PHRASES** when need be.

● 428–76

410–13

417–18

Think about format and design. Brief essays do not require **HEADINGS**; text divisions are usually marked by **TRANSITIONS** between paragraphs. In longer papers, though, heads can be helpful.

▫ 526–27

◆ 277

Organizing a Literary Analysis

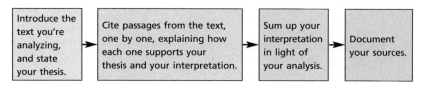

Introduce the text you're analyzing, and state your thesis. → Cite passages from the text, one by one, explaining how each one supports your thesis and your interpretation. → Sum up your interpretation in light of your analysis. → Document your sources.

IF YOU NEED MORE HELP

See Chapter 24 for guidelines on **DRAFTING,** Chapter 25 on **ASSESSING YOUR OWN WRITING,** Chapter 26 on **GETTING RESPONSE AND REVISING,** and Chapter 27 on **EDITING AND PROOFREADING.** See Chapter 28 if you are required to submit your analysis in a writing **PORTFOLIO.**

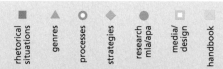

rhetorical situations

genres

processes

strategies

research mla/apa

media/ design

handbook

Memoirs 15

We write memoirs to explore our past — about shopping for a party dress with Grandma, or driving a car for the first time, or breaking up with our first love. *Memoirs* focus on events and people and places that are important to us. We usually have two goals when we write a memoir: to capture an important moment and to convey something about its significance for us. The following example is from *All Over But the Shoutin'*, the 1997 autobiography by Rick Bragg, a former reporter for the *New York Times*. Bragg grew up in Alabama, and in this memoir he recalls when, as a teenager, he paid a final visit to his dying father.

RICK BRAGG

All Over But the Shoutin'

He was living in a little house in Jacksonville, Alabama, a college and mill town that was the closest urban center — with its stoplights and a high school and two supermarkets — to the country roads we roamed in our raggedy cars. He lived in the mill village, in one of those houses the mills subsidized for their workers, back when companies still did things like that. It was not much of a place, but better than anything we had ever lived in as a family. I knocked and a voice like an old woman's, punctuated with a cough that sounded like it came from deep in the guts, told me to come on in, it ain't locked. It was dark inside, but light enough to see what looked like a bundle of quilts on the corner of a sofa. Deep inside them was a ghost of a man, his hair and beard long and going dirty gray, his face pale and cut with deep grooves. I knew I was in the right house because my daddy's only real possessions, a velvet-covered board pinned with medals, sat inside a glass cabinet on a table. But this couldn't be him.

He coughed again, spit into a can and struggled to his feet, but stopped somewhere short of standing straight up, as if a stoop was all he could manage. "Hey, Cotton Top," he said, and then I knew. My daddy, who was supposed to be a still-young man, looked like the walking dead, not just old but damaged, poisoned, used up, crumpled up and thrown in a corner to die. I thought that the man I would see would be the trim, swaggering, high-toned little rooster of a man who stared back at me from the pages of my mother's photo album, the young soldier clowning around in Korea, the arrow-straight, good-looking boy who posed beside my mother back before the fields and mophandle and the rest of it took her looks. The man I remembered had always dressed nice even when there was no cornmeal left, whose black hair always shone with oil, whose chin, even when it wobbled from the beer, was always angled up, high.

I thought he would greet me with that strong voice that sounded so fine when he laughed and so evil when, slurred by a quart of corn likker, he whirled through the house and cried and shrieked, tormented by things we could not see or even imagine. I thought he would be the man and monster of my childhood. But that man was as dead as a man could be, and this was what remained, like when a snake sheds its skin and leaves a dry and brittle husk of itself hanging in the Johnson grass.

"It's all over but the shoutin' now, ain't it, boy," he said, and when he let the quilt slide from his shoulders I saw how he had wasted away, how the bones seemed to poke out of his clothes, and I could see how it killed his pride to look this way, unclean, and he looked away from me for a moment, ashamed.

He made a halfhearted try to shake my hand but had a coughing   5
fit again that lasted a minute, coughing up his life, his lungs, and after that I did not want to touch him. I stared at the tops of my sneakers, ashamed to look at his face. He had a dark streak in his beard below his lip, and I wondered why, because he had never liked snuff. Now I know it was blood.

I remember much of what he had to say that day. When you don't see someone for eight, nine years, when you see that person's life red on their lips and know that you will never see them beyond this day, you listen close, even if what you want most of all is to run away.

"Your momma, she alright?" he said.

I said I reckon so.

rhetorical situations

genres

processes

strategies

research mla/apa

media/ design

handbook

"The other boys? They alright?"

I said I reckon so. 10

Then he was quiet for a minute, as if trying to find the words to a question to which he did not really want an answer.

"They ain't never come to see me. How come?"

I remember thinking, fool, why do you think? But I just choked down my words, and in doing so I gave up the only real chance I would ever have to accuse him, to attack him with the facts of his own sorry nature and the price it had cost us all. The opportunity hung perfectly still in the air in front of my face and fists, and I held my temper and let it float on by. I could have no more challenged him, berated him, hurt him, than I could have kicked some three-legged dog. Life had kicked his ass pretty good.

"How come?"

I just shrugged. 15

For the next few hours — unless I was mistaken, having never had one before — he tried to be my father. Between coughing and long pauses when he fought for air to generate his words, he asked me if I liked school, if I had ever gotten any better at math, the one thing that just flat evaded me. He asked me if I ever got even with the boy who blacked my eye ten years ago, and nodded his head, approvingly, as I described how I followed him into the boys' bathroom and knocked his dick string up to his watch pocket, and would have dunked his head in the urinal if the aging principal, Mr. Hand, had not had to pee and caught me dragging him across the concrete floor.

He asked me about basketball and baseball, said he had heard I had a good game against Cedar Springs, and I said pretty good, but it was two years ago, anyway. He asked if I had a girlfriend and I said, "One," and he said, "Just one?" For the slimmest of seconds he almost grinned and the young, swaggering man peeked through, but disappeared again in the disease that cloaked him. He talked and talked and never said a word, at least not the words I wanted.

He never said he was sorry.

He never said he wished things had turned out different.

He never acted like he did anything wrong. 20

Part of it, I know, was culture. Men did not talk about their feelings in his hard world. I did not expect, even for a second, that he would bare his soul. All I wanted was a simple acknowledgment that he was wrong, or at least too drunk to notice that he left his pretty wife and sons alone again and again, with no food, no money, no way to get any, short of begging, because when she tried to find work he yelled, screamed, refused. No, I didn't expect much.

After a while he motioned for me to follow him into a back room where he had my present, and I planned to take it and run. He handed me a long, thin box, and inside was a brand-new, well-oiled Remington .22 rifle. He said he had bought it some time back, just kept forgetting to give it to me. It was a fine gun, and for a moment we were just like anybody else in the culture of that place, where a father's gift of a gun to his son is a rite. He said, with absolute seriousness, not to shoot my brothers.

I thanked him and made to leave, but he stopped me with a hand on my arm and said wait, that ain't all, that he had some other things for me. He motioned to three big cardboard egg cartons stacked against one wall.

Inside was the only treasure I truly have ever known.

I had grown up in a house in which there were only two books, the   25 King James Bible and the spring seed catalog. But here, in these boxes, were dozens of hardback copies of everything from Mark Twain to Sir Arthur Conan Doyle. There was a water-damaged Faulkner, and the nearly complete set of Edgar Rice Burroughs's *Tarzan*. There was poetry and trash, Zane Grey's *Riders of the Purple Sage,* and a paperback with two naked women on the cover. There was a tiny, old copy of *Arabian Nights*, threadbare Hardy Boys, and one Hemingway. He had bought most of them at a yard sale, by the box or pound, and some at a flea market. He did not even know what he was giving me, did not recognize most of the writers. "Your momma said you still liked to read," he said.

There was Shakespeare. My father did not know who he was, exactly, but he had heard the name. He wanted them because they were pretty, because they were wrapped in fake leather, because they looked like rich folks' books. I do not love Shakespeare, but I still have those books. I would not trade them for a gold monkey.

"They's maybe some dirty books in there, by mistake, but I know you ain't interested in them, so just throw 'em away," he said. "Or at least, throw 'em away before your momma sees 'em." And then I swear to God he winked.

I guess my heart should have broken then, and maybe it did, a little. I guess I should have done something, anything, besides mumble

"Thank you, Daddy." I guess that would have been fine, would not have betrayed in some way my mother, my brothers, myself. But I just stood there, trapped somewhere between my long-standing, comfortable hatred, and what might have been forgiveness. I am trapped there still.

Bragg's memoir illustrates all the features that make a memoir good: how the son and father react to each other creates the kind of suspense that keeps us reading; vivid details and rich dialogue bring the scene to life. His later reflections make the significance of that final meeting very clear.

Key Features / Memoirs

A good story.   Your memoir should be interesting, to yourself and others. It need not be about a world-shaking event, but your topic — and how you write about it — should interest your readers. At the center of most good stories stands a conflict or question to be resolved. The most compelling memoirs feature some sort of situation or problem that needs resolution. That need for resolution is another name for suspense. It's what makes us want to keep reading.

Vivid details.   Details bring a memoir to life by giving readers mental images of the sights, sounds, smells, tastes, and textures of the world in which your story takes place. The goal is to show as well as tell, to take readers there. When Bragg describes a "voice like an old woman's, punctuated with a cough that sounded like it came from deep in the guts," we can hear his dying father ourselves. A memoir is more than simply a report of what happened; it uses vivid details and dialogue to bring the events of the past to life, much as good fiction brings to life events that the writer makes up or embellishes.

Clear significance.   Memories of the past are filtered through our view from the present: we pick out some moments in our lives as significant, some as more important or vivid than others. Over time, our interpretations change, and our memories themselves change.

A good memoir conveys something about the significance of its subject. As a writer, you need to reveal something about what the incident means to you. You don't, however, want to simply announce the significance as if you're tacking on the moral of the story. Bragg tells us that he's "trapped between [his] long-standing, comfortable hatred, and what might have been forgiveness," but he doesn't come right out and say that's why the incident is so important to him.

A BRIEF GUIDE TO WRITING MEMOIRS

Choosing an Event to Write About

220–21 ○

LIST several events or incidents from your past that you consider significant in some way. They do not have to be earthshaking; indeed, they may involve a quiet moment that only you see as important—a brief encounter with a remarkable person, a visit to a special place, a memorable achievement (or failure), something that makes you laugh whenever you think about it. Writing about events that happened at least a few years ago is often easier than writing about recent events because you can more easily step back and see those events with a clear perspective. To choose the event that you will write about, consider how well you can recall what happened, how interesting it will be to readers, and whether you want to share it with an audience.

Considering the Rhetorical Situation

3–4 ■

PURPOSE   What is the importance of the memory you are trying to convey? How will this story help your readers (and you yourself) understand you, as you were then and as you are now?

5–8 ■

AUDIENCE   Who are your readers? What do you want them to think of you after reading your memoir? How can you help them understand your experience?

| STANCE | What impression do you want to give, and how can your words contribute to that impression? What tone do you want to project? Sincere? Serious? Humorous? Detached? Self-critical? | 12–14 |

| MEDIA / DESIGN | Will your memoir be a print document? A speech? Will it be posted on a website? Will you include illustrations, audio or video clips, or other visual texts? | 15–17 |

Generating Ideas and Text

Think about what happened. Take a few minutes to write out an account of the incident: **WHAT** happened, **WHERE** it took place, **WHO** else was involved, what was said, how you feel about it, and so on. Can you identify any tension or conflict that will make for a compelling story? If not, you might want to rethink your topic.

222–23

Consider its significance. Why do you still remember this event? What effect has it had on your life? What makes you want to tell someone else about it? Does it say anything about you? What about it might interest someone else? If you have trouble answering these questions, you should probably find another topic. But in general, once you have defined the significance of the incident, you can be sure you have a story to tell—and a reason for telling it.

Think about the details. The best memoirs connect with readers by giving them a sense of what it was like to be there, leading them to experience in words and images what the writer experienced in life. Spend some time **DESCRIBING** the incident, writing what you see, hear, smell, touch, and taste when you envision it. Do you have any photos or memorabilia or other **VISUAL** materials you might include in your memoir? Try writing out **DIALOGUE**, things that were said (or, if you can't recall exactly, things that might have been said). Look at what you come up with—is there detail enough to bring the scene to life? Anything that might be called vivid? If you don't have enough detail, you might reconsider whether you recall

324–32
528–32
333–37

enough about the incident to write about it. If you have trouble coming up with plenty of detail, try **FREEWRITING, LISTING,** or **LOOPING.**

219–21 ◐

Ways of Organizing Memoirs

[Tell about the event from beginning to end]

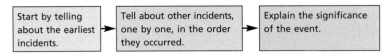

| Start by telling about the earliest incidents. | → | Tell about other incidents, one by one, in the order they occurred. | → | Explain the significance of the event. |

[Start at the end and tell how the event came about]

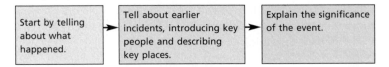

| Start by telling about what happened. | → | Tell about earlier incidents, introducing key people and describing key places. | → | Explain the significance of the event. |

IF YOU NEED MORE HELP

226–28 ◐
229–34
235–41
242–46
247–58

See Chapter 24 for guidelines on **DRAFTING,** Chapter 25 on **ASSESSING YOUR OWN WRITING,** Chapter 26 on **GETTING RESPONSE AND REVISING,** and Chapter 27 on **EDITING AND PROOFREADING.** See Chapter 28 if you are required to submit your memoir in a writing **PORTFOLIO.**

Profiles 16

Profiles are written portraits—of people, places, events, or other things. We find profiles of celebrities, travel destinations, and offbeat festivals in magazines and newspapers, on radio and TV. A profile presents a subject in an entertaining way that conveys its significance, showing us something or someone that we may not have known existed or that we see every day but don't know much about. Here, for example, is a profile of a festival that takes place in the town where *Napoleon Dynamite* was filmed. It originally appeared in the *New York Times* in 2006.

LAURA M. HOLSON

Rural Idaho Town Seeks to Turn Film's Cult Status into Prosperity

The Big J Burger on State Street here could hardly be mistaken for a hip Hollywood club. But on Saturday afternoon, a 16-year-old wearing moon boots and a T-shirt with the slogan "Vote for Pedro" jumped out of his seat and began mixing it up on an improvised dance floor. With a boom box blaring behind him, he shimmied between the restaurant's tables to the 1999 dance hit "Canned Heat" while more than 100 people whooped and cheered.

The dancer, Bryan Demke, from Fort Worth, was recreating a pivotal moment from the 2004 cult movie *Napoleon Dynamite* which was filmed in Preston. And the crowd attending the second annual Napoleon Dynamite festival loved it. "You rock!" shouted a young girl, raising her cellphone to take a picture. "I love you, Napoleon!" added another, blowing the dancer a kiss.

"I thought the movie was stupid," said a smiling Craig Smith, who showed up with his brother Gordon and teenage son Kyle. "But that kid is killing me."

More than 300 people traveled from as far away as California and Connecticut for the chance to embrace their own inner Napoleon. The movie, written by the husband and wife team of Jared and Jerusha Hess, was directed by Mr. Hess, a native of Preston who lives in Salt Lake City. Now Preston, with a population of 5,000 in the mostly rural county, hopes to capitalize on the film's cult status.

Other towns have done the same and prospered. *Field of Dreams* 5 turned little-known Dyersville, Iowa, into a tourist haven when that movie was released in 1989. Now about 65,000 people visit yearly. The Santa Ynez Valley in California became a popular vacation spot after *Sideways* was released two years ago. Even Metropolis, Illinois, experienced an increase in visitors after *Superman Returns* was released in theaters [in June 2006].

Preston, however, may be the unlikeliest backlot in recent memory. *Napoleon Dynamite* was filmed for $400,000, featured no Hollywood stars, and won no big awards. But the film, distributed by Fox Searchlight Pictures, struck a chord with moviegoers, particularly college students, garnering $44 million at the domestic box office.

"Some of the people here don't like it, but they are accepting it," said Penny Christensen, the executive director of the Preston Area Chamber of Commerce, who organized the first festival after 15,000 visitors stopped by her office last year asking for a map of the movie's sites. "I mean, why shouldn't we show off our town?"

Napoleon Dynamite is the story of an awkward small-town outsider trying to survive high school. He is a member of the Future Farmers of America (called F.F.A.) where he is milk taste-tester. He eats tater tots for lunch in the school cafeteria, plays tether ball, and dances alone in his bedroom after school. Napoleon finds newfound popularity after he shows off his Michael Jackson moves in the school auditorium, helping his friend, Pedro Sanchez, win the election for class president.

Gordon Smith, a fire sprinkler salesman, drove an hour and a half from his home in Utah to attend the festival with his daughter, Mariah. Like his brother Craig, he did not care for the movie at first, but it took on a new meaning after several viewings.

"I can relate to it," he said. "In high school it's the cool kids and 10 everybody else. I was part of the 'everybody else' crowd. But in the movie the geeks, like Napoleon, support each other. You know, there was a very good message."

The movie also made local stars of some of Mr. Hess's family friends, including Dale Critchlow, the 76-year-old cattle farmer who was signing photographs for fans lined up along State Street in downtown Preston on Saturday.

"I was putting hay in the barn when my daughter brought Jared over and said, 'Before you say no, listen to what he has to say,' " said Mr. Critchlow, recalling when Mr. Hess asked him to play Lyle in the film. "He said, 'I have a favor to ask. I want you to be in my movie.' I said, 'What do I have to do?' Jared said, 'Shoot a cow.' I said, 'Huh? O.K., I can do that.' "

Mr. Critchlow did not really shoot the cow and he was not paid for the scene. (None of the locals said they were paid.) Instead what he gained was celebrity.

"I have never had that kind of attention in my life," he said, as several onlookers listened intently. Just last week Mr. Critchlow said the cow's owner called and asked him to pose for a photograph, gun in hand, with the cow. The owner, he said, wants to sell the cow on the Internet.

While Mr. Critchlow was a favorite of autograph seekers on Saturday, 15 fans at the festival dressed up as more recognizable characters from the film. (None of the main actors, including Jon Heder, who played Napoleon, attended.) At a look-alike contest held Saturday night at the Preston High School Auditorium, there were five Napoleons, two Rex Kwon Dos (a character who teaches Napoleon and his brother Kip self-defense), and one each of Pedro, Kip, and Deb, a classmate with a crush on Napoleon.

"If you don't get it, you just don't get it," said Ryan Grisso, who dressed up as Rex in red, white, and blue star-spangled pants, a patriotic kerchief on his head, and a blue knit shirt with the name "Rex" stitched on it (he came in second). On Friday Mr. Grisso arrived from San Francisco with his wife, Coline, and mother-in-law, Lila Ludahl McConnel, who lives 350 miles away in Caldwell, Idaho. He said they would have attended the festival last year but his wife was having a baby.

During the tater tot eating contest — where entrants were given one pound of the crispy potato lumps to down — Mr. Grisso's mother-in-law playfully slipped a few tots down the front of her green shirt. "I told them I wasn't playing to win," Ms. McConnel explained with a laugh after the shirt-stuffing was witnessed by a judge. "I know it's silly, but it's terribly fun."

A tater tot eating contest at the second annual Napoleon Dynamite festival.

But what is fun can be profitable too. Mr. Demke, the Napoleon impersonator, earns money performing at football and basketball games. What he liked best about being Napoleon was what any awkward teenager craves—the ability to speak without ridicule. In January Mr. Demke said he was performing at a basketball game between Oklahoma University and the University of Texas when an attractive woman wearing a tiara asked for a signed photograph. "I thought, 'What kind of idiot wears a tiara to a basketball game?' " he recalled.

So, channeling Napoleon, Mr. Demke posed the question. "She laughed," he said, then introduced herself as Jennifer Berry, the new Miss America. "I felt so stupid. She thought I was playing in character. I was grateful she was a fan of the movie."

But while visitors wholeheartedly embrace all that is *Napoleon* 20 *Dynamite*, some in Preston fear the movie portrayed them as backward and unsophisticated. And not everyone in the mostly Mormon town likes the throngs of tourists showing up to take photographs of their favorite movie sites.

"I thought it was funny, but I was concerned people would think it was a hick town," said Monte Henderson, a cattle farmer who was in the Happiness Is Scrapbooking store on Friday with his wife, Linda. "I have to admit I related to it, though. I mean, I was part of the F.F.A."

Ms. Henderson added: "I drive a school bus, and I can't tell you how many times we've had to tell the kids to reel their little rubber men in from out the window," referring to a scene where Napoleon threw a rubber doll attached to a string out a bus window and watched it bounce on the pavement.

If the festival thrives, it will be because of Ms. Christensen at the chamber. This year's attendance paled compared to last year's 6,000 attendees. Already the town is considering scrapping the $10 admission. That would be a boon to the likes of Tyra Andrews, winner of the tether ball game, who practiced all year and showed up at the festival with ten family members.

But what would really give the festival a jolt is the same thing many in Hollywood would like to see: a blockbuster sequel. (The studio has not decided whether to go ahead or not.) Joyce Williams, who owns Happiness Is Scrapbooking, said she recently was talking to a customer service representative from Hewlett-Packard who asked her where she lived. Ms. Williams said she told the agent "where *Napoleon Dynamite* was made."

"Oh, I know that place," the representative exclaimed. "My kids 25 love the movie. We'd love to come visit."

This profile starts with an unusual subject, a small-town festival that celebrates a cult film. The writer engages our interest with descriptions of several events, including a tater tot–eating contest and a look-alike contest, and interviews with several attendees and townspeople.

Key Features / Profiles

An interesting subject.   The subject may be something unusual, or it may be something ordinary shown in an intriguing way. You might profile an interesting person (Dale Critchlow, for instance, the farmer who has a small role in *Napoleon Dynamite*), a place (the town of Preston itself, or, perhaps, Preston High School), or an event (a festival celebrating a cult film).

Any necessary background.   A profile usually includes just enough information to let readers know something about the subject's larger context. Holson sums up the plot of *Napoleon Dynamite* in one brief paragraph and says very little about the town of Preston, only that it's a small town in "mostly rural" Idaho.

An interesting angle.   A good profile captures its subject from a particular angle. Holson doesn't try to tell us everything about the Napoleon Dynamite festival; rather, she focuses on how the townspeople are reacting to their sudden fame from this small, quirky film. The complete schedule of events is irrelevant to Holson's goal: to show how *Napoleon Dynamite* has affected a rural Idaho town.

A firsthand account.   Whether you are writing about a person, place, or event, you need to spend time observing and interacting with your subject. With a person, interacting means watching and conversing. Journalists tell us that "following the guy around," getting your subject to do something and talk about it at the same time, yields excellent material for a profile. When one writer met Theodor Geisel (Dr. Seuss) before profiling him, she asked him not only to talk about his characters but also to draw one—resulting in an illustration for her profile. With a place or event, interacting may mean visiting and participating, although sometimes you may gather even more information by playing the role of the silent observer.

Engaging details.   You need to include details that bring your subject to life. These may include *specific information* ("More than 300 people traveled from as far away as California and Connecticut"); *sensory images* ("Ryan Grisso, who dressed up as Rex in red, white, and blue star-spangled pants, a patriotic kerchief on his head, and a blue knit shirt with the name 'Rex' stitched on it"); *figurative language* (visitors came "for the chance to embrace their own inner Napoleon"); *dialogue* ("I said, 'What do I have to do?' Jared said, 'Shoot a cow.' "); and *anecdotes* ("During the tater tot eating contest. . . . Mr. Grisso's mother-in-law playfully slipped a few tots down the front of her green shirt"). Choose details that show rather than tell—that let your audience see and hear your subject rather than merely read an abstract description of it. And be sure all the details create some *dominant impression* of your subject: the impression we get out of this festival, for example, is of a low-key, lighthearted event that nevertheless could contribute to the economy of the community.

A BRIEF GUIDE TO WRITING PROFILES

Choosing a Suitable Subject

A person, a place, an event—whatever you choose, make sure it's something that arouses your curiosity and that you're not too familiar with. Knowing your subject too well can blind you to interesting details. **LIST** five to ten interesting subjects that you can experience firsthand. Obviously, you can't profile a person who won't be interviewed or a place or activity that can't be observed. So before you commit to a topic, make sure you'll be able to carry out firsthand research and not find out too late that the people you need to interview aren't willing or that places you need to visit are off-limits.

220–21

Considering the Rhetorical Situation

PURPOSE Why are you writing the profile? What angle will best achieve your purpose? How can you inform *and engage* your audience?

3–4

AUDIENCE Who is your audience? How familiar are they with your subject? What expectations of your profile might they have? What background information or definitions do you need to provide? How interested will they be—and how can you get their interest?

5–8

STANCE What view of your subject do you expect to present? Sympathetic? Critical? Sarcastic? Will you strive for a carefully balanced perspective?

12–14

MEDIA / DESIGN Will your profile be a print document? Will it be published on the Web? Will it be an oral presentation? Can (and should) you include images or any other visuals?

15–17

Generating Ideas and Text

Visit your subject. If you're writing about an amusement park, go there; if you're profiling the man who runs the carousel, make an appointment to meet and interview him. Get to know your subject—if you profile Ben and Jerry, sample the ice cream! Take along a camera if there's anything you might want to show visually in your profile. Find helpful hints for OBSERVING and INTERVIEWING in the chapter on finding sources.

394–96

Explore what you already know about your subject. Why do you find this subject interesting? What do you know about it now? What do you expect to find out about it from your research? What preconceived ideas about or emotional reactions to this subject do you have? Why do you have them? It may be helpful to try some of the activities in the chapter on GENERATING IDEAS AND TEXT.

219–25

If you're planning to interview someone, prepare questions. Holson likely asked townspeople such questions as, "How do you feel about the festival? Did you like the movie?" See the INTERVIEWING guidelines in Chapter 43 for help with planning questions.

394–95

Do additional research. You may be able to write a profile based entirely on your field research. You may, though, need to do some library or Web RESEARCH as well, to deepen your understanding, get a different perspective, or fill in gaps. Often the people you interview can help you find sources of additional information; so can the sponsors of events and those in charge of places. To learn more about a city park, for instance, contact the government office that maintains it.

373

Analyze your findings. Look for patterns, images, recurring ideas or phrases, and engaging details. Compare your preconceptions with your findings. Look for contrasts or discrepancies: between a subject's words and actions, between the appearance of a place and what goes on there, between your expectations and your research findings. Holson may have expected to meet *Napoleon Dynamite* fans—but not townspeople who don't

support the festival. You may find the advice in the **READING STRATEGIES** chapter helpful here.

352–66

Come up with an angle. What's most memorable about your subject? What most interests you? What will interest your audience? Holson focuses on how *Napoleon Dynamite* has affected the people of Preston—whether they welcome the movie's fans, worry about how their town is perceived, or hope to make money off their town's unexpected fame. Sometimes you'll know your angle from the start; other times you'll need to look further into your topic. You might try **CLUSTERING, CUBING, FREEWRITING,** and **LOOPING,** activities that will help you look at your topic from many different angles.

219–22

Note details that support your angle. Use your angle to focus your research and generate text. Try **DESCRIBING** your subject as clearly as you can, **COMPARING** your subject with other subjects of its sort, writing **DIALOGUE** that captures your subject. Holson, for instance, quotes a local farmer who appeared in *Napoleon Dynamite* as saying, "I have never had that kind of attention in my life." Engaging details will bring your subject to life for your audience. Together, these details should create a dominant impression of your subject.

324–32
306–13
333–37

Ways of Organizing a Profile

[As a narrative]

One common way to organize a profile is by **NARRATING.** For example, if you are profiling a chess championship, you may write about it chronologically, creating suspense as you move from start to finish.

343–51

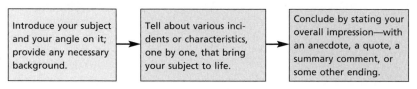

| Introduce your subject and your angle on it; provide any necessary background. | → | Tell about various incidents or characteristics, one by one, that bring your subject to life. | → | Conclude by stating your overall impression—with an anecdote, a quote, a summary comment, or some other ending. |

[As a description]

324–32

Sometimes you may organize a profile by **DESCRIBING** — a person or a place, for instance. The profile of the Napoleon Dynamite festival is organized this way.

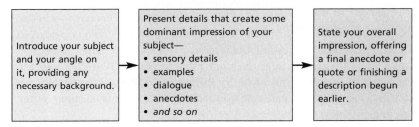

Introduce your subject and your angle on it, providing any necessary background.

Present details that create some dominant impression of your subject—
• sensory details
• examples
• dialogue
• anecdotes
• *and so on*

State your overall impression, offering a final anecdote or quote or finishing a description begun earlier.

IF YOU NEED MORE HELP

226–28
229–34
235–41
242–46
247–58

See Chapter 24 for guidelines on **DRAFTING,** Chapter 25 on **ASSESSING YOUR OWN WRITING,** Chapter 26 on **GETTING RESPONSE AND REVISING,** and Chapter 27 on **EDITING AND PROOFREADING.** See Chapter 28 if you are required to submit your profile in a writing **PORTFOLIO.**

Proposals 17

Contractors bid on building projects. Musicians and educators apply for grants. Researchers seek funding. Student leaders call for lights on bike paths. You offer to pay half the cost of a car and insurance if your parents will pay the other half. Lovers propose marriage; friends propose sharing dinner and a movie. These are all examples of proposals: ideas put forward for consideration that say, "Here is a solution to a problem" or "This is what ought to be done." All proposals are arguments: when you propose something, you are trying to persuade others to see a problem in a particular way and to accept your solution to the problem. For example, here is a proposal for reducing the costs of college textbooks, written by an accounting professor at the University of Texas who is chairman of the university's Co-op Bookstore and himself a textbook author. It originally appeared on the Op-Ed page of the *New York Times* in August 2007.

MICHAEL GRANOF

Course Requirement: Extortion

By now, entering college students and their parents have been warned: textbooks are outrageously expensive. Few textbooks for semester-long courses retail for less than $120, and those for science and math courses typically approach $180. Contrast this with the $20 to $30 cost of most hardcover best sellers and other trade books.

Perhaps these students and their parents can take comfort in knowing that the federal government empathizes with them, and in an attempt to ease their pain Congress asked its Advisory Committee on Student Financial Assistance to suggest a cure for the problem. Unfortunately, though, the committee has proposed a remedy that would only worsen the problem.

The committee's report, released in May, mainly proposes strengthening the market for used textbooks — by encouraging college bookstores to guarantee that they will buy back textbooks, establishing online book swaps among students, and urging faculty to avoid switching textbooks from one semester to the next. The fatal flaw in that proposal (and similar ones made by many state legislatures) is that used books are the cause of, not the cure for, high textbook prices.

Yet there is a way to lighten the load for students in their budgets, if not their backpacks. With small modifications to the institutional arrangements between universities, publishers, and students, textbook costs could be reduced — and these changes could be made without government intervention.

Today the used-book market is exceedingly well organized and efficient. Campus bookstores buy back not only the books that will be used at their university the next semester but also those that will not. Those that are no longer on their lists of required books they resell to national wholesalers, which in turn sell them to college bookstores on campuses where they will be required. This means that even if a text is being adopted for the first time at a particular college, there is almost certain to be an ample supply of used copies.

As a result, publishers have the chance to sell a book to only one of the multiple students who eventually use it. Hence, publishers must cover their costs and make their profit in the first semester their books are sold — before used copies swamp the market. That's why the prices are so high.

As might be expected, publishers do what they can to undermine the used-book market, principally by coming out with new editions every three or four years. To be sure, in rapidly changing fields like biology and physics, the new editions may be academically defensible. But in areas like algebra and calculus, they are nothing more than a transparent attempt to ensure premature textbook obsolescence. Publishers also try to discourage students from buying used books by bundling the text with extra materials like workbooks and CDs that

are not reusable and therefore cannot be passed from one student to another.

The system could be much improved if, first of all, colleges and publishers would acknowledge that textbooks are more akin to computer software than to trade books. A textbook's value, like that of a software program, is not in its physical form, but rather in its intellectual content. Therefore, just as software companies typically "site license" to colleges, so should textbook publishers.

Here's how it would work: A teacher would pick a textbook, and the college would pay a negotiated fee to the publisher based on the number of students enrolled in the class. If there were 50 students in the class, for example, the fee might be $15 per student, or $750 for the semester. If the text were used for ten semesters, the publisher would ultimately receive a total of $150 ($15 $\times$ 10) for each student enrolled in the course, or as much as $7,500.

In other words, the publisher would have a stream of revenue 10 for as long as the text was in use. Presumably, the university would pass on this fee to the students, just as it does the cost of laboratory supplies and computer software. But the students would pay much less than the $900 a semester they now typically pay for textbooks.

Once the university had paid the license fee, each student would have the option of using the text in electronic format or paying more to purchase a hard copy through the usual channels. The publisher could set the price of hard copies low enough to cover only its production and distribution costs plus a small profit, because it would be covering most of its costs and making most of its profit by way of the license fees. The hard copies could then be resold to other students or back to the bookstore, but that would be of little concern to the publisher.

A further benefit of this approach is that it would not affect the way courses are taught. The same cannot be said for other recommendations from the Congressional committee and from state legislatures, like placing teaching materials on electronic reserve, urging faculty to adopt cheaper "no frills" textbooks, and assigning mainly electronic textbooks. While each of these suggestions may have merit, they force faculty to weigh students' academic interests against their fiscal concerns and encourage them to rely less on new textbooks.

Neither colleges nor publishers are known for their cutting-edge innovations. But if they could slightly change the way they do business, they would make a substantial dent in the cost of higher education and provide a real benefit to students and their parents.

This proposal clearly defines the problem — some textbooks cost a lot — and explains why. It proposes a solution to the problem of high textbook prices and offers reasons why this solution will work better than others. Its tone is reasonable and measured, yet decisive.

Key Features / Proposals

A well-defined problem.   Some problems are self-evident or relatively simple, and you would not need much persuasive power to make people act — as with the problem "This university discards too much paper." While some people might see nothing wrong with throwing paper away, most are likely to agree that recycling is a good thing. Other issues are controversial: some people see them as problems while others do not, such as this one: "Motorcycle riders who do not wear helmets risk serious injury and raise health-care costs for everyone." Some motorcyclists believe that wearing or not wearing a helmet is a personal choice; you would have to present arguments to convince your readers that not wearing a helmet is indeed a problem needing a solution. Any written proposal must establish at the outset that there is a problem — and that it's serious enough to require a solution.

A recommended solution.   Once you have defined the problem, you need to describe the solution you are suggesting and to explain it in enough detail for readers to understand what you are proposing. Sometimes you might suggest several solutions, weigh their merits, and choose the best one.

A convincing argument for your proposed solution.   You need to con-vince readers that your solution is feasible — and that it is the best way to solve the problem. Sometimes you'll want to explain in detail how your proposed solution would work. See, for example, how the textbook pro-posal details the way a licensing system would operate.

Anticipate questions.   You may need to consider any questions readers may have about your proposal — and to show how its advantages out-weigh any disadvantages. Had the textbook proposal been written for col-lege budget officers, it would have needed to anticipate and answer ques-tions about the costs of implementing the proposed solution.

A call to action.   The goal of a proposal is to persuade readers to accept your proposed solution. This solution may include asking readers to take action.

An appropriate tone.   Since you're trying to persuade readers to act, your tone is important — readers will always react better to a reasonable, respectful presentation than to anger or self-righteousness.

A BRIEF GUIDE TO WRITING PROPOSALS

Deciding on a Topic

Choose a problem that can be solved. Complex, large problems, such as poverty, hunger, or terrorism, usually require complex, large solutions. Most of the time, focusing on a smaller problem or a limited aspect of a large problem will yield a more manageable proposal. Rather than tack-ling the problem of world poverty, for example, think about the problem faced by families in your community that have lost jobs and need help until they find employment.

Considering the Rhetorical Situation

3–4 **PURPOSE** Do you have a vested interest in the solution your readers adopt, or do you simply want to eliminate the problem, whatever solution might be adopted?

5–8 **AUDIENCE** How can you reach your readers? Do you know how receptive or resistant to change they are likely to be? Do they have the authority to enact your proposal?

12–14 **STANCE** How can you show your audience that your proposal is reasonable and should be taken seriously? How can you demonstrate your own authority and credibility?

15–17 **MEDIA / DESIGN** How will you deliver your proposal? In print? Online? As a speech? Would visuals help support your proposal?

Generating Ideas and Text

Explore potential solutions to the problem. Many problems can be solved in more than one way, and you need to show your readers that you've examined several potential solutions. You may develop solutions to your problem on your own; more often, though, you'll need to do 373 **RESEARCH** to see how others have solved — or tried to solve — similar problems. Don't settle on a single solution too quickly — you'll need to 306–13 **COMPARE** the advantages and disadvantages of several solutions in order to argue convincingly for one.

Decide on the most desirable solution(s). One solution may be head and shoulders above others — but be open to rejecting all the possible solutions on your list and starting over if you need to, or to combining two or more potential solutions in order to come up with an acceptable fix.

Think about why your solution is the best one. Why did you choose your solution? Why will it work better than others? What has to be done

to enact it? What will it cost? What makes you think it can be done? Writing out answers to these questions will help you argue for your solution — to show that you have carefully and objectively outlined a problem, analyzed the potential solutions, and weighed their merits — and to show the reasons the solution you propose is the best.

Ways of Organizing a Proposal

You can organize a proposal in various ways, but always you will begin by establishing that there is a problem. You may then consider several solutions before recommending one particular solution. Sometimes, however, you might suggest only a single solution.

[Several possible solutions]

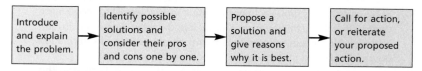

[A single solution]

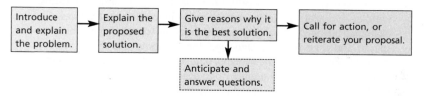

TOPIC PROPOSALS

Instructors often ask students to write topic proposals to ensure that their topics are appropriate or manageable. If you get your instructor's response to a good proposal before you write it, your finished product will likely be much better than if you try to guess the assignment's demands. Some

116–24 ▲

instructors may also ask for an **ANNOTATED BIBLIOGRAPHY** showing that appropriate sources of information are available—more evidence that the project can be carried out. Here a first-year student proposes a topic for an assignment in a writing course in which she has been asked to take a position on a global issue.

JENNIFER CHURCH

Biodiversity Loss and Its Effect on Medicine

The loss of biodiversity—the variety of organisms found in the world—is affecting the world every day. Some scientists estimate that we are losing approximately one hundred species per day and that more than a quarter of all species may vanish within fifty years. I recently had the issue of biodiversity loss brought to my attention in a biological sciences course that I am taking this quarter. I have found myself interested in and intrigued by the subject and have found an abundance of information both in books and on the Internet.

In this paper, I will argue that it is crucial for people to stop this rapid loss of our world's biodiversity. Humans are the number-one cause of biodiversity loss in the world. Whether through pollution or toxins, we play a crucial role in the extinction of many different species. For example, 80 percent of the world's medicine comes from biological species and their habitats. One medicine vanishing due to biodiversity loss is TAXOL. Found in the Wollemi pine tree, TAXOL is one of the most promising drugs for the treatment of ovarian and breast cancer. If the Wollemi pine tree becomes extinct, we will lose this potential cure.

I will concentrate primarily on biodiversity and its effects on the medical field. If we keep destroying the earth's biodiversity at the current rate, we may lose many opportunities to develop medicines we need to survive. The majority of my information will be found on the Internet, because there are many reliable Web sites from all around the world that address the issue of biodiversity loss and medicine.

Church defines and narrows her topic (from biodiversity loss to the impact of that loss on medicine), discusses her interest, outlines her argument, and discusses

her research strategy. Her goal is to convince her instructor that she has a realistic writing project and a clear plan.

Key Features / Topic Proposals

You'll need to explain what you want to write about, why you want to explore it, and what you'll do with your topic. Unless your instructor has additional requirements, here are the features to include:

A concise discussion of the subject.   Topic proposals generally open with a brief discussion of the subject, outlining any important areas of controversy or debate associated with it and clarifying the extent of the writer's current knowledge of it. In its first two paragraphs, Church's proposal includes a concise statement of the topic she wishes to address.

A clear statement of your intended focus.   State what aspect of the topic you intend to write on as clearly as you can, narrowing your focus appropriately. Church does so by stating her intended topic — loss of biodiversity — and then showing how she will focus on the importance of biodiversity to the medical field.

A rationale for choosing the topic.   Tell your instructor why this topic interests you and why you want to write about it. Church both states what made her interested in her topic and hints at a practical reason for choosing it: plenty of information is available.

Mention of resources.   To show your instructor that you can achieve your goal, you need to identify the available research materials.

IF YOU NEED MORE HELP

See Chapter 24 for guidelines on **DRAFTING,** Chapter 25 on **ASSESSING YOUR OWN WRITING,** Chapter 26 on **GETTING RESPONSE AND REVISING,** and Chapter 27 on **EDITING AND PROOFREADING.** See Chapter 28 if you are required to submit your proposal in a writing **PORTFOLIO.**

226–28
229–34
235–41
242–46
247–58

18 Reflections

Sometimes we write essays just to think about something—to speculate, ponder, probe; to play with an idea, develop a thought; or simply to share something. Reflective essays are our attempt to think something through by writing about it and to share our thinking with others. If such essays make an argument, it is about things we care or think about more than about what we believe to be "true." Have a look at one example by Jonathan Safran Foer, a novelist who lives in Brooklyn. This essay originally appeared on the Op-Ed page of the *New York Times* in 2006.

JONATHAN SAFRAN FOER

My Life as a Dog

For the last twenty years, New York City parks without designated dog runs have permitted dogs to be off-leash from 9 p.m. to 9 a.m. Because of recent complaints from the Juniper Park Civic Association in Queens, the issue has been revisited. On December 5, the Board of Health will vote on the future of off-leash hours.

Retrievers in elevators, Pomeranians on No. 6 trains, bull mastiffs crossing the Brooklyn Bridge . . . it is easy to forget just how strange it is that dogs live in New York in the first place. It is about as unlikely a place for dogs as one could imagine, and yet 1.4 million of them are among us. Why do we keep them in our apartments and houses, always at some expense and inconvenience? Is it even possible, in a city, to provide a good life for a dog, and what is a "good life"? Does the health board's vote matter in ways other than the most obvious?

I adopted George (a Great Dane/Lab/pit/greyhound/ridgeback/whatever mix—a.k.a. Brooklyn shorthair) because I thought it would be fun. As it turns out, she is a major pain an awful lot of the time.

rhetorical situations

genres

processes

strategies

research mla/apa

media/ design

handbook

She mounts guests, eats my son's toys (and occasionally tries to eat my son), is obsessed with squirrels, lunges at skateboarders and Hasids,* has the savant-like ability to find her way between the camera lens and subject of every photo taken in her vicinity, backs her tush into the least interested person in the room, digs up the freshly planted, scratches the newly bought, licks the about-to-be-served, and occasionally relieves herself on the wrong side of the front door. Her head is resting on my foot as I type this. I love her.

Our various struggles — to communicate, to recognize and accommodate each other's desires, simply to coexist — force me to interact with something, or rather someone, entirely "other." George can respond to a handful of words, but our relationship takes place almost entirely outside of language. She seems to have thoughts and emotions, desires and fears. Sometimes I think I understand them; often I don't. She is a mystery to me. And I must be one to her.

Of course our relationship is not always a struggle. My morning walk with George is very often the highlight of my day — when I have my best thoughts, when I most appreciate both nature and the city, and in a deeper sense, life itself. Our hour together is a bit of compensation for the burdens of civilization: business attire, email, money, etiquette, walls, and artificial lighting. It is even a kind of compensation for language. Why does watching a dog be a dog fill one with happiness? And why does it make one feel, in the best sense of the word, human?

It is children, very often, who want dogs. In a recent study, when asked to name the ten most important "individuals" in their lives, 7- and 10-year-olds included two pets on average. In another study, 42 percent of 5-year-olds spontaneously mentioned their pets when asked, "Whom do you turn to when you are feeling, sad, angry, happy, or wanting to share a secret?" Just about every children's book in my local bookstore has an animal for its hero. But then, only a few feet away in the cookbook section, just about every cookbook includes recipes for cooking animals. Is there a more illuminating illustration of our paradoxical relationship with the nonhuman world?

In the course of our lives, we move from a warm and benevolent relationship with animals (learning responsibility through caring for

*Hasids: a Jewish sect whose members dress distinctively. [Editor's note]

our pets, stroking and confiding in them) to a cruel one (virtually all animals raised for meat in this country are factory farmed — they spend their lives in confinement, dosed with antibiotics and other drugs).

How do you explain this? Is our kindness replaced with cruelty? I don't think so. I think in part it's because the older we get, the less exposure we have to animals. And nothing facilitates indifference or forgetfulness so much as distance. In this sense, dogs and cats have been very lucky: they are the only animals we are intimately exposed to daily.

Folk parental wisdom and behavioral studies alike generally view 10 the relationships children have with companion animals as beneficial. But one does not have to be a child to learn from a pet. It is precisely my frustrations with George, and the inconveniences she creates, that reinforce in me how much compromise is necessary to share space with other beings.

The practical arguments against off-leash hours are easily refuted. One doesn't have to be an animal scientist to know that the more a dog is able to exercise its "dogness" — to run and play, to socialize with other dogs — the happier it will be. Happy dogs, like happy people, tend not to be aggressive. In the years that dogs have been allowed to run free in city parks, dog bites have decreased 90 percent. But there is another argument that is not so easy to respond to: some people just don't want to be inconvenienced by dogs. Giving dogs space necessarily takes away space from humans.

We have been having this latter debate, in different forms, for ages. Again and again we are confronted with the reality — some might say the problem — of sharing our space with other living things, be they dogs, trees, fish, or penguins. Dogs in the park are a present example of something that is often too abstracted or far away to gain our consideration.

The very existence of parks is a response to this debate: earlier New Yorkers had the foresight to recognize that if we did not carve out places for nature in our cities, there would be no nature. It was recently estimated that Central Park's real estate would be worth more than $500 billion. Which is to say we are half a trillion dollars inconvenienced by trees and grass. But we do not think of it as an inconvenience. We think of it as balance.

Living on a planet of fixed size requires compromise, and while we are the only party capable of negotiating, we are not the only party at the table. We've never claimed more, and we've never had less. There has never been less clean air or water, fewer fish or mature trees. If we are not simply ignoring the situation, we keep hoping for (and expecting) a technological solution that will erase our destruction, while allowing us to continue to live without compromise. Maybe zoos will be an adequate replacement for wild animals in natural habitats. Maybe we will be able to recreate the Amazon somewhere else. Maybe one day we will be able to genetically engineer dogs that do not wish to run free. Maybe. But will those futures make us feel, in the best sense of the word, human?

I have been taking George to Prospect Park twice a day for more 15 than three years, but her running is still a revelation to me. Effortlessly, joyfully, she runs quite a bit faster than the fastest human on the planet. And faster, I've come to realize, than the other dogs in the park. George might well be the fastest land animal in Brooklyn. Once or twice every morning, for no obvious reason, she'll tear into a full sprint. Other dog owners can't help but watch her. Every now and then someone will cheer her on. It is something to behold.

A vote regarding off-leash hours for dogs sparks Foer's reflection on the relationship between dogs and humans. He begins by thinking about his relationship with his own dog, then goes on to consider the paradoxical nature of our treatment of animals in general. From there, he moves into a larger discussion of the compromises we make to "share space with other beings." Finally, he brings his reflection back to the personal, describing the joy of watching his dog be herself, off-leash.

Key Features / Reflections

A topic that intrigues you. A reflective essay has a dual purpose: to ponder something you find interesting or puzzling and to share your thoughts with an audience. Your topic may be anything that interests you.

You might write about someone you have never met and are curious about, an object or occurrence that makes you think, a place where you feel comfortable or safe. Your goal is to explore the meaning that the person, object, event, or place has for you in a way that will interest others. One way to do that is by making connections between your personal experience and more general ones that readers may share. Foer writes about his experience with his dog, but in so doing he raises questions and offers insights about the way everyone relates to others, human and nonhuman alike.

Some kind of structure.   A reflective essay can be structured in many ways, but it needs to *be* structured. It may seem to wander, but all its paths and ideas should relate, one way or another. The challenge is to keep your readers' interest as you explore your topic and to leave readers satisfied that the journey was pleasurable, interesting, and profitable. Foer brings his essay full-circle, introducing the vote on the off-leash law in his opening, then considering our complex relationship with dogs, and, after suggesting some of the compromises we make to share our world with other nonhuman living things, closing with an indelible image of the joy that freedom from a leash brings.

Specific details.   You'll need to provide specific details to help readers understand and connect with your subject, especially if it's an abstract or unfamiliar one. Foer offers a wealth of details about his dog: "She mounts guests, eats my son's toys (and occasionally tries to eat my son), is obsessed by squirrels, lunges at skateboarders and Hasids." Anecdotes can bring your subject to life: "Once or twice every morning, for no obvious reason, she'll tear into a full sprint. Other dog owners can't help but watch her. Every now and then someone will cheer her on." Reflections may be about causes, such as why dogs make us feel more human; comparisons, such as when Foer compares animals as pets and as food; and examples: "virtually all animals raised for meat in this country are factory farmed."

A questioning, speculative tone.   In a reflective essay, you are working toward answers, not providing them neatly organized and ready for consumption. So your tone is usually tentative and open, demonstrating a willingness to entertain, accept, and reject various ideas as your essay progresses from beginning to end. Foer achieves this tone by looking at people's relationships with dogs from several different perspectives as well as by asking questions for which he provides no direct answers.

A BRIEF GUIDE TO WRITING REFLECTIONS

Deciding on a Topic

Choose a subject you want to explore. Write a list of things that you think about, wonder about, find puzzling or annoying. They may be big things—life, relationships—or little things—quirks of certain people's behavior, curious objects, everyday events. Try **CLUSTERING** one or more of those things, or begin by **FREEWRITING** to see what comes to mind as you write.

221–22
219–20

Considering the Rhetorical Situation

PURPOSE	What's your goal in writing this essay? To introduce a topic that interests you? Entertain? Provoke readers to think about something? What aspects of your subject do you want to ponder and reflect on?
AUDIENCE	Who is the audience? How familiar are they with your subject? How will you introduce it in a way that will interest them?
STANCE	What is your attitude toward the topic you plan to explore? Questioning? Playful? Critical? Curious? Something else?
MEDIA / DESIGN	Will your essay be a print document? An oral presentation? Will it be posted on a website? Would it help to have any visuals?

3–4

5–8

12–14

15–17

Generating Ideas and Text

Explore your subject in detail.   Reflections often include descriptive details. Foer, for example, **DESCRIBES** the many ways he encounters dogs in New York: "Retrievers in elevators, Pomeranians on No. 6 trains, bull mastiffs crossing the Brooklyn Bridge." Those details provide a base for the speculations to come. You may also make your point by **DEFINING, COMPARING,** even **CLASSIFYING.** Virtually any organizing pattern will help you explore your subject.

324–32

314–23
306–13
300–305

Back away.   Ask yourself why your subject matters: why is it important or intriguing or significant? You may try **LISTING** or **OUTLINING** possibilities, or you may want to start **DRAFTING** to see where the writing takes your thinking. Your goal is to think on paper (or screen) about your subject, to play with its possibilities.

220–21
223–24
226–28

Think about how to keep readers with you.   Reflections may seem loose or unstructured, but they must be carefully crafted so that readers can follow your train of thought. It's a good idea to sketch out a rough **THESIS** to help focus your thoughts. You may not include the thesis in the essay itself, but every part of the essay should in some way relate to it.

273–75

Ways of Organizing a Reflective Essay

Reflective essays may be organized in many ways because they mimic the way we think, associating one idea with another in ways that make sense but do not necessarily form a "logical" progression. In general, you might consider organizing a reflection using this overall strategy:

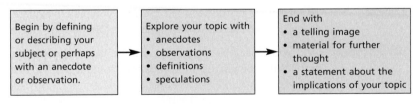

Begin by defining or describing your subject or perhaps with an anecdote or observation. → Explore your topic with
- anecdotes
- observations
- definitions
- speculations
→ End with
- a telling image
- material for further thought
- a statement about the implications of your topic

Another way to organize this type of essay is as a series of brief reflections that together create an overall impression:

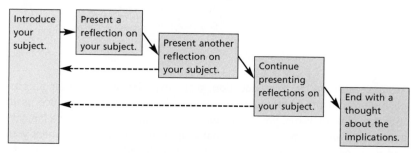

IF YOU NEED MORE HELP

See Chapter 24 for guidelines on **DRAFTING,** Chapter 25 on **ASSESSING YOUR OWN WRITING,** Chapter 26 on **GETTING RESPONSE AND REVISING,** and Chapter 27 on **EDITING AND PROOFREADING.** See Chapter 28 if you are required to submit your reflection in a writing **PORTFOLIO.**

226–28
229–34
235–41
242–46
247–58

19 Résumés and Job Letters

Résumés summarize our education, work experience, and other accomplishments for prospective employers. Application letters introduce us to those employers. When you send a letter and résumé applying for a job, you are making an argument for why that employer should want to meet you, and perhaps hire you. In a way, the two texts together serve as an advertisement selling your talents and abilities to someone who likely has to sift through many applications to decide whom to invite for an interview. That's why résumés and application letters require a level of care that few other documents do. In the same way, sending a thank-you letter following an interview completes your presentation of yourself to potential employers. Résumés, application letters, and thank-you letters are obviously very different genres—yet they share one common purpose and are done for the same audience. Thus, they are presented together in this chapter.

RÉSUMÉS

This chapter covers two kinds of résumés, print ones and scannable ones. *Print résumés* are presented on paper to be read by people. You usually design a print résumé to highlight key information typographically, using italic or bold type for headings, for instance. *Scannable résumés* can be delivered on paper or via email, but they are formatted to be read by a computer. Therefore, you need to use a single typeface without any bold or italics or even indents, and you need to write the résumé using keywords that you hope will match words found in the computer's job description database.

Following are two résumés—the first one print and the second one scannable—both written by a college student applying for an internship before his senior year.

rhetorical situations

genres

processes

strategies

research mla/apa

media/ design

handbook

Print Résumé

Samuel Praeger
28 Murphy Lane
Springfield, OH 45399
937-555-2640
spraeger22@webmail.com

name in boldface

OBJECTIVE   To obtain an internship with a public relations firm

objective tailored to specific job sought

EDUCATION
Fall 2005–present   Wittenberg University, Springfield, OH
- B.A. in Psychology expected in May 2009
- Minor in East Asian Studies

EXPERIENCE
2007–present   Department of Psychology, Wittenberg University
Research Assistant
- Collect and analyze data
- Interview research participants

work experience in reverse chronological order

Summer
2007   Landis and Landis Public Relations, Springfield, OH
Events Coordinator
- Organized local charity events
- Coordinated database of potential donors
- Produced two radio spots for event promotion

Summers
2005, 2006   Springfield Aquatic Club, Springfield, OH
Assistant Swim Coach
- Instructed children ages 5–18 in competitive swimming

HONORS
2008   Psi Chi National Honor Society in Psychology

2006–2008   Community Service Scholarship, Wittenberg University

ACTIVITIES   Varsity Swim Team, Ronald McDonald House Fund-raiser

SKILLS   Microsoft Office; SPSS for Windows; Eudora Pro; PowerPoint; fluency in Japanese language

REFERENCES   Available upon request

format to fill entire page

Scannable Résumé

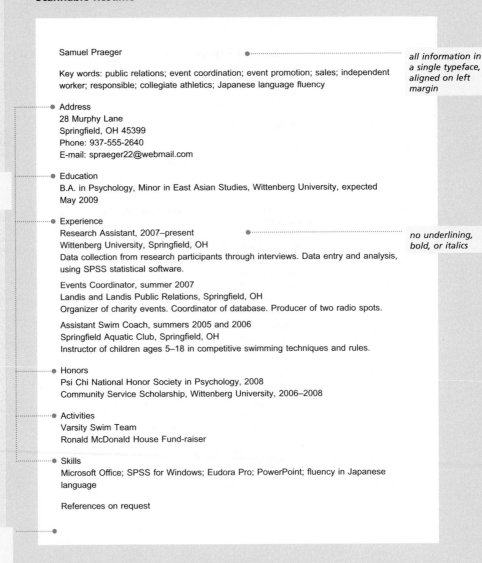

Samuel Praeger

all information in a single typeface, aligned on left margin

Key words: public relations; event coordination; event promotion; sales; independent worker; responsible; collegiate athletics; Japanese language fluency

key words to aid computer searching

Address
28 Murphy Lane
Springfield, OH 45399
Phone: 937-555-2640
E-mail: spraeger22@webmail.com

Education
B.A. in Psychology, Minor in East Asian Studies, Wittenberg University, expected May 2009

Experience
Research Assistant, 2007–present
Wittenberg University, Springfield, OH
Data collection from research participants through interviews. Data entry and analysis, using SPSS statistical software.

no underlining, bold, or italics

Events Coordinator, summer 2007
Landis and Landis Public Relations, Springfield, OH
Organizer of charity events. Coordinator of database. Producer of two radio spots.

Assistant Swim Coach, summers 2005 and 2006
Springfield Aquatic Club, Springfield, OH
Instructor of children ages 5–18 in competitive swimming techniques and rules.

Honors
Psi Chi National Honor Society in Psychology, 2008
Community Service Scholarship, Wittenberg University, 2006–2008

Activities
Varsity Swim Team
Ronald McDonald House Fund-raiser

Skills
Microsoft Office; SPSS for Windows; Eudora Pro; PowerPoint; fluency in Japanese language

References on request

printed on white paper; not folded or stapled

rhetorical situations · genres · processes · strategies · research mla/apa · media/design · handbook

Samuel Praeger's résumé is arranged chronologically, and because he was look-ing for work in a certain field, the résumé is targeted, focusing on his related work and skills and leaving out any references to high school (that he is in college allows readers to assume graduation from high school) or his past job as a house painter, which is not relevant. The print version describes his work responsibilities using action verbs to highlight what he actually did—pro-duced, instructed, and so on—whereas the scannable version converts the verbs to nouns—producer, instructor. The scannable version is formatted in a single standard typeface, with no italics, boldfacing, or other typographic variation.

Key Features / Résumés

An organization that suits your goals and experience. There are con-ventional ways of organizing a résumé but no one way. You can organize a résumé chronologically or functionally, and it can be targeted or not. A *chronological résumé* is the most general, listing pretty much all your aca-demic and work experience from the most recent to the earliest. A *tar-geted résumé* will generally announce the specific goal up top, just beneath your name, and will offer information selectively, showing only the expe-rience and skills relevant to your goal. A *functional résumé* is organized around various kinds of experience and is not chronological. You might write a functional résumé if you wish to demonstrate a lot of experience in more than one area and perhaps if you wish to downplay dates.

Succinct. A résumé should almost always be short—one page if at all possible. Entries should be parallel but do not need to be written in com-plete sentences—"Produced two radio spots," for instance, rather than "I produced two radio spots." *Print résumés* often use action verbs ("instructed," "produced") to emphasize what you accomplished; *scannable résumés* use nouns instead ("instructor," "producer").

A design that highlights key information. It's important for a résumé to look good and to be easy to scan. *On a print résumé*, typography, white space, and alignment matter. Your name should be bold at the top. Major sections should be labeled with headings, all of which should be in one slightly larger or bolder font. And you need to surround each section and the text as a whole with adequate white space to make the parts easy to read—and to make the entire document look professional. *On a scannable résumé,* you should use one standard typeface throughout and *not* use any italics, boldface, bullets, or indents.

A BRIEF GUIDE TO WRITING RÉSUMÉS

Considering the Rhetorical Situation

3–4	**PURPOSE**	Are you seeking a job? An internship? Some other position? How will the position for which you're applying affect what you include on your résumé?
5–8	**AUDIENCE**	What sort of employee is the company or organization seeking? What experience and qualities will the person doing the hiring be looking for?
12–14	**STANCE**	What personal and professional qualities do you want to convey? Think about how you want to come across—as eager? polite? serious? ambitious?—and choose your words accordingly.
15–17	**MEDIA / DESIGN**	Are you planning to send your résumé and letter on paper? As an email attachment? In a scannable format? Whatever your medium, be sure both documents are formatted appropriately and proofread carefully.

Generating Ideas and Text for a Résumé

Consider how you want to present yourself. Begin by gathering the information you will need to include. As you work through the steps of

putting your résumé together, think about the method of organization that works best for your purpose—chronological, targeted, or functional.

- *Contact information.* At the top of your résumé, list your full name, a permanent address (rather than your school address), a permanent telephone number with area code, and your email address (which should sound professional; addresses like *hotbabe334@aol.com* do not make a good first impression on potential employers).

- *Your education.* Start with the most recent: degree, major, college attended, and minor (if any). You may want to list your GPA (if it's over 3.0) and any academic honors you've received. If you don't have much work experience, list education first.

- *Your work experience.* As with education, list your most recent job first and work backward. Include job title, organization name, city and state, start and end dates, and responsibilities. Describe them in terms of your duties and accomplishments. If you have extensive work experience in the area in which you're applying, list that first.

- *Community service, volunteer, and charitable activities.* Many high school students are required to perform community service, and many students participate in various volunteer activities that benefit others. List what you've done, and think about the skills and aptitudes that participation helped you develop or demonstrate.

- *Other activities, interests, and abilities.* What do you do for fun? What skills do your leisure activities require? (For example, if you play complicated games on the Internet, you probably have a high level of knowledge about computers. You should describe your computer skills in a way that an employer might find useful.)

Define your objective. Are you looking for a particular job for which you should create a targeted résumé? Are you preparing a generic chronological résumé to use in a search for work of any kind? Defining your objective as specifically as possible helps you decide on the form the résumé will take and the information it will include.

Choose contacts.   Whether you list references on your résumé or offer to provide them on request, ask people to serve as references for you before you send out a résumé. It's a good idea to provide each reference with a one-page summary of relevant information about you (for example, give professors a list of courses you took with them, including the grades you earned and the titles of papers you wrote).

Choose your words carefully.   Remember, your résumé is a sales document—you're trying to present yourself as someone worth a second look. Focus on your achievements, using action verbs that say what you've done. If, however, you're composing a scannable résumé, use nouns rather than verbs, and use terms that will function as key words. Key words help the computer match your qualifications to the organization's needs. People in charge of hiring search the database of résumés by entering key words relating to the job for which they are seeking applicants. Key words for a lab technician, for example, might include *laboratory, technician, procedures, subjects, experimental*—among many others. To determine what key words to list on your résumé, read job ads carefully, and use the same words the ads do—as long as they accurately reflect your experience. Be honest—employers expect truthfulness, and embellishing the truth can cause you to lose a job later.

Consider key design elements.   Make sure your résumé is centered on the page and that it looks clean and clear. It's usually best to use a single, simple **FONT** (serif for print, sans serif for scannable) throughout and to print on white or off-white paper. Limit paper résumés to no more—and no less—than one full page. If you plan to send a scannable résumé or post it on a website, create a version that does *not* contain bullets, indents, italics, or underlining, since downloading can cause those elements to get lost or garbled.

524–25

Edit and proofread carefully. Your résumé must be perfect. Show it to others, and proofread again. You don't want even one typo.

Ways of Organizing a Résumé

If you don't have much work experience or if you've just gone back to school to train for a new career, put education before work experience; if you have extensive work experience in the area in which you're applying, list work before education.

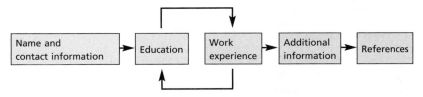

APPLICATION AND THANK-YOU LETTERS

The application letter argues that the writer should be taken seriously as a candidate for a job or some other opportunity. Generally, it is sent together with a résumé, so it doesn't need to give that much information. It does, however, have to make a favorable impression: the way it's written and presented can get you in for an interview—or not. On the following page is an application letter that Samuel Praeger wrote seeking a position at the end of his junior year. Praeger tailored his letter to one specific reader at a specific organization. The letter cites details, showing that it is not a generic application letter being sent to many possible employers. Rather, it identifies a particular position—the public relations internship—and stresses the fit between his credentials and the position. He also states his availability.

Application Letter

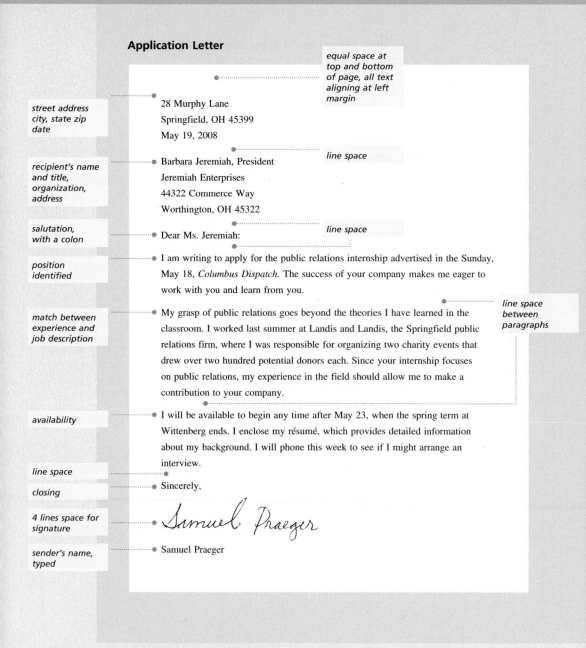

equal space at top and bottom of page, all text aligning at left margin

street address
city, state zip
date

28 Murphy Lane
Springfield, OH 45399
May 19, 2008

line space

recipient's name and title, organization, address

Barbara Jeremiah, President
Jeremiah Enterprises
44322 Commerce Way
Worthington, OH 45322

line space

salutation, with a colon

Dear Ms. Jeremiah:

position identified

I am writing to apply for the public relations internship advertised in the Sunday, May 18, *Columbus Dispatch*. The success of your company makes me eager to work with you and learn from you.

match between experience and job description

My grasp of public relations goes beyond the theories I have learned in the classroom. I worked last summer at Landis and Landis, the Springfield public relations firm, where I was responsible for organizing two charity events that drew over two hundred potential donors each. Since your internship focuses on public relations, my experience in the field should allow me to make a contribution to your company.

line space between paragraphs

availability

I will be available to begin any time after May 23, when the spring term at Wittenberg ends. I enclose my résumé, which provides detailed information about my background. I will phone this week to see if I might arrange an interview.

line space

closing

Sincerely,

4 lines space for signature

Samuel Praeger

sender's name, typed

Samuel Praeger

rhetorical situations | genres | processes | strategies | research mla/apa | media/design | handbook

Thank-You Letter

equal space at top and bottom of page, all text aligning at left margin

28 Murphy Lane · · · · · · · · · · · · · · *street address*
Springfield, OH 45399 · · · · · · · · · · · · · · *city, state zip*
June 1, 2008 · · · · · · · · · · · · · · *date*

line space

Barbara Jeremiah, President · · · · · · · · · · · · · · *recipient's name and title,*
Jeremiah Enterprises · · · · · · · · · · · · · · *organization,*
44322 Commerce Way · · · · · · · · · · · · · · *address*
Worthington, OH 45322

line space

Dear Ms. Jeremiah: · · · · · · · · · · · · · · *salutation, with a colon*

Thank you for the opportunity to meet with you yesterday. I enjoyed talking · · · · · · · · · · · · · · *thanks and confirmation of*
with you and meeting the people who work with you, and I continue to be very · · · · · · · · · · · · · · *interest*
line space between paragraphs interested in becoming an intern with Jeremiah Enterprises.

As we discussed, I worked with a public relations firm last summer, and since · · · · · · · · · · · · · · *brief review of qualifications*
then I have completed three courses in marketing and public relations that relate
directly to the work I would be doing as an intern.

I enclose a list of references, as you requested. · · · · · · · · · · · · · · *enclosures*

Thank you again for your time. I hope to hear from you soon. · · · · · · · · · · · · · · *repeat thanks*

line space

Sincerely, · · · · · · · · · · · · · · *closing*

Samuel Praeger · · · · · · · · · · · · · · *4 lines space for signature*

Samuel Praeger · · · · · · · · · · · · · · *sender's name, typed*

Sending a thank-you letter is a way of showing appreciation for an interview and restating your interest in the position. It also shows that you have good manners and understand proper business etiquette. On the previous page is a letter Samuel Praeger sent to the person who interviewed him for an internship, thanking the interviewer for her time and the opportunity to meet her, indicating his interest in the position, and reiterating his qualifications.

Key Features / Application and Thank-You Letters

A succinct indication of your qualifications. In an application letter, you need to make clear why you're interested in the position or the organization—and at the same time give some sense of why the person you're writing to should at least want to meet you. In a thank-you letter, you should remind the interviewer of your qualifications.

A reasonable and pleasing tone. When writing application and thank-you letters, you need to go beyond simply stating your accomplishments or saying thank-you. Through your words, you need to demonstrate that you will be the kind of employee the organization wants. Presentation is also important—your letter should be neat and error-free.

A conventional, businesslike format. Application and thank-you letters typically follow a prescribed format. The most common is the block format shown in the examples. It includes the writer's address, the date, the recipient's name and address, a salutation, the message, a closing, and a signature.

A BRIEF GUIDE TO WRITING JOB LETTERS

Generating Ideas and Text for Application and Thank-You Letters

Focus. Application and thank-you letters are not personal and should not be chatty. Keep them focused: when you're applying for a position,

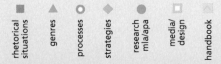

include only information relevant to the position. Don't make your audience wade through irrelevant side issues. Stay on topic.

State the reason for the letter. Unlike essays, which develop a thesis over several paragraphs, or emails, which announce their topic in a subject line, letters need to explicitly introduce their reason for being written, usually in the first paragraph. When you're applying for something or thanking someone, say so in the first sentence: "I am writing to apply for the Margaret Branscomb Peabody Scholarship for students majoring in veterinary science." "Thank you for meeting with me."

Think of your letter as an argument. When you're asking for a job, you're making an **ARGUMENT**. You're making a claim—that you're qualified for a certain position—and you need to support your claim with reasons and evidence. Praeger, for example, cites his education and his work experience—and he offers to supply references who will support his application.

283–99

Choose an appropriate salutation. If you know the person's name and title, use it: "Dear Professor Turnigan." If you don't know the person's title, one good solution is to address him or her by first and last name: "Dear Julia Turnigan." If, as sometimes happens, you must write to an unknown reader, your options include "To Whom It May Concern" and the more old fashioned "Dear Sir or Madam." Another option might be to omit the salutation completely in such situations and instead use a subject line, for example: "Subject: Public Relations Internship Application." Whenever possible, though, write to a specific person; call the organization and ask whom to write to. Once you've had an interview, write to your interviewer.

Proofread. Few writing situations demand greater perfection than professional letters—especially job letters. Employers receive dozens, sometimes hundreds, of applications, and often can't look at them all. Typos, grammar errors, and other forms of sloppiness prejudice readers against applicants: they're likely to think that if this applicant can't take the time and care to **PROOFREAD**, how badly does he or she want this position? To compete, strive for perfection.

245–46

Ways of Organizing an Application or Thank-You Letter

Application and thank-you letters should both follow a conventional organization, though you might vary the details somewhat. Here are two standard organizations.

[Application letter]

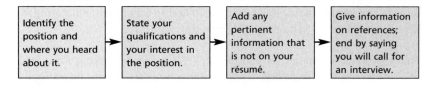

| Identify the position and where you heard about it. | → | State your qualifications and your interest in the position. | → | Add any pertinent information that is not on your résumé. | → | Give information on references; end by saying you will call for an interview. |

[Thank-you letter]

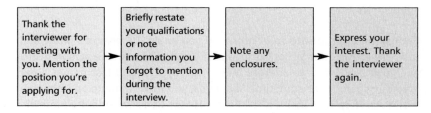

| Thank the interviewer for meeting with you. Mention the position you're applying for. | → | Briefly restate your qualifications or note information you forgot to mention during the interview. | → | Note any enclosures. | → | Express your interest. Thank the interviewer again. |

IF YOU NEED MORE HELP

See Chapter 24 for guidelines on **DRAFTING**, Chapter 25 on **ASSESSING YOUR OWN WRITING**, Chapter 26 on **GETTING RESPONSE AND REVISING**, and Chapter 27 on **EDITING**.

226–28 ◯
229–34
235–41
242–46

■ rhetorical situations
▲ genres
◯ processes
◆ strategies
● research mla/apa
□ media/ design
▨ handbook

Mixing Genres **20**

Musicians regularly mix genres, blending, for instance, reggae, hip-hop, and jazz to create a unique sound. Like musicians, writers often combine different genres in a single text. An **EVALUATION** of mining practices might include a **PROFILE** of a coal company CEO. A **PROPOSAL** to start a neighborhood watch might begin with a **REPORT** on crime in the area. Here's a column that mixes genres written by Anna Quindlen for *Newsweek* magazine in 2007.

125–32
161–70
171–79
59–82

ANNA QUINDLEN

Write for Your Life

The new movie *Freedom Writers* isn't entirely about the themes the trailers suggest. It isn't only about gang warfare and racial tensions and tolerance. It isn't only about the difference one good teacher can make in the life of one messed-up kid. *Freedom Writers* is about the power of writing in the lives of ordinary people. That's a lesson everyone needs. The movie, and the book from which it was taken, track the education of a young teacher named Erin Gruwell, who shows up shiny-new to face a class of what are called, in pedagogical jargon, "at risk" students. It's a mixed bag of Latino, Asian, and black teenagers with one feckless white kid thrown in. They ignore, belittle, and dismiss her as she proffers lesson plans and reading materials seriously out of step with the homelessness, drug use, and violence that are the stuff of their precarious existences.

    And then one day, she gives them all marbled composition books and the assignment to write their lives, ungraded, unjudged, and the world breaks open.

Textual Analysis

"My probation officer thinks he's slick; he swears he's an expert on gangs."

"Sorry, diary, I was going to try not to do it tonight, but the little baggy of white powder is calling my name."

"If you pull up my shirtsleeves and look at my arms, you will see 5 black and blue marks."

"The words 'Eviction Notice' stopped me dead in my tracks."

"When I was younger, they would lock me up in the closet because they wanted to get high and beat up on each other."

Ms. G, as the kids called her, embraced a concept that has been lost in modern life: writing can make pain tolerable, confusion clearer and the self stronger.

How is it, at a time when clarity and strength go begging, that we have moved so far from everyday prose? Social critics might trace this back to the demise of letter writing. The details of housekeeping and child rearing, the rigors of war and work, advice to friends and family: none was slated for publication. They were communications that gave shape to life by describing it for others.

Report

But as the letter fell out of favor and education became profes- 10 sionalized, with its goal less the expansion of the mind than the acquisition of a job, writing began to be seen largely as the purview of writers. Writing at work also became so stylistically removed from the story of our lives that the two seemed to have nothing in common. Corporate prose conformed to an equation: information × polysyllabic words + tortured syntax = aren't you impressed?

And in the age of the telephone most communication became evanescent, gone into thin air no matter how important or heartfelt. Think of all those people inside the World Trade Center saying goodbye by phone. If only, in the blizzard of paper that followed the collapse of the buildings, a letter had fallen from the sky for every family member and friend, something to hold on to, something to read and reread. Something real. Words on paper confer a kind of immortality. Wouldn't all of us love to have a journal, a memoir, a letter, from those we have loved and lost? Shouldn't all of us leave a bit of that behind?

Reflection

The age of technology has both revived the use of writing and provided ever more reasons for its spiritual solace. Emails are letters, after all, more lasting than phone calls, even if many of them r 2 cursory 4 u. And the physical isolation they and other arms-length cyber-advances create makes talking to yourself more important than ever. That's also what writing is: not just a legacy, but therapy. As the novelist Don DeLillo once said, "Writing is a form of personal freedom. It frees us from the mass identity we see in the making all around us. In the end, writers will write not to be outlaw heroes of some underculture but mainly to save themselves, to survive as individuals."

That's exactly what Gruwell was after when she got the kids in her class writing, in a program that's since been duplicated at other schools. Salvation and survival for teenagers whose chances of either seemed negligible. "Growing up, I always assumed I would either drop out of school or get pregnant," one student wrote. "So when Ms. G started talking about college, it was like a foreign language to me." Maybe that's the moment when that Latina girl began to speak that foreign language, when she wrote those words down. Today she has a college degree.

Argument

One of the texts Erin Gruwell assigned was *The Diary of a Young* 10 *Girl* by Anne Frank. A student who balked at reading a book about someone so different, so remote, went on to write: "At the end of the book, I was so mad that Anne died, because as she was dying, a part of me was dying with her." Of course Anne never dreamed her diary would be published, much less read by millions of people after her death at the hands of the Nazis. She wrote it for the same reason the kids who called themselves Freedom Writers wrote in those composition books: to make sense of themselves. That's not just for writers. That's for people.

Quindlen argues that writing helps us understand ourselves and our world. She uses several genres to help advance her argument — textual analysis of the film Freedom Writers, *a brief report on the decline of letter writing, and a reflection on the technologies we use to write. Together, these genres help her develop her argument that writing helps us "make sense of [our]selves."*

Key Features / Texts That Mix Genres

One primary genre. Your writing situation will often call for a certain genre that is appropriate for your purpose — an argument, a proposal, a report, a textual analysis, and so forth. Additional genres then play supporting roles. Quindlen's essay, for example, primarily argues a position and mixes in other genres, including report and reflection, to elaborate her argument and bring it to life.

A clear focus.   A text that mixes genres approaches the topic several different ways, but each genre must contribute to your main point. One genre may serve as the introduction, and others may be woven throughout the text in other ways, but all must address some aspect of the topic and support the central claim. Quindlen's analysis of the film *Freedom Writers*, for example, supports her claim that writing is one way we learn about ourselves.

Careful organization.   A text that combines several genres requires careful organization—the various genres must fit together neatly and clearly. Quindlen opens by analyzing the theme of *Freedom Writers*, noting that it's about "the power of writing in the lives of ordinary people." She then switches genres, reporting on how "we have moved so far from everyday prose" and then reflecting on the consequences of that move.

Clear transitions.   When a text includes several genres, those genres need to be connected in some way. Transitions do that, and in so doing, they help readers make their way through the text. Transitions may include words such as "in addition" and "however," and they may also consist of phrases that sum up an idea and move it forward. See, for example, how Quindlen ends one paragraph by quoting Don DeLillo as saying that writers write "to save themselves, to survive as individuals" and then begins the next paragraph by referring to DeLillo's words, saying "That's exactly what Gruwell was after."

Some Typical Ways of Mixing Genres

It's possible to mix almost any genres together. Following are some of the most commonly mixed genres and how they combine with other genres.

Memoirs.   Sometimes a personal anecdote can help support an **ARGUMENT**   ▲ 83–110
or enhance a **REPORT**. Stories from your personal experience can help read-   59–82
ers understand your motivations for arguing a certain position and can
enhance your credibility as a writer.

Profiles.   One way to bring a **REPORT** on an abstract topic to life is to   ▲ 59–82
include a profile of a person, place, or event. For example, if you were writing a report for your boss on the need to hire more sales representatives,
including a profile of one salesperson's typical day might drive home the
point that your sales force is stretched too thin.

Textual analyses.   You might need to analyze a speech or other document as part of an **ARGUMENT,** especially on a historical or political topic.   ▲ 83–110
For instance, you might analyze speeches by Abraham Lincoln and Jefferson Davis if you're writing about the causes of the Civil War, or an
advertisement for cigarettes if you're making an argument about teen
smoking.

Evaluations.   You might include an evaluation of something when you
write a **PROPOSAL** about it. For example, if you were writing a proposal for   ▲ 171–79
additional student parking on your campus, you would need to evaluate
the current parking facilities to discuss their inadequacy.

A BRIEF GUIDE TO WRITING TEXTS THAT MIX GENRES

Considering the Rhetorical Situation

PURPOSE   Why are you writing this text? To inform? Persuade?   ▊ 3–4
                     Entertain? Explore an idea? Something else? What genres
                     will help you achieve your purpose?

AUDIENCE   Who are your readers? Which genres will help these read-   ▊ 5–8
                     ers understand your point? Will starting with a memoir
                     or profile draw them in? Will some analysis help them

understand the topic? Will a profile make the topic less abstract or make them more sympathetic to your claim?

9–11 ■ **GENRE** What is your primary genre? What other genres might support that primary genre?

12–14 ■ **STANCE** What is your stance on your topic—objective? opinionated? something else? Will including a textual analysis or report help you establish an objective or analytical tone? Will some reflection or a brief memoir show your personal connection to your topic?

15–17 ■ **MEDIA / DESIGN** Will your text be a print document? An oral presentation? Will it be published on the Web? Should you include illustrations? Audio or video clips? Do you need to present any information that would be best shown in a chart or graph?

Generating Ideas and Text

Identify your primary genre. If you're writing in response to an assignment, does it specify a particular genre? Look for key verbs that name specific genres—for example, *analyze*, *argue*, *evaluate*, and so on. Be aware that other verbs imply certain genres: *explain*, *summarize*, *review*, and *describe* ask for a report; *argue*, *prove*, and *justify* signal that you need to argue a position; and *evaluate* and *propose* specify evaluations and proposals.

3–4 ■
5–8 ■

If the choice of genre is up to you, consider your **PURPOSE** and **AUDIENCE** carefully to determine what genre is most appropriate. Consult the appropriate genre chapter to identify the key features of your primary genre and to generate ideas and text.

Determine if other genres would be helpful. As you write a draft, you may identify a need—for a beginning that grabs readers' attention, for a satisfying ending, for ways to make an abstract concept more concrete or to help in analyzing something. At this point, you may want to try mixing one or more genres within your draft. Determine what genre will help you achieve your purpose and consult the appropriate genre chapter for advice on writing in that genre. Remember, however, that you're mixing genres into your draft to support and enhance it—so your supporting genres may not be as developed as complete texts in that genre would be and may not include all the key features. For example, if you include a brief memoir as part of an argument, it should include a good story and vivid details—but its significance may well be stated as part of the argument, rather than revealed through the storytelling itself.

Integrate the genres.   Your goal is to create a focused, unified, coherent text. So you need to make sure that your genres work together to achieve that goal. Make sure that each genre fulfills a purpose within the text—for example, that a textual analysis within an argument provides evidence to support your claim, or that the profile you include in a report provides a clear illustration of the larger subject. Also, use **TRANSITIONS** to help readers move from section to section in your text.

◆ 277

Multi-Genre Projects

Sometimes a collection of texts can together represent an experience or advance an argument. For example, you might document a trip to the Grand Canyon in an album that contains journal entries written during the trip, photographs, a map of northern Arizona showing the Canyon, postcards, an essay on the geology of the Canyon, and a souvenir coin stamped with an image of the Canyon. Each represents a different way of experiencing the Grand Canyon, and together they offer a multifaceted way to understand your trip.

You might also write in several different genres on the same topic. If you begin by **ARGUING** that the government should provide universal health care, for example, writing a **MEMOIR** about a time you were ill could help you explore a personal connection to the topic. Composing a **PROFILE** of a doctor might give you new insights into the issue, and writing a **PROPOSAL** for how universal health care could work might direct you to potential

◆ 283–99
▲ 153–60
161–70
171–79

solutions. You could assemble all these texts in a folder, with a title page and table of contents so that readers can see how it all fits together—or you could create a **WEBSITE,** combining text, images, video, sound, and links to other sites.

546–56

IF YOU NEED MORE HELP

See Chapter 24 for guidelines on **DRAFTING,** Chapter 25 on **ASSESSING YOUR OWN WRITING,** Chapter 29 on **BEGINNING AND ENDING,** and Chapter 30 on **GUIDING YOUR READER.**

226–28 ○
229–34
261–71 ◆
272–77

part 3

Processes

To create anything, we generally break the work down into a series of steps. We follow a recipe (or the directions on a box) to bake a cake; we break a song down into different parts and the music into various chords to arrange a piece of music. So it is when we write. We rely on various processes to get from a blank page to a finished product. The chapters that follow offer advice on some of these processes—from WRITING AS INQUIRY and GENERATING IDEAS to DRAFTING to GETTING RESPONSE to EDITING to COMPILING A PORTFOLIO, and more.

Processes

Writing as Inquiry 21

Sometimes we write to say what we think. Other times, however, we write in order to figure out what we think. Much of the writing you do in college will be the latter. Even as you learn to write, you will be writing to learn. This chapter is about writing with a spirit of inquiry — approaching writing projects with curiosity, moving beyond the familiar, keeping your eyes open, tackling issues that don't have easy answers. It's about starting with questions and going from there — and taking risks. As Mark Twain once said, "Sail away from the safe harbor. . . . Explore. Dream. Discover." This chapter offers strategies for doing just that with your writing.

Starting with Questions

The most important thing is to start with questions — with what you don't know rather than with what you do know. Your goal is to learn about your subject and then to learn more. If you're writing about a topic you know well, you want to expand on what you already know. In academic writing, good topics arise from important questions, issues, and problems that are already being discussed. As a writer, you need to find out what's being said about your topic and then see your writing as a way of entering that larger conversation.

So start with questions, and don't expect to find easy answers. If there were easy answers, there would be no reason for discussion — or for you to write. For purposes of inquiry, the best questions can't be answered by looking in a reference book. Instead, they are ones that help you explore what you think — and why. As it happens, many of the strategies in this book can help you ask questions of this kind. Following are some questions to get you started.

rhetorical situations

genres

processes

strategies

research mla/apa

media/ design

handbook

314–23
How can it be DEFINED?　What is it, and what does it do? Look it up in a dictionary; check Wikipedia. Remember, though, that these are only starting points. How *else* can it be defined? What more is there to know about it? If your topic is being debated, chances are that its very definition is subject to debate. If, for instance, you're writing about gay marriage, how you define marriage will affect how you approach the topic.

324–32
How can it be DESCRIBED?　What details should you include? From what vantage point should you describe your topic? If, for example, your topic were the physiological effects of running a marathon, what would those effects be — on the lungs, heart muscles, nerves, brain, and so on? How would you describe the physical experience of running over twenty-six miles from the runner's point of view?

338–42
How can it be EXPLAINED?　What does it do? How does it work? If you were investigating the use of performance-enhancing drugs by athletes, for example, what exactly is the effect of these drugs? What makes them dangerous — and are they always dangerous or only in certain conditions? Why are they illegal — and should they be illegal?

306–13
What can it be COMPARED with?　Again with the use of performance-enhancing drugs by athletes as an example, how does taking such supplements, or doping, compare with wearing high-tech footwear or uniforms? Does such a comparison make you see doping in a new light?

278–82
What may have CAUSED it? What might be its EFFECTS?　Who or what does it affect? What causes hyperactivity in children, for example? What are the symptoms of hyperactivity? Are some children more likely than others to develop hyperactivity? Why? If children with hyperactive behavior are not treated, what might be the consequences? If they are treated with drugs, how might their lives as adults be affected?

300–305
How can it be CLASSIFIED?　Is it a topic or issue that can be placed into categories of similar topics or issues? What categories can it be placed into? Are there legal and illegal performance-enhancing supplements (creatine and steroids, for instance), and what's the difference? Are some safe and others less safe? Classifying your topic in this way can help you consider its complexities.

rhetorical situations　genres　processes　strategies　research mla/apa　media/ design　handbook

How can it be ANALYZED?   What parts can the topic be divided into? For
example, if you were exploring the health effects of cell phone use, you
might ask what evidence suggests that cell phone radiation causes cancer?
What cancers are associated with cell phone use? What do medical experts
and phone manufacturers say? How can cell phone users reduce their risk?

278–82

How can it be INTERPRETED?   What does it really mean? How do you
interpret it, and how does your interpretation differ from others? What
evidence supports your interpretation, and what argues against it? Imagine you were exploring the topic of sports injuries among young women.
Do these injuries reflect a larger cultural preoccupation with competition?
A desire to win college scholarships? Something else?

38–58

What expectations does it raise?   What will happen next? What makes
you think so? If this happens, how will it affect those involved? For
instance, will the governing bodies of professional sports require more
blood testing than they do now? Will such tests be unfair to athletes taking drugs for legitimate medical needs?

What are the different POSITIONS on it?   What controversies or disagreements exist, and what evidence is offered for the various positions? What
else might be said? Are there any groups or individuals who seem especially authoritative? If so, you might want to explore what they have said.

83–110

What are your own feelings about it?   What interests you about the
topic? How much do you already know about it? For example, if you're an
athlete, how do you feel about competing against others who may have
taken supplements? If a friend has problems with drugs, do those problems affect your thinking about doping in sports? How do you react to
what others say about the topic? What else do you want to find out?

Are there other ways to think about it?   Is what seems true in this case
also true in others? How can you apply this subject in another situation?
Will what works in another situation also work here? What do you have
to do to adapt it? Imagine you were writing about traffic fatalities. If replacing stop signs with roundabouts reduced traffic fatalities in England, could
roundabouts also reduce accidents in the U.S.?

222–23

You can also start with the journalist's **QUESTIONS:** *Who? What? When? Where? Why? How?* Asking questions from these various perspectives can help you deepen your understanding of your topic by leading you to see it from many angles.

Keeping a Journal

One way to get into the habit of using writing as a tool for inquiry is to keep a journal. You can use a journal to record your observations, reactions, whatever you wish. Some writers find journals especially useful places to articulate questions or speculations. You may be assigned by teachers to do certain work in a journal, but in general, you can use a journal to write for yourself. Jot down ideas, speculate, digress — go wherever your thoughts lead you.

Keeping a Blog

554–56

You may also wish to explore issues or other ideas online in the form of a **BLOG**. Most blogs have a comments section that allows others to read and respond to what you write, leading to potentially fruitful discussions. You can also include links to other websites, helping you connect various strands of thought and research. The blogs of others, along with online discussion forums and groups, may also be useful sources of opinion on your topic, but keep in mind that they probably aren't authoritative research sources. There are a number of search engines that can help you find blog posts related to specific topics, including *Google Blog Search, Ice Rocket, Technorati,* and *Blog-Search.* You can create your own blog on sites such as *Blogger, LiveJournal,* or *Xanga.*

rhetorical situations | genres | processes | strategies | research mla/apa | media/ design | handbook

Collaborating 22

Whether you're working in a group, participating in a Listserv or wiki, or exchanging drafts with a classmate for peer review, you likely spend a lot of time collaborating with others. Even if you do much of your writing sitting alone at a computer, you probably get help from others at various stages in the writing process — and provide help as well. The fact is that two heads can be better than one — and learning to work well with a team is as important as anything else you'll learn in college. This chapter offers some guidelines for collaborating successfully with other writers.

Some Ground Rules for Working in a Group

- Make sure everyone is facing everyone else and is physically part of the group. Doing that makes a real difference in the quality of the interactions — think how much better conversation works when you're sitting around a table than it does when you're sitting in a row.

- Thoughtfulness, respect, and tact are key, since most writers (as you know) are sensitive and need to be able to trust those commenting on their work. Respond to the writing of others as you would like others to respond to yours.

- Each meeting needs an agenda — and careful attention paid to time. Appoint one person as timekeeper to make sure all necessary work gets done in the available time.

- Appoint another person to be group leader or facilitator. That person needs to make sure everyone gets a chance to speak, no one dominates the discussion, and the group stays on task.

416–17

- Appoint a third member of the group to keep a record of the group's discussion. He or she should jot down the major points as they come up and afterward write a **SUMMARY** of the discussion that the group members approve.

Group Writing Projects

Creating a document with a team is common in business and industry and in some academic fields as well. Collaboration of this kind presents new challenges and different kinds of responsibilities. Here are some tips for making group projects work well:

- *Define the task as clearly as possible,* and make sure everyone understands and agrees with the stated goals.
- *Divide the task into parts.* Decide which parts can be done by individuals, which can be done by a subgroup, and which need to be done by everyone together.
- *Assign each group member certain tasks.* Try to match tasks to each person's skills and interests, and divide the work equally.
- *Establish a deadline for each task.* Allow time for unforeseen problems before the project deadline.
- *Try to accommodate everyone's style of working.* Some people value discussion; others want to get right down to the writing. There's no best way to get work done; everyone needs to be conscious that his or her way is not the only way.
- *Work for consensus — not necessarily total agreement.* Everyone needs to agree that the plan is doable and appropriate — if not exactly the way you would do if you were working alone.
- *Make sure everyone performs.* In some situations, your instructor may help, but in others the group itself may have to develop a way to make sure that the work gets done well and fairly. During the course of the project, it's sometimes helpful for each group member to write an assessment both of the group's work and of individual members' contributions.

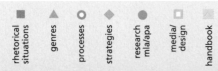

Online Collaboration

Sometimes you'll need or want to work with one or more people online. Working together online offers many advantages, including the ability to collaborate without being in the same place at the same time. Nonetheless, working online presents some challenges that differ from those of face-to-face group work. When sharing writing or collaborating with others online, consider the following suggestions:

- As with all online communication, remember that you need to choose your words carefully to avoid flaming another group member or inadvertently hurting someone's feelings. Without facial expressions, gestures, and other forms of body language and without tone of voice, your words carry all the weight.
- Remember that the **AUDIENCE** for what you write may well extend beyond your group — your work might be forwarded to others, so there is no telling who else might read it.

    5–8

- Decide as a group how best to deal with the logistics of exchanging drafts and comments. You can cut and paste text directly into email, send it as an attachment to a message, or post it to a newsgroup or course bulletin board. You may need to use a combination of methods, depending on each group member's access to equipment and software.

Writing Conferences

Conferences with instructors or writing tutors can be an especially helpful kind of collaboration. These one-on-one sessions often offer the most strongly focused assistance you can get — and truly valuable instruction. Here are some tips for making the most of conference time:

- *Come prepared.* Bring all necessary materials, including the draft you'll be discussing, your notes, any outlines — and, of course, any questions.
- *Be prompt.* Your instructor or tutor has set aside a block of time for you, and once that time is up, there's likely to be another student writer waiting.

- *Listen carefully, discuss your work seriously, and try not to be defensive.* Your instructor or tutor is only trying to help you produce the best piece possible. If you sense that your work is being misunderstood, explain what you're trying to say. Don't get angry! If a sympathetic reader who's trying to help can't understand what you mean, maybe you haven't conveyed your meaning well enough.

- *Take notes.* During the conference, jot down key words and suggestions. Immediately afterward, flesh out your notes so you'll have a complete record of what was said.

- *Reflect on the conference.* Afterward, think about what you learned. What do you have to do now? Think about questions you will ask at your next conference.

rhetorical situations

genres

processes

strategies

research mla/apa

media/ design

handbook

Generating Ideas and Text 23

All good writing revolves around ideas. Whether you're writing a job-application letter, a sonnet, or an essay, you'll always spend time and effort generating ideas. Some writers can come up with a topic, put their thoughts in order, and flesh out their arguments in their heads; but most of us need to write down our ideas, play with them, tease them out, and examine them from some distance and from multiple perspectives. This chapter offers activities that can help you do just that. *Freewriting, looping, listing,* and *clustering* can help you explore what you know about a subject; *cubing* and *questioning* nudge you to consider a subject in new ways; and *outlining, letter-writing, journal-keeping,* and *discovery drafting* offer ways to generate a text.

Freewriting

An informal method of exploring a subject by writing about it, freewriting ("writing freely") can help you generate ideas and come up with materials for your draft. Here's how to do it:

1. Write as quickly as you can without stopping for 5–10 minutes (or until you fill a page or screen).

2. If you have a subject to explore, write it at the top of the page and then start writing, but if you stray, don't worry—just keep writing. If you don't have a subject yet, just start writing and don't stop until the time is up. If you can't think of anything to say, write that ("I can't think of anything to say") again and again until you do—and you will!

3. Once the time is up, read over what you've written, and underline passages that interest you.

4. Then write some more, starting with one of those underlined passages as your new topic. Repeat the process until you've come up with a usable topic.

Looping

Looping is a more focused version of freewriting; it can help you explore what you know about a subject. You stop, reflect on what you've written, and then write again, developing your understanding in the process. It's good for clarifying your knowledge and understanding of a subject and finding a focus. Here's what you do:

1. Write for 5–10 minutes, jotting down whatever you know about your subject. This is your first loop.

2. Read over what you wrote, and then write a single sentence summarizing the most important or interesting idea. You might try completing one of these sentences: "I guess what I was trying to say was . . . ." or "What surprises me most in reading what I wrote is . . . ." This will be the start of another loop.

3. Write again for 5–10 minutes, using your summary sentence as your beginning and your focus. Again, read what you've written, and then write a sentence capturing the most important idea—in a third loop.

Keep going until you have enough understanding of your topic to be able to decide on a tentative focus—something you can write about.

Listing

Some writers find it useful to keep lists of ideas that occur to them while they are thinking about a topic. Follow these steps:

1. Write a list of potential ideas about a topic, leaving space to add ideas that might occur to you later. Don't try to limit your list—include anything that interests you.

2. Look for relationships among the items on your list: what patterns do you see?

3. Finally, arrange the items in an order that makes sense for your purpose and can serve as the beginning of an outline for your writing.

Clustering

Clustering is a way of generating and connecting ideas visually. It's useful for seeing how various ideas relate to one another and for developing subtopics. The technique is simple:

1. Write your topic in the middle of a sheet of paper and circle it.

2. Write ideas relating to that topic around it, circle them, and connect them to the central circle.

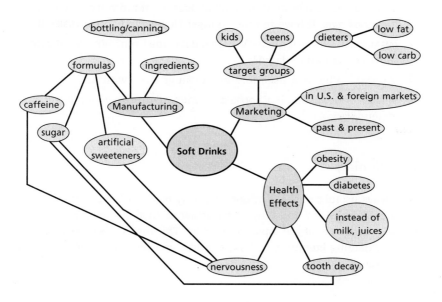

3. Write down ideas, examples, facts, or other details relating to each idea, and join them to the appropriate circles.

4. Keep going until you can't think of anything else relating to your topic.

You should end up with various ideas about your topic, and the clusters will allow you to see how they relate to one another. In the example cluster on the topic of "soft drinks" from page 221, note how some ideas link not only to the main topic or related topics but also to other ideas.

Cubing

A cube has six sides. You can examine a topic as you might a cube, looking at it in these six ways:

324–32
- **DESCRIBE** it. What's its color? Shape? Age? Size? What's it made of?

306–13
- **COMPARE** it to something else. What is it similar to or different from?

300–305
- Associate it with other things. What does it remind you of? What connections does it have to other things? How would you **CLASSIFY** it?

278–82
- **ANALYZE** it. How is it made? Where did it come from? Where is it going? How are its parts related?

- Apply it. What is it used for? What can be done with it?

83–110
- **ARGUE** for or against it. Choose a position relating to your subject, and defend it.

Questioning

211–14
It's always useful to ask **QUESTIONS.** One way is to start with What? Who? When? Where? How? and Why? A particular method of exploring a topic is to ask questions as if the topic were a play. This method is especially useful for exploring literature, history, the arts, and the social sciences. Start with these questions:

rhetorical situations
genres
processes
strategies
research mla/apa
media/ design
handbook

- **What?** What happens? How is it similar to or different from other actions?

- **Who?** Who are the actors? Who are the participants, and who are the spectators? How do the actors affect the action, and how are they affected by it?

- **When?** When does the action take place? How often does it happen? What happens before, after, or at the same time? Would it be different at another time? Does the time have historical significance?

- **Where?** What is the setting? What is the situation, and what makes it significant?

- **How?** How does the action occur? What are the steps in the process? What techniques are required? What equipment is needed?

- **Why?** Why did this happen? What are the actors' motives? What end does the action serve?

Outlining

You may create an *informal outline* by simply listing your ideas and numbering them in the order in which you want to write about them. You might prefer to make a *working outline*, to show the hierarchy of relationships among your ideas. While still informal, a working outline distinguishes your main ideas and your support, often through simple indentation:

> First main idea
>> Supporting evidence or detail
>> Supporting evidence or detail
>
> Second main idea
>> Supporting evidence or detail
>> Supporting evidence or detail

A *formal outline* shows the hierarchy of your ideas through a system of indenting, numbering, and lettering. Remember that when you divide a point into more specific subpoints, you should have at least two of them—you can't divide something into only one part. Also, try to keep items at each level parallel in structure. Formal outlines work this way:

Thesis statement
    I. First reason
      A. Supporting evidence
        1. Detail of evidence
        2. Detail of evidence
      B. Supporting evidence
   II. Another reason

Writing out a formal outline can be helpful when you're dealing with a complex subject; as you revise your drafts, though, be flexible and ready to change your outline as your understanding of your topic develops.

Letter Writing

Sometimes the prospect of writing a report or essay can be intimidating. You may find that simply explaining your topic to someone will help you get started. In that case, write a letter to someone you know—your best friend, a parent or grandparent, a sibling—in which you discuss your subject. Explain it in terms that your reader can understand. Use the unsent letter to rehearse your topic; make it a kind of rough draft that you can then revise and develop to suit your actual audience.

Keeping a Journal

Some writers find that writing in a journal helps them generate ideas. Jotting down ideas, thoughts, feelings, or the events of your day can provide a wealth of topics, and a journal can also be a good place to explore what you think and why you think as you do.

Discovery Drafting

Some writers do best by jumping in and writing. Here are the steps to take if you're ready to write a preliminary **DRAFT**:

⚪ 226–28

1. Write your draft quickly, in one sitting if possible.

2. Assume that you are writing to discover what you want to say and how you need to say it — and that you will make substantial revisions in a later part of the process.

3. Don't worry about grammatical or factual correctness — if you can't think of a word, leave a blank to fill in later. If you're unsure of a date or spelling, put a question mark in parentheses as a reminder to check it later. Just write.

IF YOU NEED MORE HELP

See also each of the **GENRE** chapters for specific stategies for generating text in each genre.

▲ 19

---

24 Drafting

At some point, you need to write out a draft. By the time you begin drafting, you've probably written quite a bit—in the form of notes, lists, outlines, and other kinds of informal writing. This chapter offers some hints on how to write a draft—and reminds you that as you draft, you may well need to get more information, rethink some aspect of your work, or follow new ideas that occur to you as you write.

Establishing a Schedule with Deadlines

375 Don't wait until the last minute to write. Computers crash, printers jam. Life intervenes in unpredictable ways. You increase your chances of success immensely by setting and meeting **DEADLINES:** Research done by ____ ; rough draft done by ____ ; revisions done by ____ ; final draft edited, proofread, and submitted by ____ . How much time you need varies with each writing task—but trying to compress everything into twenty-four or forty-eight hours before the deadline is asking for trouble.

Getting Comfortable

When are you at your best? When do you have your best ideas? For major writing projects, consider establishing a schedule that lets you write when you stand the best chance of doing good work. Schedule breaks for exercise and snacks. Find a good place to write, a place where you've got a good surface on which to spread out your materials, good lighting, a comfortable chair, and the right tools (pen, paper, computer) for the job. Often, however, we must make do: you may have to do your drafting in a busy computer lab or classroom. The trick is to make yourself as comfortable as you can manage. Sort out what you *need* from what you *prefer*.

Starting to Write

All of the above advice notwithstanding, don't worry so much about the trappings of your writing situation that you don't get around to writing. Write. Start by **FREEWRITING**, start with a first sentence, start with awful writing that you know you'll discard later—but write. That's what gets you warmed up and going.

219–20

Write quickly in spurts.   Write quickly with the goal of writing a complete draft, or a complete section of a longer draft, in one sitting. If you need to stop in the middle, jot down some notes about where you were headed when you stopped so that you can easily pick up your train of thought when you begin again.

Break down your writing task into small segments.   Big projects can be intimidating. But you can always write one section or, if need be, one paragraph or even a single sentence—and then another and another. It's a little like dieting. If I think I need to lose twenty pounds, I get discouraged and head for the doughnuts; but if I decide that I'll lose one pound and I lose it, well, I'll lose another—*that* I can do.

Expect surprises.   Writing is a form of thinking; the words you write lead you down certain roads and away from others. You may end up somewhere you didn't anticipate. Sometimes that can be a good thing—but sometimes you can write yourself into a dead end or out onto a tangent. Just know that this is natural, part of every writer's experience, and it's okay to double back or follow a new path that opens up before you.

Expect to write more than one draft.   A first sentence, first page, or first draft represents your attempt to organize into words your thoughts, ideas, feelings, research findings, and more. It's likely that some of that first try will not achieve your goals. That's okay—having writing on paper or on screen that you can change, add to, and cut means you're part of the way there. As you revise, you can fill in gaps and improve your writing and thinking.

Dealing with Writer's Block

You may sit down to write but find that you can't—nothing occurs to you; your mind is blank. Don't panic; here are some ways to get started writing again:

- Think of the assignment as a problem to be solved. Try to capture that problem in a single sentence: "How do I . . . ?" "What is the best way to . . . ?" "What am I trying to do in . . . ?" Think of a solution to the problem, and then stop thinking about it. If you can't solve it, do something else; give yourself time. Many of us find the solution in the shower, after a good night's sleep.

- Stop trying: take a walk, take a shower, do something else. Come back in a half hour, refreshed.

219–21 • Get a fresh piece of paper and **FREEWRITE,** or try **LOOPING** or **LISTING.** What are you trying to say? Just let whatever comes come—you may write yourself out of your box.

221–22 • Try a different medium: try **CLUSTERING,** or draw a chart of what you want to say; draw a picture; doodle.

373 • Do some **RESEARCH** on your topic to see what others have said about it.

235–41 • Talk to someone about what you are trying to do; if there's a writing center at your school, talk to a tutor: **GET RESPONSE.** If there's no one to talk to, talk to yourself. It's the act of talking—using your mouth instead of your hands—that can free you up.

IF YOU NEED MORE HELP

219–25
229–34
235–41 See the chapter on **GENERATING IDEAS AND TEXT** if you find you need more material. And once you have a draft, see the chapters on **ASSESSING YOUR OWN WRITING** and **GETTING RESPONSE AND REVISING** for help evaluating your draft.

Assessing Your Own Writing **25**

In school and out, our work is continually assessed by others. Teachers determine whether our writing is strong or weak; supervisors decide whether we merit raises or promotions; even friends and relatives size up the things we do in various ways. As writers, we need to assess our work — to step back and see it with a critical eye. By developing standards of our own and being conscious of the standards others use, we can assess — and shape — our writing, making sure it does what we want it to do. This chapter will help you assess your own written work.

Assessing the Writing You Do for Yourself

We sometimes write not for an audience but for ourselves — to generate ideas, reflect, make sense of things. The best advice on assessing such writing is *don't*. If you're writing to explore your thoughts, understand a subject, record the events of your day, or just for the pleasure of putting words on paper, shut off your internal evaluator. Let the words flow without worrying about them. Let yourself wander without censoring yourself or fretting that what you're writing is incorrect or incomplete or incoherent. That's okay.

One measure of the success of personal writing is its length. FREEWRITING, LISTING, CUBING, JOURNAL KEEPING, and other types of informal writing are like warm-up exercises to limber you up and get you thinking. If you don't give those writing exercises enough time and space, they may not do what you want them to. I've found, for example, that my students' best insights most often appear at the end of their journal entries. Had they stopped before that point, they never would have had those good ideas.

219–25

A way to study the ideas in your personal writing is to highlight useful patterns in different colors. For example, journal entries usually involve some questioning and speculating, as well as summarizing and paraphrasing. Try color coding each of these, sentence by sentence, phrase by phrase: yellow for summaries or paraphrases, green for questions, blue for speculations. Do any colors dominate? If, for example, your text is mostly yellow, you may be restating the course content too much and perhaps need to ask more questions. If you're generating ideas for an essay, you might assign colors to ideas or themes to see which ones are most promising.

Assessing the Writing You Do for Others

What we write for others must stand on its own because we usually aren't present when it is read—we rarely get to explain to readers why we did what we did and what it means. So we need to make our writing as good as we can before we submit, post, display, or publish it. It's a good idea to assess your writing in two stages, first considering how well it meets the needs of your particular rhetorical situation, then studying the text itself to check its focus, argument, and organization. Sometimes some simple questions can get you started:

> What works?
> What still needs work?
> Where do you need to say more (or less)?

Considering the Rhetorical Situation

3–4 ■　**PURPOSE**　What is your purpose for writing? If you have multiple purposes, list them, and then note which ones are the most important. How does your draft achieve your purpose(s)? If you're writing for an assignment, what are the requirements of the assignment and does your draft meet those requirements?

rhetorical situations　genres　processes　strategies　research mla/apa　media/design　handbook

AUDIENCE   To whom are you writing? What do those readers need and expect, as far as you can tell? Does your draft answer their needs? Do you define any terms and explain any concepts they won't know?

5–8

GENRE   What is the genre, and what are the key features of that genre? Does your draft include each of those features?

9–11

STANCE   Is it clear where you stand on your topic? Does your writing project the personality, voice, and tone that you want? Look at the words you use — how do they represent you as a person?

12–14

MEDIA / DESIGN   At this point, your text is not likely to be designed, but think about the medium (print? spoken? electronic?) and whether your writing suits it. What design requirements can you anticipate? Lists? Headings? Charts? Visuals?

15–17

Examining the Text Itself

Look carefully at your text to see how well it says what you want it to say. Start with the broadest aspect, its focus, and then examine its reasons and evidence, organization, and clarity, in that order. If your writing lacks focus, the revising you'll do to sharpen the focus is likely to change everything else; if it needs more reasons and evidence, the organization may well change.

Consider your focus.   Your writing should have a clear point, and every part of the writing should support that point. Here are some questions that can help you see if your draft is adequately focused:

- What is your **THESIS?** Even if it is not stated directly, you should be able to summarize it for yourself in a single sentence.

273–75

- Is your thesis narrow or broad enough to suit the needs and expectations of your audience?

- How does the **BEGINNING** focus attention on your main point?

261–66

- Does each paragraph support or develop that point? Do any paragraphs or sentences stray from your focus?

267–70
- Does the **ENDING** leave readers thinking about your main point? Is there another way of concluding the essay that would sharpen your focus?

Consider the support you provide for your argument. Your writing needs to give readers enough information to understand your points, fol-

283–99
low your **ARGUMENT**, and see the logic of your thinking. How much information is enough will vary according to your audience. If they already know a lot about your subject or are likely to agree with your point of view, you may need to give less detail. If, however, they are unfamiliar with your topic or are skeptical about your views, you will probably need to provide much more information to help them understand your position.

286–93
- What **REASONS** and **EVIDENCE** do you give to support your thesis? Where might more information be helpful or useful?

314–23
- What key terms and concepts do you **DEFINE**? Are there any other terms your readers might need to have explained?

324–32
- Where might you include more **DESCRIPTION** or other detail?

306–13
- Do you make any **COMPARISONS**? Especially if your readers will not be familiar with your topic, it can help to compare it with something more familiar.

343–51
- If you include **NARRATIVE**, how is it relevant to your point?

259
- See Part 4 for other useful **STRATEGIES**.

Consider the organization. As a writer, you need to lead readers through your text, carefully structuring your material so that they will be able to follow your argument.

223–24
- Analyze the structure by **OUTLINING** it. An informal outline will do since you mainly need to see the parts, not the details.

- Does your genre require an abstract, a works-cited list, or any other elements?

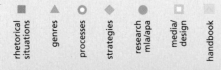

- What **TRANSITIONS** help readers move from idea to idea and paragraph to paragraph?

  277

- Would **HEADINGS** help orient readers?

  526–27

Check for clarity.   Nothing else matters if readers can't understand what you write. So clarity matters. Following are some questions that can help you see whether your meaning is clear and your text is easy to read:

- Does your **TITLE** announce the subject of your text and give some sense of what you have to say? If not, would it strengthen your argument if the title were more direct?

  272–73

- Do you state your **THESIS** directly? If not, how will readers understand your main point? Try stating your thesis outright, and see if it makes your argument easier to follow.

  273–75

- Does your **BEGINNING** tell readers what they need to understand your text, and does your **ENDING** help them make sense of what they've just read?

  261–71

- How does each paragraph relate to the ones before and after? Do you make those relationships clear — or do you need to add **TRANSITIONS**?

  277

- Do you vary your sentences? If all the sentences are roughly the same length and follow the same subject-verb-object pattern, your text probably lacks any clear emphasis and might even be difficult to read.

- Are **VISUALS** clearly labeled, positioned near the text they relate to, and referred to clearly in the text?

  528–32

- If you introduce materials from other **SOURCES,** have you clearly distinguished quoted, paraphrased, or summarized ideas from your own?

  408–19

- Have a look at the words you use. Concrete words are generally easier to understand than abstract words. If you use too many abstract words, consider changing some of them to concrete terms. Do you **DEFINE** all the words that your readers may not know?

  314–23

- Does your punctuation make your writing more clear, or less? Incorrect punctuation can make writing difficult to follow or, worse, change the intended meaning. As a best-selling punctuation manual reminds us, there's a considerable difference between "eats, shoots, and leaves" and "eats shoots and leaves."

Thinking about Your Process

Your growth as a writer depends on how well you understand what you do when you write, so that you can build on good habits. After you finish a writing project, considering the following questions can help you see the process that led to its creation—and find ways to improve the process next time.

- How would you tell the story of your thinking? Try writing these sentences: "When I first began with my topic, I thought _____. But, as I did some thinking, writing, and research about the topic, my ideas changed and I thought _____."

- At some point in your writing, did you have to choose between two or more alternatives? What were they, and how did you choose?

- What was the most difficult problem you faced while writing? How did you go about trying to solve it?

- Whose advice did you seek while researching, organizing, drafting, revising, and editing? What advice did you take, and what did you ignore? Why?

Getting Response and Revising **26**

If we want to learn to play a song on the guitar, we play it over and over again until we get it right. If we play basketball or baseball, we likely spend hours shooting foul shots or practicing a swing. Writing works the same way. Making our meaning clear can be tricky, and you should plan on revising and if need be rewriting in order to get it right. When we speak with someone face-to-face or on the phone or text message a friend, we can get immediate response and adjust or restate our message if we've been misunderstood. When we write, that immediate response is missing, so we need to seek out responses from readers to help us revise. This chapter includes a list of things for those readers to consider, along with various strategies for susequent revising and rewriting.

Getting Response

Sometimes the most helpful eyes belong to others: readers you trust, including trained writing-center tutors. They can often point out problems (and strengths) that you simply cannot see in your own work. Ask your readers to consider the specific elements in the list below, but don't restrict them to those elements. Caution: If a reader says nothing about any of these elements, don't be too quick to assume that you needn't think about them yourself.

- What did you think when you first saw the **TITLE?** Is it interesting? Informative? Appropriate? Will it attract other readers' attention? 272–73

- Does the **BEGINNING** grab readers' attention? If so, how does it do so? Does it give enough information about the topic? Offer necessary background information? How else might the piece begin? 261–66

- Is there a clear **THESIS?** What is it? 273–75

284
425–27
- Is there sufficient **SUPPORT** for the thesis? Is there anywhere you'd like to have more detail? Is the supporting material sufficiently **DOCUMENTED?**

- Does the text have a clear pattern of organization? Does each part relate to the thesis? Does each part follow from the one preceding it? Was the text easy to follow? How might the organization be improved?

267–70
- Is the **ENDING** satisfying? What did it leave you thinking? How else might it end?

12–14
- What is the writer's **STANCE?** Can you tell the writer's attitude toward the subject and audience? What words convey that attitude? Is it consistent throughout?

1
5–8
3–4
9–11
- How well does the text address the rest of its **RHETORICAL SITUATION?** Does it meet the needs and expectations of its **AUDIENCE?** Where might readers need more information, guidance, or clarification? Does it achieve its **PURPOSE?** Does every part of the text help achieve the purpose? Could anything be cut? Should anything be added? Does the text meet the requirements of its **GENRE?** Should anything be added, deleted, or changed to meet those requirements?

Revising

Once you have studied your draft with a critical eye and, if possible, gotten responses from other readers, it's time to revise. Major changes may be necessary, and you may need to generate new material or do some rewriting. But assume that your draft is good raw material that you can revise to achieve your purposes. Revision should take place on several levels, from global (whole-text issues) to particular (the details). Work on your draft in that order, starting with the elements that are global in nature and gradually moving to smaller, more particular aspects. This allows you to use your time most efficiently and take care of bigger issues first. In fact, as you deal with the larger aspects of your writing, many of the smaller ones will be taken care of along the way.

375
Give yourself time to revise.   When you have a due date, set **DEADLINES** for yourself that will give time — preferably several days but as much

as your schedule permits — to work on the text before it has to be delivered. Also, get some distance. Often when you're immersed in a project, you can't see the big picture because you're so busy creating it. If you can, get away from your writing for a while and think about something else. When you return to it, you're more likely to see it freshly. If there's not time to put a draft away for several days or more, even letting it sit overnight or for a few hours can help.

As you revise, assume that nothing is sacred. Bring a critical eye to all parts of a draft, not only to those parts pointed out by your reviewers. Content, organization, sentence patterns, individual words — all are subject to improvement. Be aware that a change in one part of the text may require changes in other parts.

At the same time, don't waste energy struggling with writing that simply doesn't work; you can always discard it. Look for the parts of your draft that do work — the parts that match your **PURPOSE** and say what you want to say. Focus your efforts on those bright spots, expanding and developing them.

■ 3–4

Revise to sharpen your focus.   Examine your **THESIS** to make sure it matches your **PURPOSE** as you now understand it. Read each paragraph to ensure that it contributes to your main point; you may find it helpful to **OUTLINE** your draft to help you see all the parts. One way to do this is to print out a copy of your draft, highlight or underline one sentence in each paragraph that expresses the paragraph's main idea, and cross out everything else. Examine the sentences that remain: Does one state the thesis of the entire essay? Do the rest relate to the thesis? Are they in the best order? If not, you need to either modify the parts of the draft that don't advance your thesis or revise your thesis to reflect your draft's focus and to rearrange your points so they advance your discussion more effectively.

◆ 273–75
■ 3–4
⊙ 223–24

Read your **BEGINNING AND ENDING** carefully; make sure that the first paragraphs introduce your topic and provide any needed contextual information and that the final paragraphs provide a satisfying conclusion.

◆ 261–70

Revise to strengthen the argument.   If readers find some of your claims unconvincing, you need to provide more information or more support. You may need to define terms you've assumed they will understand, offer

259

219–25

373

additional examples, or provide more detail by describing, explaining processes, adding dialogue, or using some other **STRATEGIES**. Make sure you show as well as tell! You might try freewriting, clustering, or other ways of **GENERATING IDEAS AND TEXT**. If you need to provide additional evidence, you might need to do additional **RESEARCH**.

Revise to improve the organization.   If you've outlined your draft, number each paragraph, and make sure each one follows from the one before. If anything seems out of place, move it, or if necessary, cut it completely.

277

526–27

9–11

Check to see if you've included appropriate **TRANSITIONS** or **HEADINGS** to help readers move through the text, and add them as needed. Check to make sure your text meets the requirements of the **GENRE** you're writing in.

Revise for clarity.   Be sure readers will be able to understand what you're saying. Look closely at your **TITLE** to be sure it gives a sense of what

272–73

273–75

the text is about, and at your **THESIS** to be sure readers will recognize your main point. If you don't state a thesis directly, consider whether you should. Be sure you provide any necessary background information

314–23

408–19

and **DEFINE** any key terms. Make sure you've integrated any **QUOTATIONS**, **PARAPHRASES**, or **SUMMARIES** into your text clearly. Be sure all paragraphs are focused around one main point and that the sentences in each paragraph contribute to that point. Finally, consider whether there are any

528–30

data that would be more clearly presented in a **CHART**, **TABLE**, or **GRAPH**.

One way to test whether your text is clear is to switch audiences: say what you're trying to say as if you were talking to an eight-year-old. You probably don't want to write that way, but the act of explaining your ideas to a young audience or readers who know nothing about your topic can help you discover any points that may be unclear.

Read and reread — and reread.   Take some advice from writing theorist Donald Murray:

> Nonwriters confront a writing problem and look away from the text to rules and principles and textbooks and handbooks and models. Writers look at the text, knowing that the text itself will reveal what needs to be done and what should not yet be done or may never be done.

rhetorical situations

genres

processes

strategies

research mla/apa

media/ design

handbook

The writer reads and rereads and rereads, standing far back and reading quickly from a distance, moving in close and reading slowly line by line, reading again and again, knowing that the answers to all writing problems lie within the evolving text.

—Donald Murray, *A Writer Teaches Writing*

Rewriting

Some writers find it useful to try rewriting a draft in various ways or from various perspectives just to explore possibilities. Try it! If you find that your original plan works best for your purpose, fine. But you may find that another way will work better. Especially if you're not completely satisfied with your draft, consider the following ways of rewriting. Experiment with your rhetorical situation:

- Rewrite your draft from different points of view, through the eyes of different people perhaps or through the eyes of an animal or even from the perspective of an object. See how the text changes (in the information it presents, its perspective, its voice).

- Rewrite for a different **AUDIENCE**. How might an email detailing a recent car accident be written to a friend, the insurance adjuster, a parent?   5–8

- Rewrite in a different **STANCE**. If the first draft was temperate and judicious, be extreme; if it was polite, be more direct. If the first draft was in standard English, rewrite it in the language your relatives use.   12–14

- Rewrite the draft in a different **GENRE** or **MEDIUM**. Rewrite an essay as a letter, story, poem, speech. Which genre and medium work best to reach your intended audience and achieve your purpose?   9–11   15–17

Ways of rewriting a narrative

- Rewrite one scene completely in **DIALOGUE**.   333–37

- Start at the end of the story and work back to the beginning, or start in the middle and fill in the beginning as you work toward the end.

Ways of rewriting a textual analysis

306–13 • **COMPARE** the text you're analyzing with another text (which may be in a completely different genre—film, TV, song lyrics, computer games, poetry, fiction, whatever).

• Write a parody of the text you're analyzing. Be as silly and as funny as you can while maintaining the structure of the original text. Alternatively, write a parody of your analysis, using evidence from the text to support an outrageous analysis.

Ways of rewriting a report

5–8 • Rewrite for a different **AUDIENCE.** For example, explain a concept to your grandparents; describe the subject of a profile to a visitor from another planet.

• Be silly. Rewrite the draft as if for *The Daily Show* or *The Onion*, or rewrite it as if it were written by Bart Simpson.

Ways of rewriting an argument

83–110 • Rewrite taking another **POSITION.** Argue as forcefully for that position as you did for your actual one, acknowledging and refuting your original position. Alternatively, write a rebuttal to your first draft from the perspective of someone with different beliefs.

343–51 • Rewrite your draft as a **STORY**—make it real in the lives of specific individuals. (For example, if you were writing about abortion rights, you could write a story about a young pregnant woman trying to decide what she believes and what to do.) Or rewrite the argument as a fable or parable.

• Rewrite the draft as a letter responding to a hostile reader, trying at least to make him or her understand what you have to say.

• Rewrite the draft as an angry letter to someone, or as a table-thumping dinner-with-the-relatives discussion. Write from the most extreme position possible.

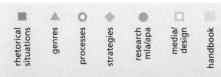

rhetorical situations   genres   processes   strategies   research mla/apa   media/ design   handbook

- Write an **ANALYSIS** of your argument in which you identify, as carefully and as neutrally as you can, the various positions people hold on the issue.

278–82

Once you've rewritten a draft in any of these ways, see whether there's anything you can use. Read each draft, considering how it might help you achieve your purpose, reach your audience, convey your stance. Revise your actual draft to incorporate anything you think will make your text more effective, whether it's other **GENRES** or a different perspective.

19

27 Editing and Proofreading

Your ability to produce clear, error-free writing shows something about your ability as a writer and also leads readers to make assumptions about your intellect, work habits, even your character. Readers of job-application letters and résumés, for example, may reject applications if they contain a single error for no other reason than it's an easy way to narrow the field of potential candidates. In addition, they may well assume that applicants who present themselves sloppily in an application will do sloppy work on the job. This is all to say that you should edit and proofread your work carefully.

Editing

Editing is the stage when you work on the details of your paragraphs, sentences, words, and punctuation to make your writing as clear, precise, correct—and effective—as possible. Your goal is not to achieve "perfection" (whatever that may be) so much as to make your writing as effective as possible for your particular purpose and audience. Check a good writing handbook for detailed advice, but the following guidelines can help you check your drafts systematically for some common errors with paragraphs, sentences, and words.

Editing paragraphs

275–76

* Does each paragraph focus on one point? Does it have a **TOPIC SENTENCE** that announces that point, and if so, where is it located? If it's not the first sentence, should it be? If there's no clear topic sentence, should there be one?

rhetorical situations

genres

processes

strategies

research mla/apa

media/ design

handbook

- Does every sentence in the paragraph relate to the main point of that paragraph? If any sentences do not, consider whether they should be deleted, moved, or revised.

- Is there enough detail to develop the paragraph's main point? How is the point developed—as a narrative? a definition? some other **STRATEGY?**

◆ 259

- Where have you placed the most important information—at the beginning? the end? in the middle? The most emphatic spot is at the end, so in general that's where to put information you want readers to remember. The second most emphatic spot is at the beginning.

- Are any paragraphs especially long or short? Consider breaking long paragraphs if there's a logical place to do so—maybe an extended example should be in its own paragraph, for instance. If you have paragraphs of only a sentence or two, see if you can add to them or combine them with another paragraph.

- Check the way your paragraphs fit together. Does each one follow smoothly from the one before? Do you need to add any **TRANSITIONS** or other links?

◆ 277

- Does the **BEGINNING** paragraph catch readers' attention? In what other ways might you begin your text?

◆ 261–66

- Does the final paragraph provide a satisfactory **ENDING?** How else might you conclude your text?

◆ 267–70

Editing sentences

- Is each sentence **COMPLETE?** Does it have someone or something (the subject) performing some sort of action or expressing a state of being (the verb)? Does each sentence begin with a **CAPITAL LETTER** and **END** with a period, question mark, or exclamation point?

HB-4

HB-81

HB-65

- Check your use of the active **VOICE** ("The choir sang 'Amazing Grace.'") and the passive ("'Amazing Grace' was sung by the choir.") Some kinds of writing call for the passive voice, and sometimes it is more appropriate than the active voice, but in general, you'll do well to edit out any use of the passive voice that's not required.

HB-18

HB-28

- Check for **PARALLELISM**. Items in a list or series should be parallel in form—all nouns (lions, tigers, bears), all verbs (hopped, skipped, jumped), all clauses (he came, he saw, he conquered), and so on.

HB-46

- Do many of your sentences begin with **IT** or **THERE?** Sometimes these words help introduce a topic, but too often they make your text vague or even conceal needed information. Why write "There are reasons we voted for him" when you can say "We had reasons to vote for him"?

- Are your sentences varied? If they all start with a subject or are all the same length, your writing might be dull and maybe even hard to read. Try varying your sentence openings by adding **TRANSITIONS**, introductory **PHRASES**, or dependent **CLAUSES**. Vary sentence lengths by adding detail to some or combining some sentences.

277
Glossary

HB-57–63

- Make sure you've used **COMMAS** correctly. Is there a comma after each introductory element? ("After an interview, you should send a thank-you note. However, an email note is generally frowned upon.") Do commas set off nonrestrictive elements—parts that aren't needed to understand the sentence? ("He always drives Dodges, which are made in America.") Are compound sentences connected with a comma? ("I'll eat broccoli steamed, but I prefer it roasted.")

Editing words

- Are you sure of the meaning of every word? Use a dictionary; be sure to look up words whose meanings you're not sure about. And remember your audience—do you use any terms they'll need to have **DEFINED**?

314–23
HB-39

- Is any of your language too **GENERAL** or vague? Why write that you competed in a race, for example, if you could say you ran the 4 × 200 relay?

13
12–14

- What about the **TONE**? If your **STANCE** is serious (or humorous or critical or something else), make sure that your words all convey that tone.

HB-24

- Do all pronouns have clear **ANTECEDENTS**? If you write "he" or "they" or "it" or "these," will readers know whom or what the words refer to?

HB-38

- Have you used any **CLICHÉS**—expressions that are used so frequently that they are no longer fresh? "Live and let live," avoiding something "like the plague," and similar expressions are so predictable that your writing will almost always be better off without them.

- Be careful with **LANGUAGE THAT REFERS TO OTHERS.** Make sure that your words do not stereotype any individual or group. Mention age, gender, race, religion, sexual orientation, and so on only if they are relevant to your subject. When referring to an ethnic group, make every effort to use the terms members of the group prefer.

HB-53–55

- Edit out language that might be considered **SEXIST.** Do you say "he" when you mean "he and she"? Have you used words like *manpower* or *policeman* to refer to people who may be female? If so, substitute less gendered words such as *personnel* or *police officer*. Do your words reflect any gender stereotypes—for example, that all engineers are male, or all nurses female? If you mention someone's gender, is it even necessary? If not, eliminate the unneeded words.

HB-54

- How many of your verbs are forms of **BE** and **DO?** If you rely too much on these words, try replacing them with more specific verbs. Why write "She did a story" when you could say "She wrote a story"?

HB-38–39

- Do you ever confuse **ITS** and **IT'S?** Use *it's* when you mean *it is* or *it has*. Use *its* when you mean *belonging to it*.

HB-43

Proofreading

Proofreading is the final stage of the writing process, the point where you clean up your work to present it to your readers. Proofreading is like checking your appearance in a mirror before going into a job interview: being neat and well groomed looms large in creating a good first impression, and the same principle applies to writing. Misspelled words, missing pages, mixed-up fonts, and other lapses send a negative message about your work—and about you. Most readers excuse an occasional error, but by and large readers are an intolerant bunch: too many errors will lead them to declare your writing—and maybe your thinking—flawed. There goes your credibility. So proofread your final draft with care to ensure that your message is taken as seriously as you want it to be.

Up to this point, you've been told *not* to read individual words on the page and instead to read for meaning. Proofreading demands the opposite: you must slow down your reading so that you can see every word, every punctuation mark.

- Use your computer's grammar checker and spelling checker, but only as a first step, and know that they're not very reliable. Computer programs don't read writing; instead, they rely on formulas and banks of words, so what they flag (or don't flag) as mistakes may or may not be accurate. If you were to write, "Sea you soon," *sea* would not be flagged as misspelled because it is a word and it's spelled correctly even though it's the wrong word in that sentence.

- To keep your eyes from jumping ahead, place a ruler or piece of paper under each line as you read. Use your finger or a pencil as a pointer.

- Some writers find it helpful to read the text one sentence at a time, beginning with the last sentence and working backward.

- Read your text out loud to yourself—or better, to others, who may *hear* problems you can't see. Alternatively, have someone else read your text aloud to you while you follow along on the page or screen.

- Ask someone else to read your text. The more important the writing is, the more important this step.

- If you find a mistake after you've printed out your text and are unable to print out a corrected version, make the change as neatly as possible in pencil or pen.

Compiling a Portfolio 28

Artists maintain portfolios of their work to show gallery owners, collectors, and other potential buyers. Money managers work with investment portfolios of stocks, bonds, and various mutual funds. And often as part of a writing class, student writers compile portfolios of their work. As with a portfolio of paintings or drawings, a portfolio of writing includes a writer's best work and, sometimes, preliminary and revised drafts of that work, along with a statement by the writer articulating why he or she considers it good. The *why* is as important as the work, for it provides you with an occasion for assessing your overall strengths and weaknesses as a writer. This chapter offers guidelines to help you compile both a *writing portfolio* and a *literacy portfolio*, a project that writing students are sometimes asked to complete as part of a literacy narrative.

Considering the Rhetorical Situation

As with the writing you put in a portfolio, the portfolio itself is generally intended for a particular audience but could serve a number of different purposes. It's a good idea, then, to consider these and the other elements of your rhetorical situation when you begin to compile a portfolio.

PURPOSE Why are you creating this portfolio? To create a record of your writing? As the basis for a grade in a course? To organize your research? To explore your literacy? For something else? 3–4

AUDIENCE Who will read your portfolio? What will your readers expect it to contain? How can you help them understand the context or occasion for each piece of writing you include? 5–8

9–11 **GENRE** What genres of writing should the portfolio contain? Do you want to demonstrate your ability to write one particular type of writing or in a variety of genres? Will your statement about the portfolio be in the form of a letter or an essay?

12–14 **STANCE** How do you want to portray yourself in this portfolio? What items should you include to create this impression? What stance do you want to take in your written assessment of its contents? Thoughtful? Enthusiastic? Something else?

15–17 **MEDIA / DESIGN** Will your portfolio be in print? Or will it be electronic? Whichever medium you use, how can you help readers navigate its contents? What design elements will be most appropriate to your purpose and medium?

A WRITING PORTFOLIO

What to Include in a Writing Portfolio

A portfolio developed for a writing course typically contains examples of your best work in that course, including any notes, outlines, preliminary drafts, and so on, along with your own assessment of your performance in that course. You might include any of the following items:

- freewriting, outlines, and other work you did to generate ideas
- drafts, rough and revised
- in-class writing assignments
- source material—copies of articles, websites, observation notes, interview transcripts, and other evidence of your research
- tests and quizzes
- responses to your drafts
- conference notes, error logs, lecture notes, other course materials
- reflections on your work

rhetorical situations genres processes strategies research mla/apa media/ design handbook

What you include will vary depending on what your instructor asks for. You may be asked to include three of your best papers or everything you've written. You may also be asked to choose certain items for evaluation or perhaps to show work in several different genres. In any case, you will need to choose, and to do that you will need to have criteria for making your choices. Don't base your decision solely on grades (unless grades are one criterion); your portfolio should reflect *your* assessment of your work, not your instructor's. What do you think is your best work? Your most interesting work? Your most ambitious work? Whatever criteria you use, you are the judge.

Organizing a Portfolio

Your instructor may provide explicit guidelines for organizing your portfolio. If not, here are some guidelines. If you set up a way to organize your writing at the start of the course, you'll be able to keep track of it throughout the course, making your job at term's end much easier. Remember that your portfolio presents you as a writer, presumably at your best. It should be neat, well organized, and easy to navigate.

Paper portfolios.   Choose something in which to gather your work. You might use a two-pocket folder, a three-ring binder, or a file folder, or you may need a box, basket, or some other container to accommodate bulky or odd-shaped items. You might also put your drafts on a computer disk, with each file clearly named.

  Label everything. Label each piece at the top of the first page, specifying the assignment, the draft, and the date: "Proposal, Draft 1, 2/12/08"; "Text Analysis, Final Draft, 10/10/08"; "Portfolio Self-Assessment, Final Draft, 12/11/08"—and so on. Write this information neatly on the page, or put it on a Post-it note. For each assignment, arrange your materials chronologically, with your earliest material (freewriting, for example) on the bottom, and each successive item (source materials, say, then your outline, then your first draft, and so on) on top of the last, ending with your final draft on top. That way readers can see how your writing progressed from earliest work to final draft.

Electronic portfolios. You might also create an electronic portfolio, or e-portfolio, that includes a home page with links to your portfolio's contents. There are several tools that can help you create an e-portfolio:

- *Online tools.* Several websites offer free tools to help you create a preformatted e-portfolio. For example, Google provides templates you can use to build an e-portfolio, uploading documents, images, and videos from your computer.

- *Blogging tools.* You can create an e-portfolio using a blogging platform, like WordPress, which allows you to upload files and create a network of linked pages. Readers can then comment on your e-portfolio, just as they might on your blog entries.

- *Wikis.* Wiki-based e-portfolios differ from blog-based ones in the level of interactivity they allow. In addition to commenting, readers may—if you allow them—make changes and add information. PBWiki is one free provider, as is WikiSpaces, although WikiSpaces pages may contain advertisements.

- *Courseware.* Your school may use a courseware system, such as Blackboard or Web CT, that allows you to create a portfolio of your work.

- *Web-authoring programs.* If you're interested in constructing a Web-based e-portfolio, you can do so using a program such as Adobe Dreamweaver and Microsoft FrontPage or a tool such as Tripod Site Builder or Yahoo! Geocities' HTML editor.

It's also possible to create an electronic portfolio using Microsoft Word, Excel, or PowerPoint. The programs available for your use and the requirements for posting your portfolio on the Web vary from school to school and instructor to instructor; ask your instructor or your school's help desk for assistance (and see the chapter on **ELECTRONIC TEXT** for general guidance).

546–56

Most electronic portfolio tools help you to first create a basic home page that includes your name, the portfolio's title, links to the various sections of the portfolio, and an introduction. Before you start creating pages and links, though, you should create a map to organize your portfolio and then add your files to the portfolio, following the map. Here's a sample map for a writing course e-portfolio that includes three major assignments (a literacy narrative, a textual analysis, and a film evaluation), and an overall self-assessment of the portfolio's contents. Each box represents a different page; each line represents a link.

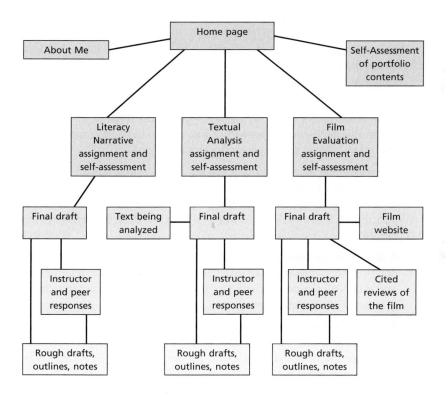

Reflecting on Your Writing Portfolio

The most important part of your portfolio is your written statement reflecting on your work. This is an occasion to step back from the work at hand and examine it with a critical eye. It is also an opportunity to assess your work and to think about what you're most proud of, what you most enjoyed doing, what you want to improve. It's your chance to think about and say what you've learned. Some instructors may ask you to write out your assessment in essay form; others will want you to put it in letter form, which usually allows for a more relaxed and personal tone. Whatever form it takes, your statement should cover the following ground:

- *An evaluation of each piece of writing in the portfolio.* Consider both strengths and weaknesses, and give examples from your writing to support what you say. What would you change if you had more time? Which is your favorite piece, and why? Your least favorite?

- *An assessment of your overall writing performance.* What do you do well? What still needs improvement? What do you *want* your work to say about you? What *does* your work say about you?

- *A discussion of how the writing you did in this course has affected your development as a writer.* How does the writing in your portfolio compare with writing you did in the past? What do you know now that you didn't know before? What can you do that you couldn't do before?

- *A description of your writing habits and process.* What do you usually do? How well does it work? What techniques seem to help you most, and why? Which seem less helpful? Cite passages from your drafts that support your conclusions.

- *An analysis of your performance in the course.* How did you spend your time? Did you collaborate with others? Did you have any conferences with your instructor? Did you visit the writing center? Consider how these or any other activities contributed to your success.

rhetorical situations　genres　processes　strategies　research mla/apa　media/ design　handbook

A Sample Self-Assessment

Here is a letter written by Nathaniel Cooney as part of his portfolio for his first-year writing class at Wright State University.

2 June 2008

Dear Reader,

It is my hope that in reading this letter, you will gain an understanding of the projects contained in this portfolio. I enclose three works that I have submitted for an introductory writing class at Wright State University, English 102, Writing in Academic Discourse: an informative report, an argument paper, and a genre project based largely on the content of the argument paper. I selected the topics of these works for two reasons: First, they address issues that I believe to be relevant in terms of both the intended audience (peers and instructors of the course) and the times when they were published. Second, they speak to issues that are important to me personally. Below I present general descriptions of the works, along with my review of their strengths and weaknesses.

My purpose in writing the informative report "Higher Standards in Education Are Taking Their Toll on Students" was to present a subject in a factual manner and to support it with well-documented research. My intent was not to argue a point. However, because I chose a narrowly focused topic and chose information to support a thesis, the report tends to favor one side of the issue over the other. Because as a student I have a personal stake in the changing standards in the formal education system, I chose to research recent changes in higher education and their effects on students. Specifically, I examine students' struggles to reach a standard that seems to be moving farther and farther beyond their grasp.

I believe that this paper could be improved in two areas. The first is a bias that I think exists because I am a student presenting information from the point of view of a student. It is my hope, however, that my inclusion of unbiased sources lessens this problem somewhat and, furthermore, that it presents the reader with a fair and accurate collection of facts and examples that supports the thesis. My second area of concern is the overall balance in the paper between outside sources supporting my own thoughts and outside sources supporting opposing points of view. Rereading the paper, I notice many places where I may have worked too hard to include sources to support my ideas. I do not necessarily see that as a bad thing, however, because, as I stated earlier, the outside sources work to counterbalance my own bias and provide the reader with additional information. I do think, though, that the paper might be improved if I were to reach a better balance between the amount of space dedicated to the expression of my ideas and the amount of space dedicated to the presentation of source materials.

The second paper, "Protecting Animals That Serve," is an argument intended not only to take a clear position on an issue but also to argue for that position and convince the reader that it is a valid one. That issue is the need for legislation guaranteeing that certain rights of service animals be protected. I am blind and use a guide dog. Thus, this issue is especially important to me. During the few months that I have had him, my guide dog has already encountered a number of situations where intentional or negligent treatment by others has put him in danger. At the time I was writing the paper, a bill was being written in the Ohio House of Representatives that, if passed, would protect service animals and establish consequences for those who violated the law. The purpose of the paper, therefore, was to present the reader with information about service animals, establish the need for the legislation in Ohio and nationwide, and argue for passage of such legislation.

I think that the best parts of my argument are the introduction and the conclusion. In particular, I think that the conclusion does a good job of not only bringing together the various points, but also conveying the significance of the issue for me and for others. In contrast, I think that the area most in need of further attention is the body of the paper. While I think the content is strong, I believe the overall organization could be improved. The connections between ideas are unclear in places, particularly in the section that acknowledges opposing viewpoints. This may be due in part to the fact that I had difficulty understanding the reasoning behind the opposing argument.

The argument paper served as a starting point for the genre project, for which the assignment was to revise one paper written for this class in a different genre. My genre project consists of a poster and a brochure. As it was for the argument paper, my primary goal was to convince my audience of the importance of a particular issue and viewpoint—specifically, to convince my audience to support House Bill 369, the bill being introduced in the Ohio Legislature that would create laws to protect the rights of service animals in the state.

Perhaps both the greatest strength and the greatest weakness of the genre project is my use of graphics. Because of my blindness, I was limited in my use of some graphics. Nevertheless, the pictures were carefully selected to capture the attention of readers, and, in part, to appeal to their emotions as they viewed and reflected on the material.

I noticed two other weaknesses in this project. First, I think that in my effort to include the most relevant information in the brochure, I may have included too many details. Because space is limited, brochures generally include only short, simple facts. Although I tried to keep the facts short and simple, I also tried to use the space that I had to provide as much supporting information as I could. This may have resulted in too much information, given the genre. Second, I dedicated one portion of the poster to a poem I wrote. While the thoughts it conveys are extremely important to me, I was somewhat unsatisfied with its style. I tried to avoid a simple rhyme scheme, but the words kept making their way back to that format. I kept the poem as it was on the advice of others, but I still believe that it could be better.

Despite its weakness, the poem also adds strength to the project in its last stanzas. There, I ask readers to take a side step for a moment, to consider what their lives would be like if they were directly affected by the issue, and to reflect on the issue from that perspective. I hope that doing so personalized the issue for readers and thus strengthened my argument.

I put a great deal of time, effort, and personal reflection into each project. While I am hesitant to say that they are finished and while I am dissatisfied with some of the finer points, I am satisfied with the overall outcome of this collection of works. Viewing it as a collection, I am also reminded that writing is an evolving process and that even if these works never become exactly what I envisioned them to be, they stand as reflections of my thoughts at a particular time in my life. In that respect, they need not be anything but what they already are, because what they are is a product of who I was when I wrote them. I hope that you find the papers interesting and informative and that as you read them, you, too, may realize their significance.

Respectfully,

Nathaniel J. Cooney

Enclosures (3)

Cooney describes each of the works he includes and considers their strengths and weaknesses, citing examples from his texts to support his assessment.

A LITERACY PORTFOLIO

As a writing student, you may be asked to think back to the time when you first learned to read and write or to remember significant books or other texts you've read and perhaps to put together a portfolio that chronicles your development as a reader and writer. You may also be asked to put together a literacy portfolio as part of a written narrative assignment.

What you include in such a portfolio will vary depending on what you've kept over the years and what your family has kept. You may have all of your favorite books, stories you dictated to a preschool teacher, notebooks in which you practiced cursive writing. Or you may have almost nothing. What you have or don't have is unimportant in the end: what's important is that you gather what you can and arrange it in a way that shows how you think about your development and growth as a literate person. What has been your experience with reading and writing? What's your earliest memory of learning to write? If you love to read, what led you to love it? Who was most responsible for shaping your writing ability? Those are some of the questions you'll ask if you write a **LITERACY NARRATIVE.** You might also compile a literacy portfolio as a good way to generate ideas and text for that assignment.

▲ 21–37

What to Include in a Literacy Portfolio

- school papers
- drawings and doodles from preschool
- favorite books
- photographs you've taken
- drawings
- poems
- letters
- journals and diaries
- lists
- reading records or logs

- marriage vows
- legal documents
- speeches you've given
- awards you've received

Organizing a Literacy Portfolio

You may wish to organize your material chronologically, but there are other methods of organization to consider as well. For example, you might group items according to where they were written (at home, at school, at work), by genre (stories, poems, essays, letters, notes), or even by purpose (pleasure, school, work, church, and so on). Arrange your portfolio in the way that best conveys who you are as a literate person. Label each item you include, perhaps with a Post-it note, to identify what it is, when it was written or read, and why you've included it in your portfolio.

Reflecting on Your Literacy Portfolio

- Why did you choose each item?
- Is anything missing? Are there any other important materials that should be here?
- Why is the portfolio arranged as it is?
- What does the portfolio show about your development as a reader and writer?
- What patterns do you see? Are there any common themes you've read or written about? Any techniques you rely on? Any notable changes over time?
- What are the most significant items—and why?

part 4

Strategies

Whenever we write, we draw on many different strategies to articulate what we have to say. We may DEFINE
key terms, DESCRIBE people or places, and EXPLAIN how
something is done. We may COMPARE one thing
to another. Sometimes we may choose a pertinent story
to NARRATE, and we may even want to include some
DIALOGUE. The chapters that follow offer advice on how
to use these AND OTHER BASIC STRATEGIES for developing
and organizing the texts you write.

Strategies

Beginning and Ending **29**

Whenever we pick up something to read, we generally start by looking at the first few words or sentences to see if they grab our attention, and based on them we decide whether to keep reading. Beginnings, then, are important, both attracting readers and giving them some information about what's to come. When we get to the end of a text, we expect to be left with a sense of closure, of satisfaction—that the story is complete, our questions have been answered, the argument has been made. So endings are important, too. This chapter offers advice on how to write beginnings and endings.

Beginning

How you begin depends on your **RHETORICAL SITUATION,** especially your purpose and audience. Academic audiences generally expect your introduction to establish context, explaining how the text fits into some larger conversation, addresses certain questions, or explores an aspect of the subject. Most introductions also offer a brief description of the text's content, often in the form of a thesis statement. The following opening of an essay about "the greatest generation" does all of this:

> Tom Brokaw called the folks of the mid-twentieth century the greatest generation. So why is the generation of my grandparents seen as this country's greatest? Perhaps the reason is not what they accomplished but what they endured. Many of the survivors feel people today "don't have the moral character to withstand a depression like that." This paper will explore the Great Depression through the eyes of ordinary Americans in the most impoverished region in the country, the

■ 1

American South, in order to detail how they endured and how the government assisted them in this difficult era.

—Jeffrey DeRoven, "The Greatest Generation:
The Great Depression and the American South"

If you're writing for a nonacademic audience or genre—for a newspaper or a website, for example—your introduction may need to entice your readers to read on by connecting your text to their interests through shared experiences, anecdotes, or some other attention-getting device. Cynthia Bass, writing a newspaper article about the Gettysburg Address on its 135th anniversary, connects that date—the day her audience would read it—to Lincoln's address. She then develops the rationale for thinking about the speech and introduces her specific topic: debates about the writing and delivery of the Gettysburg Address:

November 19 is the 135th anniversary of the Gettysburg Address. On that day in 1863, with the Civil War only half over and the worst yet to come, Abraham Lincoln delivered a speech now universally regarded as both the most important oration in U.S. history and the best explanation—"government of the people, by the people, for the people"—of why this nation exists.

We would expect the history of an event so monumental as the Gettysburg Address to be well established. The truth is just the opposite. The only thing scholars agree on is that the speech is short—only ten sentences—and that it took Lincoln under five minutes to stand up, deliver it, and sit back down.

Everything else—when Lincoln wrote it, where he wrote it, how quickly he wrote it, how he was invited, how the audience reacted—has been open to debate since the moment the words left his mouth.

—Cynthia Bass, "Gettysburg Address: Two Versions"

Ways of Beginning

Explain the larger context of your topic.   Most essays are part of an ongoing conversation, so you might begin by outlining the positions to which your writing responds, as the following example from an essay about prejudice does:

The war on prejudice is now, in all likelihood, the most uncontroversial social movement in America. Opposition to "hate speech," formerly identified with the liberal left, has become a bipartisan piety. In the past year, groups and factions that agree on nothing else have agreed that the public expression of any and all prejudices must be forbidden. On the left, protesters and editorialists have insisted that Francis L. Lawrence resign as president of Rutgers University for describing blacks as "a disadvantaged population that doesn't have that genetic, hereditary background to have a higher average." On the other side of the ideological divide, Ralph Reed, the executive director of the Christian Coalition, responded to criticism of the religious right by calling a press conference to denounce a supposed outbreak of "name-calling, scapegoating, and religious bigotry." Craig Rogers, an evangelical Christian student at California State University, recently filed a $2.5 million sexual-harassment suit against a lesbian professor of psychology, claiming that anti-male bias in one of her lectures violated campus rules and left him feeling "raped and trapped."

In universities and on Capitol Hill, in workplaces and newsrooms, authorities are declaring that there is no place for racism, sexism, homophobia, Christian-bashing, and other forms of prejudice in public debate or even in private thought. "Only when racism and other forms of prejudice are expunged," say the crusaders for sweetness and light, "can minorities be safe and society be fair." So sweet, this dream of a world without prejudice. But the very last thing society should do is seek to utterly eradicate racism and other forms of prejudice.

—Jonathan Rauch, "In Defense of Prejudice"

State your thesis. Sometimes the best beginning is a clear **THESIS** stating your position, like the following statement in an essay arguing that under certain circumstances torture is necessary:

273–75

It is generally assumed that torture is impermissible, a throwback to a more brutal age. Enlightened societies reject it outright, and regimes using it risk the wrath of the United States.

I believe this attitude is unwise. There are situations in which torture is not merely permissible but morally mandatory. Moreover, these situations are moving from the realm of imagination to fact.

—Michael Levin, "The Case for Torture"

Forecast your organization.   You might begin by briefly outlining the way in which you will organize your text. The following example offers background on the subject and an analysis of immigration patterns in the United States, and describes the points that the writer's analysis will discuss:

> This paper analyzes the new geography of immigration during the twentieth century and highlights how immigrant destinations in the 1980s and 1990s differ from earlier settlement patterns. The first part of the analysis uses historical U.S. Census data to develop a classification of urban immigrant "gateways" that describes the ebb and flow of past, present, and likely future receiving areas. The remainder of the analysis examines contemporary trends to explore the recent and rapid settlement of the immigrant population in America's metropolitan gateways.
>
> —Audrey Singer, "The Rise of New Immigrant Gateways"

Offer background information.   If your readers may not know as much as you do about your topic, giving them information to help them understand your position can be important, as David Guterson does in an essay on the Mall of America:

> Last April, on a visit to the new Mall of America near Minneapolis, I carried with me the public-relations press kit provided for the benefit of reporters. It included an assortment of "fun facts" about the mall: 140,000 hot dogs sold each week, 10,000 permanent jobs, 44 escalators and 17 elevators, 12,750 parking places, 13,300 short tons of steel, $1 million in cash disbursed weekly from 8 automatic-teller machines. Opened in the summer of 1992, the mall was built on the 78-acre site of the former Metropolitan Stadium, a five-minute drive from the Minneapolis–St. Paul International Airport. With 4.2 million square feet of floor space—including twenty-two times the retail footage of the average American shopping center—the Mall of America was "the largest fully enclosed combination retail and family entertainment complex in the United States."
>
> —David Guterson, "Enclosed. Encyclopedic. Endured: The Mall of America"

Define key terms or concepts.   The success of an argument often hinges on how key terms are **DEFINED.** You may wish to provide definitions up front, as this page from an advocacy website, *Health Care without Harm*, does in a report on the hazards of fragrances in health-care facilities:

314–23

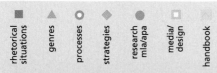

To many people, the word "fragrance" means something that smells nice, such as perfume. We don't often stop to think that scents are chemicals. Fragrance chemicals are organic compounds that volatilize, or vaporize into the air — that's why we can smell them. They are added to products to give them a scent or to mask the odor of other ingredients. The volatile organic chemicals (VOCs) emitted by fragrance products can contribute to poor indoor air quality (IAQ) and are associated with a variety of adverse health effects.

— Health Care without Harm, "Fragrances"

Connect your subject to your readers' interests or values. You'll always want to establish common ground with your readers, and sometimes you may wish to do so immediately, in your introduction, as in this example:

We all want to feel safe. Most Americans lock their doors at night, lock their cars in parking lots, try to park near buildings or under lights, and wear seat belts. Many invest in expensive security systems, carry pepper spray or a stun gun, keep guns in their homes, or take self-defense classes. Obviously, safety and security are important issues in American life.

— Andy McDonie, "Airport Security: What Price Safety?"

Start with something that will provoke readers' interest. Anna Quindlen opens an essay on feminism with the following eye-opening assertion:

Let's use the F word here. People say it's inappropriate, offensive, that it puts people off. But it seems to me it's the best way to begin, when it's simultaneously devalued and invaluable.
Feminist. Feminist, feminist, feminist.

— Anna Quindlen, "Still Needing the F Word"

Start with an anecdote. Sometimes a brief **NARRATIVE** helps bring a topic to life for readers. See, for example, how an essay on the dozens, a type of verbal contest played by some African Americans, begins:

343–51

Alfred Wright, a nineteen-year-old whose manhood was at stake on Longwood Avenue in the South Bronx, looked fairly calm as another teenager called him Chicken Head and compared his mother to Shamu the whale.
He fingered the gold chain around his thin neck while listening to a detailed complaint about his sister's sexual abilities. Then he slowly

took the toothpick out of his mouth; the jeering crowd of young men quieted as he pointed at his accuser.

"He was so ugly when he was born," Wright said, "the doctor smacked his mom instead of him."

—John Tierney, "Playing the Dozens"

Ask a question.   Instead of a thesis statement, you might open with a question about the topic your text will explore, as this study of the status of women in science does:

Are women's minds different from men's minds? In spite of the women's movement, the age-old debate centering around this question continues. We are surrounded by evidence of de facto differences between men's and women's intellects — in the problems that interest them, in the ways they try to solve those problems, and in the professions they choose. Even though it has become fashionable to view such differences as environmental in origin, the temptation to seek an explanation in terms of innate differences remains a powerful one.

—Evelyn Fox Keller, "Women in Science: A Social Analysis"

Jump right in.   Occasionally you may wish to start as close to the key action as possible. See how one writer jumps right into his profile of a blues concert:

Long Tongue, the Blues Merchant, strolls onstage. His guitar rides side-saddle against his hip. The drummer slides onto the tripod seat behind the drums, adjusts the high-hat cymbal, and runs a quick, off-beat tattoo on the tom-tom, then relaxes. The bass player plugs into the amplifier, checks the settings on the control panel, and nods his okay. Three horn players stand off to one side, clustered, lurking like brilliant sorcerer-wizards waiting to do magic with their musical instruments.

—Jerome Washington, "The Blues Merchant"

Ending

Endings are important because they're the last words readers read. How you end a text will depend in part on your RHETORICAL SITUATION. You may end by wrapping up loose ends, or you may wish to give readers some-

rhetorical situations   genres   processes   strategies   research mla/apa   media/ design   handbook

thing to think about. Some endings do both, as Cynthia Bass does in a report on the debate over the Gettysburg Address. In her two final paragraphs, she first summarizes the debate and then shows its implications:

> What's most interesting about the Lincoln-as-loser and Lincoln-as-winner versions is how they marshal the same facts to prove different points. The invitation asks Lincoln to deliver "a few appropriate remarks." Whether this is a putdown or a reflection of the protocol of the time depends on the "spin" — an expression the highly politicized Lincoln would have readily understood — which the scholar places on it.
>
> These diverse histories should not in any way diminish the power or beauty of Lincoln's words. However, they should remind us that history, even the history of something as deeply respected as the Gettysburg Address, is seldom simple or clear. This reminder is especially useful today as we watch expert witnesses, in an effort to divine what the founders meant by "high crimes and misdemeanors," club one another with conflicting interpretations of the same events, the same words, the same precedents, and the same laws.
>
> — Cynthia Bass, "Gettysburg Address: Two Versions"

Bass summarizes the dispute about Lincoln's Address and then moves on to discuss the role of scholars in interpreting historical events. Writing during the Clinton impeachment hearings, she concludes by pointing out the way in which expert government witnesses often offer conflicting interpretations of events to suit their own needs. The ending combines several strategies to bring various strands of her essay together, leaving readers to interpret her final words themselves.

Ways of Ending

Restate your main point.   Sometimes you'll simply **SUMMARIZE** your central idea, as in this example from an essay arguing that we have no "inner" self and that we should be judged by our actions alone:

416–17

> The inner man is a fantasy. If it helps you to identify with one, by all means, do so; preserve it, cherish it, embrace it, but do not present it to others for evaluation or consideration, for excuse or exculpation, or, for that matter, for punishment or disapproval.

> Like any fantasy, it serves your purposes alone. It has no standing in the real world which we share with each other. Those character traits, those attitudes, that behavior — that strange and alien stuff sticking out all over you — *that's the real you!*
>
> —Willard Gaylin, "What You See Is the Real You"

Discuss the implications of your argument. The following conclusion of an essay on the development of Post-it notes leads readers to consider how failure sometimes leads to innovation:

> Post-it notes provide but one example of a technological artifact that has evolved from a perceived failure of existing artifacts to function without frustrating. Again, it is not that form follows function but, rather, that the form of one thing follows from the failure of another thing to function as we would like. Whether it be bookmarks that fail to stay in place or taped-on notes that fail to leave a once-nice surface clean and intact, their failure and perceived failure is what leads to the true evolution of artifacts. That the perception of failure may take centuries to develop, as in the case of loose bookmarks, does not reduce the importance of the principle in shaping our world.
>
> —Henry Petroski, "Little Things Can Mean a Lot"

 343–51

End with an anecdote, maybe finishing a **NARRATIVE** that was begun earlier in your text or adding one that illustrates the point you are making. See how Sarah Vowell uses a story to end an essay on students' need to examine news reporting critically:

> I looked at Joanne McGlynn's syllabus for her media studies course, the one she handed out at the beginning of the year, stating the goals of the class. By the end of the year, she hoped her students would be better able to challenge everything from novels to newscasts, that they would come to identify just who is telling a story and how that person's point of view affects the story being told. I'm going to go out on a limb here and say that this lesson has been learned. In fact, just recently, a student came up to McGlynn and told her something all teachers dream of hearing. The girl told the teacher that she was listening to the radio, singing along with her favorite song, and halfway

rhetorical situations genres processes strategies research mla/apa media/ design handbook

through the sing-along she stopped and asked herself, "What am I singing? What do these words mean? What are they trying to tell me?" And then, this young citizen of the republic jokingly complained, "I can't even turn on the radio without thinking anymore."

—Sarah Vowell, "Democracy and Things Like That"

Refer to the beginning.   One way to bring closure to a text is to bring up something discussed in the beginning; often the reference adds to or even changes the original meaning. For example, Amy Tan opens an essay on her Chinese mother's English by establishing herself as a writer and lover of language who uses many versions of English in her writing:

> I am not a scholar of English or literature. I cannot give you much more than personal opinions on the English language and its variations in this country or others.
>
> I am a writer. And by that definition, I am someone who has always loved language. I am fascinated by language in daily life. I spend a great deal of my time thinking about the power of language—the way it can evoke an emotion, a visual image, a complex idea, or a simple truth. Language is the tool of my trade. And I use them all—all the Englishes I grew up with.

At the end of her essay, Tan repeats this phrase, but now she describes language not in terms of its power to evoke emotions, images, and ideas, but in its power to evoke "the essence" of her mother. When she began to write fiction, she says,

> [I] decided I should envision a reader for the stories I would write. And the reader I decided upon was my mother, because these were stories about mothers. So with this reader in mind—and in fact she did read my early drafts—I began to write stories using all the Englishes I grew up with: the English I spoke to my mother, which for lack of a better term might be described as "simple"; the English she used with me, which for lack of a better term might be described as "broken"; my translation of her Chinese, which could certainly be described as "watered down"; and what I imagined to be her translation of her Chinese if she could speak in perfect English, her internal language, and for that I sought to preserve the essence, but neither an English nor a

Chinese structure. I wanted to capture what language ability tests can never reveal: her intent, her passion, her imagery, the rhythms of her speech and the nature of her thoughts.

—Amy Tan, "Mother Tongue"

Note how Tan not only repeats "all the Englishes I grew up with", but also provides parallel lists of what those Englishes can do for her: "evoke an emotion, a visual image, a complex idea, or a simple truth" on the one hand, and, on the other, capture her mother's "intent, her passion, her imagery, the rhythms of her speech and the nature of her thoughts."

Propose some action, as in the following conclusion of a report on the consequences of binge drinking among college students:

> The scope of the problem makes immediate results of any interventions highly unlikely. Colleges need to be committed to large-scale and long-term behavior-change strategies, including referral of alcohol abusers to appropriate treatment. Frequent binge drinkers on college campuses are similar to other alcohol abusers elsewhere in their tendency to deny that they have a problem. Indeed, their youth, the visibility of others who drink the same way, and the shelter of the college community may make them less likely to recognize the problem. In addition to addressing the health problems of alcohol abusers, a major effort should address the large group of students who are not binge drinkers on campus who are adversely affected by the alcohol-related behavior of binge drinkers.
>
> —Henry Wechsler et al., "Health and Behavioral Consequences of Binge Drinking in College: A National Survey of Students at 140 Campuses"

Considering the Rhetorical Situation

As a writer or speaker, think about the message that you want to articulate, the audience you want to reach, and the larger context you are writing in.

3–4 ■ **PURPOSE**	Your purpose will affect the way you begin and end. If you're trying to persuade readers to do something, you may want to open by clearly stating your thesis and end by calling for a specific action.

rhetorical situations　genres　processes　strategies　research mla/apa　media/ design　handbook

AUDIENCE   Who do you want to reach, and how does that affect the way you begin and end? You may want to open with an intriguing fact or anecdote to entice your audience to read a profile, for instance, whereas readers of a report may expect it to conclude with a summary of your findings.

5–8

GENRE   Does your genre require a certain type of beginning or ending? Arguments, for example, often provide a statement of the thesis near the beginning; proposals typically end with a call for some solution.

9–11

STANCE   What is your stance, and can your beginning and ending help you convey that stance? For example, beginning an argument on the distribution of AIDS medications to underdeveloped countries with an anecdote may demonstrate concern for the human costs of the disease, whereas starting with a statistical analysis may suggest the stance of a careful researcher. Ending a proposal by weighing the advantages and disadvantages of the solution you propose may make you seem reasonable.

12–14

MEDIA / DESIGN   Your medium may affect the way you begin and end. A Web text, for instance, may open with a home page listing a menu of the site — and giving readers a choice of where they will begin. With a print text, you get to decide how it will begin and end.

15–17

IF YOU NEED MORE HELP

See also the guides to writing in chapters 6–9 for ways of beginning and ending a **LITERACY NARRATIVE,** an essay **ANALYZING TEXT,** a **REPORT,** or an **ARGUMENT.**

33–34
55–56
78–79
107–8

30 Guiding Your Reader

Traffic lights, street signs, and lines on the road help drivers find their way. Readers need similar guidance—to know, for example, whether they're reading a report or an argument, an evaluation or a proposal. They also need to know what to expect: What will the report be about? What perspective will it offer? What will this paragraph cover? What about the next one? How do the two paragraphs relate to each other? When you write, you need to provide cues to help your readers navigate your text and understand the points you're trying to make. This chapter offers advice on guiding your reader and, specifically, on using *titles, thesis statements, topic sentences*, and *transitions*.

Titles

A title serves various purposes, naming a text and providing clues to the content. It also helps readers decide whether they want to read further, so it's worth your while to come up with a title that attracts interest. Some titles include subtitles. You generally have considerable freedom in choosing a title, but always you'll want to consider the **RHETORICAL SITUATION** to be sure your title serves your purpose and appeals to the audience you want to reach.

Some titles simply announce the subject of the text:

"Black Men and Public Space"
"In the *24* World, Family Is the Main Casualty"
"Why Colleges Shower Their Students with A's"
The Greatest Generation

rhetorical situations genres processes strategies research mla/apa media/ design handbook

Some titles provoke readers or otherwise entice them to read:

"Kill 'Em! Crush 'Em! Eat 'Em Raw!"
"Thank God for the Atom Bomb"
"What Are Homosexuals For?"

Sometimes writers add a subtitle to explain or illuminate the title:

Aria: Memoir of a Bilingual Childhood
"Health and Behavioral Consequences of Binge Drinking in College:
    A National Survey of Students at 140 Campuses"
"From Realism to Virtual Reality: Images of America's Wars"

Sometimes when you're starting to write, you'll think of a title that helps you generate ideas and write. More often, though, a title is one of the last things you'll write, when you know what you've written and can craft a suitable name for your text.

Thesis Statements

A thesis identifies the topic of your text along with the claim you are making about it. A good thesis helps readers understand an essay. Working to create a sharp thesis can help you focus both your thinking and your writing. Here are three steps for moving from a topic to a thesis statement:

1. **State your topic as a question.**   You may have an idea for a topic, such as "gasoline prices," "analysis of the Dove 'real women' ad campaign," or "famine." Those may be good topics, but they're not thesis statements, primarily because none of them actually makes a statement. A good way to begin moving from topic to thesis statement is to turn your topic into a question:

What causes fluctuations in gasoline prices?

Are ads picturing "real women" who aren't models effective?

What can be done to prevent famine in Africa?

2. Then turn your question into a position. A thesis statement is an assertion—it takes a stand or makes a claim. Whether you're writing a report or an argument, you are saying, "This is the way I see . . . " "My research shows . . . ," or "This is what I believe about . . . ." Your thesis statement announces your position on the question you are raising about your topic, so a relatively easy way of establishing a thesis is to answer your own question:

> Gasoline prices fluctuate for several reasons.
>
> Ads picturing "real women" instead of models are effective because women can easily identify with them.
>
> The most recent famine in Eritrea could have been avoided if certain measures had been taken.

3. Narrow your thesis. A good thesis is specific, guiding you as you write and showing your audience exactly what your essay will cover. The preceding thesis statements need to be qualified and focused—they need to be made more specific. For example:

> Gasoline prices fluctuate because of production procedures, consumer demand, international politics, and oil companies' policies.
>
> Dove skin-firming products' ad campaign featuring "real women" works because consumers can identify with the women's bodies and admire their confidence in displaying them.
>
> The 1984 famine in Eritrea could have been avoided if farmers had received training in more effective methods and had had access to certain technology and if Western nations had provided more aid more quickly.

222–23

A good way to narrow a thesis is to ask **QUESTIONS** about it: *Why* do gasoline prices fluctuate? *How* could the Eritrea famine have been avoided? The answers will help you craft a narrow, focused thesis.

4. Qualify your thesis. Sometimes you want to make a strong argument and to state your thesis bluntly. Often, however, you need to acknowledge that your assertions may be challenged or may not be unconditionally true. In those cases, consider limiting the scope of your thesis by adding to it such terms as *may, probably, apparently, very likely, sometimes,* and *often.*

Gasoline prices *very likely* fluctuate because of production procedures, consumer demand, international politics, and oil companies' policies.

Dove skin-firming products' ad campaign featuring "real women" may work because consumers can identify with the women's bodies and admire their confidence in displaying them.

The 1984 famine in Eritrea could *probably* have been avoided if farmers had received training in more effective methods and had had access to certain technology and if Western nations had provided more aid more quickly.

Thesis statements are typically positioned at or near the end of a text's introduction, to let readers know at the outset what is being claimed and what the text will be aiming to prove. A thesis doesn't necessarily forecast your organization, which may be more complex than the thesis itself. For example, Carolyn Stonehill's research paper, "It's in Our Genes: The Biological Basis of Human Mating Behavior," contains this thesis statement:

While cultural values and messages clearly play a part in the process of mate selection, the genetic and psychological predispositions developed by our ancestors play the biggest role in determining to whom we are attracted.

However, the paper that follows includes sections on "Women's Need to Find a Capable Mate" and "Men's Need to Find a Healthy Mate," in which the "genetic and psychological predispositions" are discussed, followed by sections titled "The Influence of the Media on Mate Selection" and "If Not Media, Then What?" which discuss "cultural values and messages." The paper delivers what the thesis delivers without following the order in which the thesis presents the topics.

Topic Sentences

Just as a thesis statement announces the topic and position of an essay, a topic sentence states the subject and focus of a paragraph. Good paragraphs focus on a single point, which is summarized in a topic sentence. Usually, but not always, the topic sentence begins the paragraph:

> *Graduating from high school or college is an exciting, occasionally even traumatic event.* Your identity changes as you move from being a high school teenager to a university student or a worker; your connection to home loosens as you attend school elsewhere, move to a place of your own, or simply exercise your right to stay out later. You suddenly find yourself doing different things, thinking different thoughts, fretting about different matters. As recent high school graduate T. J. Devoe puts it, "I wasn't really scared, but having this vast range of opportunity made me uneasy. I didn't know *what* was gonna happen." Jenny Petrow, in describing her first year out of college, observes, "It's a tough year. It was for all my friends."
>
> —Sydney Lewis, *Help Wanted: Tales from the First Job Front*

Sometimes the topic sentence may come at the end of the paragraph or even at the end of the preceding paragraph, depending on the way the paragraphs relate to one another. Other times a topic sentence will summarize or restate a point made in the previous paragraph, helping readers understand what they've just read as they move on to the next point. See how the linguist Deborah Tannen does this in the first paragraphs of an article on differences in men's and women's conversational styles:

> I was addressing a small gathering in a suburban Virginia living room — a women's group that had invited men to join them. Throughout the evening, one man had been particularly talkative, frequently offering ideas and anecdotes, while his wife sat silently beside him on the couch. Toward the end of the evening, I commented that women frequently complain that their husbands don't talk to them. This man quickly concurred. He gestured toward his wife and said, "She's the talker in our family." The room burst into laughter; the man looked puzzled and hurt. "It's true," he explained. "When I come home from work I have nothing to say. If she didn't keep the conversation going, we'd spend the whole evening in silence."
>
> *This episode crystallizes the irony that although American men tend to talk more than women in public situations, they often talk less at home.* And this pattern is wreaking havoc with marriage.
>
> —Deborah Tannen, "Sex, Lies, and Conversation:
> Why Is It So Hard for Men and Women to Talk to Each Other?"

Transitions

Transitions help readers move from thought to thought — from sentence to sentence, paragraph to paragraph. You are likely to use a number of transitions as you draft; when you're **EDITING,** you should make a point of checking transitions. Here are some common ones:

242–45

- **To show causes and effects:** accordingly, as a result, because, consequently, hence, so, then, therefore, thus

- **To show comparisons:** also, in the same way, like, likewise, similarly

- **To show contrasts or exceptions:** although, but, even though, however, in contrast, instead, nevertheless, nonetheless, on the contrary, on the one hand . . . on the other hand, still, yet

- **To show examples:** for example, for instance, indeed, in fact, of course, such as

- **To show place or position:** above, adjacent to, below, beyond, elsewhere, here

- **To show sequence:** again, also, and, and then, besides, finally, furthermore, last, moreover, next, too

- **To show time:** after, as soon as, at first, at the same time, before, eventually, finally, immediately, later, meanwhile, next, simultaneously, so far, soon, then, thereafter

- **To signal a summary or conclusion:** as a result, as we have seen, finally, in a word, in any event, in brief, in conclusion, in other words, in short, in the end, in the final analysis, on the whole, therefore, thus, to summarize

---

IF YOU NEED MORE HELP

See also Chapter 51 on **PRINT TEXT** for ways of creating visual signals for your readers.

523–33

31 Analyzing Causes and Effects

Analyzing causes helps us think about why something happened, whereas thinking about effects helps us consider what might happen. When we hear a noise in the night, we want to know what caused it. Children poke sticks into holes to see what will happen. Researchers try to understand the causes of diseases. Writers often have occasion to consider causes or effects as part of a larger topic or sometimes as a main focus: in a 171–79 **PROPOSAL,** we might consider the effects of reducing tuition or the causes 153–60 of recent tuition increases; in a **MEMOIR,** we might explore why the person we had a date with failed to show up. Often we can only speculate about probable causes or likely effects. In writing about causes and effects, then, 283–99 we are generally **ARGUING** for those we consider plausible or probable. This chapter will help you analyze causes and effects in writing—and to do so in a way that suits your rhetorical situation.

Determining Plausible Causes and Effects

What causes ozone depletion? Sleeplessness? Obesity? And what are their effects? Those are of course large, complex topics, but whenever you have reason to ask why something happened or what could happen, there will likely be several possible causes and just as many predictable effects. There may be obvious causes, though often they will be less important than others that are harder to recognize. (Eating too much may be an obvious cause of being overweight, but *why* people eat too much has several less obvious causes: portion size, advertising, lifestyle, and physiological disorders are only a few possibilities.) Similarly, short-term effects are often less important than long-term ones. (A stomachache may be an effect of eating too much candy, but the chemical imbalance that can result from consuming too much sugar is a much more serious effect.)

rhetorical situations

genres

processes

strategies

research mla/apa

media/ design

handbook

LISTING, CLUSTERING, and **OUTLINING** are useful processes for analyzing causes. And at times you might need to do some **RESEARCH** to identify possible causes or effects and to find evidence to support your analysis. When you've identified potential causes and effects, you need to analyze them. Which causes and effects are primary? Which seem to be secondary? Which are most relevant to your **PURPOSE** and are likely to convince your **AUDIENCE?** You will probably have to choose from several possible causes and effects for your analysis because you won't want or need to include all of them.

219–24
373

3–4
5–8

Arguing for Causes or Effects

Once you've identified several possible causes or predictable effects, you need to **ARGUE** that some are more plausible than others. You must provide convincing support for your argument because you cannot *prove* that X causes Y or that Y will be caused by Z; you can show only, with good reasons and appropriate evidence, that X is *likely* to cause Y or that Y will *likely* follow from Z. See, for example, how an essay on the psychological basis for risk taking speculates about two potential causes for the popularity of extreme sports:

283–99

> Studies now indicate that the inclination to take high risks may be hardwired into the brain, intimately linked to arousal and pleasure mechanisms, and may offer such a thrill that it functions like an addiction. The tendency probably affects one in five people, mostly young males, and declines with age. It may ensure our survival, even spur our evolution as individuals and as a species. Risk taking probably bestowed a crucial evolutionary advantage, inciting the fighting and foraging of the hunter-gatherer. . . .
>
> As psychologist Salvadore Maddi, PhD, of the University of California at Davis warns, "High-risk takers may have a hard time deriving meaning and purpose from everyday life." Indeed, this peculiar form of dissatisfaction could help explain the explosion of high-risk sports in America and other postindustrial Western nations. In unstable cultures, such as those at war or suffering poverty, people rarely seek out additional thrills. But in a rich and safety-obsessed country like America, land of guardrails, seat belts, and personal-injury lawsuits,

everyday life may have become too safe, predictable, and boring for those programmed for risk taking.

—Paul Roberts, "Risk"

Roberts suggests that genetics is one likely cause of extreme sports and that an American obsession with safety is perhaps a cause of their growing popularity. Notice, however, that he presents these as likely or possible, not certain, by choosing his words carefully: "studies now *indicate*"; "the inclination to take high risks *may* be hardwired"; "[R]isk taking *probably* bestowed a crucial evolutionary advantage"; "this . . . dissatisfaction *could help* explain." Like Roberts, you will almost always need to qualify what you say about causes and effects—to say that something *could explain* (rather than saying it "explains") or that it *suggests* (rather than "shows"). Plausible causes and effects can't be proved definitively, so you need to acknowledge that your argument is not the last word on the subject.

Ways of Organizing an Analysis of Causes and Effects

Your analysis of causes and effects may be part of a proposal or some other genre of writing, or you may write a text whose central purpose is to analyze causes or speculate about effects. While there are many ways to organize an analysis of causes and effects, three common ways are to state a cause and then discuss its effects, to state an effect and then discuss its causes, and to identify a chain of causes and effects.

Identify a cause and then discuss its effects.   If you were writing about global warming, you might first show that many scientists fear it will have several effects, including drastic climate changes, the extinction of various kinds of plants, and elevated sea levels.

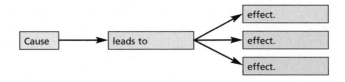

Identify an effect and then trace its causes.   If you were writing about school violence, for example, you might argue that it is a result of sloppy dress, informal teacher-student relationships, low academic standards, and disregard for rules.

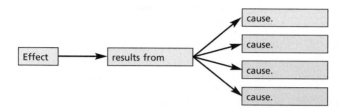

Identify a chain of causes and effects.   You may sometimes discuss a chain of causes and effects. If you were writing about the right to privacy, for example, you might consider the case of Megan's law. A convicted child molester raped and murdered a girl named Megan; the crime caused New Jersey legislators to pass the so-called Megan's law (an effect), which requires that convicted sex offenders be publicly identified. As more states enact versions of Megan's law, concern for the rights of those who are identified is developing—the effect is becoming a cause of further effects.

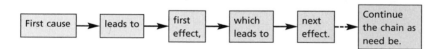

Considering the Rhetorical Situation

As a writer or speaker, you need to think about the message that you want to articulate, the audience you want to reach, and the larger context you are writing in.

PURPOSE   Your purpose may be to analyze causes. But sometimes you'll have another goal that calls for such analysis—a business report, for example, might need to explain what caused a decline in sales.

3–4

5–8 ■ **AUDIENCE** Who is your intended audience, and how will analyzing causes help you reach them? Do you need to tell them why some event happened or what effects resulted?

9–11 ■ **GENRE** Does your genre require you to analyze causes? Proposals, for example, often need to consider the effects of a proposed solution.

12–14 ■ **STANCE** What is your stance, and could analyzing causes or effects show that stance? Could it help demonstrate your seriousness or show that your conclusions are reasonable?

15–17 ■ **MEDIA / DESIGN** You can rely on words to analyze causes, but sometimes a drawing will help readers *see* how causes lead to effects.

IF YOU NEED MORE HELP

209–58 ○ See also the **PROCESSES** chapters for help generating ideas, drafting, and so on if you need to write an entire text whose purpose is to analyze causes or speculate about effects.

Arguing 32

Tennis fans argue about who's better, Venus or Serena. Political candidates argue that they have the most experience or best judgment. A toilet paper ad argues that you should "be kind to your behind." As you likely realize, we are surrounded by arguments, and much of the work you do as a college student requires you to read and write arguments. When you write a **LITERARY ANALYSIS,** for instance, you argue for a particular interpretation. In a **PROPOSAL,** you argue for a particular solution to a problem. Even a **PROFILE** argues that a subject should be seen in a certain way. This chapter offers advice on some of the key elements of making an argument, from developing an arguable thesis and identifying good reasons and evidence that supports those reasons to building common ground and dealing with viewpoints other than your own.

143–52
171–79
161–70

Reasons for Arguing

We argue for many reasons, and they often overlap: to convince others that our position on a subject is reasonable, to influence the way they think about a subject, to persuade them to change their point of view or to take some sort of action. In fact, many composition scholars and teachers believe that all writing makes an argument.

   As a student, you'll be called upon to make arguments continually: when you participate in class discussions, when you take an essay exam, when you post a comment to a Listserv or a blog. In all these instances, you are adding your opinions to some larger conversation, arguing for what you believe — and why.

Arguing Logically: Claims, Reasons, and Evidence

The basic building blocks of argument are claims, reasons, and evidence that supports those reasons. Using these building blocks, we can construct a strong logical argument.

Claims. Good arguments are based on arguable claims—statements that reasonable people may disagree about. Certain kinds of statements cannot be argued:

- *Verifiable statements of fact.* Most of the time, there's no point in arguing about facts like "The earth is round" or "George H. W. Bush is America's 41st president." Such statements contain no controversy, no potential opposition—and so no interest for an audience. However, you might argue about the basis of a fact. For example, until recently it was a fact that our solar system had nine planets, but when further discoveries led to a change in the definition of *planet*, Pluto no longer qualified.

- *Issues of faith or belief.* By definition, matters of faith cannot be proven or refuted. If you believe in reincarnation or don't believe there is an afterlife, there's no way I can convince you otherwise. However, in a philosophy or religion course you may be asked to argue, for example, whether or not the universe must have a cause.

- *Matters of simple opinion or personal taste.* If you think cargo pants are ugly, no amount of arguing will convince you to think otherwise. If you own every Beyoncé CD and think she's the greatest singer ever, you won't convince your Beatles-loving parents to like her too. If matters of taste are based on identifiable criteria, though, they may be argued in an **EVALUATION,** where "Tom Cruise is a terrible actor" is more than just your opinion—it's an assertion you can support with evidence from his performances.

 125–32

You may begin with an opinion: "I think wearing a helmet makes riding a bike more dangerous, not less." As it stands, that statement can't be considered a claim—it needs to be made more reasonable and informed. To do that, you might reframe it as a question—"Do bike riders who wear helmets get injured more often than those who don't?"—that may be answered as you do research and start to write. Your opinion or question should lead

rhetorical situations   genres   processes   strategies   research mla/apa   media/ design   handbook

you to an arguable claim, however, one that could be challenged by another thoughtful person. In this case, for example, your research might lead you to a focused, qualified claim: *Contrary to common sense, wearing a helmet while riding a bicycle increases the chances of injury, at least to adult riders.*

Qualifying a claim.   According to an old saying, there are two sides to every story. Much of the time, though, arguments don't sort themselves neatly into two sides, pro and con. No matter what your topic, your argument will rarely be a simple matter of being for or against; in most cases, you'll want to qualify your claim — that it is true in certain circumstances, with certain conditions, with these limitations, and so on. Qualifying your claim shows that you're reasonable and also makes your topic more manageable by limiting it. The following questions can help you qualify your claim.

- *Can it be true in some cases?* For example, most high school students should be urged to graduate, but students who cannot succeed there should be allowed to drop out.

- *Can it be true at some times or under certain circumstances?* For instance, cell phones and computer monitors should be recycled, but only by licensed, domestic recyclers.

- *Can it be true for some groups or individuals?* For example, nearly everyone should follow a low-carb diet, but some people, such as diabetics, should avoid it.

SOME WORDS FOR QUALIFYING A CLAIM

sometimes	nearly	it seems/seemingly
rarely	usually	some
in some cases	more or less	perhaps
often	for the most part	possibly
routinely		

Drafting a thesis statement.   Once your claim is focused and appropriately qualified, it can form the core of your essay's **THESIS STATEMENT**, which announces your position and forecasts the path your argument will

273–75

follow. For example, here is the opening paragraph of an essay by the executive director of the National Congress of American Indians arguing that the remains of Native Americans should be treated with the same respect given to others. The author outlines the context of her argument and then presents her thesis (here, in italics):

> What if museums, universities and government agencies could put your dead relatives on display or keep them in boxes to be cut up and otherwise studied? What if you believed that the spirits of the dead could not rest until their human remains were placed in a sacred area? The ordinary American would say there ought to be a law — and there is, for ordinary Americans. *The problem for American Indians is that there are too many laws of the kind that make us the archeological property of the United States and too few of the kind that protect us from such insults.*
>
> —Susan Shown Harjo, "Last Rites for Indian Dead: Treating Remains Like Artifacts Is Intolerable"

Reasons. Your claim must be supported by reasons that your audience will accept. A reason can usually be linked to a claim with the word *because*:

CLAIM	+	*BECAUSE*	+	REASON
MP3 players harm society		*because*		they isolate users from other people.

Keep in mind that you likely have a further reason, a rule or principle that underlies the reason you link directly to your claim. In this argument, the underlying reason is that isolation from other people is bad. If your audience doesn't accept that principle, you may have to back it up with further reasons or evidence.

To come up with good reasons, start by stating your position and then answering the question *why?*

CLAIM: MP3 players harm society. *Why?*
REASON: (Because) They isolate users from other people. *Why?*
UNDERLYING REASON: Isolation from other people is bad.

As you can see, this exercise can continue indefinitely as the underlying reasons grow more and more general and abstract. You can do the same with other positions:

> **CLAIM:** Smoking should be banned. *Why?*
> **REASON:** (Because) It is harmful to smokers and also to nonsmokers.
> **UNDERLYING REASON:** People should be protected from harmful substances.

Evidence.   Evidence to support your reasons can come from various sources. In fact, you may need to use several kinds of evidence to persuade your audience that your claim is true. Some of the most common types of evidence include facts, statistics, examples, authorities, anecdotes, scenarios, case studies, textual evidence, and visuals.

Facts are ideas that are proven to be true. Facts can include observations or scholarly research (your own or someone else's), but they need to be accepted as true. If your audience accepts the facts you present, they can be powerful means of persuasion. For example, an essay on junk email offers these facts to demonstrate the seasonal nature of spam:

> The flow of spam is often seasonal. It slows in the spring, and then, in the month that technology specialists call "black September" — when hundreds of thousands of students return to college, many armed with new computers and access to fast Internet connections — the levels rise sharply.
>
> — Michael Specter, "Damn Spam"

Specter offers this fact with only a general reference to its origin ("technology specialists"), but given what most people know — or think they know — about college students, it rings true. A citation from a study published by a "technology specialist" would offer even greater credibility.

Statistics are numerical data, usually produced through research, surveys, or polls. Statistics should be relevant to your argument, as current as possible, accurate, and from a reliable source. An argument advocating that Americans should eat less meat presents these data to support the writer's contention that we eat far too much of it:

Americans are downing close to 200 pounds of meat, poultry, and fish per capita per year (dairy and eggs are separate, and hardly insignificant), an increase of 50 pounds per person from 50 years ago. We each consume something like 110 grams of protein a day, about twice the federal government's recommended allowance; of that, about 75 grams come from animal protein. (The recommended level is itself considered by many dietary experts to be higher than it needs to be.) It's likely that most of us would do just fine on around 30 grams of protein a day, virtually all of it from plant sources.

— Mark Bittman, "Rethinking the Meat-Guzzler"

Bittman's statistics demonstrate the extent to which Americans have increased their meat consumption over the last half-century, the proportion of our diets that comes from meat, and, by comparison, how much protein our bodies require—and summarize the heart of his argument in stark numeric terms.

Examples are specific instances that illustrate general statements. In a book on life after dark in Europe, a historian offers several examples to demonstrate his point that three hundred years ago, night—without artificial lighting—was treacherous:

Even sure-footed natives on a dark night could misjudge the lay of the land, stumbling into a ditch or off a precipice. In Aberdeenshire, a fifteen-year-old girl died in 1739 after straying from her customary path through a churchyard and tumbling into a newly dug grave. The Yorkshireman Arthur Jessop, returning from a neighbor's home on a cold December evening, fell into a stone pit after losing his bearings.

— A. Roger Ekirch, *At Day's Close: Night in Times Past*

Ekirch illustrates his point and makes it come alive for readers by citing two specific individuals' fates.

Authorities are experts on your subject. To be useful, authorities must be reputable, trustworthy, and qualified to address the subject. You should **EVALUATE** any authorities you consult carefully to be sure they have the credentials necessary for readers to take them seriously. When you cite

400–403 ●

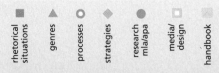

experts, you should clearly identify them and the origins of their authority in a **SIGNAL PHRASE,** as does the author of an argument that deforested
land can be reclaimed:

417–18

> Reed Funk, professor of plant biology at Rutgers University, believes
> that the vast areas of deforested land can be used to grow millions of
> genetically improved trees for food, mostly nuts, and for fuel. Funk
> sees nuts used to supplement meat as a source of high-quality protein
> in developing-country diets.
>
> —Lester R. Brown, *Plan B 2.0: Rescuing a Planet*
> *under Stress and a Civilization in Trouble*

Brown cites Funk, an expert on plant biology, to support his argument that
humans need to rethink the global economy in order to create a sustain-
able world. Without the information on Funk's credentials, though, readers would have no reason to take his proposal seriously.

Anecdotes are brief **NARRATIVES** that your audience will find believable and
that contribute directly to your argument. Anecdotes may come from your
personal experience or the experiences of others. In a speech almost two
years after Hurricane Katrina devastated New Orleans, then-presidential
candidate Barack Obama used an anecdote to personalize his criticism of
the assistance given to the city's poor:

343–51

> Yes, parts of New Orleans are coming back to life. But we also know
> that over 25,000 families are still living in small trailers; that thousands
> of homes sit empty and condemned; and that schools and hospitals
> and firehouses are shuttered. We know that even though the street-
> cars run, there are fewer passengers; that even though the parades
> sound their joyful noise, there is too much violence in the shadows.
>
> To confront these challenges we have to understand that Katrina
> may have battered these shores — but it also exposed silent storms that
> have ravaged parts of this city and our country for far too long. The
> storms of poverty and joblessness; inequality and injustice.
>
> When I was down in Houston visiting evacuees a few days after
> Katrina, I met a woman in the Reliant Center who had long known
> these storms in her life.

> She told me, "We had nothing before the hurricane. Now we got less than nothing."
>
> We had nothing before the hurricane. Now we got less than nothing. I think about her sometimes. I think about how America left her behind. And I wonder where she is today.
>
> America failed that woman long before that failure showed up on our television screens. We failed her again during Katrina. And—tragically—we are failing her for a third time. That needs to change. It's time for us to restore our trust with her; it's time for America to rebuild trust with the people of New Orleans and the Gulf Coast.
>
> —Barack Obama, "Rebuilding Trust with New Orleans"

Obama uses the anecdote about the woman he met at the Reliant Center to make specific and personal his claim that the federal government neglected its duty to rebuild New Orleans as well as to reduce poverty and increase employment more generally.

Scenarios are hypothetical situations. Like anecdotes, "what if" scenarios can help you describe the possible effects of particular actions or offer new ways of looking at a particular state of affairs. For example, a mathematician presents this light-hearted scenario about Santa Claus in a tongue-in-cheek argument that Christmas is (almost) pure magic:

> Let's assume that Santa only visits those who are children in the eyes of the law, that is, those under the age of 18. There are roughly 2 billion such individuals in the world. However, Santa started his annual activities long before diversity and equal opportunity became issues, and as a result he doesn't handle Muslim, Hindu, Jewish and Buddhist children. That reduces his workload significantly to a mere 15% of the total, namely 378 million. However, the crucial figure is not the number of children but the number of homes Santa has to visit. According to the most recent census data, the average size of a family in the world is 3.5 children per household. Thus, Santa has to visit 108,000,000 individual homes. (Of course, as everyone knows, Santa only visits good children, but we can surely assume that, on an average, at least one child of the 3.5 in each home meets that criterion.)
>
> —Keith Devlin, "The Mathematics of Christmas"

Devlin uses this scenario, as part of his mathematical analysis of Santa's yearly task, to help demonstrate that Christmas is indeed magical—because if you do the math, it's clear that Santa's task is physically impossible.

Case studies and observations feature detailed reporting about subject. Case studies are in-depth, systematic examinations of an occasion, a person, or a group. For example, in arguing that class differences exist in the United States, sociologist Gregory Mantsios presents studies of three "typical" Americans to show "enormous class differences" in their lifestyles.

Observations offer detailed descriptions of a subject. Here's an observation of the emergence of a desert stream that flows only at night:

> At about 5:30 water came out of the ground. It did not spew up, but slowly escaped into the surrounding sand and small rocks. The wet circle grew until water became visible. Then it bubbled out like a small fountain and the creek began.
>
> —Craig Childs, *The Secret Knowledge of Water*

Childs presents this and other observations in a book that argues (among other things) that even in harsh, arid deserts, water exists, and knowing where to find it can mean the difference between life and death.

Textual evidence includes QUOTATIONS, PARAPHRASES, and SUMMARIES. Usually, the relevance of textual evidence must be stated directly, as excerpts from a text may carry several potential meanings. For example, here is an excerpt from a student essay analyzing the function of the raft in *Huckleberry Finn* as "a platform on which the resolution of conflicts is made possible":

● 408–19

> [T]he scenes where Jim and Huck are in consensus on the raft contain the moments in which they are most relaxed. For instance, in chapter twelve of the novel, Huck, after escaping capture from Jackson's Island, calls the rafting life "solemn" and articulates their experience as living "pretty high" (Twain 75–76). Likewise, subsequent to escaping the unresolved feud between the Grangerfords and Shepherdsons in chapter eighteen, Huck is unquestionably at ease on the raft: "I was

powerful glad to get away from the feuds. . . . We said there warn't no home like a raft, after all. Other places do seem so cramped up and smothery, but a raft don't. You feel mighty free and easy and comfortable on a raft" (Twain 134).

— Dave Nichols, "'Less All Be Friends': Rafts as Negotiating Platforms in Twain's *Huckleberry Finn*"

Huck's own words support Nichols's claim that he can relax on a raft. Nichols strengthens his claim by quoting evidence from two separate pages, suggesting that Huck's opinion of rafts pervades the novel.

Visuals can be a useful way of presenting evidence. Remember, though, that charts, graphs, photos, drawings, and other **VISUAL TEXTS** seldom speak for themselves and thus must be explained in your text. Below, for example, is a photograph of a poster carried by demonstrators at the 2008 Beijing Summer Olympics, protesting China's treatment of Tibetans. If you were to use this photo in an essay, you would need to explain that the poster combines the image of a protester standing before a tank during the 1989 Tiananmen Square uprising with the Olympic logo, making clear to your readers that the protesters are likening China's treatment of Tibetans to its brutal actions in the past.

528–32 ▢

Choosing appropriate evidence. The kinds of evidence you provide to support your argument depends on your RHETORICAL SITUATION. If your purpose is, for example, to convince readers to accept the need for a proposed solution, you'd be likely to include facts, statistics, and anecdotes. If you're writing for an academic audience, you'd be less likely to rely on anecdotes, preferring authorities, textual evidence, statistics, and case studies instead. And even within academic communities different disciplines and genres may focus primarily on different kinds of evidence. If you're not sure what counts as appropriate evidence, ask your instructor for guidance.

Convincing Readers You're Trustworthy

For your argument to be convincing, you need to establish your own credibility with readers — to demonstrate your knowledge about your topic, to show that you and your readers share some common ground, and to show yourself to be evenhanded in the way you present your argument.

Building common ground. One important element of gaining readers' trust is to identify some common ground, some values you and your audience share. For example, to introduce a book arguing for the compatibility of science and religion, author Chet Raymo offers some common memories:

> Like most children, I was raised on miracles. Cows that jump over the moon; a jolly fat man that visits every house in the world in a single night; mice and ducks that talk; little engines that huff and puff and say, "I think I can"; geese that lay golden eggs. This lively exercise of credulity on the part of children is good practice for what follows — for believing in the miracle stories of traditional religion, yes, but also for the practice of poetry or science.
>
> — Chet Raymo, *Skeptics and True Believers: The Exhilarating Connection between Science and Religion*

Raymo presents childhood stories and myths that are part of many people's shared experiences to help readers find a connection between two realms that are often seen as opposed.

Incorporating other viewpoints. To show that you have carefully considered the viewpoints of others, including those who may agree or disagree with you, you should incorporate those viewpoints into your argument by acknowledging, accommodating, or refuting them.

Acknowledging other viewpoints. One essential part of establishing your credibility is to acknowledge that there are viewpoints different from yours and to represent them fairly and accurately. Rather than weakening your argument, acknowledging possible objections to your position shows that you've thought about and researched your topic thoroughly. For example, in an essay about his experience growing up homosexual, writer Andrew Sullivan acknowledges that not every young gay man or woman has the same experience:

> I should add that many young lesbians and homosexuals seem to have had a much easier time of it. For many, the question of sexual identity was not a critical factor in their life choices or vocation, or even a factor at all.
>
> —Andrew Sullivan, "What Is a Homosexual?"

Thus does Sullivan qualify his assertions, making his own stance appear to be reasonable.

Accommodating other viewpoints. You may be tempted to ignore views you don't agree with, but in fact it's important to acknowledge those views, to demonstrate that you are aware of them and have considered them carefully. You may find yourfself conceding that opposing views have some merit and qualifying your claim or even making them part of your own argument. See, for example, how a philosopher arguing that torture is sometimes "not merely permissible but morally mandatory" addresses a major objection to his position:

> The most powerful argument against using torture as a punishment or to secure confessions is that such practices disregard the rights of the individual. Well, if the individual is all that important—and he is—it is correspondingly important to protect the rights of individuals

threatened by terrorists. If life is so valuable that it must never be taken, the lives of the innocents must be saved even at the price of hurting the one who endangers them.

—Michael Levin, "The Case for Torture"

Levin folds his critics' argument into his own by acknowledging that the individual is indeed important and then asserting that if the life of one person is important, the lives of many people must be even more important.

Refuting other arguments. Often you may need to refute other arguments and make a case for why you believe they are wrong. Are the values underlying the argument questionable? Is the reasoning flawed? Is the evidence inadequate or faulty? For example, an essay arguing for the elimination of college athletics scholarships includes this refutation:

Some argue that eliminating athletics scholarships would deny opportunity and limit access for many students, most notably black athletes. The question is, access to what? The fields of competition or an opportunity to earn a meaningful degree? With the six-year graduation rates of black basketball players hovering in the high 30-percent range, and black football players in the high 40-percent range, despite years of "academic reform," earning an athletics scholarship under the current system is little more than a chance to play sports.

—John R. Gerdy, "For True Reform, Athletics Scholarships Must Go"

Gerdy bases his refutation on statistics showing that for more than half of African American college athletes, the opportunity to earn a degree by playing a sport is an illusion.

When you incorporate differing viewpoints, be careful to avoid the FALLACIES of attacking the person making the argument or refuting a competing position that no one seriously entertains. It is also important that you not distort or exaggerate opposing viewpoints. If *your* argument is to be persuasive, other arguments should be represented fairly.

◆ 296–98

Appealing to Readers' Emotions

Logic and facts, even when presented by someone reasonable and trust-worthy, may not be enough to persuade readers. Many successful arguments include an emotional component that appeals to readers' hearts as well as to their minds. Advertising often works by appealing to its audience's emotions, as in this paragraph from a Volvo ad:

> Choosing a car is about the comfort and safety of your passengers, most especially your children. That's why we ensure Volvo's safety research examines how we can make our cars safer for everyone who travels in them — from adults to teenagers, children to babies. Even those who aren't even born yet.
>
> —Volvo.com

This ad plays on the fear that children — or a pregnant mother — may be injured or killed in an automobile accident.

Keep in mind that emotional appeals can make readers feel as though they are being manipulated and, consequently, less likely to accept an argument. For most kinds of academic writing, use emotional appeals sparingly.

Checking for Fallacies

Fallacies are arguments that involve faulty reasoning. It's important to avoid fallacies in your writing because they often seem plausible but are usually unfair or inaccurate and make reasonable discussion difficult. Here are some of the most common fallacies:

- **Ad hominem** arguments attack someone's character rather than addressing the issues. (*Ad hominem* is Latin for "to the man.") It is an especially common fallacy in political discourse and elsewhere: "Jack Turner has no business talking about the way we run things in this city. He's lived here only five years and is just another flaky liberal." The length of time Turner has lived in the city has no bearing on the

worth of his argument; neither does his political stance, which his opponent characterizes unfairly.

- **Bandwagon appeals** argue that because others think or do something, we should, too. For example, an advertisement for a rifle association suggests that "67 percent of voters support laws permitting concealed weapons. You should, too." It assumes that readers want to be part of the group and implies that an opinion that is popular must be correct.

- **Begging the question** is a circular argument. It assumes as a given what is trying to be proved, essentially supporting an assertion with the assertion itself. Consider this statement: "Affirmative action can never be fair or just because you cannot remedy one injustice by committing another." This statement begs the question because to prove that affirmative action is unjust, it assumes that it is an injustice.

- **Either-or** arguments, also called *false dilemmas*, are oversimplifications. Either-or arguments assert that there can be only two possible positions on a complex issue. For example, "Those who oppose our actions in this war are enemies of freedom" inaccurately assumes that if someone opposes the war in question, he or she opposes freedom. In fact, people might have many other reasons for opposing the war.

- **False analogies** compare things that resemble each other in some ways but not in the most important respects. For example: "Trees pollute the air just as much as cars and trucks do." Although it's true that plants emit hydrocarbons, and hydrocarbons are a component of smog, they also produce oxygen, whereas motor vehicles emit gases that combine with hydrocarbons to form smog. Vehicles pollute the air; trees provide the air that vehicles' emissions pollute.

- **Faulty causality,** also known as *post hoc, ergo propter hoc* (Latin for "after this, therefore because of this"), assumes that because one event followed another, the first event caused the second—for example, "Legalizing same-sex marriage in Sweden led to an increase in the number of children born to unwed mothers." The statement contains no evidence to show that the first event caused the second. The birth rate could have been affected by many factors, and same-sex marriage may not even be among them.

- *Hasty generalizations* are conclusions based on insufficient or inappropriately qualified evidence. This summary of a research study is a good example: "Twenty randomly chosen residents of Brooklyn, New York, were asked whether they found graffiti tags offensive; fourteen said yes, five said no, and one had no opinion. Therefore, 70 percent of Brooklyn residents find tagging offensive." In Brooklyn, a part of New York City with a population of over two million, twenty residents is far too small a group from which to draw meaningful conclusions. To be able to generalize, the researcher would have had to survey a much greater percentage of Brooklyn's population.

- *Slippery slope* arguments assert that one event will inevitably lead to another, often cataclysmic event without presenting evidence that such a chain of causes and effects will in fact take place. Here's an example: "If the state legislature passes this 2 percent tax increase, it won't be long before all the corporations in the state move to other states and leave thousands unemployed." According to this argument, if taxes are raised, the state's economy will be ruined — not a likely scenario, given the size of the proposed increase.

Considering the Rhetorical Situation

To argue effectively, you need to think about the message that you want to articulate, the audience you want to persuade, the effect of your stance, and the larger context you are writing in.

3–4	**PURPOSE**	What do you want your audience to do? To think something? To act? To change their minds? To consider alternative views? To accept your position as plausible? To see that you have thought carefully about an issue and researched it appropriately?
5–8	**AUDIENCE**	Who is your intended audience? What do they likely know and believe about your topic? How personal is it for them? To what extent are they likely to agree or disagree with you? Why? What common ground can you find with them?

How will you incorporate other positions? What kind of evidence are they likely to accept?

GENRE   What genre will help you achieve your purpose? A position paper? An evaluation? A review? A proposal? An analysis?   ▮ 9–11

STANCE   How do you want your audience to perceive you? As an authority on your topic? As someone much like them? As calm? Reasonable? Impassioned or angry? Something else? What's your attitude toward your topic, and why? What argument strategies will help you to convey that stance?   ▮ 12–14

MEDIA / DESIGN   What media will you use, and how do your media affect your argument? If you're writing on paper, does your argument call for photos or charts? If you're giving an oral presentation, should you put your reasons and support on slides? If you're writing on the Web, should you add links to sites representing other positions or containing evidence that supports your position?   ▮ 15–17

33 Classifying and Dividing

Classification and division are ways of organizing information: various pieces of information about a topic may be classified according to their similarities, or a single topic may be divided into parts. We might classify different kinds of flowers as annuals or perennials, for example, and classify the perennials further as dahlias, daisies, roses, and peonies. We might also divide a flower garden into distinct areas: for herbs, flowers, and vegetables. Writers often use classification and division as ways of developing and organizing material. This book, for instance, classifies comparison, definition, description, and several other common ways of thinking and writing as strategies. It divides the information it provides about writing into seven parts: "Rhetorical Situations," "Genres," "Processes," and so on. Each part further divides its material into various chapters. Even if you never write a book, you will have occasion to classify and divide material

116–24 ▲
38–58

in **ANNOTATED BIBLIOGRAPHIES** and essays **ANALYZING TEXTS** and other kinds of writing. This chapter offers advice for classifying and dividing information for various writing purposes—and in a way that suits your own rhetorical situation.

Classifying

When we classify something, we group it with similar things. A linguist would classify French and Spanish and Italian as Romance languages, for example—and Russian, Polish, and Bulgarian as Slavic languages. In a hilarious (if totally phony) news story from *The Onion* about a church bake

rhetorical situations · genres · processes · strategies · research mla/apa · media/ design · handbook sale, the writer classifies the activities observed there as examples of the seven deadly sins:

> GADSDEN, AL — The seven deadly sins — avarice, sloth, envy, lust, gluttony, pride, and wrath — were all committed Sunday during the twice-annual bake sale at St. Mary's of the Immaculate Conception Church.
>
> — *The Onion,* "All Seven Deadly Sins Committed at Church Bake Sale"

The article goes on to categorize the participants' behavior in terms of the sins, describing one parishioner who commits the sin of pride by bragging about her cookies, others who commit the sin of envy by envying the popularity of the prideful parishioner's baked goods (the consumption of which leads to the sin of gluttony). In all, the article notes, "347 individual acts of sin were committed at the bake sale," and every one of them can be classified as one of the seven deadly sins.

Dividing

As a writing strategy, division is a way of breaking something into parts — and a way of making the information easy for readers to follow and understand. See how this example about children's ways of nagging divides their tactics into seven categories:

> James U. McNeal, a professor of marketing at Texas A&M University, is considered America's leading authority on marketing to children. In his book *Kids as Customers* (1992), McNeal provides marketers with a thorough analysis of "children's requesting styles and appeals." He [divides] juvenile nagging tactics into seven major categories. A *pleading* nag is one accompanied by repetitions of words like "please" or "mom, mom, mom." A *persistent* nag involves constant requests for the coveted product and may include the phrase "I'm gonna ask just one more time." *Forceful* nags are extremely pushy and may include subtle threats, like "Well, then, I'll go and ask Dad." *Demonstrative* nags are the most high risk, often characterized by full-blown tantrums in public places, breath

holding, tears, a refusal to leave the store. *Sugar-coated* nags promise affection in return for a purchase and may rely on seemingly heartfelt declarations, like "You're the best dad in the world." *Threatening* nags are youthful forms of blackmail, vows of eternal hatred and of running away if something isn't bought. *Pity* nags claim the child will be heartbroken, teased, or socially stunted if the parent refuses to buy a certain item. "All of these appeals and styles may be used in combination," McNeal's research has discovered, "but kids tend to stick to one or two of each that prove most effective . . . for their own parents."

—Eric Schlosser, *Fast Food Nation:*
The Dark Side of the All-American Meal

Here the writer announces the division scheme of "seven major categories." Then he names each tactic and describes how it works. And notice the italics: each nagging tactic is italicized, making it easy to recognize and follow. Take away the italics, and the divisions would be less visible.

Creating Clear and Distinct Categories

When you classify or divide, you need to create clear and distinct categories. If you're writing about music, you might divide it on the basis of the genre (hip-hop, rock, classical, gospel), artist (male or female, group or solo), or instruments (violins, trumpets, bongos, guitars). These categories must be distinct, so that no information overlaps or fits into more than one category, and they must include every member of the group you're discussing. The simpler the criteria for selecting the categories, the better. The nagging categories in the example from *Fast Food Nation* are based on only one criterion: a child's verbal behavior.

Highlight your categories. Sometimes you may want to highlight your categories visually to make them easier to follow. Eric Schlosser does that by italicizing each category: the *pleading* nag, the *persistent* nag, the *forceful* nag, and so on. Other **DESIGN** elements—bulleted lists, pie charts, tables, images—might also prove useful.

524–32 ▫

See, for instance, how the humorist Dave Barry uses a two-column list to show two categories of males — "men" and "guys" — in his *Complete Guide to Guys*:

Men	Guys
Vince Lombardi	Joe Namath
Oliver North	Gilligan
Hemingway	Gary Larson
Columbus	Whichever astronaut hit the first golf ball on the moon
Superman	Bart Simpson
Doberman pinschers	Labrador retrievers
Abbott	Costello
Captain Ahab	Captain Kangaroo
Satan	Snidely Whiplash
The pope	Willard Scott
Germany	Italy
Geraldo	Katie Couric

—Dave Barry, *Dave Barry's Complete Guide to Guys: A Fairly Short Book*

Sometimes you might show categories visually, like the illustration on the following page from a news story about the many new varieties of Oreo cookies. In the article, the reporter David Barboza classifies Oreos with words:

There is the Double Delight Oreo . . . , the Uh Oh Oreo (vanilla cookie with chocolate filling), Oreo Cookie Barz, Football Oreos, Oreos Cookies and Creme Pie, Oreos in Kraft Lunchables for kids, and Oreo cookies with a variety of cream fillings (mint, chocolate, coffee) and sizes (six-pack, twelve-pack, snack pack, and more).

**DOUBLE DELIGHT
MINT 'N CREME**
Introduced in 2003

**DOUBLE DELIGHT
PEANUT BUTTER &
CHOCOLATE**
2003

**DOUBLE DELIGHT
COFFEE 'N CREME**
2003

UH OH OREO
(Vanilla cookie, chocolate filling)
2003

CHOCOLATE CREME OREO
2001

FOOTBALL OREO
(Football design on biscuit)
Seasonal

DOUBLE STUFF
1974

ORIGINAL
1912

Piling on the Cookies

In the Oreo's first eight decades, Nabisco tried only a handful of variations on the original. But in recent years, it has stretched the line to more than two dozen by varying the size, the filling, the biscuit recipe — nearly everything but the brand name. Here are some examples now on store shelves.

—David Barboza, "Permutations Push Oreo Far Beyond Cookie Aisle"

The illustration, for an article that shows Oreos to be a "hyperevolving, perpetually repackaged, category-migrating" cookie, makes that classification easy to see—and gets our attention in the first place.

Considering the Rhetorical Situation

As a writer or speaker, you need to think about the message that you want to articulate, the audience you want to reach, and the larger context you are writing in.

PURPOSE	Your purpose for writing will affect how you classify or divide information. Dave Barry classifies males as "men" and "guys" to get a laugh, whereas J. Crew might divide sweaters into cashmere, wool, and cotton to help shoppers find and buy things from their website.	3–4
AUDIENCE	What audience do you want to reach, and will classifying or dividing your material help them follow your discussion?	5–8
GENRE	Does your genre call for you to categorize or divide information? A long report might need to be divided into sections, for instance.	9–11
STANCE	Your stance may affect the way you classify information. Dave Barry classifies males as "men" and "guys" to reflect a humorist's stance; if he were a psychologist, he might categorize them as "Oedipal," "hormonal," and "libidinal."	12–14
MEDIA / DESIGN	You can classify or divide in paragraph form, but sometimes a pie chart or list will show the categories better.	15–17

IF YOU NEED MORE HELP

See also **CLUSTERING, CUBING,** and **LOOPING,** three methods of generating ideas that can be especially helpful for classifying material. And see all the **PROCESSES** chapters for guidelines on drafting, revising, and so on if you need to write a classification essay.

220–22
209–58

34 Comparing and Contrasting

Comparing things looks at their similarities; contrasting them focuses on their differences. It's a kind of thinking that comes naturally and that we do constantly — for example, comparing Houston with Dallas, PCs with Macs, or three paintings by Renoir. And once we start comparing, we generally find ourselves contrasting — Houston and Dallas have differences as well as similarities.

As a student, you'll often be asked to compare and contrast paintings or poems or other things. As a writer, you'll have cause to compare and contrast in most kinds of writing. In a **PROPOSAL,** for instance, you will need to compare your solution with other possible solutions; or in an **EVALUATION,** such as a movie review, you might contrast the film you're reviewing with some other film. This chapter offers advice on ways of comparing and contrasting things for various writing purposes and for your own rhetorical situations.

Most of the time, we compare obviously similar things: cars we might purchase, three competing political philosophies, two versions of a film. Occasionally, however, we might compare things that are less obviously similar. See how John McMurtry, an ex–football player, compares football with war in an essay arguing that the attraction football holds for spectators is based in part on its potential for violence and injury:

> The family resemblance between football and war is, indeed, striking. Their languages are similar: "field general," "long bomb," "blitz," "take a shot," "front line," "pursuit," "good hit," "the draft," and so on. Their principles and practices are alike: mass hysteria, the art of intimidation, absolute command and total obedience, territorial aggression, censorship, inflated insignia and propaganda, blackboard maneuvers and strategies, drills, uniforms, marching bands, and train-

171–79

125–32

rhetorical situations

genres

processes

strategies

research mla/apa

media/ design

handbook

ing camps. And the virtues they celebrate are almost identical: hyper-aggressiveness, coolness under fire, and suicidal bravery.

— John McMurtry, "Kill 'Em! Crush 'Em! Eat 'Em Raw!"

McMurtry's comparison helps focus readers' attention on what he's arguing about football in part because it's somewhat unexpected. But the more unlikely the comparison, the more you might be accused of comparing apples and oranges. It's important, therefore, that the things we compare be legitimately compared — as is the case in the following comparison of the health of the world's richest and poorest people:

World Health Organization (WHO) data indicate that roughly 1.2 billion people are undernourished, underweight, and often hungry. At the same time, roughly 1.2 billion people are overnourished and overweight, most of them suffering from excessive caloric intake and exercise deprivation. So while 1 billion people worry whether they will eat, another billion should worry about eating too much.

Disease patterns also reflect the widening gap. The billion poorest suffer mostly from infectious diseases — malaria, tuberculosis, dysentery, and AIDS. Malnutrition leaves infants and small children even more vulnerable to such infectious diseases. Unsafe drinking water takes a heavier toll on those with hunger-weakened immune systems, resulting in millions of fatalities each year. In contrast, among the billion at the top of the global economic scale, it is diseases related to aging and lifestyle excesses, including obesity, smoking, diets rich in fat and sugar, and exercise deprivation, that cause most deaths.

— Lester R. Brown, *Plan B 2.0: Rescuing a Planet Under Stress and a Civilization in Trouble*

While the two groups of roughly a billion people each undoubtedly have similarities, this selection from a book arguing for global action on the environment focuses on the stark contrasts.

Two Ways of Comparing and Contrasting

Comparisons and contrasts may be organized in two basic ways: block and point by point.

The block method. One way is to discuss separately each item you're comparing, giving all the information about one item and then all the information about the next item. A report on Seattle and Vancouver, for example, compares the firearm regulations in each city using a paragraph about Seattle and then a paragraph about Vancouver:

> Although similar in many ways, Seattle and Vancouver differ markedly in their approaches to the regulation of firearms. In Seattle, handguns may be purchased legally for self-defense in the street or at home. After a thirty-day waiting period, a permit can be obtained to carry a handgun as a concealed weapon. The recreational use of handguns is minimally restricted.
>
> In Vancouver, self-defense is not considered a valid or legal reason to purchase a handgun. Concealed weapons are not permitted. Recreational uses of handguns (such as target shooting and collecting) are regulated by the province, and the purchase of a handgun requires a restricted-weapons permit. A permit to carry a weapon must also be obtained in order to transport a handgun, and these weapons can be discharged only at a licensed shooting club. Handguns can be transported by car, but only if they are stored in the trunk in a locked box.
>
> —John Henry Sloan et al., "Handgun Regulations, Crime, Assaults, and Homicide: A Tale of Two Cities"

The point-by-point method. The other way to compare things is to focus on specific points of comparison. A later part of the Seattle-Vancouver study compares the two cities' gun laws and how they're enforced, discussing each point one at a time. (We've underlined each point.) The authors discuss one point, comparing the two cities; then they go on to the next point, again comparing the cities:

> Although they differ in their approach to firearm regulations, both cities aggressively enforce existing gun laws and regulations, and convictions for gun-related offenses carry similar penalties. For example, <u>the commission of a class A felony (such as murder or robbery) with a firearm</u> in Washington State adds a minimum of two years of confinement to the sentence for the felony. In the province of British Columbia, the same offense generally results in one to fourteen years of imprisonment in addition to the felony sentence. <u>Similar percent-</u>

ages of homicides in both communities eventually lead to arrest and police charges. In Washington, under the Sentencing Reform Act of 1981, murder in the first degree carries a minimum sentence of twenty years of confinement. In British Columbia, first-degree murder carries a minimum sentence of twenty-five years, with a possible judicial parole review after fifteen years. Capital punishment was abolished in Canada during the 1970s. In Washington State, the death penalty may be invoked in cases of aggravated first-degree murder, but no one has been executed since 1963.

Using Graphs and Images to Present Comparisons

Some comparisons can be easier to understand if they're presented visually, as a **CHART**, **GRAPH**, or **ILLUSTRATION**. See how this chart shows comparative information about Vancouver and Seattle that can be easily understood at a glance and clearly categorized. It would be possible to show the same material in paragraph form, but it's much easier to see and read in this chart:

528–32

Seattle and Vancouver: Basic Demographic Information	Seattle, Washington	Vancouver, British Columbia
Population (1980)	493,846	430,826
Unemployment rate	5.8%	6.0%
High-school graduates	79.0%	66.0%
Median household income (U.S. dollars)	$16,254	$16,681

— John Henry Sloan et al., "Handgun Regulations, Crime, Assaults, and Homicide: A Tale of Two Cities"

The following bar graph, from an economics textbook, compares the incomes of various professions in the United States, both with one another and with the average U.S. income (defined as 100 percent). Again, it would be possible to write out this information in a paragraph—but it is much easier to understand it this way:

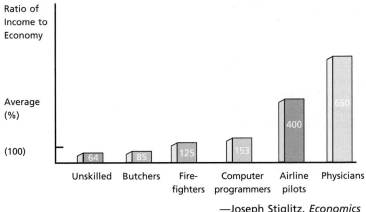

Ratio of Income to Economy

Average (%)

(100)

64 — Unskilled
85 — Butchers
125 — Fire-fighters
153 — Computer programmers
400 — Airline pilots
660 — Physicians

—Joseph Stiglitz, *Economics*

Sometimes photographs can make a comparison. The two photos below show a woman before and after she had her hair dyed. The caption suggests that the story is more complicated than the photos alone can tell, however; for the full story, we need words.

"GO BLONDE! 'I tried it before and it came out orange!' "

—iVillage.com

rhetorical situations
genres
processes
strategies
research mla/apa
media/ design
handbook

Using Figurative Language to Make Comparisons

Another way we make comparisons is with figurative language: words and phrases used in a nonliteral way to help readers see a point. Three kinds of figurative language that make comparisons are similes, metaphors, and analogies. When Robert Burns wrote that his love was "like a red, red rose," he was comparing his love with a rose and evoking an image—in this case, a simile—that helps us understand his feelings for her. A simile makes a comparison using *like* or *as*. In the following example, from an article in the food section of the *New York Times*, a restaurant critic uses several similes (underlined) to help us visualize an unusual food dish:

> Once upon a time, possibly at a lodge in Wyoming, possibly at a butcher shop in Maurice, Louisiana, or maybe even at a plantation in South Carolina, an enterprising cook decided to take a boned chicken, a boned duck, and a boned turkey, stuff them one inside the other <u>like Russian dolls</u>, and roast them. He called his masterpiece turducken. . . .
>
> A well-prepared turducken is a marvelous treat, a free-form poultry terrine layered with flavorful stuffing and moistened with duck fat. When it's assembled, it looks <u>like a turkey</u> and it roasts <u>like a turkey</u>, but when you go to carve it, you can slice through it <u>like a loaf of bread</u>. In each slice you get a little bit of everything: white meat from the breast; dark meat from the legs, duck, carrots, bits of sausage, bread, herbs, juices, and chicken, too.
>
> —Amanda Hesser, "Turkey Finds Its Inner Duck (and Chicken)"

Metaphors make comparisons without such connecting words as *like* or *as*. See how desert ecologist Craig Childs uses a metaphor to help us understand the nature of water during a flood in the Grand Canyon:

> Water splashed off the desert and ran all over the surface, looking for the quickest way down. It was too swift for the ground to absorb. When water flows like this, it will not be clean tap water. It will be <u>a gravy of debris</u>, snatching everything it finds.
>
> —Craig Childs, *The Secret Knowledge of Water*

Calling the water "a gravy of debris" allows us to see the murky liquid as it streams through the canyon.

Analogies are extended similes or metaphors that compare something unfamiliar with something more familiar. Arguing that corporations should not patent parts of DNA whose function isn't yet clear, a genetics professor uses the familiar image of a library to explain an unfamiliar concept:

> It's like having a library of books and randomly tearing pages out. You may know which books the pages came from but that doesn't tell you much about them.
>
> —Peter Goodfellow, quoted in John Vidal and John Carvel, "Lambs to the Gene Market"

Sometimes analogies are used for humorous effect as well as to make a point, as in this passage from a critique of history textbooks:

> Another history text—this one for fifth grade—begins with the story of how Henry B. Gonzalez, who is a member of Congress from Texas, learned about his own nationality. When he was ten years old, his teacher told him he was an American because he was born in the United States. His grandmother, however, said, "The cat was born in the oven. Does that make him bread?"
>
> —Frances FitzGerald, *America Revised: History Schoolbooks in the Twentieth Century*

The grandmother's question shows how an intentionally ridiculous analogy can be a source of humor—and can make a point memorably.

Considering the Rhetorical Situation

As a writer or speaker, you need to think about the message that you want to articulate, the audience you want to reach, and the larger context you are writing in.

3–4 ■

PURPOSE Sometimes your purpose for writing will be to compare two or more things. Other times, you may want to compare several things for some other purpose—to compare your views with those of others in an argument essay, or to compare one text with another as you analyze them.

AUDIENCE Who is your audience, and will comparing your topic with a more familiar one help them to follow your discussion? 5–8

GENRE Does your genre require you to compare something? Evaluations often include comparisons—one book to another in a review, or ten different cell phones in *Consumer Reports*. 9–11

STANCE Your stance may affect any comparisons you make. How you compare two things—evenhandedly, or clearly favoring one over the other, for example—will reflect your stance. 12–14

MEDIA / DESIGN Some things you will want to compare with words alone (lines from two poems, for instance), but sometimes you may wish to make comparisons visually (two images juxtaposed on a page, or several numbers plotted on a line graph). 15–17

IF YOU NEED MORE HELP

See **LOOPING** and **CUBING,** two methods of generating ideas that can be especially helpful for comparing and contrasting. If you're writing an essay whose purpose is to compare two or more things, see also the **PROCESSES** chapters for help drafting, revising, and so on. 220–22
209–58

35 Defining

Defining something says what it is — and what it is not. A terrier, for example, is a kind of dog. A fox terrier is a small dog now generally kept as a pet but once used by hunters to dig for foxes. Happiness is a jelly doughnut, at least according to Homer Simpson. All of those are definitions. As writers, we need to define any terms our readers may not know. And sometimes you'll want to stipulate your own definition of a word in order to set the terms of an **ARGUMENT** — as Homer Simpson does with a definition that's not found in any dictionary. This chapter details strategies for using definitions in your writing to suit your own rhetorical situations.

283–99

Formal Definitions

Sometimes to make sure readers understand you, you will need to provide a formal definition. If you are using a technical term that readers are unlikely to know or if you are using a term in a specific way, you need to say then and there what the word means. The word *mutual*, for example, has several dictionary meanings:

> mu•tu•al . . .
>
> **1a:** directed by each toward the other or the others <*mutual* affection> **b:** having the same feelings one for the other <they had long been *mutual* enemies> **c:** shared in common <enjoying their *mutual* hobby> **d:** joint
>
> **2:** characterized by intimacy
>
> **3:** of or relating to a plan whereby the members of an organization share in the profits and expenses; *specifically*: of, relating to, or taking the form of an insurance method in which the policyholders constitute the members of the insuring company
>
> —Merriam-Webster.com

314

rhetorical situations

genres

processes

strategies

research mla/apa

media/ design

handbook

The first two meanings are commonly understood and probably require no definition. But if you were to use *mutual* in the third sense, it might—depending on your audience. A general audience would probably need the definition; an audience from the insurance industry would not. A website that gives basic financial advice to an audience of non-specialists, for instance, offers a specific definition of the term *mutual fund*:

> *Mutual funds* are financial intermediaries. They are companies set up to receive your money and then, having received it, to make investments with the money.
>
> —Bill Barker, "A Grand, Comprehensive
> Overview to Mutual Funds Investing"

But even writers in specialized fields routinely provide formal definitions to make sure their readers understand the way they are using certain words. See how two writers define the word *stock* as it pertains to their respective (and very different) fields:

> Stocks are the basis for sauces and soups and important flavoring agents for braises. Admittedly, stock making is time consuming, but the extra effort yields great dividends.
>
> —Tom Colicchio, *Think Like a Chef*

> Want to own part of a business without having to show up at its office every day? Or ever? Stock is the vehicle of choice for those who do. Dating back to the Dutch mutual stock corporations of the sixteenth century, the modern stock market exists as a way for entrepreneurs to finance businesses using money collected from investors. In return for ponying up the dough to finance the company, the investor becomes a part owner of the company. That ownership is represented by stock—specialized financial "securities," or financial instruments, that are "secured" by a claim on the assets and profits of a company.
>
> —The Motley Fool, "Investing Basics: Stocks"

To write a formal definition

- Use words that readers are likely to be familiar with.
- Don't use the word being defined in the definition.

- Begin with the word being defined; include the general category to which the term belongs and the attributes that make it different from the others in that category.

For example:

Term	General Category	Distinguishing Attributes
Stock is	a specialized financial "security"	that is "secured" by a claim.
Photosynthesis is	a process	by which plants use sunlight to create energy.
Astronomers are	scientists	who study celestial objects and phenomena.
Adam Sandler,	a comedian,	has starred in several movies, including *Punch-Drunk Love* and *Click.*

Note that the category and distinguishing attributes cannot be stated too broadly; if they were, the definition would be too vague to be useful. It wouldn't be helpful in most circumstances, for example, to say, "Adam Sandler is a man who has acted" or "Photosynthesis is something having to do with plants."

Extended Definitions

Sometimes you need to provide a more detailed definition. Extended definitions may be several sentences long or several paragraphs long and may include pictures or diagrams. Sometimes an entire essay is devoted to defining a difficult or important concept. Here is one writer's extended definition of stem cells:

> By definition, a stem cell is an unspecialized cell that has the ability to divide and renew itself. Under certain conditions, it can generate large numbers of daughter cells and these go on to mature into cells with special functions, such as beating heart muscle or new bone to heal a fracture.

rhetorical situations

genres

processes

strategies

research mla/apa

media/ design

handbook

Stem cells exist naturally in the body. They're in bone marrow and, although rare, in the blood stream. Stem cells also exist in other tissues and organs, such as the liver, pancreas, brain, and maybe even the heart.

Currently, stem cells come from three sources: blastocysts, which are cells isolated from the inner cell mass of a three-to-five-day-old embryo grown in a petri dish in a lab, also called embryonic stem cells; cord blood cells, which are isolated from blood taken from an umbilical cord saved immediately after birth; and adult stem cells, which are collected from a person's own tissues.

— "The Miracle of Stem Cells," *Cleveland Clinic Magazine*

That definition includes a description of the distinguishing features of stem cells and tells where they are found and where they come from. We can assume that it's written for a general audience, one that doesn't know anything about stem cells.

Abstract concepts often require extended definitions because by nature they are more complicated to define. There are many ways of writing an extended definition, depending in part on the term being defined and on your audience and purpose. The following examples show some of the methods that can be used for composing extended definitions of *democracy*.

Explore the word's origins.   Where did the word come from? When did it first come into use? In the following example, from an essay considering what democracy means in the twenty-first century, the writer started by looking at the word's first known use in English. Though it's from an essay written for a first-year writing course and thus for a fairly general audience, it's a definition that might pique any audience's interest:

According to the *Oxford English Dictionary*, the term *democracy* first appeared in English in a thirteenth-century translation of Aristotle's works — specifically, in his *Politics*, where he stated that the "underlying principle of democracy is freedom" and that "it is customary to say that only in democracies do men have a share in freedom, for that is what every democracy makes its aim." By the sixteenth century, the word was used much as it is now. One writer in 1586, for instance, defined it in this way: "where free and poore men being the greater number, are lords of the estate."

—Susanna Mejía, "What Does Democracy Mean Now?"

Here's another example, this one written for a scholarly audience, from an essay about women, participation, democracy, and the information age:

> The very word *citizenship* carries with it a connotation of place, a "citizen" being, literally, the inhabitant of a city. Over the years the word has, of course, accumulated a number of associated meanings . . . and the word has come to stand in for such concepts as participation, equality, and democracy. The fact that the concept of locality is deeply embedded in the word *citizen* suggests that it is also fundamental to our current understanding of these other, more apparently abstract words.
>
> In Western thought, the concepts of citizenship, equality, and democracy are closely interlinked and can be traced back to a common source, in Athens in the fifth century B.C. Perhaps it is no accident that it was the same culture which also gave us, in its theater, the concept of the unity of time and space. The Greek city-state has been represented for centuries as the ideal model of democracy, with free and equal access for all citizens to decision making. Leaving aside, for the moment, the question of who was included, and who excluded from this notion of citizenship, we can see that the sense of place is fundamental to this model. Entitlement to participate in the democratic process is circumscribed by geography; it is the inhabitants of the geographical entity of the city-state, precisely defined and bounded, who have the rights to citizenship. Those who are not defined as inhabitants of that specific city-state are explicitly excluded, although, of course, they may have the right to citizenship elsewhere.
>
> —Ursula Huws, "Women, Participation, and
> Democracy in the Information Society"

Provide details. What are its characteristics? What is it made of? See how a historian explores the basic characteristics of democracy in a book written for an audience of historians:

> As a historian I am naturally disposed to be satisfied with the meaning which, in the history of politics, men have commonly attributed to the word—a meaning, needless to say, which derives partly from the experience and partly from the aspirations of mankind. So regarded, the term *democracy* refers primarily to a form of government, and it has always meant government by the many as opposed to government

by the one — government by the people as opposed to government by a tyrant, a dictator, or an absolute monarch. . . . Since the Greeks first used the term, the essential test of democratic government has always been this: the source of political authority must be and remain in the people and not in the ruler. A democratic government has always meant one in which the citizens, or a sufficient number of them to represent more or less effectively the common will, freely act from time to time, and according to established forms, to appoint or recall the magistrates and to enact or revoke the laws by which the community is governed.

—Carl Becker, *Modern Democracy*

Compare it with other words. How is this concept like other similar things? How does it differ? What is it *not* like? **COMPARE AND CONTRAST** it. See how a political science textbook defines a *majoritarian democracy* by comparing its characteristics with those of a *consensual democracy*:

306–13

A majoritarian democracy is one

1. having only two major political parties, not many
2. having an electoral system that requires a bare majority to elect one clear winner in an election, as opposed to a proportional electoral system that distributes seats to political parties according to the rough share of votes received in the election
3. a strong executive (president or prime minister) and cabinet that together are largely independent of the legislature when it comes to exercising the executive's constitutional duties, in contrast to an executive and cabinet that are politically controlled by the parties in the legislature and therefore unable to exercise much influence when proposing policy initiatives.

—Benjamin Ginsberg, Theodore J. Lowi, and Margaret Weir,
We the People: An Introduction to American Politics

And here's an example in which democracy is contrasted with various other forms of governments of the past:

Caesar's power derived from a popular mandate, conveyed through established republican forms, but that did not make his government any the less a dictatorship. Napoleon called his government a demo-cratic republic, but no one, least of all Napoleon himself, doubted that he had destroyed the last vestiges of the democratic republic.

—Carl Becker, *Modern Democracy*

Give examples. See how the essayist E. B. White defines democracy by giving some everyday examples of considerate behavior, humility, and civic participation—all things he suggests constitute democracy:

It is the line that forms on the right. It is the don't in "don't shove." It is the hole in the stuffed shirt through which the sawdust slowly trickles; it is the dent in the high hat. Democracy is the recurrent sus-picion that more than half of the people are right more than half of the time. . . . Democracy is a letter to the editor.

—E. B. White, "Democracy"

White's definition is elegant because he uses examples that his readers will know. His characteristics—metaphors, really—define democracy not as a conceptual way of governing but as an everyday part of American life.

300–305 ◆
Classify it. Often it is useful to divide or **CLASSIFY** a term. The ways in which democracy unfolds are complex enough to warrant entire text-books, of course, but the following definition, from a political science textbook, divides democracy into two kinds, representative and direct:

A system of government that gives citizens a regular opportunity to elect the top government officials is usually called a representative democracy or republic. A system that permits citizens to vote directly on laws and policies is often called a direct democracy. At the national level, America is a representative democracy in which citizens select government officials but do not vote on legislation. Some states, however, have provisions for direct legislation through popular refer-endum. For example, California voters in 1995 decided to bar undocu-mented immigrants from receiving some state services.

—Benjamin Ginsberg, Theodore J. Lowi, and Margaret Weir,
We the People: An Introduction to American Politics

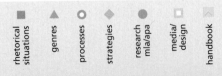

Stipulative Definitions

Sometimes a writer will stipulate a certain definition, essentially saying, "This is how I'm defining x." Such definitions are not usually found in a dictionary—and at the same time are central to the argument the writer is making. Here is one example, from an essay by Toni Morrison. Describing a scene from a film in which a newly arrived Greek immigrant, working as a shoe shiner in Grand Central Terminal, chases away an African American competitor, Morrison calls the scene an example of "race talk," a concept she then goes on to define:

> This is race talk, the explicit insertion into everyday life of racial signs and symbols that have no meaning other than pressing African Americans to the lowest level of the racial hierarchy. Popular culture, shaped by film, theater, advertising, the press, television, and literature, is heavily engaged in race talk. It participates freely in this most enduring and efficient rite of passage into American culture: negative appraisals of the native-born black population. Only when the lesson of racial estrangement is learned is assimilation complete. Whatever the lived experience of immigrants with African Americans—pleasant, beneficial, or bruising—the rhetorical experience renders blacks as noncitizens, already discredited outlaws.
>
> All immigrants fight for jobs and space, and who is there to fight but those who have both? As in the fishing ground struggle between Texas and Vietnamese shrimpers, they displace what and whom they can. Although U.S. history is awash in labor battles, political fights and property wars among all religious and ethnic groups, their struggles are persistently framed as struggles between recent arrivals and blacks. In race talk the move into mainstream America always means buying into the notion of American blacks as the real aliens. Whatever the ethnicity or nationality of the immigrant, his nemesis is understood to be African American.
>
> —Toni Morrison, "On the Backs of Blacks"

The following example is from a book review of Nancy L. Rosenblum's *Membership and Morals: The Personal Uses of Pluralism in America*, published in the *American Prospect*, a magazine for readers interested in political analysis. In it a Stanford law professor outlines a definition of "the democracy of everyday life":

> Democracy, in this understanding of it, means simply treating people as equals, disregarding social standing, avoiding attitudes of either deference or superiority, making allowances for others' weaknesses, and resisting the temptation to respond to perceived slights. It also means protesting everyday instances of arbitrariness and unfairness—from the rudeness of the bakery clerk to the sexism of the car dealer or the racism of those who vandalize the home of the first black neighbors on the block.
>
> —Kathleen M. Sullivan, "Defining Democracy Down"

Considering the Rhetorical Situation

As a writer or speaker, you need to think about the message that you want to articulate, the audience you want to reach, and the larger context you are writing in.

3–4   **PURPOSE**   Your purpose for writing will affect any definitions you include. Would writing an extended definition help you explain something? Would stipulating definitions of key terms help you shape an argument? Could an offbeat definition help you entertain your readers?

5–8   **AUDIENCE**   What audience do you want to reach, and are there any terms your readers are unlikely to know? Are there terms they might understand differently from the way you're defining them?

9–11   **GENRE**   Does your genre require you to define terms? Chances are that if you're reporting information you'll need to define some terms, and some arguments rest on the way you define key terms.

12–14   **STANCE**   What is your stance, and do you need to define key terms to show that stance clearly? How you define "fetus," for example, is likely to reveal your stance on abortion.

MEDIA / DESIGN   Your medium will affect the form your definitions take. In a print text, you will need to define terms in your text; if you're giving a speech or presentation, you might also provide images of important terms and their definitions. In an electronic text, you may be able to define terms by linking to an online dictionary definition.

15–17

IF YOU NEED MORE HELP

See also the **PROCESSES** chapters for help generating ideas, drafting, revising, and so on if you are writing a whole essay dedicated to defining a term or concept.

209–58

36 Describing

When we describe something, we indicate what it looks like — and sometimes how it sounds, feels, smells, and tastes. Descriptive details are a way of showing rather than telling, of helping readers see (or hear, smell, and so on) what we're writing about — that the sky is blue, that Miss Havisham is wearing an old yellowed wedding gown, that the chemicals in the beaker have reacted and smell like rotten eggs. You'll have occasion to describe things in most of the writing you do — from describing a favorite hat in a **MEMOIR** to detailing a chemical reaction in a **LAB REPORT.** This chapter will help you work with description — and, in particular, help you think about the use of *detail*, about *objectivity and subjectivity*, about *vantage point*, about creating a clear *dominant impression*, and about using description to fit your rhetorical situation.

153–60

133–42

Detail

The goal of using details is to be as specific as possible, providing information that will help your audience imagine the subject or make sense of it. See, for example, how Nancy Mairs, an author with multiple sclerosis, describes the disease in clear, specific terms:

> During its course, which is unpredictable and uncontrollable, one may lose vision, hearing, speech, the ability to walk, control of bladder and/or bowels, strength in any or all extremities, sensitivity to touch, vibration, and/or pain, potency, coordination of movements — the list of possibilities is lengthy and, yes, horrifying. One may also lose one's sense of humor. That's the easiest to lose and the hardest to survive without.
>
> In the past ten years, I have sustained some of these losses. Characteristic of MS are sudden attacks, called exacerbations, followed by remissions, and these I have not had. Instead, my disease has been

rhetorical situations

genres

processes

strategies

research mla/apa

media/ design

handbook

slowly progressive. My left leg is now so weak that I walk with the aid of a brace and a cane, and for distances I use an Amigo, a variation on the electric wheelchair that looks rather like an electrified kiddie car. I no longer have much use of my left hand. Now my right side is weakening as well. I still have the blurred spot in my right eye. Overall, though, I've been lucky so far.

—Nancy Mairs, "On Being a Cripple"

Mairs's gruesome list demonstrates, through *specific details*, how the disease affects sufferers generally and her in particular. We know far more after reading this text than we do from the following more general description, from a National Multiple Sclerosis Society brochure:

Multiple sclerosis is a chronic, unpredictable disease of the central nervous system (the brain, optic nerves, and spinal cord). It is thought to be an autoimmune disorder. This means the immune system incorrectly attacks the person's healthy tissue.

MS can cause blurred vision, loss of balance, poor coordination, slurred speech, tremors, numbness, extreme fatigue, problems with memory and concentration, paralysis, and blindness. These problems may be permanent, or they may come and go.

—National Multiple Sclerosis Society, *Just the Facts: 2003–2004*

Specific details are also more effective than labels, which give little meaningful information. Instead of saying that someone is a "moron" or "really smart," it's better to give details so that readers can understand the reasons behind the label: what does this person *do* or *say* that makes him or her deserve this label? See, for example, how the writer of a news story about shopping on the day after Thanksgiving opens with a description of a happy shopper:

Last Friday afternoon, the day ritualized consumerism is traditionally at its most frenetic, Alexx Balcuns twirled in front of a full-length mirror at the Ritz Thrift Shop on West Fifty-seventh Street as if inhabited by the soul of Eva Gabor in *Green Acres*. Ms. Balcuns was languishing in a $795 dyed-mink parka her grandmother had just bought her. Ms. Balcuns is six.

—Ginia Bellafante, "Staying Warm and Fuzzy during Uncertain Times"

The writer might simply have said, "A spoiled child admired herself in the mirror." Instead, she shows her subject twirling and "languishing" in a "$795 dyed-mink parka" and seemingly possessed by the soul of the actress Eva Gabor—all details that create a far more vivid description.

Sensory details help readers imagine sounds, odors, tastes, and physical sensations in addition to sights. In the following example, writer Scott Russell Sanders recalls sawing wood as a child. Note how visual details, odors, and even the physical sense of being picked up by his father mingle to form a vivid scene:

> As the saw teeth bit down, the wood released its smell, each kind with its own fragrance, oak or walnut or cherry or pine—usually pine because it was the softest, easiest for a child to work. No matter how weathered and gray the board, no matter how warped and cracked, inside there was this smell waiting, as of something freshly baked. I gathered every smidgen of sawdust and stored it away in coffee cans, which I kept in a drawer of the workbench. When I did not feel like hammering nails I would dump my sawdust on the concrete floor of the garage and landscape it into highways and farms and towns, running miniature cars and trucks along miniature roads. Looming as huge as a colossus, my father worked over and around me, now and again bending down to inspect my work, careful not to trample my creations. It was a landscape that smelled dizzyingly of wood. Even after a bath my skin would carry the smell, and so would my father's hair, when he lifted me for a bedtime hug.
>
> —Scott Russell Sanders, *The Paradise of Bombs*

Whenever you describe something, you'll select from many possible details you might use. Simply put, to exhaust all of the details to describe something is impossible—and would exhaust your readers as well. To focus your description, you'll need to determine the kinds of details that are appropriate for your subject. They will vary, depending on your **PURPOSE.** See, for example, how the details might differ in three different genres:

3–4 ■

153–60 ▲

- *For a* **MEMOIR** *about an event*, you might choose details that are significant for you, that evoke the sights, sounds, and meaning of your event.

- For a **PROFILE,** you're likely to select details that will reinforce the dominant impression you want to give, that portray the event from the perspective you want readers to see.

▲ 161–70

- For a **LAB REPORT,** you need to give certain specifics—what equipment was used, what procedures were followed, what exactly were the results.

▲ 133–42

Deciding on a focus for your description can help you see it better, as you'll look for details that contribute to that focus.

Objectivity and Subjectivity

Descriptions can be written with objectivity, with subjectivity, or with a mixture of both. Objective descriptions attempt to be uncolored by personal opinion or emotion. Police reports and much news writing aim to describe events objectively; scientific writing strives for objectivity in describing laboratory procedures and results. See, for example, the following objective account of what happened at the World Trade Center on September 11, 2001:

> **World Trade Center Disaster — Tuesday, September 11, 2001**
>
> On Tuesday, September 11, 2001, at 8:45 a.m. New York local time, One World Trade Center, the north tower, was hit by a hijacked 767 commercial jet airplane loaded with fuel for a transcontinental flight. Two World Trade Center, the south tower, was hit by a similar hijacked jet eighteen minutes later, at 9:03 a.m. (In separate but related attacks, the Pentagon building near Washington, D.C., was hit by a hijacked 757 at 9:43 a.m., and at 10:10 a.m. a fourth hijacked jetliner crashed in Pennsylvania.) The south tower, WTC 2, which had been hit second, was the first to suffer a complete structural collapse, at 10:05 a.m., 62 minutes after being hit itself, 80 minutes after the first impact. The north tower, WTC 1, then also collapsed, at 10:29 a.m., 104 minutes after being hit. WTC 7, a substantial forty-seven-story office building in its own right, built in 1987, was damaged by the collapsing towers, caught fire, and later in the afternoon also totally collapsed.
>
> — "World Trade Center," GreatBuildingsOnline.com

Subjective descriptions, on the other hand, allow the writer's opinions and emotions to come through. A house can be described as comfortable, with a lived-in look, or as rundown and in need of a paint job and a new roof. Here's a subjective description of the planes striking the World Trade Center, as told by a woman watching from a nearby building:

> Incredulously, while looking out [the] window at the damage and carnage the first plane had inflicted, I saw the second plane abruptly come into my right field of vision and deliberately, with shimmering intention, thunder full-force into the south tower. It was so close, so low, so huge and fast, so intent on its target that I swear to you, I swear to you, I felt the vengeance and rage emanating from the plane.
>
> —Debra Fontaine, "Witnessing"

Advertisers regularly use subjective as well as objective description to sell their products, as this ad for a nicotine patch demonstrates. This ad

includes an objective description of what makes smoking addictive: "Every time you smoke, the nicotine binds to these little tiny receptors in your brain. Thus, your brain becomes addicted to nicotine." However, it also presents subjective descriptions of the effects of quitting ("if you cut the brain off—well let's just say it gets a little annoyed") and the results of buying and using the product: "So your brain's happy. You're happy. Or at least you're happy that your brain's happy."

Vantage Point

Sometimes you'll want or need to describe something from a certain vantage point. Where you locate yourself in relation to what you're describing will determine what you can perceive (and so describe) and what you can't. You may describe your subject from a *stationary vantage point*, from which you (and your readers) see your subject from one angle only, as if you were a camera. This description of one of three photographs that captured a woman's death records only what the camera saw from one angle at one particular moment:

> The first showed some people on a fire escape—a fireman, a woman and a child. The fireman had a nice strong jaw and looked very brave. The woman was holding the child. Smoke was pouring from the building behind them. A rescue ladder was approaching, just a few feet away, and the fireman had one arm around the woman and one arm reaching out toward the ladder.
>
> —Nora Ephron, "The Boston Photographs"

By contrast, this description of a drive to an Italian villa uses a *moving vantage point*; the writer recounts what he saw as he passed through a gate in a city wall, moving from city to country:

> La Pietra—"the stone"—is situated one mile from the Porta San Gallo, an entry to the Old City of Florence. You drive there along the Via Bolognese, twisting past modern apartment blocks, until you come to a gate, which swings open—and there you are, at the upper end of a long lane of cypresses facing a great ocher palazzo; with olive groves spreading out on both sides over an expanse of fifty-seven acres.

There's something almost comically wonderful about the effect: here, the city, with its winding avenue; there, on the other side of a wall, the country, fertile and gray green.

—James Traub, "Italian Hours"

The description of quarries below uses *multiple vantage points* to capture the quarries from many perspectives.

Dominant Impression

With any description, your aim is to create some dominant impression—the overall feeling that the individual details add up to. The dominant impression may be implied, growing out of the details themselves. For example, Scott Russell Sanders's memory of the smell of sawdust creates a dominant impression of warmth and comfort: the "fragrance . . . as of something freshly baked," sawdust "stored . . . away in coffee cans," a young boy "lifted . . . for a bedtime hug." Sometimes, though, a writer will inform readers directly of the dominant impression, in addition to describing it. In an essay about Indiana limestone quarries, Sanders makes the dominant impression clear from the start: "they are battlefields."

> The quarries will not be domesticated. They are not backyard pools; they are battlefields. Each quarry is an arena where violent struggles have taken place between machines and planet, between human ingenuity and brute resisting stone, between mind and matter. Waste rock litters the floor and brim like rubble in a bombed city. The ragged pits might have been the basements of vanished skyscrapers. Stones weighing tens of tons lean against one another at precarious angles, as if they have been thrown there by some gigantic strength and have not yet finished falling. Wrecked machinery hulks in the weeds, grimly rusting, the cogs and wheels, twisted rails, battered engine housings, trackless bulldozers and burst boilers like junk from an armored regiment. Everywhere the ledges are scarred from drills, as if from an artillery barrage or machine-gun strafing. Stumbling onto one of these abandoned quarries and gazing at the ruins, you might be left wondering who had won the battle, men or stone.
>
> —Scott Russell Sanders, *The Paradise of Bombs*

The rest of his description, full of more figurative language ("like rubble in a bombed city," "like junk from an armored regiment," "as if from an artillery barrage or machine-gun strafing") reinforces the direct "they are battlefields" statement.

Organizing Descriptions

You can organize descriptions in many ways. When your description is primarily visual, you will probably organize it spatially: from left to right, top to bottom, outside to inside. If your description uses the other senses, you may begin with the most significant or noteworthy feature and move outward from that center, as Ephron does, or you may create a chronological description of objects as you encounter them, as Traub does in his description of his drive on pages 329–30. You might even pile up details to create a dominant impression, as Sanders and Mairs do.

Considering the Rhetorical Situation

As a writer or speaker, you need to think about the message that you want to articulate, the audience you want to reach, and the larger context you are writing in.

PURPOSE   Your purpose may affect the way you use description. If you're arguing that a government should intervene in another country's civil war, for example, describing the anguish of refugees from that war could make your argument more persuasive. If you're analyzing a painting, you will likely need to describe it.   ▮ 3–4

AUDIENCE   Who is your audience, and will they need detailed description to understand the points you wish to make?   ▮ 5–8

GENRE   Does your genre require description? A lab report generally calls for you to describe materials and results; a memoir about grandma should probably describe her — her smile, her dress, her apple pie.   ▮ 9–11

12–14 ▦
STANCE   The way you describe things can help you convey your stance. For example, the details you choose can show you to be objective (or not), careful or casual.

15–17 ▦
MEDIA / DESIGN   Your medium will affect the form your description can take. In a print or spoken text, you will likely rely on words, though you may also include visuals. In an electronic text, you can easily provide links to visuals and so may need fewer words.

IF YOU NEED MORE HELP

219–21 ◯
209–58
See also **FREEWRITING, CUBING,** and **LISTING,** three methods of generating ideas that can be especially helpful for developing detailed descriptions. Sometimes you may be assigned to write a whole essay describing something: see the **PROCESSES** chapters for help drafting, revising, and so on.

---

rhetorical situations   genres   processes   strategies   research mla/apa   media/ design   handbook

Dialogue 37

Dialogue is a way of including people's own words in a text, letting readers hear those people's voices—not just what you say about them. **MEMOIRS** and **PROFILES** often include dialogue, and many other genres do as well: **LITERARY ANALYSES** often quote dialogue from the texts they analyze, and essays **ARGUING A POSITION** might quote an authoritative source as support for a claim. This chapter provides brief guidelines for the conventions of paragraphing and punctuating dialogue and offers some good examples of how you can use dialogue most effectively to suit your own rhetorical situations.

153–60
161–70
143–52
83–110

Why Add Dialogue?

Dialogue is a way of bringing in voices other than your own, of showing people and scenes rather than just telling about them. It can add color and texture to your writing, making it memorable. Most important, however, dialogue should be more than just colorful or interesting. It needs to contribute to your rhetorical purpose, to support the point you're making. See how dialogue is used in the following excerpt from a magazine profile of the Mall of America, how it gives us a sense of the place that the journalist's own words could not provide:

> Two pubescent girls in retainers and braces sat beside me sipping coffees topped with whipped cream and chocolate sprinkles, their shopping bags gathered tightly around their legs, their eyes fixed on the passing crowds. They came, they said, from Shakopee—"It's nowhere," one of them explained. The megamall, she added, was "a buzz at first, but now it seems pretty normal. 'Cept my parents are like Twenty Questions every time I want to come here. 'Specially since the shooting."

> On a Sunday night, she elaborated, three people had been wounded when shots were fired in a dispute over a San Jose Sharks jacket. "In the *mall*," her friend reminded me. "Right here at megamall. A shooting."
> "It's like nowhere's safe," the first added.
>
> —David Guterson, "Enclosed. Encyclopedic. Endured: The Mall of America"

Of course it was the writer who decided whom and what to quote, and Guterson deliberately chose words that capture the young shoppers' speech patterns, quoting fragments ("In the *mall*. . . . Right here at mega-mall. A shooting"), slang ("a buzz at first," "my parents are like Twenty Questions"), even contractions ('cept, 'specially).

Integrating Dialogue into Your Writing

There are certain conventions for punctuating and paragraphing dialogue:

- *Punctuating.* Enclose each speaker's words in quotation marks, and put any end punctuation — periods, question marks, and exclamation marks — inside the closing quotation mark. Whether you're transcribing words you heard or making them up, you will sometimes need to add punctuation to reflect the rhythm and sound of the speech. In the last sentence of the example below, see how Chang-Rae Lee adds a comma after *well* and italicizes *practice* to show intonation — and attitude.

- *Paragraphing.* When you're writing dialogue that includes more than one speaker, start a new paragraph each time the speaker changes.

- *Signal phrases.* Sometimes you'll need to introduce dialogue with **SIGNAL PHRASES** — "I said," "she asked," and so on — to make clear who is speaking. At times, however, the speaker will be clear enough, and you won't need any signal phrases.

417–18

Here is a conversation between a mother and her son that illustrates each of the conventions for punctuating and paragraphing dialogue:

> "Whom do I talk to?" she said. She would mostly speak to me in Korean, and I would answer back in English.

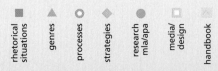

rhetorical situations   genres   processes   strategies   research mla/apa   media/design   handbook

"The bank manager, who else?"

"What do I say?"

"Whatever you want to say."

"Don't speak to me like that!" she cried.

"It's just that you should be able to do it yourself," I said.

"You know how I feel about this!"

"Well, maybe then you should consider it *practice*," I answered lightly, using the Korean word to make sure she understood.

—Chang-Rae Lee, "Coming Home Again"

Interviews

Interviews are a kind of dialogue, with different conventions for punctuation. When you're transcribing an interview, give each speaker's name each time he or she speaks, starting a new line but not indenting, and do not use quotation marks. Here are a few lines from an *OnEarth* magazine interview that science journalist Kevin Krajick conducted with Paul Anastas, professor of green chemistry at Yale:

Krajik: Many people assume chemists are evil—they inevitably cause pollution.

Anastas: People don't know we have the option of doing things green. They think that in order to have cars, computers, and other modern conveniences, we need to generate all kinds of nasty poisons. Green chemistry is disproving that myth every day.

Krajik: What's really new about it?

Anastas: We're touching on something not done historically, which is to design molecules with an eye to consequences, right from the start. You go back to the basic chemical properties—volatility, electronic properties, boiling point. That way you can design a molecule to do exactly what you want. If you just try to deal with a particular hazardous outcome—cancer or poisoning or explosions—then you're addressing things piecemeal. If you go back down to the molecular architecture, you can address a wide range of issues.

Krajik: Has green chemistry actually taken hold anywhere?

Anastas: I could give you hundreds of examples of award-winning technologies, used by companies in the United States, the United Kingdom, Japan, Italy, that have eliminated literally billions of pounds of haz-

ardous substances. It goes from the way we make pharmaceuticals or electronics to the way we raise crops or paint the bottoms of boats. That said, for every one process or product that uses green chemistry, there may be a hundred or more that have yet to be considered. So 99 percent of the work is still left.

Krajik: Give me a few examples of things we're using now, or will be using soon.

Anastas: Sure. Polylactic acid is a plastic whose molecule is made from potatoes, corn, and other plant sources. Wal-Mart put in multimillion-pound orders a year ago for cups, soup containers, food packaging — it's just getting going. Arsenic in treated lumber has been recognized as a problem, and green chemistry has come up with a water-based alternative. There's also supercritical carbon dioxide — that is, CO_2 put under high pressure so it becomes a fluid [in this form it does not contribute to greenhouse gas emissions]. It's now used in many processes that previously used some fairly toxic solvents. That includes decaffeinating coffee, which historically used methylene chloride, a cancer suspect that is also used for stripping paint.

— Kevin Krajik, "Q&A: Mastering the Molecule"

In preparing the interview for publication, Krajik had to add punctuation, which of course was not part of the oral conversation, and he probably deleted pauses and verbal expressions such as *um* and *uh*. At the same time, he kept informal constructions, such as incomplete sentences, which are typical answers to questions ("Sure.") to maintain the oral flavor of the interview and to reflect the professor's voice. Krajik may also have moved parts of the interview around, to eliminate repetition and keep related subjects together.

Considering the Rhetorical Situation

As a writer or speaker, you need to think about the message that you want to articulate, the audience you want to reach, and the larger context of your writing.

PURPOSE Your purpose will affect any use of dialogue. Dialogue can help bring a profile to life and make it memorable. Interviews with experts or first-hand witnesses can add credibility to a report or argument.

3–4

AUDIENCE Whom do you want to reach, and will dialogue help? Sometimes actual dialogue can help readers hear human voices behind facts or reason.

5–8

GENRE Does your genre require dialogue? If you're evaluating or analyzing a literary work, for instance, you may wish to include dialogue from that work. If you're writing a profile of a person or event, dialogue can help you bring your subject to life. Similarly, an interview with an expert can add credibility to a report or argument.

9–11

STANCE What is your stance, and can dialogue help you communicate that stance? For example, excerpts of an interview may allow you to challenge someone's views and make your own views clear.

12–14

MEDIA / DESIGN Your medium will affect the way you present dialogue. In a print text, you will present dialogue through written words. In an oral or electronic text, you might include actual recorded dialogue.

15–17

IF YOU NEED MORE HELP

See also the guidelines on **INTERVIEWING EXPERTS** for advice on setting up and recording interviews and those on **QUOTING, PARAPHRASING,** and **SUMMARIZING** for help deciding how to integrate dialogue into your text.

394–95
408–19

38 Explaining Processes

When you explain a process, you tell how something is (or was) done—how a bill becomes a law, how an embryo develops—or you tell someone how to do something—how to throw a curve ball, how to write a memoir. This chapter focuses on those two kinds of explanations, offering examples and guidelines for explaining a process in a way that works for your rhetorical situation.

Explaining a Process Clearly

Whether the process is simple or complex, you'll need to identify its key stages or steps and explain them one by one, in order. The sequence matters because it allows readers to follow your explanation; it is especially important when you're explaining a process that others are going to follow. Most often you'll explain a process chronologically, from start to finish. **TRANSITIONS**—words like *first*, *next*, *then*, and so on—are often necessary, therefore, to show readers how the stages of a process relate to one another and to indicate time sequences. Finally, you'll find that verbs matter; they indicate the actions that take place at each stage of the process.

277 ◆

Explaining How Something Is Done

All processes consist of steps, and when you explain how something is done, you describe each step, generally in order, from first to last. Here, for example, is an explanation of how French fries are made, from an essay published in the *New Yorker:*

> Fast-food French fries are made from a baking potato like an Idaho russet, or any other variety that is mealy, or starchy, rather than waxy. The potatoes are harvested, cured, washed, peeled, sliced, and then blanched — cooked enough so that the insides have a fluffy texture but not so much that the fry gets soft and breaks. Blanching is followed by drying, and drying by a thirty-second deep fry, to give the potatoes a crisp shell. Then the fries are frozen until the moment of service, when they are deep-fried again, this time for somewhere around three minutes. Depending on the fast-food chain involved, there are other steps interspersed in this process. McDonald's fries, for example, are briefly dipped in a sugar solution, which gives them their golden-brown color; Burger King fries are dipped in a starch batter, which is what gives those fries their distinctive hard shell and audible crunch. But the result is similar. The potato that is first harvested in the field is roughly 80 percent water. The process of creating a French fry consists, essentially, of removing as much of that water as possible — through blanching, drying, and deep-frying — and replacing it with fat.
>
> —Malcolm Gladwell, "The Trouble with Fries"

Gladwell clearly explains the process of making French fries, showing us the specific steps — how the potatoes "are harvested, cured, washed, peeled, sliced," and so on — and using clear transitions — "followed by," "then," "until," "when" — and action verbs to show the sequence. His last sentence makes his stance clear, pointing out that the process of creating a French fry consists of removing as much of a potato's water as possible "and replacing it with fat."

Explaining How to Do Something

In explaining how to do something, you are giving instruction so that others can follow the process themselves. See how Martha Stewart explains the process of making French fries. She starts by listing the ingredients and then describes the steps:

> 4 medium baking potatoes
> 2 tablespoons olive oil
> 1$^1/_2$ teaspoons salt
> $^1/_4$ teaspoon freshly ground pepper
> malt vinegar (optional)

1. Heat oven to 400 degrees. Place a heavy baking sheet in the oven. Scrub and rinse the potatoes well, and then cut them lengthwise into $^1/_2$-inch-wide batons. Place the potato batons in a medium bowl, and toss them with the olive oil, salt, and pepper.

2. When baking sheet is hot, about 15 minutes, remove from the oven. Place prepared potatoes on the baking sheet in a single later. Return to oven, and bake until potatoes are golden on the bottom, about 30 minutes. Turn potatoes over, and continue cooking until golden all over, about 15 minutes more. Serve immediately.

—Martha Stewart, *Favorite Comfort Food*

Coming from Martha Stewart, the explanation leaves out no details, giving a clear sequence of steps and descriptive verbs that tell us exactly what to do: "heat," "place," "scrub and rinse," and so on. After she gives the recipe, she even goes on to explain the process of *serving* the fries — "Serve these French fries with a bowl of malt vinegar" — and reminds us that "they are also delicious dipped in spicy mustard, mayonnaise, and, of course, ketchup."

Explaining a Process Visually

528–32 Some processes are best explained **VISUALLY**, with diagrams or photographs. See, for example, how a cookbook explains one process of shaping dough into a bagel — giving the details in words and then showing us in a drawing how to do it:

Roll each piece of dough on an unfloured counter into a 12-inch-long rope. Make a ring, overlapping the ends by 2 inches and joining them by pressing down and rolling on the overlap until it is the same thickness as the rest of the dough ring. There will be a 1-inch hole in the center.

1. Rolling the dough into a 12-inch rope

2. Making a ring by twisting one end of the dough over to overlap the other end by 2 inches

3. Pressing down and rolling the dough

—Rose Levy Beranbaum, *The Bread Bible*

Considering the Rhetorical Situation

As a writer or speaker, you need to think about the message that you want to articulate, the audience you want to reach, and the larger context you are writing in.

PURPOSE   Your purpose for writing will affect the way you explain a process. If you're arguing that we should avoid eating fast food, you might explain the process by which chicken nuggets are made. But to give information about how to fry chicken, you would explain the process quite differently.   ■ 3–4

AUDIENCE   Whom are you trying to reach, and will you need to provide any special background information? Can they be expected to be interested, or will you first need to interest them in the process?   ■ 5–8

9–11 ■ **GENRE** Does your genre require you to explain a process? In a lab report, for example, you'll need to explain the processes used in the experiment. You might want to explain the process in a profile of an activity or the process of a solution you are proposing.

12–14 ■ **STANCE** If you're giving directions for doing something, you'll want to take a straightforward "do this, then do that" perspective. If you're writing to entertain, you might want to take a clever or amusing stance.

15–17 ■ **MEDIA / DESIGN** Your medium will affect the way you explain a process. In a print text or spoken text, you can use both words and images. On the Web, you may have the option of showing an animation of the process as well.

IF YOU NEED MORE HELP

133–42 ▲
161–70
343–51 ◆
209–58 ○
See also **LAB REPORTS** if you need to explain the process by which an experiment is carried out; and **PROFILES** if you are writing about an activity that needs to be explained. See **NARRATING** for more advice on organizing an explanation chronologically. Sometimes you may be assigned to write a whole essay or report that explains a process; see **PROCESSES** for help drafting, revising, and so on.

■ rhetorical situations
▲ genres
○ processes
◆ strategies
● research mla/apa
□ media/ design
▨ handbook

Narrating 39

Narratives are stories. As a writing strategy, a good narrative can lend support to most kinds of writing—in a **POSITION PAPER** arguing for Title IX compliance, for example, you might include a brief narrative about an Olympic sprinter who might never have learned to run without Title IX. Or you can bring a **PROFILE** of a favorite coach to life with an anecdote about a pep talk he or she once gave before a championship track meet. Whatever your larger writing purpose, you need to make sure that any narratives you add support that purpose—they should not be inserted simply to tell an interesting story. You'll also need to compose them carefully—to put them in a clear *sequence*, include *pertinent detail*, and make sure they are appropriate to your particular rhetorical situation.

▲ 83–110

▲ 161–70

Sequencing

When we write a narrative, we arrange events in a particular sequence. Writers typically sequence narratives in chronological order, reverse chronological order, or as a flashback.

Use chronological order.   Often you may tell the story chronologically, starting at the beginning of an event and working through to the end, as Maya Angelou does in this brief narrative from an essay about her high school graduation:

> The school band struck up a march and all classes filed in as had been rehearsed. We stood in front of our seats, as assigned, and on a signal from the choir director, we sat. No sooner had this been accomplished than the band started to play the national anthem. We rose again and sang the song, after which we recited the pledge of allegiance. We

343

remained standing for a brief minute before the choir director and the principal signaled to us, rather desperately I thought, to take our seats.

—Maya Angelou, "Graduation"

Use reverse chronological order. You may also begin with the final action and work back to the first, as Aldo Leopold does in this narrative about cutting down a tree:

> Now our saw bites into the 1890s, called gay by those whose eyes turn cityward rather than landward. We cut 1899, when the last passenger pigeon collided with a charge of shot near Babcock, two counties to the north; we cut 1898, when a dry fall, followed by a snowless winter, froze the soil seven feet deep and killed the apple trees; 1897, another drouth year, when another forestry commission came into being; 1896, when 25,000 prairie chickens were shipped to market from the village of Spooner alone; 1895, another year of fires; 1894, another drouth year; and 1893, the year of "the Bluebird Storm," when a March blizzard reduced the migrating bluebirds to near zero.

—Aldo Leopold, *A Sand County Almanac*

188–95 ▲

RÉSUMÉS are one genre where we generally use reverse chronological order, listing the most recent jobs or degrees first and then working backward. Notice, too, that we usually write these as narratives—telling what we have done rather than just naming positions we have held:

Sept. 2007–present	*Student worker*, Department of Information Management, Central State University, Wilberforce, OH. Compile data and format reports using Excel, Word, and university database programs.
June–Sept. 2007	*Intern*, QuestPro Corporation, West Louisville, KY. Assisted in development of software programs.
Sept. 2006–June 2007	*Bagger*, Ace Groceries, Elba, KY. Bagged customers' purchases.

Use a flashback. You can sometimes put a flashback in the middle of a narrative, to tell about an incident that illuminates the larger narrative. Terry Tempest Williams does this in an essay about the startling incidence of breast cancer in her family: she recalls a dinnertime conversation with her father right after her mother's death from cancer, when she learned for the first time what caused all of the cancer in her family:

> Over dessert, I shared a recurring dream of mine. I told my father that for years, as long as I could remember, I saw this flash of light in the night in the desert. That this image had so permeated my being, I could not venture south without seeing it again, on the horizon, illuminating buttes and mesas.
>
> "You did see it," he said.
>
> "Saw what?" I asked, a bit tentative.
>
> "The bomb. The cloud. We were driving home from Riverside, California. You were sitting on your mother's lap. She was pregnant. In fact, I remember the date, September 7, 1957. We had just gotten out of the Service. We were driving north, past Las Vegas. It was an hour or so before dawn, when this explosion went off. We not only heard it, but felt it. I thought the oil tanker in front of us had blown up. We pulled over and suddenly, rising from the desert floor, we saw it, clearly, this golden-stemmed cloud, the mushroom. The sky seemed to vibrate with an eerie pink glow. Within a few minutes, a light ash was raining on the car."
>
> I stared at my father. This was new information to me.
>
> —Terry Tempest Williams, "The Clan of the One-Breasted Women"

Williams could have simply announced this information as a fact—but see how much more powerful it is when told in narrative form.

Use time markers. Time markers help readers follow a sequence of events. The most obvious time markers are those that simply label the time, as the narrative entries in a diary, journal, or log might. For example, here is the final part of the narrative kept in a diary by a doomed Antarctic explorer:

> WEDNESDAY, MARCH 21: Got within eleven miles of depot. Monday night; had to lay up all yesterday in severe blizzard. Today forlorn hope, Wilson and Bowers going to depot for fuel.

MARCH 22 and 23: Blizzard bad as ever—Wilson and Bowers unable to start—tomorrow last chance—no fuel and only one or two [days] of food left—must be near the end. Have decided it shall be natural—we shall march for the depot with or without our effects and die in our tracks.

THURSDAY, MARCH 29: Since the 21st we have had a continuous gale from W.S.W. and S.W. We had fuel to make two cups of tea apiece and bare food for two days on the 20th. Every day we have been ready to start for our depot eleven miles away, but outside the door of the tent it remains a scene of whirling drift. I do not think we can hope for any better things now. We shall stick it out to the end, but we are getting weaker, of course, and the end cannot be far. It seems a pity, but I do not think I can write more. . . .

Last Entry: For God's sake look after our people.

—Robert F. Scott, *Scott's Last Expedition: The Journals*

More often you will integrate time markers into the prose itself, as is done in this narrative about a woman preparing and delivering meals to workers at a cotton gin:

She made her plans meticulously and in secret. <u>One early evening</u> to see if she was ready, she placed stones in two five-gallon pails and carried them three miles to the cotton gin. She rested a little, and then, discarding some rocks, she walked in the darkness to the sawmill five miles farther along the dirt road. <u>On her way back</u> to her little house and her babies, she dumped the remaining rocks along the path.

<u>That same night</u> she worked into the early hours boiling chicken and frying ham. She made dough and filled the rolled-out pastry with meat. At last she went to sleep.

<u>The next morning</u> she left her house carrying the meat pies, lard, an iron brazier, and coals for a fire. <u>Just before lunch</u> she appeared in an empty lot behind the cotton gin. <u>As the dinner noon bell rang</u>, she dropped the savors into boiling fat, and the aroma rose and floated over to the workers who spilled out of the gin, covered with white lint, looking like specters.

—Maya Angelou, *Wouldn't Take Nothing for My Journey Now*

◆ 277

Use transitions.   Another way to help readers follow a narrative is with **TRANSITIONS,** words like *first, then, meanwhile, at last,* and so on. See how the following paragraphs from Langston Hughes's classic essay about meeting Jesus use transitions (and time markers) to advance the action:

> <u>Suddenly</u> the whole room broke into a sea of shouting, <u>as</u> they saw me rise. Waves of rejoicing swept the place. Women leaped in the air. My aunt threw her arms around me. The minister took me by the hand and led me to the platform.
>
> <u>When</u> things quieted down, in a hushed silence, punctuated by a few ecstatic "Amens," all the new young lambs were blessed in the name of God. <u>Then</u> joyous singing filled the room. <u>That night,</u> for the last time in my life but one — for I was a big boy twelve years old — I cried.
>
> — Langston Hughes, "Salvation"

Including Pertinent Detail

When you include a narrative in your writing, you must decide which details you need — and which ones you don't need. For example, you don't want to include so much detail that the narrative distracts the reader from the larger text. You must also decide whether you need to include any background, to set the stage for the narrative. The amount of detail you include depends on your audience and purpose: How much detail does your audience need? How much detail do you need to make your meaning clear? In an essay on the suspicion African American men often face when walking at night, a journalist deliberately presents a story without setting the stage at all:

> My first victim was a woman — white, well dressed, probably in her late twenties. I came upon her late one evening on a deserted street in Hyde Park, a relatively affluent neighborhood in an otherwise mean, impoverished section of Chicago. As I swung onto the avenue behind her, there seemed to be a discreet, uninflammatory distance between us. Not so. She cast back a worried glance. To her, the youngish black

man—a broad six feet two inches with a beard and billowing hair, both hands shoved into the pockets of a bulky military jacket—seemed menacingly close. After a few more quick glimpses, she picked up her pace and was soon running in earnest. Within seconds she disappeared into a cross street.

—Brent Staples, "Black Men and Public Space"

Words like *victim* and phrases like "came upon her" lead us to assume the narrator is scary and perhaps dangerous. We don't know why he is walking on the deserted street because he hasn't told us: he simply begins with the moment he and the woman encounter each other. For his purposes, that's all the audience needs to know at first, and details of his physical appearance that explain the woman's response come later, after he tells us about the encounter. Had he given us those details at the outset, the narrative would not have been nearly so effective. In a way, Staples lets the story sneak up on us, as the woman apparently felt he had on her.

Other times you'll need to provide more background information, as an MIT professor does when she uses an anecdote to introduce an essay about young children's experiences with electronic toys. First the writer tells us a little about Merlin, the computer tic-tac-toe game that the children in her anecdote play with. As you'll see, the anecdote would be hard to follow without the introduction:

> Among the first generation of computational objects was Merlin, which challenged children to games of tic-tac-toe. For children who had only played games with human opponents, reaction to this object was intense. For example, while Merlin followed an optimal strategy for winning tic-tac-toe most of the time, it was programmed to make a slip every once in a while. So when children discovered strategies that allowed them to win and then tried these strategies a second time, they usually would not work. The machine gave the impression of not being "dumb enough" to let down its defenses twice. Robert, seven, playing with his friends on the beach, watched his friend Craig perform the "winning trick," but when he tried it, Merlin did not slip up and the game ended in a draw. Robert, confused and frustrated, threw Merlin into the sand and said, "Cheater. I hope your brains break." He was overheard by Craig and Greg, aged six and eight, who salvaged

the by-now very sandy toy and took it upon themselves to set Robert straight. "Merlin doesn't know if it cheats," says Craig. "It doesn't know if you break it, Robert. It's not alive." Greg adds, "It's smart enough to make the right kinds of noises. But it doesn't really know if it loses. And when it cheats, it don't even know it's cheating." Jenny, six, interrupts with disdain: "Greg, to cheat you have to know you are cheating. Knowing is part of cheating."

—Sherry Turkle, "Cuddling Up to Cyborg Babies"

Opening and Closing with Narratives

Narratives are often useful as **BEGINNINGS** to essays and other kinds of writing. Everyone likes a good story, so an interesting or pithy narrative can be a good way to get your audience's attention. In the following introductory paragraph, a historian tells a gruesome but gripping story to attract our attention to a subject that might not otherwise merit our interest, bubonic plague:

261–66

> In October 1347, two months after the fall of Calais, Genoese trading ships put into the harbor of Messina in Sicily with dead and dying men at the oars. The ships had come from the Black Sea port of Caffa (now Feodosiya) in the Crimea, where the Genoese maintained a trading post. The diseased sailors showed strange black swellings about the size of an egg or an apple in the armpits and groin. The swellings oozed blood and pus and were followed by spreading boils and black blotches on the skin from internal bleeding. The sick suffered severe pain and died quickly, within five days of the first symptoms. As the disease spread, other symptoms of continuous fever and spitting of blood appeared instead of the swellings or buboes. These victims coughed and sweated heavily and died even more quickly, within three days or less, sometimes in twenty-four hours. In both types everything that issued from the body—breath, sweat, blood from the buboes and lungs, bloody urine, and blood-blackened excrement—smelled foul. Depression and despair accompanied the physical symptoms, and before the end "death is seen seated on the face."
>
> —Barbara Tuchman, "This Is the End of the World: The Black Death"

Imagine how different the preceding paragraph would be if it weren't in the form of a narrative. Imagine, for example, that Tuchman began by defining bubonic plague. Would that have gotten your interest? The piece was written for a general audience; how might it have been different if it had been written for scientists? Would they need (or appreciate) the story told here?

266–70

Narrative can be a good way of **ENDING** a text, too, by winding up a discussion with an illustration of the main point. Here, for instance, is a concluding paragraph from an essay on American values and Las Vegas weddings.

> I sat next to one . . . wedding party in a Strip restaurant the last time I was in Las Vegas. The marriage had just taken place; the bride still wore her dress, the mother her corsage. A bored waiter poured out a few swallows of pink champagne ("on the house") for everyone but the bride, who was too young to be served. "You'll need something with more kick than that," the bride's father said with heavy jocularity to his new son-in-law; the ritual jokes about the wedding night had a certain Panglossian character, since the bride was clearly several months pregnant. Another round of pink champagne, this time not on the house, and the bride began to cry. "It was just as nice," she sobbed, "as I hoped and dreamed it would be."
>
> —Joan Didion, "Marrying Absurd"

No doubt Didion makes her points about American values clearly and cogently in the essay. But concluding with this story lets us *see* (and hear) what she is saying about Las Vegas wedding chapels, which sell "'niceness,' the facsimile of proper ritual, to children who do not know how else to find it, how to make the arrangements, how to do it 'right.'"

Considering the Rhetorical Situation

As a writer or speaker, you need to think about the message that you want to articulate, the audience you want to reach, and the larger context you are writing in.

rhetorical situations   genres   processes   strategies   research mla/apa   media/design   handbook

PURPOSE Your purpose will affect the way you use narrative. For example, in an essay about seat belt laws, you might tell about the painful rehabilitation of a teenager who was not wearing a seat belt and was injured in an accident in order to persuade readers that seat belt use should be mandatory.

3–4

AUDIENCE Whom do you want to reach, and do you have an anecdote or other narrative that will help them understand your topic or persuade them that your argument has merit?

5–8

GENRE Does your genre require you to include narrative? A memoir about an important event might be primarily narrative, whereas a reflection about an event might focus more on the significance of the event than on what happened.

9–11

STANCE What is your stance, and do you have any stories that would help you convey that stance? A funny story, for example, can help create a humorous stance.

12–14

MEDIA / DESIGN In a print or spoken text, you will likely be limited to brief narratives, perhaps illustrated with photos or other images. In an electronic text, you might have the option of linking to full-length narratives or visuals available on the Web.

15–17

IF YOU NEED MORE HELP

See also the **PROCESSES** chapters if you are assigned to write a narrative essay and need help drafting, revising, and so on. Two special kinds of narratives are **LAB REPORTS** (which use narrative to describe the steps in an experiment from beginning to end) and **RÉSUMÉS** (which essentially tell the story of the work we've done, at school and on the job).

209–58
133–42
188–95

40 Reading Strategies

We read newspapers and websites to learn about the events of the day. We read cookbooks to find out how to make brownies and textbooks to learn about history, chemistry, and other academic topics. We read short stories for pleasure—and, in literature classes, to analyze plot, setting, character, and theme. And as writers, we read our own drafts to make sure they say what we mean, and we proofread our final drafts to make sure they're correct. In other words, we read in various ways for many different purposes. This chapter offers a number of strategies for reading with a critical eye—from previewing a text to annotating as you read, identifying meaningful patterns, analyzing an argument, and more.

Reading Strategically

Academic reading is challenging because it makes several demands on you at once. Textbooks present new vocabulary and concepts, and picking out the main ideas can be difficult. Scholarly articles present content and arguments you need to understand, but they often assume readers already know key concepts and vocabulary and so don't generally provide background information. As you read more texts in an academic field and participate in its conversations, the reading will become easier, but in the meantime you can develop strategies that will help you to read carefully and critically.

Different texts require different kinds of effort. Some texts can be read fairly quickly, if you're reading to get a general overview. Most of the time, though, you need to read carefully, matching the pace of your reading to the difficulty of the text. To read with a critical eye, you can't be in too much of a hurry. You'll likely need to skim the text for an overview of the basic ideas and then go back to read carefully. And then you may read the text

rhetorical situations ▲ genres ○ processes ◆ strategies ● research mla/apa □ media/ design ◈ handbook again. That is true for visual as well as verbal texts—you'll often need to get an overview of a text and then reread to pay close attention to its details.

Previewing a Text

It's usually a good idea to start by skimming a text: read the title and sub-title, any headings, the first and last paragraphs, the first sentences of all the other paragraphs. Study any illustrations and other visuals. Your goal is to get a sense of where the text is heading. At this point, don't stop to look up unfamiliar words; just underline them or put a mark in the margin, and look them up later.

Considering the Rhetorical Situation

PURPOSE What is the purpose? To entertain? Inform? Persuade readers to think something or take some action? 3–4

AUDIENCE Who is the intended audience? Are you a member of that group? If not, should you expect that you'll need to look up unfamiliar terms or concepts or that you'll run into assumptions you don't necessarily share? 5–8

GENRE What is the genre? Is it a report? An argument? An analysis? Something else? Knowing the genre can help you anticipate certain key features. 9–11

STANCE Who is the writer, and what is his or her stance? Critical? Curious? Opinionated? Objective? Passionate? Indifferent? Something else? Knowing the stance affects the way you understand a text, whether you're inclined to agree or disagree, to take it seriously, and so on. 12–14

MEDIA / DESIGN What is the medium, and how does it affect the way you read? If it's a print text, do you know anything about the publisher? If it's on the Web, who sponsors the site, and when was it last updated? Are there any design elements—such as headings, summaries, color, or boxes—that highlight key parts of the text? 15–17

Thinking about Your Initial Response

It's usually good to read a text first just to get a sense of it. Some readers find it helps to jot down brief notes about their first response to a text, noting their reaction and thinking a little about why they reacted as they did:

- *What are your initial reactions?* Describe both your intellectual reaction and any emotional reaction. Identify places in the text that caused you to react as you did. If you had no particular reaction, note that.

- *What accounts for your reaction?* Do you agree or disagree with the writer or have a different perspective? Why? Are your reactions rooted in personal experiences? Positions you hold? Particular beliefs? Some personal philosophy? As much as possible, you want to keep your opinions from coloring your analysis, so it's important to try to identify those opinions up front—and to give some thought to where they come from.

Annotating

Many readers find it helps to annotate as they read: highlighting key words, phrases, sentences; connecting ideas with lines or symbols; writing comments or questions in the margin; noting anything that seems noteworthy or questionable. Annotate as if you're having a conversation with the author, someone you take seriously but whose words you do not accept without question. Put your part of the conversation in the margin, asking questions, talking back: "What's this mean?" "So what?" "Says who?" "Where's evidence?" "Yes!" "Whoa!" or even ☺ or ☹. You may find it useful to annotate using text messaging shorthand: "intrstn," "mjr point". If you're using online sources, you may be able to copy them and annotate them electronically. If so, make your annotations a different color than the text itself.

What you annotate depends on your **PURPOSE** or what you're most interested in. If you're analyzing an argument, you would probably underline any **THESIS STATEMENT** and then the **REASONS AND EVIDENCE** that support the statement. It might help to restate those ideas in your own words,

3–4

273–75
286–93

rhetorical situations
genres
processes
strategies
research mla/apa
media/ design
handbook

in the margins — in order to put them in your own words, you need to understand them! If you are looking for meaningful patterns, you might highlight each pattern in a different color and write any questions or notes about it in that color. If you are analyzing a literary text to look for certain elements or themes or patterns, you might highlight key passages that demonstrate those things.

Annotating forces you to read for more than just the surface meaning. Especially when you are going to be writing about or responding to a text, annotating creates a record of things you may want to refer to.

There are some texts that you cannot annotate, of course: library books, materials you read on the Web, and so on. Then you will need to make notes elsewhere, and you might find it useful to keep a reading log for that purpose.

On pages 356–57 is an annotated passage from Lawrence Lessig's essay "Some Like It Hot," included in Chapter 9. These annotations rephrase key definitions, identify the essay's thesis and main ideas, ask questions, and comment on issues raised in the essay. Annotating the entire essay, which appears on pages 88–92, would provide a look at Lessig's ideas and a record of the experience of reading the essay — useful for both understanding it and analyzing it.

Playing the Believing and Doubting Game

One way to think about your response to a text is to **LIST** or **FREEWRITE** as many reasons as you can think of for believing what the writer says and then as many as you can for doubting it. First, write as if you agree with everything in the writer's argument; look at the world from his or her perspective, trying to understand the writer's premises and reasons for arguing as he or she does even if you strongly disagree. Then, write as if you doubt everything in the text: try to find every flaw in the argument, every possible way it can be refuted — even if you totally agree with it. Developed by writing theorist Peter Elbow, the believing and doubting game helps you consider new ideas and question ideas you already have — and at the same time see where you stand in relation to the ideas in the text you're reading.

◑ 219–21

Piracy—
unauthorized use
of the artistic
work of others.

"Content
industry"—new
term. Film, music,
and so on?
Doesn't include
books and maga-
zines?

Thesis: "Big
media" are all
based on piracy.

Hollywood film
industry started
in order to avoid
Edison's patents.
What were they
for? Cameras and
projectors? Is this
true?

Record-industry
piracy.

Player pianos?

If piracy means using the creative property of others without their per-mission, then the history of the content industry is a history of piracy. Every important sector of big media today—film, music, radio, and cable TV—was born of a kind of piracy. The consistent story is how each generation welcomes the pirates from the last. Each generation—until now.

The Hollywood film industry was built by fleeing pirates. Creators and directors migrated from the East Coast to California in the early twentieth century in part to escape controls that film patents granted the inventor Thomas Edison. These controls were exercised through the Motion Pictures Patents Company, a monopoly "trust" based on Edison's creative property and formed to vigorously protect his patent rights.

California was remote enough from Edison's reach that filmmakers like Fox and Paramount could move there and, without fear of the law, pirate his inventions. Hollywood grew quickly, and enforcement of federal law eventually spread west. But because patents granted their holders a truly "limited" monopoly of just seventeen years (at that time), the patents had expired by the time enough federal marshals appeared. A new industry had been founded, in part from the piracy of Edison's creative property.

Meanwhile, the record industry grew out of another kind of piracy. At the time that Edison and Henri Fourneaux invented machines for reproducing music (Edison the phonograph; Fourneaux the player piano), the law gave composers the exclusive right to control copies and public performances of their music. Thus, in 1900, if I wanted a copy of Phil Russel's 1899 hit, "Happy Mose," the law said I would have to pay for the right to get a copy of the score, and I would also have to pay for the right to perform it publicly.

But what if I wanted to record "Happy Mose" using Edison's phonograph or Fourneaux's player piano? Here the law stumbled. If I simply sang the piece into a recording device in my home, it wasn't clear that I owed the composer anything. And more important, it wasn't clear whether I owed the composer anything if I then made copies of those recordings. Because of this gap in the law, I could effectively use someone else's song without paying the composer anything. The composers (and publishers) were none too happy about this capacity to pirate.

In 1909, Congress closed the gap in favor of the composer and the recording artist, amending copyright law to make sure that composers would be paid for "mechanical reproductions" of their music. But rather than simply granting the composer complete control over the right to make such reproductions, Congress gave recording artists a right to record the music, at a price set by Congress, after the composer allowed it to be recorded once. This is the part of copyright law that makes cover songs possible. Once a composer authorizes a recording of his song, others are free to record the same song, so long as they pay the original composer a fee set by the law. So, by limiting musicians' rights—by partially pirating their creative work—record producers and the public benefit.

—Lawrence Lessig, "Some Like It Hot"

Is copyright law different for books and other printed matter?

Partial piracy? Not sure about this—when artists use a song, they pay a fee but don't need permission. The composer doesn't have complete control. So it's piracy, but not completely?

Thinking about How the Text Works: What It Says, What It Does

Sometimes you'll need to think about how a text works, how its parts fit together. You may be assigned to analyze a text, or you may just need to make sense of a difficult text, to think about how the ideas all relate to one another. Whatever your purpose, a good way to think about a text's structure is by 223–24 ○ **OUTLINING** it, paragraph by paragraph. If you're interested in analyzing its ideas, look at what each paragraph *says*; if, on the other hand, you're concerned with how the ideas are presented, pay attention to what each paragraph *does*.

What it says. Write a sentence that identifies what each paragraph says. Once you've done that for the whole text, look for patterns in the topics the writer addresses. Pay attention to the order in which the topics are presented. Also look for gaps, ideas the writer has left unsaid. Such paragraph-by-paragraph outlining of the content can help you see how the writer has arranged ideas and how that arrangement builds an argument or develops a topic. Here, for example, is such an outline of Lawrence Lessig's essay (the left column refers to paragraph numbering noted in the full version of the essay on pages 88–92):

1	Every major type of media bases its development on piracy, the unauthorized use of artists' work.
2–3	To escape patents that restricted the copying of innovations in filmmaking, the movie industry moved from the East Coast to California.
4–5	Copyright law gave composers control over the performance of their music — but because it didn't cover the recording of music and the sale of copies of the recordings, it allowed piracy in the record industry.
6	Congress eventually changed the law, allowing musicians to record a song without the composer's permission if they paid the composer a fee.
7–11	When a radio station plays a song, it pays the composer but not the recording artist, thus pirating the artist's work.

12, 13	Cable TV has pirated works, too, by paying networks nothing for their broadcasts — despite protests by broadcasters and copyright owners.
14	Congress eventually extended the copyright law to cable TV, forcing the cable companies to pay for their broadcasts at a price controlled by Congress in order to protect the innovations of the cable industry.
15	The history of the major media industries suggests that piracy is not necessarily "plainly wrong."
16, 17	Peer-to-peer file sharing, like the earlier media-industry innovations, is being used to share artistic content and avoid industry controls, but it differs from the early cable industry in that it is not selling any content.
18	P2P file sharing provides access to music that can no longer be purchased, music that copyright holders want to share, and music that is no longer copyrighted.
19	P2P file sharing, like the earlier innovations, is the result of new technology, and it raises similar questions: how can it best be used without penalizing the artists whose works are "pirated"?
20	Copyright law must balance the protection of artists' works with the innovation in technologies, a process that takes time.

What it does.   Identify the function of each paragraph. Starting with the first paragraph, ask, What does this paragraph do? Does it introduce a topic? Provide background for a topic to come? Describe something? Define something? Entice me to read further? Something else? What does the second paragraph do? The third? As you go through the text, you may identify groups of paragraphs that have a single purpose. For an example, look at this functional outline of Lessig's essay (again, the numbers on the left refer to the paragraphs):

1	Defines the key term, *piracy*, and illustrates the thesis using the history of four media industries in the United States.
2–3	Tells the history of the first medium, film, by focusing on piracy as a major factor in its development.
4–6	Tells the history of the second medium, the recording industry, again by focusing on the role of piracy in its development.

7–11	Tells the history of the third medium, radio, focusing on the role of piracy in its development.
12–14	Tells the history of the fourth medium, cable TV, focusing on the role of piracy in its development.
15	Offers conclusions about piracy based on the similar roles played by piracy in the histories of the four media.
16–17	Compares the current controversy over piracy in peer-to-peer file sharing on the Internet with the role of piracy in the earlier media.
18	Describes the benefits of P2P file sharing.
19–20	Compares those benefits with those of the other media and offers a conclusion in the form of a problem to be solved.

Summarizing

416–17

Summarizing a text can help you both to see the relationships among its ideas and to understand what it's saying. When you **SUMMARIZE**, you restate a text's main ideas in your own words, leaving out most examples and other details. Here's a summary of Lawrence Lessig's essay:

> In his essay "Some Like It Hot," Lawrence Lessig argues that the development of every major media industry is based on piracy, the unauthorized use of artists' or inventors' work. First, the film industry flourished by evading restrictions on the copying of innovations in filmmaking. Then, the recording industry benefited from copyright laws that gave composers control over the performance of their music but not over the recording of it or the sale of the recordings. A law passed in 1909 in effect allows musicians to record a song without the composer's permission if they pay the composer a fee. According to Lessig, radio broadcasters benefit from piracy, too, every time they play a song recorded by someone other than the composer: they pay the composer a fee but not the recording artist. Finally, when it first started operating, cable TV benefited from piracy — by paying the networks nothing for their broadcasts. Congress eventually extended the copyright law, forcing cable companies to pay for the content they broadcast — but at a price controlled by Congress so that the networks wouldn't be able

to drive the cable companies out of business. Peer-to-peer file sharing, like the early media industries, is being used to share artistic content and avoid industry controls on that sharing. It benefits the public by allowing access to music that is out of print, that copyright holders want to share, and that is no longer copyrighted. Therefore, Lessig argues, the public needs to figure out how to make file-sharing work without penalizing musicians by pirating their songs. Copyright law must balance the protection of artists' work with the encouragement of technological innovation.

Identifying Patterns

Look for notable patterns in the text: recurring words and their synonyms, as well as repeated phrases, metaphors and other images, and types of sentences. Some writers find it helps to highlight patterns in various colors. Does the author rely on any particular writing strategies: **NARRATION?** **COMPARISON?** Something else?

343–51
306–13

It might be important to consider the kind of evidence offered: Is it more opinion than fact? Nothing but statistics? If many sources are cited, is the information presented in any predominant patterns: as **QUOTATIONS?** **PARAPHRASES? SUMMARIES?** Are there repeated references to certain experts or sources?

418–19

In visual texts, look for patterns of color, shape, and line. What's in the foreground, and what's in the background? What's completely visible, partly visible, or invisible? In both verbal and visual texts, look for omissions and anomalies. What isn't there that you would expect to find? Is there anything that doesn't really fit in?

If you discover patterns, then you need to consider what, if anything, they mean in terms of what the writer is saying. What do they reveal about the writer's underlying premises and beliefs? What do they tell you about the writer's strategies for persuading readers to accept the truth of what he or she is saying?

See how color coding William Safire's essay on the Gettysburg Address reveals several patterns in the language Safire uses. In this excerpt from the essay, which appears in full in Chapter 7, religious references are colored yellow; references to a "national spirit," green; references to life, death, and rebirth, blue; and places where he directly addresses the reader, gray.

> But the selection of this poetic political sermon as the oratorical centerpiece of our observance need not be only an exercise. . . . now, as then, a national spirit rose from the ashes of destruction.
>
> Here is how to listen to Lincoln's all-too-familiar speech with new ears.
>
> In those 266 words, you will hear the word *dedicate* five times. . . .
>
> Those five pillars of dedication rested on a fundament of religious metaphor. From a president not known for his piety — indeed, often criticized for his supposed lack of faith — came a speech rooted in the theme of national resurrection. The speech is grounded in conception, birth, death, and rebirth.
>
> Consider the barrage of images of birth in the opening sentence. . . .
>
> Finally, the nation's spirit rises from this scene of death: "that this nation, under God, shall have a new birth of freedom." Conception, birth, death, rebirth. The nation, purified in this fiery trial of war, is resurrected. Through the sacrifice of its sons, the sundered nation would be reborn as one. . . .
>
> Do not listen on Sept. 11 only to Lincoln's famous words and comforting cadences. Think about how Lincoln's message encompasses but goes beyond paying "fitting and proper" respect to the dead and the bereaved. His sermon at Gettysburg reminds "us the living" of our "unfinished work" and "the great task remaining before us" — to resolve that this generation's response to the deaths of thousands of our people leads to "a new birth of freedom."

The color coding helps us to see patterns in Safire's language, just as Safire reveals patterns in Lincoln's words. He offers an interpretation of Lincoln's address as a "poetic political sermon," and the words he uses throughout support that interpretation. At the end, he repeats the assertion that Lincoln's address is a sermon, inviting us to consider it differently. Targeting different textual elements, such as commands to the reader ("Consider," "Do not listen," "Think about"), offers additional

information on how Safire wishes to position himself in relation to his readers.

Count up the parts. This is a two-step process. First, you count things: how many of this, how many of that. Look for words, phrases, or sentences that seem important, or select a few typical paragraphs on which to focus. After you count, see what you can conclude about the writing. You may want to work with others, dividing up the counting.

- *Count words.* Count one-, two-, three-syllable words, repeated words, active and passive verbs, prepositions, jargon or specialized terms.

- *Count sentences.* Count the number of words in each sentence, the average number of words per sentence; figure the percentage of sentences above and below average. Count the number of sentences in each paragraph. Count the number of simple sentences, compound sentences, complex sentences, and fragments. Mark the distinct rhythms (tap out the beat as you read aloud). Count repeated phrases.

- *Count paragraphs.* Count the number of paragraphs, the average number of words and sentences per paragraph, the shortest and longest paragraphs. Consider the position of the longest and shortest paragraphs. Find parallel paragraph structures.

- *Count images.* List, circle, or underline verbal or visual images, similes, metaphors, and other figures of speech. Categorize them by meaning as well as type.

What do your findings tell you about the text? What generalizations can you make about it? Why did the author choose the words or images he or she used and in those combinations? What do those words tell you about the writer—or about his or her stance? Do your findings suggest a strategy, a plan for your analysis? For instance, Safire counts the number of times Lincoln uses *dedicate* and images of birth, death, and rebirth to argue something about Lincoln's speech and what it should mean to Safire's audience on the anniversary of 9/11.

Analyzing the Argument

All texts make some kind of argument, claiming something and then offering reasons and evidence as support for the claim. As a critical reader, you need to look closely at the argument a text makes—you need to recognize all the claims it makes, consider the support it offers for those claims, and decide how you want to respond. What do you think, and why? Here are some of the aspects of a text you'll need to consider when you analyze an argument:

- *What is the claim?* What is the main point the writer is trying to make? Is there a clearly stated THESIS, or is it merely implied?

- *What support does the writer offer for the claim?* What REASONS are given to support the claim? What EVIDENCE backs up those reasons? Facts? Statistics? Testimonials by authorities? Examples? Pertinent anecdotes? Are the reasons plausible and sufficient?

- *How evenhandedly does the writer present the issues?* Is there any mention of counterarguments? If so, how does the writer deal with them? By REFUTING them? By ACKNOWLEDGING them and responding to them reasonably? Does the writer treat other arguments respectfully? Dismissively? Are his or her own arguments appropriately qualified?

- *What authorities or sources of outside information does the writer use?* How are they used? How credible are they? Are they in any way biased or otherwise unreliable? Are they current?

- *How does the writer address you as the reader?* Does the writer assume that readers know something about what is being discussed? Does his or her language include you or exclude you? (Hint: If you see the word *we*, do you feel included?) Do you sense that you and the author share any beliefs or attitudes?

Check for fallacies. FALLACIES are arguments that involve faulty reasoning. Because they often seem plausible, they can be persuasive. It is important, therefore, that you question the legitimacy of such reasoning when you run across it.

273–75

286–93

294–95

296–98

Considering the Larger Context

All texts are part of ongoing conversations with other texts that have dealt with the same topic. An essay arguing for handgun trigger locks is part of an ongoing conversation about gun control, which is itself part of a conversation on individual rights and responsibilities. Academic texts document their sources in part to show their relationship to the ongoing scholarly conversations on a particular topic. Academic reading usually challenges you to become aware of those conversations. And, in fact, any time you're reading to learn, you're probably reading for some larger context. Whatever your reading goals, being aware of that larger context can help you better understand what you're reading. Here are some specific aspects of the text to pay attention to:

- *Who else cares about this topic?* Especially when you're reading in order to learn about a topic, the texts you read will often reveal which people or groups are part of the conversation — and might be sources of further reading. For example, an essay describing the formation of Mammoth Cave could be of interest to geologists, spelunkers, travel writers, or tourists. If you're reading such an essay while doing research on the cave, you should consider how the audience addressed determines the nature of the information provided — and its suitability as a source for your research.

- *Ideas.* Does the text refer to any concepts or ideas that give you some sense that it's part of a larger conversation? An argument on airport security measures, for example, is part of larger conversations about government response to terrorism, the limits of freedom in a democracy, and the possibilities of using technology to detect weapons and explosives, among others.

- *Terms.* Is there any terminology or specialized language that reflects the writer's allegiance to a particular group or academic discipline? If you run across words like *false consciousness*, *ideology*, and *hegemony*, for example, you might guess the text was written by a Marxist scholar.

- *Citations.* Whom does the writer cite? Do the other writers have a particular academic specialty, belong to an identifiable intellectual school, share similar political leanings? If an article on politics cites Michael Moore and Barbara Ehrenreich in support of its argument, you might assume the writer holds liberal opinions; if it cites Rush Limbaugh and Sean Hannity, the writer is likely a conservative.

400–403

229–34

235–41

242–46

IF YOU NEED MORE HELP

See also the chapter on **EVALUATING SOURCES** for help analyzing the reliability of a text, and see the chapters on **ASSESSING YOUR OWN WRITING, GETTING RESPONSE AND REVISING,** and **EDITING AND PROOFREADING** for advice on reading your own writing.

Taking Essay Exams 41

Essay exams present writers with special challenges. You must write quickly, on a topic presented to you on the spot, to show your instructor what you know about a specific body of information. This chapter offers advice on how to take essay exams.

Considering the Rhetorical Situation

PURPOSE   In an essay exam, your purpose is to show that you have mastered certain material, and that you can analyze and apply it in an essay. You may need to make an argument, or simply to convey information on a topic.

3–4

AUDIENCE   Will your course instructor be reading your exam, or a TA? Sometimes standardized tests are read by groups of trained readers. What specific criteria will your audience use to evaluate your writing?

5–8

GENRE   Does the essay question specify or suggest a certain genre? In a literature course, you may need to write a compelling literary analysis of a passage. In a history course, you may need to write an argument for the significance of a key historical event. In an economics course, you may need to contrast the economies of the North and South before the Civil War. If the essay question doesn't specify a genre, look for key words such as *argue*, *evaluate*, or *explain*, which point to a certain genre.

9–11

12–14 ▪   **STANCE**   In an essay exam, your stance is usually unemotional, thoughtful, and critical.

15–17 ▪   **MEDIA / DESIGN**   Since essay exams are usually handwritten on lined paper or in an exam booklet, legible handwriting is a must.

Analyzing Essay Questions

Essay questions usually include key verbs that specify the kind of writing you'll need to do—argue a position, compare two texts, and so on. Following are some of the most common kinds of writing you'll be asked to do on an essay exam.

38–58 ▲

- *Analyze:* Break an idea, theory, text, or event into its parts and examine them. For example, a world history exam might ask you to **ANALYZE** European imperialism's effect on Africa in the late nineteenth century, and discuss how Africans responded.

- *Apply:* Consider how an idea or concept might work out in practice. For instance, a film studies exam might ask you to apply the concept of auterism—a theory of film that sees the director as the primary creator, whose body of work reflects a distinct personal style—to two films by Robert Altman. An economics exam might ask you to apply the concept of opportunity costs to a certain supplied scenario.

283–99 ◆

- *Argue/prove/justify:* Offer reasons and evidence to support a position. A philosophy exam, for example, might ask you to **ARGUE** whether or not all stereotypes contain a "kernel of truth," and whether believing a stereotype is ever justified.

300–305 ◆

- *Classify:* Group something into categories. For example, a marketing exam might ask you to **CLASSIFY** shoppers in categories based on their purchasing behavior, motives, attitudes, or lifestyle patterns.

- *Compare/contrast:* Explore the similarities and/or differences between two or more things. An economics exam, for example, might ask you to **COMPARE** the effectiveness of patents and tax incentives in encouraging technological advances.

306–13

- *Critique:* **ANALYZE** and **EVALUATE** a text or argument, considering its strengths and weaknesses. For instance, an evolutionary biology exam might ask you to critique John Maynard Smith's assertion that "scientific theories say nothing about what is right, but only about what is possible" in the context of the theory of evolution.

38–58
125–32

- *Define:* Explain what a word or phrase means. An art history exam, for example, might ask you to **DEFINE** negative space, and to discuss the way various artists use it in their work.

314–23

- *Describe:* Tell about the important characteristics or features of something. For example, a sociology exam might ask you to **DESCRIBE** Erving Goffman's theory of the presentation of self in ordinary life, focusing on roles, props, and setting.

324–32

- *Evaluate:* Determine something's significance or value. A drama exam, for example, might ask you to **EVALUATE** the setting, lighting, and costumes in a filmed production of *Macbeth*.

125–32

- *Explain:* Provide reasons and examples to clarify an idea, argument, or event. For instance, a rhetoric exam might ask you to explain the structure of the African American sermon and discuss its use in writings of Frederick Douglass and Martin Luther King Jr.

- *Summarize/review:* Give the major points of a text or idea. A political science exam, for example, might ask you to **SUMMARIZE** John Stuart Mill's concept of utilitarianism and its relation to freedom of speech.

416–17

- *Trace:* Explain a sequence of ideas or order of events. For instance, a geography exam might ask you to trace the patterns of international migration since 1970, and discuss how these patterns differ from those of the 1870s.

Some Guidelines for Taking Essay Exams

Before the exam

354–55
- **Read** over your class notes and course texts strategically, **ANNOTATING** them to keep track of details you'll want to remember.

215–16
- **Collaborate** by forming a **STUDY GROUP** that meets throughout the term to help one another master the course content.

404–6
- **Review** key ideas, events, terms, and themes. Look for common themes and **CONNECTIONS** in lecture notes, class discussions, and any readings — they'll lead you to important ideas.

- **Ask** your instructor about the form the exam will take: how long it will be, what kind of questions will be on it, how it will be evaluated, and so on. Working with a study group, write questions you think your instructor might ask, and then answer the questions together.

219–20
- **Warm up** just before the exam by **FREEWRITING** for ten minutes or so to gather your thoughts.

During the exam

- **Scan the questions** to determine how much each part of the test counts and how much time you should spend on it. For example, if one essay is worth 50 points and two others are worth 25 points each, you'll want to spend half your time on the 50-point question.

- **Read over** the entire test before answering any questions. Start with the question you feel most confident answering, which may or may not be the first question on the test.

- **Don't panic.** Know yourself and your first reaction to the testing situation. Sometimes when I first read an essay question, my mind goes blank, but after a few moments, I start to recall the information I need.

- **Plan.** Although you won't have much time for revising or editing, you still need to plan and allow yourself time to make some last-minute changes before you turn in the exam. So apportion your time. For a three-question essay test in a two-hour test period, you might divide your time like this:

Total Exam Time — 120 minutes
Generating ideas — 20 minutes (6–7 minutes per question)
Drafting — 85 minutes (45 for the 50-point question,
                         20 for each 25-point question)
Revising, editing, proofreading — 15 minutes

Knowing that you have built in time at the end of the exam period can help you remain calm as you write, as you can use that time to fill in gaps or reconsider answers you feel unsure about.

- *Jot down the main ideas* you need to cover in answering the question on scratch paper or on the cover of your exam book, number those ideas in the order you think makes sense — and you have an outline for your essay. If you're worried about time, plan to write the most important parts of your answers early on. If you don't complete your answer, refer your instructor to your outline to show where you were headed.

- *Turn the essay question into your introduction,* like this:

  Question: How did the outcomes of World War II differ from those of World War I?

  Introduction: The outcomes of World War II differed from those of World War I in three major ways: World War II affected more of the world and its people than World War I, distinctions between citizens and soldiers were eroded, and the war's brutality made it impossible for Europe to continue to claim cultural superiority over other cultures.

- *State your thesis explicitly,* provide **REASONS** and **EVIDENCE** to support your thesis, and use transitions to move logically from one idea to the next. Restate your main point in your conclusion. You don't want to give what one professor calls a "garbage truck answer," dumping everything you know into a blue book and expecting the instructor to sort it all out.

◆ 286–93

- *Write on every other line* and only on one side of each page so that you'll have room to make additions or corrections. If you're typing on a computer, double space.

- *If you have time left, go over your exam,* looking for ideas that need elaboration as well as for grammatical and punctuation errors.

After the exam. If your instructor doesn't return your exam, consider asking for a conference to go over your work so you can learn what you did well and where you need to improve — important knowledge to take with you into your next exam.

rhetorical situations

genres

processes

strategies

research mla/apa

media/ design

handbook

part 5

Doing Research

We do research all the time, for many different reasons. We search the Web for information about a new computer, ask friends about the best place to get coffee, try on several pairs of jeans before deciding which ones to buy. You have no doubt done your share of library research before now, and you probably have visited a number of schools' websites before deciding which college you wanted to attend. Research, in other words, is something you do every day. The following chapters offer advice on the kind of research you'll need to do for your academic work and, in particular, for research papers and other written documents.

Doing Research

Developing a Research Plan **42**

When you need to do research, it's sometimes tempting to jump in and start looking for information right away. To do research well, however—to find appropriate sources and use them wisely—you need to work systematically. You need a research plan. This chapter will help you establish such a plan and then get started.

Establishing a Schedule

Doing research is complex and time-consuming, so it's good to establish a schedule for yourself. Research-based writing projects usually require you to come up with a topic (or to analyze the requirements of an assigned topic). You'll need to do preliminary research to come up with a research question to guide your research efforts. Once you do some serious, focused research to find the information you need, you'll be ready to turn your research question into a tentative thesis and sketch out a rough outline. After doing whatever additional research you need to fill in your outline, you'll write a draft—and get some response to that draft. Perhaps you'll need to do additional research before revising. Finally, you'll need to edit and proofread. And so you'll want to start by establishing a schedule, perhaps using the form on the next page.

Getting Started

Once you have a schedule, you can get started. The sections that follow offer advice on considering your rhetorical situation, coming up with a topic, and thinking about what you already know about it; doing prelim-

rhetorical situations

genres

processes

strategies

research mla/apa

media/ design

handbook

Scheduling a Research Project

	Complete by:
Analyze your rhetorical situation.	_____
Choose a possible topic.	_____
Do preliminary research.	_____
Come up with a research question.	_____
Schedule interviews and other field research.	_____
Find and read library and Web sources.	_____
Do any field research.	_____
Come up with a tentative thesis and outline.	_____
Write out a draft.	_____
Get response.	_____
Do any additional research.	_____
Revise.	_____
Prepare a list of works cited.	_____
Edit.	_____
Prepare the final draft.	_____
Proofread.	_____
Submit the final draft.	_____

inary research, and creating a working bibliography; developing a research question, devising a tentative thesis and a rough outline, and keeping track of your sources. The chapters that follow offer guidelines for **FINDING SOURCES, EVALUATING SOURCES,** and **SYNTHESIZING IDEAS.**

384–99
400–405
404–7

Considering the Rhetorical Situation

As with any writing task, you need to start by considering your purpose, your audience, and the rest of your rhetorical situation:

PURPOSE　　Is this project part of an assignment—and if so, does it specify any one purpose? If not, what is your broad purpose? To inform? Argue? Entertain? A combination?　　■ 3–4

AUDIENCE　　To whom are you writing? What does your audience likely know about your topic, and is there any background information you'll need to provide? What opinions or attitudes do your readers likely hold? What kinds of evidence will they find persuasive? How do you want them to respond to your writing?　　■ 5–8

GENRE　　Are you writing to report on something? To compose a profile? To make a proposal? An argument? What are the requirements of your genre in terms of the number and kind of sources you must use?　　■ 9–11

STANCE　　What is your attitude toward your topic? What accounts for your attitude? How do you want to come across? Curious? Critical? Positive? Something else?　　■ 12–14

MEDIA / DESIGN　　What medium will you use? Print? Spoken? Electronic? Will you need to compose any charts, photographs, video, presentation software slides, or other visuals?　　■ 15–17

Coming Up with a Topic

If you need to choose a topic, consider your interests. What do you want to learn about? What do you have questions about? What topics from your courses have you found intriguing? What community, national, or global issues do you care about? If your topic is assigned, you still need to make sure you understand exactly what it asks you to do. Read the assignment carefully, looking for key words: does it ask you to **ANALYZE, COMPARE, EVALUATE, SUMMARIZE?** If the assignment offers broad guidelines but allows you to choose within them, identify the requirements and the range of possibilities, and define your topic within those constraints. For

◆ 278–82
306–13
▲ 125–32
● 416–17

example, in an American history course, your instructor might ask you to "discuss social effects of the Civil War." To define a suitable topic, you might choose to explore such topics as poverty among Confederate soldiers or former slaveholders, the migration of members of those groups to Mexico or northern cities, the establishment of independent black churches, the growth of sharecropping among former slaves, or the spread of the Ku Klux Klan — to name a few possibilities. Once you have a broad topic, you might try **FREEWRITING, LOOPING, LISTING,** or **CLUSTERING** to find an angle to research.

219–22 ◯

Narrow the topic.   As you consider possible topics, look to narrow your focus on a topic to make it specific enough for you to research and cover in a paper. For example:

> **Too general:** ethanol
>
> **Still too general:** ethanol and the environment
>
> **Better:** the potential environmental effects of increasing the use of gasoline mixed with ethanol

If you limit your topic, you can address it with specific information that you'll be more easily able to find and manage. In addition, a limited topic will be more likely to interest your audience than a broad subject that forces you to use abstract, general statements. For example, it's much harder to write well about "the environment" than it is to address a topic that covers a single environmental issue.

Think about what you know about your topic.   Chances are you already know something about your topic, and articulating that knowledge can help you see possible ways to focus your topic or come up with potential sources of information. **FREEWRITING, LISTING, CLUSTERING,** and **LOOPING** are all good ways of tapping your knowledge of your topic. Consider where you might find information about it: Have you read about it in a textbook? Heard stories about it on the news? Visited websites focused on it? Do you know anyone who knows about this topic?

219–22 ◯

Doing Some Preliminary Research

Doing some preliminary research can save you time in the long run. Scholarly sources usually focus on narrow, specialized aspects of subjects. To define the focus for your research, you first need to explore sources that will provide an overview of your topic.

One way to begin is to look at **REFERENCE WORKS** — sources that deal with the general topic and that include summaries or overviews of the scholarship in a field. General encyclopedias can give you some background, but they aren't suitable as sources for college work; use them as a starting point, to give you some basic information about your topic and help you see some of the paths you might follow. The same is true of the results you're likely to get from skimming websites on the subject. Discipline-specific encyclopedias can be more helpful, as they usually present subjects in much greater depth and provide more scholarly references that might suggest starting points for your research. Even if you know a lot about a subject, doing preliminary research can open you to new ways of seeing and approaching it, increasing your options for developing and narrowing your topic.

388–89

At this stage, pay close attention to the terms used to discuss your topic. These terms could be keywords that you can use to search for information on your topic in library catalogs, in databases, and on the Web.

Keeping a Working Bibliography

A working bibliography is a record of all the sources you consult. You should keep such a record so that you can find sources easily when you need them and then cite any that you use. You can keep a working bibliography on index cards or in a notebook, or in many cases you can print out or photocopy the data you find useful. To save time later, include all the bibliographic information you'll need to document the sources you use. If possible, follow the **DOCUMENTATION** style you'll use when you write.

425–27

On the next page is most of the basic information you'll want to include for each source in your working bibliography. Go to wwnorton.com/write/fieldguide for templates you can use to keep track of this information.

Information for a Working Bibliography

FOR A BOOK

Library call number
Author(s) or editor(s)
Title and subtitle
Publication information: city, publisher, year of publication
Other information: edition, volume number, translator, and so on
If your source is an essay in a collection, include its author, title, and page numbers.

FOR AN ARTICLE IN A PERIODICAL

Author(s)
Title and subtitle
Name of periodical
Volume number, issue number, date
Page numbers

FOR A WEB SOURCE

URL
DOI if provided
Author(s) or editor(s) if available
Name of site
Sponsor of site
Date site was first posted or last updated
Date you accessed site
If the source is an article or book reprinted on the Web, include its title, the title and publication information of the periodical or book where it was first published, and any page numbers.

FOR A SOURCE FROM AN ELECTRONIC DATABASE

Publication information for the source
Name of database
Item number, if there is one
Name of subscription service and its URL
Library where you accessed source
Date you accessed source

rhetorical situations | genres | processes | strategies | research mla/apa | media/design | handbook

Coming Up with a Research Question

Once you've surveyed the territory of your topic, you'll likely find that your understanding of your topic has become broader and deeper. You may find that your interests have changed and your research has led to surprises and additional research. That's okay: as a result of exploring avenues you hadn't anticipated, you may well come up with a better topic than the one you'd started with. At some point, though, you need to come up with a research question—a specific question that you will then work to answer through your research.

To write a research question, review your analysis of the **RHETORICAL SITUATION,** to remind yourself of any time constraints or length considerations. Generate a list of questions beginning with *What? When? Where? Who? How? Why? Would? Could?* and *Should?* Here, for example, are some questions about the tentative topic "the potential environmental effects of increasing the use of gasoline mixed with ethanol":

◼ 1

What are the environmental effects of producing and burning ethanol, gasoline, and diesel fuel?

When was ethanol introduced as a gasoline additive?

Where is ethanol produced, and how does this affect the energy costs of transporting it?

Who will benefit from increased ethanol use?

How much energy does producing ethanol require?

Why do some environmental groups oppose the use of ethanol?

Would other alternative energy sources be more energy-efficient?

Could ethanol replace gasoline completely in passenger vehicles?

Should ethanol use be increased?

Select one question from your list that you find interesting and that suits your rhetorical situation. Use the question to guide your research.

Drafting a Tentative Thesis

Once your research has led you to a possible answer to your research question, try formulating that answer as a tentative **THESIS**. You need not be

◆ 273–75

committed to the thesis; in fact, you should not be. The object of your research should be to learn about your topic, not to find information that simply supports what you already think you believe. Your tentative thesis may (and probably will) change as you learn more about your subject, consider the many points of view on it, and reconsider your topic and, perhaps, your goal: what you originally planned to be an informational report may become an argument, or the argument you planned to write may become a report. However tentative, a thesis allows you to move forward by clarifying your purpose for doing research. Here are some tentative thesis statements on the topic of ethanol:

> Producing ethanol uses more fossil fuels than burning it saves.
>
> The federal government should require the use of ethanol as a gasoline additive.
>
> Ethanol is a more environmentally friendly fuel than gasoline, but it's not as "green" as liquid propane gas.

As with a research question, a tentative thesis should guide your research efforts — but be ready to revise it as you learn still more about your topic. Research should be a process of inquiry in which you approach your topic with an open mind, ready to learn and possibly change. If you hold too tightly to a tentative thesis, you risk focusing only on evidence that supports your view, making your writing biased and unconvincing.

Creating a Rough Outline

223–24

After you've created a tentative thesis, write out a rough **OUTLINE** for your research paper. Your rough outline can be a simple list of topics you want to explore, something that will help you structure your research efforts and organize your notes and other materials. As you read your sources, you can use your outline to keep track of what you need to find and where the information you do find fits into your argument. Then you'll be able to see if you've covered all the ideas you intended to explore — or whether you need to rethink the categories on your outline.

Keeping Track of Your Sources

- *Staple together copies and printouts of print materials.* It's easy for individual pages to get shuffled or lost on a desk or in a backpack. Keep a stapler handy, and fasten pages together as soon as you copy them or print them out.
- *Store website URLs* as *favorites* (in Internet Explorer) or *bookmarks* (in Firefox).
- *Label everything.* Label your copies with the source's author and title.
- *Highlight sections you plan to use.* When you sit down to draft, your goal will be to find what you need quickly, so as soon as you decide you might use a source, highlight the paragraphs or sentences that you think you'll use. If your instructor wants copies of your sources to see how you used them, you've got them ready.
- *Use your rough outline to keep track of what you've got.* In the margin of each highlighted section, write the number or letter of the outline division to which the section corresponds. (It's a good idea to write it in the same place consistently so you can flip through a stack of copies and easily see what you've got.) Alternatively, attach sticky notes to each photocopy, using a different color for each main heading in your outline.
- *Keep everything in a file folder or box.* That way, even though your research material may not look organized, it will all be in one place—and if you highlight, number, and use sticky notes, your material will be organized and you'll be better prepared to write a draft. This folder or box will also serve you well if you are required to create a portfolio that includes your research notes, photocopies of sources, and drafts.

IF YOU NEED MORE HELP

See the guidelines on **FINDING SOURCES** once you're ready to move on to in-depth research and those on **EVALUATING SOURCES** for help thinking critically about the sources you find.

384–99
400–403

43 Finding Sources

To analyze media coverage of the 2008 Democratic National Convention, you examine news stories and blogs published at the time. To write an essay interpreting a poem by Maya Angelou, you study the poem and read several critical interpretations in literary journals. To write a report on career opportunities in psychology, you interview a graduate of your university who is working in a psychology clinic. In each of these cases, you go beyond your own knowledge to consult additional sources of information.

This chapter offers guidelines for locating a range of sources—print and online, general and specialized, published and firsthand. Keep in mind that as you do research, finding and **EVALUATING SOURCES** are two activities that usually take place simultaneously. So this chapter and the next one go hand in hand.

400–403

Kinds of Sources

Primary and secondary sources.   Your research will likely lead you to both primary and secondary sources. *Primary sources* include historical documents, literary works, eyewitness accounts, field reports, diaries, letters, and lab studies, as well as any original research you do through interviews, observation, experiments, or surveys. *Secondary sources* include scholarly books and articles, reviews, biographies, textbooks, and other works that interpret or discuss primary sources. Novels and poems are primary sources; articles interpreting them are secondary sources. The

Declaration of Independence is a primary historical document; a historian's description of the events surrounding the Declaration's writing is secondary. A published report of scientific findings is primary; a critique of that report is secondary.

Whether a work is considered primary or secondary sometimes depends on your topic and purpose: if you're analyzing a poem, a critic's article interpreting the poem is a secondary source—but if you're investigating that critic's work, the article would be a primary source for your own study and interpretation.

Primary sources are useful because they offer subjects for firsthand study, whereas secondary sources can help you understand and evaluate primary source material.

Print and online sources.   Some sources are available only in print; some are available only online. But many print sources are also available on the Web. You'll find print sources in your school's library, but chances are that many of the books in your library's reference section will also be available online. And when it comes to finding sources, it's likely that you'll *search* for most sources online, through the library's website (rather than through a commercial search engine, which may lead you to unreliable sources). In general, there are four kinds of sources you'll want to consult, each of which is discussed in this chapter:

GENERAL REFERENCE WORKS, for encyclopedias, dictionaries, and the like ● 388

THE LIBRARY CATALOG, for books   389–90

INDEXES AND DATABASES, for periodicals   390–93

SEARCH ENGINES AND SUBJECT DIRECTORIES, for material on the Web   393–94

On the next page is a sample search page from the catalog of one university library. This catalog, like most, allows you to search by book title, journal title, author, subject, call number, and keyword. In addition, the links at the top of the page permit you to search through various indexes and databases and take advantage of interlibrary loan (for materials that your library doesn't have) and various tutorials.

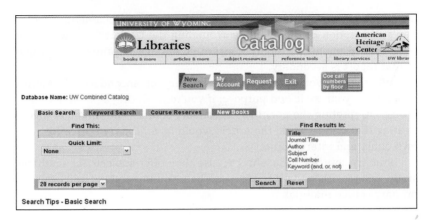

Part of a library catalog search page.

Searching Electronically

Whether you're searching for books, articles in periodicals, or material available on the Web, chances are you'll conduct much of your search electronically. Most materials produced since the 1980s can be found electronically, most library catalogs are online, and most periodical articles can be found by searching electronic indexes and databases. In each case, you can search for authors, titles, or subjects.

When you're searching for subjects, you'll need to come up with *keywords* that will lead you to the information you're looking for. Usually if you start with only one keyword, you'll end up with far too many results—tens of thousands of references when you're searching the Web—so the key to searching efficiently is to come up with keywords that will focus your searches on the information you need. Some search engines will let you enter more than one word and will identify only those sources that contain all the words you entered. Other search engines will let you type in more than one word and will identify those sources that contain at least one of those words but not necessarily all of them. Most search engines

have "advanced search" options that will help you focus your research. Specific commands will vary among search engines and within databases, but here are some of the most common ones:

- Type quotation marks around words to search for an exact phrase— "Thomas Jefferson"—unless you're using a search engine that includes a field to search for exact phrases, in which case you won't need the quotation marks. If your exact-phrase search doesn't yield good results, try removing the quotation marks.

- Type AND to find sources that include more than one keyword: Jefferson AND Adams. Some search engines require a plus sign instead: +Jefferson+Adams.

- Type OR if you're looking for sources that include one of several terms: Jefferson OR Adams OR Madison.

- Type NOT to find sources *without* a certain word: Jefferson NOT Adams. Some search engines call for a minus sign (actually, a hyphen) instead: +Jefferson-Adams will result in sources in which the name Jefferson appears but the name Adams does not.

- Type an asterisk—or some other symbol—to search for words in different forms—teach* will yield sources containing *teacher* and *teaching*, for example. Check the search engine's search tips to find out what symbol to use.

- Some search engines allow you to ask questions in conversational language: What did Thomas Jefferson write about slavery?

- Be more general (*education Japan* instead of *secondary education Japan*) when you get too few sources; be more specific (*homeopathy* instead of *medicine*) when you get far too many sources.

- If you don't get results with one set of keywords, substitute synonyms (if *folk medicine* doesn't generate much information, try *home remedy*). Or look through the sources that turn up in response to other terms to see what keywords you might use in subsequent searches. Searching requires flexibility, in the words you use and the methods you try.

Reference Works

The reference section of your school's library is the place to find encyclo-pedias, dictionaries, atlases, almanacs, bibliographies, and other reference works in print. Many of these sources are also online and can be accessed from any computer that is connected to the Internet. Others are available only in the library. Remember, though, that whether in print or online, reference works are only a starting point, a place where you can get an overview of your topic.

General reference works. Consult encyclopedias for general back-ground information on a subject, dictionaries for definitions of words, atlases for maps and geographic data, and almanacs for statistics and other data on current events. These are some works you might consult:

The New Encyclopaedia Britannica

The Columbia Encyclopedia

Webster's Third New International Dictionary

Oxford English Dictionary

National Geographic Atlas of the World

Statistical Abstract of the United States

The World Almanac and Book of Facts

Caution: Wikipedia is a popular online research tool, but since anyone can edit its entries, you can't be certain of its accuracy. Avoid using it.

Specialized reference works. You can also go to specialized reference works, which provide in-depth information on a single field or topic. These may also include authoritative bibliographies, leading you to more spe-cific works. A reference librarian can refer you to specialized encyclope-dias in particular fields; you'll find a list of some at wwnorton.com/write/fieldguide.

Bibliographies. Bibliographies provide an overview of what has been published on a topic, listing published works along with the information you'll need to find each work. Some are annotated with brief summaries of each work's contents. You'll find bibliographies at the end of scholarly articles and books, and you can also find book-length bibliographies, both in the reference section of your library and online. Check with a reference librarian for bibliographies on your research topic.

Books / Searching the Library Catalog

The library catalog is your primary source for finding books. Most library catalogs are computerized and can be accessed through the library's website. You can search by author, title, subject, or keyword. The image below shows the result of a keyword search for material on art in Nazi Germany. This search revealed that the library has nineteen books on

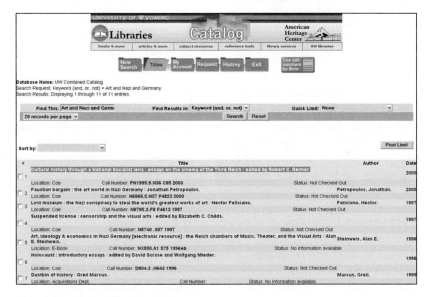

List of books on a library catalog screen.

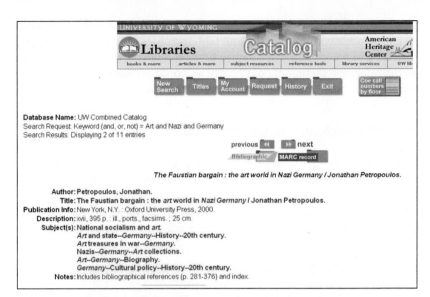

Information about a book on a library catalog screen.

the topic; to access information on each one, the researcher must simply click on the title. The image above shows detailed information for one source: bibliographic data about author, title, and publication; related subject headings (which may lead to other useful materials in the library) — and more. Library catalogs also supply a call number, which identifies the book's location on the library's shelves.

Periodicals / Searching Indexes and Databases

To find journal and magazine articles, you will need to search periodical indexes and databases. Indexes provide listings of articles organized by topics; databases provide the full texts. Some databases also provide indexes of bibliographic citations, so you can track down the actual articles. Some indexes are in print and can be found in the reference section

of the library; many are online. Some databases are available for free; most of the more authoritative ones, however, are available only by subscription and so must be accessed through a library.

Print indexes. You'll need to consult print indexes to find articles published before the 1980s. Here are six useful ones:

The Readers' Guide to Periodical Literature (print, 1900–; online, 1983–)

Magazine Index (print, 1988–; online via InfoTrac, 1973–)

The New York Times Index (print and online, 1851–)

Humanities Index (print, 1974–; online, 1984–)

Social Sciences Index (print, 1974–; online, 1983–)

General Science Index (print, 1978–; online, 1984–)

General electronic indexes and databases. A reference librarian can help you determine which databases will be most helpful to you, but here are some useful ones:

Academic Search Complete is a multidisciplinary index and database containing the full text of articles in more than 4,400 journals and indexing of over 9,300 journals, with abstracts of their articles.

EBSCOhost provides interlinked databases of abstracts and full-text articles from a variety of periodicals.

FirstSearch offers access to more than 10 million full-text, full-image articles in dozens of databases covering many disciplines.

InfoTrac offers over 20 million full-text articles in a broad spectrum of disciplines and on a wide variety of topics from nearly 6,000 scholarly and popular periodicals, including the *New York Times*.

JSTOR archives scanned copies of entire publication runs of scholarly journals in many disciplines, but it does not include current issues of the journals.

LexisNexis Academic Universe contains full-text publications and articles from a large number of sources—newspapers, business and legal resources, medical texts, and reference sources such as *The World Almanac* and the Roper public opinion polls.

ProQuest provides access to full-text articles from thousands of periodicals and newspapers from 1986 to the present, with many entries updated daily, and a large collection of dissertations and theses.

SIRS Researcher contains records of articles from selected domestic and international newspapers, magazines, journals, and government publications.

Single-subject indexes and databases. These are just a sample of what's available; check with a reference librarian for indexes and databases in the subject you're researching.

America: History and Life indexes scholarly literature on the history of the United States and Canada.

BIOSIS Previews provides abstracts and indexes for more than 5,500 sources on biology, botany, zoology, environmental studies, and agriculture.

ERIC is the U.S. Department of Education's Educational Resource Information Center database.

Historical Abstracts includes abstracts of articles on the history of the world, excluding the United States and Canada, since 1450.

Humanities International Index contains bibliographic references to more than 1,700 journals dealing with the humanities.

MLA International Bibliography indexes scholarly articles on modern languages, literature, folklore, and linguistics.

PsychINFO indexes scholarly literature in a number of disciplines relating to psychology.

Web-based indexes and databases. The following are freely available on the Internet:

Infomine contains "useful Internet resources such as databases, electronic journals, electronic books, bulletin boards, mailing lists, online library card catalogs, articles, directories of researchers, and many other types of information."

Librarians' Internet Index is a searchable, annotated subject directory of more than 20,000 websites selected and evaluated by librarians for their usefulness to users of public libraries.

The World Wide Web Virtual Library is a catalog of websites on a wide range of subjects, compiled by volunteers with expertise in particular subject areas.

CSA Discovery Guides provide comprehensive information on current issues in biomedicine, engineering, the environment, the social sciences, and the humanities, with an overview of each subject, key citations with abstracts, and links to websites.

The Voice of the Shuttle: Web Site for Humanities Research offers information on subjects in the humanities, organized to mirror the way the humanities are organized for research and teaching as well as the way they are adapting to social, cultural, and technological changes.

The Library of Congress offers online access to information on a wide range of subjects, including academic subjects, as well as prints, photographs, and government documents.

JURIST is a university-based online gateway to authoritative legal instruction, information, scholarship, and news.

The Web

The Web provides access to countless sites containing information posted by governments, educational institutions, organizations, businesses, and individuals. Websites are different from other sources in several ways: (1) they often provide entire texts, not just citations of texts, (2) their content varies greatly in its reliability, and (3) they are not stable: what you see on a site today may be different (or gone) tomorrow. Anyone who wants to can post texts on the Web, so you need to **EVALUATE** carefully what you find there.

400–403

Because it is so vast and dynamic, finding what you want on the Web can be a challenge. The primary way of finding information on the Web is with a search engine. There are several ways of searching the Web:

- *Keyword searches.* Google, HotBot, AltaVista, Lycos, and Yahoo! all scan the Web looking for keywords that you specify.

- *Subject directories.* Google, Yahoo!, and some other search engines offer directories that arrange information by topics, much like a library cataloging system. Such directories allow you to broaden or narrow your search if you need to—for example, a search for "birds" can be broadened to "animals" or narrowed to "blue-footed booby."

- *Metasearches.* Copernic Agent, SurfWax, and Dogpile are metasearch engines that allow you to use several search engines simultaneously.

- *Academic searches.* You may find more suitable results for academic writing at Google Scholar (scholar.google.com), a search engine that finds scholarly literature, including peer-reviewed papers, technical reports, and abstracts, or at Scirus (scirus.com), which finds peer-reviewed documents on scientific, technical, and medical topics.

Each search engine and metasearch engine has its own protocols for searching; most have an "advanced search" option that will help you search more productively. Remember, though, that you need to be careful about evaluating sources that you find on the Web because the Web is unregulated and no one independently verifies the information posted on its sites.

Doing Field Research

Sometimes you'll need to do your own research, to go beyond the information you find in published sources and gather data by doing field research. Three kinds of field research you might want to consider are interviews, observations, and questionnaires.

Interviewing experts.   Some kinds of writing—a profile of a living person, for instance—almost require that you conduct an interview. And sometimes you may just need to find information that you haven't been able to find in published sources. To get firsthand information on the experience of serving as a soldier in Iraq, you might interview your cousin who served a tour of duty there; to find current research on pesticide residues

rhetorical situations

genres

processes

strategies

research mla/apa

media/ design

handbook

in food, you might need to interview a toxicologist. Whatever your goal, you can conduct interviews face-to-face, over the telephone, or by mail or email. In general, you will want to use interviews to find information you can't find elsewhere. Below is some advice on planning and conducting an interview.

Before the interview

1. Once you identify someone you want to interview, email or phone to ask for an appointment, stating your **PURPOSE** for the interview and what you hope to learn.
2. Once you've set up the appointment, send a note or email confirming the time and place. If you wish to record the interview, be sure to ask for permission to do so. If you plan to conduct the interview by mail or email, state when you will send your questions.
3. Write out questions. Plan questions that invite extended response: "What accounts for the recent spike in gasoline prices?" forces an explanation, whereas "Is the recent spike in gas prices a direct result of global politics?" is likely to elicit only a yes or a no.

3–4

At the interview

4. Record the full name of the person you interview, along with the date, time, and place of the interview; you'll need this information to cite and document the interview accurately.
5. Take notes, even if you are recording the interview.
6. Keep track of time: don't take more than you agreed to beforehand unless both of you agree to keep talking. End by saying thank you and offering to provide a copy of your final product.

After the interview

7. Flesh out your notes with details as soon as possible after the interview, while you still remember them. What did you learn? What surprised you? Summarize both the interviewee's words and your impressions.
8. Be sure to send a thank-you note or email.

Observation.   Some writing projects are based on information you get by observing something. For a sociology paper, you may observe how students behave in large lectures. For an education course, you may observe one child's progress as a writer over a period of time. The following advice can help you conduct observations.

Before observing

3–4

1. Think about your research **PURPOSE:** What are you looking for? What do you expect to find? How will your presence as an observer affect what you observe? What do you plan to do with what you find?
2. If necessary, set up an appointment. You may need to ask permission of the people you wish to observe. Be honest and open about your goals and intentions; college students doing research assignments are often welcomed where others may not be.

While observing

3. You may want to divide each page of your notepaper down the middle vertically and write only on the left side of the page, reserving the right side for information you will fill in later.

324–27

4. Note **DESCRIPTIVE DETAILS** about the setting. What do you see? What do you hear? Do you smell anything? Get down details about color, shape, size, sound, and so on. Consider photographing or making a sketch of what you see.

324–32

5. Who is there, and what are they doing? **DESCRIBE** what they look like, and make notes about what they say. Note any significant demographic details—about gender, race, occupation, age, dress, and so on.

343–51

6. What is happening? Who's doing what? What's being said? Write down these kinds of **NARRATIVE** details.

After observing

7. As soon as possible after you complete your observations, use the right side of your pages to fill in gaps and note additional details.

278–82

8. **ANALYZE** your notes, looking for patterns. Did some things appear or happen more than once? Did anything stand out? Surprise or puzzle you? What did you learn?

Questionnaires and surveys.   Written or online questionnaires and surveys can provide information or opinions from a large number of people. For a political science course, you might conduct a survey to ask students who they plan to vote for. Or, for a marketing course, you might distribute a questionnaire asking what they think about an advertising campaign. The advice in this section will help you create useful questionnaires and surveys.

Define your goal.   The goal of a questionnaire or survey should be limited and focused, so that every question will contribute to your research question. Also, people are more likely to respond to a brief, focused survey.

Define your sample.   A survey gets responses from a representative sample of the whole group. The answers to these questions will help you define that sample:

1. Who should answer the questions? The people you contact should represent the whole population. For example, if you want to survey undergraduate students at your school, your sample should reflect your school's enrollment in terms of gender, year, major, age, ethnicity, and so forth.
2. How many people make up a representative sample? In general, the larger your sample, the more the answers will reflect those of the whole group. But if your population is small — 200 students in a history course, for example — your sample must include a large percentage of that group.

Decide on a medium.   Will you ask the questions face-to-face? Over the phone? On a website? By mail? Oral questionnaires work best for simple surveys or to gather impersonal information. You're more likely to get responses to more personal questions with written or Web-based questionnaires. **DESIGN** issues differ, depending on the medium: written or Web-based surveys should be neat and easy to read, while phone interviews may require well-thought-out scripts that anticipate possible answers and make it easy to record these answers.

521

Design good questions.   The way you ask questions will determine the answers you get, so take care to write questions that are clear and unambiguous. Here are some typical question types:

- *Multiple-choice*

  What is your current age?

  ____ 15–20   ____ 21–25   ____ 26–30   ____ 31–35   ____ Other

- *Rating scale*

  How would you rate the service at the campus bookstore?

  ____ Excellent   ____ Good   ____ Fair   ____ Poor

- *Agreement scale*

  How much do you agree with the following statements?

	Strongly Agree	Agree	Disagree	Strongly Disagree
The bookstore has sufficient numbers of textbooks available.	❏	❏	❏	❏
Staff at the bookstore are knowledgeable.	❏	❏	❏	❏
Staff at the bookstore are courteous and helpful.	❏	❏	❏	❏

- *Open-ended*

  How often do you visit the campus bookstore?

  How can the campus bookstore improve its service?

Include all potential alternatives when phrasing questions to avoid biasing the answers. And make sure each question addresses only one issue — for example, "bookstore staff are knowledgeable and courteous" could lead to the response "knowledgeable, agree; courteous, disagree."

When arranging questions, place easier ones at the beginning and harder ones near the end (but if the questions seem to fall into a natural order, follow it). Make sure each question asks for information you will need — if a question isn't absolutely necessary, omit it.

Include an introduction.   Start by stating your survey's purpose and how the results will be used. It's also a good idea to offer an estimate of the time needed to complete the questions.

Test the survey or questionnaire.   Make sure your questions elicit the kinds of answers you need by asking three or four people who are part of your target population to answer them. They can help you find unclear instructions, questions that aren't clear or that lack sufficient alternatives, or other problems that you should correct to make sure your results are useful. But if you change the questionnaire as a result of their responses, don't include their answers in your total.

IF YOU NEED MORE HELP

See **EVALUATING SOURCES** for help determining their usefulness. See also Chapter 46 for help **TAKING NOTES** on your sources.

400–403
408–9

44 Evaluating Sources

Searching the *Health Source* database for information on the incidence of meningitis among college students, you find seventeen articles. A Google search on the same topic produces over ten thousand hits. How do you decide which sources to read? This chapter presents advice on evaluating sources—first to determine whether a source is useful for your purposes and then to read with a critical eye the ones you choose.

Considering the Reliability of Print and Online Sources

Books and journals that have been published in print have most likely been evaluated by editors, publishers, or expert reviewers before publication. Magazines and newspapers have probably been fact-checked; not so most websites—anyone who wishes to post something on the Web can do so. In addition, Web sources come and go and are easily changed. So print sources (including journals available online) are always more stable and often more trustworthy.

Considering Whether a Source Serves Your Purpose

3–4

Think about your **PURPOSE.** Are you trying to persuade readers to believe or do something? To inform them about something? If the former, it will be especially important to find sources representing various stances; if the latter, you may need sources that are more factual or informative. Reconsider

5–8

your **AUDIENCE.** What kinds of sources will they find persuasive? If you're writing for readers in a particular field, what counts as evidence in that field? Following are some questions that can help you select useful sources:

- *Is it relevant?* How does the source relate to your purpose? What will it add to your work? Look at the title and at any introductory material — a preface, abstract, or introduction — to see what it covers.

- *What are the author's credentials?* What are the author's qualifications to write on the subject? Is he or she associated with a particular position on the issue? If the source is a book or a periodical, see whether it mentions other works this author has written. If it's a website, see whether an author is identified. If one is, you might do a Web search to see what else you can learn about him or her.

- *What is the* STANCE? Consider whether a source covers various points of view or advocates one particular point of view. Does its title suggest a certain slant? If it's a website, you might check to see whether it includes links to other sites of one or many perspectives. You'll want to consult sources with a variety of viewpoints.

  12–14

- *Who is the publisher?* If it's a book, what kind of company published it; if an article, what kind of periodical did it appear in? Books published by university presses and articles in scholarly journals are reviewed by experts before they are published. Books and articles written for general audiences typically do not undergo rigorous review — and they may lack the kind of in-depth discussion that is useful for research.

- *If it's a website, who is the sponsor?* Is the site maintained by an organization? An interest group? A government agency? An individual? If the site doesn't give this information, look for clues in the URL: *edu* is used mostly by colleges and universities, *gov* by government agencies, *org* by nonprofit organizations, *mil* by the military, and *com* by commercial organizations.

- *What is the level?* Can you understand the material? Texts written for a general audience might be easier to understand but are not likely to be authoritative enough for academic work. Texts written for scholars will be more authoritative but may be hard to comprehend.

- *When was it published?* See when books and articles were published. Check to see when websites were last updated. (If the site lists no date, see if links to other sites still work.) Recent does not necessarily mean better—some topics may require very current information whereas others may call for older sources.

- **Is it available?** Is it a source you can get hold of? If it's a book and your school's library doesn't have it, can you get it through interlibrary loan?

- **Does it include other useful information?** Is there a bibliography that might lead you to other sources? How current are the sources it cites?

Reading Sources with a Critical Eye

- **What ARGUMENTS does the author make?** Does the author present a number of different positions, or does he or she argue for a particular position? Do you need to **ANALYZE THE ARGUMENT?**

110000 ▲

283–99 ◆

- **How persuasive do you find the argument?** What reasons and evidence does the author provide in support of any position(s)? Are there citations or links—and if so, are they credible? Is any evidence presented without citations? Do you find any of the author's assumptions questionable? How thoroughly does he or she consider opposing arguments?

- **What is the author's STANCE?** Does the author strive for objectivity, or does the language reveal a particular bias? Is the author associated with a special interest that might signal a certain perspective? Does he or she consider opposing views? Do the sources cited reflect multiple viewpoints, or only one?

12–14 ■

- **Does the publisher bring a certain stance to the work?** Book publishers, periodicals, or websites that are clearly liberal or conservative or advance a particular agenda will likely express views reflecting their **STANCE.**

12–14 ■

- **Do you recognize ideas you've run across in other sources?** Does it leave out any information that other sources include?

- **Does this source support or challenge your own position—or does it do both?** Does it support your thesis? Offer a different argument altogether? Does it represent a position you may need to **ACKNOWLEDGE** or

104 ▲

REFUTE? Don't reject a source that challenges your views; your sources should reflect a variety of views on your topic, showing that you've considered the subject thoroughly.

△ 105

- *What can you tell about the intended* **AUDIENCE** *and* **PURPOSE?** Are you a member of the audience addressed—and if not, does that affect the way you interpret what you read? Is the main purpose to inform readers about a topic or to argue a certain point?

■ 5–8
3–4

IF YOU NEED MORE HELP

See **QUOTING, PARAPHRASING, AND SUMMARIZING** for help in taking notes on your sources and deciding how to use them in your writing. See also **ACKNOWLEDGING SOURCES, AVOIDING PLAGIARISM** for advice on giving credit to the sources you use.

● 408–19
420–24

45 Synthesizing Ideas

38–58 ▲

To **ANALYZE** the works of a poet, you show how she uses similar images in three different poems to explore a recurring concept. To solve a crime, a detective studies several eyewitness accounts to figure out who did it.

306–13 ◆

To trace the history of photojournalism, a professor **COMPARES** the uses of photography during the Civil War and during the war in Vietnam. These are all cases where someone *synthesizes*—brings together material from two or more sources in order to generate new information or to support a new perspective. When you do research, you need to go beyond what your sources say; you need to use what they say to inspire and support *what you want to say*. This chapter focuses on how to synthesize ideas you find in other sources as the basis for your own ideas.

Reading for Patterns and Connections

Your task as a writer is to find as much information as you can on your topic—and then to sift through all that you have found to determine and support what you yourself will write. In other words, you'll need to synthesize ideas and information from the sources you've consulted to figure out first what arguments *you* want to make and then to provide support for those arguments.

When you synthesize, you group similar bits of information together, looking for patterns or themes or trends and trying to identify the key points. For example, researching the effectiveness of the SAT writing exam you find several sources showing that scores correlate directly

■ rhetorical situations
▲ genres
○ processes
◆ strategies
● research mla/apa
□ media/ design
⌃ handbook

with length and that a majority of U. S. colleges and universities have decided not to count the results of the test in their admission decisions. You can infer that the test is not yet seen as an effective measure of writing ability.

Here are some tips for reading to identify patterns and connections:

- Take notes and jot down a brief **SUMMARY** of each source to help you see relationships, patterns, and connections among your sources. Take notes on your own thoughts, too.

416–17

- Read all your sources with an open mind. Withhold judgment, even of sources that seem wrong-headed or implausible. Don't jump to conclusions.

- Pay attention to your first reactions. You'll likely have many ideas to work with, but your first thoughts can often lead somewhere that you will find interesting. Try **FREEWRITING, CLUSTERING,** or **LISTING** to see where they lead.

219–22

- Try to think creatively, and pay attention to thoughts that flicker at the edge of your consciousness, as they may well be productive.

- Be playful. Good ideas sometimes come when we let our guard down or take ideas to extremes just to see where they lead.

Ask yourself these questions about your sources:

- What sources make the strongest arguments? What makes them so strong?

- Do some arguments recur in several sources?

- Which arguments do you agree with? Disagree with? Of those you disagree with, which ones seem strong enough that you need to **ACKNOWLEDGE** them in your text?

294

- Are there any disagreements among your sources?

- Are there any themes you see in more than one source?

- Are any data — facts, statistics, examples — or experts cited in more than one source?

- What have you learned about your topic? How have your sources affected your thinking on your topic? Do you need to adjust your **RESEARCH QUESTION**? If so, how?

381

- Have you discovered new questions you need to investigate?

1–17

- Keep in mind your **RHETORICAL SITUATION**—have you found the information you need that will achieve your **PURPOSE,** appeal to your **AUDIENCE,** and suit your **GENRE** and **MEDIUM?**

What is likely to emerge from this questioning is a combination of big ideas—new ways of understanding your topic, insights into recent scholarship about it—and smaller ones—how two sources agree with one another but not completely, how the information in one source supports or undercuts the argument of another. These ideas and insights will become the basis for your own ideas, and for what *you* have to say about the topic.

Synthesizing Information to Support Your Own Ideas

59–82

38–58
83–110

If you're doing research to write a **REPORT,** your own ideas will be communicated primarily through the information you include from the sources you cite and how you organize that information. If you're writing a **TEXTUAL ANALYSIS,** your synthesis may focus on the themes, techniques, or other patterns you find. If you're writing a research-based **ARGUMENT,** on the other hand, your synthesis of sources must support that argument. No matter what your genre, the challenge is to synthesize information from your research to develop ideas about your topic and then to support those ideas.

Entering the Conversation

As you read and think about your topic, you will come to an understanding of the concepts, interpretations, and controversies relating to your topic—and you'll become aware that there's a larger conversation going

rhetorical situations

genres

processes

strategies

research mla/apa

media/ design

handbook

on. When you begin to find connections among your sources, you will begin to see your own place in that conversation, to discover your own ideas, your own stance on your topic. This is the exciting part of a research project, for when you write out your own ideas on the topic, you will find yourself entering that conversation. Remember that your **STANCE** as an author needs to be clear: simply stringing together the words and ideas of others isn't enough. You need to show readers how your source materials relate to one another and to your thesis.

12–14

IF YOU NEED MORE HELP

See Chapter 46, **QUOTING, PARAPHRASING, AND SUMMARIZING,** for help in integrating source materials into your own text. See also Chapter 47 on **ACKNOWLEDGING SOURCES, AVOIDING PLAGIARISM** for advice on giving credit to the sources you cite.

408–19
420–24

46 Quoting, Paraphrasing, and Summarizing

In an oral presentation about the rhetoric of Abraham Lincoln, you quote a memorable line from the Gettysburg Address. For an essay on the Tet Offensive in the Vietnam War, you paraphrase arguments made by several commentators and summarize some key debates about that war. Like all writers, when you work with the ideas and words of others, you need to clearly distinguish those ideas and words from your own and give credit to their authors. This chapter will help you with the specifics of quoting, paraphrasing, and summarizing source materials that you wish to use in your writing.

Taking Notes

When you find material you think will be useful, take careful notes. How do you determine how much or how little to record? You need to write down enough information so that when you refer to it later, you will be reminded of the main points and have a precise record of where the information comes from.

- *Use index cards, a computer file, or a notebook,* labeling each entry with the information that will allow you to keep track of where it comes from—author, title, and the pages or the URL. You needn't write down full bibliographic information (you can abbreviate the author's name and title) since you'll include that information in your **WORKING BIBLIOGRAPHY**.

379–80

rhetorical situations genres processes strategies research mla/apa media/ design handbook

- *Take notes in your own words, and use your own sentence patterns.* If you make a note that is a detailed **PARAPHRASE,** label it as such so that you'll know to provide appropriate **DOCUMENTATION** if you use it.

413–16
425–27

- *If you find wording that you'd like to quote,* be sure to enclose it in quotation marks to distinguish your source's words from your own. Double-check your notes to be sure any quoted material is accurately quoted—and that you haven't accidentally **PLAGIARIZED** your sources.

420–24

- *Label each note with a subject heading.*

Here's an example of one writer's notes:

Source: Steingraber, "Pesticides" (976)

—1938: pathbreaking experiments showed that dogs exposed to aromatic amines developed cancer of the bladder.

—aromatic amines: chemicals used in coal-derived synthetic dyes

—Mauve the first synthetic dye—invented in 1854—then synthetic dyes replaced most natural dyes made with plants

—Bladder cancer common among textile workers who used dyes

—Steingraber: "By the beginning of the twentieth century, bladder cancer rates among this group of workers had skyrocketed, and the dog experiments helped unravel this mystery."

—1921: International Labor Organization labels a.a. as carcinogenic (before experiments)

—Dog experiments also helped explain: early 20th century: metal workers, machinists, and workers in the tire industry developed bladder cancer—cutting oils contained aromatic amines to inhibit rust used a.a. accelerants.

—Sandra Steingraber: biologist and ecologist

Deciding Whether to Quote, Paraphrase, or Summarize

When it comes time to **DRAFT,** you'll need to decide *how* to use the sources you've found—in other words, whether to quote, paraphrase, or summa-

226–28

410–13

rize. You might follow this rule of thumb: **QUOTE** texts when the wording is worth repeating or makes a point so well that no rewording will do it justice, when you want to cite the exact words of a known authority on your topic, when his or her opinions challenge or disagree with those of

413–16

others, or when the source is one you want to emphasize. **PARAPHRASE** sources that are not worth quoting but contain details you need to include.

416–17

SUMMARIZE longer passages whose main points are important but whose details are not.

Quoting

Quoting a source is a way of weaving someone else's exact words into your text. You need to reproduce the source exactly, though you can modify it to omit unnecessary details (with ellipses) or to make it fit smoothly into your text (with brackets). You also need to distinguish quoted material from your own by enclosing short quotations in quotation marks, setting off

417–18

longer quotes as a block, and using appropriate **SIGNAL PHRASES.**

Incorporate short quotations into your text, enclosed in quotation marks.

428–76
477–519

If you are following **MLA STYLE,** this rule holds for four typed lines or fewer; if you are following **APA STYLE,** short means no more than forty words.

> Gerald Graff (2003) argues that colleges make the intellectual life seem more opaque than it needs to be, leaving many students with "the misconception that the life of the mind is a secret society for which only an elite few qualify" (p. 1).

If you are quoting three lines or less of poetry, run them in with your text, enclosed in quotation marks. Separate lines with slashes, leaving one space on each side of the slashes.

> Emma Lazarus almost speaks for the Statue of Liberty with the words inscribed on its pedestal: "Give me your tired, your poor, / Your huddled masses yearning to breathe free, / The wretched refuse of your teeming shore" (58).

Set off long quotations block style.   If you are using MLA style, set off quotations of five or more typed lines by indenting the quote one inch (or ten spaces) from the left margin. If you are using APA style, indent quotes of forty or more words one-half inch (or five spaces) from the left margin. In either case, do not use quotation marks, and put any parenthetical citation *after* any end punctuation.

> Nonprofit organizations such as Oxfam and Habitat for Humanity rely on visual representations of the poor. What better way to get our attention, asks rhetorician Diana George:
>
>> In a culture saturated by the image, how else do we convince Americans that — despite the prosperity they see all around them — there is real need out there? The solution for most nonprofits has been to show the despair. To do that they must represent poverty as something that can be seen and easily recognized: fallen down shacks and trashed out public housing, broken windows, dilapidated porches, barefoot kids with stringy hair, emaciated old women and men staring out at the camera with empty eyes. (210)

If you are quoting four or more lines of poetry, they need to be set off block style in the same way.

Indicate any omissions with ellipses.   You may sometimes delete words from a quotation that are unnecessary for your point. Insert three ellipsis marks (leaving a space before the first and after the last one) to indicate the deletion. If you omit a sentence or more in the middle of a quotation, put a period before the three ellipsis dots. Be careful not to distort the source's meaning, however.

> Faigley points out that Gore's "Information Superhighway" metaphor "associated the economic prosperity of the 1950s and . . . 1960s facilitated by new highways with the potential for vast . . . commerce to be conducted over the Internet" (253).

> According to Welch, "Television is more acoustic than visual. . . . One can turn one's gaze way from the television, but one cannot turn one's ears from it without leaving the area where the monitor leaks its aural signals into every corner" (102).

Indicate additions or changes with brackets.   Sometimes you'll need to change or add words in a quote—to make the quote fit grammatically within your sentence, for example, or to add a comment. In the following example, the writer changes the passage "one of our goals" to fit the grammar of her sentences:

> Writing about the dwindling attention among some composition scholars to the actual teaching of writing, Susan Miller notes that "few discussions of writing pedagogy take it for granted that one of [their] goals is to teach how to write" (480).

Here's an example of brackets used to add explanatory words to a quotation:

> Barbosa observes that even Buarque's lyrics have long included "many a metaphor of *saudades* [yearning] so characteristic of *fado* music" (207).

A note about punctuating quotes.   When you incorporate a quotation into your text, you have to think about the end punctuation in the quoted material and also about any punctuation you need to add when you insert the quote into your own sentence.

Periods and commas. With brief quotations, put periods or commas inside the quotation marks, except when you have a parenthetical citation at the end, in which case you put the period after the parentheses.

> "Country music," Tichi says, "is a crucial and vital part of the American identity" (23).

With long quotes set off block style, however, there are no quotation marks, so the period goes *before* the citation, as shown in the example on page 411.

Question marks and exclamation points. These go *inside* closing quotation marks if they are part of the quoted material but outside when they are not. If there's a parenthetical citation at the end, it immediately follows the closing quotation mark, and any punctuation that's part of your sentence comes after.

> Speaking at a Fourth of July celebration in 1852, Frederick Douglass asked, "What have I, or those I represent, to do with your national independence?" (35).

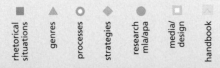

Who can argue with W. Charisse Goodman's observation that media images persuade women that "thinness equals happiness and fulfillment" (53)?

Colons and semicolons. These always go outside the quotation marks.

It's hard to argue with W. Charisse Goodman's observation that media images persuade women that "thinness equals happiness and fulfillment"; nevertheless, American women today are more overweight than ever (53).

Paraphrasing

When you paraphrase, you restate information from a source in your own words, using your own sentence structures. Paraphrase when the source material is important but the original wording is not. Because it includes all the main points of the source, a paraphrase is usually about the same length as the original.

Here is a paragraph about synthetic dyes and cancer, followed by three example paraphrases. The first two demonstrate some of the challenges of paraphrasing:

ORIGINAL SOURCE

In 1938, in a series of now-classic experiments, exposure to synthetic dyes derived from coal and belonging to a class of chemicals called aromatic amines was shown to cause bladder cancer in dogs. These results helped explain why bladder cancers had become so prevalent among dyestuffs workers. With the invention of mauve in 1854, synthetic dyes began replacing natural plant-based dyes in the coloring of cloth and leather. By the beginning of the twentieth century, bladder cancer rates among this group of workers had skyrocketed, and the dog experiments helped unravel this mystery. The International Labor Organization did not wait for the results of these animal tests, however, and in 1921 declared certain aromatic amines to be human carcinogens. Decades later, these dogs provided a lead in understanding why tire-industry workers, as well as machinists and metalworkers, also began falling victim to bladder cancer: aromatic amines had been added to rubbers and cutting oils to serve as accelerants and antirust agents.

—Sandra Steingraber, "Pesticides, Animals, and Humans"

UNACCEPTABLE PARAPHRASE: WORDING TOO CLOSE

Now-classic experiments in 1938 showed that when dogs were exposed to aromatic amines, chemicals used in synthetic dyes derived from coal, they developed bladder cancer. Similar cancers were prevalent among dyestuffs workers, and these experiments helped to explain why. Mauve, a synthetic dye, was invented in 1854, after which cloth and leather manufacturers replaced most of the natural plant-based dyes with synthetic dyes. By the early twentieth century, this group of workers had skyrocketing rates of bladder cancer, a mystery the dog experiments helped to unravel. As early as 1921, though, before the test results proved the connection, the International Labor Organization had labeled certain aromatic amines carcinogenic. Even so, decades later many metalworkers, machinists, and tire-industry workers began developing bladder cancer. The animal tests helped researchers understand that rubbers and cutting oils contained aromatic amines as accelerants and antirust agents (Steingraber 976).

This paraphrase borrows too much of the language of the original or changes it only slightly, as the underlined words and phrases show.

UNACCEPTABLE PARAPHRASE: SENTENCE STRUCTURE TOO CLOSE

In 1938, several pathbreaking experiments showed that being exposed to synthetic dyes that are made from coal and belong to a type of chemicals called aromatic amines caused dogs to get bladder cancer. These results helped researchers identify why cancers of the bladder had become so common among textile workers who worked with dyes. With the development of mauve in 1854, synthetic dyes began to be used instead of dyes based on plants in the dyeing of leather and cloth. By the end of the nineteenth century, rates of bladder cancer among these workers had increased dramatically, and the experiments using dogs helped clear up this oddity. The International

Labor Organization anticipated the results of these tests on animals, though, and in 1921 labeled some aromatic amines carcinogenic. Years later these experiments with dogs helped researchers explain why workers in the tire industry, as well as metalworkers and machinists, also started dying of bladder cancer: aromatic amines had been put into rubbers and cutting oils as rust inhibitors and accelerants (Steingraber 976).

This paraphrase uses original language but follows the sentence structure of Steingraber's text too closely.

ACCEPTABLE PARAPHRASE

Biologist Sandra Steingraber explains that pathbreaking experiments in 1938 demonstrated that dogs exposed to aromatic amines (chemicals used in coal-derived synthetic dyes) developed cancers of the bladder that were similar to cancers common among dyers in the textile industry. After mauve, the first synthetic dye, was invented in 1854, leather and cloth manufacturers replaced most natural dyes made from plants with synthetic dyes, and by the early 1900s textile workers had very high rates of bladder cancer. The experiments with dogs proved the connection, but years before, in 1921, the International Labor Organization had labeled some aromatic amines carcinogenic. Even so, years later many metalworkers, machinists, and workers in the tire industry started to develop unusually high rates of bladder cancer. The experiments with dogs helped researchers understand that the cancers were caused by aromatic amines used in cutting oils to inhibit rust and in rubbers as accelerants (976).

Some guidelines for paraphrasing

- *Use your own words and sentence structure.* It is acceptable to use some words from the original, but the phrasing and sentence structures should be your own.

- *Put in quotation marks any of the source's original phrasing that you use.* Quotation marks distinguish the source's phrases from your own.

- *Indicate the source of your paraphrase.* Although the wording may be yours, the ideas and information come from another source; be sure to name the author and include an **IN-TEXT CITATION** to avoid the possibility of **PLAGIARISM.**

MLA 432–38 ⬤

APA 480–85

420–24 ⬤

Summarizing

A summary states the main ideas found in a source concisely and in your own words. Unlike a paraphrase, a summary does *not* present all the details, so it is generally as brief as possible. Summaries may boil down an entire book or essay into a single sentence, or they may take a paragraph or more to present the main ideas. Here, for example, is a summary of the Steingraber paragraph:

> Steingraber explains that experiments with dogs demonstrated that aromatic amines, chemicals used in synthetic dyes, cutting oils, and rubber, cause bladder cancer (976).

In the context of an essay, the summary might take this form:

> Medical researchers have long relied on experiments using animals to expand understanding of the causes of disease. For example, biologist and ecologist Sandra Steingraber notes that in the second half of the nineteenth century, the rate of bladder cancer soared among textile workers. According to Steingraber, experiments with dogs demonstrated that synthetic chemicals in dyes used to color the textiles caused the cancer (976).

Some guidelines for summarizing

- *Include only the main ideas; leave out the details.* A summary should include just enough information to give the reader the gist of the original. It is always much shorter than the original, sometimes even as brief as one sentence.

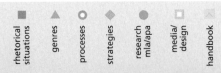

- *Use your own words.* If you quote from the original, enclose the word or phrase in quotation marks.

- *Indicate the source.* Although the wording may be yours, the ideas and information come from another source. Name the author, either in a signal phrase or parentheses, and include an appropriate **IN-TEXT CITATION** to avoid the possibility of **PLAGIARISM**.

432–38 MLA
480–85 APA
420–24

Incorporating Source Materials into Your Text

You need to introduce quotations, paraphrases, and summaries clearly, usually letting readers know who the author is — and, if need be, something about his or her credentials. Consider this sentence:

> Professor and textbook author Elaine Tyler May argues that many high school history books are too bland to interest young readers (531).

The beginning ("Professor and textbook author Elaine Tyler May argues") functions as a *signal phrase*, telling readers who is making the assertion and why she has the authority to speak on the topic — and making clear that everything between the signal phrase and the parenthetical citation comes from that source. Since the signal phrase names the author, the parenthetical citation includes only the page number; had the author not been identified in the signal phrase, she would have been named in the parentheses:

> Even some textbook authors believe that many high school history books are too bland to interest young readers (May 531).

Signal phrases.　A signal phrase tells readers who says or believes something. The verb you use can be neutral — *says* or *thinks* — or it can suggest something about the **STANCE** — the source's or your own. The example above referring to the textbook author uses the verb *claims*, suggesting that what she says is arguable (or that the writer believes it is). How would it change your understanding if the signal verb were *observes* or *suggests*?

12–14

SOME COMMON SIGNAL VERBS

acknowledges	claims	disagrees	observes
admits	comments	disputes	points out
advises	concludes	emphasizes	reasons
agrees	concurs	grants	rejects
argues	confirms	illustrates	reports
asserts	contends	implies	responds
believes	declares	insists	suggests
charges	denies	notes	thinks

Verb tenses. MLA and APA have different conventions regarding the verbs that introduce signal phrases. MLA requires present-tense verbs (*writes, asserts, notes*) in signal phrases to introduce a work you are quoting, paraphrasing, or summarizing.

> In *Poor Richard's Almanack*, Benjamin Franklin <u>notes</u>, "He that cannot obey, cannot command" (739).

If, however, you are referring to the act of writing or saying something rather than simply quoting someone's words, you might not use the present tense. The writer of the following sentence focuses on the year in which the source was written—therefore, the verb is necessarily in the past tense:

> Back in 1941, Kenneth Burke <u>wrote</u> that "the ethical values of work are in its application of the competitive equipment to cooperative ends" (316).

If you are following APA style, use the past tense or present-perfect tense to introduce sources composed in the past.

> Dowdall, Crawford, and Wechsler (1998) <u>observed</u> that women attending women's colleges are less likely to engage in binge drinking than are women who attend coeducational colleges (p. 713).

APA requires the present tense, however, to discuss the results of an experiment or to explain conclusions that are generally agreed on.

> The findings of this study <u>suggest</u> that excessive drinking has serious consequences for college students and their institutions.

> The authors of numerous studies <u>agree</u> that smoking and drinking among adolescents are associated with lower academic achievement.

IF YOU NEED MORE HELP

See the section on **ACKNOWLEDGING SOURCES, AVOIDING PLAGIARISM** for help in giving credit to the sources you use. See also the **SAMPLE RESEARCH PAPERS** to see how sources are cited in MLA and APA styles.

● 420–24
● 467–76 MLA
508–19 APA

47 Acknowledging Sources, Avoiding Plagiarism

Whenever you do research-based writing, you find yourself entering a conversation—reading what many others have had to say about your topic, figuring out what you yourself think, and then putting what you think in writing—"putting in your oar," as the rhetorician Kenneth Burke once wrote. As a writer, you need to *acknowledge* any words and ideas that come from others—to give credit where credit is due, to recognize the various authorities and many perspectives you have considered, to show readers where they can find your sources, and to situate your own arguments in the ongoing conversation. Using other people's words and ideas without acknowledgment is *plagiarism,* a serious academic and ethical offense. This chapter will show you how to acknowledge the materials you use and avoid plagiarism.

Acknowledging Sources

When you insert in your text information that you've obtained from others, your reader needs to know where your source's words or ideas begin and end. Therefore, you should introduce a source by naming the author in a **SIGNAL PHRASE**, and follow it with a brief parenthetical **IN-TEXT CITATION** or by naming the source in a parenthetical citation. (You need only a brief citation here, since your readers will find full bibliographic information in your list of **WORKS CITED** or **REFERENCES**.)

417–18
MLA 432–38
APA 480–85
MLA 439–67
APA 486–508

Sources that need acknowledgment. You almost always need to acknowledge any information that you get from a specific source. Material you should acknowledge includes the following:

420

- *Direct quotations.* Any quotations from another source must be enclosed in quotation marks, cited with brief bibliographic information in parentheses, and usually introduced with a signal phrase that tells who wrote it and provides necessary contextual information, as in the following sentence:

  > In a dissenting opinion on the issue of racial preferences in college admissions, Supreme Court justice Ruth Bader Ginsburg argues, "The stain of generations of racial oppression is still visible in our society, and the determination to hasten its removal remains vital" (*Gratz v. Bollinger*).

- *Arguable statements and information that may not be common knowledge.* If you state something about which there is disagreement or for which arguments can be made, cite the source of your statement. If in doubt about whether you need to give the source of an assertion, provide it. As part of an essay on "fake news" programs like *The Daily Show*, for example, you might make the following assertion:

  > The satire of *The Daily Show* complements the conservative bias of Fox News, since both have abandoned the stance of objectivity maintained by mainstream news sources, notes Michael Hoyt, executive editor of the *Columbia Journalism Review* (43).

  Others might argue with the contention that the Fox News Channel offers biased reports of the news, so the source of this assertion needs to be acknowledged. In the same essay, you might present information that should be cited because it's not widely known, as in this example:

  > According to a report by the Pew Research Center, 21 percent of Americans under thirty got information about the 2004 presidential campaign primarily from "fake news" and comedy shows like *The Daily Show* and *Saturday Night Live* (2).

- *The opinions and assertions of others.* When you present the ideas, opinions, and assertions of others, cite the source. You may have rewrit-

ten the concept in your own words, but the ideas were generated by someone else and must be acknowledged, as they are here:

> Social philosopher David Boonin, writing in the *Journal of Social Philosophy,* asserts that, logically, laws banning marriage between people of different races are not discriminatory since everyone of each race is affected equally by them. Laws banning same-sex unions are discriminatory, however, since they apply only to people with a certain sexual orientation (256).

- *Any information that you didn't generate yourself.* If you did not do the research or compile the data yourself, cite your source. This goes for interviews, statistics, graphs, charts, visuals, photographs — anything you use that you did not create. If you create a chart using data from another source, you need to cite that source.

- *Collaboration with and help from others.* In many of your courses and in work situations, you'll be called on to work with others. You may get help with your writing at your school's writing center or from fellow students in your writing courses. Acknowledging such collaboration or assistance, in a brief informational note, is a way of giving credit—and saying thank you. See guidelines for writing notes in the **MLA** and **APA** sections of this book.

439

486

Sources that don't need acknowledgment.   Widely available information and common knowledge do not require acknowledgment. What constitutes common knowledge may not be clear, however. When in doubt, provide a citation, or ask your instructor whether the information needs to be cited. You generally do not need to cite the following sources:

- *Information that most readers are likely to know.* You don't need to acknowledge information that is widely known or commonly accepted as fact. For example, in a literary analysis, you wouldn't cite a source saying that Harriet Beecher Stowe wrote *Uncle Tom's Cabin;* you can assume your readers already know that. On the other hand, you should cite the source from which you got the information that the book was first published in installments in a magazine and then, with revisions, in book form, because that information isn't common knowledge. As you do research in areas you're not familiar with, be aware that what constitutes common knowledge isn't always clear; the history of the novel's publication would be known to Stowe scholars and would likely need no acknowledgment in an essay written for them. In this case, too, if you aren't sure whether to acknowledge information, do so.

- *Information and documents that are widely available.* If a piece of information appears in several sources or reference works or if a document has been published widely, you needn't cite a source for it. For example, the date when astronauts Neil Armstrong and Buzz Aldrin landed a spacecraft on the moon can be found in any number of reference works. Similarly, the Declaration of Independence and the Gettysburg Address are reprinted in thousands of sources, so the ones where you found them need no citation.

- *Well-known quotations.* These include such famous quotations as Lady Macbeth's "Out, damned spot!" and John F. Kennedy's "Ask not what your country can do for you; ask what you can do for your country." Be sure, however, that the quotation is correct; Winston Churchill is said to have told a class of schoolchildren, "Never, ever, ever, ever, ever, ever, ever give up. Never give up. Never give up. Never give up." His actual words, however, taken from a longer speech, are much different and begin "Never give in."

- *Material that you created or gathered yourself.* You need not cite photographs that you took, graphs that you composed based on your own findings, or data from an experiment or survey that you conducted — though you should make sure readers know that the work is yours.

A good rule of thumb: *when in doubt, cite your source.* You're unlikely to be criticized for citing too much — but you may invite charges of plagiarism by citing too little.

Avoiding Plagiarism

When you use the words or ideas of others, you need to acknowledge who and where the material came from; if you don't credit those sources, you are guilty of plagiarism. Plagiarism is often committed unintentionally —

as when a writer paraphrases someone else's ideas in language that is close to the original. It is essential, therefore, to know what constitutes plagiarism: (1) using another writer's words or ideas without in-text citation and documentation, (2) using another writer's exact words without quotation marks, and (3) paraphrasing or summarizing someone else's ideas using language or sentence structures that are too close to theirs.

408–9

To avoid plagiarizing, take careful **NOTES** as you do your research, clearly labeling as quotations any words you quote directly and being careful to use your own phrasing and sentence structures in paraphrases and summaries. Be sure you know what source material you must **DOCUMENT**, and give credit to your sources, both in the text and in a list of **REFERENCES** or **WORKS CITED**. Be especially careful with material found online—copying source material right into a document you are writing is all too easy to do. You must acknowledge information you find on the Web just as you must acknowledge all other source materials.

425–27
APA 486–508
MLA 439–67

And you must recognize that plagiarism has consequences. Scholars' work will be discredited if it too closely resembles another's. Journalists found to have plagiarized lose their jobs, and students routinely fail courses or are dismissed from their school when they are caught cheating—all too often by submitting as their own essays that they have purchased from online "research" sites. If you're having trouble completing an assignment, seek assistance. Talk with your instructor, or if your school has a writing center, go there for advice on all aspects of your writing, including acknowledging sources and avoiding plagiarism.

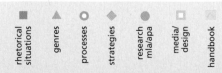

Documentation **48**

In everyday life, we are generally aware of our sources: "I read it in the *Post.*" "Amber told me it's your birthday." "If you don't believe me, ask Mom." Saying how we know what we know and where we got our information is part of establishing our credibility and persuading others to take what we say seriously.

The goal of a research project is to study a topic, combining what we learn from sources with our own thinking and then composing a written text. When we write up the results of a research project, we cite the sources we use, usually by quoting, paraphrasing, or summarizing, and we acknowledge those sources, telling readers where the ideas came from. The information we give about sources is called documentation, and we provide it not only to establish our credibility as researchers and writers but also so that our readers, if they wish to, can find the sources themselves.

Understanding Documentation Styles

The Norton Field Guide covers the documentation styles of the Modern Language Association (MLA) and the American Psychological Association (APA). MLA style is used chiefly in the humanities; APA is used mainly in the social sciences. Both are two-part systems, consisting of (1) brief in-text parenthetical documentation for quotations, paraphrases, or summaries and (2) more-detailed documentation in a list of sources at the end of the text. MLA and APA require that the end-of-text documentation provide the following basic information about each source you cite:

- author, editor, or organization providing the information
- title of work
- place of publication
- name of organization or company that published it
- date when it was published
- for online sources, date when you accessed the source

MLA and APA are by no means the only documentation styles. Many other publishers and organizations have their own style, among them the University of Chicago Press and the Council of Science Editors. We focus on MLA and APA here because those are styles that college students are often required to use. On the following page are examples of how the two parts — the brief parenthetical documentation in your text and the more detailed information at the end — correspond. The top of the next page shows the two parts according to the MLA system; the bottom, the two parts according to the APA system.

As the examples show, when you cite a work in your text, you can name the author either in a signal phrase or in parentheses. If you name the author in a signal phrase, give the page number(s) in parentheses; when the author's name is not given in a signal phrase, include it in the parentheses.

The examples here and throughout this book are color-coded to help you see the crucial parts of each citation: tan for author and editor, yellow for title, and gray for publication information: city of publication, name of publisher, year of publication, page number(s), and so on. Comparing the MLA and APA styles of listing works cited or references reveals some differences: MLA includes an author's first name while APA gives only the initial; MLA puts the date at the end while APA places it right after the author's name; MLA underlines titles of long works while APA italicizes them; MLA capitalizes most of the words in the title and subtitle while APA capitalizes only the first words and proper nouns of each. Overall, however, the styles provide similar information: each gives author, title, and publication data.

author   title   publication

MLA Style

IN-TEXT DOCUMENTATION

As Lester Faigley puts it, "The world has become a bazaar from which to shop for an individual 'lifestyle' " (12).

As one observer suggests, "The world has become a bazaar from which to shop for an individual 'lifestyle' " (Faigley 12).

WORKS-CITED DOCUMENTATION

Faigley, Lester. <u>Fragments of Rationality: Postmodernity and the Subject of Composition</u>. Pittsburgh: U of Pittsburgh P, 1992.

APA Style

IN-TEXT DOCUMENTATION

As Faigley (1992) suggested, "The world has become a bazaar from which to shop for an individual 'lifestyle'" (p. 12).

As one observer has noted, "The world has become a bazaar from which to shop for an individual 'lifestyle'" (Faigley, 1992, p. 12).

REFERENCE-LIST DOCUMENTATION

Faigley, L. (1992). *Fragments of rationality: Postmodernity and the subject of composition*. Pittsburgh, PA: University of Pittsburgh Press.

49 MLA Style

Modern Language Association style calls for (1) brief in-text documentation and (2) complete documentation in a list of works cited at the end of your text. The models in this chapter draw on the *MLA Handbook for Writers of Research Papers*, 6th edition, by Joseph Gibaldi (2003). Additional information is available at www.mla.org.

A DIRECTORY TO MLA STYLE

author   title   publication

Notes   439

MLA List of Works Cited   439

author　　　　title　　　　publication

MLA IN-TEXT DOCUMENTATION

Brief documentation in your text makes clear to your reader what you took from a source and where in the source you found the information.

408–19 In your text, you have three options for citing a source: QUOTING, PARAPHRASING, and SUMMARIZING. As you cite each source, you will need to decide whether or not to name the author in a signal phrase—"as Toni Morrison writes"—or in parentheses—"(Morrison 24)."

The first examples in this chapter show basic in-text citations of a work by one author. Variations on those examples follow. All of the examples are color-coded to help you see how writers using MLA style work authors and page numbers—and sometimes titles—into their texts. The examples also illustrate the MLA style of using quotation marks around titles of short works and underlining titles of long works. (Your instructor may prefer italics to underlining; find out if you're not sure.)

1. AUTHOR NAMED IN A SIGNAL PHRASE

If you mention the author in a signal phrase, put only the page number(s) in parentheses. Do not write *page* or *p*.

> McCullough describes John Adams as having "the hands of a man accustomed to pruning his own trees, cutting his own hay, and splitting his own firewood" (18).

> McCullough describes John Adams's hands as those of someone used to manual labor (18).

2. AUTHOR NAMED IN PARENTHESES

If you do not mention the author in a signal phrase, put his or her last name in parentheses along with the page number(s). Do not use punctuation between the name and the page number(s).

> Adams is said to have had "the hands of a man accustomed to pruning his own trees, cutting his own hay, and splitting his own firewood" (McCullough 18).

author   title   publication

One biographer describes John Adams as someone who was not a stranger to manual labor (McCullough 18).

Whether you use a signal phrase and parentheses or parentheses only, try to put the parenthetical citation at the end of the sentence or as close as possible to the material you've cited without awkwardly interrupting the sentence. Notice that in the first example above, the parenthetical reference comes after the closing quotation marks but before the period at the end of the sentence.

3. TWO OR MORE WORKS BY THE SAME AUTHOR

If you cite multiple works by one author, you have four choices. You can mention the author in a signal phrase and give the title and page reference in parentheses. Give the full title if it's brief; otherwise, give a short version.

Kaplan insists that understanding power in the Near East requires "Western leaders who know when to intervene, and do so without illusions" (Eastward 330).

You can mention both author and title in a signal phrase and give only the page reference in parentheses.

In Eastward to Tartary, Kaplan insists that understanding power in the Near East requires "Western leaders who know when to intervene, and do so without illusions" (330).

You can indicate author, title, and page reference only in parentheses, with a comma between author and title.

Understanding power in the Near East requires "Western leaders who know when to intervene, and do so without illusions" (Kaplan, Eastward 330).

Or you can mention the title in a signal phrase and give the author and page reference in parentheses.

> Eastward to Tartary argues that understanding power in the Near East requires "Western leaders who know when to intervene, and do so without illusions" (Kaplan 330).

4. AUTHORS WITH THE SAME LAST NAME

If your works-cited list includes works by authors with the same last name, you need to give the author's first name in any signal phrase or the author's first initial in the parenthetical reference.

> Edmund Wilson uses the broader term imaginative, whereas Anne Wilson chooses the narrower adjective magical.

> Imaginative applies not only to modern literature (E. Wilson) but also to writing of all periods, whereas magical is often used in writing about Arthurian romances (A. Wilson).

5. AFTER A BLOCK QUOTATION

When quoting more than three lines of poetry, more than four lines of prose, or dialogue from a drama, set off the quotation from the rest of your text, indenting it one inch (or ten spaces) from the left margin. Do not use quotation marks. Place any parenthetical documentation *after* the final punctuation.

> In Eastward to Tartary, Kaplan captures ancient and contemporary Antioch for us:
>
> > At the height of its glory in the Roman-Byzantine age, when it had an amphitheater, public baths, aqueducts, and sewage pipes, half a million people lived in Antioch. Today the population is only 125,000. With sour relations between Turkey and Syria, and unstable politics throughout the Middle East,

author   title   publication

> Antioch is now a backwater—seedy and tumbledown, with
> relatively few tourists. I found it altogether charming. (123)

6. TWO OR MORE AUTHORS

For a work by two or three authors, name all the authors, either in a signal phrase or in the parentheses.

> Carlson and Ventura's stated goal is to introduce Julio Cortázar, Marjorie
> Agosín, and other Latin American writers to an audience of
> English-speaking adolescents (v).

For a work with four or more authors, you have the option of mentioning all their names or just the name of the first author followed by *et al.*, which means "and others."

> One popular survey of American literature breaks the contents into sixteen
> thematic groupings (Anderson, Brinnin, Leggett, Arpin, and Toth A19–24).

> One popular survey of American literature breaks the contents into
> sixteen thematic groupings (Anderson et al. A19–24).

7. ORGANIZATION OR GOVERNMENT AS AUTHOR

If the author is an organization, cite the organization either in a signal phrase or in parentheses. It's acceptable to shorten long names.

> The U.S. government can be direct when it wants to be. For example, it
> sternly warns, "If you are overpaid, we will recover any payments not
> due you" (Social Security Administration 12).

8. AUTHOR UNKNOWN

If you don't know the author of a work, as you won't with many reference books and with most newspaper editorials, use the work's title or a shortened version of the title in the parentheses (examples are on page 436).

The explanatory notes at the front of the literature encyclopedia point out that writers known by pseudonyms are listed alphabetically under those pseudonyms (<u>Merriam-Webster's</u> vii).

A powerful editorial in last week's paper asserts that healthy liver donor Mike Hurewitz died because of "frightening" faulty postoperative care ("Every Patient's Nightmare").

9. LITERARY WORKS

When referring to literary works that are available in many different editions, cite the page numbers from the edition you are using, followed by information that will let readers of any edition locate the text you are citing.

NOVELS

Give the page and chapter number.

In <u>Pride and Prejudice,</u> Mrs. Bennett shows no warmth toward Jane and Elizabeth when they return from Netherfield (105; ch. 12).

VERSE PLAYS

Give the act, scene, and line numbers; separate them with periods.

Macbeth continues the vision theme when he addresses the Ghost with "Thou hast no speculation in those eyes / Which thou dost glare with" (3.3.96–97).

POEMS

Give the part and the line numbers (separated by periods). If a poem has only line numbers, use the word line(s) in the first reference.

Whitman sets up not only opposing adjectives but also opposing nouns in "Song of Myself" when he says, "I am of old and young, of the foolish as much as the wise, / . . . a child as well as a man" (16.330–32).

One description of the mere in <u>Beowulf</u> is "not a pleasant place!" (line 1372). Later, the label is "the awful place" (1378).

author   title   publication

10. WORK IN AN ANTHOLOGY

If you're citing a work that is included in an anthology, name the author(s) of the work, not the editor of the anthology—either in a signal phrase or in parentheses.

> "It is the teapots that truly shock," according to Cynthia Ozick in her essay on teapots as metaphor (70).

> In In Short: A Collection of Creative Nonfiction, readers will find both an essay on Scottish tea (Hiestand) and a piece on teapots as metaphors (Ozick).

11. SACRED TEXT

When citing sacred texts such as the Bible or the Qur'an, give the title of the edition used, and in parentheses give the book, chapter, and verse (or their equivalent), separated by periods. MLA style recommends that you abbreviate the names of the books of the Bible in parenthetical references.

> The wording from The New English Bible follows: "In the beginning of creation, when God made heaven and earth, the earth was without form and void, with darkness over the face of the abyss, and a mighty wind that swept over the surface of the waters" (Gen. 1.1–2).

12. MULTIVOLUME WORK

If you cite more than one volume of a multivolume work, each time you cite one of the volumes, give the volume and the page numbers in parentheses, separated by a colon.

> Sandburg concludes with the following sentence about those paying last respects to Lincoln: "All day long and through the night the unbroken line moved, the home town having its farewell" (4: 413).

If your works-cited list includes only a single volume of a multivolume work, the only number you need to give in your parenthetical reference is the page number.

13. TWO OR MORE WORKS CITED TOGETHER

If you're citing two or more works closely together, you will sometimes need to provide a parenthetical citation for each one.

> Tanner (7) and Smith (viii) have looked at works from a cultural perspective.

If the citation allows you to include both in the same parentheses, separate the references with a semicolon.

> Critics have looked at both Pride and Prejudice and Frankenstein from a cultural perspective (Tanner 7; Smith viii).

14. SOURCE QUOTED IN ANOTHER SOURCE

When you are quoting text that you found quoted in another source, use the abbreviation *qtd. in* in the parenthetical reference.

> Charlotte Brontë wrote to G. H. Lewes: "Why do you like Miss Austen so very much? I am puzzled on that point" (qtd. in Tanner 7).

15. WORK WITHOUT PAGE NUMBERS

For works without page numbers, give paragraph or section numbers, using the abbreviation *par.* or *sec.* If you are including the author's name in the parenthetical reference, add a comma.

> Russell's dismissals from Trinity College at Cambridge and from City College in New York City are seen as examples of the controversy that marked the philosopher's life (Irvine, par. 2).

16. AN ENTIRE WORK OR ONE-PAGE ARTICLE

If your text is referring to an entire work rather than a part of it or a one-page-long article, identify the author in a signal phrase or in parentheses. There's no need to include page numbers.

> Kaplan considers Turkey and Central Asia explosive.

> At least one observer considers Turkey and Central Asia explosive (Kaplan).

author   title   publication

NOTES

Sometimes you may need to give information that doesn't fit into the text itself—to thank people who helped you, provide additional details, or refer readers to other sources not cited in your text. Such information can be given in a *footnote* (at the bottom of the page) or an *endnote* (on a separate page with the heading *Notes* just before your works-cited list. Put a super-script number at the appropriate point in your text, signaling to readers to look for the note with the corresponding number. If you have multiple notes, number them consecutively throughout your paper.

TEXT

This essay will argue that small liberal arts colleges should not recruit athletes and, more specifically, that giving student athletes preferential treatment undermines the larger educational goals.[1]

NOTE

[1] I want to thank all those who have contributed to my thinking on this topic, especially my classmates and my teachers Marian Johnson and Diane O'Connor.

MLA LIST OF WORKS CITED

A works-cited list provides full bibliographic information for every source cited in your text. The list should be alphabetized by authors' last names (or sometimes by editors' or translators' names). Works that do not have an identifiable author or editor are alphabetized by title. See pages 475–76 for a sample works-cited list.

Books

BASIC FORMAT FOR A BOOK

For most books, you'll need to provide information about the author; the title and any subtitle; and the place of publication, publisher, and date. You'll find this information on the book's title page and copy-right page.

> Greenblatt, Stephen. <u>Will in the World: How Shakespeare Became Shakespeare</u>. New York: Norton, 2004.

A FEW DETAILS TO NOTE

- **TITLES**: Capitalize the first and last words of titles, subtitles, and all principal words. Do not capitalize *a*, *an*, *the*, *to*, or any prepositions or coordinating conjunctions unless they begin a title or subtitle.
- **PLACE OF PUBLICATION**: If more than one city is given, use only the first.
- **PUBLISHER**: Use a shortened form of the publisher's name (Norton for W. W. Norton & Company, Princeton UP for Princeton University Press).
- **DATES**: If more than one year is given, use the most recent one.

1. ONE AUTHOR

> Author's Last Name, First Name. <u>Title</u>. Publication City: Publisher, Year of publication.

> Anderson, Curtis. <u>The Long Tail: Why the Future of Business Is Selling Less of More</u>. New York: Hyperion, 2006.

When the title of a book itself contains the title of another book (or other long work), do not underline that title.

> Walker, Roy. <u>Time Is Free: A Study of</u> Macbeth. London: Dakers, 1949.

When the title of a book contains the title of a short work, the title of the short work should be enclosed in quotation marks, and the entire title should be underlined.

> Thompson, Lawrance Roger. <u>"Fire and Ice": The Art and Thought of Robert Frost</u>. New York: Holt, 1942.

Note: include the author's middle name or initials, if listed.

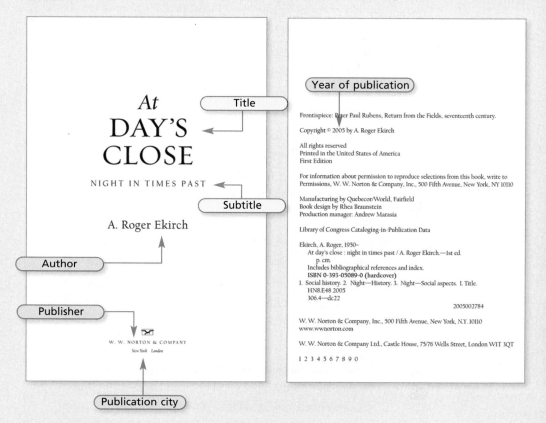

Documentation Map (MLA)

Book

Frontispiece: Roger Paul Rubens, Return from the Fields, seventeenth century.

Copyright © 2005 by A. Roger Ekirch

All rights reserved
Printed in the United States of America
First Edition

For information about permission to reproduce selections from this book, write to
Permissions, W. W. Norton & Company, Inc., 500 Fifth Avenue, New York, NY 10110

Manufacturing by Quebecor/World, Fairfield
Book design by Rhea Braunstein
Production manager: Andrew Marasia

Library of Congress Cataloging-in-Publication Data

Ekirch, A. Roger, 1950–
    At day's close : night in times past / A. Roger Ekirch.—1st ed.
        p. cm.
    Includes bibliographical references and index.
    ISBN 0-393-05089-0 (hardcover)
1. Social history. 2. Night—History. 3. Night—Social aspects. I. Title.
    HN8.E48 2005
    306.4—dc22

                                                        2005002784

W. W. Norton & Company, Inc., 500 Fifth Avenue, New York, N.Y. 10110
www.wwnorton.com

W. W. Norton & Company Ltd., Castle House, 75/76 Wells Street, London W1T 3QT

1 2 3 4 5 6 7 8 9 0

Title

Subtitle

Author

Publisher

Publication city

Year of publication

At
DAY'S
CLOSE

NIGHT IN TIMES PAST

A. Roger Ekirch

W. W. NORTON & COMPANY
New York   London

439–47
for more on
citing books
MLA style

Author's Last Name, First Name. <u>Title: Subtitle</u>. Publication City:
    Publisher, Year of publication.

Ekirch, A. Roger. <u>At Day's Close: Night in Times Past</u>. New York: Norton,
    2005.

2. TWO OR MORE WORKS BY THE SAME AUTHOR(S)

Give the author's name in the first entry, and then use three hyphens in the author slot for each of the subsequent works, listing them alphabetically by the first important word of each title.

> Author's Last Name, First Name. Title That Comes First Alphabetically. Publication City: Publisher, Year of publication.

> ---. Title That Comes Next Alphabetically. Publication City: Publisher, Year of publication.

> Kaplan, Robert D. The Coming Anarchy: Shattering the Dreams of the Post Cold War. New York: Random, 2000.

> ---. Eastward to Tartary: Travels in the Balkans, the Middle East, and the Caucasus. New York: Random, 2000.

3. TWO AUTHORS

> First Author's Last Name, First Name, and Second Author's First and Last Names. Title. Publication City: Publisher, Year of publication.

> Malless, Stanley, and Jeffrey McQuain. Coined by God: Words and Phrases That First Appear in the English Translations of the Bible. New York: Norton, 2003.

4. THREE AUTHORS

> First Author's Last Name, First Name, Second Author's First and Last Names, and Third Author's First and Last Names. Title. Publication City: Publisher, Year of publication.

> Sebranek, Patrick, Verne Meyer, and Dave Kemper. Writers INC: A Guide to Writing, Thinking, and Learning. Burlington: Write Source, 1990.

5. FOUR OR MORE AUTHORS

You may give each author's name or the name of the first author only, followed by et al., Latin for "and others."

author   title   publication

First Author's Last Name, First Name, Second Author's First and Last
Names, Third Author's First and Last Names, and Final Author's First
and Last Names. <u>Title</u>. Publication City: Publisher, Year of publication.

Anderson, Robert, John Malcolm Brinnin, John Leggett, Gary Q. Arpin,
and Susan Allen Toth. <u>Elements of Literature: Literature of the
United States</u>. Austin: Holt, 1993.

First Author's Last Name, First Name, et al. <u>Title</u>. Publication City:
Publisher, Year of publication.

Anderson, Robert, et al. <u>Elements of Literature: Literature of the United
States</u>. Austin: Holt, 1993.

6. ORGANIZATION OR GOVERNMENT AS AUTHOR

Sometimes the author is a corporation or government organization.

Organization Name. <u>Title</u>. Publication City: Publisher, Year of
publication.

Diagram Group. <u>The Macmillan Visual Desk Reference</u>. New York:
Macmillan, 1993.

National Assessment of Educational Progress. <u>The Civics Report Card</u>.
Princeton: ETS, 1990.

7. ANTHOLOGY

Editor's Last Name, First Name, ed. <u>Title</u>. Publication City: Publisher, Year
of publication.

Hall, Donald, ed. <u>The Oxford Book of Children's Verse in America</u>. New
York: Oxford UP, 1985.

If there is more than one editor, list the first editor last-name-first and
the others first-name-first.

Kitchen, Judith, and Mary Paumier Jones, eds. <u>In Short: A Collection of
Brief Creative Nonfiction</u>. New York: Norton, 1996.

8. WORK(S) IN AN ANTHOLOGY

> Author's Last Name, First Name. "Title of Work." <u>Title of Anthology</u>.
> Ed. Editor's First and Last Names. Publication City: Publisher, Year of
> publication. Pages.

> Achebe, Chinua. "Uncle Ben's Choice." <u>The Seagull Reader: Literature</u>.
> Ed. Joseph Kelly. New York: Norton, 2005. 23–27.

To document two or more selections from one anthology, list each selection by author and title, followed by a cross-reference to the anthology. In addition, include on your works-cited list an entry for the anthology itself (see no. 7 on page 443).

> Author's Last Name, First Name. "Title of Work." Anthology Editor's Last
> Name. Pages.

> Hiestand, Emily. "Afternoon Tea." Kitchen and Jones. 65–67.

> Ozick, Cynthia. "The Shock of Teapots." Kitchen and Jones. 68–71.

You don't include the anthology separately if you're using only one selection from it.

9. AUTHOR AND EDITOR

Start with the author if you've cited the text itself.

> Author's Last Name, First Name. <u>Title</u>. Ed. Editor's First and Last Names.
> Publication City: Publisher, Year of publication.

> Austen, Jane. <u>Emma</u>. Ed. Stephen M. Parrish. New York: Norton, 2000.

Start with the editor if you've cited his or her work.

> Editor's Last Name, First Name, ed. <u>Title</u>. By Author's First and Last Names.
> Publication City: Publisher, Year of publication.

> Parrish, Stephen M., ed. <u>Emma</u>. By Jane Austen. New York: Norton, 2000.

10. NO AUTHOR OR EDITOR

> Title. Publication City: Publisher, Year of publication.

> <u>2008 New York City Restaurants</u>. New York: Zagat, 2008.

author   title   publication

11. TRANSLATION

Start with the author to emphasize the work itself.

> Author's Last Name, First Name. <u>Title</u>. Trans. Translator's First and Last
> Names. Publication City: Publisher, Year of publication.

> Dostoevsky, Fyodor. <u>Crime and Punishment</u>. Trans. Richard Pevear and
> Larissa Volokhonsky. New York: Vintage, 1993.

Start with the translator to emphasize the translation.

> Translator's Last Name, First Name, trans. <u>Title</u>. By Author's First and Last
> Names. Publication City: Publisher, Year of publication.

> Pevear, Richard, and Larissa Volokhonsky, trans. <u>Crime and Punishment</u>.
> By Fyodor Dostoevsky. New York: Vintage, 1993.

12. FOREWORD, INTRODUCTION, PREFACE, OR AFTERWORD

> Part Author's Last Name, First Name. Name of Part. <u>Title of Book</u>.
> By Author's First and Last Names. Publication City: Publisher, Year
> of publication. Pages.

> Tanner, Tony. Introduction. <u>Pride and Prejudice</u>. By Jane Austen.
> London: Penguin, 1972. 7–46.

13. MULTIVOLUME WORK

If you cite all the volumes of a multivolume work, give the number of volumes after the title.

> Author's Last Name, First Name. <u>Title of Complete Work</u>. Number of vols.
> Publication City: Publisher, Year of publication.

> Sandburg, Carl. <u>Abraham Lincoln: The War Years</u>. 4 vols. New York:
> Harcourt, 1939.

If you cite only one volume, give the volume number after the title.

> Sandburg, Carl. <u>Abraham Lincoln: The War Years</u>. Vol. 2. New York:
> Harcourt, 1939.

14. ARTICLE IN A REFERENCE BOOK

Provide the author's name if the article is signed. If the reference work is well known, give only the edition and year of publication.

> Author's Last Name, First Name. "Title of Article." <u>Title of Reference Book</u>. Edition number. Year of publication.

> "Histrionics." <u>Merriam-Webster's Collegiate Dictionary.</u> 11th ed. 2003.

If the reference work is less familiar or more specialized, give full publication information. If it has only one volume or is in its first edition, omit that information.

> Author's Last Name, First Name. "Title of Article." <u>Title of Reference Book</u>. Ed. Editor's First and Last Name. Edition number. Number of vols. Publication City: Publisher, Year of publication.

> Campbell, James. "The Harlem Renaissance." <u>The Oxford Companion to Twentieth-Century Poetry</u>. Ed. Ian Hamilton. Oxford: Oxford UP, 1994.

15. BOOK IN A SERIES

> Editor's Last Name, First Name, ed. <u>Title of Book</u>. By Author's First and Last Names. Series Title abbreviated. Publication City: Publisher, Year of publication.

> Wall, Cynthia, ed. <u>The Pilgrim's Progress</u>. By John Bunyan. Norton Critical Ed. New York: Norton, 2007.

16. SACRED TEXT

If you have cited a specific edition of a religious text, you need to include it in your works-cited list.

> <u>Title</u>. Editor's First and Last Names, ed. (if any) Publication City: Publisher, Year of publication.

author   title   publication

The New English Bible with the Apocrypha. New York: Oxford UP, 1971.

The Torah: A Modern Commentary. W. Gunther Plaut, ed. New York: Union of American Hebrew Congregations, 1981.

17. EDITION OTHER THAN THE FIRST

Author's Last Name, First Name. Title. Name or number of ed. Publication City: Publisher, Year of publication.

Gibaldi, Joseph. MLA Handbook for Writers of Research Papers. 6th ed. New York: MLA, 2003.

Hirsch, E. D., Jr., ed. What Your Second Grader Needs to Know: Fundamentals of a Good Second-Grade Education. Rev. ed. New York: Doubleday, 1998.

18. REPUBLISHED WORK

Give the original publication date after the title, followed by the publication information of the republished edition.

Author's Last Name, First Name. Title. Year of original edition. Publication City: Current Publisher, Year of republication.

Bierce, Ambrose. Civil War Stories. 1909. New York: Dover, 1994.

Periodicals

BASIC FORMAT FOR AN ARTICLE

For most articles, you'll need to provide information about the author, the article title and any subtitle, the periodical title, any volume or issue number, the date, and inclusive page numbers.

Weinberger, Jerry. "Pious Princes and Red-Hot Lovers: The Politics of Shakespeare's Romeo and Juliet." Journal of Politics 65 (2003): 370–75.

A FEW DETAILS TO NOTE

- **AUTHORS:** If there is more than one author, list the first author last-name-first and the others first-name-first.

- **TITLES:** Capitalize the first and last words of titles and subtitles and all principal words. Do not capitalize *a*, *an*, *the*, *to*, or any prepositions or coordinating conjunctions unless they begin a title or subtitle. For periodical titles, omit any initial *A*, *An*, or *The*.

- **DATES:** Abbreviate the names of months except for May, June, or July: Jan., Feb., Mar., Apr., Aug., Sept., Oct., Nov., Dec. Journals paginated by volume or issue call only for the year (in parentheses).

- **PAGES:** If an article does not fall on consecutive pages, give the first page with a plus sign (55+).

19. ARTICLE IN A JOURNAL PAGINATED BY VOLUME

Author's Last Name, First Name. "Title of Article." Title of Journal
　　Volume (Year): Pages.

Cooney, Brian C. "Considering Robinson Crusoe's 'Liberty of Conscience'"
　　in an Age of Terror." College English 69 (2007): 197–215.

20. ARTICLE IN A JOURNAL PAGINATED BY ISSUE

Author's Last Name, First Name. "Title of Article." Title of Journal
　　Volume.Issue (Year): Pages.

Weaver, Constance, Carol McNally, and Sharon Moerman. "To
　　Grammar or Not to Grammar: That Is Not the Question!" Voices
　　from the Middle 8.3 (2001): 17–33.

21. ARTICLE IN A MONTHLY MAGAZINE

Author's Last Name, First Name. "Title of Article." Title of Magazine
　　Month Year: Pages.

Fellman, Bruce. "Leading the Libraries." Yale Alumni Magazine
　　Feb. 2002: 26–31.

author　·　　　title　　　publication

Documentation Map (MLA)
Article in a Journal

Title of article →

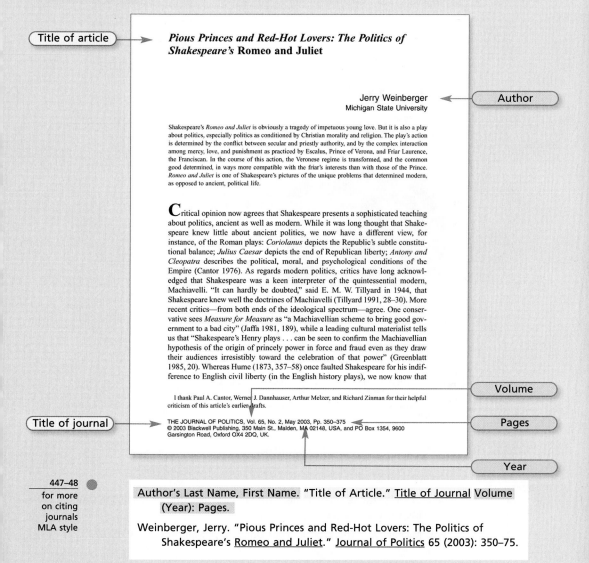

Pious Princes and Red-Hot Lovers: The Politics of Shakespeare's Romeo and Juliet

Jerry Weinberger ← Author
Michigan State University

Shakespeare's *Romeo and Juliet* is obviously a tragedy of impetuous young love. But it is also a play about politics, especially politics as conditioned by Christian morality and religion. The play's action is determined by the conflict between secular and priestly authority, and by the complex interaction among mercy, love, and punishment as practiced by Escalus, Prince of Verona, and Friar Laurence, the Franciscan. In the course of this action, the Veronese regime is transformed, and the common good determined, in ways more compatible with the friar's interests than with those of the Prince. *Romeo and Juliet* is one of Shakespeare's pictures of the unique problems that determined modern, as opposed to ancient, political life.

Critical opinion now agrees that Shakespeare presents a sophisticated teaching about politics, ancient as well as modern. While it was long thought that Shakespeare knew little about ancient politics, we now have a different view, for instance, of the Roman plays: *Coriolanus* depicts the Republic's subtle constitutional balance; *Julius Caesar* depicts the end of Republican liberty; *Antony and Cleopatra* describes the political, moral, and psychological conditions of the Empire (Cantor 1976). As regards modern politics, critics have long acknowledged that Shakespeare was a keen interpreter of the quintessential modern, Machiavelli. "It can hardly be doubted," said E. M. W. Tillyard in 1944, that Shakespeare knew well the doctrines of Machiavelli (Tillyard 1991, 28–30). More recent critics—from both ends of the ideological spectrum—agree. One conservative sees *Measure for Measure* as "a Machiavellian scheme to bring good government to a bad city" (Jaffa 1981, 189), while a leading cultural materialist tells us that "Shakespeare's Henry plays . . . can be seen to confirm the Machiavellian hypothesis of the origin of princely power in force and fraud even as they draw their audiences irresistibly toward the celebration of that power" (Greenblatt 1985, 20). Whereas Hume (1873, 357–58) once faulted Shakespeare for his indifference to English civil liberty (in the English history plays), we now know that

I thank Paul A. Cantor, Werner J. Dannhauser, Arthur Melzer, and Richard Zinman for their helpful criticism of this article's earlier drafts.

THE JOURNAL OF POLITICS, Vol. 65, No. 2, May 2003, Pp. 350–375.
© 2003 Blackwell Publishing, 350 Main St., Malden, MA 02148, USA, and PO Box 1354, 9600 Garsington Road, Oxford OX4 2DQ, UK.

Title of journal →   ← Volume
← Pages
← Year

447–48
for more
on citing
journals
MLA style

Author's Last Name, First Name. "Title of Article." Title of Journal Volume (Year): Pages.

Weinberger, Jerry. "Pious Princes and Red-Hot Lovers: The Politics of Shakespeare's Romeo and Juliet." Journal of Politics 65 (2003): 350–75.

Documentation Map (MLA)
Article in a Magazine

PERSPECTIVES
Essays by leading thinkers
in celebration of the dog

Title of article →

The Wolf in Your Dog

Author → By Michael W. Fox, DVM, PhD

*Though in their deep heart's core,
there is a commonality of origin,
spirit, emotional intelligence and
empathetic sensibility, the wild wolf
looks through us, while the dog
looks to us.*

OF ALL THE MYRIAD MEMBERS OF THE ANIMAL KINGDOM, the domesticated dog (*Canis lupus familiaris*) is closest to us. With individual exceptions in other species, this canine species is the most understanding, if not also the most observant, of human behavior—of our actions and intentions. This is why dogs are so responsive to us, even mirroring or mimicking our behavior. And it is why dogs are so trainable.

Fear in unsocialized and abused dogs interferes with their attentiveness to and interpretation of human behavior and intentions. This is one reason wild species like the coyote and wolf, even when born and raised in captivity, are difficult to train. The wolf "Tiny," whom I bottle-raised and intensely socialized during her formative early days, never really lost her fear and distrust of strangers.

Tiny did not start mirroring human behavior until she was close to nine years old. At this point, she began to mimic the human-to-human greeting grin, revealing her front teeth as she curled her lips into a snarly smile. In my experience, dogs

who can do this do so at a much earlier age, even as early as four to six months.

In comparing socialized (human-bonded) wolves and dogs in terms of how they have related to me as well as to my family members, friends and strangers, I would say that the main difference between the two species is the fear factor. Differences in trainability hinge on this; as I theorize in my new book (*Dog Body, Dog Mind*), domestication has altered the tuning of the dog's adrenal and autonomic nervous systems. This tuning (which dampens adrenal fright, flight and fight reactions and possibly alters brain serotonin levels), is accomplished through selective breeding for docility, and by gentle handling during the critical period for socialization. According to the earlier research of my mentors—Drs. John Paul Scott and John L. Fuller of the Jackson Laboratory in Bar Harbor, Maine—pups with no human contact during this critical socialization period (which ends around 12 to 16 weeks of age) are wild and unapproachable.

Title of magazine
Pages

Month and year → Mar/Apr 2008 | **Bark** 85

448, 451
for more
on citing
magazines
MLA style

Author's Last Name, First Name. "Title of Article." <u>Title of Magazine</u> Day Month Year: Pages.

Fox, Michael W. "The Wolf in Your Dog." <u>Bark</u> Mar./Apr. 2008: 85–87.

author   title   publication

22. ARTICLE IN A WEEKLY MAGAZINE

Author's Last Name, First Name. "Title of Article." <u>Title of Magazine</u>
    Day Month Year: Pages.

Walsh, Bryan. "Not a Watt to Be Wasted." <u>Time</u> 17 Mar. 2008: 46–47.

23. ARTICLE IN A DAILY NEWSPAPER

Author's Last Name, First Name. "Title of Article." <u>Name of Newspaper</u>
    Day Month Year: Pages.

Springer, Shira. "Celtics Reserves Are Whizzes vs. Wizards." <u>Boston Globe</u>
    14 Mar. 2005: D4+.

If you are documenting a particular edition of a newspaper (indicated on
the front page), specify the edition (late ed., natl. ed., etc.) in between the
date and the section and page reference.

Svoboda, Elizabeth. "Faces, Faces Everywhere." <u>New York Times</u> 13 Feb.
    2007, natl. ed.: D1+.

24. UNSIGNED ARTICLE

"Title of Article." <u>Name of Publication</u> Day Month Year: Page(s).

"Being Invisible Closer to Reality." <u>Atlanta Journal-Constitution</u> 11 Aug.
    2008: A3.

25. EDITORIAL

"Title." Editorial. <u>Name of Publication</u> Day Month Year: Page.

"Gas, Cigarettes Are Safe to Tax." Editorial. <u>Lakeville Journal</u> 17 Feb.
    2005: A10.

26. LETTER TO THE EDITOR

Author's Last Name, First Name. "Title (if any)." Letter. <u>Name of</u>
    <u>Publication</u> Day Month Year: Page.

Festa, Roger. "Social Security: Another Phony Crisis." Letter. <u>Lakeville</u>
    <u>Journal</u> 17 Feb. 2005: A10.

27. REVIEW

> Author's Last Name, First Name. "Title (if any) of Review." Rev. of <u>Title of Work</u>, by Author's First and Last Names. <u>Title of Periodical</u> Day Month Year: Pages.

> Frank, Jeffrey. "Body Count." Rev. of <u>The Exception</u>, by Christian Jungersen. <u>New Yorker</u> 30 July 2007: 86–87.

Electronic Sources

BASIC FORMAT FOR AN ELECTRONIC SOURCE

Not every electronic source gives you all the data that MLA would like to see in a works-cited entry. Ideally, you will be able to list the author's name, the title, any information about print publication, information about electronic publication (title of site, editor, date of first electronic publication and / or most recent revision, name of the sponsoring institution), date of access, and URL. Of those nine pieces of information, you will find seven in the following example.

> Johnson, Charles W. "How Our Laws Are Made." <u>Thomas: Legislative Information on the Internet</u> 30 June 2003. Lib. of Congress. 21 June 2008 <http://www.senate.gov/reference/resources/pdf/howourlawsaremade.pdf>.

A FEW DETAILS TO NOTE

- **AUTHORS:** If there is more than one author, list the first author last-name-first and the others first-name-first.
- **TITLES:** Capitalize the first and last words of titles and subtitles, and all principal words. Do not capitalize *a, an, the, to,* or any prepositions or coordinating conjunctions unless they begin a title or subtitle. For periodical titles, omit any initial *A, An,* or *The.*

- **DATES:** Abbreviate the names of months except for May, June, or July: Jan., Feb., Mar., Apr., Aug., Sept., Oct., Nov., Dec. Although MLA asks for the date when materials were first posted or most recently updated, you won't always be able to find that information. You'll also find that it will vary—you may find only the year, not the day and month. The date you must include is the date on which you accessed the electronic source.

- **URL:** Give the address of the website in angle brackets. When a URL will not fit on one line, break it only after a slash (and do not add a hyphen). If a URL is very long, consider giving the URL of the site's home page or search page instead. Also keep in mind that if you are accessing an online source through a library's subscription to a database provider (such as EBSCO), you may not see the URL itself. In that case, end your documentation with a period after your access date.

28. ENTIRE WEBSITE

PROFESSIONAL WEBSITE

Title of Site. Ed. Editor's First and Last Names. Date posted or last
  updated. Sponsoring Institution. Day Month Year of access <URL>.

Stanford Encyclopedia of Philosophy. Ed. Edward N. Zalta. 2007.
  Metaphysics Research Lab, Center for the Study of Language and
  Information, Stanford U. 25 July 2008 <http://plato.stanford.edu>.

PERSONAL WEBSITE

Author's Last Name, First Name. Home page. Date posted or last
  updated. Day Month Year of access <URL>.

Fallows, James. Home page. 2008. 20 June 2008 <http://
  jamesfallows.theatlantic.com>.

29. DOCUMENT FROM A WEBSITE

Author's Last Name, First Name. "Title of Document." <u>Title of Website.</u>
   Ed. Editor's First and Last Names. Date posted or last updated.
   Sponsoring Institution. Day Month Year of access <URL>.

Buff, Rachel Ida. "Becoming American." <u>Immigration History Research
   Center</u>. 24 March 2008. U of Minnesota. 4 April 2008 <http://
   www.ihrc.umn.edu/index.php?entry=119161>.

30. HOME PAGE FOR AN ACADEMIC DEPARTMENT

Academic Department. Dept. home page. School. Day Month Year of
   access <URL>.

English Language and Literatures. Dept. home page. Wright State U
   College of Liberal Arts. 16 Jan. 2008 <http://www.wright.edu/cola/
   Dept/eng/>.

31. HOME PAGE FOR AN ACADEMIC COURSE

Instructor's Last Name, First Name. Title of Course. Course home page.
   Dates of course. Dept. name, School. Day Month Year of access <URL>.

Woolf, Linda M. Political Psychology. Course home page. Aug. 2008–Dec.
   2008. Dept. of Psychology, Webster U. 26 Aug. 2008
   <http://www.webster.edu/~woolflm/polpsych.html>.

32. ONLINE BOOK OR PART OF A BOOK

Author's Last Name, First Name. "Title of Short Work." <u>Title of
   Long Work</u>. Original year of publication. <u>Database</u>. Date of
   electronic publication. Day Month Year of access <URL>.

Anderson, Sherwood. "The Philosopher." <u>Winesburg, Ohio</u>. 1919.
   <u>Bartleby.com: Great Books Online</u>. 1999. 7 Apr. 2008 <http://
   www.bartleby.com/156/5.html>.

author   title   publication

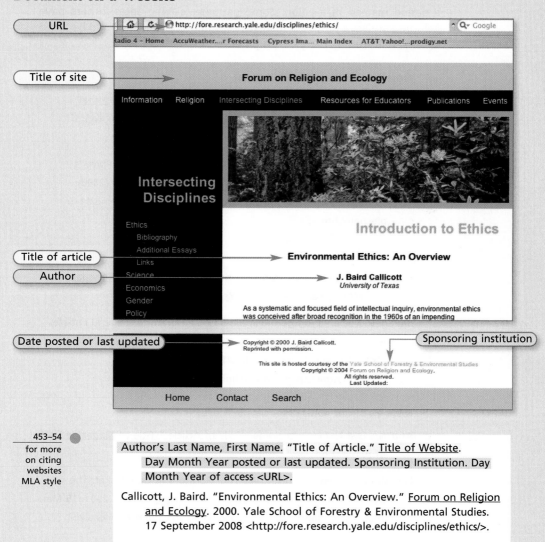

Documentation Map (MLA)
Document on a Website

URL — http://fore.research.yale.edu/disciplines/ethics/ ⌄ Q▾ Google

Radio 4 – Home   AccuWeather....r Forecasts   Cypress Ima...   Main Index   AT&T Yahoo!...prodigy.net

Title of site → **Forum on Religion and Ecology**

Information   Religion   Intersecting Disciplines   Resources for Educators   Publications   Events

Intersecting Disciplines

Ethics
  Bibliography
  Additional Essays
  Links
Science
Economics
Gender
Policy

Introduction to Ethics

Title of article → **Environmental Ethics: An Overview**

Author → **J. Baird Callicott**
University of Texas

As a systematic and focused field of intellectual inquiry, environmental ethics was conceived after broad recognition in the 1960s of an impending

Date posted or last updated — Copyright © 2000 J. Baird Callicott.
Reprinted with permission.

Sponsoring institution →

This site is hosted courtesy of the Yale School of Forestry & Environmental Studies.
Copyright © 2004 Forum on Religion and Ecology.
All rights reserved.
Last Updated:

Home   Contact   Search

453–54
for more
on citing
websites
MLA style

Author's Last Name, First Name. "Title of Article." <u>Title of Website</u>. Day Month Year posted or last updated. Sponsoring Institution. Day Month Year of access <URL>.

Callicott, J. Baird. "Environmental Ethics: An Overview." <u>Forum on Religion and Ecology</u>. 2000. Yale School of Forestry & Environmental Studies. 17 September 2008 <http://fore.research.yale.edu/disciplines/ethics/>.

33. ARTICLE IN AN ONLINE PERIODICAL

If a source does not number pages or paragraphs, follow the year with a period instead of a colon. Some periodicals have dates; others have volume and issue numbers instead — volume 10, issue 3 should be listed as 10.3, followed by the year (in parentheses).

FROM AN ONLINE SCHOLARLY JOURNAL

Author's Last Name, First Name. "Title of Article." Title of Journal
Date or Volume.Issue (Year): Pages or pars. Day Month Year of
access <URL>.

Gleckman, Jason. "Shakespeare as Poet or Playwright? The Player's
Speech in Hamlet." Early Modern Literary Studies 11.3 (2006):
13 pars. 24 June 2008 <http://www.chass.utoronto.ca/emls/11-3/
glechaml.htm>.

FROM AN ONLINE NEWSPAPER

Author's Last Name, First Name. "Title of Article." Title of Newspaper
Day Month Year. Day Month Year of access <URL>.

Banerjee, Neela. "Proposed Religion-Based Program for Federal Inmates
Is Canceled." New York Times 28 October 2006. 24 June 2008
<http://www.nytimes.com/2006/10/28/us/
28prison.html?scp=96&sq=religion&st=nyt>.

FROM AN ONLINE MAGAZINE

Author's Last Name, First Name. "Title of Article." Title of Magazine Date
of publication. Day Month Year of access <URL>.

Landsburg, Steven E. "Putting All Your Potatoes in One Basket: The
Economic Lessons of the Great Famine." Slate 13 Mar. 2001. 15 Mar.
2006 <http://slate.msn.com/Economics/01-03-13/Economics.asp>.

author   title   publication

34. BLOG POST

The MLA does not provide guidelines for documenting a blog post. The below guidelines are based on those for documenting electronic sources.

> Author's Last Name, First Name. "Title of Blog Entry." <u>Title of Blog</u>. Blog. Day Month Year posted. Day Month Year of access <URL>.

> Gladwell, Malcolm. "Enron and Newspapers." <u>Gladwell.com</u>. Blog. 4 Jan. 2007. 26 Aug. 2008 <http://gladwell.typepad.com/gladwellcom/ 2007/01/enron_and_newsp.html>.

35. ARTICLE ACCESSED THROUGH A SUBSCRIPTION SERVICE

Library subscription services, such as InfoTrac and EBSCO, and personal subscription services, such as America Online, provide access to texts for a fee.

FROM A LIBRARY SUBSCRIPTION SERVICE

> Author's Last Name, First Name. "Title of Article." <u>Title of Periodical</u> Date or Volume.Issue (Year): Pages or pars. <u>Database</u>. Name of service. Library. Day Month Year of access <URL of service>.

> Ott, Brian L. " 'I'm Bart Simpson, Who the Hell Are You?': A Study in Postmodern Identity (Re)Construction." <u>Journal of Popular Culture</u> 37.1 (2003): 56–82. <u>Academic Search Complete</u>. EBSCO. Paul Laurence Dunbar Library, Wright State U. 24 March 2008 <http://search.ebscohost.com>.

FROM A PERSONAL SUBSCRIPTION SERVICE

> Author's Last Name, First Name. "Title of Document." <u>Title of Longer Work</u>. Date of work. Service. Day Month Year of access. Keyword: Word.

> Stewart, Garrett. "Bloomsbury." <u>World Book Online</u>. 2003. America Online. 13 Mar. 2007. Keyword: Worldbook.

Documentation Map (MLA)
Article in a Database

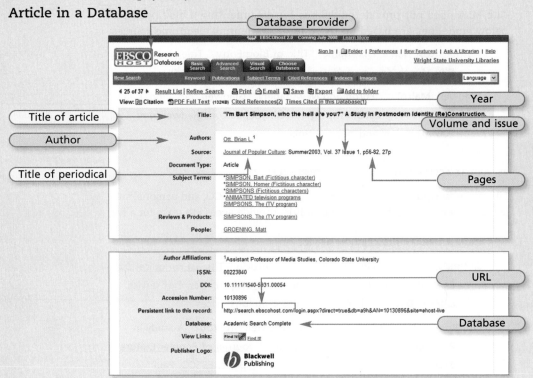

Database provider

Title of article

Author

Title of periodical

Year

Volume and issue

Pages

URL

Database

457
for more
on citing an
article in a
database
MLA style

Author's Last Name, First Name. "Title of Article." Title of Periodical
Volume.Issue (Year): Pages. Database. Database provider. Library.
Day Month Year of access <URL>.

Ott, Brian L. "'I'm Bart Simpson, Who the Hell Are You?' A Study in
Postmodern Identity (Re)Construction." Journal of Popular Culture
37.1 (2003): 56–82. Academic Search Complete. EBSCO. Paul
Laurence Dunbar Lib., Wright State U. 24 March 2008 <http://
search.ebscohost.com>.

author   title   publication

36. ONLINE EDITORIAL

"Title of Editorial." Editorial. <u>Title of Site</u> Day Month Year of publication. Day Month Year of access <URL>.

"Keep Drinking Age at 21." Editorial. <u>ChicagoTribune.com</u> 25 Aug. 2008. 28 Aug. 2008 <http://newsblogs.chicagotribune.com/vox_pop/ 2008/08/keep-the-drinki.html>.

37. ONLINE LETTER TO THE EDITOR

Author's Last Name, First Name. Letter. <u>Title of Site</u> Day Month Year posted. Day Month Year of access <URL>.

Hartman, Berl. Letter. <u>Boston Globe: Boston.com</u> 26 Aug. 2008. 29 Aug. 2008 <http://www.boston.com/bostonglobe/editorial_opinion/letters/ articles/2008/08/26/find_real_solutions_for_rising_gas_prices/>.

38. ONLINE REVIEW

Author's Last Name, First Name. "Title (if any) of Review." Rev. of <u>Title of Work</u>, by Author's First and Last Names. <u>Title of Website</u> Day Month Year posted. Day Month Year of access <URL>.

Foundas, Scott. "Heath Ledger Peers into the Abyss in <u>The Dark Knight</u>." Rev. of <u>The Dark Knight</u>, dir. Christopher Nolan. <u>VillageVoice.com</u> 16 Jul. 2008. 26 Aug. 2008 <http://www.villagevoice.com/ 2008-07-16/film/heath-ledger-dark-knight/>.

39. EMAIL

Writer's Last Name, First Name. "Subject Line." Email to the author. Day Month Year of message.

Smith, William. "Teaching Grammar—Some Thoughts." Email to the author. 19 Nov. 2007.

40. POSTING TO AN ELECTRONIC FORUM

> Writer's Last Name, First Name. "Title of Posting." Online posting. Day Month
> Year of posting. Name of Forum. Day Month Year of access <URL>.

> Schafer, Judith Kelleher. "Re: Manumission." Online posting. 27 Jan.
> 2004. H-Net List on Slavery. 29 Jan. 2006 <http://h-net.msu.edu/
> cgi-bin/logbrowse.pl?trx=lm&list=H-Slavery>.

41. ARTICLE IN AN ONLINE REFERENCE WORK

> "Title of Article." Title of Reference Work. Date of work. Sponsor of
> work. Day Month Year of access <URL>.

> "Dubai." MSN Encarta. 2008. Microsoft Corporation. 20 June 2008
> <http://encarta.msn.com/encyclopedia_761574406/Dubai.html>.

42. ENTRY IN A WIKI, NO AUTHOR

The MLA does not provide guidelines for documenting a wiki entry. The
below guidelines are based on those for documenting electronic sources.

> "Title of Entry." Title of Wiki. Day Month Year updated. Sponsoring
> Institution. Day Month Year of access <URL>.

> "Planet." Wikipedia. 28 Aug. 2008. Wikimedia Foundation. 2 Sept. 2008
> <http://en.wikipedia.org/wiki/PLANET>.

43. CD-ROM

FOR A SINGLE-ISSUE CD-ROM

> Title. CD-ROM. Any pertinent information about the edition, release, or
> version. Publication City: Publisher, Year of publication.

> Othello. CD-ROM. Princeton: Films for the Humanities and Sciences, 1998.

If you are citing only part of the CD-ROM, name the part as you would a
part of a book.

> "Snow Leopard." Encarta Encyclopedia 2007. CD-ROM. Seattle: Microsoft,
> 2007.

FOR A PERIODICAL ON A CD-ROM

Author's Last Name, First Name. "Title of Article." <u>Title of Periodical</u>. Date or Volume.Issue (Year): Page. <u>Database</u>. CD-ROM. Database provider. Month Year of CD-ROM.

Hwang, Suein L. "While Many Competitors See Sales Melt, Ben & Jerry's Scoops Out Solid Growth." <u>Wall Street Journal</u>. 25 May 1993: B1. <u>ABI-INFORM</u>. CD-ROM. ProQuest. June 1993.

44. PODCAST

The MLA does not provide guidelines for documenting a podcast. The below guidelines are based on those for documenting electronic sources.

Performer or Host's Last Name, First Name. "Title of Podcast." Podcast. Host's First and Last Name. <u>Title of Program</u>. Day Month Year posted. Sponsoring Institution. Day Month Year of access <URL>.

Blumberg, Alex, and Adam Davidson. "The Giant Pool of Money." Podcast. Ira Glass. <u>This American Life</u>. 9 May 2008. Chicago Public Radio. 18 Sept. 2008 <http://www.thisamericanlife.org/ Radio_Episode.aspx?sched=1242>.

Other Kinds of Sources

This section shows how to prepare works cited entries for categories other than books, periodicals, and writing found on the Web and CD-ROMs. The categories are in alphabetical order. Two of them — art and cartoon — cover works that do not originate on the Web but make their way there. From these examples, you can figure out a documentation style for any texts that you may come across on the Web.

A FEW DETAILS TO NOTE

- **AUTHORS**: If there is more than one author, list the first author last-name-first and the others first-name-first. Do likewise if you begin an entry with performers, speakers, and so on.

- **TITLES:** Capitalize the first and last words of titles and subtitles, and all principal words. Do not capitalize *a, an, the, to,* or any prepositions or coordinating conjunctions unless they begin a title or subtitle. For periodical titles, omit any initial *A, An,* or *The.*

- **DATES:** Abbreviate the names of months except for May, June, or July: Jan., Feb., Mar., Apr., Aug., Sept., Oct., Nov., Dec. Journals paginated by volume or issue need only the year (in parentheses).

45. ADVERTISEMENT

Product or Company. Advertisement. <u>Title of Periodical</u> Date or
   Volume.Issue (Year): Page.

Empire BlueCross BlueShield. Advertisement. <u>Fortune</u> 8 Dec. 2003: 208.

46. ART

Artist's Last Name, First Name. <u>Title of Art</u>. Year. Institution, City.

Van Gogh, Vincent. <u>The Potato Eaters</u>. 1885. Van Gogh Museum,
   Amsterdam.

ART ON THE WEB

Warhol, Andy. <u>Self-Portrait</u>. 1979. J. Paul Getty Museum, Los Angeles.
   29 Mar. 2007 <http://getty.edu/art/collections/objects/oll4421.html>.

47. CARTOON

Artist's Last Name, First Name. "Title of Cartoon (if titled)." Cartoon. <u>Title
   of Periodical</u> Date or Volume.Issue (Year): Page.

Chast, Roz. "The Three Wise Men of Thanksgiving." Cartoon. <u>New Yorker</u>
   1 Dec. 2003: 174.

CARTOON ON THE WEB

Horsey, David. Cartoon. <u>Seattle Post-Intelligencer</u> 20 Apr. 2008. 21 Apr.
   2008 <http://seattlepi.nwsource.com/horsey/viewbydate.asp?
   ID=1749>.

48. DISSERTATION

Treat a published dissertation as you would a book, but after its title, add the abbreviation *Diss.*, the name of the institution, and the date of the dissertation. If the dissertation is published by University Microfilms International (UMI), include the order number, as in the example below.

> Author's Last Name, First Name. Title. Diss. Institution, Year.
> Publication City: Publisher, Year.

> Goggin, Peter N. A New Literacy Map of Research and Scholarship in
> Computers and Writing. Diss. Indiana U of Pennsylvania, 2000. Ann
> Arbor: UMI, 2001. 9985587.

For unpublished dissertations, put the title in quotation marks and end with the degree-granting institution and the year.

> Kim, Loel. "Students Respond to Teacher Comments: A Comparison of
> Online Written and Voice Modalities." Diss. Carnegie Mellon U, 1998.

49. FILM, VIDEO, OR DVD

> Title. Dir. Director's First and Last Names. Perf. Lead Actors' First and Last
> Names. Distributor, Year of release.

> Casablanca. Dir. Michael Curtiz. Perf. Humphrey Bogart, Ingrid Bergman,
> and Claude Rains. Warner, 1942.

If you want to emphasize a particular person's contribution (for example, when discussing a director or screenwriter's work), include the name before the title.

> Cody, Diablo, scr. Juno. Dir. Jason Reitman. Perf. Ellen Page, Michael
> Cera, Jennifer Garner, Jason Bateman. Fox Searchlight, 2007.

If it's a video or DVD, give that information before the name of the distributor.

> Easter Parade. Dir. Charles Walters. Perf. Judy Garland and Fred Astaire.
> DVD. MGM, 1948.

If it's an online video from YouTube or a similar site, give that information and follow it with website access information.

Title. Dir. Director's First and Last Names (if available). Name of website. Day Month Year of release. Day Month Year of access <URL>.

Bounce! Dir. PivotMasterDX. YouTube. 14 June 2008. 21 June 2008 <http://www.youtube.com/watch?v=ZjALYqj0dPw>.

50. INTERVIEW

BROADCAST INTERVIEW

Subject's Last Name, First Name. Interview. Title of Program. Network. Station, City. Day Month Year.

Gates, Henry Louis, Jr. Interview. Fresh Air. NPR. WNYC, New York. 9 Apr. 2002.

PUBLISHED INTERVIEW

Subject's Last Name, First Name. Interview. or "Title of Interview." Title of Periodical Date or Volume.Issue (Year): Pages.

Brzezinski, Zbigniew. "Against the Neocons." American Prospect Mar. 2005: 26–27.

Stone, Oliver. Interview. Esquire Nov. 2004: 170.

PERSONAL INTERVIEW

Subject's Last Name, First Name. Personal interview. Day Month Year.

Roddick, Andy. Personal interview. 17 August 2008.

51. LETTER

UNPUBLISHED LETTER

Author's Last Name, First Name. Letter to the author. Day Month Year.

Quindlen, Anna. Letter to the author. 11 Apr. 2002.

author   title   publication

PUBLISHED LETTER

> Letter Writer's Last Name, First Name. Letter to First and Last Names.
> Day Month Year of letter. <u>Title of Book</u>. Ed. Editor's First and
> Last Names. Publication City: Publisher, Year of publication. Pages.

> White, E. B. Letter to Carol Angell. 28 May 1970. <u>Letters of E. B. White</u>.
> Ed. Dorothy Lobarno Guth. New York: Harper, 1976. 600.

52. MAP

> <u>Title of Map</u>. Map. Publication City: Publisher, Year of publication.

> <u>Toscana</u>. Map. Milan: Touring Club Italiano, 1987.

53. MUSICAL COMPOSITION

> Composer's Last Name, First Name. "Title of Short Composition." or <u>Title
> of Long Composition</u>. Year of composition (optional).

> Ellington, Duke. "Mood Indigo." 1931.

If you are identifying a composition by form, number, key, and opus, do
not underline that information or enclose it in quotation marks.

> Beethoven, Ludwig van. String quartet no. 13 in B flat, op. 130. 1825.

54. SOUND RECORDING

> Artist's Last Name, First Name. <u>Title of Long Work</u>. Other pertinent
> details about the artists. Manufacturer, Year of release.

> Beethoven, Ludwig van. <u>Missa Solemnis</u>. Perf. Westminster Choir and
> New York Philharmonic. Cond. Leonard Bernstein. Sony, 1992.

Whether you list the composer, conductor, or performer first depends on
where you want to place the emphasis. If you are citing a specific song,
put it in quotation marks before the name of the recording, which should
be underlined.

> Brown, Greg. "Canned Goods." <u>The Live One</u>. Red House, 1995.

For a spoken-word recording, you may begin with the writer, speaker, or producer, depending on your emphasis.

> Dale, Jim, narr. <u>Harry Potter and the Deathly Hallows</u>. By J.K. Rowling. Audio CD. Random House Audio, 2007.

55. ORAL PRESENTATION

> Speaker's Last Name, First Name. "Title of Lecture." Sponsoring Institution. Site, City. Day Month Year.

> Cassin, Michael. "Nature in the Raw—The Art of Landscape Painting." Berkshire Institute for Lifetime Learning. Clark Art Institute, Williamstown. 24 Mar. 2005.

56. PAPER FROM PROCEEDINGS OF A CONFERENCE

> Author's Last Name, First Name. "Title of Paper." <u>Title of Conference Proceedings</u>. Date, City. Ed. Editor's First and Last Names. Publication City: Publisher, Year. Pages.

> Zolotow, Charlotte. "Passion in Publishing." <u>A Sea of Upturned Faces: Proceedings of the Third Pacific Rim Conference on Children's Literature</u>. 1986, Los Angeles. Ed. Winifred Ragsdale. Metuchen: Scarecrow P, 1989. 236–49.

57. PERFORMANCE

> <u>Title</u>. By Author's First and Last Names. Other appropriate details about the performance. Site, City. Day Month Year.

> <u>Take Me Out</u>. By Richard Greenberg. Dir. Scott Plate. Perf. Caleb Sekeres. Dobama Theatre, Cleveland. 17 Aug. 2007.

58. TELEVISION OR RADIO PROGRAM

> "Title of Episode." <u>Title of Program</u>. Other appropriate information about the writer, director, actors, etc. Network. Station, City. Day Month Year of broadcast.

author   title   publication

"Tabula Rasa." <u>Criminal Minds</u>. Writ. Dan Dworkin. Dir. Steve Boyum.
NBC. WCNC, Charlotte. 14 May 2008.

59. PAMPHLET

Author's Last Name, First Name. <u>Title of Pamphlet</u>. Publication City:
Publisher, Year.

Bowers, Catherine. <u>Can We Find a Home Here? Answering Questions of
Interfaith Couples</u>. Boston: UUA Publications, n.d.

60. LEGAL SOURCE

The name of a legal case is underlined in the text, but not in a works-cited
entry.

Names of the first plaintiff and the first defendant. Number of case.
Name of court. Day Month Year of decision.

District of Columbia v. Heller. No. 07-290. Supreme Ct. of the US. 26 June
2008.

For acts of law, include both the Public Law number and the Statutes at
Large cataloging number.

Name of law. Public law number. Day Month Year enacted. Statutes at
Large cataloging number.

Military Commissions Act. Pub. L. 109-366. 17 Oct. 2006. Stat. 120.2600.

SAMPLE RESEARCH PAPER, MLA STYLE

Dylan Borchers wrote the following essay, which reports information, for
a first-year writing course. It is formatted according to the guidelines of
the *MLA Handbook for Writers of Research Papers,* 6th edition (2003). While
the MLA guidelines are used widely in literature and other disciplines in
the humanities, exact documentation requirements may vary from discipline to discipline and course to course. If you're unsure about what your
instructor wants, ask for clarification.

Dylan Borchers

Professor Bullock

English 102, Section 4

20 January 2007

Against the Odds:

Harry S. Truman and the Election of 1948

"Thomas E. Dewey's Election as President Is a Foregone
Conclusion," read a headline in the New York Times during the
presidential election race between incumbent Democrat Harry S.
Truman and his Republican challenger, Thomas E. Dewey. Earlier,
Life magazine had put Dewey on its cover with the caption "The
Next President of the United States" (qtd. in "1948 Truman-Dewey
Election"). In a Newsweek survey of fifty prominent political writers,
each one predicted Truman's defeat, and Time correspondents
declared that Dewey would carry 39 of the 48 states (Donaldson
210). Nearly every major media outlet across the United States
endorsed Dewey and lambasted Truman. As historian Robert H.
Ferrell observes, even Truman's wife, Bess, thought he would be
beaten (270).

The results of an election are not so easily predicted, as the
famous photograph on page 2 shows. Not only did Truman win the
election, but he won by a significant margin, with 303 electoral
votes and 24,179,259 popular votes, compared to Dewey's 189
electoral votes and 21,991,291 popular votes (Donaldson 204-07). In
fact, many historians and political analysts argue that Truman

---

Put your last name and the page number in the upper-right corner of each page.

Center the title.

Double-space throughout.

If you name the author of a source in a signal phrase, give the page numbers in parentheses.

Borchers   2

Fig. 1. President Harry S. Truman holds up an Election Day edition of the <u>Chicago Daily Tribune</u>, which mistakenly announced "Dewey Defeats Truman." St. Louis, 4 Nov. 1948 (Rollins).

would have won by an even greater margin had third-party Progressive candidate Henry A. Wallace not split the Democratic vote in New York State and Dixiecrat Strom Thurmond not won four states in the South (McCullough 711). Although Truman's defeat was heavily predicted, those predictions themselves, Dewey's passiveness as a campaigner, and Truman's zeal turned the tide for a Truman victory.

In the months preceding the election, public opinion polls predicted that Dewey would win by a large margin. Pollster Elmo Roper stopped polling in September, believing there was no reason to continue, given a seemingly inevitable Dewey landslide. Although the margin narrowed as the election drew near, the other

Insert illustrations close to the text to which they relate. Label with figure number, caption, and parenthetical source citation.

Indent paragraphs $\frac{1}{2}$-inch or 5 spaces.

Give the author and page numbers in parentheses when no signal phrase is used.

pollsters predicted a Dewey win by at least 5 percent (Donaldson 209). Many historians believe that these predictions aided the president in the long run. First, surveys showing Dewey in the lead may have prompted some of Dewey's supporters to feel overconfident about their candidate's chances and therefore to stay home from the polls on Election Day. Second, these same surveys may have energized Democrats to mount late get-out-the-vote efforts ("1948 Truman-Dewey Election"). Other analysts believe that the overwhelming predictions of a Truman loss also kept at home some Democrats who approved of Truman's policies but saw a Truman loss as inevitable. According to political analyst Samuel Lubell, those Democrats may have saved Dewey from an even greater defeat (Hamby, Man of the People 465). Whatever the impact on the voters, the polling numbers had a decided effect on Dewey.

Historians and political analysts alike cite Dewey's overly cautious campaign as one of the main reasons Truman was able to achieve victory. Dewey firmly believed in public opinion polls. With all indications pointing to an easy victory, Dewey and his staff believed that all he had to do was bide his time and make no foolish mistakes. Dewey himself said, "When you're leading, don't talk"

If you quote text quoted in another source, cite that source in a parenthetical reference.

(qtd. in McCullough 672). Each of Dewey's speeches was well-crafted and well-rehearsed. As the leader in the race, he kept his remarks faultlessly positive, with the result that he failed to deliver a solid message or even mention Truman or any of Truman's policies. Eventually, Dewey began to be perceived as aloof and stuffy. One

Borchers   4

observer compared him to the plastic groom on top of a wedding cake (Hamby, "Harry S. Truman"), and others noted his stiff, cold demeanor (McCullough 671-74).

As his campaign continued, observers noted that Dewey seemed uncomfortable in crowds, unable to connect with ordinary people. And he made a number of blunders. One took place at a train stop when the candidate, commenting on the number of children in the crowd, said he was glad they had been let out of school for his arrival. Unfortunately for Dewey, it was a Saturday ("1948: The Great Truman Surprise"). Such gaffes gave voters the feeling that Dewey was out of touch with the public.

Again and again through the autumn of 1948, Dewey's campaign speeches failed to address the issues, with the candidate declaring that he did not want to "get down in the gutter" (qtd. in McCullough 701). When told by fellow Republicans that he was losing ground, Dewey insisted that his campaign not alter its course. Even _Time_ magazine, though it endorsed and praised him, conceded that his speeches were dull (McCullough 696). According to historian Zachary Karabell, they were "notable only for taking place, not for any specific message" (244). Dewey's numbers in the polls slipped in the weeks before the election, but he still held a comfortable lead over Truman. It would take Truman's famous whistle-stop campaign to make the difference.

Few candidates in U.S. history have campaigned for the presidency with more passion and faith than Harry Truman. In the

If you cite two or more works closely together, provide a parenthetical citation for each one.

autumn of 1948, he wrote to his sister, "It will be the greatest campaign any President ever made. Win, lose, or draw, people will know where I stand" (91). For thirty-three days, Truman traveled the nation, giving hundreds of speeches from the back of the <u>Ferdinand Magellan</u> railroad car. In the same letter, he described the pace: "We made about 140 stops and I spoke over 147 times, shook hands with at least 30,000 and am in good condition to start out again tomorrow for Wilmington, Philadelphia, Jersey City, Newark, Albany and Buffalo" (91). McCullough writes of Truman's campaign:

> No President in history had ever gone so far in quest of support from the people, or with less cause for the effort, to judge by informed opinion. . . . As a test of his skills and judgment as a professional politician, not to say his stamina and disposition at age sixty-four, it would be like no other experience in his long, often difficult career, as he himself understood perfectly. More than any other event in his public life, or in his presidency thus far, it would reveal the kind of man he was. (655)

He spoke in large cities and small towns, defending his policies and attacking Republicans. As a former farmer and relatively late bloomer, Truman was able to connect with the public. He developed an energetic style, usually speaking from notes rather than from a prepared speech, and often mingled with the crowds that met his train. These crowds grew larger as the campaign

Set off quotations of four or more lines by indenting 1 inch (or 10 spaces).

Put parenthetical references after final punctuation in block quotations.

Borchers   6

progressed. In Chicago, over half a million people lined the streets as he passed, and in St. Paul the crowd numbered over 25,000. When Dewey entered St. Paul two days later, he was greeted by only 7,000 supporters ("1948 Truman-Dewey Election"). Reporters brushed off the large crowds as mere curiosity seekers wanting to see a president (McCullough 682). Yet Truman persisted, even if he often seemed to be the only one who thought he could win. By going directly to the American people and connecting with them, Truman built the momentum needed to surpass Dewey and win the election.

The legacy and lessons of Truman's whistle-stop campaign continue to be studied by political analysts, and politicians today often mimic his campaign methods by scheduling multiple visits to key states, as Truman did. He visited California, Illinois, and Ohio 48 times, compared with 6 visits to those states by Dewey. Political scientist Thomas M. Holbrook concludes that his strategic campaigning in those states and others gave Truman the electoral votes he needed to win (61, 65).

The 1948 election also had an effect on pollsters, who, as Elmo Roper admitted, "couldn't have been more wrong" (qtd. in Karabell 255). Life magazine's editors concluded that pollsters as well as reporters and commentators were too convinced of a Dewey victory to analyze the polls seriously, especially the opinions of undecided voters (Karabell 256). Pollsters assumed that undecided voters would vote in the same proportion as decided voters -- and that

If you cite a work with no known author, use the title in your parenthetical reference.

turned out to be a false assumption (Karabell 258). In fact, the lopsidedness of the polls might have led voters who supported Truman to call themselves undecided out of an unwillingness to associate themselves with the losing side, further skewing the polls' results (McDonald, Glynn, Kim, and Ostman 152). Such errors led pollsters to change their methods significantly after the 1948 election.

> *In a work by four or more authors, either cite them all or name the first one followed by et al.*

After the election, many political analysts, journalists, and historians concluded that the Truman upset was in fact a victory for the American people, who, the New Republic noted, "couldn't be ticketed by the polls, knew its own mind and had picked the rather unlikely but courageous figure of Truman to carry its banner" (qtd. in McCullough 715). How "unlikely" is unclear, however; Truman biographer Alonzo Hamby notes that "polls of scholars consistently rank Truman among the top eight presidents in American history" (Man of the People 641). But despite Truman's high standing, and despite the fact that the whistle-stop campaign is now part of our political landscape, politicians have increasingly imitated the style of the Dewey campaign, with its "packaged candidate who ran so as not to lose, who steered clear of controversy, and who made a good show of appearing presidential" (Karabell 266). The election of 1948 shows that voters are not necessarily swayed by polls, but it may have presaged the packaging of candidates by public relations experts, to the detriment of public debate on the issues in future presidential elections.

Borchers 8

Works Cited

Donaldson, Gary A. <u>Truman Defeats Dewey</u>. Lexington: UP of
    Kentucky, 1999.

Ferrell, Robert H. <u>Harry S. Truman: A Life</u>. Columbia: U of Missouri P,
    1994.

Hamby, Alonzo L., ed. "Harry S. Truman (1945-1953)."
    <u>AmericanPresident.org</u>. 11 Dec. 2003. Miller Center of Public
    Affairs, U of Virginia. 12 Jan. 2007 <http://
    www.americanpresident.org/history/harrytruman>.

---. <u>Man of the People: A Life of Harry S. Truman</u>. New York: Oxford
    UP, 1995.

Holbrook, Thomas M. "Did the Whistle-Stop Campaign Matter?" <u>PS:
    Political Science and Politics</u> 35 (2002): 59-66.

Karabell, Zachary. <u>The Last Campaign: How Harry Truman Won the
    1948 Election</u>. New York: Knopf, 2000.

McCullough, David. <u>Truman</u>. New York: Simon & Schuster, 1992.

McDonald, Daniel G., Carroll J. Glynn, Sei-Hill Kim, and Ronald E.
    Ostman. "The Spiral of Silence in the 1948 Presidential
    Election." <u>Communication Research</u> 28 (2001): 139-55.

"1948 Truman-Dewey Election." <u>Electronic Government Project:
    Eagleton Digital Archive of American Politics</u>. 2004. Eagleton
    Inst. of Politics, Rutgers, State U of New Jersey. 11 Jan. 2007
    <http://www.eagleton.rutgers.edu/>.

1"

Center the heading.

Double-space throughout.

Alphabetize the list by authors' last names or by title for works with no author.

Begin each entry at the left margin; indent subsequent lines $\frac{1}{2}$-inch or 5 spaces.

If you cite more than one work by a single author, list them alphabetically by title, and use 3 hyphens instead of repeating the author's name after the first entry.

Borchers   9

"1948: The Great Truman Surprise." <u>Media and Politics Online</u>

<u>Projects: Media Coverage of Presidential Campaigns</u>. 29 Oct.

2003. Dept. of Political Science and International Affairs,

Kennesaw State U. 11 Jan. 2007 <http://www.kennesaw.edu/

pols.3380/pres/1948.html>.

Rollins, Byron. Untitled photograph. "The First 150 Years: 1948." <u>AP</u>

<u>History</u>. Associated Press. 10 Jan. 2007 <http://www.ap.org/

pages/history/timeline/1948.htm>.

Truman, Harry S. "Campaigning, Letter, October 5, 1948." <u>Harry S.</u>

<u>Truman</u>. Ed. Robert H. Ferrell. Washington: CQ P, 2003. 91.

Check to be sure that every source you use is on the list of works cited.

APA Style **50**

American Psychological Association (APA) style calls for (1) brief documentation in parentheses near each in-text citation and (2) complete documentation in a list of references at the end of your text. The models in this chapter draw on the *Publication Manual of the American Psychological Association*, 5th edition (2001). Additional information is available at www.apastyle.org.

A DIRECTORY TO APA STYLE

author   title   publication

APA IN-TEXT DOCUMENTATION

Brief documentation in your text makes clear to your reader precisely what you took from a source and, in the case of a quotation, precisely where (usually, on which page) in the source you found the text you are quoting.

Paraphrases and summaries are more common than quotations in APA-style projects. The chapter on quoting, paraphrasing, and summarizing covers all three kinds of citations. It also includes a list of words you can use in signal phrases to introduce quotations, paraphrases, and summaries. As you cite each source, you will need to decide whether to name the author in a signal phrase — "as McCullough (2001) wrote" — or in parentheses — "(McCullough, 2001)."

The first examples in this chapter show basic in-text documentation for a work by one author. Variations on those examples follow. All of the examples are color-coded to help you see how writers using APA style work authors and page numbers — and sometimes titles — into their texts.

1. AUTHOR NAMED IN A SIGNAL PHRASE

If you are quoting, you must give the page number(s). You are not required to give the page number(s) with a paraphrase or a summary, but APA encourages you to do so, especially if you are citing a long or complex work; most of the models in this chapter do include page numbers. Check with your instructors to find out their preferences.

AUTHOR QUOTED

Put the date in parentheses right after the author's name; put the page in parentheses as close to the quotation as possible.

> McCullough (2001) described John Adams as having "the hands of a man accustomed to pruning his own trees, cutting his own hay, and splitting his own firewood" (p. 18).

author title publication

> John Adams had "the hands of a man accustomed to pruning his own trees, cutting his own hay, and splitting his own firewood," according to McCullough (2001, p. 18).

Notice that in the first example, the parenthetical reference with the page number comes *after* the closing quotation marks but *before* the period at the end of the sentence.

AUTHOR PARAPHRASED

Put the date in parentheses right after the author's name; follow the date with the page.

> McCullough (2001, p. 18) described John Adams's hands as those of someone used to manual labor.

> John Adams's hands were those of a laborer, according to McCullough (2001, p. 18).

2. AUTHOR NAMED IN PARENTHESES

If you do not mention an author in a signal phrase, put his or her name, a comma, and the year of publication in parentheses as close as possible to the quotation, paraphrase, or summary.

AUTHOR QUOTED

Give the author, date, and page in one parentheses, or split the information between two parentheses.

> Adams is said to have had "the hands of a man accustomed to pruning his own trees, cutting his own hay, and splitting his own firewood" (McCullough, 2001, p. 18).

> One biographer (McCullough, 2001) has said John Adams had "the hands of a man accustomed to pruning his own trees, cutting his own hay, and splitting his own firewood" (p. 18).

AUTHOR PARAPHRASED OR SUMMARIZED

Give the author, date, and page in one parentheses toward the beginning or the end of the paraphrase.

> One biographer (McCullough, 2001, p. 18) described John Adams as someone who was not a stranger to manual labor.

> John Adams's hands were those of a laborer (McCullough, 2001, p. 18).

3. AUTHORS WITH THE SAME LAST NAME

If your reference list includes more than one person with the same last name, include initials in all documentation to distinguish the authors from one another.

> Eclecticism is common in contemporary criticism (J. M. Smith, 1992, p. vii).

> J. M. Smith (1992, p. vii) has explained that eclecticism is common in contemporary criticism.

4. AFTER A BLOCK QUOTATION

If a quotation runs forty or more words, set it off from the rest of your text and indent it one-half inch (or five spaces) from the left margin without quotation marks. Place the page number(s) in parentheses *after* the end punctuation.

> Kaplan (2000) captured ancient and contemporary Antioch for us:
>> At the height of its glory in the Roman-Byzantine age, when it had an amphitheater, public baths, aqueducts, and sewage pipes, half a million people lived in Antioch. Today the population is only 125,000. With sour relations between Turkey and Syria, and unstable politics throughout the Middle East, Antioch is now a backwater—seedy and tumbledown, with relatively few tourists. (p. 123)
> Antioch's decline serves as a reminder that the fortunes of cities can change drastically over time.

5. TWO AUTHORS

Always mention both authors. Use *and* in a signal phrase, but use an ampersand (&) in parentheses.

> Carlson and Ventura (1990, p. v) wanted to introduce Julio Cortázar, Marjorie Agosín, and other Latin American writers to an audience of English-speaking adolescents.

> According to the Peter Principle, "In a hierarchy, every employee tends to rise to his level of incompetence" (Peter & Hull, 1969, p. 26).

6. THREE OR MORE AUTHORS

In the first reference to a work by three to five persons, name all contributors. In subsequent references, name the first author followed by *et al.* Whenever you refer to a work by six or more contributors, name only the first author, followed by *et al.* Use *and* in a signal phrase, but use an ampersand (&) in parentheses.

> Faigley, George, Palchik, and Selfe (2004, p. xii) have argued that where there used to be a concept called *literacy*, today's multitude of new kinds of texts has given us *literacies*.

> It's easier to talk about a good movie than a good book (Sebranek, Meyer, & Kemper, 1990, p. 143).

> Peilen et al. (1990, p. 75) supported their claims about corporate corruption with startling anecdotal evidence.

7. ORGANIZATION OR GOVERNMENT AS AUTHOR

If an organization has a long name that is recognizable by its abbreviation, give the full name and the abbreviation the first time you cite the source. In subsequent citations, use only the abbreviation. If the organization does not have a familiar abbreviation, use the full name each time you refer to it. (See the next page for examples.)

FIRST CITATION

(American Psychological Association [APA], 2008)

SUBSEQUENT CITATIONS

(APA, 2008)

8. AUTHOR UNKNOWN

With reference books and newspaper editorials, among other things, you may not know the author of a work. Use the complete title if it is short; if it is long, use the first few words of the title under which the work appears in the reference list.

> *Webster's New Biographical Dictionary* (1988) identifies William James as "American psychologist and philosopher" (p. 520).

> A powerful editorial asserted that healthy liver donor Mike Hurewitz died because of "frightening" faulty postoperative care ("Every Patient's Nightmare," 2007).

9. TWO OR MORE WORKS CITED TOGETHER

If you need to cite multiple works in the same parentheses, list them in the same order that they appear in your reference list, separated by semicolons.

> Many researchers have argued that what counts as "literacy" is not necessarily learned at school (Heath, 1983; Moss, 2003).

10. SOURCE QUOTED IN ANOTHER SOURCE

When you need to cite a source that was quoted in another source, let the reader know that you used a secondary source by adding the words *as cited in.*

author   title   publication

During the meeting with the psychologist, the patient stated repeatedly that he "didn't want to be too paranoid" (as cited in Oberfield & Yasik, 2004, p. 294).

11. WORK WITHOUT PAGE NUMBERS

Instead of page numbers, some electronic works have paragraph numbers, which you should include if you are referring to a specific part of such a source. Use the ¶ symbol or the abbreviation *para*. In sources with neither page nor paragraph numbers, refer readers to a particular part of the source if possible, perhaps indicating a heading and the paragraph under the heading.

Russell's dismissals from Trinity College at Cambridge and from City College in New York City have been seen as examples of the controversy that marked the philosopher's life (Irvine, 2006, para. 2).

12. AN ENTIRE WORK

You do not need to give a page number if you are directing readers' attention to an entire work. Identify the author in a signal phrase or in parentheses, and cite the year of publication in parentheses.

Kaplan (2000) considered Turkey and Central Asia explosive.

13. PERSONAL COMMUNICATION

Cite email, telephone conversations, interviews, personal letters, and other personal texts as *personal communication*, along with the person's initial(s), last name, and the date. You do not need to include such personal communications in your reference list.

The author and editors seriously considered alternative ways of demonstrating documentation styles (F. Weinberg, personal communication, November 14, 2007).

L. Strauss (personal communication, December 6, 2006) told about visiting Yogi Berra when they both lived in Montclair, New Jersey.

NOTES

APA recognizes that there are instances when writers of research papers may need to use *content notes* to give an explanation or information that doesn't fit into the paper proper. To signal a content note, place a superscript numeral in your text at the appropriate point. Your readers will know to look for a note beginning with the same superscript numeral on a separate page with the heading *Notes*, after your paper but before the reference list. If you have multiple notes, number them consecutively throughout your paper. Indent the first line of each note five spaces, and flush all subsequent lines left.

Here is an example showing text and an accompanying content note from a book called *In Search of Solutions: A New Direction in Psychotherapy* (2003).

TEXT WITH SUPERSCRIPT

An important part of working with teams and one-way mirrors is taking the consultation break, as at Milan, BFTC, and MRI.[1]

CONTENT NOTE

[1]It is crucial to note here that, while working within a team is fun, stimulating, and revitalizing, it is not necessary for successful outcomes. Solution-oriented therapy works equally well when working solo.

APA REFERENCE LIST

A reference list provides full bibliographic information for every source cited in your text with the exception of personal communication. This list should be alphabetized by authors' last names (or sometimes by editors' names). Works that do not have an identifiable author or editor are alphabetized by title. See pages 518–19 for a sample reference list.

author   title   publication

Books

BASIC FORMAT FOR A BOOK

For most books, you'll need to provide information about the author; the date of publication; the title and any subtitle; and the place of publication and publisher. You'll find this information on the book's title page and copyright page.

> Diamond, J. (2005). *Collapse: How societies choose to fail or succeed.*
> New York: Viking.

A FEW DETAILS TO NOTE

- **DATES**: If more than one year is given, use the most recent one.

- **TITLES**: Capitalize only the first word and proper nouns and proper adjectives in titles and subtitles.

- **PLACE OF PUBLICATION**: Give city followed by state (abbreviated) or province or country (for example, Dubuque, IA). Omit state, province, or country for larger cities such as London, New York, and Tokyo. If more than one city is given, use the first.

- **PUBLISHER**: Use a shortened form of the publisher's name (Little, Brown for Little, Brown and Company), but retain *Association*, *Books*, and *Press* (American Psychological Association, Princeton University Press).

1. ONE AUTHOR

> Author's Last Name, Initials. (Year of publication). *Title.* Publication City:
> Publisher.

> Young, K. S. (1998). *Caught in the net: How to recognize the signs of Internet addiction — and a winning strategy for recovery.* New York: Wiley.

Documentation Map (APA)
Book

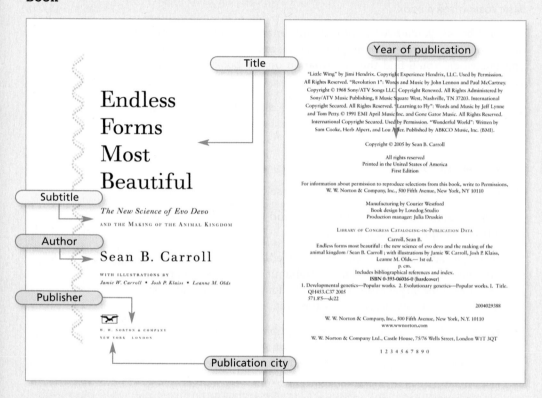

487–92
for more on
citing books
APA style

Author's Last Name, Initials. (Year of publication). *Title: Subtitle.*
    Publication City: Publisher.

Carroll, S. B. (2005). *Endless forms most beautiful: The new science of evo
    devo and the making of the animal kingdom.* New York: Norton.

author   title   publication

2. TWO OR MORE WORKS BY THE SAME AUTHOR

If the works were published in different years, list them chronologically.

> Lewis, B. (1995). *The Middle East: A brief history of the last 2,000 years.*
> New York: Scribner.

> Lewis, B. (2003). *The crisis of Islam: Holy war and unholy terror.* New
> York: Modern Library.

If the works were published in the same year, list them alphabetically by title, adding "a," "b," and so on to the years.

> Kaplan, R. D. (2000a). *The coming anarchy: Shattering the dreams of the
> post cold war.* New York: Random House.

> Kaplan, R. D. (2000b). *Eastward to Tartary: Travels in the Balkans, the
> Middle East, and the Caucasus.* New York: Random House.

3. TWO OR MORE AUTHORS

For two to six authors, use this format.

> First Author's Last Name, Initials, Next Author's Last Name, Initials, & Last
> Author's Last Name, Initials. (Year of publication). *Title.* Publication
> City: Publisher.

> Leavitt, S. D., & Dubner, S. J. (2006). *Freakonomics: A rogue economist
> explores the hidden side of everything.* New York: William Morrow.

> Sebranek, P., Meyer, V., & Kemper, D. (1990). *Writers INC: A guide to
> writing, thinking, and learning.* Burlington, WI: Write Source.

For a work by seven or more authors, name just the first six authors. After the sixth name, add the abbreviation *et al.*

4. ORGANIZATION OR GOVERNMENT AS AUTHOR

Sometimes a corporation or government organization is both author and publisher. If so, use the word *Author* as the publisher (see page 490).

> Organization Name or Government Agency. (Year of publication). *Title*. Publication City: Publisher.

Catholic News Service. (2002). *Stylebook on religion 2000: A reference guide and usage manual*. Washington, DC: Author.

U.S. Social Security Administration. (2008). *Social Security: Retirement benefits*. Washington, DC: Author.

5. AUTHOR AND EDITOR

> Author's Last Name, Initials. (Year of edited edition). *Title*. (Editor's Initials Last Name, Ed.). Publication City: Publisher. (Original work[s] published year[s])

Dick, P. F. (2008). *Five novels of the 1960s and 70s*. (J. Lethem, Ed.). New York: Library of America. (Original works published 1964–1977)

6. EDITED COLLECTION

> First Editor's Last Name, Initials, Next Editor's Last Name, Initials, & Final Editor's Last Name, Initials. (Eds.). (Year of edited edition). *Title*. Publication City: Publisher.

Raviv, A., Oppenheimer, L., & Bar-Tal, D. (Eds.). (1999). *How children understand war and peace: A call for international peace education*. San Francisco: Jossey-Bass.

7. WORK IN AN EDITED COLLECTION

> Author's Last Name, Initials. (Year of publication). Title of article or chapter. In Initials Last Name (Ed.), *Title* (pp. pages). Publication City: Publisher.

Harris, I. M. (1999). Types of peace education. In A. Raviv, L. Oppenheimer, & D. Bar-Tal (Eds.), *How children understand war and peace: A call for international peace education* (pp. 46–70). San Francisco: Jossey-Bass.

author   title   publication

8. UNKNOWN AUTHOR

> *Title*. (Year of publication). Publication City: Publisher.

> *Webster's new biographical dictionary*. (1988). Springfield, MA: Merriam-
> Webster.

If the title page of a work lists the author as *Anonymous*, treat the reference-list entry as if the author's name were Anonymous, and alphabetize it accordingly.

9. EDITION OTHER THAN THE FIRST

> Author's Last Name, Initials. (Year). *Title* (name or number ed.).
> Publication City: Publisher.

> Burch, D. (2008). *Emergency navigation: Find your position and shape your
> course at sea even if your instruments fail* (2nd ed.). Camden, ME:
> International Marine/McGraw-Hill.

10. TRANSLATION

> Author's Last Name, Initials. (Year of publication). *Title* (Translator's First
> Initial Last Name, Trans.). Publication City: Publisher. (Original work
> published Year)

> Hugo, V. (2008). *Les misérables* (J. Rose, Trans.). New York: Modern
> Library. (Original work published 1862)

11. MULTIVOLUME WORK

> Author's Last Name, Initials. (Year). *Title* (Vols. numbers). Publication City:
> Publisher.

> Nastali, D. P. & Boardman, P. C. (2004). *The Arthurian annals: The tradition
> in English from 1250 to 2000* (Vols. 1–2). New York: Oxford University
> Press USA.

ONE VOLUME OF A MULTIVOLUME WORK

> Author's Last Name, Initials. (Year). *Title of whole work: Vol. number.
> Title of volume*. Publication City: Publisher.

Spiegelman, A. (1986). *Maus: Vol. 1. My father bleeds history.* New York: Random House.

12. ARTICLE IN A REFERENCE BOOK

UNSIGNED

Title of entry. (Year). In *Title of reference book* (Vol. number, name or number ed., pp. pages). Publication City: Publisher.

Macrophage. (2003). In *Merriam-Webster's collegiate dictionary* (10th ed., p. 698). Springfield, MA: Merriam-Webster.

SIGNED

Author's Last Name, Initials. (Year). Title of entry. In *Title of reference book* (Vol. number, pp. pages). Publication City: Publisher.

Wasserman, D. E. (2006). Human exposure to vibration. In *International encyclopedia of ergonomics and human factors* (Vol. 2, pp. 1800–1801). Boca Raton, FL: CRC.

Periodicals

BASIC FORMAT FOR AN ARTICLE

For most articles, you'll need to provide information about the author; the date; the article title and any subtitle, the periodical title; and any volume or issue number and inclusive page numbers. Here is an example of an entry for an article in a journal.

Ferguson, N. (2005). Sinking globalization. *Foreign Affairs, 84*(2), 64–77.

A FEW DETAILS TO NOTE

- **AUTHORS**: Give each author's last name first followed by initials. When there are seven or more authors, name the first six and add *et al.* after the sixth name.

author   title   publication

- **DATES**: For journals, give year only. For magazines and newspapers, give year followed by a comma and then month or month and day. Do not abbreviate months.

- **TITLES**: Capitalize only the first word and proper nouns and proper adjectives in titles and subtitles of articles. Capitalize the first and last words and all principal words of periodical titles. Do not capitalize *a*, *an*, *the*, or any prepositions or coordinating conjunctions unless they begin the title of the periodical.

- **VOLUME AND ISSUE**: For journals and magazines, give volume or volume and issue, as explained in more detail below. For newspapers, do not give volume or issue.

- **PAGES**: For a journal or magazine article, do not use *p.* or *pp.* even though you do use that designation for a newspaper article. If an article does not fall on consecutive pages, give all the page numbers (for example, 45, 75–77 for a journal or magazine; pp. C1, C3, C5–C7 for a newspaper).

13. **ARTICLE IN A JOURNAL PAGINATED BY VOLUME**

Author's Last Name, Initials. (Year). Title of article. *Title of Journal, volume*, pages.

Yaffe, K., Fox, P., Newcomer, R., Sands, L., Lindquist, K., Dane, K., et al. (2002). Patient and caregiver characteristics and nursing home placement in patients with dementia. *Journal of American Medical Association, 287*, 2090–2097.

14. **ARTICLE IN A JOURNAL PAGINATED BY ISSUE**

Author's Last Name, Initials. (Year). Title of article. *Title of Journal, volume*(issue), pages.

Weaver, C., McNally, C., & Moerman, S. (2001). To grammar or not to grammar: That is *not* the question! *Voices from the Middle, 8*(3), 17–33.

Documentation Map (APA)
Article in a Journal

Title of article →

Asperger Syndrome and Medication Treatment

Author →

Luke Y. Tsai

Asperger syndrome (AS) is a neurobiological disorder whose core clinical symptoms include impairment in social interaction, impairments in verbal and nonverbal communication, and restricted, repetitive, and stereotyped patterns of behavior, interests, and activities. AS is often accompanied by coexisting neuropsychiatric disorders, including anxiety disorder, affective disorder, obsessive–compulsive disorder, Tourette syndrome, attention-deficit/hyperactivity disorder, and sleep disorders. These clinical features provide the rationale for the use of psychotropic medications (psychopharmacotherapy) in individuals with AS. This article describes the clinical indications for psychopharmacotherapy and provides guidelines for monitoring the effectiveness of medication treatment and for preventing and monitoring the development of side effects and/or adverse effects of psychotropic medications.

Early detection and effective treatment of these coexisting neuropsychiatric disorders or medication-induced side effects are critical. Like most medications, psychotherapeutic agents can correct or compensate for some malfunctions in the human body or systems. They do not cure AS, but they can lessen the challenges to persons with AS and their family members and improve patients' quality of life.

This article was written to summarize the current state of knowledge of when and how medication can be used as part of a comprehensive treatment of individuals with AS. Building on an overview of the comorbid neuropsychiatric disorders of AS, the article outlines a process of medical assessment of these disorders and concludes with guidelines for psychopharmacological treatment. These recommendations are developed mainly from the author's experience with persons with AS, as well as from limited published clinical studies.

Behavioral and biological studies have generated evidence to suggest neurobiologic etiologies of Asperger syndrome (AS). At present, however, no specific biological marker or markers have been identified as causing AS. Hence, no treatment modality specifically based on cause has been developed to "cure" individuals with AS. Nevertheless, there is potential for some medications to be helpful in ameliorating psychiatric or behavioral symptoms that can interfere with an individual's ability to participate in educational, social, work, and family systems, as well as to enhance positive responses to other forms of intervention in persons with AS.

Many of the behavioral problems or disturbed emotions reported may be clinical manifestations of coexisting neuropsychiatric disorders or side effects induced by psychotherapeutic medications. Strong data have shown that psychotherapeutic medications can be quite effective as first-line treatments for certain neuropsychiatric disorders that may develop in individuals with AS. These neuropsychiatric disorders include attention-deficit/hyperactivity disorder (ADHD), obsessive–compulsive disorder (OCD), tic disorders, affective disorder, anxiety disorder, seizure disorders, and sleep disorders. The psychopharmacological field has also compiled knowledge of side effects that may be produced by these medications.

Comorbid Neuropsychiatric Disorders of AS

Information about comorbid neuropsychiatric disorders of AS is limited because professionals in the United States have only recognized AS as a distinct clinical entity for a relatively short time. Furthermore, there is no established method for clinicians to assess comorbid neuropsychiatric disorders in this population. Nonetheless, AS has been associated with reported cases of other psychiatric disorders, such as Tourette syndrome (Berthier, Bayes, & Tolosa, 1993; Kadesjo & Gillberg, 2000; Marriage et al., 1993; Ringman & Jankovic, 2000; Searcy et al., 2000), ADHD (Ghaziuddin & Butler, 1998), affective illness or mood disorders (Duggal, 2001; Frazier, Doyle, Chiu, & Coyle, 2002; Ghaziuddin & Butler, 1998; Tantam, 1988, 1991; Wing, 1981), anxiety disorder (Tantam, 1991), OCD (Tantam, 1991), and schizophrenia (Tantam, 1991).

Green, Gilchrist, Burton, and Cox (2000) examined psychiatric and social functioning in 20 individuals with AS ages 11 to 19 years with full-scale IQ scores abo[...] searchers found that 35% of the adolescents r[...]

Title of journal

Year

FOCUS ON AUTISM AND OTHER DEVELOPMENTAL DISABILITIES
VOLUME 22, NUMBER 3, FALL 2007
PAGES 138–148

Volume and issue

Pages

Author's Last Name, Initials. (Year). Title of article. *Title of Journal, volume*(issue), pages.

Tsai, L. Y. (2007). Asperger syndrome and medication treatment. *Focus on Autism and Other Developmental Disabilities, 22*(3), 138–148.

author   title   publication

Documentation Map (APA)

Article in a Magazine

Author's Last Name, Initials. (Year, Month Day). Title of article. *Title of Magazine, volume*(issue), page(s).

Cullen, L. T. (2008, March 24). Freshen up your drink. *Time, 171*(12), 65.

496
for more
on citing
magazines
APA style

15. ARTICLE IN A MAGAZINE

If a magazine is published weekly, include the day and the month. If there is a volume number, include it after the magazine title.

> Author's Last Name, Initials. (Year, Month Day). Title of article. *Title of Magazine, volume*, page(s).

> Gregory, S. (2008, June 30). Crash course: Why golf carts are more hazardous than they look. *Time, 171*, 53.

If a magazine is published monthly, include the month(s) only.

> Fox D. (2008, February). Did life begin in ice? *Discover, 52*, 58–60.

16. ARTICLE IN A NEWSPAPER

If page numbers are consecutive, separate them with a dash. If not, separate them with a comma.

> Author's Last Name, Initials. (Year, Month Day). Title of article. *Title of Newspaper*, p(p). page(s).

> Schneider, G. (2005, March 13). Fashion sense on wheels. *The Washington Post*, pp. F1, F6.

17. ARTICLE BY AN UNKNOWN AUTHOR

List an article whose author is unknown by the title of the article.

IN A MAGAZINE

> Title of article. (Year, Month Day). *Title of Magazine, volume*, page(s).

> Hot property: From carriage house to family compound. (2004, December). *Berkshire Living, 1*, 99.

IN A NEWSPAPER

> Title of article. (Year, Month Day). *Title of Newspaper*, p(p). page(s).

> Clues in salmonella outbreak. (2008, June 21). *New York Times*, p. A13.

author   title   publication

18. REVIEW

IN A JOURNAL

Author's Last Name, Initials. (Year). Title of review [Review of *Title of Work*]. *Title of Journal, volume*(issue), page(s).

Geller, J. L. (2005). The cock and bull of Augusten Burroughs [Review of the books *Running with scissors*, *Dry: A memoir*, and *Magical thinking*]. *Psychiatric Services, 56,* 364–365.

IN A MAGAZINE

Author's Last Name, Initials. (Year, Month Day). Title of review [Review of *Title of Work*]. *Title of Magazine, volume*, page(s).

Brandt, A. (2003, October). Animal planet [Review of the book *Intelligence of apes and other rational beings*]. *National Geographic Adventure, 5,* 47.

IN A NEWSPAPER

Author's Last Name, Initials. (Year, Month Day). Title of review [Review of *Title of Work*]. *Title of Newspaper*, p(p). page(s).

Morris, C. A. (2005, March 24). Untangling the threads of the Enron fraud [Review of the book *Conspiracy of fools: A true story*]. *The New York Times*, p. B9.

If the review does not have a title, include just the bracketed information about the work being reviewed.

Jarratt, S. C. (2000). [Review of the book *Lend me your ear: Rhetorical constructions of deafness*]. *College Composition and Communication, 52,* 300–302.

19. LETTER TO THE EDITOR

IN A JOURNAL

Use the appropriate style for a journal paginated by volume or by issue (examples are on page 493).

Author's Last Name, Initials. (Year). Title of letter [Letter to the editor].
  Title of Journal, volume, page(s).

Rosner, W. (2001). An extraordinarily inaccurate assay for free testosterone
  is still with us [Letter to the editor]. *Journal of Clinical Endocrinology
  and Metabolism,* 86, 2903.

IN A MAGAZINE

Author's Last Name, Initials. (Year, Month Day). Title of letter [Letter to
  the editor]. *Title of Magazine, volume,* page(s).

Jorrin, M. (2008, September 1). Mowing it [Letter to the editor]. *The New
  Yorker, 84,* 16.

IN A NEWSPAPER

Author's Last Name, Initials. (Year, Month Day). Title of letter [Letter to
  the editor]. *Title of Newspaper,* p(p). page(s).

Hitchcock, G. (2008, August 3). Save our species [Letter to the editor]. *San
  Francisco Chronicle,* p. P-3.

Electronic Sources

BASIC FORMAT FOR AN ELECTRONIC SOURCE

Not every electronic source gives you all the data that APA would like to
see in a reference entry. Ideally, you will be able to list author's or editor's
name; date of first electronic publication or most recent revision, title of
document; information about print publication if any; information about
electronic publication (title of site, date of your access of the site or
retrieval of the document, name of the sponsoring institution); and URL
(address of document or site) or DOI (Digital Object Identifier, a string of
letters and numbers that identifies an online document). Of those nine
pieces of information, you will find seven in the following example.

author   title   publication

Johnson, C. W. (2000). How our laws are made. In *Thomas: Legislative information on the Internet*. Retrieved March 5, 2007, from the Library of Congress website: http://thomas.loc.gov/home/holam.txt

A FEW DETAILS TO NOTE

- **AUTHORS**: List all authors last-name-first and initials. When there's more than one author, use an ampersand (&). When there are seven or more authors, name the first six and add *et al.* after the sixth name.

- **TITLES**: For websites and electronic documents, articles, or books, capitalize only the first word of titles and subtitles, proper nouns, and proper adjectives; for titles of periodicals, capitalize the first and last words and all principal words of the periodical title, but do not capitalize *a, an, the, to,* or any prepositions or coordinating conjunctions unless they begin a title or subtitle.

- **DATES**: After the author, give the year of the document's original publication on the Web or of its most recent revision. If neither of those years is clear, use *n.d.* to mean "no date". For undated content or content that may change—like an "about us" statement or blog post—include the month (not abbreviated), day, and year that you retrieved the document. For content that's unlikely to change—like a published journal article or book excerpt—you don't need to include the retrieval date.

- **URL OR DOI**: A DOI provides a permanent link to an online document, so when it's available, include the DOI instead of the URL in the reference. A DOI is often found on the first page of an article, but sometimes you'll need to click on a button labeled "Article" or "CrossRef" to find it. If you do not identify the sponsoring institution ("the Library of Congress website" in the example on page 000), you do not need a colon before the URL or DOI. Don't include any punctuation at the end of the URL or DOI. If online material is presented in frames and no DOI is available, provide the URL of the home page or menu page.

20. NONPERIODICAL WEBSITE

COMPLETE SITE

Author's or Editor's Last Name, Initials. (Ed. if appropriate). (Year). *Title of site*. Retrieved Month Day, Year, from URL

Ockerbloom, J. M. (Ed.). (2005). *The online books page*. Retrieved March 28, 2007, from http://digital.library.upenn.edu/books

If you cannot find an author's or editor's name, use the name of the organization that created the website. Alternatively, begin with the title of the site, placing it before the year, as in the following example. For the year give the most recent update. The URL should lead to the site's home page.

Mental help net. (2007). Retrieved March 28, 2007, from http://mentalhelp.net

PART OF SITE

Author's Last Name, Initials. (Year). Title of page or article. In *Title of site*. Retrieved Month Day, Year (if necessary), from URL or DOI

Schwartz, A. N. (2008). Stuff, why is it so difficult to part with? In *Obsessive compulsive disorder*. Retrieved from http://www.mentalhelp.net/poc/view_doc.php?type=weblog&wlid=5&id=436&cn=6

LARGE AND COMPLEX SITE

Introduce the URL or DOI by naming the host organization and the relevant collection, department, or institute within the organization.

Author's or Editor's Last Name, Initials. (Ed. if appropriate). (Year). *Title of site*. Retrieved Month Day, Year, from Host Organization website: URL

Salda, M. N. (Ed.). (2005). *The little red riding hood project*. Retrieved March 12, 2007, from University of Southern Mississippi, De Grummond Children's Literature Research Collection website: http://www.usm.edu/english/fairytales/lrrh/lrrhhome.htm

Documentation Map (APA)

Part of a Website

URL

Title of site

Title of page or article

Author

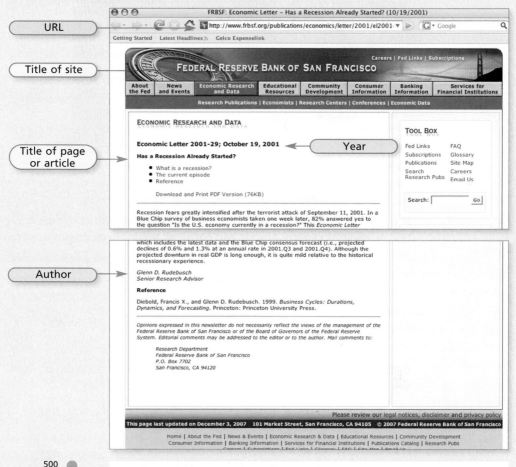

500
for more
on citing
websites
APA style

Author's Last Name, Initials. (Year). Title of page or article. In *Title of site*.
    Retrieved Month Day, Year, from URL

Rudebusch, G. D. (2001). Has a recession already started? In *Federal
    Reserve Bank of San Francisco*. Retrieved April 3, 2008, from http://
    www.frbsf.org/publications/economics/letter/2001/el2001-29.html

21. ARTICLE IN AN ONLINE PERIODICAL OR DATABASE

When available, include both the volume number and issue number. If a document can only be accessed with a subscription, provide the URL of the home page or menu page.

AN ARTICLE IN AN ONLINE PERIODICAL WITH NO PRINT VERSION

Author's Last Name, Initials. (Year, Month Day). Title of article. *Title of Periodical, Volume*(issue). Retrieved Month Day, Year (if necessary), from URL or DOI

Bohannon, J. (2008, June 20). Slaying monsters for science. *Science, 320*(5883). doi:10.1126/science.320.5883.1592c

AN ARTICLE IN PRINT AND IN AN ONLINE PERIODICAL

If an article appears online in the same format and with the same content as its print version, simply add *[Electronic version]*; you do not need to give the URL or DOI.

Author's Last Name, Initials. (Year, Month Day). Title of article [Electronic version]. *Title of Newspaper*, p(p). page(s).

Collins, G. (2008, June 21). Vice is nice [Electronic version]. *The New York Times*, p. A27.

Give the URL or DOI if the online version of a periodical article differs from the print version.

Author's Last Name, Initials. (Year, Month Day). Title of article. *Title of Newspaper*, p. page. Retrieved from URL

Collins, G. (2008, June 21). Vice is nice. *The New York Times*, p. A27. Retrieved from http://www.nytimes.com/2008/06/21/opinion/21collins.html

author   title   publication

Documentation Map (APA)
Article in a Database

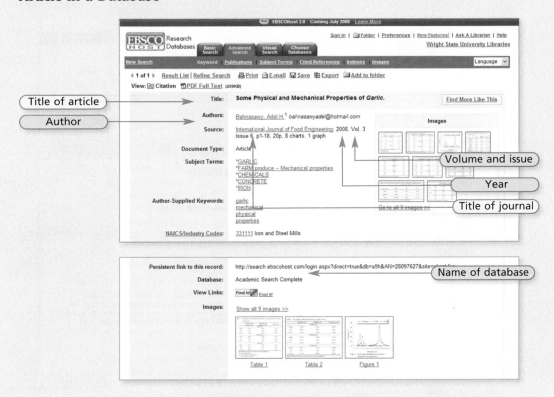

502, 505
for more
on citing an
article in a
database
APA style

Author's Last Name, Initials. (Year). Title of article. *Title of Journal,
volume*(issue). Retrieved Month Day, Year, from Name of database.

Bahnasawy, A. H. (2008). Some physical and mechanical properties of
garlic. *International Journal of Food Engineering, 3*(6). Retrieved
March 25, 2008, from Academic Search Complete database.

Documentation Map (APA)
Article in a Database with DOI

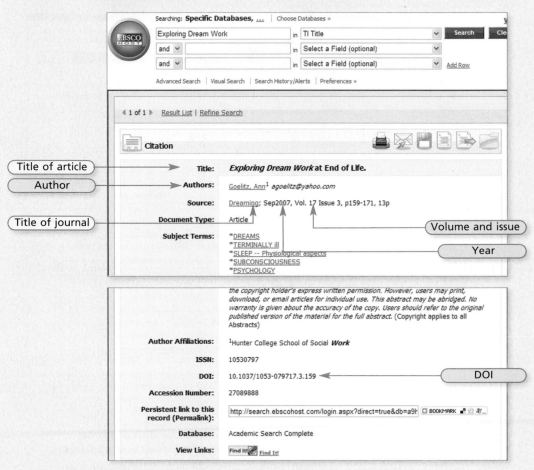

502, 505
for more
on citing an
article in a
database
APA style

Author's Last Name, Initials. (Year). Title of article. *Title of Journal, volume*(issue). doi

Goerlitz, A. (2007). Exploring dream work at end of life. *Dreaming, 17*(3). doi: 10.1037/1053-0797.17.3.159

author   title   publication

AN ONLINE ARTICLE ACCESSED THROUGH A DATABASE

Follow the format for a journal (as below), magazine, newspaper, or other source. In most cases, you don't need to include the database name; only provide it if you're citing a rare book or other hard-to-find document that you located in a database and no DOI is provided.

> Author's Last Name, Initials. (Year). Title of article. *Title of Journal,*
> *volume*(issue), pages. Retrieved from Name of database
> (if necessary) or DOI.

> White, D. E. (1999). The "Joineriana": Anna Barbauld, the Aikin
> family circle, and the dissenting public sphere. *Eighteenth-Century*
> *Studies, 32*(4), 511–533. Retrieved from Project Muse database.

22. ARTICLE IN AN ONLINE REFERENCE WORK

For online reference works like dictionaries or encyclopedias, provide the URL of the home page or menu page if no DOI is provided.

> Author's Last Name, Initials. (Year). Title of entry. In *Title of reference*
> *work.* Retrieved from URL or DOI.

> Smith, R. L. (2008). Ecology. In *MSN Encarta.* Retrieved from http://
> encarta.msn.com

23. CHAPTER OR SECTION OF A WEB DOCUMENT

> Author's Last Name, Initials. (Year). Title of chapter or section. In *Title of*
> *work* (chap. chapter or section number). Retrieved Month Day, Year,
> from URL

> Greenspun, P. (1993). Freezing to death in the Canadian Rockies. In *Trav-*
> *els with Samantha* (chap. VI). Retrieved September 2, 2008, from
> http://philip.greenspun.com/samantha/samantha=VI

24. ELECTRONIC DISCUSSION SOURCES

List online postings only if they are archived and can be retrieved.

Author's Last Name, Initials. (Year, Month Day). Subject line of message [Msg number, if any]. Message posted to Name of Organization electronic mailing list, archived at URL

Baker, J. (2005, February 15). Huffing and puffing [Msg 89]. Message posted to the American Dialect Society electronic mailing list, archived at http://listserv.linguistlist.org/archives/ads-1.html

Do not include email or other nonarchived discussions in your list of references. Simply cite the sender's name in your text. See no. 13 on page 485 for guidelines on identifying such sources in your text.

25. ONLINE VIDEO

Last Name, Initials (Writer), & Last Name, Initials (Producer). (Year, Month Day posted). *Title* [Descriptive label]. Retrieved Month Day, Year, from URL

Coulter, J. (Songwriter & Performer), & Booth, M. S. (Producer). (2006, September 23). *Code Monkey* [Music video]. Retrieved May 18, 2007, from http://www.youtube.com/watch?v=v4Wy7gRGgeA

Other Kinds of Sources

26. FILM, VIDEO, OR DVD

Last Name, Initials (Producer), & Last Name, Initials (Director). (Year). *Title* [Motion picture]. Country: Studio.

Wallis, H. B. (Producer), & Curtiz, M. (Director). (1942). *Casablanca* [Motion picture]. United States: Warner.

27. MUSIC RECORDING

Composer's Last Name, Initials. (Year of copyright). Title of song. On *Title of album* [Medium]. City: Label.

author   title   publication

Veloso, C. (1997). Na baixado sapateiro. On *Livros* [CD]. Los Angeles:
Nonesuch.

If the music is performed by someone other than the composer, put that
information in brackets following the title. When the recording date is different from the copyright date, put it in parentheses after the label.

Cahn, S., & Van Heusen, J. (1960). The last dance [Recorded by F. Sinatra].
On *Sinatra reprise: The very good years* [CD]. Burbank, CA: Reprise
Records. (1991)

28. PROCEEDINGS OF A CONFERENCE

Author's Last Name, Initials. (Year of publication). Title of paper. In
Proceedings Title (pp. pages). Publication City: Publisher.

Heath, S. B. (1997). Talking work: Language among teens. In *Symposium
about Language and Society–Austin* (pp. 27–45). Austin: Department
of Linguistics at the University of Texas.

29. TELEVISION PROGRAM

Last Name, Initials (Writer), & Last Name, Initials (Director). (Year). Title
of episode [Descriptive label]. In Initials Last Name (Producer), *Series
title*. City: Network.

Mundy, C. (Writer), & Bernaro, E. A. (Director). (2007). In birth and death
[Television series episode]. In E. A. Bernaro (Executive Producer),
Criminal minds. New York: NBC.

30. SOFTWARE OR COMPUTER PROGRAM

Title and version number [Computer software]. (Year). Publication City:
Publisher.

The Sims 2: Holiday edition [Computer software]. (2005). Redwood City,
CA: Electronic Arts Inc.

31. DISSERTATION ABSTRACT

PRINT

Author's Last Name, Initials. (Year). Title of dissertation (Doctoral
dissertation, Name of institution, Year degree granted). *Title of
Source, volume*(issue), page(s).

Palenski, J. E. (1981). Running away: A sociological analysis (Doctoral
dissertation, New York University, 1981). *Dissertation Abstracts
International, 41*(12), 5251.

ONLINE

Author's Last Name, Initials. (Year). *Title of dissertation* (publication
number) [Abstract]. Retrieved from Name of database.

Knapik, M. (2008). *Adolescent online trouble-talk: Help-seeking in
cyberspace* (AAT NR38024) [Abstract]. Retrieved from Dissertation
Abstracts (Online) database.

32. UNPUBLISHED DISSERTATION

Author's Last Name, Initials. (Year). *Title of dissertation.* Unpublished
doctoral dissertation, Institution, Location.

Connell, E. (1996). *The age of experience: Edith Wharton and the "divorce
question" in early twentieth-century America.* Unpublished doctoral
dissertation, University of Virginia, Charlottesville, Virginia.

SAMPLE RESEARCH PAPER, APA STYLE

Carolyn Stonehill wrote the following paper for a first-year writing course.
It is formatted according to the guidelines of the *Publication Manual of
the American Psychological Association*, 5th edition (2001). While APA guidelines are used widely in linguistics and the social sciences, exact requirements may vary from discipline to discipline and course to course. If you're
unsure about what your instructor wants, ask for clarification.

author   title   publication

It's in Our Genes   1

Insert a short-ened title and page number in the upper-right corner of each page, including the title page.

It's in Our Genes:

The Biological Basis of Human Mating Behavior

Carolyn Stonehill

English 102, Section 22

Professor Bertsch

February 24, 2007

Center the full title, your name, the name and section number of the course, your instructor's name, and the date, unless your instructor requires different information.

It's in Our Genes   2

Abstract

While cultural values and messages certainly play a part in the process of mate selection, the genetic and psychological predispositions developed by our ancestors play the biggest role in determining to whom we are attracted. Women are attracted to strong, capable men with access to resources to help rear children. Men find women attractive based on visual signs of youth, health, and, by implication, fertility. While perceptions of attractiveness are influenced by cultural norms and reinforced by advertisements and popular media, the persistence of mating behaviors that have no relationship to societal realities suggests that they are part of our biological heritage.

Unless your instructor speci-fies another length, limit your abstract to 120 words or fewer.

author   title   publication

It's in Our Genes:

The Biological Basis of Human Mating Behavior

Consider the following scenario: It's a sunny afternoon on campus, and Jenny is walking to her next class. Out of the corner of her eye, she catches sight of her lab partner, Joey, parking his car. She stops to admire how tall, muscular, and stylishly dressed he is, and she does not take her eyes off him as he walks away from his shiny new BMW. As he flashes her a pearly white smile, Jenny melts, then quickly adjusts her skirt and smooths her hair.

This scenario, while generalized, is familiar: Our attraction to people—or lack of it—often depends on their physical traits. But why this attraction? Why does Jenny respond the way she does to her handsome lab partner? Why does she deem him handsome at all? Certainly Joey embodies the stereotypes of physical attractiveness prevalent in contemporary American society. Advertisements, television shows, and magazine articles all provide Jenny with signals telling her what constitutes the ideal American man. Yet she is also attracted to Joey's new sports car even though she has a new car herself. Does Jenny find this man striking because of the influence of her culture, or does her attraction lie in a more fundamental part of her constitution? Evolutionary psychologists, who apply principles of evolutionary biology to research on the human mind, would say that Jenny's responses in this situation are due largely to mating strategies developed by her prehistoric ancestors. Driven by the need to reproduce and propagate the species, these ancestors of ours formed patterns of mate selection so effective in providing for their needs and those of their offspring that they are mimicked even in today's society. While cultural values and messages clearly play a part in the process of mate selection, the genetic and psychological predispositions developed by our ancestors play the biggest role in determining to whom we are attracted.

Provide headings to help readers follow the organization.

Women's Need to Find a Capable Mate

Pioneering evolutionary psychologist Trivers (as cited in Allman, 1993) observed that having and rearing children requires women to invest far more resources than men because of the length of pregnancy, the dangers of childbirth, and the duration of infants'

Refer to authors by last name. In general, use the past tense or the present perfect in signal phrases.

dependence on their mothers (p. 56). According to Fisher (as cited in Frank, 2001), one of the leading advocates of this theory, finding a capable mate was a huge preoccupation of all prehistoric reproductive women, and for good reason: "A female couldn't carry a baby in one arm and sticks and stones in the other arm and still feed and protect herself on the very dangerous open grasslands, so she began to need a mate to help her rear her young" (p. 85). So because of this it became advantageous for the woman to find a strong, capable man with access to resources, and it became suitable for the man to find a healthy, reproductively sound woman to bear and care for his offspring. According to evolutionary psychologists, these are the bases upon which modern mate selection is founded, and there are many examples of this phenomenon to be found in our own society.

author   title   publication

It's in Our Genes   5

One can see now why Jenny might be attracted by Joey's display of resources — his BMW. In our society, men with good job prospects, a respected social position, friends in high places, or any combination thereof have generally been viewed as more desirable mates than those without these things because they signal to women that the men have resources (Buss & Schmitt, 1993, p. 226). Compared with males, females invest more energy in bearing and raising children, so it is most advantageous for females to choose mates with easy access to resources, the better to provide for their children.

If the author is not named in a signal phrase, include the name in parentheses, along with the date and the page number.

Men's Need to Find a Healthy Mate

For men, reproductive success depends mainly on the reproductive fitness of their female counterpart: No amount of available resources can save a baby miscarried in the first month of gestation. Because of this need for a healthy mate, men have evolved a particular attraction "radar" that focuses on signs of a woman's health and youth, markers that are primarily visual (Weiten, 2001, p. 399). Present-day attractiveness ratings are based significantly on this primitive standard: "Some researchers have suggested that cross-cultural standards of beauty reflect an evolved preference for physical traits that are generally associated with youth, such as smooth skin, good muscle tone, and shiny hair" (Boyd & Silk, 2000, p. 625). This observation would explain why women of our time are preoccupied with plastic surgery, makeup, and — in Jenny's case — a quick hair check as a potential date

Use ampersands in parenthetical references — but use and in signal phrases.

approaches. As Cunningham, Roberts, Barbee, Druen, and Wu (1995) noted, "A focus on outer beauty may have stemmed from a need for desirable inner qualities," such as health, strength, and fertility, and "culture may build on evolutionary dynamics by specifying grooming attributes that signal successful adaptation" (pp. 262–263).

If an author is named in a signal phrase, include the publication date in parentheses after the name.

The Influence of the Media on Mate Selection

There is, however, a good deal of opposition to evolutionary theory. Some critics say that the messages fed to us by the media are a larger influence on the criteria of present-day mate selection than any sort of ancestral behavior. Advertisements and popular media have long shown Americans what constitutes a physically ideal mate: In general, youthful, well-toned, symmetrical features are considered more attractive than aging, flabby, or lopsided ones. Evolutionary psychologists argue that research has not determined what is cause and what is effect. Cosmides and Tooby (1997) offered the following analogy to show the danger of assigning culture too powerful a causal role:

Indent quotations of 40 or more words 5 to 7 spaces, about $\frac{1}{2}$-inch from the left margin.

For example, people think that if they can show that there is information in the culture that mirrors how people behave, then *that* is the cause of their behavior. So if they see that men on TV have trouble crying, they assume that their example is *causing* boys to be afraid to cry. But which is cause and which effect? Does the fact that men don't cry much on TV *teach* boys to not cry, or does it merely *reflect* the way boys normally develop? In the absence of research on the particular topic,

author   title   publication

It's in Our Genes   7

there is no way of knowing. ("Nature and Nurture: An

Adaptationist Perspective," para. 16)

We can hypothesize, then, that rather than media messages determining our mating habits, our mating habits determine the media messages. Advertisers rely on classical conditioning to interest consumers in their products. For instance, by showing an image of a beautiful woman while advertising a beauty product, advertisers hope that consumers will associate attractiveness with the use of that particular product (Weiten, 2001). In order for this method to be effective, however, the images depicted in conjunction with the beauty product must be ones the general public already finds attractive, and an image of a youthful, clear-skinned woman would, according to evolutionary psychologists, be attractive for reasons of reproductive fitness. In short, what some call media influence is not an influence at all but merely a mirror in which we see evidence of our ancestral predispositions.

If Not Media, Then What?

Tattersall (2001), a paleoanthropologist at the American Museum of Natural History, offered another counterargument to the evolutionary theory of mate selection. First, he argued that the behavior of organisms is influenced not only by genetics, but also by economics and ecology working together (p. 663). Second, he argued that no comparisons can be made between modern human behavior and that of our evolutionary predecessors because the appearance of *Homo sapiens* presented a sudden, qualitative change

To cite a specific part of an unpaginated website, count paragraphs from the beginning of the document or, as is done here, from a major heading.

from the Neanderthals — not a gradual evolution of behavioral traits:

> As a cognitive and behavioral entity, our species is truly unprecedented. Our consciousness is an emergent quality, not the result of eons of fine-tuning of a single instrument. And, if so, it is to this recently acquired quality of uniqueness, not to the hypothetical "ancestral environments," that we must look in the effort to understand our often unfathomable behaviors. (p. 665)

The key to Tattersall's argument is this "emergent quality" of symbolic thought; according to his theories, the ability to think symbolically is what separates modern humans from their ancestors and shows the impossibility of sexual selection behaviors having been passed down over millions of years. Our sexual preferences, Tattersall said, are a result of our own recent and species-specific development and have nothing whatsoever to do with our ancestors.

Opponents of the evolutionary theory, though, fail to explain how "unfathomable" mating behaviors can exist in our present society for no apparent or logical reason. Though medicine has advanced to the point where fertility can be medically enhanced, Singh (1993) observed that curvy women are still viewed as especially attractive because they are perceived to possess greater fertility — a perception that is borne out by several studies of female fertility, hormone levels, and waist-to-hip ratio (p. 304). Though

author   title   publication

It's in Our Genes   9

more and more women are attending college and achieving high-paying positions, women are still "more likely than men to consider economic prospects a high priority in a mate" (Sapolsky, 2001–2002, p. 18). While cultural norms and economic conditions influence our taste in mates, as Singh (1993) showed in observing that "the degree of affluence of a society or of an ethnic group within a society may, to a large extent, determine the prevalence and admiration of fatness [of women]" (pp. 304–305), we still react to potential mates in ways determined in Paleolithic times. The key to understanding our mating behavior does not lie only in an emergent modern quality, nor does it lie solely in the messages relayed to us by society; rather, it involves as well the complex mating strategies developed by our ancestors.

Begin list of references on a new page; center the heading.

References

Alphabetize the list by author's last name.

Allman, W. F. (1993, July 19). The mating game. *U.S. News & World Report,* 56–63.

Boyd, R., & Silk, J. B. (2000). *How humans evolved.* (2nd ed.). New York: Norton.

Indent all lines after the first line of each entry 5 spaces or $\frac{1}{2}$-inch.

Buss, D. M., & Schmitt, D. P. (1993). Sexual strategies theory: An evolutionary perspective on human mating. *Psychological Review, 100*(2), 204–232.

Be sure every source listed is cited in the text; don't list sources consulted but not cited.

Cosmides, L., & Tooby, J. (1997). *Evolutionary psychology: A primer.* Retrieved February 2, 2007, from University of California, Santa Barbara, Center for Evolutionary Psychology website: http://www.psych.ucsb.edu/research/cep/primer.html

Cunningham, M. R., Roberts, A. R., Barbee, A. P., Druen, P. B., & Wu, C.-H. (1995). "Their ideas of beauty are, on the whole, the same as ours": Consistency and variability in the cross-cultural perception of female physical attractiveness. *Journal of Personality and Social Psychology, 68,* 261–279.

Frank, C. (2001, February). Why do we fall in—and out of—love? Dr. Helen Fisher unravels the mystery. *Biography,* 95–97, 112.

Sapolsky, R. M. (2001–2002, December–January). What do females want? *Natural History,* 18–21.

Singh, D. (1993). Adaptive significance of female physical attractiveness: Role of waist-to-hip ratio. *Journal of Personality and Social Behavior, 65,* 293–307.

author   title   publication

It's in Our Genes   11

Tattersall, I. (2001). Evolution, genes, and behavior. *Zygon: Journal of Religion & Science, 36,* 657–666. Retrieved from the Psychology and Behavioral Sciences Collection database.

Weiten, W. (2001). *Psychology: Themes & variations.* (5th ed.). San Bernardino, CA: Wadsworth.

part 6

Media / Design

Consciously or not, we design all the texts we write, choosing typefaces, setting up text as lists or charts, deciding whether to add headings — and then whether to center them or flush them left. Sometimes our genre calls for certain design elements — essays begin with titles, letters begin with salutations ("Dear Auntie Em"). Other times we design texts to meet the demands of particular audiences, formatting documentation in MLA or APA or some other style, setting type larger for young children, and so on. And always our designs will depend upon our medium. A memoir might take the form of an essay in a book, be turned into a bulleted list for a PowerPoint presentation, or include links to images or other pages if presented on a website. The chapters in this part offer advice for working with PRINT texts, SPOKEN texts, and ELECTRONIC texts.

Media / Design

Print Text 51

USA Today reports on a major news story with an article that includes a large photo and a colorful graph; the *New York Times* covers the same story with an article that is not illustrated but has a large headline and a pull quote highlighting one key point. Your psychology textbook includes many photos, tables, charts, and other visuals to help readers understand the subject matter. When you submit an essay for a class, you choose a typeface and you may make the type larger—or smaller—as need be. In all these instances, the message is in some way "designed." This chapter offers advice on designing print texts to suit your purpose, audience, genre, and subject. Much of the advice also holds for **ELECTRONIC TEXTS** and for visuals that accompany **SPOKEN TEXTS**.

546–56

534–45

Considering the Rhetorical Situation

As with all writing tasks, your rhetorical situation affects the way you design a print text.

PURPOSE
Consider how you can design your text to help achieve your purpose. If you're reporting certain kinds of information, for instance, you may want to present some data in a chart or table; if you're trying to get readers to care about an issue, a photo or pull quote—a brief selection of text "pulled out" and reprinted in a larger typeface—might help you do so.

3–4

AUDIENCE
Do you need to do anything designwise for your intended audience? Change the type size? Add headings? Tables? Color?

5–8

rhetorical situations · genres · processes · strategies · research mla/apa · media/design · handbook

9–11 ▣
GENRE   Does your genre have any design requirements? Must (or can) it have headings? Illustrations? Tables or graphs? A certain size paper?

12–14 ▣
STANCE   How can your design reflect your attitude toward your audience and subject? Do you need a businesslike typeface, or a playful one? Will illustrations help you convey a certain tone?

Some Elements of Design

Whatever your text, you have various design decisions to make. What typeface(s) should you use? How should you arrange your text on the page? Should you include any headings? The following guidelines will help you consider each of these questions.

Type.   You can choose from among many typefaces, and the one you choose will affect your text—how well readers can read it and how they will perceive your **TONE** and **STANCE.** Times Roman will make a text look businesslike or academic; *Comic Sans* will make it look playful. For most academic writing, you'll want to use 10- or 11- or 12-point type, and you'll usually want to use a serif face (such as Times Roman or Bookman), which is generally easier to read than a sans serif face (such as Arial, Verdana, or Century Gothic). It's usually a good idea to use a serif face for your main text, reserving sans serif for headings and parts you want to highlight. Decorative typefaces (such as *Magneto*, *Amaze*, *Chiller*, and *Jokerman*) should be used sparingly and only when they're appropriate for your audience, purpose, and the rest of your **RHETORICAL SITUATION.** If you use more than one typeface in a text, use each one consistently: one face for **HEADINGS,** one for captions, one for the main body of your text. And don't go overboard—you won't often have reason to use more than two or, at most, three typefaces in any one text.

13 ▣
12–14

1 ▣
526–27 ▢

Every typeface has regular, **bold**, and *italic* fonts. In general, choose regular for the main text, bold for major headings, and italic for titles of

books and other long works and, occasionally, to emphasize words or brief phrases. Avoid italicizing or boldfacing entire paragraphs. If you are following **MLA**, **APA**, or some other style, be sure your use of fonts conforms to its requirements.

428–76
477–519

Finally, consider the line spacing of your text. Generally, academic writing is double-spaced, whereas **LETTERS** and **RÉSUMÉS** are usually single-spaced. Some kinds of **REPORTS** may call for single-spacing; check with your instructor if you're not sure. In addition, you'll often need to add an extra space to set off parts of a text—items in a list, for instance, or headings.

189–200
59–82

Layout.   Layout is the way text is arranged on a page. An academic essay, for example, will usually have a title centered at the top, one-inch margins all around, and double-spacing. A text can be presented in paragraphs—or in the form of **LISTS**, **TABLES**, **CHARTS**, **GRAPHS**, and so on. Sometimes you need to include other elements as well: headings, images and other graphics, captions, lists of works cited.

525–26
528–30

Paragraphs.   Dividing text into paragraphs focuses information for readers and helps them process the information by dividing it into manageable chunks. If you're writing a story for a newspaper with narrow columns, for example, you'll divide your text into shorter paragraphs than you would if you were writing an academic essay. In general, indent paragraphs five spaces when your text is double-spaced; either indent or skip a line between paragraphs that are single-spaced.

Lists.   Put information into list form that you want to set off and make easily accessible. Number the items in a list when the sequence matters (in instructions, for example); use bullets when the order is not important. Set off lists with an extra line of space above and below, and add extra space between the items on a list if necessary for legibility. Here's an example:

Darwin's theory of how species change through time derives from three postulates, each of which builds on the previous one:

1. The ability of a population to expand is infinite, but the ability of any environment to support populations is always finite.

2. Organisms within populations vary, and this variation affects the ability of individuals to survive and reproduce.

3. The variations are transmitted from parents to offspring.

—Robert Boyd and Joan B. Silk, *How Humans Evolved*

Do not set off text as a list unless there's a good reason to do so, however. Some lists are more appropriately presented in paragraph form, especially when they give information that is not meant to be referred to more than once. In the following example, there is no reason to highlight the information by setting it off in a list—and bad news is softened by putting it in paragraph form:

> I regret to inform you that the Scholarship Review Committee did not approve your application for a Board of Rectors scholarship, for the following reasons: your grade-point average did not meet the minimum requirements; your major is not among those eligible for consideration; and the required letter of recommendation was not received before the deadline.

Presented as a list, that information would be needlessly emphatic.

Headings.　Headings make the structure of a text easier to follow and help readers find specific information. Some genres require standard headings—announcing an **ABSTRACT,** for example, or a list of **WORKS CITED.** Other times you will want to use headings to provide an overview of a section of text. You may not need any headings with brief texts, and when you do, you'll probably want to use one level at most, just to announce major topics. Longer texts and information-rich genres, such as pamphlets or detailed **REPORTS,** may require several levels of headings. If you decide to include headings, you will need to decide how to phrase them, what typefaces and fonts to use, and where to position them.

111–15
475–76
59–82

Phrase headings concisely.　Make your headings succinct and parallel in structure. You might make all the headings nouns (**Mushrooms**), noun phrases (**Kinds of Mushrooms**), gerund phrases (**Recognizing Kinds of Mushrooms**), or questions (**How Do I Identify Mushrooms?**). Whatever form you decide on, use it consistently for each heading. Sometimes your

phrasing will depend on your purpose. If you're simply helping readers find information, use brief phrases:

Head	**Forms of Social Groups among Primates**
Subhead	***Solitary Social Groups***
Subhead	***Monogamous Social Groups***

If you want to address your readers directly with the information in your text, consider writing your headings as questions:

How can you identify morels?
Where can you find morels?
How can you cook morels?

Make headings visible.   Headings need to be visible, so consider printing them in a bold, italic, or underlined font—or use a different typeface. For example, you could print your main text in a serif font like Times Roman and your headings in a sans serif font like Arial or make the headings larger than the regular text. When you have several levels of headings, use capitalization, boldface, and italics to distinguish among the various levels. For example:

FIRST-LEVEL HEAD
Second-Level Head
Third-Level Head

Be aware, though, that APA and MLA formats expect headings to be in the same typeface as the main text; APA requires that each level of heading appear in a specific style: all uppercase, uppercase and lowercase, italicized uppercase and lowercase, and so on.

Position headings appropriately.   If you're following **APA** format, center first- and second-level headings. If you're following **MLA** format, align headings at the left margin without any extra space above or below. If you are not following a prescribed format, you get to decide where to position your headings: centered, flush with the left margin, or even alongside the text, in a wide left-hand margin. Position each level of head consistently throughout your text.

477–519
428–76

White space.   Use white space to separate the various parts of a text. In general, use one-inch margins for the text of an essay or report. Unless you're following MLA or APA format, include space above headings, above and below lists, and around photos, graphs, and other images to set them apart from the rest of the text. See the two **SAMPLE RESEARCH PAPERS** in this book for examples of the formats required by MLA and APA.

MLA 467–76
APA 508–19

Visuals

Visuals can sometimes help you to make a point in ways that words alone cannot. Be careful, however, that any visuals you use contribute to your point—not simply act as decoration. This section discusses how to use photos, graphs, charts, tables, and diagrams effectively.

Select visuals that are appropriate for your rhetorical situation.   There are various kinds of visuals: photographs, line graphs, bar graphs, pie charts, tables, diagrams, flowcharts, drawings, and more. Which ones you use, if any, will depend on your content, your **GENRE,** and your **RHETORICAL SITUATION.** A newspaper article on housing prices might include a bar graph or line graph, and also some photographs; a report on the same topic written for an economics class would probably have graphs but no photos. See the examples on the facing page, along with advice for using each one.

19
1

Some guidelines for using visuals

- Use visuals as an element of your text's content, one that is as important as your words to your message. Therefore, avoid clip art, which is primarily intended as decoration.

- Position visuals in your text as close as possible to your discussion of the topic to which they relate.

- Number all visuals, using a separate sequence for figures (photos, graphs, and drawings) and tables: *Figure 1, Figure 2*; *Table 1, Table 2.*

- Refer to the visual before it appears, identifying it and summarizing its point. For example: "As Figure 1 shows, Japan's economy grew dramatically between 1965 and 1980."

Photographs can support an argument, illustrate events and processes, present other points of view, and help readers "place" your information in time and space.

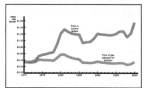

Line graphs are a good way of showing changes in data over time. Each line here shows a different set of data; plotting the two lines together allows readers to compare the data at different points in time.

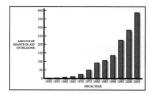

Bar graphs are useful for comparing quantitative data, measurements of how much or how many. The bars can be horizontal or vertical.

Pie charts can be used for showing how a whole is divided into parts or how something is apportioned.

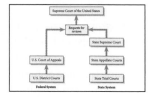

Tables are useful for displaying information concisely, especially when several items are being compared.

Diagrams, flowcharts, and drawings are ways of showing relationships and processes.

- Provide a title or caption for each visual to identify it and explain its significance for your text. For example: "Table 1. Japanese economic output, 1965–80."

425–27

- **DOCUMENT** the source of any visuals you found in another source: "Figure 1. Two Tokyo shoppers display their purchases. (Ochiro, 1967)." Document any tables you create with data from another source. You need not document visuals you create yourself, such as drawings or photos, or data from your own experimental or field research.

- Obtain permission to use any visuals you found in another source that will appear in texts you publish in any form other than for a course.

- Label visuals clearly to ensure that your audience will understand what they show. For example, label each section of a pie chart to show what it represents.

When you choose visuals and integrate them into your texts, follow the same procedures you use with other source materials.

Evaluate visuals as you would any text. Make sure visuals relate directly to your subject, support your assertions, and add information that words alone can't provide as clearly or easily. Evaluate visuals as you would other source materials: Is the photographer named? Do charts and graphs identify the source of the data they portray? Where was the visual published? How was the visual used in its original context? Does the information in the visual match, complement, or contradict the information in your other sources?

Include any necessary source information. Make sure visuals are accompanied by background and citation information: graphs and tables should cite the source of the data they present, and captions of photos should identify the photographer and date.

Use visuals ethically. You may want to crop a photograph, cutting it to show only part. See, for example, the photo on the facing page of two children in medieval costumes and the cropped version that shows only the boy.

You might have reason to crop the photo to accompany a profile or memoir about the boy, but you would not want to eliminate the girl from the photo

in an account of their school's medieval festival. If you crop or otherwise alter a photograph, keep your **PURPOSE** in mind.

3–4

But altering photographs in a way that misrepresents someone or something is a serious breach of ethics. In 1997, when O. J. Simpson was arrested for the murder of his ex-wife, both *Time* and *Newsweek* used the same mug shot on their covers. *Time*, however, digitally darkened Simpson's skin, making him look "blacker." This sort of manipulation misleads readers, creating visual lies that can inappropriately influence how readers interpret both the text and the subject. If you alter a photo, be sure the image represents the subject accurately—and tell your readers how you have changed it.

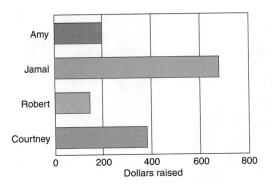

Fig. 1. Fund-raising results for the class gift.

Charts and graphs can mislead, too. Changing the scale on a bar graph, for example, can change the effect of the comparison, making the quantities being compared seem very similar or very different, as the two bar graphs of identical data show in figures 1 and 2.

Depending on the fund-raising goal implied by each bar graph ($800 or $5,000) and the increments of the dollars raised ($200 or $1,000), the two graphs send very different messages, though the dollars raised by each fund-raiser remain the same. Just as you shouldn't edit a quotation or a photograph in a way that might misrepresent its meaning, you should not present data in a way that could mislead readers.

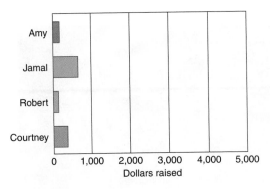

Fig. 2. Fund-raising results for the class gift.

Evaluating a Design

Does the design suit its PURPOSE ?   Do the typeface and any visuals help convey the text's message, support its argument, or present information? Is there any key information that should be highlighted in a list or chart?

3–4

How well does the design meet the needs of its AUDIENCE ?   Will the overall appearance of the text appeal to the intended readers? Is the typeface large enough for them to read? Are there headings to help them find their way through the text? Are there the kind of visuals they are likely to expect? Are the visuals clearly labeled and referred to in the main text so that readers know why they're there?

5–8

How well does the text meet the requirements of its GENRE ?   Can you tell by looking at the text that it is an academic essay, a lab report, a résumé? Do its typeface, margins, headings, and page layout meet the requirements of **MLA, APA,** or whatever style is being followed? Are visuals appropriately labeled and cited?

9–11

428–76
477–519

How well does the design reflect the writer's STANCE ?   Do the page layout and typeface convey the appropriate tone — serious, playful, adventuresome, conservative, and so on? Do the visuals reveal anything about the writer's position or beliefs? For instance, does the choice of visuals show any particular bias?

12–14

52 Spoken Text

In a marketing class, you give a formal presentation as part of a research project. As a candidate for student government, you deliver several speeches to various campus groups. At a good friend's wedding, you make a toast to the married couple. In school and out, you may be called on to speak in public, to compose and deliver spoken texts. This chapter offers guidelines to help you prepare and deliver effective spoken texts, along with the visual aids you often need to include. We'll start with two good examples.

ABRAHAM LINCOLN

Gettysburg Address

Given by the sixteenth president of the United States, at the dedication of the Gettysburg battlefield as a memorial to those who died in the Civil War, this is one of the most famous speeches ever delivered in the United States.

Four score and seven years ago our fathers brought forth on this continent, a new nation, conceived in Liberty, and dedicated to the proposition that all men are created equal.

Now we are engaged in a great civil war, testing whether that nation, or any nation so conceived and so dedicated, can long endure. We are met on a great battle-field of that war. We have come to dedicate a portion of that field, as a final resting place for those who here gave their lives that that nation might live. It is altogether fitting and proper that we should do this.

But, in a larger sense, we can not dedicate—we can not consecrate—we can not hallow—this ground. The brave men, living and

rhetorical situations

genres

processes

strategies

research mla/apa

media/ design

handbook

dead, who struggled here, have consecrated it, far above our poor power to add or detract. The world will little note, nor long remember what we say here, but it can never forget what they did here. It is for us the living, rather, to be dedicated here to the unfinished work which they who fought here have thus far so nobly advanced. It is rather for us to be here dedicated to the great task remaining before us—that from these honored dead we take increased devotion to that cause for which they gave the last full measure of devotion—that we here highly resolve that these dead shall not have died in vain—that this nation, under God, shall have a new birth of freedom—and that government of the people, by the people, for the people, shall not perish from the earth.

You won't likely be called on to deliver such an address, but the techniques Lincoln used—brevity, rhythm, recurring themes—are ones you can use in your own spoken texts. The next example represents the type of spoken text we are sometimes called on to deliver at important occasions in the lives of our families.

JUDY DAVIS

Ours Was a Dad . . .

This short eulogy was given at the funeral of the writer's father, Walter Boock. Judy Davis lives in Davis, California, where she is the principal of North Davis Elementary School.

Elsa, Peggy, David, and I were lucky to have such a dad. Ours was a dad who created the childhood for us that he did not have for himself. The dad who sent us airborne on the soles of his feet, squealing with delight. The dad who built a platform in the peach tree so we could eat ourselves comfortably into peachy oblivion. The dad who assigned us chores and then did them with us. The dad who felt our pain when we skinned our knees.

Ours was the dad who took us camping, all over the U.S. and Canada, but most of all in our beloved Yosemite. The one who awed us with his ability to swing around a full pail of water without spilling a drop and let us hold sticks in the fire and draw designs in the night air with hot orange coals.

Our dad wanted us to feel safe and secure. On Elsa's eighth birthday, we acquired a small camping trailer. One very blustery night in Minnesota, Mom and Dad asleep in the main bed, David suspended in the hammock over them, Peggy and Elsa snuggled in the little dinette bed, and me on an air mattress on the floor, I remember the most incredible sense of well-being: our family all together, so snug, in that little trailer as the storm rocked us back and forth. It was only in the morning that I learned about the tornado warnings. Mom and Dad weren't sleeping; they were praying that when morning came we wouldn't find ourselves in the next state.

Ours was the dad who helped us with homework at the round oak table. He listened to our oral reports, taught us to add by looking for combinations of 10, quizzed us on spelling words, and when our written reports sounded a little too much like the *World Book* encyclopedia, he told us so.

Ours was the dad who believed our round oak table that seated　5 twelve when fully extended should be full at Thanksgiving. Dad called the chaplain at the airbase, asked about homesick boys, and invited them to join our family. Or he'd call International House in Berkeley to see if someone from another country would like to experience an American Thanksgiving. We're still friends with the Swedish couple who came for turkey forty-five years ago. Many people became a part of our extended family around that table. And if twelve around the table were good, then certainly fourteen would be better. Just last fall, Dad commissioned our neighbor Randy to make yet another leaf for the table. There were fourteen around the table for Dad's last Thanksgiving.

Ours was a dad who had a lifelong desire to serve. He delivered Meals on Wheels until he was eighty-three. He delighted in picking up the day-old doughnuts from Mr. Rollen's shop to give those on his route an extra treat. We teased him that he should be receiving those meals himself! Even after walking became difficult for him, he continued to drive and took along an able friend to carry the meals to the door.

Our family, like most, had its ups and downs. But ours was a dad who forgave us our human failings as we forgave him his. He died in

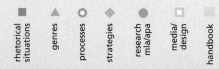

peace, surrounded by love. Elsa, Peggy, David, and I were so lucky to have such a dad.

This eulogy, in honor of the writer's father, provides concrete and memorable details that give the audience a clear image of the kind of man he was. The repetition of the phrase "ours was a dad" provides a rhythm and unity that moves the text forward, and the use of short, conventional sentences makes the text easy to understand — and deliver.

Key Features / Spoken Text

A clear structure.   Spoken texts need to be clearly organized so that your audience can follow what you're saying. The **BEGINNING** needs to engage their interest, make clear what you will be talking about, and perhaps forecast the central parts of your talk. The main part of the text should focus on a few main points and only as many as your listeners can be expected to handle. (Remember, they can't go back to reread!) The **ENDING** is especially important: it should leave your audience with something to remember, think about, or do. Davis ends as she begins, saying that she and her sisters and brother "were so lucky to have such a dad." Lincoln ends by challenging his audience to "the great task remaining before us . . . that we . . . resolve that these dead shall not have died in vain — that this nation, under God, shall have a new birth of freedom — and that government of the people, by the people, for the people, shall not perish from the earth."

261–66

266–70

Signpost language to keep your audience on track.   You may need to provide cues to help your listeners follow your text, especially **TRANSITIONS** that lead them from one point to the next. Sometimes you'll also want to stop and **SUMMARIZE** a complex point to help your audience keep track of your ideas and follow your development of them.

277

416–17

A tone to suit the occasion.   Lincoln spoke at a serious, formal event, the dedication of a national cemetery, and his address is formal and even solemn. Davis's eulogy is more informal in **TONE,** as befits a speech given

13

for friends and loved ones. In a presentation to a panel of professors, you probably would want to take an academic tone, avoiding too much slang and speaking in complete sentences. If you had occasion to speak on the very same topic to a neighborhood group, however, you would likely want to speak more casually.

Sound. Remember that spoken texts have the added element of sound. Be aware of how your words and phrases sound. Even if you're never called on to deliver a Gettysburg Address, you will find that repetition and parallel structure can lend power to a presentation, making it easier to follow — and more likely to be remembered. "We can not dedicate, we can not consecrate — we can not hallow": these are words said more than one hundred years ago, but who among us does not know where they're from? The repetition of "we can not" and the parallel forms of the three verbs are one reason they stay with us. These are structures any writer can use. See how the repetition of "ours was a dad" in Davis's eulogy creates a rhythm that engages listeners and at the same time unifies the text.

Visual aids. Sometimes you will want or need to use visuals — PowerPoint or other presentation software, transparencies, flip charts, and so on — to present certain information and to highlight key points.

Considering the Rhetorical Situation

As with any writing, you need to consider your purpose, audience, and the rest of your rhetorical situation:

3–4 ■	**PURPOSE**	What is your primary purpose? To inform? Persuade? Entertain? Evoke an emotional response? Something else?
5–8 ■	**AUDIENCE**	Think about whom you'll be addressing and how well you know your audience. Will they be interested, or will you need to get them interested? Are they likely to be friendly?

How can you get and maintain their attention, and how can you establish common ground? Will they know about your subject, or will you need to provide background and define key terms?

GENRE   The genre of your text will affect the way you structure it. If you're making an argument, for instance, you'll need to consider counterarguments—and to anticipate questions from members of the audience who hold other opinions. If you're giving a report, you may have reason to prepare handouts with detailed information you don't have time to cover.   9–11

STANCE   Consider the attitude you want to express—is it serious? thoughtful? passionate? well-informed? funny? something else?—and choose your words accordingly.   12–14

Delivering a Spoken Text

The success of a spoken text often hinges on how you deliver it. As you practice delivering your spoken texts, bear in mind the following points.

Speak clearly.   When delivering a spoken text, your first goal is to be understood by your audience. If listeners miss important words or phrases because you don't form your words distinctly, your talk will not succeed. Make sure your pace matches your audience's needs—sometimes you may need to speak slowly to explain complex material; other times you may need to speed up to keep an audience's attention.

Pause for emphasis.   In writing, you have white space and punctuation to show readers where an idea or discussion ends. When speaking, you need to be the one to pause to signal the end of a thought, to give listeners a moment to consider something you've said, or to get them ready for a surprising or amusing statement.

Try not to read your presentation.   Speech textbooks often advise that you never read your speech. For some of us, though, that's just not possible. If you can speak well from notes or an outline, great—you're likely to do well. If you must have a complete text in front of you, though, try to write it as if you were talking. Then, practice by reading it into a tape recorder; listen for spots that sound as if you're reading, and work on your delivery to sound more relaxed.

Stand up straight, and look at your audience.   Try to maintain some eye contact with your audience. If that's uncomfortable, fake it: pick a spot on the wall just above the head of a person in the last row of chairs, and focus on it. You'll appear as if you're looking at your audience even if you're not looking them in the eye. And if you stand up straight, you'll project the sense that you have confidence in what you're saying. If you appear to believe in your words, others will, too.

Use gestures for emphasis.   If you're not used to speaking in front of a group, you may let your nervousness show by holding yourself stiffly, elbows tucked in. To overcome some of that nervousness, take some deep breaths, try to relax, move your arms as you would if you were talking to a friend. Use your hands for emphasis. Most public speakers use one hand to emphasize points and both to make larger gestures. Watch politicians on C-SPAN to see how people who speak on a regular basis use their hands and bodies as part of their overall delivery.

Practice.   Practice, practice, and then practice some more. Pay particular attention to how much time you have—and don't go over your time limit. If possible, deliver your speech to an audience of friends to test their response.

Visual Aids

When you give an oral presentation, you'll often want or need to include some visuals to help listeners follow what you're saying. Especially when you're presenting complex information, it helps to let them see it as well as hear it. Remember, though, that visuals are a means of conveying information, not mere decoration.

Deciding on the appropriate visual.　Presentation software, overhead transparencies, flip charts, and posters are some of the most common kinds of visuals. Presentation software and overhead transparencies are useful for listing main points and for projecting illustrations, tables, and graphs. Overhead transparencies, like whiteboards and chalkboards, allow you to create visuals as you speak. Sometimes you'll want to distribute handouts to provide lists of works cited or copies of any slides you show.

Whatever you decide to use, make sure that the necessary equipment is available—and that it works. If at all possible, check out the room and the equipment before you give your presentation. If you bring your own equipment, make sure electrical outlets are in reach of your power cords.

Also make sure that your visuals will be seen. You may have to rearrange the furniture or the screen in the room to make sure everyone can see. And finally: *have a backup plan.* Computers fail; projector bulbs burn out; marking pens run dry. Whatever visuals you plan, have an alternative plan in case any of these things happen.

Using presentation software.　Programs such as Microsoft PowerPoint allow you to create slides that you then project via a computer. These programs enable you to project graphs, charts, photographs, sound—and plain text. Here are some tips for using presentation software effectively:

- *Use* LISTS *rather than paragraphs.* Use slides to emphasize your main points, not to reproduce your talk onscreen. Be aware that you can project the list all at once or one item at a time.

  525–26

- *Don't put too much information on a slide.* How many bulleted points you include will depend on how long each one is, but you want to be sure that you don't include more words than listeners will be able to read as you present each slide.

- *Be sure your* TYPE *is large enough for your audience to read it.* In general, you don't want to use any type smaller than 18 points, and you'll want something larger than that for headings. Projected slides are easier to read in sans serif fonts like Arial, Helvetica, and Tahoma instead of serif fonts like Times Roman. Avoid using all caps—all-capped text is hard to read.

  524–25

Dewey

○ Appeared overconfident
○ Ran a lackluster, "safe" campaign
○ Was perceived as stuffy and aloof
○ Made several blunders
○ Would not address issues

Truman

○ Conducted whistle-stop campaign
○ Made hundreds of speeches
○ Spoke energetically
○ Connected personally with voters
○ Focused on key states

Slides made with presentation software.

- *Choose colors carefully.* Your text must contrast strongly with the background. Dark text on a light background is easier to read than the reverse. And remember that not everyone sees all colors; be sure your audience does not need to recognize colors in order to get your meaning. Red-green contrasts are especially hard to see and should be avoided.

 rhetorical situations
 genres
 processes
 strategies
 research mla/apa
 media/ design
handbook

- *Use bells and whistles sparingly, if at all.* Presentation software offers lots of decorative backgrounds, letters that fade in or dance across the screen, and, literally, bells and whistles. These can be more distracting than helpful; avoid using them unless they help you make your point.

- *Mark your text.* In your notes, mark each place where you need to click a mouse to call up the next slide.

The example on page 542 shows two slides from a PowerPoint presentation that Dylan Borchers created for an oral presentation based on his essay exploring the U.S. presidential election campaign of 1948. These slides offer an outline of Borchers' main points; the speech itself fills in the details. The design is simple and uncluttered, and the large font and high contrast between type and background make the slides easy to read, even from across a large room.

Overhead transparencies.   Transparency slides can hold more information than slides created with presentation software, but someone must place each transparency on the projector one at a time. To minimize the number of slides you will need, you can place a lot of information on each transparency and use a blank sheet of paper to cover and reveal each point as you discuss it. Here are some tips for using transparencies effectively:

- *Use a white background and large type.* If you're typing your text, use black type. Use type that is at least 18 points, and use larger type for headings. As with presentation software, fonts like Arial and Tahoma are easiest to read from a distance. If you're making handwritten transparencies, you might write in several colors.

- *Write legibly and large.* If you want to write as you speak and have trouble writing in a straight line, place a sheet of lined paper under the blank slide. Use a blank sheet to cover any unused part of the slide so that you don't smudge the ink on the slide as you write.

- *Position slides carefully.* You might want to mark the top right corner of each transparency to make sure you put it where it needs to go on the projector. And have someplace to put the transparencies before and after you use them.

Dewey

- Appeared overconfident
- Ran a lackluster, "safe" campaign
- Was perceived as stuffy and aloof
- Made several blunders
- Would not address issues

Truman

- Conducted whistle-stop campaign
- Made hundreds of speeches
- Spoke energetically
- Connected personally with voters
- Focused on key states

An overhead transparency.

Compare the sample transparency slide shown above with the Power-Point slides on page 542—you'll see that they provide identical information.

Handouts.   When you want to give your audience information they can refer to later—reproductions of your visuals, bibliographic information about your sources, printouts of your slides—do so in the form of a hand-

out. Refer to the handout in your presentation, but unless it includes material your audience needs to consult as you talk, don't distribute the handouts until you are finished because they can distract listeners from your presentation. Clearly label everything you give out, including your name and the date and title of the presentation.

IF YOU NEED MORE HELP

See also the guidelines in Chapter 51 on designing **PRINT TEXT** for additional help creating visuals. If you are working with a group, see Chapter 22 on **COLLABORATING.**

523–33
215–18

53 Electronic Text

College singing groups create websites to publicize their concerts and sell their CDs. Political commentators post their opinions on blogs; readers of the blogs post responses. Job seekers post scannable résumés. And for most of us, email and text messaging are parts of everyday life. In the future, you'll likely have occasion to write many other electronic texts. Such texts differ in a few obvious ways from print texts—websites open with home pages rather than with plain introductory paragraphs, for instance—but like print texts, they have certain key features and are composed in the context of particular rhetorical situations. This chapter offers some very basic advice for thinking about the rhetorical situations and key features of texts that you post online.

Considering the Rhetorical Situation

As with any writing task, you need to consider your particular rhetorical situation when you write something to post online. In fact, you may need to consider it especially carefully, since in most cases the makeup of an online audience is pretty much impossible to predict—there's often no telling who might read what you write or how efficient your readers' computer systems will be at dealing with different types and sizes of files.

3–4 ■ **PURPOSE**   Why are you writing? To fulfill an assignment? Answer a question? Find or provide information? Get in touch with someone? In email, you may want to state your topic, and even your purpose, in the subject line. On a website, you will need to make the site's purpose clear on its home page.

rhetorical situations   genres   processes   strategies   research mla/apa   media/design   handbook

AUDIENCE

What kind of readers are you aiming to reach, and what might they be expecting from you? What are they likely to know about your topic, and what information will you need to provide? What are their technical limitations — can they receive files the size of the one you want to send? If you're constructing a website, what kind of home page will appeal to your intended audience?

5–8

    What do you want them to do? Read what you write? Forward what you write to others? Write something themselves? Remember, however, that you can never be sure where your original readers will forward your email or who will visit a website; don't put any writing online that you don't feel comfortable having lots of different people read.

GENRE

Are you reporting information? Evaluating something? Arguing a point? Proposing an action?

9–11

STANCE

What overall impression do you want to convey? If you're constructing a website for a group, how does the group wish to be seen? Should the site look academic? Hip? Professional? If you want to demonstrate a political stance, remember that the links you provide can help you to do so. (Remember too that if you want to show a balanced political stance, the links should reflect a range of different viewpoints.)

12–14

DESIGN

Your medium will affect your design choices. If you're writing email, you'll want to format it to be as simple as possible — different colors and fonts are not necessarily recognized by every email program, so it's best to write in black type using a standard font. It's best also to keep your paragraphs short so readers can see each point without a lot of scrolling. If you're constructing a website, you'll need to create a consistent design scheme using color and type to signal key parts of the site.

15–17

Key Features / Email

Email is such a constant form of communicating that it can feel and read more like talking than writing. But writing it is, and it has certain features and conventions that readers expect and that writers need to be aware of.

An explicit subject line.   Your subject line should state your topic clearly: "Reminder: emedia meeting at 2" rather than "Meeting" or "Hi" (though the latter is appropriate for informal messages to friends). People get so much email that they need to see a reason to read yours. In addition, most computer viruses are sent via unsolicited email messages, so many people—or their spam filters—delete all messages from unknown senders or with suspicious or vague subject lines. A clear subject line increases the chances that your message will be read.

A tone appropriate to the situation.   Email messages should be written in the same tone you'd use if you were writing the same text on paper. You can be informal when writing to friends, but you should be more formal when writing to people you don't know, especially in professional or academic contexts (to your boss or your instructor). Be aware that your tone starts with your salutation (*Hi Lisa* to a friend, *Dear Professor Alikum* to a teacher). And of course your tone is reflected in the register and conventions of your writing. You can use email shorthand with friends (gtg, cul8r), but professional and academic email should observe professional and academic conventions (complete sentences, correct spelling and punctuation).

Brevity.   Email works best when it's brief. Short paragraphs are easier to read on screen than long ones—you don't want readers to have to do too much scrolling to see the point you're trying to make. When you need to email a longer text, you may want to send it as an attachment that readers can open separately. If you don't know for sure whether your recipients will be able to open an attachment, check with them first before sending it.

Speed and reach.   This one's not a textual feature as much as it is a reminder to be careful before you hit *send*. Email travels so fast—and can be so easily forwarded to people you never imagined would read what

rhetorical situations   genres   processes   strategies   research mla/apa   media/ design   handbook

you've written — that you want to be good and sure that your email neither says something you'll regret later (don't send email when you're
angry!) nor includes anything you don't want the whole world, or at least
part of it, reading (don't put confidential or sensitive information in email).

Key Features / Websites

The writing you do for the Web differs from that which you do on paper
in the way that you organize and present it — and in the way your readers will approach what you write. Here are some of the features that char-
acterize most websites, along with general advice to help you think about
each feature when you write for the Web.

A home page.   The home page functions much like the first page of an
essay, giving the name of the site, indicating something about its purpose,
and letting readers know what they'll find on the site. It also gives the name
of the site's author or sponsor and includes information about when the
site was last updated. Plan the text for a home page so that it fits on one
screen, and make it simple enough graphically that it downloads quickly.

A clear organizational structure.   Web texts are presented as a number
of separate pages, and when you compose a website you need to organize the pages so that readers can get to them. Unlike print text, in which
the writer determines where a text begins and ends and what order it
follows in between, most online texts are organized so that readers can
choose which pages they'll look at and in what order. There's no sure way
that you can know what sequence they'll follow. Here are three common
ways of organizing a website:

As a sequence.   A simple way to organize a site is as a linear sequence
of pages.

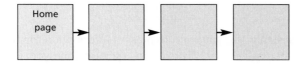

Use this organization if you want readers to view pages in a specific sequence. Though it still doesn't guarantee that they'll follow your sequence, it certainly increases the chances that they'll do so.

As a hierarchy. A hierarchical design groups related pages in the same way an outline organizes related topics in an essay.

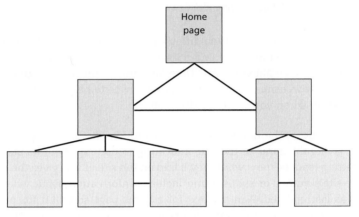

Use a hierarchy to guide readers through complex information while allowing them to choose what to read within categories.

As a web. A web design allows readers to view pages in just about any order they wish.

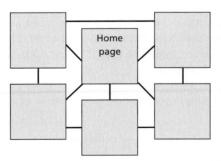

Use a web design when you want to present information that readers can browse for themselves, with little or no guidance from you.

An explicit navigation system. Just as a book has a table of contents, so a website has a navigation menu. The navigation menu shows what's on your site, usually in a menu of the main parts that readers can click on to get to the pages. The navigation menu should appear in the same place on every page. One item on the menu should be a button that lets readers return to the home page.

A consistent design. Design is important—for creating a visual tone for the site, highlighting features or information, and providing a clear focus and emphasis. You need to create a clear color scheme (all links in one color, for example, to distinguish them from the rest of the text) and a consistent **PAGE DESIGN** (for example, a navigation bar at the top of each page and a background color that stays the same and doesn't detract from the content); in addition, you need to use **TYPE** consistently (for example, one font for the main text, another for the headings).

524–28
524–25

You can also use color and type to create emphasis or to highlight particular types of information. Though you can't know which pages readers will go to, careful site design can help you control what's on the page they'll see first. You can also include **IMAGES**—drawings, photos, maps, and the like. Be sure, however, that the illustrations you include support or add to your point, that they are not mere decoration. Take care also that you don't include so many graphics that the site takes a long time to open.

528–32

Finally, your design should reflect the appropriate tone and **STANCE.** Formal, informal, academic, whimsical, whatever—your choice of type and color and images can convey this stance.

12–14

Links. Websites include links among the pages on the site as well as to material elsewhere on the Web. Links allow you to bring material from other sources into your text—you can link to the definition of a key term, for instance, rather than defining it yourself, or you can link to a **SOURCE** rather than summarizing or paraphrasing it. You can also provide a list of links to related sites. When you're writing a text for a website, you can link to some of the details, giving readers the choice of whether they want or need to see an illustration, detailed description, map, and so on. For example, page 552 shows how my literacy narrative (see pages 24–26) might look as a Web text.

384–99

Sample Web text, with links

Amanda K. Hartman was born in 1882 in West Virginia. She left home at 14 for Cleveland, Ohio, where she worked as a seamstress. In her 30s she married Frederick Hartman, a German immigrant. Together they had one child, Louise. After her husband's death in 1955, Amanda obtained a realtor's license and sold real estate for many years.

She read widely, preferring Greek and Roman history and philosophy. Between 1952 and 1956, she and her husband shared a large house with my parents, giving her ample opportunity to read to me. She taught me to read by reading to me for hours on end, every day. She died at the age of 93.

My family was blue-collar, working-class, and—my grandmother excepted—not very interested in books or reading. But my parents took pride in my achievement and told stories about my precocious literacy, such as the time at a restaurant when the waitress bent over as I sat in my booster chair and asked, "What would you like, little boy?" I'm told I gave her a withering look and said, "I'd like to see a menu."

There was a more serious aspect to reading so young, however. At that time the murder trial of Dr. Sam Sheppard, a physician whose wife had been bludgeoned to death in their house, was the focus of lurid coverage in the Cleveland newspapers. Daily news stories recounted the grisly details of both the murder and the trial testimony, in which Sheppard maintained his innocence. (The story would serve as the inspiration for the TV series and Harrison Ford movie, The Fugitive.)

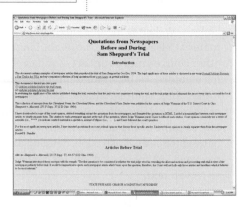

 rhetorical situations
 genres
 processes
 strategies
 research mla/apa
 media/ design
handbook

How text on the Web links to details from other sources.   As the text on the facing page shows, links from my narrative might include a brief biography of my grandmother, *Court TV's* account of the Sheppard murder case, a site presenting excerpts of news coverage of the trial, and a poster from *The Fugitive*. Such links allow me to stay focused on my own narrative while offering readers the opportunity to explore issues mentioned in my story in as much depth as they want.

A Sample Site

Here and on page 554 are examples from a home page, a content page, and a linked page from a website created by Colleen James, a student at Illinois State University, as part of an online portfolio of work for a course in hypertext.

Home page

What is a Weblog?
  ∟ Short overview
  ∟ Example sites
  ∟ Weblog portals
  ∟ Articles & books

Creating a Weblog
  ∟ The basics & tips
  ∟ Using livejournal
  ∟ Using diaryland
  ∟ Using blogger.com
  ∟ Other blogging tools

Uses for a Weblog
  ∟ Traditional weblog
  ∟ Online journal
  ∟ Miscellaneous uses
  ∟ Some content tips

Other Stuff
  ∟ About me & this site
  ∟ Send me an email

High contrast between text and simple background makes reading easy.

Careful organization: Text has been divided into brief sections grouped logically.

Table of contents contains links to each section, permitting easy navigation within sections.

Illustration and title clearly describe the site's contents.

Content page

Explicit navigation system: Links to pages in the site appear at the same place on each page.

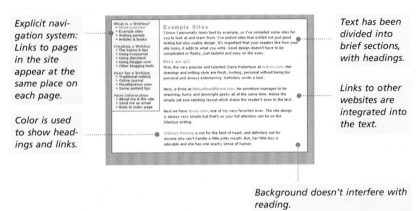

Color is used to show headings and links.

Text has been divided into brief sections, with headings.

Links to other websites are integrated into the text.

Background doesn't interfere with reading.

Linked page

Consistent design helps readers know where they are and how to navigate the site.

Links to other parts of the site help readers navigate.

High contrast between text and simple background makes reading easy.

Blogs

Blogs are journals that are kept online. They generally include written entries, photos, links to other blogs or websites of interest to the writer

(or "blogger"), and space for readers to post comments. Sites such as blog-ger.com, vox.com, or livejournal.com will walk you through the process of creating a blog. Julia Gilkinson's blog, below, created for her writing class at Edinboro University, consists of two columns: the larger, right-hand col-umn contains her postings, each of which is titled and includes the date and time it was posted. Below each posting are comments readers have made in response to her post and a link inviting more comments. The left-hand column presents a list of Julia's postings and, under the heading "about me," a link to her profile. This blog consists entirely of class-related writing, but a similar structure can be used for virtually any blog content, whether personal or professional. In fact, many companies use blogs as their primary websites.

blog archive

▼ 2007 (3)
  ▼ September (2)
    Common Hour
    Presentation
    My Freshman Year: Life in
    the Dorms
  ▶ August (1)

about me

Julia Gilkinson

View my
complete profile

monday, september 17, 2007

● ● ● **My Freshman Year: Life in the Dorms**

Our lives become so stressful because of all the choices that we are given. The community is always in flux no one organization stays alive long enough to make its mark on the University. I enjoyed the second chapter because I can now see how everything will fall into place for me. I have been given so many choices to make for myself that I become overwhelmed. I did not expect to like this book because now I can relate to it. She makes well constructed points and gives countless examples to prove her point. Each example one freshman can relate to doing or witnessing. I truly enjoyed when she talked about the underlying values of college -these of course being fun, expressiveness, individuality, freedom, and spontaneity. I can see how college in their room because they are becoming their own person and straying independent of the family. Especially in myself, the only pictures of my family that I have are on my phone. The only picture of family that I have in my room is of my great grandmother's and myself...

Posted by juliagulia at 2:57 PM

1 comments:

Ⓑ Wendy Austin said...
Interesting that you said "I did not expect to like this book, but I did." I'll be curious to see what you think of it toward the end of the class after you've read the rest of it.

September 25, 2007 9:46 AM

Post a Comment

Newer Post   Home   Older Post

Subscribe to: Post Comments (Atom)

When you create or respond to a blog:

- Remember that, unlike entries in a private journal or diary, blog postings are public, so you shouldn't post anything that you wouldn't want your parents, friends, or employer to read. Some bloggers have forgotten that rule and paid serious consequences: for example, in 2002 Heather Armstrong criticized her employer on her blog, dooce.com. Her employer discovered her post and fired her, leading to the slang term *dooced:* fired for the contents of one's blog.

- Assume that what you post in a blog is permanent. Because your content is stored on a computer server and may be copied and pasted by others, it is likely to be available even if you edit or delete it. So your friends, family, and employer—anyone—may read a posting years in the future, even if the blog no longer exists.

- Since what you write in a blog will be both public and permanent, it's especially important to think twice before posting when you're angry or upset. In the heat of the moment, it's easy to write an entry or comment that you'll regret later. Give yourself some time to cool down before you post what will be immediately read by others.

IF YOU NEED MORE HELP

523–33

259

See **Chapter 51, PRINT TEXT,** for more information on text design elements, such as fonts and effective use of white space. When writing electronic texts, be aware that the way you use various **STRATEGIES** may change—for example, you may create a link to a dictionary definition of a term instead of defining it within the text.

part 7

Handbook

"Pfft, English, who needs that? I'm never going to England." So says the illustrious Homer Simpson on an early episode called "The Way We Was." Maybe Homer can ignore the conventions of English grammar and usage, but that's not the case for the rest of us. If we want the world to take seriously what we think and say, we need to pay attention to our grammar and language. We need to edit our SENTENCES so they're clear, choose our WORDS carefully, and use PUNCTUATION purposefully. This handbook provides guidelines to help you edit what you write.

Handbook

Sentences S

rhetorical
situations

genres

processes

strategies

research
mla/apa

media/
design

handbook

S-1 Complete Sentences

In casual situations, we often use a kind of shorthand, because we know our audience will fill in the gaps. When we say to a dinner guest, "Coffee?" he knows we mean, "Would you like some coffee?" When we email a friend, "7:00 at Starbucks?" our friend will understand that we are asking, "Should we meet at 7:00 at Starbucks?" In more formal writing or speaking situations, though, our audience may not share the same context, so to be sure we're understood we usually need to present our ideas in complete sentences. This section reviews the parts of a sentence.

S-1a Elements of a Sentence

Subjects and predicates

A sentence contains a subject and a predicate. The subject, usually a **NOUN** or **PRONOUN,** names the topic of the sentence; the predicate, which always includes a **VERB,** says what the subject is or does.

Glossary

HB-24–28

HB-11–24

      s p
▶ Birds fly.

      s   p
▶ Birds are feathered vertebrates.

The subject and the predicate each may contain only one word. Usually, however, both the subject and the predicate contain more than one word.

        s   p
▶ Birds of many kinds fly south in the fall.

A sentence may contain more than one subject or verb.

     s   s   v
▶ Birds and butterflies fly south in the fall.

     s   v   v
▶ Birds fly south in the fall and return north in the spring.

■ rhetorical situations

▲ genres

○ processes

◆ strategies

● research mla/apa

□ media/ design

▨ handbook

At times, the subject comes after the verb.

      V   ┌─S─┐
▶ Here comes the sun.

Expressing subjects explicitly

English requires an explicit subject in every **CLAUSE**, even if all of the clauses in a sentence are about the same subject.

HB-6

               it
▶ Although the dinner cost too much, impressed my guests.

    The second clause needs the subject *it*, which refers back to *dinner.*

The only exception is commands, in which the subject is understood to be *you.*

▶ Eat smaller portions at each meal.

Sentences beginning with *there* or *it*.   In some cases where the verb precedes the subject, the **EXPLETIVE** *there* or *it* is needed before the verb.

Glossary

    There is
▶ I̶s̶ no place like home.

    It is
▶ I̶s̶ both instructive and rewarding to work with young children.

You can also rephrase the sentence to avoid using the expletive.

    Working with young children is
▶ I̶s̶ both instructive and rewarding. t̶o̶ ̶w̶o̶r̶k̶ ̶w̶i̶t̶h̶ ̶y̶o̶u̶n̶g̶ ̶c̶h̶i̶l̶d̶r̶e̶n̶.

If English is not your first language, be aware that English does not emphasize a subject by repeating it in the same clause.

▶ My friend Jing Jing s̶h̶e̶ changed her name to Jane.

▶ The European students who were visiting on a school trip t̶h̶e̶y̶ were detained at the airport for three hours.

Clauses

A clause is a group of words containing a subject and predicate. An independent clause can function alone as a sentence: *Birds fly*. A subordinate clause begins with a **SUBORDINATING WORD** such as *as*, *because*, or *which* and thus cannot stand alone as a sentence: *because birds fly*.

HB-8

INDEPENDENT CLAUSE   SUBORDINATE CLAUSE

▶ My yard is now quiet because most of the birds flew south.

Phrases

A phrase is a word group that lacks a subject, a verb, or both and therefore cannot stand alone as a sentence. Some common ones include prepositional, appositive, participial, gerund, and infinitive phrases.

HB-39–40

A prepositional phrase starts with a **PREPOSITION** such as *at*, *from*, *of*, or *in* and usually ends with a noun: *at school*, *from home*, *in bed*.

▶ The last week *of her life* I spent *at home*.
—Valerie Steiker, "Our Mother's Face"

An appositive phrase follows and gives further information about a noun or pronoun. Appositives function as nouns.

▶ I knew I was in the right house because my daddy's only real possessions, *a velvet-covered board pinned with medals*, sat inside a glass cabinet on a table.
—Rick Bragg, "All Over But the Shoutin' "

A participial phrase contains the present or past participle of a verb plus any **OBJECTS**, **MODIFIERS**, and **COMPLEMENTS**.

Glossary

▶ *Charting a riskier course for teen drama*, creator Kevin Williamson has steered the series into delicate issues such as verbally abusive parents, manic depression, and, most recently, homosexuality.
—Ben Leever, "In Defense of *Dawson's Creek*: Teen Heroes Inspire Youths Seeking Answers"

▶ A study from Princeton *issued at the same time as the Duke study* showed that women in the sciences reported less satisfaction in their jobs and less of a sense of belonging than their male counterparts.
> —Anna Quindlen, "Still Needing the F Word"

A gerund phrase includes the -*ing* form of a verb plus any objects, modifiers, and complements.

▶ For roller coasters, *being the star of summer amusement park rides certainly has its ups and downs.*
> —Cathi Eastman and Becky Burrell, "The Science of Screams: Laws of Physics Instill Thrills in Roller Coasters"

An infinitive phrase includes an infinitive (*to* plus the base form of a verb: *to read, to write*) and any objects, modifiers, and complements.

▶ *To commit more troops* seemed crazy when we couldn't win the war.

▶ The point of ribbon decals is *to show support for the troops.*

S-2 Sentence Fragments

Sentence fragments show up often in advertising: "Got milk?" "Good to the last drop." "Not bad for something that tastes good too." We use them in informal speech and text messages as well. But some readers consider fragments too informal, and in many academic writing situations it's best to avoid them altogether. This section helps you identify and edit out fragments.

S-2a Identifying Fragments

A sentence fragment is a group of words that is capitalized and punctuated as a sentence but is not a sentence. A sentence needs at least one

HB-4

HB-11–24

independent clause, which contains a **SUBJECT** and **VERB** and does not start with a subordinating word.

NO SUBJECT	The catcher batted fifth. Fouled out, ending the inning.
	Who fouled out?
NO VERB	The first two batters walked. Manny Ramirez again.
	What did Ramirez do again?
SUBORDINATE CLAUSE	Although the Yankees loaded the bases.
	There is a subject (*Yankees*) and a verb (*loaded*), but *although* makes this a subordinate clause. What happened after the Yankees loaded the bases?

SOME SUBORDINATING WORDS

after	before	though	whether
although	if	unless	while
as	since	until	who
as if	so that	when	which
because	that	where	why

Writers often use sentence fragments for emphasis or to be informal.

FOR EMPHASIS	Throughout my elementary and middle school years, I was a strong student, always on the honor roll. I never had a GPA below 3.0. I was smart, and I knew it. *That is, until I got the results of the proficiency test.*
	—Shannon Nichols, " 'Proficiency' "
TO BE INFORMAL	The SAT writing test predicts how successful a student will be in college. *Since when?*

S-2b Editing Fragments

Since some readers regard fragments as errors, it's generally better to write complete sentences. Here are four ways to make fragments into

sentences: (1) remove the subordinating word, (2) add a subject, (3) add a verb, or (4) attach the fragment to a nearby sentence.

Remove the subordinating word

▶ I'm thinking about moving to a large city. ~~Because~~ I dislike the lack of privacy in my country town of three thousand.

Add a subject

▶ The catcher batted fifth. *He fouled* ~~Fouled~~ out, ending the inning.

Add a verb

▶ The first two batters walked. Manny Ramirez *walked* again.

Sometimes a fragment contains a verb form, such as a present or past participle, that cannot function as the main verb of a sentence. In these cases, you can either substitute an appropriate verb form or add a **HELPING VERB**.

HB-16–17

▶ As the game progressed, the fans' excitement diminished. The pitcher's arm ~~weakening,~~ *weakened,* and the fielders ~~making~~ *made* a number of errors.

▶ The media influence the election process. Political commercials *are* appearing on television more frequently than in years past.

Attach the fragment to a nearby sentence

▶ Some candidates spread nasty stories/ ~~About~~ *about* their opponents.

▶ These negative stories can deal with many topics/ ~~Such~~ *, such* as marital infidelity, sources of campaign funds, and drug use.

▶ Put off by negative campaigning/ ~~Some~~ *, some* people decide not to vote at all.

S-3 Comma Splices and Fused Sentences

When you join two independent clauses using only a comma, you've created a comma splice: "He dropped the bucket, the paint spilled on his feet." Without the comma—"He dropped the bucket the paint spilled on his feet"—it's a fused sentence. You'll sometimes see comma splices and fused sentences in ads or literary works, but they're generally regarded as errors in academic writing. This section shows how to recognize comma splices and fused sentences and edit them out of your writing.

S-3a Identifying Comma Splices and Fused Sentences

A comma splice occurs when an **INDEPENDENT CLAUSE** follows another independent clause with only a comma between them.

HB-6

> **COMMA SPLICE**   T. S. Eliot is best known for his poetry, he also wrote and produced several plays.

A fused sentence occurs when one independent clause follows another with no punctuation in between.

> **FUSED SENTENCE**   The school board debated the issue for three days they were unable to reach an agreement.

S-3b Editing Comma Splices and Fused Sentences

There are several ways to edit comma splices or fused sentences: (1) make the clauses into two sentences, (2) add a comma and a **COORDINATING CONJUNCTION**, (3) add a semicolon, or (4) recast one clause as a **SUBORDINATE CLAUSE**.

HB-31

HB-6

Make the clauses two sentences

▶ T. S. Eliot is best known for his poetry, ̸he also wrote several plays.
                                        . *He*

Add a comma and a coordinating conjuction

▶ The school board debated the issue for three days ⋀*, but* they were unable to reach an agreement.

Add a semicolon

If the relationship between the two clauses is clear without a coordinating conjunction, you can simply join them with a semicolon.

▶ Psychologists study individuals' behavior/⋀; sociologists focus on group-level dynamics.

When clauses are linked by a **TRANSITION** such as *therefore* or *as a result*, the transition needs to be preceded by a semicolon and followed by a comma.

◆ 277

▶ The hill towns experienced heavy spring and summer rain/⋀; therefore, the fall foliage fell far short of expectations.

Recast one clause as a subordinate clause

Add a **SUBORDINATING WORD** to clarify the relationship between the two clauses.

▧ HB-8

▶ ~~Initial~~ ⋀*Although initial* critical responses to *The Waste Land* were mixed, the poem has been extensively anthologized, read, and written about.

S-4 Verbs

Verbs are the engines of sentences, giving energy, action, and life to writing. "I Googled it" is much more vivid than "I found it on the Internet"—and the difference is the verb. Sometimes a verb can obscure meaning, however, as when a politician avoids taking responsibility by saying, "Mistakes were made." Our choice of verbs shapes our writing in important ways, and this section reviews ways of using verbs appropriately and effectively.

S-4a Verb Tenses

To express time, English verbs have three simple tenses—present, past, and future. In addition, each of these verb tenses has perfect and progressive forms that indicate more complex time frames. The present perfect, for example, indicates an action that began in the past but is continuing into the present. The lists that follow show each of these tenses for the regular verb *talk* and the irregular verb *write*.

Simple tenses

PRESENT	PAST	FUTURE
I talk	I talked	I will talk
I write	I wrote	I will write

Use the simple present to indicate actions that take place in the present or that occur habitually. Use the simple past to indicate actions that were completed in the past. Use the simple future to indicate actions that will take place in the future.

▶ Every few years the Republicans *propose* a tax cut.
　　　　　—David Brooks, "The Triumph of Hope over Self-Interest"

▶ One day my mother *came* home from Coffee Dan's with an awful story.
　　　　　—Mike Rose, "Potato Chips and Stars"

▶ Prohibiting English *will do* for the language what Prohibition *did* for liquor.
　　　　　—Dennis Baron, "Don't Make English Official—Ban It Instead"

Use the present tense to express scientific or general facts even when the rest of the sentence is in the past tense.

▶ Agatston showed that South Beach dieters ~~lost~~ *lose* about ten pounds in the first two weeks.

In general, use the present tense to write about literature.

▶ Macbeth *evokes* the theme of vision when he *says* to the Ghost, "Thou hast no speculation in those eyes / Which thou dost glare with" (3.3.96–97).

▶ As in many fantasy novels and fairy tales, the central character *is* on a quest; however, the narrative of Harry's quest *unfolds* more like a classic mystery.   —Philip Nel, "Fantasy, Mystery, and Ambiguity"

In **APA STYLE**, use the past tense or the present perfect to report results and the present tense to give your own insights into or conclusions about the results.

● 477–519

▶ The bulk of the data collected in this study *validated* the research of Neal Miller; the subjects *appeared* to undergo operant conditioning of their smooth muscles in order to relax their frontalis muscles and increase their skin temperatures. Subjects 3 and 6 each *failed* to do this in one session; subject 7 *failed* to do this several times. This finding *is* difficult to explain precisely.   —Sarah Thomas, "The Effect of Biofeedback Training on Muscle Tension and Skin Temperature"

Perfect tenses

PRESENT PERFECT	PAST PERFECT	FUTURE PERFECT
I have talked	I had talked	I will have talked
I have written	I had written	I will have written

Use the present perfect to indicate actions that took place at no specific time in the past or that began in the past and continue into the present.

▶ As a middle-class black I *have* often *felt* myself contriving to be "black."
                    —Shelby Steele, "On Being Black and Middle Class"

Use the past perfect for an action that was completed before another action began.

▶ By the time I was born, the Vietnam War *had* already ended.

The war ended before the writer was born.

Use the future perfect to indicate actions that will be completed at a specific time in the future.

▶ By this time next year, you *will have graduated*.

Progressive tenses

PRESENT PROGRESSIVE	PAST PROGRESSIVE	FUTURE PROGRESSIVE
I am talking	I was talking	I will be talking
I am writing	I was writing	I will be writing

PRESENT PERFECT PROGRESSIVE	PAST PERFECT PROGRESSIVE	FUTURE PERFECT PROGRESSIVE
I have been talking	I had been talking	I will have been talking
I have been writing	I had been writing	I will have been writing

Use progressive tenses to indicate continuing action.

▶ Congress *is considering*, and may soon pass, legislation making English the official language of the United States.
　　　　　　　　—Dennis Baron, "Don't Make English Official—Ban It Instead"

▶ The night after Halloween, we *were watching* TV when the doorbell rang.
　　　　　　　　—David Sedaris, "Us and Them"

▶ As they do every year on the Friday before exams, the Kenyon Kokosingers *will be singing* next Friday evening in Rosse Hall.

▶ Willie joined the Grace Church Boy Choir when he was ten, and he *has been singing* ever since.

S-4b Verb Forms

There are four forms of a verb: the base form, the past, the past participle, and the present participle. Samples of each appear in the lists below. All of the various tenses are generated with these four forms.

The past tense and past participle of all regular verbs is formed by adding -ed or -d to the base form (*talked, lived*). Irregular verbs are not as predictable; see the list of some common ones below. The present participle consists of the base form plus -ing (*talking, living*).

BASE FORM	On Thursdays, we *visit* a museum.
PAST TENSE	Last week, we *visited* the Museum of Modern Art.
PAST PARTICIPLE	I have also *visited* the Metropolitan Museum, but I've not yet *been* to the Cloisters.
PRESENT PARTICIPLE	We will be *visiting* the Cooper-Hewitt Museum tomorrow to see the cutlery exhibit.

Some common irregular verbs

BASE FORM	PAST TENSE	PAST PARTICIPLE	PRESENT PARTICIPLE
be	was/were	been	being
choose	chose	chosen	choosing
do	did	done	doing
eat	ate	eaten	eating
fall	fell	fallen	falling
give	gave	given	giving
go	went	gone	going
hang (suspend)	hung	hung	hanging
know	knew	known	knowing
lay	laid	laid	laying
lie (recline)	lay	lain	lying
make	made	made	making
prove	proved	proved, proven	proving
rise	rose	risen	rising
set	set	set	setting
sit	sat	sat	sitting
teach	taught	taught	teaching
write	wrote	written	writing

Some writers get confused about when to use the past tense and when to use a past participle. One simple rule is to use the past tense if

there is no helping verb and to use a past participle if there is a helping verb.

> *went*
> ▶ For vacation last spring, my family ~~gone~~ to Turkey.

> *eaten*
> ▶ After two weeks in Istanbul, we had ~~ate~~ a lot of Turkish delight.

Helping verbs

Glossary
HB-12–14
HB-19–20

Do, have, be, and **MODALS** such as *can* and *may* all function as helping
verbs in order to express certain **VERB TENSES** and **MOODS**. *Do, have,* and
be change form to indicate tenses; modals do not. The appropriate forms
of main verbs and helping verbs are discussed in this section.

FORMS OF *DO*	do, does, did
FORMS OF *HAVE*	have, has, had
FORMS OF *BE*	be, am, is, are, was, were, been
MODALS	can, could, may, might, must, shall, should, will, would, ought to

Do, does, or *did* requires the base form of the main verb.

> ▶ That professor *did take* class participation into account when calculating
> grades.

> ▶ Sometimes even the smartest students *do* not *like* to answer questions out
> loud in class.

Have, has, or *had* requires the past participle of the main verb.

> ▶ I *have written* to my senator to express my views on global warming.

> ▶ When all of the visitors *had gone,* the security guards locked the building
> for the night.

HB-18–19

Forms of *be* are used with a present participle to express a continuing
action or with a past participle to express the **PASSIVE VOICE**.

CONTINUING ACTION

▶ The university *is considering* a change in its policy on cell phone use.

▶ I *was studying* my notes from last week as I walked to class.

PASSIVE VOICE

▶ Six classes per semester *is considered* a heavy course load.

▶ Ancient Greek *was studied* by many university students in the early twentieth century, but it is not a popular major today.

Modals are used with the base form of the main verb.

▶ After each class, small groups of students *will meet* for focused discussion.

▶ Each student *should participate* in every group session.

Gerunds and infinitives

A gerund is a verb form ending in -ing that functions as a noun: *hopping, skipping, jumping.*

▶ Although many people like *driving,* some prefer *walking.*

An infinitive is *to* plus the base form of a verb: *to hop, to skip, to jump.*

▶ Although many people like *to drive,* some prefer *to walk.*

In general, use infinitives to express intentions or desires, and use gerunds to express plain facts.

▶ I planned *to learn* Spanish, Japanese, and Arabic.

▶ I also really wanted *to know* Russian.

▶ Unfortunately, I ended up *studying* only Spanish and Arabic—and *speaking* only Spanish.

> *putting*
> Just in time for Thanksgiving, the painters finished ~~to put~~ up the wallpaper.

With several verbs—*forget, remember, stop,* and a few others—the choice of an infinitive or gerund changes the meaning.

> I stopped to eat lunch.

In other words, I paused to eat lunch.

> I stopped eating lunch.

In other words, I no longer ate lunch.

HB-39–40

Always use a gerund after a **PREPOSITION**.

> *swimming.*
> The water is too cold for ~~to swim.~~

S-4c Active and Passive Voice

Verbs can be active or passive. When a verb is in the active voice, the subject performs the action (*she caught the ball*). When a verb is in the passive voice, the subject receives the action (*the ball was thrown to her*).

ACTIVE   The wealthiest 1 percent of the American population *holds* 38 percent of the total national wealth.
                    —Gregory Mantsios, "Class in America—2003"

PASSIVE   By the 1970s, Leslie had developed a distinctive figural style in which subjects *are shown* in frontal, confrontational poses, at close range.
                    —David S. Rubin, "It's the Same Old Song"

Active verbs tend to be more direct and easier to understand, but the passive voice can be useful when you specifically want to emphasize the recipient of the action.

▶ In a sense, little girls *are urged* to please adults with a kind of coquettishness, while boys *are enjoined* to behave like monkeys toward each other.   —Paul Theroux, "Being a Man"

The passive voice is also appropriate in scientific writing when you wish to emphasize the research itself, not the researchers.

▶ The treatment order was random for each subject, and it *was reversed* for his or her second treatment.
                        —Sarah Thomas, "The Effect of Biofeedback Training on Muscle Tension and Skin Temperature"

S-4d Mood

Mood indicates a writer's attitude about a statement. There are three moods in English: indicative, imperative, and subjunctive. The indicative is used to state facts or opinions and to ask questions.

▶ Thanks to its many volunteers, Habitat for Humanity *has built* twelve houses in the region this year.

▶ What other volunteer opportunities *does* Habitat *offer*?

The imperative is used to give commands or directions.

▶ *Sit* up straight and *do* your work.

The subjunctive is used to express wishes or requests or to indicate hypothetical or unlikely conditions. It is used most often in conditional sentences, ones that often include a clause beginning with *if*. The verb used in the *if* clause depends on the likelihood that the information in the clause is true.

Facts

When there's no doubt that the information in the *if* clause is true, use the same tense in both clauses. Use the present tense in both clauses to express a scientific fact.

▶ If an earthquake *strikes* that region, forecasters *expect* a tsunami.

▶ One hundred years ago, if a hurricane *hit*, residents *had* very little warning.

Predictions

When the information in the *if* clause is probably true, use the present tense in the *if* clause and a modal such as *will* or *might* + the base form of the verb in the other clause.

▶ If you faithfully *follow* the South Beach Diet for two weeks, you *will lose* about ten pounds.

Speculations

When the information in the *if* clause is not likely to be true, use the past form in the *if* clause and *would* (or *could* or *might*) + the base form of the verb in the other clause. The past form of *be* in the subjunctive is always *were*.

▶ If doctors *discovered* a cure for cancer tomorrow, they *could save* millions of lives.

▶ If Martin Luther King Jr. *were* alive today, he *would acknowledge* progress in race relations in this country, but he *would* also *ask* significant questions.

When the *if* clause is about an event in the past that never happened, use the past perfect in the *if* clause and *would have* (or *could* or *might have*) + a past participle in the other clause.

▶ If the police officer *had separated* the witnesses, their evidence *would have been* admissible in court.

S-5 Subject-Verb Agreement

Subjects and verbs should agree: if the subject is in the third-person singular, the verb should be in the third-person singular—"Dinner is on the table." Yet sometimes it's not that clear, as when we say that "macaroni and cheese *are* available in most grocery stores" but that "macaroni and cheese *is* our family's favorite comfort food." This section focuses on subject-verb agreement.

S-5a Agreement in Number and Person

SUBJECTS and VERBS should agree with each other in number (singular or plural) and person (first, second, or third).

HB-4

HB-11–24

SINGULAR   A 1922 *ad* for Resinol soap *urges* women to "make that dream come true" by using Resinol.

PLURAL   *Boys are* the catch of the day in the Listerine ad.
—Doug Lantry, " 'Stay Sweet As You Are' "

S-5b Subjects and Verbs Separated by Other Words

A verb should agree with its subject, not with another word that falls in between.

▶ In the backyard, the *leaves* of the apple tree *rattle* across the lawn.
—Gary Soto, "The Guardian Angel"

▶ The price of soybeans ~~fluctuate~~ *fluctuates* according to demand.

S-5c Compound Subjects

Two or more subjects joined by *and* are generally plural.

▶ Obviously, safety and security *are* important issues in American life.
—Andie McDonie, "Airport Security"

However, if the parts of the subject form a single unit, they take a singular verb.

▶ Forty acres and a mule ~~are~~ *is* what General William T. Sherman promised each freed slave.

If the subjects are joined by *or* or *nor*, the verb should agree with the closer subject.

▶ Either you or she ~~are~~ *is* mistaken.

▶ Neither the teacher nor his students ~~was~~ *were* able to solve the equation.

S-5d Subjects That Follow the Verb

English verbs usually follow their subjects. Be sure the verb agrees with the subject even when the subject follows the verb, such as when the sentence begins with *there is* or *there are*.

▶ Gone, however, *is* the contrived backdrop of singularly happy, two-parent families living in upper-middle-class America.

—Ben Leever, "In Defense of *Dawson's Creek*"

▶ There *are* several possible explanations for increases in student borrowing.

—Tracey King and Ellynne Bannon, "The Burden of Borrowing"

▶ There ~~was~~ *were* too many unresolved problems for the project to begin.

S-5e Collective Nouns

Collective nouns such as *group, team, audience,* or *family* can take singular or plural verbs, depending on whether the noun refers to the group as a single unit or to the multiple members that make up the group.

▶ The choir ~~sing~~ *sings* *The Messiah* every Christmas.

▶ Gregor's family *keep* reassuring themselves that things will be just fine again.

—Scott Russell Sanders, "Under the Influence"

The individual members of the family reassure one another.

rhetorical situations · genres · processes · strategies · research mla/apa · media/design · handbook

S-5f *Everyone* and Other Indefinite Pronouns

Most **INDEFINITE PRONOUNS**, such as *anyone, anything, each, either, everybody, everything, neither, no one, one, someone,* and *something,* take a singular verb.

Glossary

▶ But . . . no one *is* selling the content that gets shared on P2P services.
— Lawrence Lessig, "Some Like It Hot"

▶ Each of the candidates ~~agree~~ *agrees* with the president.

Both, few, many, others, and *several* are always plural.

▶ Already, few *know* how to read a serious book.
— Paul West, "Borrowed Time"

All, any, enough, more, most, none, and *some* are singular when they refer to a singular noun, but they are plural whenever they refer to a plural noun.

▶ Don't assume that all of the members of a family ~~votes~~ *vote* the same way.

▶ None of the music we heard last night ~~come~~ *comes* from the baroque period.

S-5g *Who, That,* or *Which*

The **RELATIVE PRONOUNS** *who, that,* and *which* take a singular verb when they come after a singular noun and a plural verb when they come after a plural noun.

Glossary

▶ I find it refreshing to have work that *rewards* initiative and effort.
— Lars Eighner, "On Dumpster Diving"

▶ We fell in with some other hippie-groupie types who *were* obsessed with Hendrix, the Doors, Janis Joplin, and Zeppelin as well as the Stones.
— Susan Jane Gilman, "Mick Jagger Wants Me"

One of the is always followed by a plural noun, and the verb should be plural.

▶ Jaime is one of the speakers who ~~asks~~ *ask* provocative questions.
ask

> Several speakers ask provocative questions. Jaime is one. *Who* refers to *speakers*, so the verb is plural.

The only one, however, takes a singular verb.

▶ Jaime is the only one of the speakers who ~~ask~~ provocative questions.
asks

> Only one speaker asks provocative questions: Jaime. *Who* thus refers to *one*, so the verb is singular.

S-6 Pronouns

We use pronouns to take the place of nouns so we don't have to write or say the same word or name over and over. Imagine how repetitive our writing would be without pronouns: *Little Miss Muffet sat on Little Miss Muffet's tuffet eating Little Miss Muffet's curds and whey.* Luckily, we have pronouns, and this section demonstrates how to use them clearly.

S-6a Pronoun-Antecedent Agreement

A pronoun must agree with its antecedent in gender and in number.

IN GENDER　*Grandma* took *her* pie out of the oven.

IN NUMBER　*My grandparents* spent weekends at *their* cabin on White Bear Lake.

Indefinite pronouns

Glossary

INDEFINITE PRONOUNS such as *anyone, each, either, everyone, neither, no one, someone,* and *something* take a singular pronoun.

▶ Everyone in the class did ~~their~~ best.
his or her

If you find *his or her* awkward, you can rewrite the sentence.

> *All of the students*
> ▶ ~~Everyone~~ in the class did their best.
> ^

Collective nouns

Collective nouns such as *audience, committee,* or *team* take a singular pronoun when they refer to the group as a whole and a plural pronoun when they refer to members of the group as individuals.

> *its*
> ▶ The winning team drew ~~their~~ inspiration from the manager.
> ^

> *their*
> ▶ The winning team threw ~~its~~ gloves in the air.
> ^

He, his, *and other masculine pronouns*

To avoid **SEXIST LANGUAGE**, use *he, him, his,* or *himself* only when you know that the antecedent is male.

HB-54–55

> *or her.*
> ▶ Before meeting a new doctor, many people worry about not liking him/
> ^

S-6b Pronoun Reference

A pronoun needs to have a clear antecedent, a specific word to which the pronoun points.

> ▶ My grandmother spent a lot of time reading to me. She mostly read the standards, like *The Little Engine That Could,* over and over and over again.   —Richard Bullock, "How I Learned about the Power of Writing"

Ambiguous reference

A pronoun is ambiguous if it could refer to more than one antecedent.

> *the printer*
> ▶ After I plugged the printer into the computer, ~~it~~ sputtered and died.
> ^

> What sputtered and died—the computer or the printer? The edit makes the reference clear.

Implied reference

If a pronoun does not refer clearly to a specific word, rewrite the sentence to omit the pronoun or insert an antecedent.

Unclear reference of *this*, *that*, and *which*. These three pronouns must refer to specific antecedents.

▶ Ultimately, the Justice Department did not insist on the breakup of
Microsoft, ~~which~~ *an oversight that* set the tone for a liberal merger policy in the following
years.

Indefinite use of *they*, *it*, and *you*. *They* and *it* should be used only to refer to people or things that have been specifically mentioned. *You* should be used only to address your reader.

▶ *Many*
~~In many~~ European countries/ ~~they~~ don't allow civilians to carry handguns.

▶ *The*
~~On the~~ weather station/ ~~it~~ said that storms would hit Key West today.

▶ Many doctors argue that age should not be an impediment to
for people who
physical exercise ~~if you~~ have always been active.

S-6c Pronoun Case

The pronouns in the list below change case according to how they function in a sentence. There are three cases: subjective, objective, and possessive. Pronouns functioning as subjects or subject complements are in the subjective case; those functioning as objects are in the objective case; those functioning as possessives are in the possessive case.

SUBJECTIVE   *We* lived in a rented house three blocks from the school.

OBJECTIVE   I went to my room and shut the door behind *me*.

POSSESSIVE   All *my* life chocolate has made me ill.

—David Sedaris, "Us and Them"

SUBJECTIVE	OBJECTIVE	POSSESSIVE
I	me	my / mine
we	us	our / ours
you	you	your / yours
he / she / it	him / her / it	his / her / hers / its
they	them	their / theirs
who / whoever	whom / whomever	whose

In subject complements

Use the subjective case for pronouns that follow **LINKING VERBS** such as *be*, *seem*, *become*, and *feel*.

Glossary

▶ In fact, Li was not the one who broke the code; it was ~~me.~~ *I.*

If *It was I* sounds awkward, revise the sentence further: *I did it.*

In compound structures

When a pronoun is part of a compound subject, it should be in the subjective case. When it's part of a compound object, it should be in the objective case.

▶ On our vacations, my grandfather and ~~me~~ *I* went fishing together.

▶ There were never any secrets between ~~he~~ *him* and ~~I.~~ *me.*

After than or as

Often comparisons with *than* or *as* leave some words out. When such comparisons include pronouns, your intended meaning determines the case of the pronoun.

▶ You trust John more than *me*.

This sentence means *You trust John more than you trust me.*

▶ You trust John more than *I*.

This sentence means *You trust John more than I trust him.*

Before gerunds

HB-17

Pronouns that come before a **GERUND** are usually in the possessive case.

> ▶ Savion's fans loved ~~him~~ tap dancing to classical music.
>   ^his^

With who and whom

Use *who* (and *whoever*) where you would use *he* or *she,* and use *whom* (and *whomever*) where you would use *him* or *her*. It can be confusing when one of these words begins a question. To figure out which case to use, try answering the question using *she* or *her*. If *she* works, use *who;* if *her* works, use *whom*.

> ▶ ~~Who~~ do the critics admire most?
>   ^Whom^

> They admire *her,* so change *who* to *whom*.

> ▶ ~~Whom~~ will begin the discussion on this thorny topic?
>   ^Who^

> *She* will begin the discussion, so change *whom* to *who*.

S-7 Parallelism

Been there, done that. Eat, drink, and be merry. For better or for worse. Out of sight, out of mind. All of these common sayings are parallel in structure, putting parallel words in the same grammatical form. Parallel structure emphasizes the connection between the elements and can make your writing rhythmic and easy to read. This section offers guidelines for maintaining parallelism in your writing.

S-7a In a Series or List

Use the same grammatical form for all items in a series or list—all nouns, all gerunds, all prepositional phrases, and so on.

▶ The seven deadly sins—*avarice*, *sloth*, *envy*, *lust*, *gluttony*, *pride*, and *wrath*—were all committed Sunday during the twice-annual bake sale at St. Mary's of the Immaculate Conception Church.   —*The Onion*

▶ After fifty years of running, biking, swimming, weight lifting, and ~~on the squash court~~ *playing squash* to stay in shape, Aunt Dorothy was unhappy to learn she had a knee problem requiring arthroscopic surgery.

S-7b With Paired Ideas

One way to emphasize the connection between two ideas is to put them in identical grammatical forms. When you connect ideas with *and*, *but*, or another **COORDINATING CONJUNCTION**, make the ideas parallel in structure, and when you link ideas with *either . . . or* or another **CORRELATIVE CONJUNCTION**, use the same grammatical structure after each part.

HB-31
HB-32

▶ Many rural residents are voting on conservation issues and ~~agree~~ *agreeing* to pay higher property taxes in order to keep community land undeveloped.

▶ General Electric paid millions of dollars to dredge the river and ~~for removing~~ *to remove* carcinogens from backyards.

▶ Sweet potatoes are highly nutritious, providing both dietary fiber and ~~as a good source of~~ vitamins A and C.

▶ Information on local cleanup efforts can be obtained not only from the town government but also ~~by going to~~ *at* the public library.

S-7c On PowerPoint Slides

PowerPoint and other presentation slides present most information in lists. Entries on these lists should be in parallel grammatical form.

During the 1946 presidential race, Truman

- Conducted a whistle-stop campaign
- Made hundreds of speeches
- *Spoke energetically*
  ~~Energetic speaker~~
- Connected personally with voters

S-7d On a Résumé

Entries on a résumé should be grammatically and typographically parallel. Each entry in the example below has the date on the left; the job title in bold followed by the company on the first line; the city and state on the second line; and the duties performed on the remaining lines, each starting with a verb.

2008–present   **INTERN,** Benedetto, Gartland, and Co.
New York, NY
Assist in analyzing data for key accounts.
Design PowerPoint slides and presentations.

2007, summer   **SALES REPRESENTATIVE,** Vector Marketing Corporation
New York, NY
Sold high-quality cutlery, developing my own client base.

2006, summer   **TUTOR,** Grace Church Opportunity Project
New York, NY
Tutored low-income children in math and reading.

S-7e In Headings

When you add headings to a piece of writing, put them in parallel forms—all nouns, all prepositional phrases, and so on. Consider, for example, the following three headings in the chapter on developing a research plan.

Establishing a Schedule
Getting Started
Considering the Rhetorical Situation

S-7f With All the Necessary Words

Be sure to include all the words necessary to make your meaning clear and your grammar parallel.

▶ Voting gained urgency in cities, *in* suburbs, and on farms.

▶ She loved her son more than *she loved* her husband.

> The original sentence was ambiguous; it could also mean that she loved her son more than her husband did.

S-8 Coordination and Subordination

When we combine two or more ideas in one sentence, we can use coordination to emphasize each idea equally or subordination to give more emphasis to one of the ideas. Assume, for example, that you're writing about your Aunt Irene. Aunt Irene made great strawberry jam. She did not win a blue ribbon at the Iowa State Fair.

COORDINATION	Aunt Irene made great strawberry jam, but she did not win the blue ribbon at the Iowa State Fair.
SUBORDINATION	Though Aunt Irene made great strawberry jam, she did not win the blue ribbon at the Iowa State Fair.

S-8a Linking Equal Ideas

To link ideas that you consider equal in importance, use a coordinating conjunction, a pair of correlative conjunctions, or a semicolon.

COORDINATING CONJUNCTIONS

and	or	so	yet
but	nor	for	

▶ The line in front of Preservation Hall was very long, *but* a good tenor sax player was wandering up and down the street, *so* I took my place at the end of the line. —Fred Setterberg, "The Usual Story"

▶ I did not live in a neighborhood with other Latinos, *and* the public school I attended attracted very few. —Tanya Barrientos, "Se Habla Español"

Be careful not to overuse *and*. Try to use the coordinating conjunction that best expresses your meaning.

▶ Mosquitoes survived the high-tech zapping devices, ~~and~~ *but* bites were a small price for otherwise pleasant evenings in the country.

CORRELATIVE CONJUNCTIONS

| either . . . or | not only . . . but also |
| neither . . . nor | just as . . . so |

▶ *Not only* are the majority of students turning to student loans, *but* debt levels are *also* escalating.
—Tracey King and Ellynne Bannon, "The Burden of Borrowing"

277

If you use a semicolon, you might use a **TRANSITION** such as *therefore* or *however* to make the relationship between the ideas especially clear.

▶ Second, reading and spelling require much more than just phonics; spelling strategies and word-analysis skills are equally important.
—Debra Johnson, "Balanced Reading Instruction:
A Review of the Literature"

▶ As in many fantasy novels and fairy tales, the central character is on a quest; *however*, the narrative of Harry's quest unfolds more like a classic mystery. —Philip Nel, "Fantasy, Mystery, and Ambiguity"

S-8b Emphasizing One Idea over Others

HB-6–7

To emphasize one idea over others, put the most important one in an **INDEPENDENT CLAUSE** and the less important ones in **SUBORDINATE CLAUSES** or **PHRASES**.

rhetorical situations   genres   processes   strategies   research mla/apa   media/ design   handbook

▶ Because storytelling lies at the heart of Pueblo culture, it is absurd to attempt to fix the stories in time.
—Leslie Marmon Silko, "Language and Literature from a Pueblo Perspective"

▶ Even ignoring the extreme poles of the economic spectrum, we find enormous class differences in the life-styles among the haves, the have-nots, and the have-littles.   —Gregory Mantsios, "Class in America—2003"

S-9 Shifts

You're watching the news when your brother grabs the remote and changes the channel to a cartoon. The road you're driving on suddenly changes from asphalt to gravel. These shifts are jarring and sometimes disorienting. Similarly, shifts in writing—from one tense to another, for example—can confuse your readers. This section explains how to keep your writing consistent in verb tense and point of view.

S-9a Shifts in Tense

Only when you want to emphasize that actions took place at different times should you shift **VERB TENSE**.

HB-12–14

▶ My plane *will arrive* in Albuquerque two hours after it *leaves* Portland.

Otherwise, keep tenses consistent.

▶ As the concert ended, several people ~~are~~ ^{were} already on their way up the aisle, causing a distraction.

In writing about literary works, use the present tense. Be careful not to shift to the past.

▶ The two fugitives start down the river together, Huck fleeing his abusive father and Jim running away from his owner. As they ~~traveled,~~ ^{travel,} they ~~met~~ ^{meet} with many colorful characters, including the Duke and King, two actors and con artists who involve Huck and Jim in their schemes.

S-9b Shifts in Point of View

Do not shift between first person (*I, we*), second person (*you*), and third person (*he, she, it, they, one*)—or between singular and plural subjects.

▶ When ~~one has~~ *you have* a cold, you should stay home rather than risk exposing others.

Unnecessary shifts between singular and plural subjects can confuse readers.

▶ Because of late frosts, oranges have risen dramatically in price. But since ~~the orange is~~ *oranges are* such a staple, they continue to sell.

Words **W**

rhetorical situations

genres

processes

strategies

research mla/apa

media/ design

handbook

W-1 Appropriate Words

Cool. Sweet. Excellent. These three words can mean the same thing, but each has a different level of formality. We usually use informal language when we're talking with friends, and we use slang and abbreviations when we send text messages, but we choose words that are more formal for most of our academic and professional writing. Just as we wouldn't wear an old T-shirt to most job interviews, we wouldn't write in a college essay that *Beloved* is "an awesome book." This section offers you help in choosing words that are appropriate for different audiences and purposes.

W-1a Formal and Informal Words

3–4

5–8

Whether you use formal or informal language depends on your **PURPOSE** and **AUDIENCE**.

> **FORMAL**   Four score and seven years ago our fathers brought forth on this continent, a new nation, conceived in Liberty, and dedicated to the proposition that all men are created equal.
> —Abraham Lincoln, Gettysburg Address

> **INFORMAL**   Our family, like most, had its ups and downs.
> —Judy Davis, "Ours Was a Dad"
>
> Abraham Lincoln delivered the first, more formal sentence in 1863 to 20,000 people, including officials and celebrities. The second, less formal sentence was spoken in 2004 by a woman to a small gathering of family and friends at her father's funeral.

Colloquial language (*What's up? No clue*) and slang (*A-list, S'up?*) are not appropriate for formal speech and may be too informal for most academic and professional writing.

>   Many   excited   they are
> ▶ A lot of drivers are ~~hot~~ about the new hybrid cars because ~~they're~~ so fuel efficient.

► At 1:00, we ~~scarfed down~~ *ate* our lunches and then went straight back to
   work.
   ~~the grind.~~

W-1b Pretentious Language

Long or complicated words might seem to lend authority to your writing, but often they make it sound pretentious and stuffy. Use such words
sparingly and only when they best capture your meaning and suit your
RHETORICAL SITUATION.

1

► *After*
   ~~Subsequent to~~ adopting the new system, managers ~~averred~~ *claimed* that their
   staff worked ~~synergistically~~ *together* ~~in a way that exceeded parameters.~~ *better than expected.*

W-1c Jargon

Jargon is a specialized vocabulary used in a profession, trade, or field
and should be used only when you know your audience will understand
what you are saying. The following paragraph might be easily under-
standable to a computer enthusiast, but most readers would not be
familiar with terms like *HDMI, DVI,* and *1080p.*

► As far as quality is concerned, HDMI is the easiest and most convenient way
   to go about high-def. Why? Because you get audio and sound in a single,
   USB-like cable, instead of a nest of component cables or the soundless
   garden hose of DVI. Also, unless you're trying to run 1080p over 100 feet or
   somesuch, stay away from premium brands. Any on-spec cheapie HDMI
   cable will be perfect for standard living room setups.
                    —Rob Beschizza, "Which Is Better, HDMI or Component?"

When you are writing for an audience of nonspecialists, resist the temptation to use overly technical language.

> *small incision* *breastbone*
> The ~~mini-sternotomy~~ from the lower end of the ~~sternum~~ to the second
> *between her ribs* *preserved her appearance.*
> ~~intercostal~~ space ~~resulted in satisfactory cosmesis.~~

W-1d Clichés

Steer clear of clichés, expressions that are so familiar as to have become
trite (*white as snow, the grass is always greener*).

> *unconventionally.*
> The company needs a recruiter who thinks ~~outside the box.~~

> *soundly.*
> After canoeing all day, we all slept ~~like logs~~.

> *collaborates well,*
> Nita ~~is a team player,~~ so we hope she will be assigned to the project.

W-2 Precise Words

Venus edges past Jankovic. Roger Federer overpowers Andy Roddick.
In each case, the writer could have simply used the word *defeats*. But
at least to tennis fans, these newspaper headlines are a bit more precise and informative as a result of the words chosen. This section offers
guidelines for editing your own writing to make it as precise as it needs
to be.

W-2a *Be* and *do*

Try not to rely too much on *be* or *do*. Check your writing to see if you
can replace forms of these words with more precise verbs.

> *focuses on*
> David Sedaris's essay "Us and Them" ~~is about~~ his love/hate relationship
> with his family.

► Some doctors believe that ~~doing~~ *solving* crossword puzzles can delay the onset of senility and even Alzheimer's disease.

Sometimes using a form of *be* or *do* is unavoidable, such as when you are describing someone or something.

► Barnes *is* a legend among southern California Met lovers—an icon, a beacon, and a font of useful knowledge and freely offered opinions.
—Bob Merlis, "Foster Cars"

W-2b Balancing General and Specific Words

Abstract words refer to general qualities or ideas (*truth, beauty*), whereas concrete words refer to specific things we can perceive with our senses (*books, lipstick*). You'll often need to use words that are general or abstract, but remember that specific, concrete words can make your writing more precise and more vivid—and can make the abstract easier to understand.

► In Joan Didion's work, there has always been a fascination with what she once called "the unspeakable peril of the everyday"—the coyotes by the interstate, the snakes in the playpen, the fires and Santa Ana winds of California.
—Michiko Kakutani, "The End of Life As She Knew It"

The concrete *coyotes, snakes, fires,* and *winds* help explain the abstract *peril of the everyday.*

W-2c Prepositions

Prepositions are words like *at, in,* and *on* that express relationships between words. Do you live *in* a city, *on* an island, or *at* the beach? In each case, you need to use a certain preposition. You'll often need to check a dictionary to decide which preposition to use. Here are some guidelines for using *in, on,* and *at* to indicate place and time.

Prepositions of place

IN

a container, room, or area: *in* the mailbox, *in* my office, *in* the woods
a geographic location: *in* San Diego, *in* the Midwest
a printed work: *in* the newspaper, *in* chapter 3

ON

a surface: *on* the floor, *on* the grass
a street: *on* Ninth Street, *on* Western Avenue
an electronic medium: *on* DVD, *on* the radio
public transportation: *on* the bus, *on* an airplane

AT

a specific address or business: *at* 33 Parkwood Street, *at* McDonald's
a public building or unnamed business: *at* the courthouse, *at* the bakery
a general place: *at* home, *at* work

Prepositions of time

IN

a defined time period: *in* an hour, *in* three years
a month, season, or year: *in* June, *in* the fall, *in* 2007
a part of the day: *in* the morning, *in* the evening

ON

a day of the week: *on* Friday
an exact date: *on* September 12
a holiday: *on* Thanksgiving, *on* Veteran's Day

AT

a specific time: *at* 4:30 p.m., *at* sunset, *at* lunchtime, *at* night

W-2d Figurative Language

Glossary

Figures of speech such as **SIMILES** and **METAPHORS** are words used imaginatively rather than literally that can help readers understand an abstract point by comparing it to something they are familiar with or can easily imagine.

SIMILE   His body is in almost constant motion—rolling those cigarettes, rubbing an elbow, reaching for a glass—but the rhythm is tranquil and fluid, *like a cat licking its paw.*
                        —Sean Smith, "Johnny Depp: Unlikely Superstar"

METAPHOR   And so, before the professor had even finished his little story, *I had become a furnace of rage.*
                        —Shelby Steele, "On Being Black and Middle Class"

W-3 Commonly Confused Words

When you're tired, do you *lay* down or *lie* down? After dinner, do you eat *desert* or *dessert*? This section's purpose is to alert you to everyday words that can trip you up and to help you understand the differences between certain words people tend to confuse.

accept, except *Accept* means "to receive willingly": *accept an award.* *Except* as a preposition means "excluding": *all Western languages except English.*

adapt, adopt *Adapt* means "to adjust": *adapt the recipe to be dairy free.* *Adopt* means "to take as one's own": *adopt a pet from a shelter.*

advice, advise *Advice* means "recommendation": *a lawyer's advice.* *Advise* means "to give advice": *We advise you to learn your rights.*

affect, effect *Affect* as a verb means "to produce a change in": *Stress can affect people's physical health. Effect* as a noun means "result": *cause and effect.*

all right, alright *All right* is the preferred spelling.

allusion, illusion *Allusion* means "indirect reference": *an allusion to* Alice in Wonderland. *Illusion* means "false appearance": *an optical illusion.*

a lot Always two words, *a lot* means "a large number or amount" or "to a great extent": *a lot of voters; he misses her a lot.* The phrase is too informal for most academic writing.

among, between Use *among* for three or more items: *among the fifty states.* Use *between* for two items: *between you and me.*

amount, number Use *amount* for items you can measure but not count: *a large amount of water.* Use *number* for things you can count: *a number of books.*

as, as if, like *Like* introduces a noun or noun phrase: *It feels like silk.* To begin a subordinate clause, use *as* or *as if*: *Do as I say, not as I do; It seemed as if he had not prepared at all for the briefing.*

bad, badly Use *bad* as an adjective following a linking verb: *I feel bad.* Use *badly* as an adverb following an action verb: *I play piano badly.*

capital, capitol A *capital* is a city where the government of a state, province, or country is located: *Kingston was the first state capital of New York.* A *capitol* is a government building: *the dome of the capitol.*

cite, sight, site *Cite* means to quote: *Cite your sources. Sight* is the act of seeing or something that is seen: *an appalling sight.* A *site* is a place: *the site of a famous battle.*

compose, comprise The parts *compose* the whole: *Fifty states compose the Union.* The whole *comprises* the parts: *The Union comprises fifty states.*

could of In writing, use *could have* (*could've*).

council, counsel *Council* refers to a body of people: *the council's vote. Counsel* means "advice" or "to advise": *her wise counsel; she counseled victims of domestic abuse.*

criteria, criterion *Criteria* is the plural of *criterion* and takes a plural verb: *certain criteria have been established.*

data *Data*, the plural of *datum*, technically should take a plural verb (*The data arrive from many sources*), but some writers treat it as singular (*The data is persuasive*).

desert, dessert *Desert* as a noun means "arid region": *Mojave Desert.* As a verb it means "to abandon": *he deserted his post. Dessert* is a sweet served toward the end of a meal.

disinterested, uninterested *Disinterested* means "fair; unbiased": *disinterested jury. Uninterested* means "bored" or "indifferent": *uninterested in election results.*

emigrate (from), immigrate (to) *Emigrate* means "to leave one's country": *emigrate from Slovakia. Immigrate* means "to move to another country": *immigrate to Canada.*

etc. The abbreviation *etc.* is short for the Latin *et cetera*, "and other things." Avoid using *etc.* in your writing, substituting *and so on* if necessary.

everyday, every day *Everyday* is an adjective meaning "ordinary": *After the holidays, we go back to our everyday routine. Every day* means "on a daily basis": *Eat five or more servings of fruits and vegetables every day.*

fewer, less Use *fewer* when you refer to things that can be counted: *fewer calories.* Use *less* when you refer to an amount of something that cannot be counted: *less fat.*

good, well *Good* is an adjective indicating emotional health, appearance, or general quality: *She looks good in that color; a good book. Well* is used as an adjective indicating physical health after a linking verb: *She looks well despite her recent surgery. Well* as an adverb follows an action verb: *He speaks Spanish well.*

hopefully In academic writing, avoid *hopefully* to mean "it is hoped that"; use it only to mean "with hope": *to make a wish hopefully.*

imply, infer *Imply* means "to suggest": *What do you mean to imply? Infer* means "to conclude": *We infer that you did not enjoy the trip.*

its, it's *Its* is a possessive pronoun: *The movie is rated PG-13 because of its language. It's* is a contraction of "it is" or "it has": *It's an exciting action film.*

lay, lie *Lay*, meaning "to put" or "to place," always takes a direct object: *She lays the blanket down. Lie*, meaning "to recline" or "to be positioned," never takes a direct object: *She lies on the blanket.*

lead, led The verb *lead* (rhymes with *heed*) is the present tense and base form: *I will lead the way. Led* is the past tense and past participle of *lead: Yesterday I led the way.* The noun *lead* (rhymes with *head*) is a type of metal: *Use copper pipes instead of lead.*

literally   Use *literally* only when you want to stress that you don't mean *figuratively*: *While sitting in the grass, he realized that he literally had ants in his pants.*

loose, lose   *Loose* means "not fastened securely" or "not fitting tightly": *a pair of loose pants. Lose* means "to misplace" or "to not win": *lose an earring; lose the race.*

man, mankind   Use *people*, *human*, or *humankind* instead.

may of, might of, must of   In writing, use *may have, might have,* or *must have (may've, might've, must've).*

media   *Media*, a plural noun, takes a plural verb: *The media report another shooting.* The singular form is *medium: Television is a popular medium for advertising.*

percent, percentage   Use *percent* after a number: *eighty percent.* Use *percentage* after an adjective or article: *an impressive percentage, the percentage was impressive.*

principal, principle   As a noun, *principal* means "a chief official" or "a sum of money": *in the principal's office; raising the principal for a down payment.* As an adjective, it means "most important": *the principal cause of death. Principle* means "a rule by which one lives" or "a basic truth or doctrine": *Lying is against her principles; the principles of life, liberty, and the pursuit of happiness.*

raise, rise   Meaning "to grow" or "to cause to move upward," *raise* always takes a direct object: *He raised his hand.* Meaning "to get up," *rise* never takes a direct object: *The sun rises at dawn.*

the reason . . . is because   Use *because* or *the reason . . . is (that)*, but not both: *The reason for the price increase was a poor growing season* or *Prices increased because of a poor growing season.*

reason why   Instead of this redundant phrase, use *the reason* or *the reason that: Psychologists debate the reasons that some people develop depression and others do not.*

respectfully, respectively   *Respectfully* means "full of respect": *Speak to your elders respectfully. Respectively* means "in the order given": *George*

rhetorical situations

genres

processes

strategies

research mla/apa

media/ design

handbook

H. W. Bush and George W. Bush were the forty-first president and the forty-third president, respectively.

sensual, sensuous   *Sensual* suggests sexuality: *a sensual caress*. *Sensuous* involves pleasing the senses through art, music, and nature: *the violin's sensuous solo*.

set, sit   *Set*, meaning "to put" or "to place," takes a direct object: *Please set the table*. *Sit*, meaning "to take a seat," does not take a direct object: *She sits on the bench*.

should of   In writing, use *should have* (*should've*).

stationary, stationery   *Stationary* means "staying put": *a stationary lab table*. *Stationery* means "paper to write on": *the college's official stationery*.

than, then   *Than* is a conjunction used for comparing: *She is taller than her mother*. *Then* is an adverb used to indicate a sequence: *Finish your work and then reward yourself*.

that, which   Use *that* to add information that is essential for identifying something: *The horses that live on this island are endangered*. Use *which* to give additional but nonessential information: *Abaco Barb horses, which live on an island in the Bahamas, are endangered*.

their, there, they're   *Their* signifies possession: *their canoe*. *There* tells where: *Put it there*. *They're* is the contraction of *they are*: *They're too busy to come*.

to, too, two   *To* is either a preposition that tells direction (*Give it to me*) or part of an infinitive (*To err is human*). *Too* means "also" or "excessively": *The younger children wanted to help, too; too wonderful for words*. *Two* is a number: *tea for two*.

unique   Because *unique* suggests that an item or person is the only one of its kind, avoid using comparative or superlative adjectives (*more, most, less, least*), intensifiers (such as *very*), or hedges (such as *somewhat*) to modify it.

weather, whether   *Weather* refers to atmospheric conditions: *dreary weather*. *Whether* refers to a choice between options: *whether to stay home or go out*.

who's, whose   *Who's* is a contraction for *who is* or *who has: Who's the most experienced candidate for the job? Whose* asks or tells who owns something: *Whose keys are these? Jenna, whose keys were lying on the table, had left.*

would of   In writing, use *would have (would've).*

your, you're   *Your* signifies possession: *your diploma. You're* is a contraction for *you are: You're welcome.*

W-4 Unnecessary Words

At this point in time. Really unique. In a manner of speaking. Each of these phrases includes words that are unnecessary or says something that could be said more concisely. This section shows you how to edit your own writing to make every word count.

W-4a *Quite, very,* and Other Empty Words

Intensifiers such as *quite* and *very* are used to strengthen what we say. Hedges such as *apparently, possibly,* and *tend* are a way to qualify what we say. It's fine to use words of this kind when they are necessary. Sometimes, however, they are not. You shouldn't say something is "very unique," because things either are unique or they're not; there's no need to add the intensifier. And why say someone is "really smart" when you could say that he or she is "brilliant"?

▶ Accepted by five Ivy League schools, Jackson ~~seems to be facing an apparently very~~ _{is facing a} difficult decision.

W-4b *There is, it is*

Glossary

The **EXPLETIVES** *there is* and *it is* are useful ways to introduce and emphasize an idea, but often they add unnecessary words and can be replaced with stronger, more precise verbs.

▶ *must*
~~It is necessary for~~ Americans today ~~to~~ learn to speak more than
one language.

▶ *Four*
~~There are four~~ large moons and more than 30 small ones ~~that~~
orbit Jupiter.

In certain contexts, *there is* and *it is* can be the best choices. Imagine the
ending of *The Wizard of Oz* if Dorothy were to say *No place is like home*
instead of the more emphatic (and sentimental) *There's no place like home*.

W-4c Wordy Phrases

Many common phrases use several words when a single word will do.
Editing out such wordy phrases will make your writing more concise
and easier to read.

WORDY	CONCISE
as far as . . . is concerned	concerning
at the time that	when
at this point in time	now
in spite of the fact that	although, though
in the event that	if
in view of the fact that	because, since

▶ *Because*
~~Due to the fact that~~ Professor Lee retired, the animal sciences
department now lacks a neurology specialist.

W-4d Redundancies

Eliminate words and phrases that are unnecessary for your meaning.

▶ Painting the house purple ~~in color~~ will make it stand out from the many
white houses in town.

▶ Dashing ~~quickly~~ into the street to retrieve the ball, the young girl was almost hit by a car.

▶ How much wood is ~~sufficient~~ enough for the fire to burn all night?

W-5 Adjectives and Adverbs

Adjectives and adverbs are words that describe other words, adding important information and detail. When Dave Barry writes that the Beatles "were the *coolest* thing you had ever seen" and that "they were *smart*; they were *funny*; they didn't take themselves *seriously*," the adjectives and adverbs (italicized here) make clear why he "wanted *desperately* to be a Beatle." This section will help you use adjectives and adverbs in your own writing.

W-5a When to Use Adjectives and Adverbs

Adjectives tell *which*, *what kind*, or *how many* and are used to modify nouns and pronouns.

▶ *Parallel* rows of *ancient oak* trees lined the *narrow* driveway.

▶ Years of testing will be needed to prove whether geneticists' theories are *correct*.

▶ If you are craving something *sweet*, have a piece of fruit rather than a candy bar.

Adverbs tell *where, when, how, why, under what conditions, how often*, or *to what degree* and are used to modify verbs, adjectives, and other adverbs. Although many adverbs end in -ly (*tentatively, immediately*), many do not (*now, so, soon, then, very*).

▶ Emergency room personnel must respond *quickly* when an ambulance arrives.

▶ Environmentalists are *increasingly* worried about Americans' consumption of fossil fuels.

rhetorical situations genres processes strategies research mla/apa media/ design handbook

▶ If the senator had known that the news cameras were on, she would not have responded *so angrily*.

Well and good.   Use *well* as an adjective to describe physical health; use *good* to describe emotional health or appearance.

▶ Some herbs can keep you feeling ~~good~~ *well* when everyone else has the flu.

▶ Staying healthy can make you feel *good* about yourself.

Good should not be used as an adverb; use *well*.

▶ Because both Williams sisters play tennis so ~~good,~~ *well,* they frequently compete against each other in major tournaments.

Bad and badly.   Use the adjective *bad* after a **LINKING VERB** to describe an emotional state or feeling. In such cases, the adjective describes the subject.

Glossary

▶ Arguing with your parents can make you feel *bad*.

Use the adverb *badly* to describe an **ACTION VERB**.

Glossary

▶ Arguing with your parents late at night can make you sleep *badly*.

W-5b Comparatives and Superlatives

Most adjectives and adverbs have three forms: the positive, the comparative, and the superlative. The comparative is used to compare two things, and the superlative is used to compare three or more things.

COMPARATIVE   Who's the *better* quarterback, Peyton Manning or his brother Eli?

SUPERLATIVE   Many Colts fans consider Peyton to be the *greatest* quarterback ever.

The comparative and superlative of most adjectives are formed by adding the endings *-er* and *-est*: slow, *slower, slowest*. Longer adjectives and most adverbs use *more* and *most* (or *less* and *least*): helpful, *more help-ful, most helpful*.

W-5c Modifier Placement

Glossary

Place adjectives, adverbs, and other **MODIFIERS** close to the words they describe.

> *at the seminar*
> ► The doctor explained advances in cancer treatment to the families of patients. at the seminar.

The doctor, not the patients, is at the seminar.

> *Before the anesthesiologist arrived, the*
> ► The doctors assured the patient that they intended to make only two small incisions. before the anesthesiologist arrived.

The original sentence suggests that the incisions will be made without anesthesia, surely not the case.

To avoid ambiguity, position limiting modifiers such as *almost, even, just, merely,* and *only* next to the word or phrase they modify—and be careful that your meaning is clear. See how the placement of *only* results in two completely different meanings.

> *only*
> ► A triple-threat athlete, Martha only played soccer in college.

> *only*
> ► A triple-threat athlete, Martha only played soccer in college.

Dangling modifiers

Modifiers are said to be dangling when they do not clearly modify any particular word in the sentence. You can fix a dangling modifier by adding the subject that the modifier is intended to describe to the main clause or by adding a subject to the modifier itself.

rhetorical situations

genres

processes

strategies

research mla/apa

media/ design

handbook

▶ Speaking simply and respectfully, many people ~~felt comforted by the~~ *the doctor comforted*
~~doctor's~~ presentation. *with his*

The doctor was speaking, not the other people.

▶ While running to catch the bus, the shoulder strap on my fake Balenciaga *I was*
bag broke.

W-6 Articles

A, *an,* and *the* are articles, which tell whether something is indefinite or definite. Use *a* or *an* with nouns whose specific identity is not known to your audience—for example, when you haven't mentioned them before: *I'm reading a great book.* Use *the* with nouns whose specific identity is known to your audience—for instance, a noun that describes something specific, as in *the book on the table,* or something that you've mentioned before, as in *Francesca finally finished writing her book. The book will be published next year.*

W-6a When to Use *a* or *an*

Use *a* or *an* with singular count nouns whose identity is not known to your audience. Count nouns refer to things that can be counted: *one book, two books.* Use *a* before a consonant sound: *a tangerine;* use *an* before a vowel sound: *an orange.*

▶ Do you want to see *a movie* this afternoon?

▶ Yesterday we went to see *a fascinating* documentary about World War II.

▶ There was *an article* about the film in last Saturday's newspaper.

▶ I'd like to watch *an amusing* movie today rather than a serious one.

Do not use *a* or *an* before a noncount noun. Noncount nouns refer to abstractions or masses that can be quantified only with certain modifiers or units: *too much information, two cups of coffee.*

▶ These students could use *some encouragement* from their teacher.

▶ The last thing Portland needs this week is *more rain.*

W-6b When to Use *the*

Use *the* before nouns whose identity is clear to your audience and before superlatives.

▶ Our teacher warned us that *the poem she had assigned* had multiple levels of meaning.

▶ *The Secretary-General of the United Nations* will speak later this morning about *the military crackdown in Myanmar.*

▶ Some of *the fastest runners in the country* compete at *the Penn Relays.*

Do not use *the* with most singular proper nouns (*Judge Judy, Lake Titicaca*), but do use it with most plural proper nouns (*the Adirondack Mountains, the Philippines*).

Do use *the* before singular proper nouns in the following categories.

LARGER BODIES OF WATER   the Arctic Ocean, the Mississippi River

GOVERNMENT BODIES   the United States Congress, the Canadian Parliament

HISTORICAL PERIODS   the Renaissance, the Roman Empire, the Tang Dynasty

LANDMARKS   the Empire State Building, the Taj Mahal

REGIONS   the East Coast, the Middle East, the Mojave Desert

RELIGIOUS ENTITIES, TEXTS, AND LEADERS   the Roman Catholic Church, the Koran, the Dalai Lama

■ rhetorical situations
▲ genres
○ processes
◆ strategies
● research mla/apa
□ media/ design
▨ handbook

W-7 Words That Build Common Ground

A secretary objects to being called one of "the girls." The head of the English department finds the title "chairman" offensive. Why? The secretary is male, the department head is a woman, and those terms don't include them. We can build common ground—or not—by the words we choose, by including others or leaving them out. This section offers tips for using language that is positive and inclusive and that will build common ground with those we wish to reach.

W-7a Avoiding Stereotypes

Stereotypes are generalizations about groups of people and as such can offend because they presume that all members of a group are the same. The writer Geeta Kothari explains how she reacts to a seemingly neutral assumption about Indians: "Indians eat lentils. I understand this as an absolute, a decree from an unidentifiable authority that watches and judges me."

We're all familiar with stereotypes based on sex or race, but stereotypes exist about other characteristics: age, body type, education, income, occupation, physical ability, political affiliation, region, religion, sexual orientation, and more. Be careful not to make any broad generalizations about any group—even neutral or positive ones (that Asian students work hard, for example, or that Republicans are patriotic).

Also, be careful not to call attention to a person's group affiliation if that information is not relevant.

▶ The ~~gay~~ physical therapist who worked the morning shift knew when to let patients rest and when to push them.

W-7b Using Preferred Terms

When you are writing about a group of people, try to use terms that members of that group use themselves. This advice is sometimes easier said than done, because language changes—and words that were commonly used ten years ago may not be in wide use today. Americans of African ancestry, for example, were referred to many years ago as "colored" or "Negro" and then as "black"; today the preferred terminology is "African American."

When you are referring to ethnicities, it's usually best to be as specific as possible. Instead of saying someone is Latin or Hispanic, for instance, it's better to say he or she is Puerto Rican or Dominican or Cuban, as appropriate. The same is true of religions; it's better to specify a religion when you can (Sunni Muslims, Episcopalians, Orthodox Jews). And while "Native American" was once widely used, some people now prefer references to particular tribes (Dakota, Chippewa).

W-7c Editing Out Sexist Language

Sexist language is language that stereotypes or ignores women or men—or that gratuitously calls attention to someone's gender. Try to eliminate such language from your writing.

Default he

Writers once used *he, him,* and other masculine pronouns as a default to refer to people whose sex is unknown. Today such usage is not widely accepted—and is no way to build common ground. Here are some alternatives.

Use both masculine and feminine pronouns joined by *or*. (Note, however, that using this option repeatedly may become awkward.)

▶ Before anyone can leave the country, he *or she* must have a passport or other documentation.

Replace a singular noun or pronoun with a plural noun.

▶ Before ~~anyone~~ *travelers* can leave the country, ~~he~~ *they* must have a passport or other documentation.

Eliminate the pronoun altogether.

> Before ~~anyone can leave~~ the country, ~~he~~ must have a passport or other documentation.

leaving (above "anyone can leave")

a traveler (above "he")

You should also avoid nouns that include *man* when you're referring to people who may be either men or women.

INSTEAD OF	USE
man, mankind	humankind, humanity, humans
salesman	salesperson
fireman	firefighter
congressman	representative, member of congress
male nurse	nurse
female truck driver	truck driver

P Punctuation / Mechanics

rhetorical situations

genres

processes

strategies

research mla/apa

media/ design

handbook

P-1 Commas

Commas matter. Consider, for instance, the title of the best-selling book *Eats, Shoots & Leaves*. The cover of this book shows two pandas, one with a gun in its paw. Is the book about a panda that dines and then fires a gun and exits? In fact, it's a book about punctuation, and the confusion raised by its title shows how commas affect meaning. This section shows you when and where to use commas in your own writing.

P-1a To Join Independent Clauses with *and, but,* and Other Coordinating Conjunctions

Put a comma before the **COORDINATING CONJUNCTIONS** *and, but, for, nor, or, so,* and *yet* when they connect two **INDEPENDENT CLAUSES**. The comma signals that one idea is ending and another is beginning.

HB-31
HB-6

▶ I do not love Shakespeare, but I still have those books.
        —Rick Bragg, "All Over But the Shoutin' "

▶ Most people think the avocado is a vegetable, yet it is actually a fruit.

▶ They awarded the blue ribbon to Susanna, and Sarah got the red ribbon.

Without the comma, readers might first think that both girls got the blue ribbon.

Although some writers omit the comma, especially with short independent clauses, you'll never be wrong to include it.

▶ I was smart, and I knew it.   —Shannon Nichols, " 'Proficiency' "

You do not need a comma between the verbs when a single subject performs two actions—but you need commas when a third verb is added.

▶ I enrolled in a three-month submersion program in Mexico and emerged able to speak like a sixth-grader with a C average.
        —Tanya Barrientos, "Se Habla Español"

▶ Augustine wrote extensively about his mother/but mentioned his father only briefly.

▶ Kim had bought the sod, delivered it, and rolled it out before we got home.

P-1b To Set Off Introductory Words

HB-6–7

Use a comma after an introductory word, **PHRASE**, or **CLAUSE** to mark the end of the introduction and the start of the main part of the sentence.

▶ Consequently, our celebration of Howard Stern, Don Imus, and other heroes of "shock radio" might be evidence of a certain loss of moral focus.
　　　　　　　　　　　　　　　　　　—Stephen L. Carter, "Just Be Nice"

▶ On the other hand, opponents of official English remind us that without legislation we have managed to get over ninety-seven percent of the residents of this country to speak the national language.
　　　　　　　—Dennis Baron, "Don't Make English Official—Ban It Instead"

▶ Even ignoring the extreme poles of the economic spectrum, we find enormous class differences in the life-styles among the haves, the have-nots, and the have-littles.　　—Gregory Mantsios, "Class in America—2003"

▶ When Miss Emily Grierson died, our whole town went to her funeral.
　　　　　　　　　　　　　　　　　—William Faulkner, "A Rose for Emily"

Some writers don't use a comma after a short introductory word, phrase, or clause, but it's never wrong to include one.

P-1c To Separate Items in a Series

Use a comma to separate the items in a series.

▶ I spend a great deal of time thinking about the power of language—the way it can evoke an emotion, a visual image, a complex idea, or a simple truth.　　　　　　　　　　　　　　　　—Amy Tan, "Mother Tongue"

rhetorical situations　　genres　　processes　　strategies　　research mla/apa　　media/ design　　handbook

Though some writers leave out the comma between the final two items in a series, this omission can confuse readers. It's never wrong to include the final comma.

▶ Nadia held a large platter of sandwiches—egg salad, peanut butter, ham, and cheese.

Without the last comma, it's not clear whether there are three or four kinds of sandwiches on the platter.

P-1d To Set Off Nonrestrictive Elements

A nonrestrictive element is one that isn't needed to understand the sentence; it should be set off with commas. A restrictive element is one that is needed to understand the sentence and therefore should not be set off with commas.

NONRESTRICTIVE

The inspiration for strawberry shortcake can be traced to American Indians, who prepared a sweetened bread from strawberries and cornmeal.

—*Martha Stewart Living*

The detail about the Indians' preparation of sweetened bread adds information, but it is not essential to the meaning of the sentence and thus is set off with a comma.

RESTRICTIVE

Navajo is the Athabaskan language that is spoken in the Southwest by the Navajo people.

The detail about where Navajo is spoken is essential: Navajo is not the only Athabaskan language; it is the Athabaskan language that is spoken in the Southwest.

Restrictive and nonrestrictive elements can be clauses, phrases, or single words.

CLAUSES

▶ He always drove Chryslers, which are made in America.

▶ He always drove cars that were made in America.

PHRASES

▶ I fumble in the dark, trying to open the mosquito netting around my bed.
— Chanrithy Him, "When Broken Glass Floats"

▶ I see my mother clutching my baby sister.
— Chanrithy Him, "When Broken Glass Floats"

WORDS

▶ At 8:59, Flight 175 passenger Brian David Sweeney tried to call his wife, Julie.
— The 9/11 Commission, "The Hijacking of United 175"

▶ At 9:00, Lee Hanson received a second call from his son Peter.
— The 9/11 Commission, "The Hijacking of United 175"

Sweeney had only one wife, so her name provides extra but nonessential information. Hanson presumably had more than one son, so it is essential to specify which son called.

P-1e To Set Off Parenthetical Information

Information that interrupts the flow of a sentence needs to be set off with commas.

▶ Bob's conduct, most of us will immediately respond, was gravely wrong.
— Peter Singer, "The Singer Solution to World Poverty"

▶ With as little as two servings of vegetables a day, it seems to me, you can improve your eating habits.

P-1f To Set Off Transitional Expressions

277

TRANSITIONS such as *thus, nevertheless, for example,* and *in fact* help connect sentences or parts of sentences. They are usually set off with commas. When a transition connects two independent clauses, it is preceded by either a period or a semicolon and is followed by a comma.

► [S]torytelling always includes the audience, the listeners. In fact, a great deal of the story is believed to be inside the listener; the storyteller's role is to draw the story out of the listeners.

—Leslie Marmon Silko, "Language and Literature from a Pueblo Indian Perspective"

► There are few among the poor who speak of themselves as lower class; instead, they refer to their race, ethnic group, or geographic location.

—Gregory Mantsios, "Class in America—2003"

P-1g To Set Off Direct Quotations

Use commas to set off quoted words from the speaker or the source.

► Pa shouts back, "I just want to know where the gunfire is coming from."

—Chanrithy Him, "When Broken Glass Floats"

► "My children," my mother answered in a clear, curt tone, "will be at the top of their classes in two weeks."   —Tanya Barrientos, "Se Habla Español"

► "Death and life are in the power of the tongue," says the proverb.

P-1h To Set Off Direct Address, *Yes* or *No,* Interjections, and Tag Questions

DIRECT ADDRESS	"Yes, Virginia, there really is a Santa Claus."
YES OR **NO**	No, you cannot replace the battery on your iPhone. Apple has to do it for you.
INTERJECTION	Oh, a Prius. How long did you have to wait to get it?
TAG QUESTION	That wasn't so hard, was it?

P-1i With Addresses, Place Names, and Dates

▶ Send contributions to Human Rights Campaign, 1640 Rhode Island Ave., Washington, DC 20036.

▶ Athens, Georgia, has been famous since the 1970s for its thriving music scene.

▶ On July 2, 1937, the aviator Amelia Earhart disappeared over the Pacific Ocean while trying to make the first round-the-world flight at the equator.

Omit the commas, however, if you invert the date (*On 2 July 1937*) or if you give only the month and year (*In July 1937*).

P-1j Checking for Unnecessary Commas

Commas have so many uses that it's easy to add them when they are not needed. Here are some situations when you should not use a comma.

Between subject and verb

▶ What the organizers of the 1969 Woodstock concert did not anticipate/ was the turnout.

▶ The event's promoters/ turned down John Lennon's offer to play with his Plastic Ono Band.

Between verb and object

▶ Pollsters wondered/ how they had so poorly predicted the winner of the 1948 presidential election.

▶ Virtually every prediction indicated/ that Thomas Dewey would defeat Harry Truman.

After a coordinating conjunction

▶ The College Board reported a decline in SAT scores and/ attributed the decline to changes in "student test-taking patterns."

rhetorical situations
genres
processes
strategies
research mla/apa
media/ design
handbook

▶ The SAT was created to provide an objective measure of academic potential, but/ studies in the 1980s found racial and socioeconomic biases in some test questions.

After like *or* such as

▶ Many American-born authors, such as/ Henry James, Ezra Pound, and F. Scott Fitzgerald, lived as expatriates in Europe.

With a question mark or an exclamation point

▶ Why would any nation have a monarch in an era of democracy?/ you might ask yourself.

▶ "O, be some other name!/" exclaims Juliet.

P-2 Semicolons

Semicolons offer one way to connect two closely related thoughts. Look, for example, at Martha Stewart's advice about how to tell if fruit is ripe: "A perfectly ripened fruit exudes a subtle but sweet fragrance from the stem end, appears plump, and has deeply colored skin; avoid those that have wrinkles, bruises, or tan spots." Stewart could have used a period, but the semicolon shows the connection between what to look for and what to avoid when buying peaches or plums.

P-2a Between Independent Clauses

Closely related independent clauses are most often joined with a **COMMA** plus *and* or another **COORDINATING CONJUNCTION**. If the two clauses are closely related and don't need a conjunction to signal the relationship, they may be linked with a semicolon.

HB-57–63

HB-31

▶ The silence deepened; the room chilled.
                    —Wayson Choy, "The Ten Thousand Things"

▶ The life had not flowed out of her; it had been seized.
— Valerie Steiker, "Our Mother's Face"

Note that a period would work in either of the examples above, but the semicolon suggests a stronger connection between the two independent clauses.

277

Another option is to use a semicolon with a **TRANSITION** that clarifies the relationship between the two independent clauses. Put a comma after the transition.

▶ There are few among the poor who speak of themselves as lower class; instead, they refer to their race, ethnic group, or geographic location.
— Gregory Mantsios, "Class in America—2003"

P-2b In a Series with Commas

Use semicolons to separate items in a series when one or more of the items contain commas.

▶ There are images of a few students: Erwin Petschaur, a muscular German boy with a strong accent; Dave Sanchez, who was good at math; and Sheila Wilkes, everyone's curly-haired heartthrob.
— Mike Rose, "Potato Chips and Stars"

P-2c Checking for Mistakes with Semicolons

Use a comma, not a semicolon, to set off an introductory clause.

▶ When the sun finally sets; everyone gathers at the lake to watch the fireworks.

HB-74–75

Use a **COLON**, not a semicolon, to introduce a list.

▶ Every American high school student should know that the U.S. Constitution contains three sections; preamble, articles, and amendments.

rhetorical situations

genres

processes

strategies

research mla/apa

media/ design

handbook

P-3 End Punctuation

She married him. She married him? She married him! In each of these three sentences, the words are the same, but the end punctuation completely changes the meaning, from a simple statement to a bemused question to an emphatic exclamation. This section will help you use periods, question marks, and exclamation points in your writing.

P-3a Periods

Use a period to end a sentence that makes a statement.

▶ Rose Emily Meraglio came to the United States from southern Italy as a little girl in the early 1920s and settled with her family in Altoona, Pennsylvania. —Mike Rose, "The Working Life of a Waitress"

An indirect question, which reports something someone else has asked, ends with a period, not a question mark.

▶ Presidential candidates are often asked how they will provide affordable health care to all Americans?.

When a sentence ends with an abbreviation that has its own period, do not add another period.

▶ She signed all her letters Eileen Kinch, Ph.D./

P-3b Question Marks

Use a question mark to end a direct question.

▶ Did I think that because I was a minority student jobs would just come looking for me? What was I thinking?
                —Richard Rodriguez, "None of This Is Fair"

Use a period rather than a question mark to end an indirect question.

▶ Aunt Vivian often asked what Jesus would do⌃.

P-3c Exclamation Points

Use an exclamation point to express strong emotion or add emphasis to a statement or command. Exclamation points should be used sparingly, however, or they may undercut your credibility.

▶ "Keith," we shrieked as the car drove away, "Keith, we love you!"
—Susan Jane Gilman, "Mick Jagger Wants Me"

When the words themselves are emotional, an exclamation point is often unnecessary and a period is sufficient.

▶ It was so close, so low, so huge and fast, so intent on its target that I swear to you, I swear to you, I felt the vengeance and rage emanating from the plane.
—Debra Fontaine, "Witnessing"

P-4 Quotation Marks

"YMCA" "Two thumbs up!" "Frankly, my dear, I don't give a damn." These are just some of the ways that quotation marks are used—to punctuate a song title, to cite praise for a movie, to set off dialogue. In college writing, you will use quotation marks frequently to acknowledge when you are you are using words you've taken from others. This section will show you how to use quotation marks correctly and appropriately.

P-4a Direct Quotations

Use quotation marks to enclose words spoken or written by others.

▶ "Nothing against Tom, but Johnny may be the bigger star now," says director John Waters.   —Sean Smith, "Johnny Depp: Unlikely Superstar"

▶ Newt Gringrich and Jesse Jackson have both pounded nails and raised funds for Habitat for Humanity. This is what Millard Fuller calls the "theology of the hammer."

　　　　　　　　　　　—Diana George, "Changing the Face of Poverty"

When you introduce or follow a quotation with words like *he said* or *she claimed*, you need a comma between the verb and the quoted material.

▶ When my mother reported that Mr. Tomkey did not believe in television, my father said, "Well, good for him. I don't know that I believe in it either."

　　　"That's exactly how I feel," my mother said, and then my parents watched the news, and whatever came on after the news.

　　　　　　　　　　　　　　　—David Sedaris, "Us and Them"

You do not need any punctuation between *that* and a quotation.

▶ We were assigned to write one essay agreeing or disagreeing with George Orwell's statement that/ "the slovenliness of our language makes it easier for us to have foolish thoughts."

In dialogue, insert a new pair of quotation marks to signal each change of speaker.

▶ At the school's office the registrar frowned when we arrived.

　　　"You people. Your children are always behind, and you have the nerve to bring them in late?"

　　　"My children," my mother answered in a clear, curt tone, "will be at the top of their classes in two weeks."

　　　　　　　　　　　　　　—Tanya Barrientos, "Se Habla Español"

P-4b Long Quotations

Long quotations should be set off without quotation marks as **BLOCK QUOTATIONS**. If you are following **MLA STYLE**, set off five or more typed lines of prose (or four or more lines of poetry) as a block, indented ten spaces (or one inch) from the left margin.

411

428–76

Biographer David McCullough describes Truman's railroad campaign as follows:

> No president in history had ever gone so far in quest of support from the people, or with less cause for the effort, to judge by informed opinion. . . . As a test of his skills and judgment as a professional politician, not to say his stamina and disposition at age sixty-four, it would be like no other experience in his long, often difficult career, as he himself understood perfectly. (655)

477–519

If you are following **APA STYLE,** format a quotation of forty words or more block style, indented five spaces (or one-half inch) from the left.

> In an article in *The Nation*, Maggie Cutler questions the common assumption that media violence causes some children's violent behavior:
> Do temperamentally violent kids seek out shows that express feelings they already have, or are they in it for the adrenaline boost? Do the sort of parents who let kids pig out on gore tend to do more than their share of other hurtful things that encourage violent behavior?

P-4c Titles of Short Works

Use quotation marks to enclose the titles of articles, chapters, essays, short stories, poems, songs, and episodes of television series. Titles of books, films, newspapers, and other longer works should be in **ITALICS** rather than enclosed in quotation marks.

HB-82–84

▶ In "Unfriendly Skies Are No Match for El Al," Vivienne Walt, a writer for *USA Today,* describes her experience flying with this airline.
> —Andy McDonie, "Airport Security"

Note that the title of the newspaper is italicized, whereas the newspaper article title takes quotation marks.

▶ With every page of Edgar Allan Poe's story "The Tell-Tale Heart," my own heart beat faster.

▶ Rita Dove's poem "Dawn Revisited" contains vivid images that appeal to the senses of sight, sound, smell, and taste.

rhetorical situations · genres · processes · strategies · research mla/apa · media/design · handbook

P-4d Single Quotation Marks

When you quote a passage that already contains quotation marks, whether they enclose a quotation or a title, change the inner ones to single quotation marks.

▶ Debra Johnson notes that according to Marilyn J. Adams, "effective reading instruction is based on 'direct instruction in phonics, focusing on the orthographic regularities of English.' "

▶ Certain essays and stories are so good (or so popular) that they are included in almost every anthology. The 2004 edition of *The Norton Reader* notes, for example, "Some essays—Martin Luther King Jr.'s 'Letter from Birmingham Jail' and Jonathan Swift's 'A Modest Proposal,' for example—are constant favorites."

P-4e With Other Punctuation

The following examples show how to use other punctuation marks inside or outside quotation marks.

Commas and periods

Put commas and periods inside closing quotation marks.

▶ "On the newsstand, the cover is acting as a poster, an ad for what's inside," she said. "The loyal reader is looking for what makes the magazine exceptional."
    —Katharine Q. Seelye, "Lucid Numbers on Glossy Pages!"

When there is parenthetical **DOCUMENTATION** after an end quotation mark, the period goes after the parentheses.
425–27

▶ Dewey himself said, "When you're leading, don't talk" (qtd. in McCullough 672).
    —Dylan Borchers, "Against the Odds"

Semicolons and colons

Put semicolons and colons outside closing quotation marks.

▶ No elder stands behind our young to say, "Folks have fought and died for
your right to pierce your face, so do it right"; no community exists that can
model for a young person the responsible use of the "right"; for the right,
even if called self-expression, comes from no source other than desire.

—Stephen L. Carter, "Just Be Nice"

▶ According to James Garbarino, author of *Lost Boys: Why Our Sons Turn
Violent and How We Can Save Them*, it makes no sense to talk about
violent media as a direct cause of youth violence. Rather, he says, "it
depends": Media violence is a risk factor that, working in concert with
others, can exacerbate bad behavior.

—Maggie Cutler, "Whodunit—The Media?"

Question marks and exclamation points

Put question marks and exclamation points inside closing quotation
marks if they are part of the quotation but outside if they apply to the
whole sentence.

▶ Then she began to talk more loudly. "What he want, I come to New York
tell him front of his boss, you cheating me?"

—Amy Tan, "Mother Tongue"

▶ How many people know the words to "Louie, Louie"?

P-4f Checking for Mistakes with Quotation Marks

HB-36–37

Avoid using quotation marks to identify **SLANG**, to indicate irony, or
to emphasize a word. Remove the quotation marks or substitute a better word.

SLANG   Appearing ~~"~~hip~~"~~ is important to many parents in New York.

IRONY   Natalie was more interested in ~~"facilitating"~~ *delegating tasks* than in doing
work herself.

EMPHASIS   The woman explained that she is /only/ a masseuse, not the owner of the health club.

Do not enclose indirect quotations in quotation marks.

▶ Even before winning her fourth Wimbledon singles title, Venus Williams said that /she expected to play well./

P-5 Apostrophes

McDonald's: "*I'm lovin' it*" proclaims a recent advertisement, demonstrating two common uses of the apostrophe: to show ownership (*McDonald's*) and to mark missing letters (*I'm, lovin'*). This section offers guidelines on these and other common uses for apostrophes.

P-5a Possessives

Use an apostrophe to make a word possessive: *Daniel Craig's eye, someone else's problem, the children's playground.*

Singular nouns.   To form the possessive of most singular nouns, add an apostrophe and -s.

▶ Some bloggers are getting press credentials for this summer's Republican Convention.   —Lev Grossman, "Meet Joe Blog"

▶ The magical thinking of denial became Ms. Didion's companion.
—Michiko Kakutani, "The End of Life As She Knew It"

▶ Bill Gates's philanthropic efforts focus on health care and education.

If adding -'s makes a word hard to pronounce, use only an apostrophe.

▶ Euripides' plays are more realistic than those of Aeschylus and Sophocles.

Plural nouns.   To form the possessive of a plural noun not ending in -s, add an apostrophe and -s. For plural nouns that end in -s, add only an apostrophe.

▶ Are women**'s** minds different from men**'s** minds?
—Evelyn Fox Keller, "Women in Science"

▶ In the wake of his parents**'** recent divorce, he didn't turn to drugs or alcohol but instead fell back on his friends and is now directing a movie he wrote.   —Ben Leever, "In Defense of *Dawson's Creek*"

▶ Did you hear that Laurence Strauss is getting married? The reception will be at the Strausses**'** home.

***Something, everyone,* and other indefinite pronouns.**   To form the possessive of an indefinite pronoun, add an apostrophe and -s. Indefinite pronouns do not refer to specific persons or things: *anyone, everything, nobody,* and so on.

▶ Clarabelle was everyone**'s** favorite clown.

Joint possession.   To show that two or more individuals possess something together, use the possessive form for the last noun only.

▶ Carlson and Ventura**'s** book is an introduction to Latino writers for English-speaking adolescents.

To show individual possession, make each noun possessive.

▶ The winners of the screenwriter**'s** and director**'s** Oscars were easy to predict.

Compound nouns.   To show possession for a compound noun, make the last word possessive.

▶ The surgeon general**'s** report persuaded many Americans to stop smoking.

P-5b Contractions

An apostrophe in a contraction indicates where letters have been omitted.

▶ "Let's do it, Susie," she said. "We're really going to do it."
—Susan Jane Gilman, "Mick Jagger Wants Me"

Let's is a contraction of *let us; we're* is a contraction of *we are.*

P-5c Plurals

Most writers add an apostrophe and -s to pluralize numbers, letters, and words discussed as words, but usage is changing and some writers now leave out the apostrophe. Either way is acceptable, as long as you are consistent. Notice that you need to italicize the number, letter, or word but not the plural ending.

▶ The resolution passed when there were more *aye*'s than *nay*'s.

▶ The winning hand had three *7*'s.

▶ The admissions officers at Brown spoke enthusiastically about their no-grades option—and then told us we needed mostly *A*'s to get in.

Most writers omit the apostrophe when pluralizing decades.

▶ During the 1950s, the civil rights movement and environmentalism began to develop in the United States.

To make an abbreviation plural, add only an -s.

▶ How many computers and TVs does the average American family have in its home?

▶ The United States has been seeking comprehensive free trade agreements (FTAs) with the Middle Eastern nations most firmly on the path to reform.
—The 9/11 Commission, "Prevent the Continued Growth of Islamist Terrorism"

P-5d Checking for Mistakes with Apostrophes

Do not use an apostrophe in the following situations.

With plural nouns that are not possessive

> ▶ Both ~~cellist's~~ *cellists* played encores.

With his, hers, ours, yours, *and* theirs

> ▶ Look at all the lettuce. ~~Our's~~ *Ours* is organic. Is ~~your's?~~ *yours?*

With the possessive its

> ▶ It's an unusual building; ~~it's~~ *its* style has been described as postmodern, but it fits beautifully with the gothic buildings on our campus.

> It's is a contraction meaning it is; its is the possessive form of it.

P-6 Other Punctuation Marks

Some carpenters can do their jobs using only a hammer and a saw, but most rely on additional tools. The same is true of writers: you can get along with just a few punctuation marks, but having some others in your toolbox—colons, dashes, parentheses, brackets, ellipses, and slashes—can help you say what you want to say in your writing and can help readers follow what you write. This section can help you use these other punctuation marks effectively.

P-6a Colons

Colons are used to direct readers' attention to words that follow the colon—an explanation or elaboration, a list, a quotation, and so on.

▶ What I remember best, strangely enough, are the two things I couldn't understand and over the years grew to hate: grammar lessons and mathematics.   —Mike Rose, "Potato Chips and Stars"

▶ I sized him up as fast as possible: tight black velvet pants pulled over his boots, black jacket, a red-green-yellow scarf slashed around his neck.
                              —Susan Jane Gilman, "Mick Jagger Wants Me"

▶ She also voices some common concerns: "The product should be safe, it should be easily accessible, and it should be low-priced."
                              —Dara Mayers, "Our Bodies, Our Lives"

▶ Fifteen years after the release of the Carnegie report, College Board surveys reveal data are no different: test scores still correlate strongly with family income.   —Gregory Mantsios, "Class in America—2003"

Colons are also used after the salutation in a business letter, in ratios, between titles and subtitles, between city and publisher in bibliographies, and between chapter and verse in biblical references.

▶ Dear President Michaels:

▶ For best results, add water to the powder in a 3:1 ratio.

▶ *The Last Campaign: How Harry Truman Won the 1948 Election*

▶ New York: Norton, 2008.

▶ "Death and life are in the power of the tongue" (Proverbs 18:21).

P-6b Dashes

You can create a dash by typing two hyphens (--) with no spaces before or after or by selecting the em dash from the symbol menu of your word processor.

Use dashes to set off material you want to emphasize. Unlike colons, dashes can appear not only after an independent clause but also at other points in a sentence. To set off material at the end of a sentence, use one dash; to set off material in the middle of the sentence, place a dash before and after the words you want to emphasize.

▶ After that, the roller coaster rises and falls, slowing down and speeding up—all on its own.
—Cathi Eastman and Becky Burrell, "The Science of Screams"

▶ It did not occur to me—possibly because I am an American—that there could be people anywhere who had never seen a Negro.
—James Baldwin, "Stranger in the Village"

Dashes are often used to signal a shift in tone or thought.

▶ Was it Dorothy Parker who said, "The best way to keep children home is to make the home atmosphere pleasant—and let the air out of the tires"?

Keep in mind that dashes are most effective if they are used only when material needs particular emphasis. Too many dashes can interfere with the flow and clarity of your writing.

P-6c Parentheses

Use parentheses to enclose supplemental details and digressions.

▶ When I was a child, attending grade school in Washington, D.C., we took classroom time to study manners. Not only the magic words "please" and "thank you" but more complicated etiquette questions, like how to answer the telephone ("Carter residence, Stephen speaking") and how to set the table (we were quizzed on whether knife blades point in or out).
—Stephen L. Carter, "Just Be Nice"

▶ In their apartments they have the material possessions that indicate success (a VCR, a color television), even if it means that they do without necessities and plunge into debt to buy these items.
—Diana George, "Changing the Face of Poverty"

▶ Before participating in the trials, Seeta and Ratna (not their real names) knew nothing about H.I.V.
—Dara Mayers, "Our Bodies, Our Lives"

P-6d Brackets

Put brackets around words that you insert or change in a QUOTATION.

412

▶ As Senator Reid explained, "She [Nancy Pelosi] realizes that you cannot make everyone happy."

If you are quoting a source that contains an error, put the Latin word *sic* in brackets after the error to indicate that the mistake is in the original source.

▶ Warehouse has been around for 30 years and has 263 stores, suggesting a large fan base. The chain sums up its appeal thus: "styley [*sic*], confident, sexy, glamorous, edgy, clean and individual, with it's [*sic*] finger on the fashion pulse."

—Anne Ashworth, "Chain Reaction: Warehouse"

P-6e Ellipses

Ellipses are three spaced dots that indicate an omission or a pause. Use ellipses to show that you have omitted words within a QUOTATION. If you omit a complete sentence or more in the middle of a quoted passage, put a period before the three dots.

411

▶ The Lux ad's visual content . . . supports its verbal message. Several demure views of Irene Dunne emphasize her "pearly-smooth skin," the top one framed by a large heart shape. In all the photos, Dunne wears a feathery, feminine collar, giving her a birdlike appearance: she is a bird of paradise or an ornament. At the bottom of the ad, we see a happy Dunne being cuddled and admired by a man.

▶ The Lux ad's visual content, like Resinol's, supports its verbal message. Several demure views of Irene Dunne emphasize her "pearly-smooth skin," the top one framed by a large heart shape. . . . At the bottom of the ad, we see a happy Dunne being cuddled and admired by a man.

—Doug Lantry, " 'Stay Sweet As You Are': An Analysis of Change and Continuity in Advertising Aimed at Women"

P-6f Slashes

In quoting two or three lines of poetry, use slashes to show where one line ends and the next begins. Put a space before and after each slash.

> ▶ In the opening lines of the poem, he warns the reader to "Lift not the painted veil which those who live **/** Call Life" (1–2).
> 　　　　　　—Stephanie Huff, "Metaphor and Society in Shelley's 'Sonnet' "

411 ●

When you quote more than three lines of poetry, set them up as a **BLOCK QUOTATION, MLA STYLE.**

> The chorus warns Oedipus,
> 　　　We look at this man's words and yours, my king,
> 　　　and we find both have spoken them in anger.
> 　　　We need no angry words but only thought
> 　　　how we may best hit the God's meaning for us. (446–449)

P-7 Hyphens

If your mother gives you much needed advice, has she given you a great deal of advice that you needed, or advice that you needed badly? What about a psychiatry experiment that used thirty five year old subjects: were there 35 subjects who were a year old? 30 subjects who were 5 years old? Or an unspecified number of 35-year-old subjects? In each case, hyphens could clear up the confusion. This section provides tips for when to use hyphens and when to omit them.

P-7a Compound Words

Compound words can be two words (*ground zero*), hyphenated (*self-esteem*), or one word (*outsource*). Check a dictionary, and if a compound word is not there, assume that it is two words.

Compound adjectives

A compound adjective is made up of two or more words. Most compound adjectives take a hyphen before a noun.

▶ a well-known trombonist

▶ a foul-smelling river

Do not use a hyphen to connect an -ly adverb and an adjective.

▶ a carefully executed plan

A compound adjective after a noun is usually easy to read without a hyphen; insert a hyphen only if the compound is unclear without it.

▶ The river has become foul smelling in recent years.

Prefixes and suffixes

A hyphen usually isn't needed after a prefix or before a suffix (*preschool, antislavery, counterattack, catlike, citywide*). However, hyphens are necessary in the following situations.

WITH *GREAT-*, *SELF-*, *-ELECT* great-aunt, self-hate, president-elect

WITH CAPITAL LETTERS anti-American, post-Soviet literature

WITH NUMBERS post-9/11, the mid-1960s

TO AVOID DOUBLE AND TRIPLE LETTERS anti-intellectualism, ball-like

TO CLARIFY MEANING re-creation (a second creation) *but* recreation (play)

Numbers

Simple fractions and spelled-out numbers from 21 to 99 take hyphens.

▶ three-quarters of their income

▶ thirty-five-year-old subjects

P-7b At the End of a Line

Use a hyphen to divide a multisyllabic word that does not fit on one line. (A one-syllable word is never hyphenated.) Divide words between syllables as given in a dictionary, after a prefix, or before a suffix. Divide compound words between the parts of the compound if possible. Do not leave only one letter at the end or the beginning of a line.

op-er-a-tion   knot-ty   main-stream

Dividing Internet addresses

428–76   **MLA STYLE** suggests that you divide an Internet address only after a slash, with no hyphen (readers might think the hyphen is part of the address).

P-8 Capitalization

Capital letters are an important signal, either that a new sentence is beginning or that a specific person, place, or brand is being discussed. Capitalize *Carol* and it's clear that you're referring to a person; write *carol*, and readers will know you're writing about a song sung at Christmas. This section offers guidelines to help you know what to capitalize and when.

P-8a Proper Nouns and Common Nouns

Proper nouns begin with a capital letter, whereas common nouns begin with a lowercase letter.

PROPER NOUNS	COMMON NOUNS
Sanjay Gupta	a doctor
Senator Biden	a U.S. senator
Uncle Daniel	my uncle

PROPER NOUNS	COMMON NOUNS
France	a republic
Mississippi River	a river
the West Coast	a coast
Christianity	a religion
Allah	a god
the Torah	a sacred text
Central Intelligence Agency	an agency
U.S. Congress	the U.S. government
Ohio University	a university
Composition 101	a writing course
World War II	a war
July	summer
the Middle Ages	the fourteenth century
Kleenex	tissues

Adjectives derived from proper nouns, especially the names of people and places, are usually capitalized: *Shakespearean, Swedish, Chicagoan.* There are exceptions to this rule, however, such as *french fries, roman numeral,* and *congressional.* Consult your dictionary if you are unsure whether an adjective should be capitalized.

Many dictionaries capitalize the terms *Internet, Net,* and *World Wide Web,* but you'll see variations such as *Website* and *website.* Whether you capitalize or not, be consistent throughout a paper.

P-8b Titles before a Person's Name

A professional title is capitalized when it appears before a person's name but not when it appears after a proper noun or alone.

Senator Dianne Feinstein   Dianne Feinstein, the California senator

P-8c The First Word of a Sentence

Capitalize the first word of each sentence of your own and each quoted sentence, with one exception: when *that* introduces the quotation, you need not capitalize the first word.

▶ Writing about the English language, George Orwell noted, "It becomes ugly and inaccurate because our thoughts are foolish."

▶ Writing about the English language, George Orwell noted that "it becomes ugly and inaccurate because our thoughts are foolish."

Interrupted quotations

Capitalize the second part of an interrupted quotation only if it begins a new sentence.

▶ "It was just as nice," she sobbed, "as I hoped and dreamed it would be."
—Joan Didion, "Marrying Absurd"

▶ "On the newsstand, the cover is acting as a poster, an ad for what's inside," she said. "The loyal reader is looking for what makes the magazine exceptional."   —Katharine Q. Seelye, "Lurid Numbers on Glossy Pages!"

P-8d Titles and Subtitles

Capitalize the first and last words and all other important words of a title and subtitle. Do not capitalize less important words such as ARTICLES, COORDINATING CONJUNCTIONS, and PREPOSITIONS.

HB-51–52
HB-31
HB-39–40

"Give Peace a Chance"

Vanity Fair

Naked Economics: Undressing the Dismal Science

P-9 Italics

Italic type tells us to read words a certain way. Think of the difference between fresh air and *Fresh Air*, or between time and *Time*. In each case, the italicized version tells us it's a specific radio show or magazine. This section provides guidelines on using italics in your writing.

P-9a Titles of Long Works

Titles and subtitles of long works should appear in italics (or under-lined). A notable exception is sacred writing such as the Qur'an or the Old Testament.

BOOKS   *The Norton Field Guide to Writing, War and Peace*
PERIODICALS   *Newsweek, Teen Vogue, College English*
NEWSPAPERS   *Los Angeles Times*
PLAYS   *Medea, Six Degrees of Separation*
LONG POEMS   *The Odyssey, Paradise Lost*
FILMS AND VIDEOS   *Good Night and Good Luck, Warplane*
MUSICAL WORKS OR ALBUMS   *The Four Seasons, Rubber Soul*
RADIO AND TV SERIES   *Fresh Air, Survivor*
PAINTINGS, SCULPTURES   the *Mona Lisa*, Michelangelo's *David*
DANCES BY A CHOREOGRAPHER   Mark Morris's *Gloria*
SOFTWARE   *Microsoft Visual Studio 6.0*
SHIPS, SPACESHIPS   *Queen Mary, Challenger*

A short work, such as a short story, an article, an episode of a series, or a song, takes **QUOTATION MARKS**.

HB-66–71

P-9b Words as Words

Italicize a word you are discussing as a word. The same practice applies to numbers as numbers, letters as letters, and symbols as symbols.

▶ In those 236 words, you will hear the word *dedicate* five times.
—William Safire, "A Spirit Reborn"

▶ Most American dictionaries call for one *t* in the word *benefited.*

▶ All computer codes consist of some combination of *0*'s and *1*'s.

Some writers use quotation marks rather than italics to signal words discussed as words.

> He asks me for my name and I supply it, rolling the double "r" in "Barrientos" like a pro.   —Tanya Barrientos, "Se Habla Español"

P-9c Non-English Words

Use italics for an unfamiliar word or phrase in a language other than English. Do not italicize proper nouns.

> *Verstehen*, a concept often associated with Max Weber, is the sociologist's attempt to understand human actions from the actor's point of view.

If the word or phrase has become part of everyday English or has an entry in English-language dictionaries, it does not need italics.

> An ad hoc committee should be formed to assess the university's use of fossil fuels and ways to incorporate alternative energy sources.

> The plot of *Jane Eyre* follows the conventions of a bildungsroman, or a coming-of-age story.

P-9d For Emphasis

You can use italics occasionally to lend emphasis to a word or phrase, but do not overuse them.

> It is, perhaps, as much what Shakespeare did *not* write as what he did that seems to indicate something seriously wrong with his marriage.
>   —Stephen Greenblatt, "Shakespeare on Marriage"

> Despite a physical beauty that had . . . hordes of teenage girls (and a few boys) dreaming of touching his hair *just once*, Depp escaped from the Hollywood star machine.   —Sean Smith, "Johnny Depp"

P-10 Abbreviations

MTV. USA. OC. DNA. fwiw. D.I.Y. These are some common abbreviations, shortcuts to longer words and phrases. This section will help you use abbreviations appropriately in academic writing.

You can use common abbreviations such as *DNA, NAFTA*, and *HIV* in academic writing if you are sure your readers will recognize them. If your readers might not be familiar with an abbreviation, include the full name the first time with the abbreviation in parentheses immediately after. Throughout the rest of the paper, you can use the abbreviations alone.

▶ In a recent press release, officials from the international organization Médicins Sans Frontières (MSF) stressed the need for more effective tuberculosis drugs.

P-10a With Names

Most titles are abbreviated when they're used before or after a name.

Mr. Ed Stanford	Ed Stanford, Jr.
Dr. Ralph Lopez	Ralph Lopez, MD
Prof. Susan Miller	Susan Miller, PhD

Do not abbreviate job titles that are not attached to a name.

▶ The ~~RN~~ who worked with trauma victims specialized in cardiac care.
    nurse

P-10b With Numbers

The following abbreviations can be used when attached to a number.

632 BC ("before Christ")

344 BCE ("before the common era")

AD 800 ("*anno Domini*")

800 CE ("common era")

10:30 AM (or a.m.)

7:00 PM (or p.m.)

Notice that *BC*, *BCE*, and *CE* follow the date, *AD* precedes the date. Remember that the above abbreviations cannot be used without a date or time.

> ▶ By early *afternoon,* ~~p.m.,~~ all prospective subjects for the experiment had checked in.

P-10c In Notes and Documentation

Abbreviations such as *etc.*, *i.e.*, and *et al.* are not acceptable in the body of a paper but are acceptable in footnotes or endnotes, in-text documentation, and bibliographies.

P-11 Numbers

Numbers may be written with numerals or words: 97 percent or ninety-seven percent. This section presents general rules for when to use numerals and when to spell numbers out.

Spell out numbers and fractions that you can write in one or two words (*thirteen, thirty-seven, thirty thousand, two-thirds*). Any number at the beginning of a sentence should be spelled out as well.

> ▶ Yohji Yamamoto designed *seventy-five* ~~75~~ pieces for his first Paris collection.

> ▶ Exceeding expectations, the number of journalists there approached ~~10,000.~~ *ten thousand.*

> ▶ *A collection of* 110 pieces ~~for a collection~~ struck the fashion editors as excessive.

Use numerals if you cannot express a number in one or two words.

▶ He designed ~~one hundred ten~~ ¹¹⁰ pieces for his first Paris collection.

▶ Among the attendees were ~~thirty-five hundred~~ ^{3,500} American design students.

For very large numbers that include a fraction or decimal, use a combination of numerals and words.

▶ One of the larger retailers had sold more than 4.5 million of its basic T-shirts the previous year.

In addition, always use numerals in the following situations.

ADDRESSES 500 Broadway, 107 175th Street

DATES December 26, 2012; 632 BCE; the 1990s

DECIMALS AND FRACTIONS 59.5, 59$^1/_2$

PARTS OF WRITTEN WORKS volume 2; chapter 5; page 82; act 3, scene 3

PERCENTAGES 66 percent (or 66%)

RATIOS 16:1 *or* 16 to 1

STATISTICS a median age of 32

Acknowledgments

IMAGE ACKNOWLEDGMENTS

45: Courtesy ResiCal, Inc.; **46:** Courtesy Unilever; **48:** © McNEIL-PPC, Inc. 2007. LISTERINE® is a registered trademark of Johnson & Johnson. Used with permission; **69:** Bettman/Corbis; **72:** Steve Morris/Air Team Images; **90:** (both) Bettmann/Corbis; **164:** Brian Nicholson/The New York Times/Redux; **292:** © Reagan Louie; **304:** Naum Kazhdan/Redux; **310:** (top) From Stiglitz, Joseph. *Economics*. New York: Norton, (bottom) www.ivillage.com; **328:** Courtesy Glaxo Smith Kline; **341:** From Beranbaum, Rose Levy. *The Bread Bible*. New York: Norton; **386, 389, 390:** Courtesy of University of Wyoming Library; **450:** (wolf) Jim Krueger, (beagle) DlILL/Corbis, text courtesy of *The Bark*; **456:** Courtesy of Forum on Religion and Ecology, Yale University and J. Baird Callicott; **458:** Reprinted with permission of EBSCO Publishing, 2008; **469:** Bettmann/Corbis; **495:** Lisa Takeuchi Cullen, "Freshen Up Your Drink": Copyright TIME INC. Reprinted by permission. TIME is a registered trademark of Time Inc. All rights reserved, (David Stern) Amanda Friedman/Icon International, (Justin Timberlake) Tobias Schwartz/Reuters; **501:** Reprinted from the Federal Reserve Bank of San Francisco Economic Letter 2001-29. The opinions expressed in this article do not necessarily reflect the views of the management of the Federal Reserve Bank of San Francisco, or of the Board of Governors of the Federal Reserve System. Glenn D. Rudebusch; **503, 504:** Reprinted with permission of EBSCO Publishing, 2008; **529:** (top) Peter Turnley/Corbis, (second image) from Stiglitz and Walsh. *Principles of Microeconomics*. 3rd ed. New York: Norton, (third image) From Ginsberg, Lowi, Weir. *We the People*. 5th ed. New York: Norton, (fourth image) From Stiglitz, Joseph. *Economics*. New York: Norton, (fifth image) From Maier, Smith, Keyssar, Kevles. *Inventing America*. New York: Norton, (sixth image) From Ginsberg, Lowi, Weir. *We the People*. 5th ed. New York: Norton; **531:** (top two) Photo: Don Nowak, (bottom two) AP Photo; **552:** (clockwise from top left) Courtesy of the author, AP Photo, Courtesy of Dr. R. Standleer, Warner Brothers/Photofest; **553:** Courtesy Illinois State University; **554:** (top) Courtesy Illinois State University, (bottom) Clare Robertson, www.loobylu.com; **555:** Courtesy Julia Gilkinson.

TEXT ACKNOWLEDGMENTS

Marjorie Agosín: "Always Living in Spanish," *The Literary Life*, p. 25. Reprinted by permission of the author.

Dave Barry: "Guys vs. Men (Table)" from *Dave Barry's Complete Guide to Guys* by Dave Barry, copyright © 1995 by Dave Barry. Used by permission of Random House, Inc. For on-line information about other Random House, Inc. books and authors, see the Internet web site at http://www.randomhouse.com.

A-1

Doug Lantry: "Stay Sweet As You Are." Reprinted by permission of the author.

Lawrence Lessig: "Some Like It Hot—Wired Magazine article," from *Free Culture* by Lawrence Lessig, copyright © 2004 by Lawrence Lessig. Used by permission of The Penguin Press, a division of Penguin Group (USA) Inc. For on-line information about other Penguin Group (USA) books and authors, see the Internet website at: http://www.penguin.com.

Joanna MacKay: "Organ Sales Will Save Lives." Reprinted by permission of the author.

Sarah McGlone: "Effect of Biofeedback Training on Muscle Tension and Skin Temperature." Reprinted by permission of the author.

Shannon Nichols: " 'Proficiency'." Reprinted by permission of the author.

Jessica Ann Olson: "Annotated Bibliography on Global Warming." Copyright © 2008 by Jessica Ann Olson. Reprinted by permission of the author.

Anna Quindlen: "Write for Your Life." Reprinted by permission of International Creative Management, Inc. Copyright © 2007 by Anna Quindlen. First appeared in *Newsweek*, January 22, 2007.

William Safire: "A Spirit Reborn," *The New York Times*, September 9, 2002. © 2002, The New York Times. Reprinted by permission.

Susan Stellin: "The Inevitability of Bumps" from *The New York Times*, 6/12/2007, © 2007 The New York Times. All rights reserved. Used by permission and protected by the Copyright Laws of the United States. The printing, copying, redistribution, or retransmission of the Material without express written permission is prohibited. www.nytimes.com.

Martha Stewart: Reprinted from *Favorite Comfort Food: Classic Favorites and Great New Recipes* by Martha Stewart. Copyright © 1999 Martha Stewart Living Omnimedia, Inc. Published by Clarkson Potter Publishers, a division of Random House, Inc.

Carolyn Stonehill: "Modern Dating, Prehistoric Style." Reprinted by permission of the author.

Gary Taubes: "What If It's All Been a Big Fat Lie?," *The New York Times*, July 7, 2002. © 2002, The New York Times. Reprinted by permission.

Luke Y. Tsai: "Asperger Syndrome and Medication Treatment," *Focus on Autism and Other Developmental Disabilities* 22.3, p. 138. Copyright © 2007, Hammill Institute on Disabilities. Reprinted by permission of Sage Publications.

Jerry Weinberger: "Pious Princes and Red-Hot Lovers: The Politics of Shakespeare's Romeo and Juliet," *The Journal of Politics* (2003), 65, p. 350. Copyright © 2003, Southern Political Science Association. Reprinted with the permission of Cambridge University Press.

Emily Yantis: "Informal Reflections on Honor." Copyright © 2008 by Emily Yantis. Reprinted by permission of the author.

Every effort has been made to gain permission for images and selections used in this book. Unless otherwise noted, all images not cited in this section have been provided by the editors and author of this publication. Rights holders of any images or selections not properly credited should contact Permissions Department, W.W. Norton & Company, Inc., 500 Fifth Avenue, New York, NY 10110, in order for a correction to be made in the next reprinting of our work.

Glossary / Index

A

a, HB-51–52

abbreviations, HB-85–86
  with names, HB-85
  in notes and documentation, HB-86
  with numbers, HB-85–86

abstract, 111–15 A GENRE of writing that summarizes a book, an article, or a paper, usually in 100–200 words. Authors in some academic fields must provide, at the top of a report submitted for publication, an abstract of its content. The abstract may then appear in a journal of abstracts, such as *Psychological Abstracts*. An *informative abstract* summarizes a complete report; a briefer *descriptive abstract* works more as a teaser; a standalone *proposal abstract* (also called a TOPIC PROPOSAL) requests permission to conduct research, write on a topic, or present a report at a scholarly conference. Key Features: SUMMARY of basic information • objective description • brevity
  brevity and, 113
  conforming to requirements, 114
  copy and paste key statements, 114
  descriptive, 112
  example of, 111–12

Note: This glossary/index defines key terms and concepts and directs you to pages in the book where you can find specific information on these and other topics. Please note the words set in SMALL CAPITAL LETTERS are themselves defined in the glossary/index.

  generating ideas and text, 114
  help with, 115
  informative, 111–12
  key features of, 113
  for last reports, 139
  objective description, 113
  organizing, 115
  paper first, abstract last, 114
  pare down to key ideas, 114
  proposal, 112–13
  rhetorical situation, 113–14
  summary of basic information, 113

academic reading, *see* textbooks, reading
Academic Search Complete, 391
accept, HB-41
acknowledging sources, 420–23
  arguable statements, 421
  avoiding plagiarism, 423–24
  collaborations, 422
  direct quotations, 421
  opinions and assertions of others, 421–22
  sources that don't need acknowledgment, 422–23
  when in doubt, 423

action verb, HB-49 A VERB that expresses a physical or mental action (*jump, consider*).

active voice, HB-18–19
adapt, HB-41
addresses, HB-62

ad hominem argument, 296–97 logical FALLACY that attacks someone's character rather than address the issues.

APA style, 477–519   A system of documenting sources in the social sciences. APA stands for the American Psychological Association. *See also* DOCU-MENTATION.

appendix   A section at the end of a written work for supplementary material that would be distracting in the main part of the text.

application letters, 188, 195–200   Letters written to apply for a job or other position. *See also* RÉSUMÉS. Key Features: succinct indication of qualifications • reasonable and pleasing tone • conventional, businesslike form

arguing, 283–99   A STRATEGY that can be used in any kind of writing to support a claim with REASONS and EVIDENCE.

arguing a position, 83–110   A GENRE of writing that uses REASONS and EVIDENCE to support a CLAIM or POSITION and, sometimes, to persuade an AUDIENCE to accept that position. Key Features: clear and arguable position • necessary background • good reason • convincing support for each reason • appeal to read-

article, HB-51–52   The word *a*, *an*, or *the*, used to indicate that a NOUN is indefinite (*a, an*) or definite (*the*).

audience, 5–8, HB-36   Those to whom a text is directed—the people who read, listen to, or view the text. Audience is a key part of every text's RHETORICAL SITUATION.

evidence, 287–93   The data you present to support your REASONS. Such data may include statistics, calculations, examples, ANECDOTES, QUOTATIONS, case studies, or anything else that will convince your reader that your reasons are compelling. Evidence should be sufficient (enough to show that the reasons have merit) and relevant (appropriate to the argument you're making).

explaining a process, 338–42   A STRATEGY for telling how something is done or how to do something. Sometimes an explanation of a process serves as the ORGANIZING principle for a whole text.

expletive   A word such as *it* or *there* that stands in for information provided later in the sentence: *It was difficult to drive on the icy road. There is plenty of food in the refrigerator.*

F

H

hasty generalization, 298   A FALLACY that reaches a conclusion based on insufficient or inappropriately qualified EVIDENCE.

home page, 549   The introductory page of a website. *See also* websites.

I

indefinite pronoun, HB-23, HB-24–25   A PRONOUN, such as *all, anyone, anything, everyone, everything, few, many, some,* and *something*, that functions like a NOUN but does not refer to or take the place of a specific noun.

K

keyword   A term that a researcher inputs when searching databases and the World Wide Web for information.

L

lab report, 133–42   A GENRE of writing that covers the process of conducting an experiment in a controlled setting. Key Features: explicit title • ABSTRACT • PURPOSE • methods • results and discussion • REFERENCES • APPENDIX • appropriate format

layout, 525   The way text is arranged on a page or screen—for example, in paragraphs, in lists, on charts, with headings, and so on.

letter writing, 224   A process of GENERATING IDEAS AND TEXT by going through the motions of writing to someone to explain a topic.

memories and, 159

narratives and, 351

portfolios and, 248

previewing a text, 353

profiles and, 167

proposals and, 176

reflections and, 185

reporting information and, 75

research plan and, 377

résumés and, 192

textual analysis and, 51

thinking about, 16

see also electronic text; print text; spoken text

Mejia, Susanna, 317

member of congress, HB-55

Membership and Morals: The Personal Uses of Plural-ism in America (Rosenblum), 321

memoir, 153–60 A GENRE that focuses on something significant from the writer's past. Key Features: good story • vivid details • clear significance

clear significance of, 157–58

details of, 159–60

example of, 153–57

generating ideas and text, 159–60

as a good story, 157

guide to, 158–60

help with, 160

key features of, 157–58

mixing genres, 205

organizing, 160

rhetorical situation, 158–59

significance of, 159

stance and, 13

topic for, 158

vivid details of, 157

Merlis, Bob, 9–10, HB-39

metaphor, 311, HB-40–41 A figure of speech that makes a comparison without using the word *like* or

as: "All the world's a stage/And all the men and women merely players" (William Shakespeare, *As You Like It* 2.7.138–39).

"Metaphor and Society in Shelley's 'Sonnet'," 144–46, HB-78

"Mick Jagger Wants Me," HB-23, HB-66, HB-75

might, HB-20

might of, HB-44

mine, HB-27

"Miracle of Stem Cells, The," 316–17

mixing genres, 201–8

audience, 205–6

design, 206

determining need for, 206–7

focus, 204

generating ideas and text, 206–7

guide to, 205–6

help with, 208

integrating the genres, 207

key features of, 203–4

multi-genre projects, 207–8

organization, 204

primary genre, 203–4, 206

purpose, 205

rhetorical situation, 205–6

stance, 206

transitions, 204

typical ways of, 204–5

MLA International Bibliography, 392

MLA style, 428–76, HB-67, HB-78, HB-80 A system of documenting sources in the humanities and fine arts. MLA stands for the Modern Language Association. *See also* DOCUMENTATION.

directory to, 428–31

endnotes or footnotes, 439

in-text documentation, 427, 428–29, 432–38

list of works cited, 427, 429–31, 439–67

books, 439–47

N

narration, 21, 343–51   A STRATEGY for presenting information as a story, for telling "what happened." It is a pattern most often associated with fiction, but it shows up in all kinds of writing. When used in an essay, a REPORT, or another academic GENRE, a narrative must support a point—not merely tell an interesting story for its own sake. It must also present events in some kind of sequence and include only pertinent detail. Sometimes narrative serves as the ORGANIZING principle for a whole text. See also LITERACY NARRATIVE.

O

print résumés, 188–92
  example of, 189
  see also résumés
print sources, 385–86
  reliability of, 400
print text, 523–33
  design elements, 524–28
  evaluating a design
  headings, 526–27
  layout, 525
  lists, 525–26
  paragraphs, 525
  rhetorical situation, 523–24, 528
  typefaces, 524–25
  visuals, *see* visuals, print text
  white space, 528
proceeding of a conference, citing
  in APA style, 507
  in MLA style, 466

process, 209–58   In writing a series of actions that may include GENERATING IDEAS AND TEXT, DRAFTING, REVISING, EDITING, and PROOFREADING a text. *See also* EXPLAINING A PROCESS *and specific processes.*

" 'Proficiency'," 26–27, 28, 32, 34, HB-8, HB-57

profile, 161–70   A GENRE that presents an engaging portrait of a person, place, or event based on first-hand FIELD RESEARCH. Key Features: interesting subject • necessary background • interesting angle • firsthand account • engaging details
  analysis of findings, 168–69
  angles, 169
  background or context, 165–66
  as a description, 170
  engaging details, 166
  example of, 9–10, 161–65
  firsthand accounts, 166
  generating ideas and text, 168–69

  guide to, 167–70
  help with, 170
  interesting angles, 166
  interesting subjects, 165
  key features of, 165–66
  mixing genres, 205
  as a narrative, 169
  preexisting knowledge and, 168
  questions to ask, 168
  research, 168
  rhetorical situation, 167
  suitable subjects, 167
  visiting your subject, 168

pronoun, HB-4, HB-24–28   A word that takes the place of a NOUN or functions the way a noun does.
  indefinite, HB-23, HB-24–25
  relative, HB-23–24

pronoun-antecedent agreement, HB-24–25
pronoun case, HB-26–28
pronoun reference, HB-25–26
proofreading, 245–46
  application letters, 199
  thank-you letters, 199
  see also editing and proofreading

proofreading, 245–46   The final PROCESS of writing, when a writer checks for correct spelling and punctuation as well as for page order, missing copy, and consistent use of typefaces and FONTS. *See also* EDITING, REVISING, and REWRITING.

proper nouns, HB-80–81, HB-84
proposal abstracts, 112–13
  organizing, 115
  see also abstracts

proposal, 171–79   A GENRE that argues for a solution to a problem or suggests some action. *See also* TOPIC PROPOSAL. Key Features: well-defined problem • recommended solution • answers to anticipated questions • call to action • appropriate TONE

purpose, 3–4, HB-36   A writer's goal: to explore; to express oneself; to entertain; to demonstrate learning; to report; to persuade; and so on. Purpose is one element of the RHETORICAL SITUATION.

Q

questioning, 211–14   A PROCESS of GENERATING IDEAS AND TEXT about a topic — asking, for example, What? Who? When? Where? How? and Why? or other questions

response, 235–36 A PROCESS of writing in which a reader responds to a writer's work by giving his or her thoughts about the writer's title, beginning, clarity of THESIS, support and DOCUMENTATION, ORGANIZING, STANCE, treatment of AUDIENCE, achievement of PURPOSE, handling of the GENRE, ending, and other matters.

résumé, 188–95, HB-30 A GENRE that summarizes someone's academic and employment history, generally written to submit to potential employers, DESIGN and word choice depend on whether a résumé is submitted as a print document or in an electronic or scannable form. Key Features: organization that suits goals and experience • succinctness • design that highlights key information (for print) or that uses only one typeface (for scannable).

Y

Z

Revision Symbols

abbr	abbreviation **HB-85**		*ital*	italics **HB-82**
adj	adjective **HB-48**		*jarg*	jargon **HB-37**
adv	adverb **HB-48**		lc	lowercase letter **HB-80**
agr	agreement **HB-20, HB-24**		*mm*	misplaced modifier **HB-50**
art	article **HB-51**		*num*	number **HB-86**
awk	awkward		¶	new paragraph
cap	capitalization **HB-80**		//	parallelism **HB-28**
case	pronoun case **HB-26**		*pass*	passive voice **HB-18**
cliché	cliché **HB-38**		*ref*	pronoun reference **HB-25**
⌣	close up space		*run-on*	comma splice or fused sentence **HB-10**
cs	comma splice **HB-10**		*sexist*	sexist language **HB-54**
def	define **314–23**		*shift*	confusing shift **HB-33**
dm	dangling modifier **HB-50**		*sl*	slang **HB-36**
doc	documentation **425–519**		#	insert space
emph	emphasis **HB-31**		*sp*	spelling
frag	sentence fragment **HB-7**		*trans*	transition **277**
fs	fused sentence **HB-10**		*vb*	verb **HB-11**
hyph	hyphen **HB-78**		*wrdy*	wordy **HB-46**
^	insert		*ww*	wrong word **HB-41**

A Directory to MLA Style

A Directory to APA Style

Handbook Menu